THE **WINE ATLAS** OF
FRANCE
AND TRAVELLER'S GUIDE
TO THE VINEYARDS

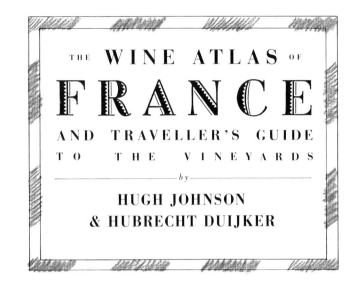

THE WINE ATLAS OF
FRANCE
AND TRAVELLER'S GUIDE
TO THE VINEYARDS

by

HUGH JOHNSON
& HUBRECHT DUIJKER

SIMON AND SCHUSTER
NEW YORK · LONDON · TORONTO · SYDNEY · TOKYO

The Wine Atlas of France

Edited and designed by Mitchell Beazley
International Ltd., Artists House,
14–15 Manette Street, London W1V 5LB

Library of Congress Cataloging-in-Publication Data

Johnson, Hugh.
  The wine atlas of France.

  Includes index.
  1. Wine and wine making–France–Guide-books.
2. France–Description and travel–1975–
Guide-books. I. Duijker, Hubrecht. II. Title.
TP553.J64   1987   641.2'22'0944   87–4582
ISBN 0-671-64232-4

Editor Dian Taylor
Art Editor Eljay Crompton
Map Editor Anita Wagner
Assistant Vibeke Schönkopf
Index Tom Blott, Alexandra Boyle
Picture Research Jackum Brown
Production Philip Collyer

Senior Executive Editor Chris Foulkes
Senior Executive Art Editor Roger Walton

Translation Rosetta Translations:
Raymond Kaye

Wine maps Thames Cartographic Services,
based on the 1985 edition of **The World Atlas of Wine**

Illustrations Polly Raynes
Sketch maps and key maps Sue Sharples,
John Laing

Typeset by Servis Filmsetting Ltd., Manchester, England
Reproduction by Gilchrist Bros. Ltd., Leeds, England
Printed by Printer Industria Grafica SA, Barcelona
DLB 22193-1987

CONTENTS

INTRODUCTION

A wine atlas of France is a logical extension of *The World Atlas of Wine*. For years I have been photocopying the relevant pages of the *World Atlas* each time I have visited France. It is a heavy book to carry, and maps of Greece and California are of limited value in the Loire valley. It has made sense to take a section on the Loire, say, or a sheaf of Bordeaux pages. In the field they have become dog-eared and wine-stained, scrawled on at tastings, corrected for new buildings or new roads.

They have been invaluable in updating the *Atlas*. But what I have been wanting, and what you now have in your hand, is the whole of French wine: maps of the vineyards, a road atlas, advice on where to go, what to see, who to meet, which hotel to dine at. A book designed more for the automobile than for the desktop. A travelling companion with rapid answers to the questions that crop up in the most rewarding country on earth for the wine lover to visit. To its writing my co-author Hubrecht Duijker has brought his unrivalled knowledge of the French wine districts, great and small, and the highways and byways that lead through them. It has been a happy and fruitful collaboration.

Why is the very thought of touring France so exciting? There are many answers, but all point in the same direction. France is the country that has perfected the art of living – public living, that is. France offers the world a polished front. She sets herself the highest standards. You can (or at least you could until recently) find perfectly baked bread in every village.

History contains certain instances of cultural identity that bear no logical explanation. One can think of the Middle East and its religious productivity; German musicality; Italian architecture – but think of France and you think of the table. The whole table. French food is chosen and prepared with a care and seriousness that has no parallel. Surely it is the same gustatory genius that made France the creator of wine at the level of luxury.

Is this really true? Were there no *crus*, no wine beyond the ordinary, until the French got to work? Not quite: the Romans were finely discriminating 1,800 years ago. German monasteries and aristocrats have maintained a Frankish wine culture for 1,200 years. But only in the land of France have the infinite potentialities of the vine progressed far beyond haphazard instances of quality.

Nobody looking closely at the Frenchman and his farm can mistake the blend of instinct and passion and pride that constitutes national genius. No other race could have conceived the painstaking process of *élevage*: the word implies finding and encouraging the best qualities of site, soil, vines, their wine and its maturation. Perhaps "breeding" is the most apposite English equivalent.

What the French have done through history, almost it seems without knowing it, is to breed quality in wine. Just as a trainer and breeder produces faster and faster horses, winegrowers in certain privileged parts of France (and they are many) have acted to speed and direct the process of evolution. Long before technology had any meaning, owners of good land were seeking a premium for its products, reinvesting it in the land itself, and from the fields in better heart growing the best grapes they could find, studying the art of making their wine better and more distinct.

For distinction – individual character – is at the heart of the matter. Were wine one single beverage, however excellent, we should drink it gratefully, but it would lose its fascination. To teach the product of each region, even each vineyard, to taste like itself, and not precisely like any other wine, has been France's contribution.

To explain just what this means, and why the wine of this slope is lighter, more perfumed, more structured or leaves its flavour longer in the mouth than the wine from the slope across the way, France has coined the term "terroir". Terroir literally means soil, but it embraces far more. It includes shelter, drainage, angle of slope in relation to the sun, microclimate, incidence of frost, and even traditional or novel practices of cultivation. All these things constitute the "terroir" that gives identity and distinction to a wine. What English word can we offer as an equivalent? The hard-worked term "environment" is perhaps the nearest.

How much of the environment that created and produces the world's favourite wines is due to the land, and how much to the people? Given the genius of the French for taking pains with what they eat and drink, would or could they have turned any other country – Spain, for example, or Italy – into the motherland of wine?

In historical terms the answer must be no. France makes great wine, and delicate, digestible, easily drinkable wine, because she has the ideal climate for it: above all, moderate summer heat, with nights growing cooler as vintage time approaches. More important even than the terroir, there are perfect natural conditions for its fermentation and cellaring. France did not need to wait for the invention of refrigeration and air conditioning. Her grapes are picked at the moment when autumn chill takes over from summer heat. Spain or most of Italy without electricity for refrigeration would be back in the Dark Ages as far as fine wine is concerned.

The north of France lies so close to the limit of practicable viticulture that it is touch and go whether in any year the grapes will reach full ripeness. To the west the mouth of the Loire, to the east Champagne and the valley of the Moselle define the line beyond which grapes are no longer a satisfactory crop. The limit is farther north in the east than in the west because of the English Channel. Successive waves of clouds coming from the Atlantic cover the sun over Brittany and Normandy for too much of the summer. They roll inland to Paris and beyond and cover Picardy and the Pas de Calais. Champagne is the nearest point to the Channel that escapes this unwelcome cloud cover. It even benefits marginally from the continental climate with its warmer summers to the east.

Does champagne with its enlivening briskness express the spirit of the French? – or is it the inevitable result of growing grapes where they scarcely have time to ripen (and certainly will not finish fermentation) before the cold weather catches up with them?

If it helps to settle the question, enthusiasm for wine goes back to the inhabitants of France in Roman times and beyond. The Gauls were fanatical about it. Tacitus reported that one amphora of Italian wine imported into Gaul would buy one Gallic slave for Rome. (An amphora held a mere 26 litres: less than three dozen modern bottles.)

Nor did the Gallic tribes wait for the colonizing Romans to arrive with wine as their pacifying opiate. Three hundred years before Julius Caesar divided all Gaul into three parts, a substantial raiding party from what is now Burgundy headed south into Italy, sacked Rome, settled in Lombardy and occupied it for several generations. They returned home vignerons, so that by the time of Roman rule wine was already established as part of Gallic culture: a part that the Romans at first encouraged, until they found that it damaged the market for their own Italian wines.

It is conventional today to think of classical antiquity as an era separated from our own by the abyss of "the dark ages". The Renaissance, we are taught, rediscovered the Greek and Roman genius and learnt to reproduce their designs. We forget that there are direct links, activities and processes that never stopped, whatever barbarian hordes swept through the abandoned forums of the Empire.

The Roman infrastructure of roads remained intact. So did the sites of most of their cities. As the Church gained power the centres of Roman administration tended to become episcopal seats, and the Roman "counties" the dioceses of the Church.

Thus the factors that decided which should be the principal vineyards of Roman Gaul never went away, but were only reinforced by the growing power of bishops and, later, monasteries. Of these Citeaux in Burgundy became, with the advent of the Cistercians in the twelfth century, the most influential. Its great walled vineyard, the Clos de Vougeot, still remains as a reminder of the resources and technology at the disposal of the medieval church. But its location was a decision taken 1,000 years before that, when the traffic on the Sâone valley highway, passing through the territory of what later became (and still is) the diocese of Autun, suggested to the citizens a use for the scrubby hillside that we now call the Côte d'Or.

There is scarcely an exception to the rule that France's great vineyards began with the Romans. The odd one out is Alsace. Ideal though the sheltered eastern Vosges have proved themselves for vines, to the Gallo-Romans they were out on a limb, with no ready marketplace and no easy transport to one. What of the river Rhine? It flowed too fast, over too many rapids, in the stretch above what is now the Franco-German border. And it flowed north, away from the export market of Italy and towards the already successful vineyards of the German Rhine and the Moselle.

If France's vineyards were established an astonishingly long time ago, so it seems were the families of grapes that were eventually to decide the flavour of the wines. According to the great historian of French winegrowing Roger Dion, the vines that helped to form the different characters of Burgundy and Bordeaux came from two widely different sources. Burgundy shares with the east of France right up to Champagne in the north the group of varieties that includes the Pinot Noir. Dion speculates that the Pinot and its cousins are the result of centuries of selection from the wild grapes of the Alpine foothills of the Dauphiné by the Gallic tribe whose alliance with Julius Caesar assured the conquest of Gaul. The Romans referred to their hardy vine as Allobrogica, the plant of the Allobrogic people.

By contrast the Bordeaux group of grapes, the Cabernets, the Merlot and the Petit Verdot, have a common ancestor in the plant known as Biturica, which was probably brought to Bordeaux from the older Roman settlements of the Ebro valley in Spain. The substantial remains of a Roman *cuvier* are still to be seen near Cenicero in Rioja. Perhaps its grapes formed the character of Bordeaux, and fashioned the style of winemaking that was to be re-exported to Rioja 1,800 years later.

What better proof can there be of the continuity of French winegrowing than the existence even today of two distinct stylistic traditions in eastern and western France, their headquarters respectively in Burgundy and Bordeaux? There is only one region where they meet and mingle, and that is along the valley of the Loire, presumably invaded with winegrowing ideas from both ends, from Burgundy near its headwaters and from Bordeaux via the Bay of Biscay.

Historians have argued the toss about why the progress of 2,000 years has not led to a more homogeneous pattern. Why have all French winegrowers not settled for the same grapes, the same techniques, the same ideal of what a good wine should be? This, after all, is what the New World has done. It has adopted the six best French vines everywhere from Australia to Oregon.

Terroir is part of the answer: the land itself chooses the crop that suits it best. Another, not to be underestimated, is local pride – even secrecy.

France up to the last century was, in practical terms, a bigger place than the entire world today. There was no hobnobbing between winemakers of different regions (unless it was among the Cistercians). There were no universities for winemakers. Tradition fed on itself. Grape varieties arose by continually taking cuttings from the best plants in your own vineyards. The date of the harvest was directed by the local authorities so that everyone in the district made the same sort of wine. These were the conditions that in the country backwaters of France bred some wonderfully individual and even eccentric traditions. They are also the reason why no wine traveller should stick solely to the "classic" areas, or be condescending about a "little" local wine that has 2,000 years of history behind it.

What is the best way, then, to turn a distant acquaintance with the wines of France to a full familiarity with the regions and their varied products? There is no substitute for travel. Much can be done by tasting the different

wines at home, more with reading about them, but only by going there can you learn to associate a certain taste with a certain cut of the landscape, colour of rooftile, grey river estuary or green-floored valley in view of the perpetual snow.

A European approach to France will be different from that of a visitor from America or Australia. Having come this far, such visitors usually argue, we would be crazy not to see it all. I confess to being that sort of tourist myself at times. Better a single vaporetto ride down the Grand Canal than not to have seen Venice at all. You can catch a glimpse, and retain a memory, of Reims, Beaune, Lyon and Bordeaux in a week, and still have a weekend left over for Paris.

Perhaps this is the logical (if expensive) way to begin an acquaintance with the variety of France. Some memory, some incident: perhaps a person, perhaps a landscape, perhaps a restaurant or even a glass of wine will stay with you and insist that you go back.

Your second journey will be less ambitious in mileage: more focussed in intent. With time to walk and explore, to look beneath the surface, the character of the region – as opposed to its famous monuments – will creep up on you.

Chablis is not a glamorous town. Visitors are invariably disappointed at first sight that such a universally known name should mean no more than a huddle of grey houses down to an unexceptional little river.

It was my good fortune, though, years ago, to visit Chablis with one of the great English wine merchants of the old school, Ronald Avery, a man as perceptive as he was eccentric. Important buyer though he was, this was no state visit. We spent as much time walking as we did tasting or sitting at table. It was early summer, fresh, but hot in the sunshine. We toiled up the slope behind the town where the Grands Crus vineyards enjoy the privilege of midday sunshine burning at right angles into their soil. It reminded me of gritty cheese.

By the time we had paced out Vaudésir and Les Clos, the two mid-slope Crus that face most directly south, I could hardly wait to taste their wines, to see if my tongue could detect the differences that my eyes (and legs) told me should be there. Back in town, in the half-light of a grower's cellar, enjoying the damp cool after the baking hillside, I imbibed a lesson about Chablis I have never forgotten. I learnt how Chablis from the valley slopes can be a drink as limpid and restoring as the water of celestial wells; how light it can be, and yet how distinct in its smell and taste, which are never of fruit, always of the soil and its stones and the turf that covers it.

I learnt to recognize a degree of extra density and what I can only call tension in the taste of wines from the better slopes. The character of Chablis seemed most sharply defined in a young Premier Cru wine. A young Grand Cru seemed overstuffed with flavour; too rich to be refreshing – and Vaudésir and Les Clos were denser than any, even with a hint of honey in their heady, ill-defined aromas. There could be no question that these were wines still in the clumsy colt stage, their forces not yet developed into harmonious coordination.

Of course we drank an older bottle, after our tasting of the wines of the new vintage. It was a Vaudésir of a famous vintage, then 15 years old. To my amazement the characteristic colour of Chablis, what I can only call a green glint in its eye, had intensified with age into a gem-like lustre. Its spring-turf perfume filled the cellar. And in its flavour all that I had found limpid and lovely about a simple young Chablis was sublimated into a major chord. This was great white burgundy. Perhaps, I sometimes think, the very greatest. And I had been led to it by the one route that truly elucidated the qualities of wine: comparison with its close relations, always moving from the good to the better, the young and closed to the gloriously open and mature.

It need not have been Chablis. The same revelation can be experienced anywhere in the world of wine to the degree that its products are categorized and refined as they are, particularly, in Burgundy. It is one of the greatest differences between France (and also Germany) and the wine countries of the New World or the less-polished regions of the old. They will perhaps have many different wines to show you, from different grape varieties and different vintages – even perhaps from different vineyards.

What no one has except the studious French (and even they not everywhere) is a classification of quality sanctioned by the experience of generations who have each, in turn, experienced what I did that summer years ago in Chablis.

I think of it each time I find myself in that uneventful town. I have walked along the towpath of the Serein on misty mornings, picking a dew-soaked dogrose from the hedge, and paced in winter under the bare poplars, sheltering my ears against the wind in the collar of my coat. What difference does it make to know the sidestreets and the lanes? It intensifies the sense of place. And a sense of place, an awareness of the terroir, is the key to the understanding of the wines of France, even more than those of any other country.

This Atlas presupposes an independently minded traveller. There are many, perhaps even the majority, who are unaccustomed to finding their own way around. Group travel offers the anonymity that glosses over ignorance of language or of the subject in hand. It is the way not to become involved; to look on as a bystander – but also to miss a great deal.

I have met tourists three days into a bus tour of Bordeaux who asked me when they were going to see the city of Beaune that they had heard so much about. (For that matter, I have heard a member of a coach party confide in the cellarmaster of a great château that she didn't like wine. He comforted her so graciously that no one could know whether it was the first, or the fiftieth, time that such a person had been misdirected into his cellars.)

Travel alone and you are exposed. It is up to you to make the running. Its success, measured in enjoyment, depends directly on the commitment you are prepared to make: commitment to communicate, and also commitment to understand. It is all too easy to arrive in Bordeaux or Burgundy with a preset package of ideas; only to ask leading questions designed to reinforce what you already believe; not to be open to learning from what you see around you, what you taste or what you are told.

As experienced travellers know, it is much easier to ask a question in a foreign language than to understand the answer. Just as you are congratulating yourself for formulating an intelligible French sentence you are faced with an enthusiastic, idiomatic, probably circuitous reply. The words are familiar; the ideas are not. Miss one negative and you have been led in completely the wrong direction. It becomes embarrassing to persist, to rephrase your question: much easier to nod and interject "oui" and "entendu" and "d'accord".

Even professionals can fall into this trap. It is, I suspect, why a surprising number of the most experienced wine-trade buyers, who travel to France several times a year, speak little French. Rather than risk misunderstanding they prefer to rely on local brokers who speak English (a number, indeed, are British or American). Experience may also have taught them that their French suppliers come to the point more directly when forced to use their often limited English than if they are encouraged to luxuriate in their mother tongue.

As an independent visitor you have some homework to do. First, in planning your itinerary. It is not normally essential to make reservations in French country hotels far in advance, unless there is some particular event drawing the crowds. Burgundy on the third weekend in November is full up for Les Trois Glorieuses. Bordeaux at Vinexpo time is so full that a special express train shuttles back and forth to Biarritz to take advantage of that resort's hotels. The key weekends at the beginning and end of August when all France is on the roads are difficult – but then it is a time to avoid travelling in France at all.

Outside famous resort areas or three-star restaurant-hotels, outside special events, and outside of big cities (above all, Paris) a telephone call a few days in advance is usually enough to secure a reasonable hotel room. Hotels below the luxury category are notably good value: it is these that are principally featured in the travel information in this book.

You will probably be more concerned about the quality of your accommodation if you plan to spend more than a night or two in one place. In this case it is worth doing more specific research, writing for brochures and confirming your reservation by letter. (See also page 17.)

Famous restaurants are generally booked up for weeks in advance in the summer season; a reservation by letter is often essential.

As to announcing your arrival at a château or a wine estate, the general rule is simple enough. The grander and more prestigious the establishment the more notice (and indeed influence) you need to be made welcome, or sometimes even to be admitted at all.

A first-growth Bordeaux château, or one of the grandest Burgundy domaines, rather reasonably likes to limit visits to those who are actual or potential customers for its very expensive wines. The conventional way of establishing your standing as a regular massive buyer of first-growth wines is to ask your supplier at home to write you a letter of introduction, which you then send in advance with a request for a visit, if possible giving a choice of dates. If your request is granted (which is normal, but not automatic) you can then expect to be received with some formality, punctually at the prearranged time, probably by the cellarmaster or maître de chai.

Courtesy on your part demands that you have done some homework about the château or domaine in question. At least be sure you know what sort of wine you can expect to find in its barrels – the appellation and its ground rules as to grape varieties. In Bordeaux this is straightforward. Most *chais* (the Bordeaux word for cellar, a building usually half-underground) contain one kind of wine only – probably from two vintages, the newest and the previous year's, waiting for the appropriate moment to be bottled. By contrast, in Burgundy one cellar often contains barrels of wine from ten different appellations, red or white. It will certainly encourage the grower to confide in you if you have prepared yourself with a reference book and know in advance where he has plots of vines, and therefore which wines from among the long list of Nuits, Beaune, Corton, Pommard and the rest you can expect to find in his barrels.

An honoured guest (certainly an established buyer) will be offered a tasting from every barrel in the cellar if time allows. The grower will almost always follow the same order, starting with his humblest wine and climbing the ladder of quality.

Your response to such a major tasting should show appropriate appreciation and result, either directly or indirectly, in some business for the grower.

Far more common, and less demanding for all parties, is the unstructured casual visit to a less prestigious establishment. Most such visits are prompted by a sign by the roadside: "Vente Directe" (direct sales) or "Dégustation Gratuite" (free tasting). An ever-open door is, of course, unlikely to be attended by the proprietor himself. In a large establishment it will be an employee; in a small one a member of the family who will offer you a little routine visit. A growers' cooperative is also usually an excellent place to make acquaintance with the wine of the region and perhaps start a trail leading to friendship.

A casual visitor is often offered just one glass – and that from a bottle already open, perhaps kept in a refrigerator. This is the moment to size up the property and decide whether you would like to know more – perhaps based on what you are tasting, perhaps on a glimpse of something more interesting in the background.

If your host goes to the length of drawing a sample direct from a barrel for you (using a pipette to suck one or two glassfuls from the bunghole), you have the right to feel flattered. He (or she) is taking trouble, and is trusting you to judge the wine in its pre-bottled state (which is almost always slightly different, for better or worse, than after it has been finally filtered into bottles).

In these circumstances taste the wine with extreme care. This is not the place to start on a course of instruction in winetasting, but the following procedure both observes the proprieties and allows you to make up your own mind about what you are tasting.

Accept the glass you are offered with both your hands, taking the foot (not the stem) in your right hand and steadying the top with your left. (An advanced ploy, recommended only to those with self-confidence, is to reach in your pocket for your own silver tastevin, which you keep there wrapped in a handkerchief, and hold it out to be filled.)

9

Spend ten seconds looking at the wine before you do anything else. Take a piece of white paper from your pocket and tip the glass you are holding (still by the foot) against it so that the colour is shown up clearly against the paper. The design of a silver tastevin, incidentally, is to maximize reflection of whatever light there is in a dark cellar through the wine.

You need not comment on the colour, but if you are feeling loquacious the safe remark is "joli robe".

Briefly swirl the wine in your glass so as to give it more contact with the air. This is much easier to do if you are holding the glass by the foot. There is no need to make your debut at this exercise in a cellar: practise at home, even with water if you like. It will soon become second nature and, more important, increase your enjoyment of every glass.

Having swirled, sniff. Two or three short sharp sniffs should be enough if you are concentrating on the matter in hand. I find it easier to concentrate on what I am smelling if I close my eyes. Being self-conscious I usually turn away or walk to one side at this moment.

Vaguely to hold the glass under your nose while chattering about something else is pure futility; you can form no impression of an aroma while you are talking (or even listening).

While you are still concentrating, take a good-sized sip, hold it in your mouth, then chew the wine as though it were bread. In a cold cellar, and especially in winter, take a very small sip: a mouthful of icy wine can make your teeth protest. As soon as you have thoroughly soaked your palate in flavour, spit the wine out. Some cellars provide a spittoon or perhaps a box of sawdust. If there is no obvious provision, spit on the floor. It is perfectly good form. If there is a doorway leading outside, I often wander over to it and spit in the open air. The pause gives time to reflect.

Having tasted, what you say or do next is a more open question. A remark of some sort is clearly called for. If you liked what you tasted, and want to prolong the encounter, homework once again comes to the rescue. Anyone in a wine region will tell you when the normal bottling time is for each vintage. Before you risk a pronouncement on what you have tasted, you might draw out your host by asking him when he expects to "faire la mise" (en bouteilles). His reply will often give you a hint of his opinion of the vintage.

It is prudent to keep your own pronouncement on a fairly general level. "Très prometteux" (very promising) is acceptably neutral. "Intéressant" is perhaps the minimum compliment within the bounds of courtesy. (I am writing, of course, not for professionals, but for amateurs who would like to feel their way closer to the subject.)

One remark that can lead to further conversation (and tasting) is to say that you would like to taste the wine again in six months' or a year's time. Does Monsieur sell his wine in London/Amsterdam/San Francisco? Does he have an agent whose address you might make a note of? (To take notes while you are tasting is not only a sign of serious purpose which will be duly noted, it is also by far the best way to add to your stock of accurate wine knowledge.)

If you like what you have just tasted, would it be a nuisance (would Monsieur be dérangé) if you bought one or two bottles to take away? If you loved his wine, could he perhaps spare you a dozen? (But this becomes expensive, and involves a surprising amount of paperwork.)

One well-tried route to competent and welcoming producers, particularly in the less-frequented parts of France, is via the local hoteliers and restaurateurs. A conversation at your hotel may lead to a telephone call by the hotelier and a genuinely friendly reception. This approach has led me to many excellent producers whose market has been primarily local (and highly discriminating).

A typical occasion was at the Hotel Bellevue at Les Roches de Condrieu, a hotel whose dining room (from within) appears to straddle the great grey flood of the Rhône. The Viognier of Condrieu is one of France's most exquisite white wines. There are very few producers, whose names are now all pretty well-known.

The Viognier we had had at dinner was excellent, and its label unknown to me. Enquiries led to a large old house across the river with no sign of a vineyard, but a tennis court where an animated foursome was in progress.

Was this, I asked between sets, Monsieur X's house? His daughter left her game to come and tell me all I needed to know, made me taste the new vintage, and put me through on the telephone to her (distant) father. I have been enjoying his wine from time to time ever since.

Sooner or later a keen wine lover will be tempted to visit all the major wine regions of France. As this book amply illustrates, each has its own way of doing things, its own attractions and drawbacks.

Champagne, at one extreme, is so highly organized to welcome visitors and dazzle them with its vast cellars and complex procedures that most tours are impersonal affairs in which you feel rather like one of the bottles being processed. If you truly love champagne, it is worth talking seriously to your supplier about a letter from the importer of a marque you would be interested to visit in more depth.

Bordeaux, although infinitely fascinating and varied to its devotees, can be rather slow going for casual visitors. One chai is not very unlike another (at least at the workaday level below the Grandest Crus). As to tasting, very young Bordeaux is not easy to appreciate.

It is worth bearing in mind, certainly as a novice, that nearly all cellar tasting is of very young wines. Rarely is the crusted bottle broached, at least on first acquaintance. There is therefore more enjoyment to be had visiting and tasting in regions where the wines are delicious in their youth. It is what makes Germany a perfect land for wine tourism. The same principle applies to Alsace, the Loire valley, the Alps, much of Southwest France and indeed almost all "minor" areas. With less monoculture of the vine, minor areas are also generally more varied and picturesque (if less rich in historical monuments).

The obvious time to plan a visit to a wine region is at vintage time, when there is most to see. Actually to see the pickers at work, the tumbrils trundling in laden with blue fruit, the fruit disappearing into hoppers; to see presses at work, to smell the heady, dangerous fumes of fermentation is the most vivid way to learn how wine is made.

It is also, for equally obvious reasons, the time when the winegrower has least time – probably, in fact, no time – for visitors. You will be tolerated, but you can scarcely expect a red carpet when every moment is full of action and anxiety. To join the picking gangs is one thing (and an excellent introduction to wine for young people). To expect them to stop and pose for you is another.

You should see one vintage somewhere (my favourite spots at vintage time are Beaujolais and Alsace). But then give consideration to other seasons. Each has its charms: spring most of all, perhaps, while the leaves are still tender green, or mid-June when the vines are in flower over most of France, filling the vineyards with a most haunting sweet perfume said to provoke young love like no other scent.

Late October, after the vintage, is an excellent time to go. Vineyards are golden and village streets still full of the scent of fermenting wine.

Later still, although days are short, empty roads and busy towns decorated for Christmas make France a friendly, convivial place to be. Even the coldest months have their attractions and snow in the vineyards can be more beautiful than heavy summer leaves. There is only the pruning to be done outdoors, and plenty of time for tasting and talk in the cellar. Hotels are almost empty and even three-star restaurants become approachable.

To revisit a corner of France, especially one that is not in every guidebook, until you have a sense of belonging is (to some people) the most rewarding way of really entering into the spirit of the place. With only a little persistence, two or three visits perhaps, your face becomes familiar, the welcome warmer when you arrive. The local Confrérie (scarcely a corner of France is without its half-serious, half simply convivial, dining club) will be delighted to enrol you as a member. You will time a holiday to coincide with one of its feasts. Before long you will be involved in exchanging schoolchildren in the summer. You will have a real link with the place that seemed so remote when it was just a name on a wine label.

HUGH JOHNSON

A CALENDAR OF WINE EVENTS

Wine fairs, festivals and other events take place all through the year in France, and it is worth taking this into account when planning your itinerary. The following calendar lists events that are held at regular intervals, but it is by no means a comprehensive survey of all the vinous celebrations organized in France. It does not, for example, cover all the *chapitres* of the dozens of wine fraternities, nor the festivals held across the country when the grape harvest is in.

In compiling this list, every effort has been made to achieve the greatest possible accuracy. However, it sometimes happens that in certain years particular events may take place at times other than those indicated here, so it is prudent to check details with regional or local tourist offices, hotels or wine producers.

Details of local wine activities are also given in the Travel Information sections throughout the *Atlas*.

JANUARY

Some time in January	Ampuis (N. Rhône)	Fête des Vins Nouveaus
First weekend	Lire (Anjou)	Wine fair
Saturday after 22 January	Côte d'Or commune	St-Vincent Tournante
Fourth weekend	Vouvray (Touraine)	Wine fair

FEBRUARY

First weekend	Bourgueil (Touraine)	Wine fair
	Vihiers (Anjou)	Wine fair
Second weekend	Saumur (Anjou)	Wine fair
	Tours-Fondettes (Touraine)	Wine fair
Third weekend	Montlouis (Touraine)	Wine fair
Last weekend	Azay-le-Rideaux (Touraine)	Wine fair
	Chalonnes-sur-Loire (Anjou)	Wine fair
Late February	St Pourçain-sur-Sioule (Massif Central)	

MARCH

Early March	Vinsobres (S. Rhône)	Festival and concours Côtes du Rhône Villages
First weekend	Le Loroux-Bottereau (Pays Nantais)	Wine fair
Second weekend	Durtal (Anjou)	Wine fair
Third weekend	Chinon (Touraine)	Wine fair
	Vallet (Pays Nantais)	Wine fair
Last weekend	Machecoul (Pays Nantais)	Wine fair
Last Sunday	Eguisheim (Alsace)	Presentation of new wines

APRIL

Some time in April	Brignoles (Provence)	Wine fair
Second Saturday	Brissac (Anjou)	Concours des Anjou-Rouge
Friday before Palm Sunday	Morey-St-Denis (Côte d'Or)	Carrefour de Dionysos
Weekend of Palm Sunday	Lugny (Mâconnais)	Foire des Vins du Haut-Mâconnais
Palm Sunday	Nuits-St-Georges (Côte d'Or)	Hospices de Nuits wine auction
Around 20 April	Villeneuve-lès-Avignon (S. Rhône)	Fête de St-Marc
Easter	Amboise (Touraine)	Wine fair
	St-Georges-sur-Cher (Touraine)	Wine fair
Around 25 April	Châteauneuf-du-Pape (S. Rhône)	Fête de St-Marc
First Sunday after Easter	Onzain (Touraine)	Wine fair
Late April	Ammerschwihr (Alsace)	Wine fair

MAY

Some time in May	Roanne (Massif Central)	Wine and cheese fair
1 May	Molsheim (Alsace)	Wine fair
	Panzoult (Touraine)	Wine fair
Around 1 May	Bagnols-sur-Cèze (S. Rhône)	Wine festival
Weekend of 1 May	Sancerre (Upper Loire)	Fête du Crottin de Chavignol
Early May	Cravant-les-Coteaux (Touraine)	Wine fair
Second weekend	Valençay (Touraine)	Wine fair
Around 20 May	La Baume-de-Transit (S. Rhône)	Tricastin wines concours
	Mâcon	Wine fair
Ascension Day	Clisson (Pays Nantais)	Wine fair
	Guebwiller (Alsace)	Wine fair
Saturday nearest 25 May	Kintzheim (Alsace)	Fête de St-Urbain
Last weekend	Dorlisheim (Alsace)	Wine festival
Late May	Bouzy (Champagne)	Heures Champenoises
End May/early June	Auch (Armagnac)	Foire aux Eaux-de-Vie d'Armagnac

JUNE

Some time in June	Perpignan (Roussillon)	Salon de la Gastronomie Fête de St-Bacchus
	Vertou (Pays Nantais)	Wine fair
Early June	La Réole (Bordeaux)	Wine fair
	Vendôme (Touraine)	Wine fair
First Sunday	Thouarcé (Anjou)	Alliance des Vins avec le Fromage
Second weekend	Troyes (Aube)	Foire de Champagne
Around 15 June	Pourrières (Provence)	Wine fair
	St-Victor-la-Coste (S. Rhône)	Côtes du Rhône and "heritage" festival
	St-Yzans-de-Médoc (Bordeaux)	Foire aux Sarments
Whitsun	Meusnes (Touraine)	Wine fair
	Sancerre (Upper Loire)	Wine fair

June continued

Late June	Bordeaux	Vinexpo (alternate years: 1989, 91, etc.)

JULY

Some time in July	Elne (Roussillon)	Fête du Vin et des Fruits
First week	Rivesaltes (Roussillon)	Fête de Rivesaltes
	Violès (S. Rhône)	Fête des Vins des Vignerons
First Saturday	Dambach-la-Ville (Alsace)	Cellars open to public
First weekend	Ohrschwihr (Alsace)	Fête du Crémant
	Thésée (Touraine)	Wine fair
Weekend before 14 July	St-Lambert-du-Lattay (Anjou)	Fête de la Vinée
14 July	Barr (Alsace)	Wine fair
	St-Marcel-d'Ardèche (S. Rhône)	Wine festival
Around 14 July	Arbois (Jura)	Fête des Vins d'Arbois
Sunday nearest 14	Lisle-sur-Tarn (Gaillac)	Wine festival
Weekend after 14	St-Aubin-de-Luigne (Anjou)	Fêtes des Vins Millisimés
Sunday after 14	Husseren-les-Châteaux (Alsace)	Fête des Guinguettes
Around 15 July	Gordes (S. Rhône)	Fête des Côtes du Ventoux
	Lézignan-Corbières (Languedoc)	Wine festival
	Vacqueyras (S. Rhône)	Fête des Côtes du Rhône
	Castillon-la-Bataille (Bordeaux)	Wine fair
Second half of July	Duras (Lot-et-Garonne)	Wine fair
Around 20 July	Buisson (S. Rhône)	Wine festival
	Mondragon (S. Rhône)	Wine festival
Third weekend	Rodern (Alsace)	Fête du Pinot Noir
	Sigoulès (Bergerac)	Wine fair
Last but one weekend	Beblenheim (Alsace)	Fête du Sonnenglanz
	Ribeauvillé (Alsace)	Wine fair
	Riquewihr (Alsace)	Fête du Riesling
Last week	Sauveterre-de-Guyenne (Bordeaux)	Wine festival
Last weekend	Kientzheim (Alsace)	Wine festival
	Mittelbergheim (Alsace)	Wine festival
Last Sunday	Verdigny (Upper Loire)	Fête des Grappes Nouvelles
Late July	Amarens (Gaillac)	Wine festival
	Maynal (Jura)	Sud-Revermont wine fair
	Minerve (Languedoc)	Minerve 1210
	Pont St-Esprit (S. Rhône)	Fête des Vins des Côtes du Rhône Gardoises
	St-Aignan-du-Cher (Touraine)	Journée du Vin
	Vire-sur-Lot (Cahors)	Fête des Vins de Cahors
	Wettolsheim (Alsace)	Wine festival
Late July/early August	Ste-Croix-du-Mont (Bordeaux)	Wine fair

AUGUST

Some time in August	Frontignan (Languedoc)	Fête du Muscat
	Narbonne (Languedoc)	Wine fair
	St-Tropez (Provence)	Wine festival

Early August	Estagel (Roussillon)	Wine festival
	Lesparre (Bordeaux)	Wine fair
	Valréas (S. Rhône)	Wine festival and lavender parade
First and second week	Colmar (Alsace)	Wine fair
First weekend	Châteauneuf-du-Pape (S. Rhône)	Fête de la Véraison
	Martigné-Briand (Anjou)	Fête des Fleurs et Vins
	Turckheim (Alsace)	Wine festival
	Westhalten (Alsace)	Wine festival
First Sunday	Bergheim (Alsace)	Fête du Gewürztraminer
	Bué (Upper Loire)	Foire aux Sorciers
	Mittelwihr (Alsace)	Fête des Amandiers
	Monein (Pyrenees)	Wine and fruit show
Around 10 August	Bédoin (S. Rhône)	Fête des Vignerons du Mont Ventoux
	Ruoms (S. Rhône)	Fête des Vignerons Ardèchois
	St Maurice-sur-Eygues (S. Rhône)	Wine festival
First Sunday after 6 August	Fréjus (Provence)	Fête du Raisin
Weekend before 15 August	Gaillac	Cocagne des Vins
Second Sunday	Heiligenstein (Alsace)	Fête du Klevner
Second weekend	Ammerschwihr (Alsace)	Fête du Kaefferkopf
	Bennwihr (Alsace)	Wine festival
	Cénac (Bergerac)	Wine fair
14 and 15 August	Dambach-la-Ville (Alsace)	Fête des Vins de France
15 August	Amboise (Touraine)	Wine fair
	Chinon (Touraine)	Wine fair
	Marlenheim (Alsace)	Mariage de l'Ami Fritz
	Orschwiller (Alsace)	Cellars open to public
	Pouilly-sur-Loire (Upper Loire)	Wine fair
Around 15 August	Chagny (Chalonnais)	Wine fair
	Madiran (Pyrenees)	Wine festival
	Mirabel-aux-Baronnies (S. Rhône)	Festival of wines and olives
	Séguret (S. Rhône)	Festival of wine and of Provence
Weekend nearest 15 August	Obernai (Alsace)	Mini wine fair
Second half of August	St-Chinian (Languedoc)	Wine festival
Last but one weekend	Scherwiller (Alsace)	Art, Artisanat et Riesling
	Gueberschwihr (Alsace)	Cellars open to the public
Last weekend	Sancerre (Upper Loire)	Foire aux Vins de France
	St-Pourçain-sur-Sioule (Massif Central)	Wine festival
	Turckheim (Alsace)	Open days at cooperative
Last Sunday	Eguisheim (Alsace)	Fête des Vignerons
Late August	Visan (S. Rhône)	Wine festival
Late August/early September	Cogolin (Provence)	Wine festival
	La Motte (Provence)	Wine festival

SEPTEMBER

Early September	Cassis (Provence)	Grape harvest festival
	Langon (Bordeaux)	Wine fair
	Meursault (Côte d'Or)	Banée et Trinquée de Meursault

	St-Péray (Central Rhône)	Rhône wine market
	Wolxheim (Alsace)	Fête du Riesling
First Saturday	Mont-Brouilly (Beaujolais)	Wine festival
First Sunday	Arbois (Jura)	Fête du Bijou
	Ribeauvillé (Alsace)	Fêtes des Ménétriers
Second Saturday	Millery (Lyonnais/Beaujolais)	Journée du Vin des Coteaux Lyonnais
Second weekend	Bar-sur-Aube (Aube)	Wine fair
Second or third weekend	Chacé and Varrains (Anjou)	Fête du Champigny
Last weekend	Dahlenheim (Alsace)	Wine festival
	Wuenheim (Alsace)	Wine festival

OCTOBER

Some time in October	Béziers (Languedoc)	Fête du Vin Nouveau
	Le Louroux-Bottereau (Pays Nantais)	Wine festival
Early October	Nantes (Pays Nantais)	Fêtes des Châtaignes et du Vin
Second Sunday	St-Fiacre-sur-Maine (Pays Nantais)	Fête du Muscadet
Around 15 October	Perpignan (Roussillon)	Fête du Vin Nouveau
Third Sunday	Marlenheim (Alsace)	Grape harvest festival
	Obernai (Alsace)	Grape harvest festival
Last weekend	Romanèche-Thorins (Beaujolais)	Fête Raclet

NOVEMBER

Early November	Fleurie (Beaujolais)	Show and sale of Beaujolais-Mâconnais *crus*
First week	Créon (Bordeaux)	Wine fair
First weekend	Nîmes (Languedoc)	Wine fair
Weekend before 11 November	St-Bris-le-Vineux (near Chablis)	Fête du Sauvignon
Second Sunday	Juliénas (Beaujolais)	Wine festival
Around 15 November	Vaison-la-Romaine (S. Rhône)	Wine fair and festival of Primeur wines
Third weekend and following Monday	Vougeot, Beaune, Meursault	Les Trois Glorieuses
Around 20 November	Ste-Cécile-les-Vignes (S. Rhône)	Festival of wine and music
Fourth Sunday	Chablis	Fête du Chablis
Last Sunday	Bois-d'Oingt (Beaujolais)	Concours and show
Late November	Chavanay (N. Rhône)	Wine market

DECEMBER

Some time in December	Cornas (Central Rhône)	Wine market
First Thursday	Ancenis (Pays Nantais)	Wine fair
First weekend	Villefranche (Beaujolais)	Concours des Vins du Beaujolais
Second Sunday	Beaujeu (Beaujolais)	Hospices de Beaujeu auction
Around 15 December	Aire-sur-l'Ardour (Pyrenees)	Wine festival
Third weekend	Régnié-Durette (Beaujolais)	Presentation of wines

THE ATLAS

HOW TO USE THIS ATLAS

France was the first of the wine-producing countries to map its vineyards. Map them, that is, with the purpose of marking out boundaries that would have legal force and would define status and quality. Today, when every wine nation has a system of mapping of greater or lesser complexity, France still stands ahead. It is the country where the place the wine comes from matters most. The better the wine, the more particular are the laws about defining and fixing its home field. In Burgundy this system reaches a pitch of sophistication. Each little plot of vines has its name and status. Other areas paint with a broader brush, but even the Vins de Pays, the newest and most junior rank, have clearly defined zones of origin.

The French appellation system gives pride of place to the concept of *terroir* – the combination of environmental factors, of which soil and site are the two most weighty, which gives a wine its character. It is assumed in this system that any competent person can make wine of a given status in a given appellation. There are quality control tests, to establish if an individual wine is worthy of the appellation, but location is given clear primacy over individual skill. That is the law; the marketplace knows different. It accords certain producers a premium over others. Partly this reflects the fact that one château is better placed than another. Partly it recognizes that Monsieur X makes better, more consistent, wine than Monsieur Y.

The painstaking precision of the French appellation contrôlée system has obvious benefits for the wine drinker. It also is of great help to the traveller, who will be able to visit, and gaze upon, the exact vineyards which are home to the most memorable names and tastes in wine. Great satisfaction can be had from walking, map in hand, along the hillside from which comes one of your favourites. Distinctions which were once academic become suddenly clear. It is possible to see how the colour and texture of the soil changes with the slope, how the low gravel dunes of the Médoc quite obviously have better drainage than the land beside the streams, how the best-known sites in Alsace are tucked into the warm, sunny corners.

There is more to France than wine, and this Atlas attempts to unify the wines of France with the landscape, the culture and the pleasures, gastronomic and otherwise, that await the traveller. It is designed to be a practical, and intended to be an inspiring, companion, both when travelling and when at home.

THE MAPS

This Atlas contains maps of several kinds. They divide into two broad sorts, which are designed to be used both separately and in tandem. First are maps whose prime job is to define vineyards or wine zones, and to show those factors of landscape which influence the position of the vineyards and the wine those vineyards produce. Call these wine maps. They come in widely varying scales and degrees of detail, depending upon the complexity of the story they are drawn to tell. The second sort of maps are touring maps. They are designed for the traveller and for those who wish to put the vineyards into their geographical context.

Each wine map is accompanied by a small key map which both shows where the wine district is, in relation to major features such as towns and rivers, and tells on which pages to find the touring map which covers the same area.

The wine maps are each enclosed by a border which contains a grid. This allows points on the map to be given a letter and number reference, each reference referring to the square extending down and to the right from the points where the lines from the letter and number intersect. Where a wine château, or other property, or a village or town, is listed in either the main index or the lists of producers within the text, these grid references are given.

The maps vary widely in scale and detail, depending upon the complexity of the area. There is a scale bar with each map. Some large areas of countryside with few and scattered vineyards have sketch maps. Here the information to be conveyed does not justify the level of detail of the more formal maps.

Sketch maps are also used for the main Vins de Pays areas: the Midi and the southern Rhône. The Vins de Pays zones overlay the existing appellation and VDQS zones: it is possible to make either, or both, wines from the same land. This makes it impossible to portray the Vins de Pays and the appellations on the same map without ridiculous complexity. The two maps which show the Vins de Pays (pages 238 and 256) cover the same area and are at the same scale as the detailed maps of the same areas (pages 232 and 252) and have the same towns and rivers marked. It is thus possible to crossrefer between the two sorts of map.

The French vineyards are in a constant state of change: Vins de Pays get promoted to VDQS (Vins Délimités de Qualité Supérieure), while the VDQS wines are themselves being phased out and promoted to Appellation Contrôlée. Inevitably, some vineyards have been added to the official lists since the maps in this Atlas were prepared. These include the following new Vins de Pays:

Côte Vermeille (Pyrénées Orientales)
Bessilles (Hérault)
Terroirs Landais (Landes)
Thézac-Pericard (Lot et Garonne – not yet officially recognized).

To crossrefer from the touring maps to the wine maps, in order to have a detailed look at a particular wine region, first refer to the appropriate zone map. The touring maps are grouped by zone, and at the start of each zone a zone key map shows all the wine districts.

A legend for the touring maps appears on page 24.

THE FIVE ZONES

France is a large country and its vineyards are fairly evenly spread over three-fourths of its area. The Atlas therefore divides the country into five zones, named for points of the compass. These zones correspond also to the traditional, and logical, divisions of France and French wine. Thus the Southwest zone, centred on Bordeaux, also covers those wine districts which traditionally traded their wine down the rivers to and through Bordeaux, and which also share the same repertoire of grape varieties. The Northeast brings together Champagne and Alsace, areas which solve the conundrums of a cool climate in subtly differing ways. The East zone links Burgundy with the Jura and Savoie, which both have grape varieties and wine styles in common with their famous neighbour.

To check which zone a wine or a place is in, turn to the zone key map on the next two pages. The two pages after that contain a general map of France and its communications. Then comes a key to the touring maps. Use these two key maps to plan a cross-country journey or a wine tour.

Each zone is self-contained, with a key map displaying the outline geography and the wine zones, a set of touring maps, and wine maps accompanied by text.

The zones are distinguished by a system of colour-coding. This runs right through the Atlas, from the contents page to the individual page numbers. Each zone has its own colour. It is thus possible to see at a glance which section of the Atlas you are in.

The zone key maps show major roads such as autoroutes as well as major towns, rivers and wine zones. The autoroutes include those projected or under construction at the time of going to press in May 1987. Such autoroutes are not numbered on the maps.

THE TEXT

The Atlas is designed to be either read consecutively or to be used for reference. Each of the five zones is divided into chapters on the wine districts, following a logical progression around or through the zone. For each district there is a wine map, an introduction, a directory of châteaux and other wine producers, and a section of travel information. It is both possible and profitable to read the district introductions, one after the other, as a straightforward description of French wine.

TRAVEL INFORMATION

The sections of travel information begin with details of local hotels and restaurants. These lists are not meant to be comprehensive: this Atlas does not attempt to supplant the many excellent existing hotel and restaurant guides. The places described are those which are either known to the authors, or which have been recommended by local wine merchants, château proprietors and other knowledgeable people. To a large extent, therefore, the lists are a guide to places local people use and consider worth telling visitors about.

Hotels and restaurants are graded according to their broad price band, not as the equivalent of a star rating for quality. Remember, too, that ownership, telephone numbers, staff, décor, etc. – and prices – of hotels and restaurants are always subject to change.

Hotels, based on the price of an average double room without breakfast, are graded as:

Class A, luxury, from 350 francs
Class B, average, from 150 to 350 francs
Class C, simple, to 150 francs.

Restaurants are based on the average price of a meal per person, excluding wine and other drinks:

Class A, luxury, from 250 francs
Class B, average, from 150 to 250 francs
Class C, simple, to 150 francs.

In France it is always wise to reserve hotel rooms in advance, and it is preferable to do this by telephone and then confirm by letter. Reserving rooms only by letter can frequently lead to disappointment, especially at the smaller hotels; you may find on arrival that there is no room available after all, or not of the type you asked for. In towns and in the bigger villages ask for a room at the rear, because of traffic noise; the same applies, of course, to country hotels near a main road or motorway. Church bells and town hall clocks, too, can be a remarkable nuisance in small French towns. Most work all night at hourly, if not more frequent, intervals.

When choosing a hotel, take a close look at the map. A recent traveller discovered what appeared to be one of the most peaceful country hotels in central France, with lawns sweeping down to a quiet river bank. The visitor found his discovery to be a little less idyllic at the rear. A railway line on an embankment ran a short stone's throw from the first-floor bedroom windows. Many valleys in the more hilly parts of France accommodate a railway and a road as well as the river. Make sure your hotel is not too close to the former.

Hotels usually hold reserved rooms until a specified time (8.00 p.m. for example). Telephone if you are likely to arrive later. Many hotels require a deposit and it is better to pay this by cheque rather than in cash: a Eurocheque is ideal. At weekends – and certainly at Sunday lunchtimes – it is essential to reserve a table in restaurants. On weekdays, too, it can be a wise precaution to telephone beforehand – if only to make sure that the restaurant in question does not happen to be closed.

In many cases the travel notes in this Atlas also contain information on local gastronomic specialities. It is pleasant to match these with the local wines.

The travel sections continue with (necessarily brief) notes on local places of interest and give, where available, dates of local wine festivals and places where detailed wine information can be sought. A calendar of wine events is on pages 11–13. Nearly every wine district in France has some body, usually a Maison du Vin, with the job of publicizing the local wine. It is to these people that it is best to go to enquire about visiting wine châteaux and about places to taste wine. They will have the most up-to-date information. Their addresses are given in this Atlas where possible. The address of the Syndicat d'Initiative for almost every town in France is given in the annual Michelin Red Guide. The overseas offices of the French Government Tourist Board should also be able to help.

PRODUCERS OF SPECIAL INTEREST

The chapter for each wine district includes a directory which lists the authors' selection of wine producers of special interest. There are hundreds of thousands of people making wine in France, and any selection must be to some extent arbitrary. Those chosen stand out as makers of good examples of the wine of their appellation. They are listed according to

their village, and there is a grid reference to the accompanying wine map if the property or its village is marked on the map. Stars next to the names of producers indicate those the authors consider especially noteworthy. As with hotels and restaurants, properties rise and fall. Owners sell, or retire, and the estate may well perform differently in new hands. Recommendations are given in good faith but must be treated with some caution. For an up-to-date assessment of the quality of many French wine châteaux, consult Hugh Johnson's annually updated *Pocket Wine Book* (*Pocket Encyclopedia of Wine* in the USA).

WINE ROUTES

The majority of the wine maps have marked on them a suggested motoring route around the vineyards. With the larger-scale maps it is also possible to use these routes on foot or on cycle. Some districts have formal routes with signposts and even roadside tasting booths. Others are more reticent, or less organized. Often the locals fear that a formal route will attract too many people (Chablis turned down such a plan for this reason), or local rivalries may make it impossible to agree on a route. In such cases we have suggested a route which takes the traveller through the most interesing and beautiful parts of the district. These routes, be they formal or informal, are marked on the wine maps in green. In some cases, there are descriptions of the route in the Travel Information text.

France has yet to adopt on any scale the German idea of vineyard footpaths. Alsace has some – presumably influenced by geographical proximity – but few exist elsewhere. This is due in part to a French reluctance to allow wandering pedestrians through their vineyards. Signposted paths may be lacking, but it is perfectly possible to penetrate most vineyards via the tracks used by the farmers. Respect, however, the walled vineyards and those obviously fenced off.

WHERE TO GO

This map is designed as a general tour planner. It divides France into five zones, corresponding to the arrangement of the Atlas as a whole. Each zone is covered by larger-scale road maps at the beginning of the relevant section.

WESTERN ZONE

Dominating this part of France is the Loire valley with its long stretch of vineyards. Its wines, characterized by a light, grapey quality, include the delicate rosé of Anjou, the subtly flinty Sancerre and the crisp, tangy Muscadet. The river winds through rich and fertile countryside, past meadows, orchards, historic old towns such as Orléans and Tours, and innumerable fairytale châteaux. To the south of the Loire lie the flat, agricultural lands of Poitou and Berry. The Atlantic coast here has many magnificent beaches, resorts and the romantic old port of La Rochelle.

SOUTHWEST ZONE

The inclusion of Bordeaux makes this the key zone in any wine tour of France. The names of the Bordeaux appellations read like a litany to Bacchus: Pauillac, Margaux, Graves, Sauternes, St-Emilion. Here is an *embarras de richesses* indeed, and much of great beauty to look at as well, including the gracious city of Bordeaux itself. To the east of Bordeaux is the wine region of Bergerac, bisected by the Dordogne river which flows lyrically down from the uplands of Périgord, an area famed for its cuisine. Go 100 kilometres south of Dordogne, and you are in the centre of the Armagnac brandy region, ringed by many intriguing appellations such as Cahors, Gaillac, Madiran and Jurançon. Farther south lie the Pyrenees and the Basque country, and in between is some of the most dramatic scenery in France: thundering gorges, fortresses on rocky pinnacles, hilltop villages – a landscape that mirrors a colourful and often violent history.

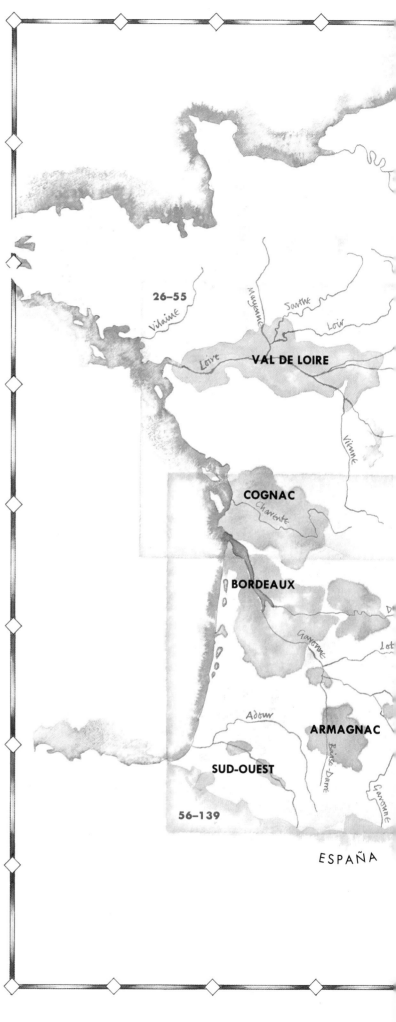

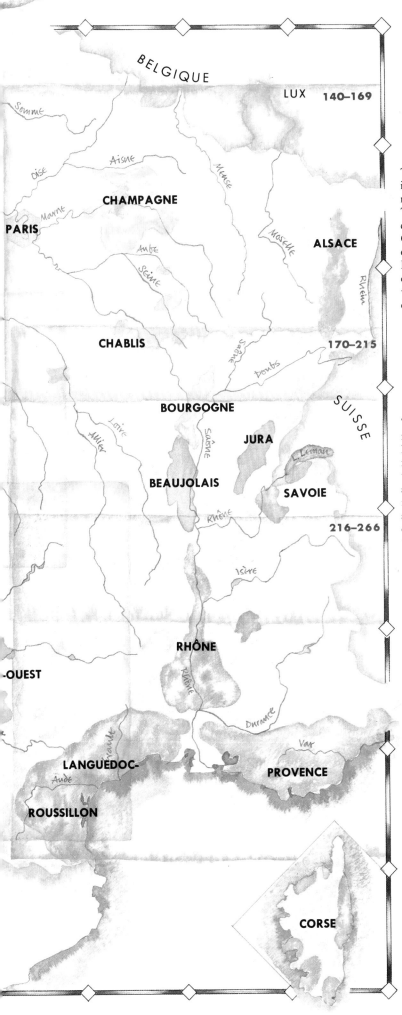

LUX **140–169**

170–215

216–266

NORTHEAST ZONE

Two major winegrowing areas, Champagne and Alsace, are incorporated in this zone. If you drive east from Paris you come first to the Champagne region, which gives its name to the undisputed emperor of sparkling wines. The complex alchemy that goes into its making can be seen at work in the cellars of the great champagne houses, mainly in Reims and Epernay. Going farther east you pass through Lorraine with its forests, lakes and elegant capital, Nancy. Beyond Lorraine lies Alsace, German by heritage, French by adoption, with a style of aromatic white wine that reflects both countries, as does the superb cuisine. Its lively capital, Strasbourg, still wears a charmingly old-world garb. This zone possesses four great Gothic cathedrals – those of Reims, Strasbourg, Metz and Troyes.

EASTERN ZONE

Travel in a diagonal line through this part of France, roughly from northwest to southeast, and you will pass through three main wine regions: Burgundy, Jura and Savoie, as well as experiencing some sharp contrasts in scenery. First comes Chablis, an outpost of Burgundy floating by itself, which produces a renowned white wine. Then comes Burgundy proper and its adjunct, Beaujolais. This is a land of long, lavish meals, countryside now softly pastoral, now rugged, old mellow towns like Beaune and Dijon, and of course many great wines. Carry on to the southeast and the scenery changes. You are in the Jura, a country of swollen rivers, lakes, wooded mountain slopes and a surprising variety of wines. Southeast again, Savoie produces white wine that is clean and fresh like the alpine scenery.

SOUTHEAST ZONE

Down the middle of this part of France the river Rhône, flanked by its famous vineyards, runs between two great uplands. To the east are the French Alps. To the west is the Massif Central, a huge, indulating plateau, wild, pastoral and haunting in its beauty. When it reaches the Camargue the Rhône fans out and flows into the Mediterranean near the great port of Marseille, between two areas where both wine and visual beauty abound. To the east lies Provence, a hilly oblong bounded on the south by the glorious Riviera coast. In the other direction, curving around the coast in a crescent to the border of Spain, is Languedoc-Roussillon, the Midi, where a third of French wine is produced. To the south is the island of Corsica, which in recent years has established itself as a source of good wines.

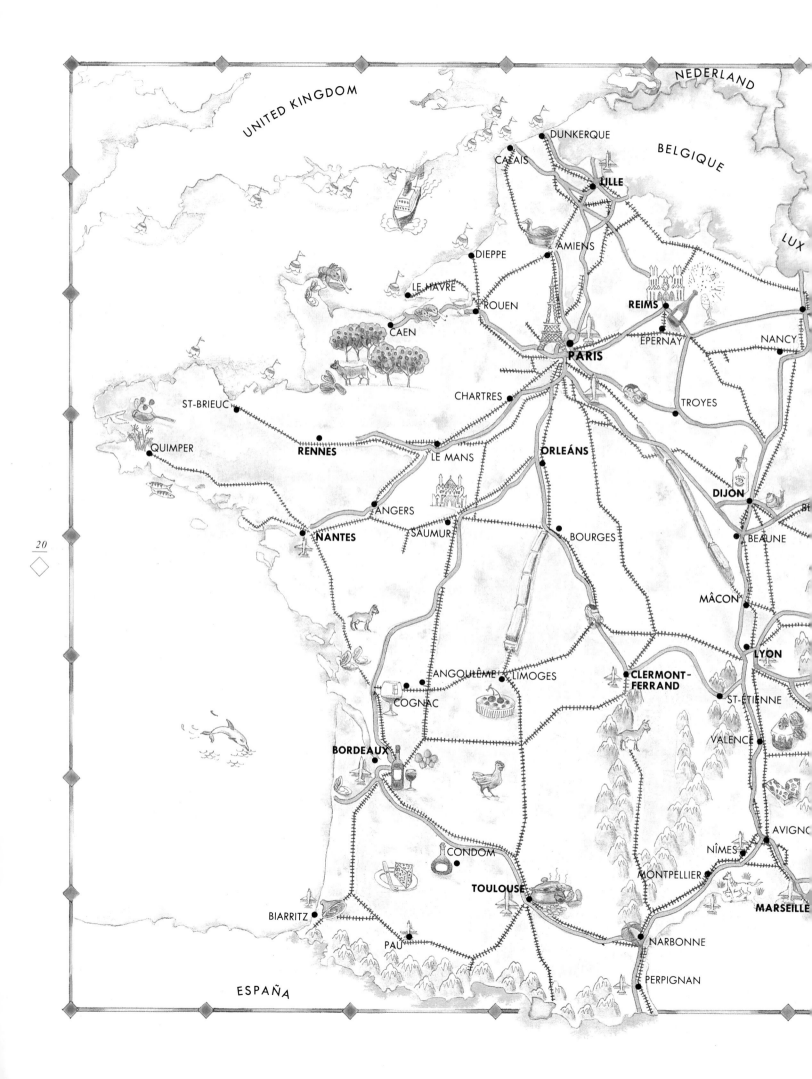

HOW TO GET THERE

France can be explored with ease and pleasure by road, rail, air or combinations of the three. The road system has been augmented in the last decade by a very good system of autoroutes – superhighways which are run by private concerns and which charge tolls. They are numbered with the prefix A. Roads with the prefix N are the *routes nationales*, non-toll highways which often date, in alignment at least, from Napoleonic times. These great roads, often ruler-straight and fringed by avenues of trees, are a legacy of the French predeliction for centralized government. They were designed to speed the passage of the King's – and Emperor's – messengers and soldiers. Consequently they tend to radiate from Paris. N roads are often crowded, more so than the autoroutes: not all traffic is prepared to pay the tolls.

Lesser roads are organized on a département basis and carry the prefix D. Some D roads are as straight and wide as many Ns, others are purely local routes. Study of the maps will show that some D roads provide attractive routes parallel to the main roads. For instance, the busy N7 follows the east bank of the upper Loire on its way from Paris to Lyon. Just across the river is another, less-frequented route made up of a chain of D roads. Such roads require a little more navigation, yet are more relaxing, more scenic and more rewarding than the *camion*-infested Ns.

The French are occasionally disposed to renumber their road system, with consequent confusion as maps and signboards fail to agree. Before planning a journey, invest in an up-to-date single-sheet map of French main roads: all the major map publishers issue them.

Travel in France becomes very difficult in high summer, especially at the weekends at the start and finish of August. It pays to avoid these periods, but if you have to travel, look out for the specially signposted holiday routes. These are diversions around known traffic black-spots. One runs east of Paris, for instance, taking traffic from the north on its way south around rather than through the capital.

Visitors from countries such as the UK and the Netherlands are often pleasantly surprised by how empty France, and French roads, can seem. It is a large country with a relatively small population, and many roads. Driving in France has a somewhat different flavour. The often straight roads, the fairly long distance between towns and the lack of traffic allows for distances to be covered at a pleasant, rhythmic pace. Many travellers find that a judicious mixture of autoroutes for speed and selected lesser roads for interest is an excellent way of covering distances in France.

Not all French roads, especially D roads, have impeccable surfaces, although conditions are much improved compared to a decade ago. This is perhaps an argument against overloading the car. It is still the practice among commercial drivers to stop for an extended lunch, which means that the roads have fewer heavy trucks between noon and 2 pm.

Speed limits are rigorously enforced and police have power to levy on-the-spot fines. Up-to-date information about speed limits, frontier formalities, road conditions and new roads can be obtained from the French National Tourist Office (offices in many capital cities) and motoring organizations.

The map, left, shows autoroutes in the course of construction as well as those open. Check the detailed maps in each zone section.

Rail services take the traveller to most parts of France. The ultra-fast TGV trains run from Paris to Lyon in two hours; to Nice in seven; and to many of the other major wine-growing regions. A network of car-carrying trains allows northerners to cross France to the Riviera or the Midi in a single night. The French rail company, SNCF, offers various tourist fares which allow unlimited travel for a set period. The SNCF has offices in major capitals abroad. It also has attractive schemes for renting cars and bicycles at stations.

Air Inter, the French national domestic airline, serves the airports marked on the map. Airports with extensive overseas connections include Paris, Nice, Strasbourg, Lyon, Bordeaux and Marseille.

For those for whom time is not a problem, the French navigable rivers and canals provide an entrée to the heart of rural France. These waterways are still in use by commercial barges, but pleasure boats can be hired and several companies run canal cruises in sybaritically equipped converted barges.

DEUTSCHLAND

RASBOURG

LHOUSE

BASEL

ÖSTERREICH

SUISSE

NEVE

ITALIA

OBLE

NICE

TOULON

CORSE

TOURING MAP KEY

The touring maps in this Atlas are designed for use by motorists and other travellers. They show the French road and rail network in considerable detail and also give a clear idea of relief by the use of hill-shading.

The key map on these pages allows identification of the various map spreads. Each page carries a colour-coded page number allowing instant identification of the zone it partly covers (see page 16 for information on the zone system).

The next two pages show a complete legend giving guidance on the symbols used on the touring maps.

The maps are at a scale of 1:750,000.

The five zones in this Atlas cover the following wine areas:

WESTERN ZONE

The Loire:
Pays Nantais,
Anjou, Saumur, Touraine,
Pouilly, Sancerre.

SOUTHWEST ZONE

Bordeaux
The Médoc: Margaux,
The Central Médoc, St-Julien,
Pauillac, St-Estèphe,
The Northern Médoc.
Bourg, Blaye, Graves,
Sauternes, Barsac,
Entre-Deux-Mers,
Premières Côtes
de Bordeaux,
St-Emilion, Pomerol,
Fronsac, Côtes
de Castillon,
Côtes de Francs.
Cognac, Bergerac,
Lot-et-Garonne.
Côtes du Frontonnais,
Côtes de Duras,
Côtes du Marmandais,
Buzet, Cahors.
Gaillac, Armagnac,
Madiran, Jurançon,
Béarn.

NORTHEAST ZONE

Champagne, The Aube,
Alsace,
Lorraine.

EASTERN ZONE

Burgundy: Chablis,
Santenay, Chassagne-
Montrachet, Puligny-
Montrachet, Meursault,
Volnay, Pommard, Beaune,
Savigny, Aloxe-Corton, Nuits-
St-Georges, Vosne-Romanée,
Vougeot, Chambolle-Musigny,
Gevrey-Chambertin, Fixin,
The Chalonnais, Mâconnais,
Beaujolais, Jura, Savoie.

SOUTHEAST ZONE

The Rhône: Hermitage,
Côte Rôtie, Condrieu,
Cornas, Châteauneuf-du-Pape,
Lirac, Tavel, Côtes du Rhône.
Provence, Languedoc:
Minervois, Corbières,
Fitou. Roussillon,
Corsica,
Vins de Pays.

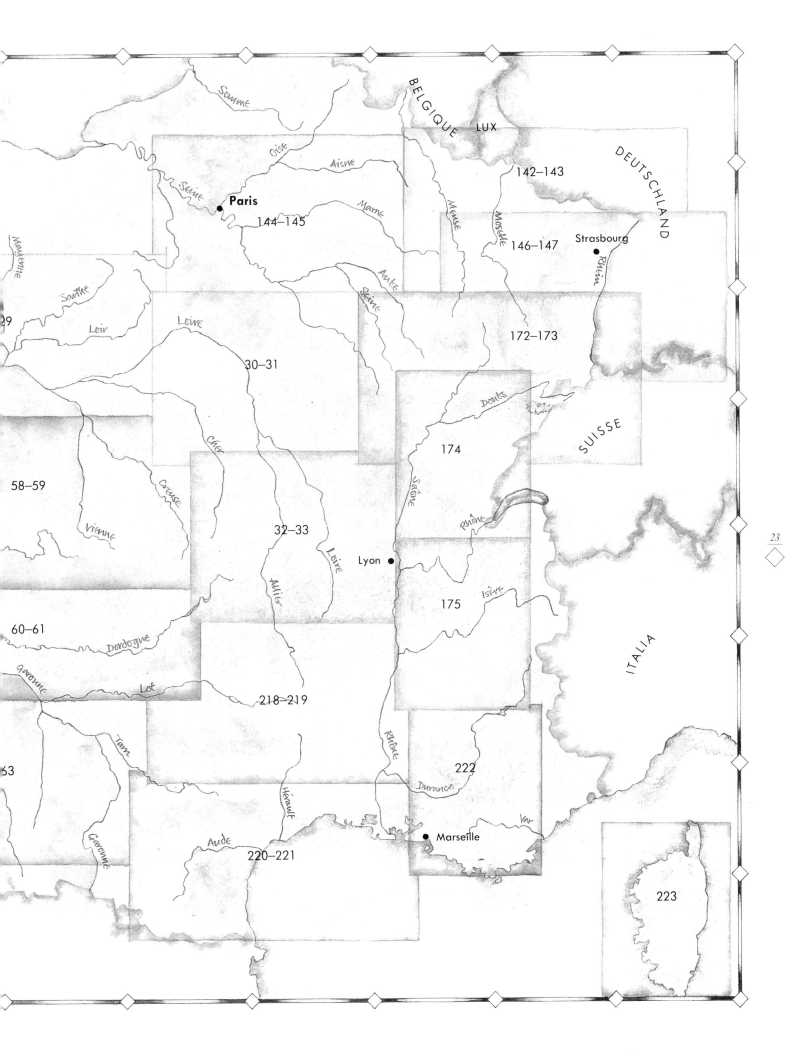

TOURING MAP LEGEND

Straßen / Roads — Routes / Strade

German	English	Symbol	French	Italian
Autobahn mit Anschlußstelle	Motorway with junction	le Mans-Est	Autoroute avec point de jonction	Autostrada con stazione
Autobahn in Bau	Motorway under construction	Datum, Date / Date, Data	Autoroute en construction	Autostrada in costruzione
Autobahn in Planung	Motorway projected	Datum, Date / Date, Data	Autoroute en projet	Autostrada in progetto
Autobahn-Nummer	Motorway number	A10	Numéro d'autoroute	Sigla ufficiale di autostrada
Raststätte mit Übernachtungsmöglichkeit	Road-side restaurant and hotel	ℍ	Hôtel	Area di ristoro in autostrada con motel
Raststätte ohne Übernachtungsmöglichkeit	Road-side restaurant	ℝ	Restaurant	Area di ristoro in autostrada
Verkaufskiosk	Snackbar		Buffet	Barosco
Tankstelle	Filling station		Poste d'essence	Stazione di rifornimento
Straße mit zwei getrennten Fahrbahnen	Dual carriage-way		Route à chaussées séparées	Strada a due carreggiate (4 corsie)
Straße mit zwei getrennten Fahrbahnen in Bau	Dual carriage-way under construction	Datum, Date / Date, Data	Route à chaussées séparées en construction	Strada a due carreggiate in costruzione
Durchgangsstraße	Thoroughfare		Route principale	Strada di grande comunicazione
Durchgangsstraße in Bau	Thoroughfare under construction	Datum, Date / Date, Data	Route principale en construction	Strada di grande comunicazione in costruzione
Wichtige Hauptstraße	Important main road		Route de commun. importante	Strada di interesse regionale
Wichtige Hauptstraße in Bau	Important main road under construction	Datum, Date / Date, Data	Route de commun. importante en construction	Strada di interesse regionale in costruzione
Hauptstraße	Main road		Route de communication	Strada principale
Hauptstraße in Bau	Main road under construction	Datum, Date / Date, Data	Route de communication en construction	Strada principale in costruzione
Sonstige Straßen	Other roads		Autres routes	Altre strade
Sonstige Straßen in Bau	Other roads under construction		Autres routes en construction	Altre strade in costruzione
Straßentunnel	Road with tunnel	⟶	Route avec tunnel	Galleria stradale
Europastraßen-Nummer	European road number	E06	Numéro de route européenne	Numero di strada europea
Straßen-Nummer	Road number	N7 49	Numéro de route	Numero di strada statale
Fernkilometer	Very long distances	180	Distances très grandes	Grandi distanze in Km.
Großkilometer	Long distances	49	Distances grandes	Medie distanze in Km.
Kleinkilometer	Short distances	10	Distances courtes	Brevi distanze in Km.
Kleinkilometer an der Autobahn zwischen den Anschlußstellen	Short distances along the motorway between junctions	12	Distances courtes sur l'autoroute entre points de jonctions	Brevi distanze in Km. tra le stazioni autostradali

Sonstige Verkehrswege / Other means of communication — Autres voies de communication / Altre vie di comunicazione

German	English	Symbol	French	Italian
Fernverkehrsbahn	Main line railway		Chemin de fer: ligne à grand trafic	Ferrovia principale
Übrige Eisenbahnen	Secondary line railway		Chemin de fer: ligne à trafic secondaire	Ferrovia secondaria
Bergbahn	Mountain railway		Chemin de fer de montagne	Ferrovia a cremagliera
Sessellift	Chair-lift		Télésiège	Seggiovia
Autoverladung per Bahn	Transport of cars by rail		Transport de voiture par chemin de fer	Trasporto auto per ferrovia
Autofähre	Car ferry	●	Bac pour automobiles	Traghetto per auto
Schiffahrtslinie	Shipping route		Ligne de navigation	Linea di navigazione
Kanal	Canal		Canal	Canale

Touristische Hinweise / Directions for tourists — Renseignements touristiques / Indicazioni turistiche

German	English	Symbol	French	Italian
Besonders sehenswertes Objekt	Place of particular interest	Reims	Curiosité très intéressante	Località particolarmente degna di nota
Sehenswertes Objekt	Place of considerable interest	Orléans	Curiosité intéressante	Località degna di nota
Landschaftlich besonders schöne Strecke	Beautiful scenery		Parcours pittoresque	Percorso pittoresco
Touristenstraße	Tourist route	Route des Crêtes	Route touristique	Strada di interesse turistico
Straße gegen Gebühr befahrbar	Toll road		Route à péage	Strada a pedaggio
Straße für Kfz. gesperrt	Road closed to motor traffic	××××	Route interdite aux véhicules à moteur	Strada vietata ai veicoli a motore
Zeitlich geregelter Verkehr	Temporal regulated traffic		Circulation réglementée	Traffico permesso ad ore stabilite
Paß mit Höhen- und Steigungsangabe, Wintersperre	Pass with height and gradient, closure in winter	1650 8% XI-IV	Col avec cote d'altitude et montée, fermeture en hiver	Passo con indicazione altimetrica, pendenza, chiusura invernale
Bedeutende Steigungen	Important gradients	15%	Montées importantes	Pedenze importanti
Bergspitze mit Höhenangabe	Mountain summit with height	2963	Pic avec cote d'altitude	Cima, altitudine in metri
Ortshöhe	Height above sea level	(630)	Cote d'altitude de la localité	Località, altitudine in metri
Besonders schöner Ausblick	Important scenic view		Point de vue remarquable	Punto panoramico
Nationalpark	National park		Parc national	Parco nazionale
Sperrgebiet	Prohibited area		Champ de Tir	Zona vietata
Grenzen	Boundaries		Frontières	Confine

Maßstab · Scale · Echelle · Scala 1 : 750 000

0 5 10 20 30 40 km
5 10 15 20 25 miles

24

Signaturen
Conventional signs

Kirche Church	
Kirchenruine Church ruin	
Kloster Monastery	
Klosterruine Monastery ruin	
Schloß, Burg Palace, castle	
Schloß-, Burgruine Palace ruin, castle ruin	
Denkmal Monument	

Signes conventionnels
Altri segni convenzionali

Eglise Chiesa	
Église en ruines Rovine di chiesa	
Monastère Monastero	
Monastère en ruines Rovine di monastero	
Château, château-fort Castello, Fortezza	
Château en ruines Rovine di castello o fortezza	
Monument Monumento	

Wasserfall Waterfall	
Höhle Cave	
Ruinenstätte Ruins	
Sonstiges Objekt Other object	
Campingplatz Camp site	
Jugendherberge Youth hostel	
Parador, Pousada Parador, Pousada	
Verkehrsflughafen Airport	
Landeplatz Airfield	

Cascade Cascata	
Grotte Grotta	
Ruines Rovine	
Autre objet Altri punti d'interesse	
Terrain de camping Campeggio	
Auberge de jeunesse Ostello per la gioventù	
Parador, Pousada Parador, Pousada	
Aéroport Aeroporto importante	
Aérodrome Aeroporto turistico	

THE DEPARTEMENTS OF FRANCE

France is divided for local government purposes into départements. All addresses include a postal code. These codes each start with two digits which refer to the département. They appear on labels and can be a useful clue to where a *vin de table* comes from — or at least where it was bottled.

WESTERN ZONE

The more modest wines of the greater part of this territory go by the evocative name of Vins de Pays du Jardin de la France. The garden of France is the Loire valley: placid, fertile, long cultivated and marvellously adorned with the castles and palaces of France's kings and queens.

A glance at the map shows the dominance of Paris to the north, sending its tentacles of highways south and west. In former times the Loire itself was the main route; travellers from Paris went south to Orléans to take a ship to Tours or Angers, or farther to Nantes and thence to Brittany or La Rochelle.

North of Nantes, with its immensely productive Muscadet vineyards, the vine gives way to the apple; south of it, good wine to thin stuff fit only for distilling into cognac. Nantes is the ocean's own vineyard, making the perfect wine for its perfect seafood; one of the happiest gastronomic marriages in France.

The lower Loire has long traditions for making sweet and surprisingly strong wines from the Chenin Blanc; wines that must be counted among France's very finest, rare though they are. Elsewhere on this map, only the little upstream outposts of Sancerre and Pouilly, growing their strong-scented Sauvignon, have any widespread reputation.

Where the Creuse and the Vienne drain the northern Massif Central, the most celebrated contribution to gastronomy is not from vines but from oaks: this is the country of the great forests of the Limousin, Tronçais and Allier, whose pungent planks season not only the great red and white wines of Burgundy and Bordeaux, but every self-respecting California or Australian wine, and not a few in Italy and Spain.

VINS DE PAYS

1 Retz
2 Marches de Bretagne
3 Charentais
4 Coteaux du Cher et de l'Arnon

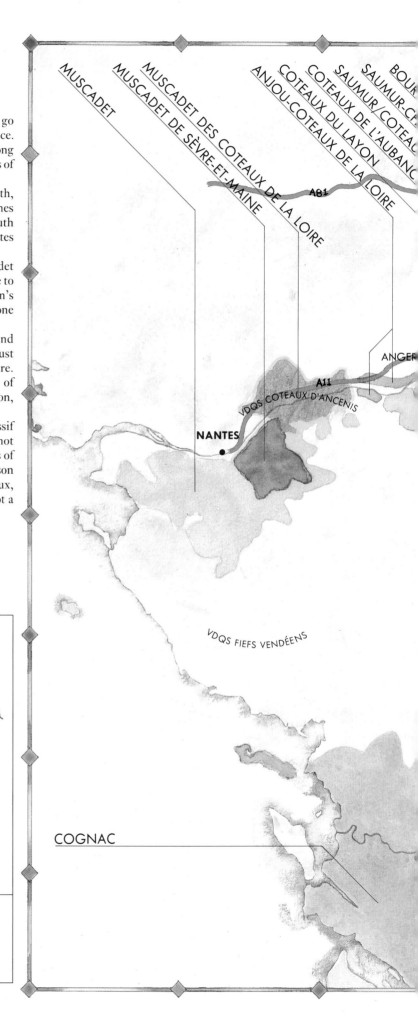

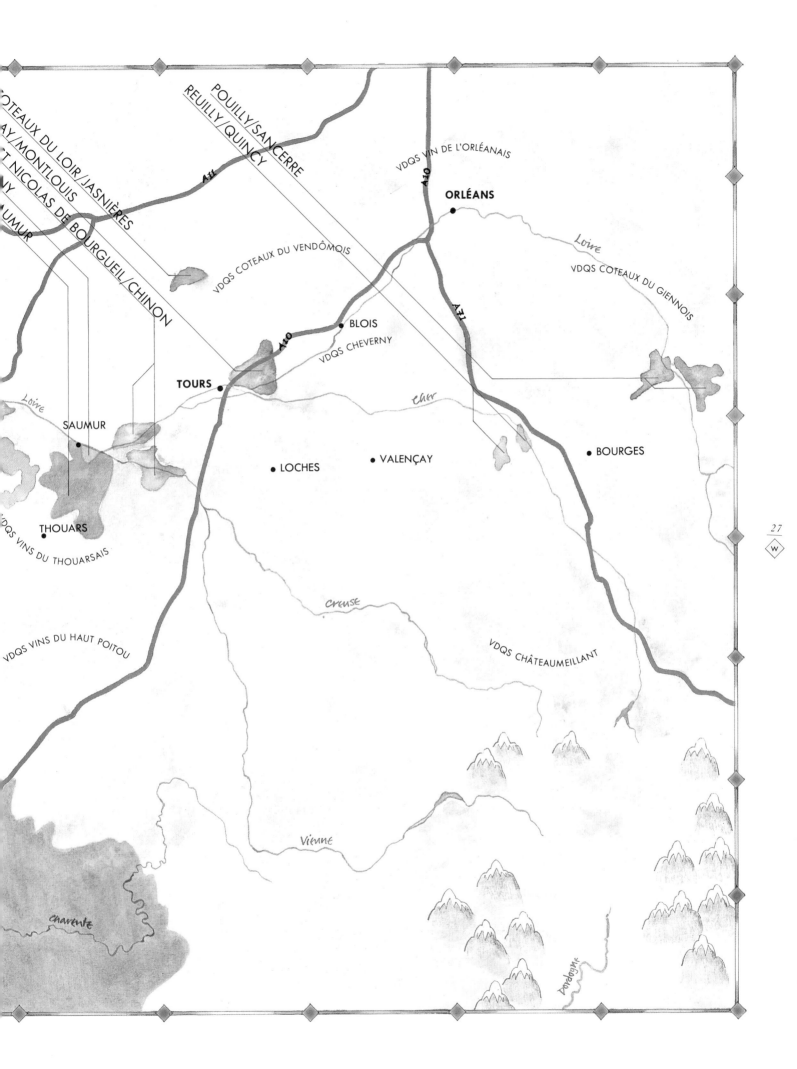

COTEAUX DU LOIR/JASNIÈRES

AY/MONTLOUIS

T NICOLAS DE BOURGUEIL/CHINON

AUMUR

POUILLY/SANCERRE

REUILLY/QUINCY

VDQS VIN DE L'ORLÉANAIS

A10

ORLÉANS

Loire

VDQS COTEAUX DU GIENNOIS

VDQS COTEAUX DU VENDÔMOIS

A11

A10

BLOIS

VDQS CHEVERNY

A71

TOURS

Loire

Cher

SAUMUR

• **BOURGES**

• LOCHES

• VALENÇAY

VDQS VINS DU THOUARSAIS

THOUARS

Creuse

VDQS CHÂTEAUMEILLANT

VDQS VINS DU HAUT POITOU

Vienne

Charente

Dordogne

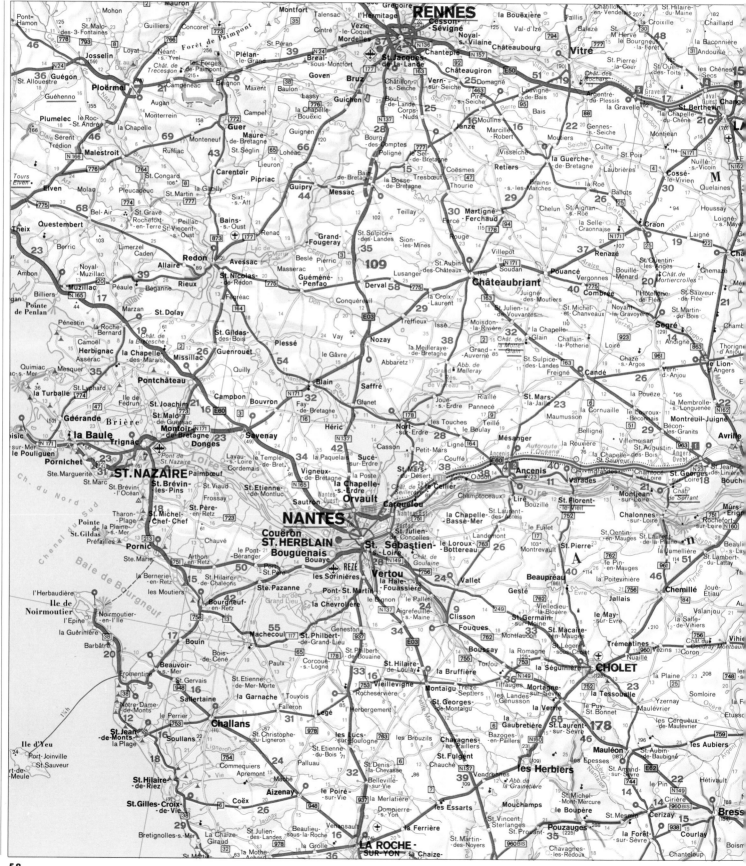

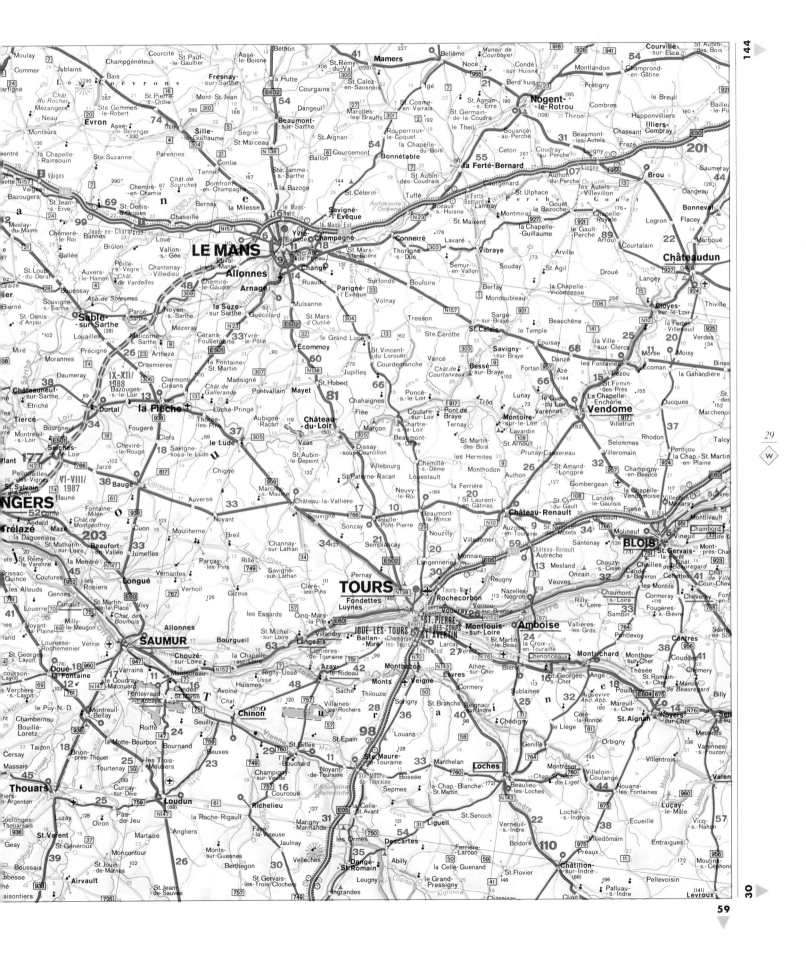

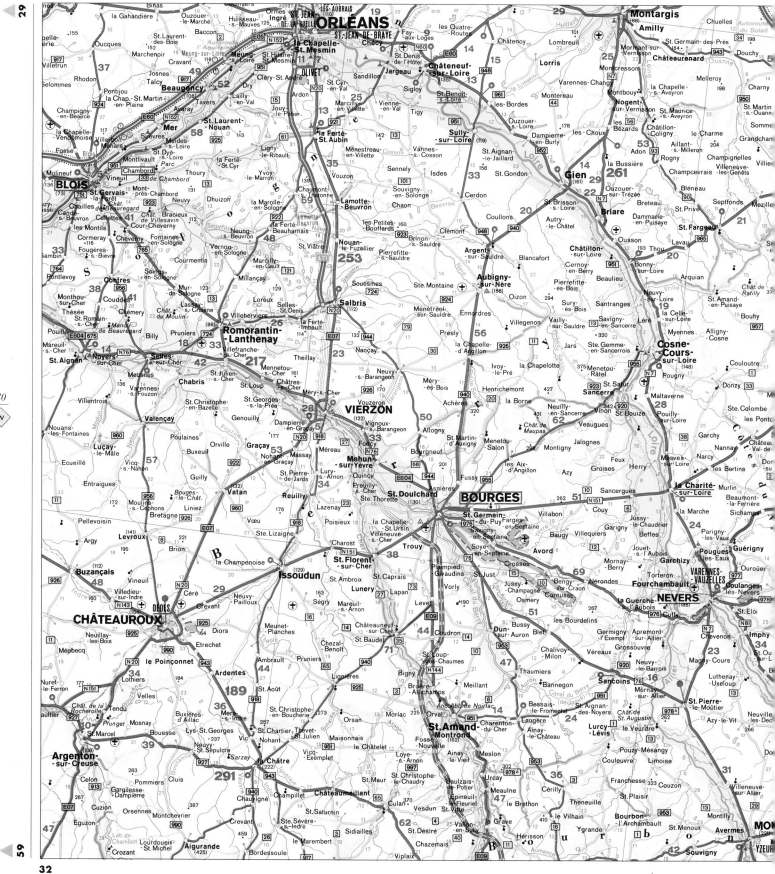

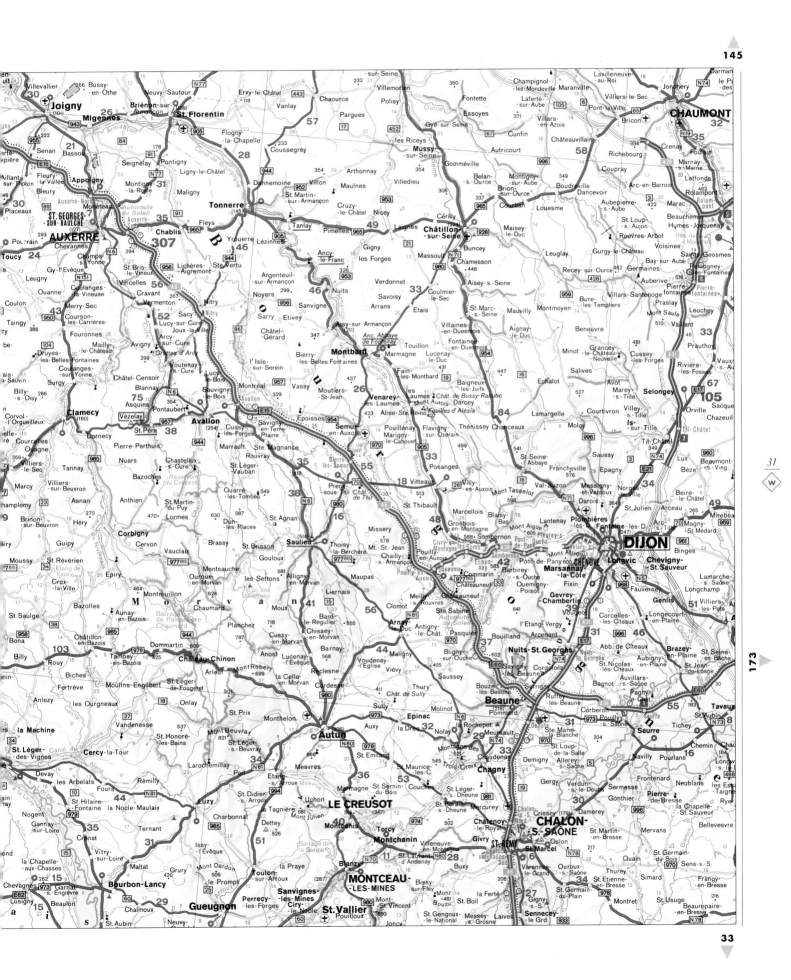

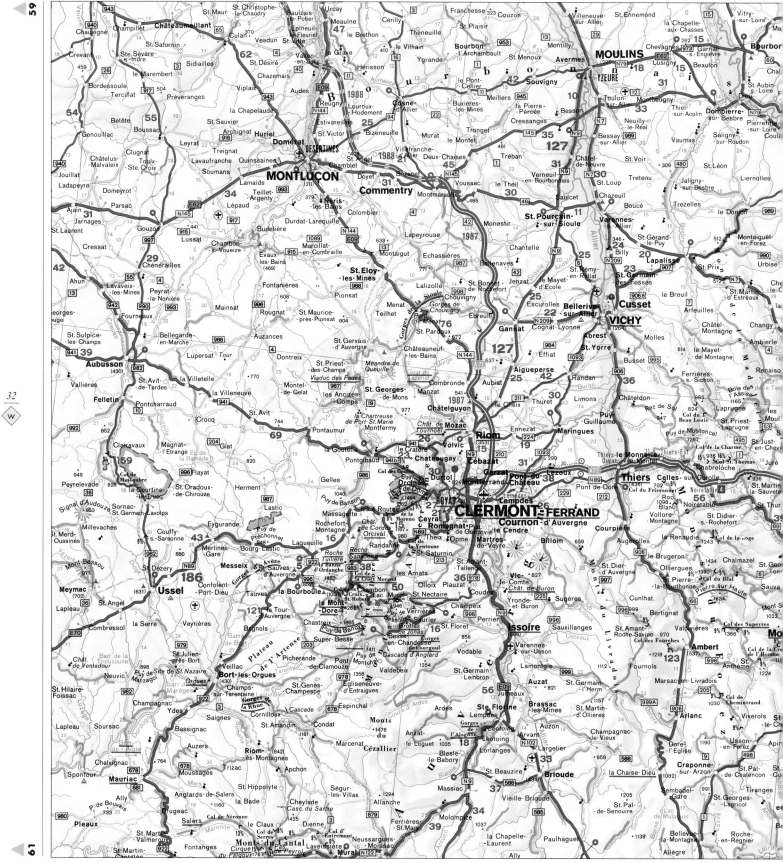

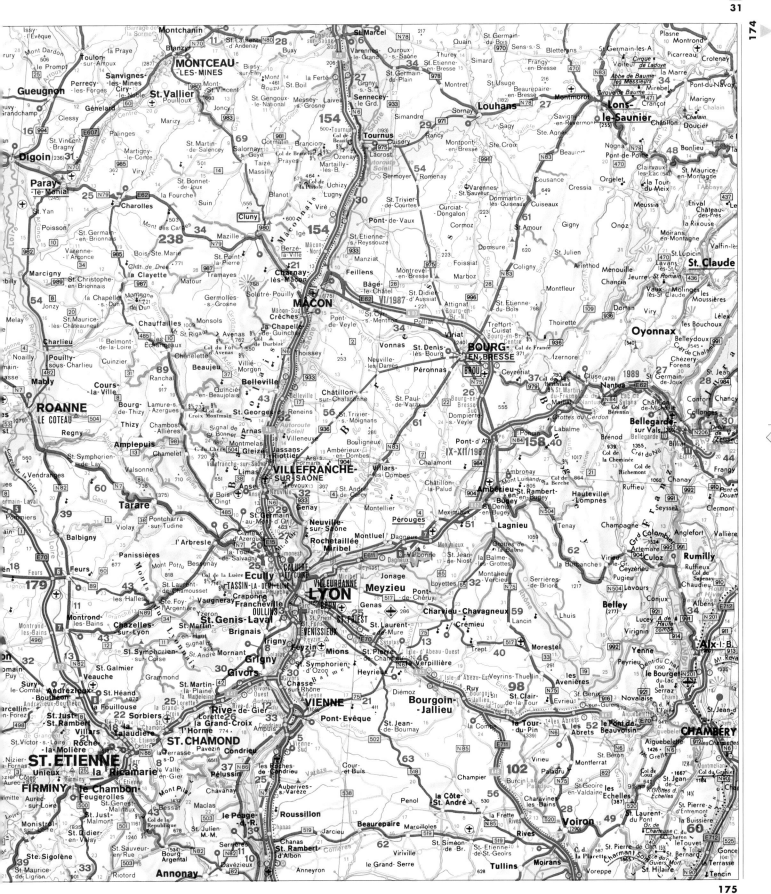

THE LOIRE

The river Loire is the connecting thread of a whole swathe of northern and central France, and of more than 80 wines, ranging from sea-sharp Muscadet to mellow, unctuous Anjou. It rises high in the Ardèche, quite a way to the south of Lyon and close to the valley of the Rhône. Its major tributary, the Allier, rises farther south still, in the mountains which fringe the Gard and the Languedoc plain. The Loire's great sweep north then west takes it past many of the great historic cities of France. It begins its course on the edge of the Midi, washes the frontiers of Normandy and reaches the sea on the edge of Brittany.

The Loire is the royal river of France. Its ample forests, benign climate and rich farmlands attracted the kings of France who built themselves first hunting lodges, then châteaux, along its banks. Nobles and courtiers followed, turning the valley into an architectural treasury. The most remarkable châteaux date from the French Renaissance period when Francis I (1515–47) built Chambord and Amboise. Amboise was where Leonardo da Vinci died after being lured to France by the royal patron.

Today the valley keeps its royal, rural peace. It is a land for lovers of tranquillity, little changed from 130 years ago when Flaubert summed up the Loire as having "in a word, more good sense then grandeur, and more wit than poetry. C'est la France!"

For most of its course the Loire flows through unspoiled agricultural country. The farming is of cattle and crops, orchards and fields of grain. Vineyards are scattered and, in proportion to the woods, fields and meadows, sparse. In few places do the Loire vineyards resemble, in scale and dominance of the countryside, those of Bordeaux or Champagne. Rarely, too, do the vineyards crowd close to the river in the manner of the Mosel or the Rhine. This is a different kind of river in a different kind of valley: a northern stream, a river of gravelly shallows, willow trees, water meadows and rapids. It is inclined to flood, spreading across wide areas of land in early spring when the snow melts in the mountains. Consequently the villages and towns are either set back from the river or perched on the few points where high ground provides a flood refuge and a bridging point. The vineyards are in side valleys or at the edge of the flood plain.

It may seem to stretch a point to ascribe unity of taste and style to the wines from such a wide band of country. But there is a discernible link. The wines of the Loire have in common a cool, northern character, an affinity with apples rather than olives, cream rather than pungent herbs. It is a character stemming from latitude and the pervasive influence of the ocean, blowing warm but cloudy weather far inland from the Bay of Biscay, reaching as far east as Pouilly and Sancerre. Bordeaux, to the south, is warmer. Burgundy, to the east, is more "continental" in its weather, more prey to cold east winds in winter and spring, and enjoying more intense heat in the summer. The Loire climate is an ideal one for the making of wine, with sufficient warmth yet without the intense, drying heat of the south or the high risk of late spring frosts of Champagne and Burgundy.

Most Loire wine is white, in part because red grapes have to struggle to ripen in these latitudes, in part due to a tradition of selling white wine for distilling. The region has collected grape varieties from its neighbours to the southwest and east, and has developed one of its own, Chenin Blanc, often called Pineau de la Loire by local growers, although it has no connection with the Pinot family, and none with the various other Pineaus which crop up across the country. Nowhere else in the world does Chenin perform such wonders. It makes a range of wines, from fresh and steel-dry to densely sweet, and is the foundation of the Saumur sparkling-wine industry.

Sauvignon shows its character on the chalk soil of Sancerre, and is spreading in Touraine, and Cabernet Franc, here vinified on its own rather than in the classic Bordeaux blend, makes soft yet brisk and flavourful reds. Chardonnay is intruding into countryside once the preserve of Chenin, and making some interesting wines as well as contributing to some Crémant de Loire *cuvées*. Gamay makes red wines in Touraine which never quite seem to manage the brisk fruitiness of their Beaujolais cousins. Malbec, also known as Cot, is a more successful Loire red grape and is often blended with Cabernet Franc.

The region's ability to offer an alternative for every course on the menu makes the Loire section a welcome one on a wine list. The sparkling wines of Saumur and Vouvray offer apéritifs, with the higher-quality Crémant de Loire in the same role. Anjou's dry Chenin Blanc wines, especially Savennières, go well with food and can also be enjoyed alone. Muscadet's marriage with seafood is perfect, and for richer fish dishes there are Sancerre, Pouilly-Fumé and the more solid Muscadets. The underrated medium-to-sweet Vouvrays partner food well, especially when the dish is rich with the cream-based sauces found in these parts.

The sweet whites fall into two classes. The gentle, sharp-but-sweet wines of the Coteaux du Layon and Coteaux de l'Aubance are enjoyable young and cold, on their own or with simple food. The grander Bonnezeaux and Quarts de Chaume wines, touched in good years with noble rot, partner the Loire's incomparable fruit – and the local specialities, fruit tarts and pies. Or, like all great sweet wines, they can be drunk on their own.

Fashion plays casually with Loire reputations and prices. Muscadet is an example of a wine unknown outside its home départements a generation ago, yet now sold worldwide – and sometimes taken rather too seriously by its promoters and buyers. Sancerre is another, a Parisian restaurant success, responding to the modish call for a white both dry and strong in personality. Anjou rosé is travelling in the opposite direction, damned by a fashionable trend away from pink wine. Vouvray, too, is in the doldrums: consumers will not take the trouble to understand its variability.

The Loire offers a wide field for the explorer, both of wine lists and of countryside. There are many appellations which are hard to find outside the region. Very little Quincy ever leaves its département, or Jasnières, or Coteaux de l'Aubance. In the process of exploration, the visitor will also find plenty of good food to go with the wines. Fish from the rivers and the sea, early vegetables from the rich valley farmlands, game from the woods, fruit from the orchards; all are used by chefs who inherit a rich tradition. The Loire's royal overlords demanded the best.

This part of France provides the gastronomic "defence in depth" so typical of the whole country: good peasant fare based on local ingredients, more refined bourgeois cooking with a regional slant, and then, at the pinnacle, a kind of aristocratic *cuisine naturelle* which dates back to Francis I. The king, fired by his Italian adventures, brought back more than a taste for culture and castles. He introduced gardeners armed with then-exotic plants such as lettuce, artichokes and peas. The new vegetables flourished, nurtured by the mild climate and stimulated by the demands of a hungry court. Today, the market gardens of the Loire supply the Parisian markets – and the local restaurants – with the best of produce.

The Travel Information sections in the pages that follow give guidance on some of the Loire's hotels and restaurants where this gastronomic exploration can be carried on. But there are many, many more places where an unpromising façade can conceal surprising delights. Look out, too, for the château-hotels that are becoming more common in France. Country hotels have their charms, but few visitors can resist the chance to stay in a genuine castle.

This, too, is the countryside for the vineyard visitor. There are few showplaces, apart from the sparkling-wine cellars of Saumur, which are admirably organized on the Champagne model. More, here, it is a question of following a *vente directe* sign to a small family cellar, tasting and buying wines which never see a shop. Most of the Loire growers operate on a small scale. The private client is central to them: often the same customers, vintage after vintage, drive down from Paris at bottling time to taste, discuss, assess and buy. To join in this pleasant process is a very happy form of commerce.

It is common practice, and followed here, to divide the Loire into four main zones. Working from west to east, from mouth to source, there comes first the Pays Nantais, the Muscadet country. Then comes Anjou-Saumur, then without a break Touraine. The Upper Loire, the fourth zone, is more fragmented, with the major concentration of vines around the twin towns of Sancerre and Pouilly. Beyond these four are outliers such as the Massif Central and Haut-Poitou away to the south.

Above: fishing boats on the lower Loire.

Far left: the château of Azay-le-Rideau.

Left: the little tributary the Layon gives its name to one of the great sweet wine districts of Anjou.

THE PAYS NANTAIS

Grapes have been grown in the Pays Nantais, the area around the town of Nantes, since Roman times, although for centuries the wines were of only local importance. This changed in the seventeenth century when the Dutch discovered that the district was a potential supplier of wines for distilling: production increased, techniques improved and the wines began to be exported. Gradually, too, the emphasis changed from red to white wines, a process that was dramatically accelerated by the notorious winter of 1709, when all the vines were killed by frost.

In the following decades almost all the vineyards were replanted with white grapes, mainly the Melon de Bourgogne which locally acquired the name Muscadet – like its wine. According to the words on a simple plaque ("Ici Berceau du Muscadet"), the first vines were planted in May 1740 at Château de la Cassemichère in La Chapelle-Heulin.

The Muscadet is an early-ripening grape that can usually be harvested in September and sometimes as early as August, before the autumn rains begin. The light structure of Muscadet wine (12.3 percent alcohol is the legal maximum) and its naturally low acidity make it liable to oxidation, so to keep the wine as fresh as possible it is often bottled *sur lie*. This means that after fermentation the new wine is not transferred to clean barrels or tanks but is left lying on its sediment (the *lie*) and from there is bottled in the spring, keeping its contact with oxygen to a minimum and at the same time extracting the maximum flavour from the grapes.

A good Muscadet *sur lie* may be very slightly sparkling from its carbon dioxide so that it tingles pleasantly on the tongue. It matches *fruits de mer* perfectly. The wine is characteristically dry, fresh and clean, light but not thin. Some Muscadets can also develop surprisingly well in bottle for up to four or five years.

About 85 percent of the Muscadet vineyards lie east and southeast of Nantes in the Sèvre et Maine district, and this is where the best wines are produced. The countryside here is gently hilly, the roads narrow and winding, the villages small and the churches often large. The climate is so mild that magnolias, fig trees and Mediterranean pines flourish in the parks and gardens. A second district, much smaller, stretches along the banks of the Loire producing Muscadet des Coteaux de la Loire. Finally there is simply Muscadet without further definition.

As well as the various Muscadets, the Pays Nantais also makes other

▲ The Lac de Grand-Lieu in the wide, flat country southwest of Nantes supplies freshwater fish, as an alternative to Atlantic seafood, to go with the local Muscadet and Gros Plant du Pays Nantais wines.

wines. The biggest in volume is Gros Plant du Pays Nantais, a simple white wine with high acidity from the Gros Plant grape (the local name for the Folle Blanche). As with Muscadet, the better Gros Plant wines are usually bottled *sur lie*.

Around Ancenis are the vineyards of Coteaux d'Ancenis, the appellation of a modest quantity of simple, uncomplicated wines, most of them light red and rosé from Gamay and a little Cabernet.

South of the Muscadet area is the Vendée, where rosé and red wines are also made, sold under the name Fiefs-Vendéens.

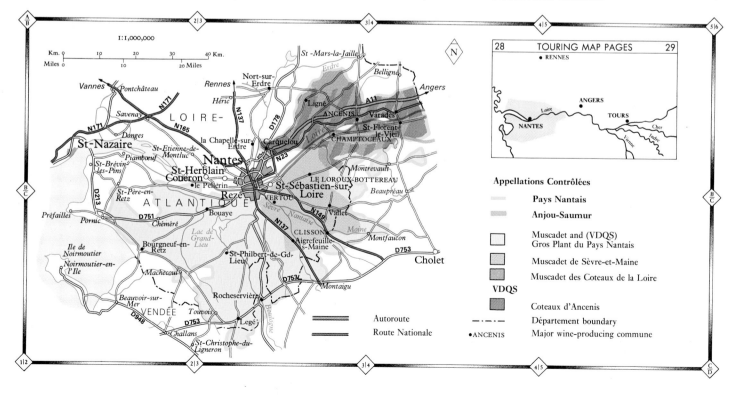

TRAVEL INFORMATION

Nantes is the capital of Brittany, so it is not surprising that the hotels and restaurants provide an abundance of fish and shellfish. Freshwater fish (salmon, pike) are also served, often with *beurre blanc*, a speciality of Nantes. The white wines of the region make an excellent accompaniment.

HOTELS

Auberge de la Lande St-Martin, 44115 Clisson, tel. 40 80 00 80. Well-appointed hotel, set among the vineyards. Sometimes rather noisy at weekends (with wedding parties, etc). The restaurant's menu includes well-prepared eel dishes and duck. Class B.

Abbaye de Villeneuve, 44400 Les Sorinières, tel. 40 04 40 25. Luxurious hotel in what was an 18th-century abbey, with a swimming pool and good cooking (including fresh Loire salmon). Hotel class A; restaurant class A/B.

RESTAURANTS

Auberge de Bel Air, 44150 Ancenis, tel. 40 83 02 87. On the road to Angers. Pleasant surroundings and service; fish specialities. Class C.

Mon Rêve, La Divatte, 44115 Basse-Goulaine, tel. 40 03 55 50. Restaurant by the river; the pike is excellent. Class C.

La Bonne Auberge, 44190 Clisson, tel. 40 78 01 90. Inventive dishes such as *filet de bar rôti aux huîtres*. Inexpensive lunch menu on weekdays. Class B.

La Mangeoire, 16 Rue des Petites-Ecuries, 44000 Nantes, tel. 40 48 70 83. Sturdy cooking (*pot au feu*) and regional wines. Class C.

Les Maraichers, 21 Rue Foure, 44000 Nantes, tel. 40 47 06 51. One of the best seafood restaurants in Nantes. Class B.

Delphin, 44470 Pont de Bellevue, tel. 40 25 60 39. Highly regarded restaurant on the Loire (try the *estouffade de turbot au Muscadet*) and an extensive wine list. Class B.

Le Manoir de la Comète, 44230 St-Sebastien-sur-Loire, tel. 40 34 15 93. In a large 19th-century manor with park and terrace. Excellent but affordable. Class B.

PLACES OF INTEREST

Ancenis Attractive little town on the river Loire where France and the Duchy of Brittany signed the treaty in 1468 by which Brittany lost its independence. Only parts of the castle where the treaty was signed remain. An impressive suspension bridge spans the river at Ancenis.

Champtoceaux Just downstream from Ancenis on the D751; has an atmospheric ruined castle with two 15th-century towers.

Clisson At the confluence of the Sèvre Nantaise and the Maine. The castle dates from the 14th century and has a wine-tasting hall.

Haute-Goulaine The splendid Château de Goulaine, just southeast of Nantes near Vertou, is the showpiece of the Muscadet region and a historic monument. It was built between the 15th and 18th centuries on the foundations of an older castle. The Marquis de Goulaine produces wine from the vineyards that surround the château.

Nantes There are more attractive towns than Nantes, but the centre is interesting. In the cathedral of St-Pierre-et-St-Paul there is the marble tomb of Francis II and his wife, and Château Ducal, near the cathedral, has three museums: the Musée des Arts Decoratifs, the Musée d'Art Populaire (folklore and costume) and the Musée de la Marine (which shows the history of the port, including the slave trade which brought prosperity to Nantes in the 18th century). The Musée Jules-Verne (3 Rue de l'Hermitage) has mementos of the writer's life and work, and the Musée des Beaux-Arts has a rich collection of paintings by artists including Georges de la Tour, Monet and Rubens.

WINE ACTIVITIES

The region is well provided with wine fairs and festivals:

First weekend in March In Le Loroux-Bottereau.

Third weekend in March (The region's biggest) in Vallet.

Last weekend in March In Machecoul.

Ascension Day In Clisson.

June In Vertou.

Beginning of October Fête des Chataignes (chestnuts) et du Vin in Nantes.

Second Sunday in October Fête du Muscadet in St-Fiacre-sur-Maine.

October Wine festival at Le Loroux-Bottereau.

November Foire de Nantes.

First Thursday in December Wine fair in Ancenis.

The Ordre des Chevaliers de Bretvins has been active since 1948; Les Gastronomes de la Mer was founded some 20 years later.

WINE INFORMATION

There is a Maison des Vins at La Haye-Fouassière, just southeast of Nantes on the N149.

PRODUCERS OF SPECIAL INTEREST

LA CHAPELLE-HEULIN, postcode 44330

Donatien Bahuaud*: Négociants marketing the carefully selected Le Master de Donatien, Château de la Cassemichère and other brands.

HAUTE-GOULAINE, postcode 44115

Marquis de Goulaine: Established at the stately Château de Goulaine (see Places of Interest).

LA HAYE-FOUASSIERE, postcode 44690

Domaine de la Louveterie*: The Landron family make very pure wines, including a Cuvée Prestige.

ST-FIACRE-SUR-MAINE, postcode 44690

Chéreau-Carré*: Distributes the estate wines from the Chéreau and Carré families. Among them are the Muscadets from Domaine du Bois Bruley, Château de Chasseloir, Château du Coing de St-Fiacre and Grand Fief de la Cormeraie; **Domaine de Gras-Moutons/Jean Dabin*; Louis Métaireau*:** Louis Métaireau has brought together a group of like-minded growers who select and sell their wines under the Métaireau brand name. They also bought Domaine du Grand Mouton. For sheer class, Métaireau wines are outstanding.

▲ A well-preserved 14th-century feudal keep dominates the little town of Clisson in the south of the Sèvre-et-Maine Muscadet district.

MOUZILLON, postcode 44330

Michel Chiron*: Excellent Clos des Roches Gaudinières; **Marcel-Joseph Guihoux*; Guilbaud Frères*:** Energetic small firm with wines that include a number of good ones from its own estates.

LE PALLET, postcode 44690

Château de la Mercredière; Marcel Sautejeau: Négociant whose own Domaine de l'Hyvernière is first class.

ROSNAY, postcode 85320

Etienne Boureau; Roger Galerneau; Gilles Jard (all for Fiefs Vendéens).

ST-COLOMBAN, postcode 44310

Château de la Roulière*: Fine Muscadet and Gros Plant.

ST-GEREON, postcode 44150

Domaine Guindon*

VALLET, postcode 44330

Joseph Hallereau*; Château la Noë*: One of the few châteaux in Muscadet, a graceful mansion built in 1836, where Jean de Malestroit produces attractive wines; **Sauvion & Fils/Château du Cléray*:** The Sauvion family produce their own elegant château wine. They also market very pure, lively Muscadets from individual estates (Les Découvertes, Lauréat, Cardinal Richard). The Sauvion Muscadets are of a very high average standard. (Another Sauvion product is Les Geneviève: Muscadet grapes soaked in *eau-de-vie* and coated in chocolate.)

VIX, postcode 85770

Domaine de la Chaignée/Mercier Frères* (Fiefs Vendéens).

ANJOU

▲ Moonrise over the western Loire. The river here is broad, although its many sandbanks make navigation difficult. Before the railways the river was, despite the drawbacks, a major highway. Boats voyaging upstream used enormous sails and the west winds from the Atlantic to stem the current.

No other Loire region offers such a wide choice of wines as Anjou. Many different districts, some only the size of a largish Bordeaux vineyard, produce dry, medium-dry and sweet white wines, as well as various kinds of rosé, red and sparkling wines. In all, Anjou has some 25 appellations, most of them south of the river Loire and the capital Angers. The countryside is as varied as the wines. Pleasant hills alternate with stark tufa ridges; green pastures and vineyards with woods, orchards and flower nurseries (the village of Doué-la-Fontaine is as famous for its roses as for its wines).

In terms of volume, Rosé d'Anjou is the most important still wine, closely followed by the rosé Cabernet d'Anjou. Both are semi-sweet, but for Cabernet d'Anjou nobler grapes are used (Cabernet Franc and Cabernet Sauvignon) and the production requirements are more strict. There is also a dry rosé, Rosé de Loire, a reasonably priced, light and refreshing summer wine. Because interest in rosé is declining, an increasing number of growers are producing red Anjou. The usual version is most often made from Cabernet Franc; Anjou Gamay is made exclusively from Gamay, the Beaujolais grape. The growing interest in red Anjou is reflected in the creation in 1986 of a new appellation, Anjou Villages. The region also produces considerable quantities of white Anjou, although the classic light, sweet Anjou Blanc is increasingly being replaced by wines made by modern methods that are dry and rich in fruit. The name Anjou also appears on bottles of sparkling white and rosé wines.

Southwest of Angers, Rochefort-sur-Loire (which is no longer on the river) is the gateway to the Coteaux du Layon. This region's speciality is naturally sweet wines from overripe grapes. The growers of the Layon valley, like those of the Sauternes district of Bordeaux, hope the grapes (Chenin Blanc, here called Pineau de la Loire) will be affected by "noble rot". A good Coteaux du Layon displays a perfect balance between sweetness and acidity and is usually further improved by maturing for a long time in bottle. Wines of great years may require a decade or two of patience. At their best, they have a fresh, grapey fragrance with floral tones and an aroma of ripe fruit such as apricots or peaches. Sometimes there is a hint of hazelnuts and spice. But the rich and creamy sweetness of a Sauternes is rarely reached, which is why, in the district itself, Coteaux du Layon wines accompany fish and poultry rather than sweet desserts.

The better types of Coteaux du Layon are allowed to use the name of their commune on the label. These are the wines of Beaulieu-sur-Layon, Chaume (the lowest production per hectare and often the highest quality), Faye-d'Anjou, Rablay-du-Layon, Rochefort-sur-Loire, St-Aubin-de-Luigné and St-Lambert-du-Lattay. There are also two Crus: the enclaves of Quarts de Chaume and Bonnezeaux, where small quantities of elegantly sweet wines with extraordinary keeping qualities are made. East of Layon flows the small and unassuming river Aubance, whose banks are lined with vineyards. Among the wines produced here is Coteaux de l'Aubance, a pleasant, mild white wine that just lacks the class to be really exciting. Anjou Coteaux de la Loire (which comes from 11 villages west of Angers) is very similar.

In Saumur and the surrounding area there are a great number of wine firms, large and small. Some handle wines from the whole Loire valley, but most produce exclusively sparkling wines. As in Champagne, the sparkle is induced by a secondary fermentation in bottle. This method was introduced in 1811 by Jean Ackerman, who had worked in Champagne and then moved to Saumur where he founded the firm Ackerman-Laurance. In 1975, sparkling Saumur – always called "Saumur d'Origine"

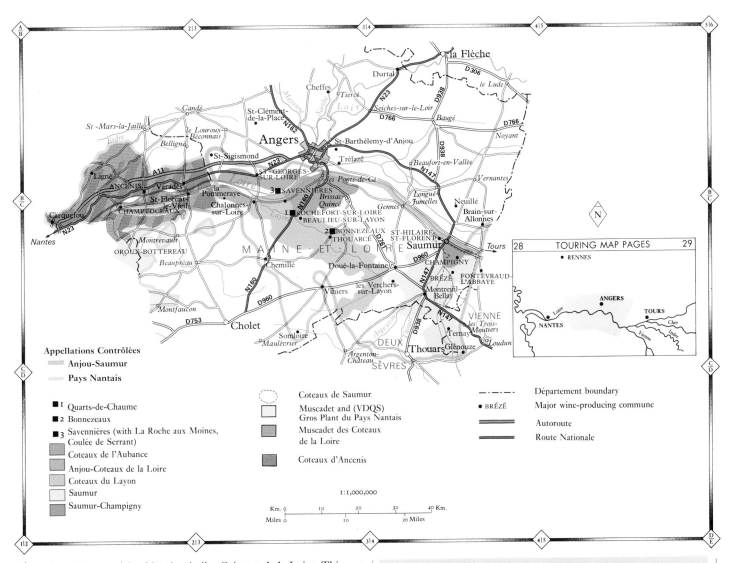

Appellations Contrôlées

░ Anjou-Saumur
░ Pays Nantais

■1 Quarts-de-Chaume
■2 Bonnezeaux
■3 Savennières (with La Roche aux Moines, Coulée de Serrant)
▨ Coteaux de l'Aubance
▨ Anjou-Coteaux de la Loire
▨ Coteaux du Layon
▨ Saumur
▨ Saumur-Champigny

◌ Coteaux de Saumur
▨ Muscadet and (VDQS) Gros Plant du Pays Nantais
▨ Muscadet des Coteaux de la Loire
▨ Coteaux d'Ancenis

–·–·– Département boundary
● BRÉZÉ Major wine-producing commune
══ Autoroute
══ Route Nationale

TOURING MAP PAGES

1:1,000,000

on the label – was joined by the similar Crémant de la Loire. This may originate not only in the 93 Saumur *mousseux* communes but may also be produced from grapes from the whole of Anjou and Touraine. The millions of bottles of wine produced every year in and around Saumur are normally stored in tufastone caves and many firms conduct guided tours for visitors. There is also a still white Saumur, rarely exciting but at its best an excellent fresh apéritif or party drink.

More often worthy of attention is the red wine of the district, the Saumur-Champigny produced in the seven communes, where it forms two thirds of the harvest. This often richly coloured, supple and slightly fruity wine is the best red in Anjou.

The Savennières district on the north bank of the Loire is justifiably famous, in spite of its very restricted size, for it is the birthplace of superb dry white wines. Often unforthcoming and acidic when young, with age they acquire a refined smoothness and their bouquet develops a subtly nuanced charm. The two Savennières Crus are Coulée de Serrant and La Roche-aux-Moines. Around the town of Thouars and the Thouet valley there is a small wine region that could have been part of Anjou if the wine growers had not preferred independence in 1936. These wines are called Vins du Thouarsais. The whites have more to offer than the reds or rosés. Farther south again, in the département of Vienne, is Haut-Poitou, a wine district that is rising fast. Under the guidance of the well-equipped cooperative at Neuville-de-Poitou the wines have greatly improved in quality. The white wines are from Sauvignon, Chardonnay and Chenin Blanc, the reds from Gamay and the rosés from the Cabernets.

TRAVEL INFORMATION

Freshwater fish such as chad, pike and salmon are prepared and served in a variety of ways in Anjou. Freshwater crayfish are also often on the menu, and the charcuterie – pork sausages, pâtés and hams – and poultry are delicious.

HOTELS

Hotel d'Anjou, 1 Boulevard Foch, 49000 Angers, tel. 41 88 99 55. Centrally located with modern comforts (including double glazing). The rather aggressively chic restaurant has a number of fish dishes on the menu and a wide range of regional wines. Hotel class A/B; restaurant class B.
Campanile, 49400 Bagneux, tel. 41 50 14 40. Straightforward comfort. Restaurant. Class B.
Auberge du Thouet, 49400 Chacé, tel. 41 50 12 04. Rural simplicity in a wine village near Saumur. Restaurant. Class B/C.

La Prieuré, 49350 Chênehutte-les-Tuffeaux, tel. 41 50 15 31. Luxury hotel a few kilometres northwest of Saumur via the D751 and D161. Most of the rooms are in the old priory; avoid the rather dreary bungalows. Pleasant views of the river and the surrounding countryside, swimming pool and excellent light (and expensive) cuisine. Class A.
Relais du Bellay, 49260 Montreuil-Bellay, tel. 41 52 35 50. Comfortable, with a swimming pool. Class B.
Le Bussy, 49730 Montsoreau, tel. 41 51 70 18. Pleasant place to stay; many rooms look out on to the local château. Class B.
Grand Hotel, 49190 Rochefort-sur-Loire, tel. 41 78 70 06. Pleasant but certainly not grand. A good base from which to visit the Coteaux du Layon and Savennières vineyards. Restaurant. Class B.
Anne d'Anjou, 31 Quai Mayaud,

49400 Saumur, tel. 41 67 30 30.
Fairly recent hotel in a beautiful
building. Very comfortable. Class B.

RESTAURANTS

Le Quéré, 9 Place de Ralliement,
49000 Angers, tel. 41 87 64 94. The
best restaurant in Anjou, named after
its Breton owner/chef Paul le Quéré.
His wife is responsible for the
excellent wine list. Class B.
Le Toussaint, 7 Rue Toussaint,
49000 Angers, tel. 41 87 46 20.
Recommended for regional cuisine at
its best. The building is 18th century,
the interior rustic, and there is a good
choice of wines. Class B.
Auberge de l'Abbaye, 49590
Fontevraud l'Abbaye, tel. 41 51 71 04.
Traditional cooking and surprisingly
agreeable prices. Class C.
La Licorne, 49590 Fontevraud-
l'Abbaye, tel. 41 51 72 49. Small
restaurant offering sophisticated
dishes. Class A.
Hostellerie de la Porte St-Jean,
49260 Montreuil-Bellay, tel.
41 52 30 41. Regional dishes and
wines, served in a dining room with a
beamed ceiling. Class C.
Jeanne de Laval, 49350 Les
Rosiers-sur-Loire, tel. 41 51 80 75.
Very good regional dishes (Loire
salmon with *beurre blanc*) and a
brilliant range of wines. Garden and
terrace. Also a deluxe hotel.
Restaurant A/B; hotel class A.
La Toque Blanche, 49350 Les
Rosiers-sur-Loire, tel. 41 51 80 75.
Typical of the many restaurants in
France where you can eat well for
little money. Class C.
Le Gambetta, 12 Rue Gambetta,
49400 Saumur, tel. 41 51 11 13.
Good food and fresh ingredients. The
menu usually has dishes prepared
with wines of the region. Class C.
Le Pullman, 52 Rue d'Orléans,
49400 Saumur, tel. 41 51 31 79.
Amusingly fitted out as a railway
carriage. Plenty of fish on the menu.
Class C.

PLACES OF INTEREST

Angers Known as "the black town"
because many of the old houses were
built of the local slate. The largest
and most important monument is the
Château du Roi René, a 13th-century
castle protected by walls and 17 high
round towers. Inside the castle walls
there is a 15th-century chapel, a large
garden (with vines) and the richest
collection of tapestries in the world,
including the 14th-century
"Apocalypse", the longest tapestry in
France. Near the castle is an old
quarter of the town and the cathedral
of St-Pierre (12th to 13th century).
The Musée Jean Lurçat (on the north
bank of the Maine, at 4 Boulevard
Arago) contains contemporary

tapestries and in the 12th-century
cellars there is a Musée du Vin.
Bagneux Near a garden and café
there is an enormous dolmen built of
20 blocks of granite.
Beaulieu-sur-Layon Panoramic
view of the river Layon. Also wine
tastings.
Brissac-Quincé The 17th-century
Château de Brissac is one of the
tallest in France. Many of the 150
rooms are richly furnished and wines
can be tasted in the cellars.
Dénezé Caves with more than 200
carvings.
Doué-la-Fontaine Medieval
quarries are now used as an
amphitheatre ("Arènes"). There is
also a zoo and a Musée des Vieux
Commerces.
Fontevraud-l'Abbaye A former
abbey with tombs of the
Plantagenets, including the great
Queen Eleanor of Aquitaine. There is
a beautiful abbey church and
remarkable kitchens in the 12th-
century octagonal Tour d'Evrault.
Louresse-Rochemenier
Underground cave dwellings, now
used as a museum.

▲ Above: the château of Saumur
broods over the little riverside town.
◄ Left: children in fancy dress for a
parade pose before Angers cathedral.

Montreuil-Bellay A small town on
the river Thouet, with ancient houses
and a magnificent partly feudal castle.
Montsoreau Picturesque little town
on the Loire.
Les Ponts-de-Cé On the river just
south of Angers. As well as the ruins
of a castle there is a Musée des
Coiffes d'Anjou (regional dress).
St-Georges-sur-Loire The stately
Château de Serrant (16th to 18th
century) has a magnificent interior,
with Flemish tapestries and a library
of 10,000 books.
St-Hilaire-St-Florent On the
Anjou-Saumur boundary: many wine
firms such as Ackerman-Laurance,
Veuve Amiot and Langlois-Chateau
have their headquarters here.

Saumur A splendid battlemented
14th-century castle dominates the
town and the surrounding
countryside. It houses two museums:
the Musée des Arts Décoratifs
(tableware, tapestries, etc) and an
equestrian museum, the Musée du
Cheval (the cavalry school with its
famous Cadre Noire is at Saumur).
In the centre of Saumur there are
half-timbered houses, a magnificent
16th-century town hall and two
Romanesque churches, both
containing Gobelin tapestries.
Savennières Church with 10th-
century side porch. On the Ile de
Béhuard near by in the Loire is a
hamlet with a 15th-century chapel
built partly into the rock.
Turquant The Moulin de la
Herpinière, a restored windmill,
houses a small wine museum.

WINE ACTIVITIES

First weekend in January Wine
fair in Liré (close to Ancenis; see
Pays Nantais).
First weekend in February Wine
fair in Vihiers.
Second weekend in February Wine
fair in Saumur.
Last weekend in February Wine
fair in Chalonnes-sur-Loire.
Second weekend in March Wine
fair in Durtal.
Second Saturday in April
Competition for Anjou-Rouge wines
in Brissac.
First Sunday in June Alliance des
Vins de Thouarcé et de Bonnezeaux
avec le Fromage, in Thouarcé.
Weekend before 14th July Fête de
la Vinée in St-Lambert-du-Lattay.
Weekend after 14 July Fête des
Vins Millésimés in St-Aubin-de-
Luigné.
First weekend in August Festival
des Fleurs et Vins in Martigné-
Briand.
**Second and third weekend in
September** Fête du Champigny in
Chacé and Varrains.
   The oldest fraternity in the district
is La Confrérie des Chevaliers du
Sacavin, founded in 1904 (Anjou
wines). There are also la Confrérie
des Vignerons de la Canette
(southern Anjou), La Confrérie des
Fins Gousiers d'Anjou (Coteaux du
Layon, Coteaux de l'Aubance), La
Commanderie du Taste-Saumur
(Saumur) and La Confrérie des
Hume-Piot du Loudunois (southern
Saumur). Haut-Poitou has La
Confrérie Vineuse des Tire-Douzils.

WINE INFORMATION

Information can be obtained from the
Maison du Vin de l'Anjou (5bis Place
Kennedy, Angers) or the Maison du
Vin de Saumur (25 Rue Beaurepaire,
Saumur).

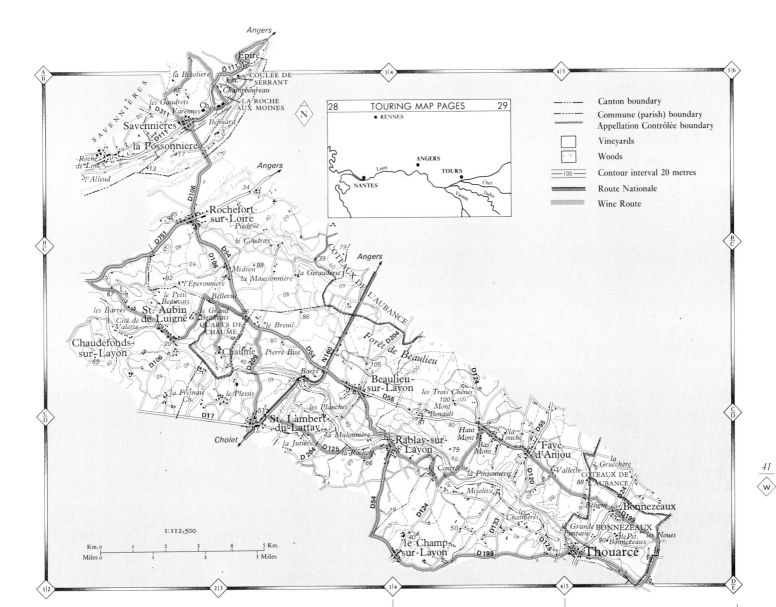

PRODUCERS OF SPECIAL INTEREST

ANJOU

DOUE-LA-FONTAINE,
postcode 49700, 39 C4

Vignobles Touchais*: Mature white Anjou, including the legendary Moulin.

MOZE-SUR-LOUET, postcode 49190

Domaine Richou*

LE PUY-NOTRE-DAME,
postcode 49260

Henri Aupuy/Clos de l'Abbaye*

LA VARENNE, postcode 49270

Aubert Frères Wine merchants.

COTEAUX DU LAYON

BEAULIEU-SUR-LAYON,
postcode 49190, 39 C3, 41 C3

Domaine Pierre-Bise*; Domaine de la Soucherie*.

CHAVAGNES-LES-EAUX,
postcode 49380

Domaine du Petit Val*: Excellent Bonnezeaux.

ROCHEFORT-SUR-LOIRE,
postcode 49190, 39 C3

Domaine des Baumard*: Biggest producer of Savennières. Also the excellent Coteaux du Layon Clos Ste-Catherine and a beautiful Quarts de Chaume; **Château de Belle Rive**: Leading Quarts de Chaume; **Château de la Guimonière*; Domaine de la Motte*.**

THOUARCE, postcode 49380, 39 C3, 41 D5

Domaine La Croix de Mission*: Very good Bonnezeux; **Château de Fesles*:** Jacques Boivin is the driving force of Bonnezeaux in terms of both quality and quantity.

SAUMUR

CHAINTRES, postcode 49400

Château de Chaintres*; Paul Filliatreau*.

PARNAY, postcode 49730

Château de Targé*

ST-CYR-EN-BOURG, postcode 49260

Cave Coopérative*

ST-HILAIRE-ST-FLORENT,
postcode 49400, 39 C4

Ackerman-Laurance; Bouvet-Ladunay*: Owned by the Champagne firm Taittinger; **Langlois-Chateau*:** Owned by the Champagne firm Bollinger; Veuve Amiot.

SAUMUR, postcode 49400, 39 C4

Gratien & Meyer*

VARRAINS, postcode 49400

Claude Daheuiller/Domaine des Varinelles*; Domaine des Roches-Neuves*.

SAVENNIERES

SAVENNIERES, postcode 49170, 39 B3, 41 B2

Domaine de Bizolière*; Château de Chamboureau*; Domaine du Closel*; Clos de Coulaine*; Clos de la Coulée de Serrant*: In a lovely situation on the north bank of the Loire. White wine needs to mature for 5 to 10 years, but even after a longer period can still surprise with its vitality; **Château d'Epiré*.**

OTHER AREAS

NEUVILLE-DE-POITOU,
postcode 86170

Cave Cooperative*: This excellent cooperative produces almost all the wines of Haut-Poitou.

OIRON, postcode 79100

Michel Gigon*: The best and most energetic producer of Vins du Thouarsais. The Chenin Blanc is the highest quality in the range.

TOURAINE

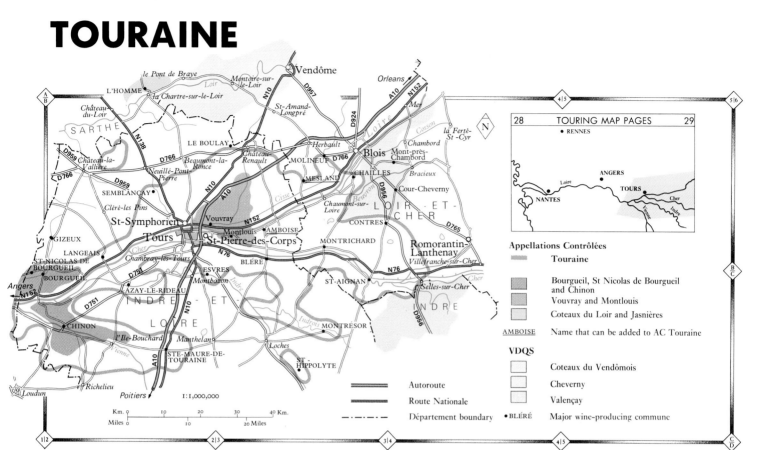

Appellations Contrôlées

Touraine

Bourgueil, St Nicolas de Bourgueil and Chinon

Vouvray and Montlouis

Coteaux du Loir and Jasnières

AMBOISE   Name that can be added to AC Touraine

VDQS

Coteaux du Vendômois

Cheverny

Valençay

• BLÉRÉ   Major wine-producing commune

Autoroute

Route Nationale

Département boundary

1:1,000,000

Km. 0   10   20   30   40 Km.

Miles 0   10   20 Miles

reen valleys, fertile fields and orchards, expanses of woodland and a mild climate have given Touraine the title of "garden of France". In this former province, which takes in the present département of Indre-et-Loire as well as parts of Loir-et-Cher and Indre, grapes have been grown for a very long time. Today the area has some 11,500 hectares (28,400 acres) of vineyards with an appellation contrôlée, stretching around and to the south of the capital, Tours.

More than a third of the vineyard area produces the local Touraine wine. The most important, and usually the best, is the white Sauvignon, a flowery, very fresh wine, at its best distinctly aromatic, that makes a reasonably priced alternative to Sancerre and Pouilly-Fumé (see the chapter on the Upper Loire). Red Touraine wine, produced in quantities roughly equal to those of the white, varies greatly in quality according to year and grower. A good Gamay de Touraine can be as fruity as a Beaujolais, a successful Cabernet de Touraine certainly has merit, and the relatively recent Tradition (a blend of Gamay, Cabernet Franc and Malbec) is sometimes of a surprising completeness. There is also sparkling Touraine.

In addition to the broad Touraine appellation three districts are distinguished: Touraine-Amboise (mainly red wines – those made from the Cot or Malbec can be particularly striking); Touraine Azay-le-Rideau (dry and semi-sweet rosé and white wines); and Touraine-Mesland (mainly red wines, often rich in colour and fruity).

The most westerly districts of Touraine are Bourgueil, St-Nicolas-de-Bourgueil and Chinon. These produce a red wine that, due in part to its grape variety (Cabernet Franc, with sometimes a little Cabernet Sauvignon), shows a certain kinship with a simple Médoc. Fruit – currants, raspberries, wild strawberries – can often be present in the perfume and taste, and in good years these Loire reds can possess a surprising vitality. Chinon offers the most finesse. Bourgueil is rather more dour and often requires years of patience. St-Nicolas-de-Bourgueil usually has a somewhat lighter structure than Bourgueil and is more accessible. In all three districts a little dry rosé is made, and Chinon also makes a rare white wine. For the visitor the district of Chinon has the most to offer, with the little town itself nestling between a vast ruined castle and the bank of the Vienne.

One of the most famous districts of Touraine is the charming Vouvray, a few kilometres east of Tours. Using only the Chenin Blanc, growers of

Vouvray and seven other communes produce dry (*sec*), semi-sweet (*demi-sec*) or very sweet (*moelleux*) wines: the degree of ripeness of the grapes determines the style. The vines often grow on plateaus of limestone and tufa, which form such thick stratum in places that not only wine cellars have been hewn out of it but also three- and four-storey dwellings. A really dry Vouvray has a high degree of acidity which makes it difficult to drink in its youth but potentially superb with age. The sweeter Vouvrays also benefit greatly from maturing in bottle. About three fifths of the vintage is processed into sparkling or slightly sparkling wine, using the champagne method; the quality can be excellent.

Almost opposite Vouvray, on the south bank of the Loire, lies the district of Montlouis. This produces the same sort of wines as Vouvray, albeit a little softer, less full – and in much smaller quantities. Other wines from Touraine or the immediate surroundings are Cheverny (mainly white, with the uncommon Romorantin the most distinctive grape and Chardonnay the best), Valençay (chiefly minor red wines), Jasnières (chalk-dry whites), Coteaux du Loir (mainly simple red and rosés) and Coteaux du Vendômois (light red, rosé and white wines).

TRAVEL INFORMATION

CHATEAUX OF THE LOIRE

Many châteaux have been built along the banks of the Loire and its tributaries. At first there were austere-looking fortifications, but from the late 15th century the military aspect faded and the châteaux became gracious lodgings for kings, their mistresses and for the wealthy nobility. Most of the châteaux and many of the medieval castles have been preserved in perfect condition and can be visited. Touraine in particular has many beautiful châteaux. The most important of them – and some from the margins of the area – are described briefly here. If there is a "sound and light" presentation (*son et lumière*) at a château in the summer, this is indicated. For opening times and similar details consult the regional or local tourist information offices. Information is also available in many of the hotels.

Amboise This partly 15th-century château rises above the little town, on a rocky plateau above the Loire. It was once five times the size it is now, and knights used to be able to ride up to its high terrace via the spiral Tour des Minimes, which has a diameter of 20 metres (66 feet). The château is furnished and has a fine

Gothic chapel. Royal residents have included Charles VIII, François I and François II. In 1516 Leonardo da Vinci accepted François I's invitation to live at Amboise; he died there in 1519. (*Son et lumière*.)

Azay-le-Rideau A brilliant example of Renaissance architecture; completed in 1529, it stands on an island in the Indre. It contains a museum devoted to the Renaissance (Flemish tapestries, furniture) and a remarkable old vaulted kitchen. (*Son et lumière*.)

Beauregard This former hunting lodge of François I has a magnificent hall with hundreds of historic portraits, a floor with blue Delft tiles and a splendidly carved ceiling. The château is of 16th-century origin and was later enlarged.

Blois The three parts of this château in the centre of the town represent three architectural styles. The best-known is François I's Renaissance wing, which has an open staircase and an Italianate look. Earlier, Louis XII had built a late-Gothic wing in brick and stone. Later, after the time of François I, Gaston d'Orléans added a wing in Classical style, the work of François Mansart. Henri III also lived in the castle (he had the Duc de Guise and his brother,

Louis II de Lorraine, the cardinal, murdered here in 1588). The château has two museums devoted to fine arts and archaeology. (*Son et lumière*.)

Bouges An 18th-century château not far from Valençay with beautiful gardens and, a particular feature, a collection of carriages.

Chambord With its 440 rooms, 84 staircases and 365 chimneys, this is the largest of the Loire châteaux. In the 16th century 1,800 men worked on it for 15 years, commissioned by François I – and it still was not fully completed. In addition to the magnificent main staircase the interior has reminders of its residents, many of them royal. Molière produced two of his plays here to the royal command of Louis XIV. (*Son et lumière*.)

Chaumont A late-15th-century castle with round towers, high on a cliff above the Loire near Amboise. It looks warlike but has a Renaissance interior, with furniture, Gobelin tapestries of the 15th and 16th centuries and an Italian tiled floor. The 19th-century stables are also worth seeing. Diane de Poitiers lived here after being driven out of Chenonceau.

Chenonceau One of the most visited of all the national monuments of France. The château is built over the

river Cher and was completed in 1521; it was given by Henri II to his mistress, Diane de Poitiers, in 1547. In the château there are French, Italian and Spanish furniture, Flemish tapestries and a vast kitchen. Diane worked for nine years on the ornamental garden. After Henri's death in 1559 she was forced by Catherine de Médicis to leave. A waxworks museum recalls the court life of former times. (*Son et lumière*).

Cheverny A luxuriously furnished 17th-century château that is still the property of the family that originally had it built. There are some 2,000 antlers in the museum of hunting and also kennels with dozens of hounds. (*Son et lumière*.)

Chinon Rising above the town are the ruins of three castles that look like one. Before they were dismantled by Cardinal Richelieu they afforded shelter to English monarchs (Henry II, Richard Lionheart) and French (such as Philippe Auguste). This is also where Joan of Arc first met Charles VII, in 1429; there is a museum devoted to her in the Tour de l'Horloge, near the castle entrance. (*Son et lumière*.)

Cinq-Mars Two large towers and a deep, dry moat remain of a feudal castle built here before the 11th century. The east tower gives a splendid view.

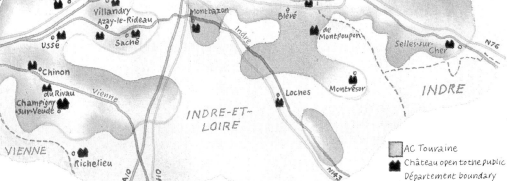

Touraine is a countryside of châteaux. The map, right, shows the most notable in the context of the Touraine AC boundary. The text above gives details of visiting these beautiful buildings.

Langeais Dark-grey, sombre castle dating from 1467. Despite its feudal exterior it possesses an interior that includes a collection of 15th- and 16th-century tapestries. Charles VIII married Anne of Brittany here in 1491.

Loches The earliest part of this château is 13th century and austere; various wings and terraces with greater charm were added later. Anne of Brittany and Agnes Sorel, the

mistress of Charles VII, lived here, and this is where Joan of Arc persuaded Charles VII to be crowned at Reims. Collections include tapestries and a triptych. (*Son et lumière*.)

Montpoupon One of the most graceful of Touraine's Renaissance châteaux, with earlier 13th-century towers, 15th-century living quarters and a museum of hunting.

Montrésor The origin of this castle goes back to the 11th century, but large parts of the present château date from the 15th. Long occupied by a Polish family, it has a collection of mementoes of Polish history.

Le Riveau Grey, feudal castle that in 1442 was further strengthened with towers and a moat. An exhibition of paintings is held here in summer and the permanent collections include antique furniture and old weapons.

Ussé The fairytale château that is said to have inspired Charles Perrault to write his *Sleeping Beauty* (*Belle au Bois Dormant*). Situated in the middle of woods overlooking the valleys of the Loire and the Indre, the château dates from the 15th and 16th centuries and has a royal suite and terraced gardens.

Valençay The statesman Talleyrand acquired this palace-like château in 1803. It was built in the 16th century and enlarged in the 17th and 18th. Visitors are welcome in the Talleyrand museum, and there is a zoo and a car museum. (*Son et lumière*.)

Villandry The gardens, laid out on three levels, are unique in Europe and more famous than the château itself. Built in 1536, this was the last of the great Renaissance châteaux.

HOTELS

Le Grand Monarque, 37190 Azay-le-Rideau, tel. 47 45 40 08. A hospitable village hotel (but the comfort of the rooms varies). Good substantial cooking including fish from the Loire with *beurre blanc*. Class B.

Le Bon Laboureur et Château, 37150 Chenonceaux, tel. 47 23 90 02. Comfortable hotel with an annexe, an inner courtyard, a terrace and a pleasant restaurant (e.g. *terrine aux quatre poissons de Loire*). Class B.

Chris' Hotel, 37500 Chinon, tel. 47 93 36 92. In a beautiful building, attractively furnished. Class B.

Hotel de France, 41700 Contres, tel. 54 79 50 14. Hotel with restaurant well situated for visiting Blois and the châteaux. Hotel class B; restaurant class C.

Luccotel, 37600 Loches, tel. 47 91 50 50. Modern hotel with restaurant in a peaceful park. Hotel class B; restaurant class C.

Domaine de Beauvois, 37330 Luynes, tel. 47 55 50 11. Château hotel offering great comfort and excellent cooking. Has a park and swimming pool. Class A.

Château de Marçay, 37500 Marçay, tel. 47 93 03 47. Beautifully restored 15th-century castle where the cooking is outstanding (e.g. *huîtres chaudes au Vouvray*). Class A.

Domaine de la Tortinière, 37250 Montbazon, tel. 47 26 00 19. Small château on a hill overlooking the Indre valley, with a swimming pool and park. The restaurant is in the orangery. Hotel class A; restaurant class B.

Le Relais de Touraine, 37250 Montbazon, tel. 47 26 01 12. Good rooms, a restaurant and a park. Class B.

▼ An inviting café in Azay-le-Rideau. The town is famous for its castle and a very early church.

Domaine des Hauts de Loire, 51150 Onzain, tel. 54 20 72 57. Luxurious rooms and apartments in a 19th-century hunting lodge, with a large park and a lake. Fine cuisine. Class A.

Château des Tertres, 41150 Onzain, tel. 54 20 83 88. Charming small château surrounded by a park. Class B.

Les Fontaines, 37210 Rochecorbon, tel. 47 52 52 80. Pleasant, quiet hotel near Tours. Breakfast is served on the terrace in good weather. Class B.

Le Bordeaux, 3 Place du Maréchal-Leclerc, 37000 Tours, tel. 47 05 40 32. Centrally located, comfortable hotel with restaurant (*matelote d'anguille au Bourgueil*). Hotel class B; restaurant class C.

Hostellerie Les Perce-Neige, 37210 Vernou-sur-Brenne, tel. 47 52 10 04. Rural peace, good cooking and friendly service. Hotel class B; restaurant class C.

▼ Chinon's picturesque town centre is medieval, dating back to the 14th century. The town is the centre of a notable red-wine district and has a fine château.

As well as freshwater fish, asparagus is a great Touraine speciality. So are *rillettes* (a coarse-textured terrine of meat – usually pork); and *rillons* (cubes of meat prepared in much the same way as *rillettes*).

RESTAURANTS

Le Mail St-Thomas, 37400 Amboise, tel. 47 47 22 52. In a villa near the château at Amboise. The cooking is fairly traditional (*foie confit au Vouvray*). Excellent wine list. Class B.

La Péniche, Promenade du Mail, 41000 Blois, tel. 54 74 37 23. A converted Loire barge. Very good cooking, based on what is in season. Class B.

Le Relais, 41250 Bracieux, tel. 54 46 41 22. Fine cuisine and marvellous local wines in a contemporary setting. A first-rate establishment. Class B.

Le Plaisir Gourmand, 37500 Chinon, tel. 47 93 20 48. The best restaurant in Chinon, in a 17th-century building with walls of tufa (volcanic rock). Dishes include *jambonette de caneton au vieux Chinon*. Class B.

Le Ste-Maxime, 37500 Chinon, tel. 47 93 05 04. *Rillettes, coq au vin*: simple, good food. Class C.

La Botte d'Asperges, 41700 Contres, tel. 54 79 50 49. Ample country dishes based on fresh ingredients (including, of course, asparagus in season). Class C.

Hotel des Trois Marchands, 41700 Cour-Cheverny, tel. 54 79 96 44. Good regional cooking. Also a hotel. Class C.

Château d'Artigny, 37250 Montbazon, tel. 47 26 24 24. Vast, luxurious hotel where a well-to-do clientele enjoys not only the comfort, the view and the swimming pool, but also the fine cuisine. Class A.

La Chancelière, 37250 Montbazon, tel. 47 26 00 67. Inspired cooking. Lunch menu with lower prices on week days. Class A/B.

Le Moulin Fleuri, 37250 Montbazon, tel. 47 26 01 12. Restored 16th-century mill by the Indre with a good restaurant and a pleasant hotel. *Demi-pension* obligatory in season. Restaurant class C; hotel class B/C.

Roc en Val, 37270 Montlouis-sur-Loire, tel. 47 50 81 96. Opened in 1986; the cooking is capable and modern. Has a park and a terrace. Class B.

Pont d'Ouchet, 41150 Onzain, tel. 54 20 70 33. Convivial restaurant and hotel. Mussels are a speciality. *Demi-pension* obligatory in season. Class C.

l'Oubliette, 37210 Rochecorbon, tel. 47 52 50 49. Restaurant built partly into the steep cliff. Good cooking and

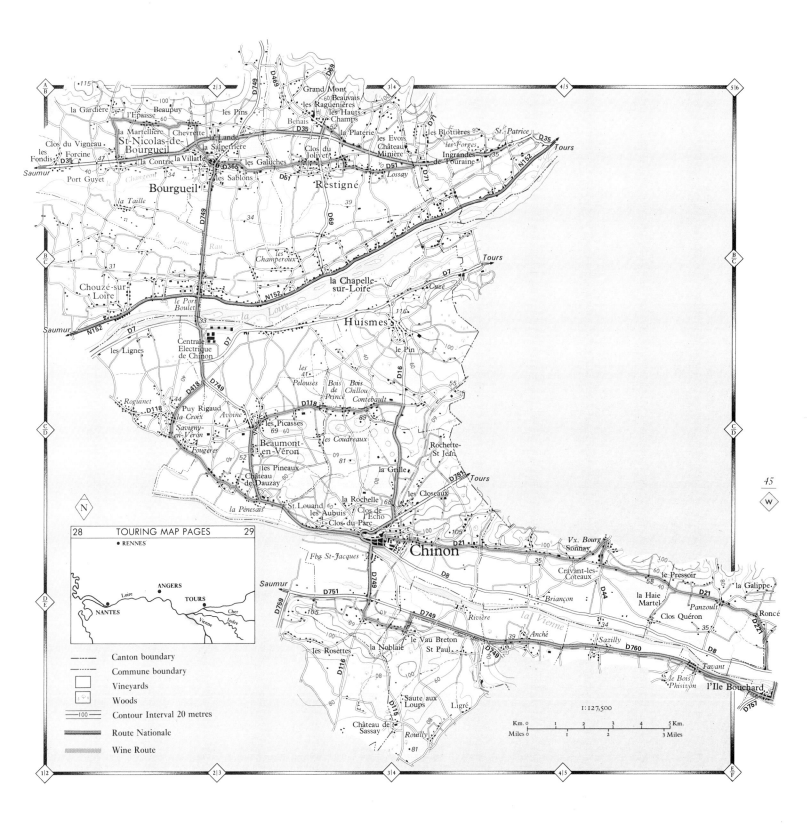

TOURING MAP PAGES

28   29

• RENNES

ANGERS

Loire

NANTES   TOURS

Cher

Vienne   Indre

- - - - - -   Canton boundary

- - - - -   Commune boundary

            Vineyards

            Woods

———100———   Contour Interval 20 metres

═══════   Route Nationale

░░░░░░░   Wine Route

1:127,500

Km. 0   1   2   3   4   5 Km.
Miles 0   1   2   3 Miles

plenty of Vouvray wines. Class C.
Auberge du XIIe Siècle, 37190
Sache, tel. 47 26 86 58.
Contemporary cooking in a medieval
setting, with a garden. Class B.
Les Jardins du Castel, 10 Rue
Croison, 37000 Tours, tel.
47 41 94 40. One of the best
restaurants in Tours; the menu offers
a wide choice. Has a garden. Class B.
La Renaissance, 62 Rue Colbert,
37000 Tours, tel. 47 77 73 25.
Optimum quality for not too much
money. Class C.
Le Cheval Rouge, 37300 Villandry,
tel. 47 50 02 07. Reliable cooking
(*navarin de la mer*, for example),
large wine cellar; also a comfortable
hotel. Class B.
Auberge du Grand Vatel, 37120
Vouvray, tel. 47 52 70 32. Rather
obtrusively decorated; a wide choice
of fish dishes (with white and red
wine). Class B.

PLACES OF INTEREST

Amboise Clos-Lucé is the large
15th-century house where Leonardo
da Vinci lived from 1516 until his
death three years later. Exhibits
include small models of his designs.
The Amboise town hall has a
museum devoted to the rich history
of the area, and the Musée de la
Poste displays many aspects of postal
transport of the past. Beside the
Loire there is a fountain designed by
Max Ernst (1968). Just south of
Amboise the Pagode de Canteloup, a
curious structure 44 metres (144 ft)
high, is all that remains of a castle.

The Château d'Amboise is described
on page 43.
Azay-le-Rideau As well as its
château (see page 43), Azay-le-Rideau
has the church of St-Symphorien,
parts of which date back to the 5th
and 6th centuries.
Blois Many Renaissance houses; a
château (see page 43); the cathedral
of St-Louis (16th to 17th century,
with a 10th-century crypt); the 12th-
to 13th-century church of St-Nicolas,
with 20th-century stained-glass
windows; and the modern basilica of
Notre-Dame-de-la-Trinité, with its
carillon of 48 bells.
Bourgueil An abbey founded in 990
can be visited. The local church has a
beautiful Gothic choir.
Chevrette Just north of Bourgueil
there is the Cave de la Dive Bouteille
with a wine exhibition and tasting
room.
Chinon Delightful little town on the
banks of the Vienne with half-
timbered houses of the 14th, 15th
and 16th centuries; the Musée du Vin
et de la Tonnellerie (a wine and
cooperage museum in a cave, with
various coin-operated models); and
the Musée des Etats Généraux (local
history, religious art). A little steam
train runs from Chinon to Richelieu
in summer. Chinon castle is
described on page 43.
Cinq-Mars-la-Pile As well as castle
ruins (see page 43) there is a
remarkable Roman column 30 metres
(98 ft) high.
Cour-Cheverny The small
Renaissance Château de Troissay has

a collection of agricultural and
domestic items. (See page 43 for the
Château de Cheverny.)
Cravant-les-Coteaux Chinon's
most important wine village. In the
Vieux-Bourg there is a small church
with Carolingian elements, now a
museum.
La Devinière The house where
François Rabelais, the 16th-century
satirist, was born; it is now a
museum.
Chartreuse du Liget Carthusian
monastery in the forest of Loches,
founded by Henry II of England as a
penance for the murder of Thomas à
Becket. There are Romanesque
frescos in the chapel of St-Jean-du-
Liget.
Loches Medieval town centre with a
castle (see page 44), the 12th-century
church of St-Ours, a keep that has
served as a prison and, in the towers
of the Porte Royale, two museums
(painting and Oriental art, and
history of the region).
Mesland Wine museum and an
11th-century church.
Montlouis Wine can be tasted in the
Cave Touristique; there is also an
exhibition of tools used in wine
growing and making.
Montrichard Atmospheric little
town on the river Cher, at the foot of
an 11th-century keep.
Richelieu Cardinal Richelieu used
stone from the castle of Chinon,
which he ordered to be dismantled,
to build the little town that bears his
name. With its grid layout it is a
textbook example of 17th-century

town planning. La Fontaine called it
"the most beautiful village in the
universe". It has a Richelieu
museum.
Rochecorbon Cave dwellings, wine
cellars and a 15th-century watch
tower (La Lanterne).
Saché Honoré de Balzac wrote *Le
Lys dans la Vallée* and other works
here; his house beside the Indre is
now a museum. A large abstract –
and controversial – work by the
American Alexander Calder is in the
village square.
St-Aignan Attractive village with a
Romanesque church, with murals.
The local château is not open to
visitors.
Savonnières Huge caves with
stalactites and stalagmites, and an
underground lake.
Selles-sur-Cher Remains of a castle,
and the 12th- to 15th-century church
of St-Eusice. A former abbey
contains the Musée Municipal
d'Histoire et des Traditions Locales,
with a collection of coopers' and
winemakers' tools.
Tavant The church has some of the
earliest known Romanesque frescos.
Tours Large university town; the
centre has old half-timbered houses,
the cathedral of St-Gatien (part
Flamboyant Gothic), the towers of
the former basilica of St-Martin (next
to the present basilica, which dates
from 1924) with 11th-century frescos,
and many museums. The Musée des
Vins de Touraine (16 Rue Nationale)
has a large collection arranged on
thematic lines. The Musée des
Beaux-Arts (Place François-Sicard) is
in the former archbishop's palace and
includes works by Rembrandt,
Rubens and Delacroix; there is a
magnificent old cedar in the fine
garden. The Château Royal (Rue
Lavoisier) has 165 figures of the
Historial de Touraine and there are
Roman excavations around the
château. The Musée de
Compagnonnage (8 Rue Nationale) is
concerned with the time of the
guilds; the museum of antiquities is
in the most beautiful of the
Renaissance buildings in Tours (25
Rue Commerce); and the Musée du
Gemmail (7 Rue du Murier) shows
how art can be created in a particular
kind of stained glass.
Villaines-les-Roches The basket-
making "capital". Also cave
dwellings.

▼ The town of Montlouis-sur-Loire lines the south bank of the river just upstream from Vouvray. Its wines are very similar, attractive still and sparkling whites, but they are less well known than those of its neighbour. The vineyards are on the plateau behind and to the south and east of the town. The Loire here is much divided up by islands: it is sometimes hard to decide which is the main stream.

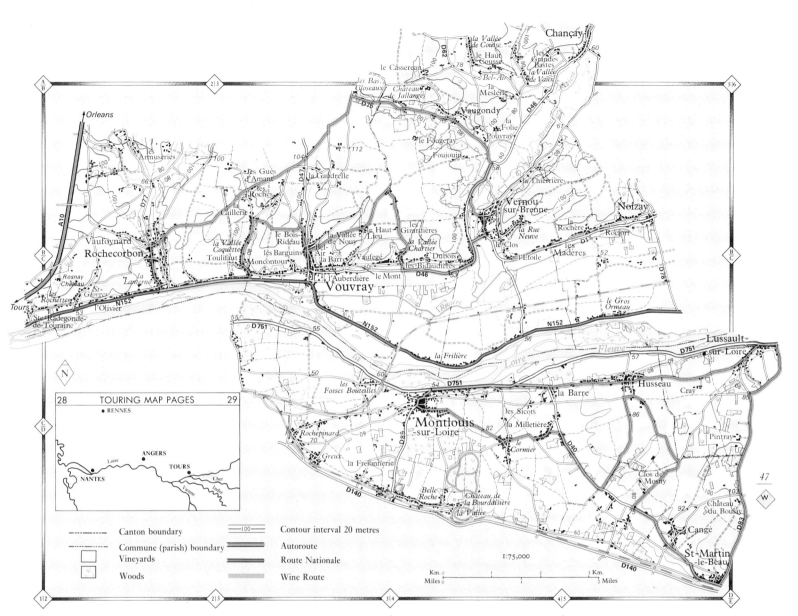

Canton boundary
Commune (parish) boundary
Vineyards
Woods
Contour interval 20 metres
Autoroute
Route Nationale
Wine Route

1:75,000

TOURING MAP PAGES
28   29
• RENNES

ANGERS
NANTES   TOURS
Loire
Cher
Vienne
Indre

47

WINE FAIRS AND FESTIVALS

Fourth weekend in January Wine fair in Vouvray.

First weekend in February Wine fair in Bourgueil.

Second weekend in February The great *foire aux vins*, Tours-Fondettes.

Third weekend in February Wine fair in Montlouis-sur-Loire.

Last weekend in February Wine fair in Azay-le-Rideau.

Third weekend in March Chinon wine fair.

Easter Wine fairs in Amboise and St-Georges-sur-Cher.

First Sunday after Easter Wine fair in Selles-sur-Cher.

Third weekend after Easter Onzain wine fair.

1 May Panzoult wine fair.

Early May Cravant-les-Coteaux wine fair.

Second weekend in May Valençay wine fair.

Whitsun Meusnes wine fair.

Early June Vendôme wine fair.

First weekend in July Thésée wine fair.

End of July Journée du Vin held in St-Aignan-sur-Cher.

15 August Wine fair in Amboise and a medieval market in Chinon.

WINE FRATERNITIES

The following wine fraternities are active in the Touraine appellation: La Confrérie des Maîtres de Chais (St-Georges-sur-Cher); La Confrérie des Tire-Douzils de la Grande Brosse (Chémery); La Confrérie des Coteaux d'Ange (Ange); La Confrérie des Vignerons du Noble Joué (Joue-les-Tours and district); Les Chevaliers des Cuers du Baril (Loches). In addition there are: La Commanderie des Grands Vins d'Amboise (Touraine-Amboise); La Confrérie des Compagnons de Grandgousier (Touraine-Mesland); Les Bons Entonneurs Rabelaisiens (Chinon); La Commanderie de la Dive Bouteille (Bourgueil and St-Nicolas-de-Bourgueil); La Confrérie des Fripe-Douzils (Ingrandes-de-Touraine, Bourgueil); La Confrérie des Chevaliers de la Chantepleure (Vouvray); La Coterie des Closiers de Montlouis (Montlouis); Les Grands Escuyers de Gâtine (Valençay); and La Confrérie des Chevaliers de la Puette et du Franc-Pinot (Coteaux du Vendômois).

WINE INFORMATION

Information can be obtained from the Comité Interprofessionnel des Vins de Touraine, 19 Square Prosper-Mérimée, Tours, and from the Maison des Vins de Blois, 84 Avenue de Verdun, Blois.

PRODUCERS OF SPECIAL INTEREST

TOURAINE

HUISSEAU-SUR-COSSON, postcode 41350

Aimé Boucher*: Firm with excellent contacts throughout the Loire valley.

MONTRICHARD, postcode 41400, 42 B3

J. M. Monmousseau: Specialist in sparkling wines (owned by Taittinger of Champagne).

OISLY, postcode 41700

Confrérie des Vignerons de Oisly et Thésée*: Cooperative of 50 growers; progressive, with modern equipment and a remarkable number of very good wines. The undisputed star is the Sauvignon de Touraine; Domaine des Corbillières/ Maurice Barbou.

ST-GEORGES-SUR-CHER, postcode 41400

Jean-Claude Bougrier: Négociant firm with its own vineyards.

TOURAINE-AMBOISE

AMBOISE, postcode 37400, 42 B3

Hubert & Thierry Denay (in Le Breuil); Domaines Girault-Artois*: Although the office and cellars are in Amboise, the vineyards are in Mesland. Mainly red wines.

TOURAINE AZAY-LE-RIDEAU

AZAY-LE-RIDEAU, postcode 37190, 42 C2

Château de l'Aulée; Robert Denis.

TOURAINE-MESLAND

MESLAND, postcode 41150, 42 B3

Philippe Brossillon

BENAIS, postcode 37140, 45 B3

Robert Caslot; Pierre-Jacques Druet; Domaine Jacques Morin (inc. Domaine Morin-Goisnard).

BOURGUEIL, postcode 37140, 42 C1, 45 B2

Clos de l'Abbaye/GAEC de la Dîme*: The vineyard that belonged to the old abbey at Bourgueil; Audebert & Fils*; Domaine des Galluches/ Jean Gambier*: Family firm handling excellent wines from Bourgueil, St-Nicolas-de-Bourgueil and Chinon.

INGRANDES-DE-TOURAINE, postcode 37140, 45 B4

Raphaël Galteau & Fils; GAEC Lamé-Delille-Boucard*; Jean Nau.

RESTIGNE, postcode 37140, 45 B3

Marcel Audebert; Caslot-Jamet; Marc Mureau*; Georges Renou.

ST-NICOLAS-DE-BOURGUEIL

ST-NICOLAS-DE-BOURGUEIL, postcode 37140, 42 C1, 45 B2

Claude & Thierry Admirault; GAEC P. Jamet & Fils; Jean-Paul Mabileau/Clos du Bourg*.

CHINON

CHINON, postcode 37500, 42 C2, 45 D4

Domaine de l'Abbaye/Michel Fontaine; Couly-Dutheil*: This family firm has made an important contribution to establishing the reputation of Chinon. Château de la Grille; Clos de la Lysardière/Georges Farget; Clos du Parc de St-Louans/Louis Faron; Plouzeau & Fils.

CRAVANT-LES-COTEAUX, postcode 37500, 45 D5

Bernard Baudry; Henri Lambert; Jean-François Olek*; Serge & Daniel Sourdais; Gérard Spelty.

LIGNE, postcode 37500, 45 E4

Donzon Père & Fils/Clos du Saint-au-Loup; Château de Ligré; Domaine de la Noblaie.

PANZOULT, postcode 37220, 45 E5

Raymond Desbourdes; Domaine du Roncée.

SAVIGNY-EN-VERON, postcode 37420, 45 D2

Jean-Maurice Raffault; Olga Raffault: Also a very good white Chinon; Raymond Raffault/Domaine du Raffault.

SAZILLY, postcode 37220, 45 E5

Charles Joguet*

VOUVRAY

ROCHECORBON, postcode 37210, 47 C2

Marc Brédif*: The property of Patrick de Ladoucette (see the Upper Loire chapter), excellent *pétillant* Vouvray; Blanc Foussy/Société Foltz: Various sparkling Touraines.

VOUVRAY, postcode 37210, 42 B2, 47 C3

Domaine Allias; Domaine des Barguins*; Cave Coopérative des Grands Vins; Cave Coopérative Château Vaudenuits; Bernard Courson; Philippe Foreau/Domaine du Clos Naudin; Bernard Fouquet; André Freslier; Domaine Huet*: Vouvrays of the very highest quality; the cellars, too, are splendid; Château Moncontour; Prince Poniatowski*: One of the best and most conscientious producers in the district with a famous Vouvray Clos Baudoin.

MONTLOUIS

HUSSEAU, postcode 37270, 47 C5

Jean-Pierre Leblois; Pierre Moreau.

MONTLOUIS-SUR-LOIRE, postcode 37270, 42 B3, 47 C4

Dominique Moyer*

SAINT-MARTIN-LE-BEAU, postcode 37270, 47 D5

Berger Frères*: Particularly fine sparkling wines and some still wines; Marcel Galliot; Jean Simier.

CHEVERNY

COUR-CHEVERNY, postcode 41700, 42 B4

GAEC Gendrier; Givierge Père & Fils; GAEC Tessier.

VALENCAY

FONTGUENAND, postcode 36600

Cave Coopérative

MEUSNES, postcode 41130

Hubert Sinson

JASNIERES & COTEAUX DU LOIR

LA CHARTRE-SUR-LE-LOIR, postcode 72340

Joël Gigou

L'HOMME, postcode 72340, 42 A2

Jean-Baptiste Pinon

COTEAUX DU VENDOMOIS

HOUSSAY, postcode 41800

GAEC Gevais Frères

THE UPPER LOIRE

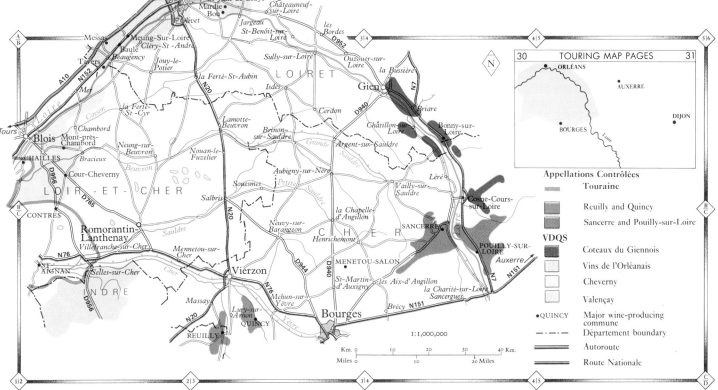

Vineyards become more scarce along the upper reaches of the Loire, yet this is where Sancerre and Pouilly-Fumé, the best-known white wines of the entire valley, have their origin. Both are made from Sauvignon Blanc, which in only a few places in the world is grown so successfully as here. In both districts it gives aromatic wines with an often powerful perfume and an exhilarating fresh taste that is the perfect accompaniment for all kinds of fish, crustaceans and shellfish (and the local goats' milk cheeses). The bouquet can sometimes have something vegetable about it and the association with asparagus is often made – although in poorer ripening years it can suggest wet wool. Traditionally it is described as "flinty", from the characteristic smell of flints being struck. Pouilly-Fumé is the firmer of the two wines, partly because of the heavier soil from which it comes, and it goes well with poultry and white meat as well as with fish and shellfish.

The village of Sancerre crowns a steep hill that rises quite unexpectedly above the peaceful green countryside and the nearby river Loire. The Romans were established here (an old gate is called the Porte César) and in the tenth century an imposing castle was built on the hill, but all that remains is the sentinel-like Tour des Fiefs. The other communes of this wine district are in many cases tucked away in the valleys. The south-facing slopes of these valleys are mainly planted with vines; on the north-facing slopes cereals are grown.

One of the most impressive vineyards of Sancerre, and of the entire Loire valley, is Clos de la Poussie at Bué: a natural amphitheatre with slopes of 60 degrees or more in places. Bué also has other remarkable vineyards, among them Clos du Chêne Marchand, Le Grand Chemarin and part of Clos du Roy, which are the origin of some of Sancerre's best wines. A fourth important wine commune – of the 14 that make up the Sancerre appellation – is Verdigny.

Sancerre also produces red and rosé wines from Pinot Noir, the Burgundian grape. Locally they are often proud of these wines, but pride is only justified in a very few cases: most lack concentration, class and character. However, they sell well and represent about a fifth of the vintage.

Pouilly is a much smaller wine district than Sancerre, with some 600 hectares (1,500 acres) compared to Sancerre's nearly 1,600 hectares (4,000 acres). For the visitor, too, it is somewhat more subdued than its neighbour across the river. For many years the busy RN7 highway ran through the centre of Pouilly-sur-Loire, but since the completion of a bypass in 1973 peace has returned to this former Roman settlement. The best vineyards lie in a band some 6 kilometres (4 miles) wide to the north of Pouilly-sur-Loire and most of the growers live in the little hamlets of Les Loges and Les Berthiers, where wine can be tasted in nearly all the houses – look for the signs "vente directe" or "dégustation" or similar notices. The district also has its own pleasantly meandering wine route. More than half the production of Pouilly-Fumé is dominated by Patrick de Ladoucette, whose family owns the stylish Château du Nozet.

In contrast to Sancerre, the Pouilly district makes no red or rosé wines but it does produce a second type of white wine, Pouilly-sur-Loire, from the Chasselas grape. It is a rather neutral but quite pleasant wine for drinking young.

Southwest of Sancerre is the modest but growing district of Menetou-Salon. Its white wines closely resemble those of Sancerre, but perhaps are a little lighter and more charming; the red and the rosé wines are even of a higher average quality. As a wine district on the way up Menetou-Salon is worth following.

Away from the Loire itself, west of Bourges and south of Vierzon, are the two small isolated districts of Reuilly and Quincy. Both take their name from villages and Sauvignon is the most widely grown grape. In Reuilly, where the ground is rich in lime, this gives a rather austere, bone-dry white wine; in Quincy the wine is more agreeable and rounded.

Reuilly's best wine is actually a dry Pinot Gris rosé: a light beige-pink in colour, it has a refreshing, amiable taste of a class that is not equalled anywhere else in the Loire valley.

At the most northerly point of the Upper Loire, around Orléans, is the district of Vin de l'Orléanais. The wines are light and not very memorable as a rule, although some growers make surprisingly good wine from the Chardonnay (called the Auvernat Blanc locally). The most characteristic wine, however, is the Gris Meunier, a softly fresh, slightly earthy red wine from Pinot Meunier.

Upstream from Orléans the Coteaux de Giennois district leads a less than brilliant existence. Most of the vineyards are around Cosne-sur-Loire (and formerly around Gien); the cooperative at Pouilly-sur-Loire vinifies a large proportion of the grapes.

▲ Two of the top Sancerre hamlets. Top: Chavignol from the top of les Monts Damnés, one of its most noted vineyards. In the distance is the equally famous la Grand Côte. Above: the sun shines on the hamlet of Reigny in its shallow, south-facing amphitheatre of vines.

TRAVEL INFORMATION

As elsewhere along the Loire, freshwater fish is very much in evidence. All the restaurants feature goats' milk cheeses, including the famous Crottin de Chavignol which is excellent with the local white wines.

HOTELS

l'Abbaye, 45190 Beaugency, tel. 38 44 67 35. In a former abbey in the lovely little town of Beaugency, west of Orléans. Good-sized rooms with a view over the river. Hotel class A; restaurant class B.

Ecu de Bretagne, 45190 Beaugency, tel. 38 44 67 60. Quiet hotel on the main square, but the rooms are rather small. There is a modern annexe. Class B.

Auberge à la Ferme, 58200 Cosne-sur-Loire, tel. 86 28 15 85. Just outside Cosne, on the D114 to Cours; rural quiet, terrace and a restaurant. Hotel class B; restaurant class C.

Le Relais Fleuri, 58150 Pouilly-sur-Loire, tel. 86 39 12 99. Pleasant little village hotel with a terrace by the river. Good, regionally based cooking in Le Coq Hardi restaurant. Hotel class B; restaurant class C.

Hotel Panoramic, 18300 Sancerre, tel. 48 54 22 44. Functional hotel for an overnight stay, with a pleasant view of the wine-growing countryside. Fairly conservative cuisine. Class B.

Les Remparts, 18300 Sancerre, tel. 48 54 10 18. Formerly the top address in Sancerre but now only to be recommended if everywhere else is full. Hotel class B; restaurant class C.

RESTAURANTS

Auberge des Templiers, 45290 Les Bézards, tel. 38 31 80 01. Eminent restaurant and hotel north of Gien, with a swimming pool. Marvellous Loire salmon and pike-perch and a well-stocked wine cellar. Class A.

Auberge La Treille, 18300 Chavignol, tel. 48 54 12 17. A good place to sample Crottin de Chavignol cheese, served in various ways (including in a warm salad). Class C.

Le Sévigné, 16 Rue du 14-Juillet, 58200 Cosne-sur-Loire, tel. 86 28 27 50. Regional cooking in an atmospheric setting. Class C.

l'Espérance, 58150 Pouilly-sur-Loire, tel. 86 39 10 68. Conservative restaurant near the river and the vineyards. Try the *écrevisses au Pouilly* and the *aiguillettes de canard au Sancerre rouge*. Also has rooms. Class B.

l'Auberge, 18300 St-Thibault, tel. 48 54 13 79. Old village inn near Sancerre (*truite au Sancerre*). Rustic décor and a garden. Also a hotel. Class C.

l'Etoile, 18300 St-Thibault, tel. 48 54 12 15. Hotel and restaurant; *demi-pension* is obligatory in season. Traditional regional cooking such as *matelote d'anguille*. Garden. Class C.

Auberge Alphonse Mellot, 18300 Sancerre, tel. 48 54 20 53. Joseph Mellot, not the firm of Alphonse Mellot, owns this restaurant, serving omelettes, goats' milk cheese, etc. Also a display of old winemaking equipment. Class C.

Restaurant de la Tour, 18300 Sancerre, tel. 48 54 00 81. The *patron* is also the chef. Pizzas are served in the cellar. Class B.

PLACES OF INTEREST

Beaugency This small town has an enormous 11th-century keep (the Donjon de César), a 12th-century church, a town hall in Renaissance style, and the 15th-century Château Dunois with a Musée des Arts et Traditions Populaires d'Orléanais (including a room dedicated to wine).

Bourges Capital of the Cher département and richly endowed: the 13th-century cathedral of St-Etienne is a Gothic masterpiece, and the Palais Jacques Coeur (15th century, in Rue Jacques-Coeur) is also splendid. The Musée du Berry (4–6 Rue des Arènes) has collections including archaeology; the Musée de l'Hôtel Lallemand (6 Rue Bourbonnoux) displays utensils, toys, etc. Bourges also has many beautiful old houses.

Châtillon-Coligny A meal in Les Bézards (see Restaurants) could be combined with a visit to Château de la Bussière, 10 km to the west, which houses the Musée International de la Pêche (fishing). The château is 15th and 16th century.

Chavignol Charming valley village, noted for its cheese (Crottin de Chavignol), its wine (Sancerre) and an elm planted by Henri IV (who declared Chavignol to be the best wine he had drunk).

Cosne-sur-Loire Once known for its wroughtiron work. The Palais de Justice contains the Musée de la Marine de Loire, devoted to the once-important riverborne traffic.

Gien This little town was badly damaged in 1940 and 1944 but has made a good recovery; the modern church of Ste-Jeanne-d'Arc is one example. The large 15th-century château has a particularly interesting Musée International de la Chasse (hunting). Gien is a pottery centre and has a museum on the theme.

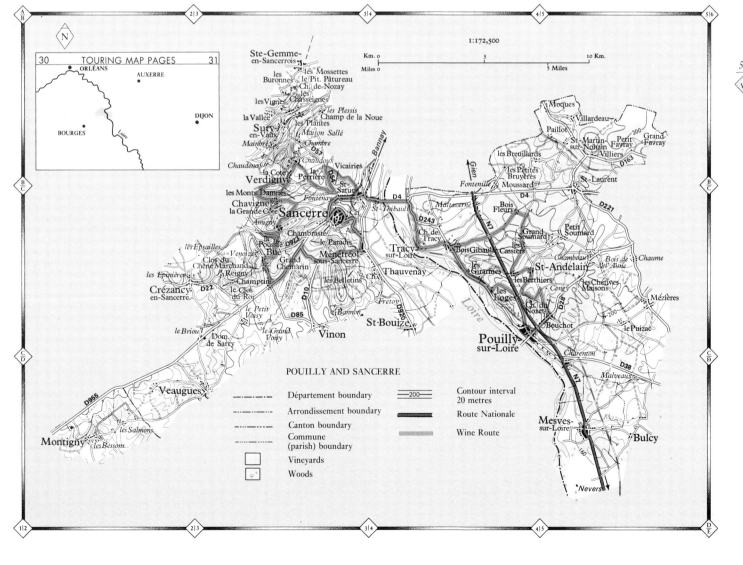

POUILLY AND SANCERRE

————————	Département boundary
— — — — —	Arrondissement boundary
– – – – –	Canton boundary
··········	Commune (parish) boundary
▢	Vineyards
▣	Woods

—200— Contour interval 20 metres

Route Nationale

Wine Route

1:172,500

Km. 0   5   10 Km.
Miles 0   5 Miles

TOURING MAP PAGES 30 31

Menetou-Râtel Not far to the west of this Sancerre village is Château Boucard, a moated 15th- to 16th-century castle with an inner courtyard.

Menetou-Salon The imposing 15th-century château built here by Jacques Coeur, finance minister to Charles VII, was renovated in the 19th century. Its contents include Flemish tapestries, and next to the castle there is a museum of old carriages.

Morogues In this commune of the Menetou-Salon district there is the Château de Maupas with its large collection of plates, and the village itself has a 14th-century church with an unusual wooden canopy and a number of old buildings. East of Morogues the Motte d'Humbligny, the highest point of the region, offers a good view.

Orléans Reminders of Joan of Arc, the Maid of Orléans, are here in plenty, in the Maison de Jeanne d'Arc (3 Place de Gaulle), and there is an equestrian statue of her in the Place du Martroi. The 13th- to 16th-century cathedral of Ste-Croix is almost as large as Notre-Dame in Paris and has two neo-Gothic towers (of the 18th century, remarkably, like Westminster Abbey). The Musée des Beaux-Arts, beside the cathedral, has a fine collection of French painting. Of the various other places of interest, the Parc Floral at Orléans-La-Source is well worth a visit, especially in June-July when its 100,000 rose bushes are in bloom.
Pouilly-sur-Loire The Musée Ernest-Guédon displays painting, sculpture and pottery.

Sancerre Attractive hilltop village with narrow, steeply sloping streets, 15th- and 16th-century houses and a market square. The Tour des Fiefs, only remnant of the castle that once dominated Sancerre, can be climbed at certain times for a panoramic view of the surrounding countryside.
Sury-en-Vaux Beautiful 13th-century church tower. The village lies in a valley in the Sancerre district.
Verdigny The Sancerre wine museum is here (the Musée du Vigneron).
Villegnon The fine Château de la Verrerie, west of Villegnon, was built by Scottish Stuarts in the 15th to 16th centuries. It has a hexagonal tower and the chapel has 16th-century frescos.

WINE ACTIVITIES

Weekend of 1 May Fête du Crottin de Chavignol, held in the Caves de la Mignonne, Sancerre.
Whitsun weekend Wine fair in the Caves de la Mignonne, Sancerre.
Last Sunday in July Fête des Grappes Nouvelles, Verdigny.
First Sunday in August Foire aux Sorciers (magicians) in Bué (and no lack of wine).
15 August Pouilly wine fair.
Last weekend of August Foire aux Vins de France in the Caves de la Mignonne, Sancerre.
Local wine fraternities are La Compagnie d'Honneur des Sorciers et Birettes (Bué, Sancerre); Les Vignerons d'Honneur (Crézancy, Sancerre); Les Chevaliers du Cep (Verdigny, Sancerre); La Confrérie des Baillis de Pouilly-sur-Loire (Pouilly); l'Ordre des Chevaliers du Paissiau (Menetou-Salon); Maîtrise des Echansons (Reuilly).

WINE INFORMATION

Sancerre has no *maison du vin*, but it does have enormous rock cellars, the Caves de la Mignonne, where information is available and wine can be tasted. These are on the southwest side of Sancerre, on the D955.

PRODUCERS OF SPECIAL INTEREST

SANCERRE

BUE, postcode 18300, 51 C3

Bailly-Reverdy*: One of the rare estates where both the white and the red Sancerre are excellent; **Jean-Paul Chaumau; Lucien Crochet***: Excellent Clos du Chêne Marchand and a good Clos du Roy; **Pierre Girault***; **Pierre Millet-Roger; Lucien Picard***; **Clos de la Poussie***: Belongs to the Cordier firm of Bordeaux; **Jean-Max Roger***: Elegant wines from an energetic grower. Jean-Max also makes an excellent Menetou-Salon.

CHAUDOUX-VERDIGNY, postcode 18300, 51 B3

André Dezat*; **Domaine des Garennes/Jacques Fleuriet***; **Bernard Reverdy & Fils***.

CHAVIGNOL, postcode 18300, 51 C3

H. Bourgeois & Fils; Francis & Paul Cotat*; **Vincent Delaporte***.

MENETREOL-SOUS-SANCERRE, postcode 18300, 51 C3

Gitton Père & Fils*: Excellently equipped property that produces a range of splendid, balanced Sancerre and Pouilly-Fumé.

STE-GEMME, postcode 18300, 51 B3

Domaine du Nozay/Philippe de Benoist*

ST-SATUR, postcode 18300, 51 C3

Domaine Laporte

SANCERRE, postcode 18300, 49 C4, 51 C3

Cave Coopérative; Alphonse Mellot*: Quality-minded merchants; **Château de Sancerre***: Belongs to the Marnier-Lapostolle family (of Grand Marnier fame); **Domaine Vacheron***: White and red wines of high standard.

SURY-EN-VAUX, postcode 18300, 51 B3

Château de Maimbray*

VERDIGNY-EN-SANCERRE, postcode 18300, 51 C3

Paul & Claude Fournier*; **Roger Neveu***; **Pierre Prieur/Domaine de Saint-Pierre***; **Bernard-Noël Reverdy***; **Jean Reverdy***; **Reverdy-Ducroux & Fils***.

POUILLY-FUME

LES BERTHIERS, postcode 58150, 51 C4

Jean-Claude Châtelain*; **Serge Dagueneau***.

LES LOGES, postcode 58150, 51 C4

Bailly Père & Fils*; **Paul Figeat***.

POUILLY SUR LOIRE, postcode 58150, 49 C4, 51 C4

Cave Coopérative; Pascal Jolivet*; A small négociant with impeccable wines; **De Ladoucette***: At Château du Nozet, built in 1850, Patrick de Ladoucette makes more than half of all Pouilly-Fumé. Part comes from the firm's own vineyard of some 65 hectares (160 acres), and must is also bought in from other growers. The Pouilly-Fumé is exquisite, but the special, very expensive Baron de L selection is of even higher standard. Other wines from De Ladoucette include Sancerre (Comte Lafon), Touraine, Bourgueil, Saumur (Baron Briare), Vouvray and Chinon (Marc Brédif) and Chablis (Baron Patrick, A. Regnard & Fils); **Domaine J. M. Masson-Blondelet***: Small family estate with expertly made wines that repeatedly win awards.

ST-ANDELAIN, postcode 58150, 51 C4

Domaine Renaud-Bossuat & Fils*

MENETOU-SALON

MENETOU-SALON, postcode 18510, 49 C3

G. Chavet & Fils*; **Domaine de Chatenoy***.

MOROGUES, postcode 18220

Henry Pellé*

QUINCY

QUINCY, postcode 18120, 49 C3

Claude Houssier*; **Pierre & Jean Mardon***: Presently owned by the Gaumior-Denis family; **Raymond Pipet***.

REUILLY

REUILLY, postcode 36260, 49 C3

Gérard Cordier*; **Claude Lafond***; **Guy Malbete***.

ORLEANAIS

MAREAU-AUX-PRES, postcode 45370

Jacky Legroux/Domaine de Chantoiseau; GAEC Clos de St-Fiacre*: The Montigny family's white Auvernat (Chardonnay) is excellent.

MEZIERES-LES-CLERY, postcode 45370, 51 C5

GAEC Valoir/Michel Javoy

AROUND THE MASSIF CENTRAL

The Auvergne is a land of uplands, deep valleys and stone-built farms. In contrast to the middle Loire valley, this countryside has an almost northern European aspect. In spring and early summer it is awash with wild flowers.

Only a limited quantity of the wines of the Massif Central and the adjoining districts is sold outside the region. Anyone who wants to taste them is almost obliged to travel around the area – which is no hardship. The Massif itself, with its granite plateaux, extinct volcanoes and hot springs, has a great deal of natural beauty, and the surrounding districts are pleasantly surprising for their tranquillity and their places of interest.

The most northerly district is St-Pourçain. It takes its name from the little town of St-Pourçain-sur-Sioule which, 325 kilometres (200 miles) from Paris, is a favourite stop for holidaymakers on their way to or from the sunny south. Wine growing in St-Pourçain once experienced a golden age. The local wine was served at the French court and also enjoyed such popularity elsewhere that in the eighteenth century the district had some 8,000 hectares (19,800 acres) of vineyards.

Today only ten percent of this area is still planted with vines, and only half of it produces St-Pourçain (a VDQS, like all the wines included in this chapter). More than half the total wine production consists of red wine from the Gamay or Pinot Noir: not, as a rule, of any great consequence, seldom rising above the level of a pleasant picnic wine. The white wines can be more interesting, especially those with a good basis of Chardonnay and Sauvignon. You then have charming, fresh wines that taste splendid with, for example, crayfish or trout.

From St-Pourçain-sur-Sioule it is some 80 kilometres (50 miles) in a southeasterly direction to the ancient city of Roanne, once a busy river port but now world-famous for the Troisgros restaurant. The fertile plain west of the town lies in the lee of spurs running from the Massif Central, with a modest amount of wine growing on their slopes. When the rivers were still important traffic arteries, wines from the Côte Roannaise were shipped to Paris in large quantities: around the beginning of the eighteenth century, 10,000 ox carts were sometimes needed to bring all the barrels down from the hillsides to the port.

But that is in the past. The wines of the Côte Roannaise today are of only local importance and the vineyard area is little greater than that of St-Pourçain. The only permitted grape is the Gamay, from which both light, fresh red wines and the more traditional styles, aged in wood and benefiting from some development in bottle, are made. Some of the growers also produce a little dry rosé.

South of Côte Roannaise, around the village of Boën-sur-Lignon, is the district of Côtes du Forez. Here, too, the only grape is the Gamay, and about three quarters of the harvest is processed by a cooperative. Red Côtes du Forez must be regarded as a simple, fresh, everyday wine that – quite rightly – does not cost very much. A workable alternative to most Beaujolais, in fact.

The vineyards of the Massif Central itself lie spread across the Puy-de-Dôme département, both north and south of the large industrial city Clermont-Ferrand. The appellation is Côtes d'Auvergne, to which the names of the subdistricts Boudes, Chanturgue, Châteaugay (by far the largest), Corent and Madargues may be added. The district comprises 54 wine communes altogether. This might lead to expectations of a large production, but in fact it remains limited to roughly 20,000 hectolitres, about the same as St-Pourçain.

The extent of the district sometimes makes the vineyards difficult to find; there are no large estates and the vines are surrounded by other crops. Gamay is the most important grape for the red wines (about three quarters of the total) but Pinot Noir can also be used. At its best, red Côtes d'Auvergne is a firm wine with tannin and some fruit. It makes an ideal table companion for Auvergne's famous charcuterie, and so does the dry rosé – the *vin gris* from Corent can be very successful. The only white grape used is the Chardonnay, which gives a light, fresh wine.

On the far side of the N144, about 60 kilometres (37 miles) south of Bourges, the district of Châteaumeillant produces fresh red and rosé wines with a modest amount of fruit. The grapes are Gamay and Pinot Noir.

TRAVEL INFORMATION

ST-POURCAIN

Most travellers just stop overnight in St-Pourçain-sur-Sioule, but the surroundings and the wines justify a longer stay. At the hotels, ask for a room at the back as the through traffic is heavy.

HOTELS

Le Chêne Vert, 35 Boulevard Ledru-Rollin, 03500 St-Pourçain-sur-Sioule, tel. 70 45 40 65. A busy place, not least because of its restaurant, where the helpings are generous and the prices agreeable. Fresh crayfish, *poulet fermier* and desserts are among the specialities. Class B.
Les Deux Ponts, 4 Le Tivoli, 03500 St-Pourçain-sur-Sioule, tel. 70 45 41 14. Large hotel with a restaurant and terrace, on an island in the little river Sioule. Class B.

RESTAURANTS

Auberge de l'Etang, 03110 Broût-Vernet, tel. 70 58 21 42. Country atmosphere. Class C.
Hotel du Commerce, 03500 Châtel-de-Neuve, tel. 70 42 07 77. Good cooking and a simple hotel. Class C.
Le Cellier, 69 Boulevard Ledru-Rollin, 03500 St-Pourçain-sur-Sioule, tel. 70 45 43 48. A tasting and sales room for local wines and cheeses. Conserves are also sold. Class C.
Maison du St-Pourçain, Quai de la Ronde, 03500 St-Pourçain-sur-Sioule, tel. 70 43 34 90. Run by the wine cooperative and catering particularly for tourist coaches. Class C.
Chez Lucien, 03500 Saulcet, tel. 70 45 44 61. For an inexpensive lunch. Saulcet is the most important wine village of the area. Class C.

THE ROANNAIS

Roanne attracts gourmets from all over the world to the three-star restaurant Troisgros, but you can also eat well at a simpler level in the area.

HOTELS

Central, 42370 Renaison, tel. 77 64 25 39. Simple hotel with a restaurant, in a wine village. Class C.
Terminus, Place de la Gare, 42300 Roanne, tel. 77 71 79 69. Functional hotel where you can stay overnight when dining at Troisgros, just a few steps away. No restaurant. Class B.

RESTAURANTS

Jacques-Coeur, 42370 Renaison, tel. 77 64 25 34. In good weather you eat in the garden. Also a hotel. Class B.
Troisgros, Place de la Gare, 42300 Roanne, tel. 77 71 66 97. In their futuristic kitchen, father Pierre and

son Michel Troisgros and their staff prepare the masterpieces that have won them a worldwide reputation. The most famous Troisgros creation is the salmon with sorrel. In the extensive wine list the emphasis is on Burgundy. Also a hotel. Class A.
Le Lion d'Or, 42370 St-André-d'Apchon, tel. 77 65 81 53. Good food, expertly prepared, and local wines. Also a hotel. Class B.
Le Tournebroche, 42640 St-Romain-la-Motte, tel. 77 64 50 40. Choose the straightforward dishes and accompany them with a Côte Roannaise. Class C.

THE COTES D'AUVERGNE

The hotels and restaurants below are all away from the industrial town Clermont-Ferrand. Auvergne cuisine with its soups, charcuterie, hams and cheeses is fairly hearty and the light, refreshing regional wines go well with it. Fresh crayfish, salmon and trout also appear frequently on menus.

HOTELS

Le Pariou, 18 Avenue Kennedy, 63500 Issoire, tel. 73 89 22 11. Pleasant place to stay where you can also eat well and enjoy the wines of the region. Has a terrace. Class C.
La Rose des Vents, 63530 Luzet, tel. 73 33 50 77. Holiday hotel quietly situated in the neighbourhood of Volvic. Swimming pool and restaurant. Class B.

RESTAURANTS

Les Petits Ventres, 6 Rue Anne-Dubourg, 63200 Riom, tel. 73 38 21 65. A restaurant of quality. Class B.
Le Rivalet, 63320 Montaigut-le-Blanc, tel. 73 96 73 92. The village is west of Champeix, which in turn lies west of a number of wine communes (Nerschers, for example). Regional dishes. Class B.
Auberge de Tralume, 63730 Montpeyroux, tel. 73 96 60 09. One of the best restaurants of the Puy-de-Dôme département, with *ris de veau aux écrevisses* among its specialities. Also a quiet hotel with a few rooms. Restaurant class A; hotel class B.
La Belle Meunière, 25 Avenue de la Vallée, 63130 Royat, tel. 73 35 80 17. A *belle époque* dining room and traditional cuisine; also a hotel. The spa town of Royat lies just west of Clermont-Ferrand. Class B.
Le Pont des Soupirs, 63130 Royat, tel. 73 35 82 66 (on the D68, in westerly direction). Substantial, not markedly regional cooking. Class B.
Royat, Boulevard Dr Roumeuf, 63130 Royat, tel. 73 35 82 72. Modern. Also a hotel. Class B.

PLACES OF INTEREST

ST-POURCAIN

Most of the villages below are on the wine route that runs west from St-Pourçain-sur-Sioule.
Besson Remains of the 13th-century Château de Fourchaud, and a Romanesque church.
Chantelle Former castle of the dukes of Bourbon. There is a signposted walk along the Gorges de Bouble.
Chareil-Chintrat A 16th-century château with wall paintings.
Etroussat The Château de Douzon has a beautiful garden in classical French style.
St-Pourçain-sur-Sioule Parts of the church in the centre of this small town date from the 12th century and behind the church there is a Musée de la Vigne et du Vin.
Saulcet Wine village with a 13th-century church.

COTE ROANNAISE AND COTES DU FOREZ

Ambierle This Roannais commune amid the vineyards has a beautiful 15th-century monastery church with paintings attributed to the Flemish master Rogier van der Weyden.
Roanne People come here mainly to eat at the Troisgros restaurant, but the Musée Joseph-Déchelette with its archaeological finds is worth visiting. The Loire gorges lie to the south of Roanne.
St-Etienne-le-Molard Village near Boën-sur-Lignon, the centre of the Côtes du Forez. The remarkable La Bastie d'Urfé is here, a château with a fairytale shell grotto.
St-Hâon-le-Châtel Old fortified village on the Roanne wine slopes.
Thelins Just south of Boën-sur-Lignon: the Château de Goutelas dates partly from the 15th century and now serves as a regional cultural centre.

COTES D'AUVERGNE

Busséol East of the wine villages of Corent and Orcet lies Busséol with its formidable castle and unusual garden. The castle dates from 1170 and is the oldest such structure still intact in Auvergne.
Châteaugay Well-known wine village, situated on a hill around a 14th- to 16th-century castle. The castle has a wine-tasting hall.
Châtelguyon A spa, known for its springs and beautiful parks.
Chazeron In summer the attractive château has a *son et lumière*.
Clermont-Ferrand The vast Michelin tyre-manufacturing complex

is here. In the old part of the town there is one of the most beautiful Romanesque churches in France, the Notre-Dame-du-Port.
Issoire The large, 12th-century church of St-Austremoine is a perfect example of the Romanesque Auvergnat style. Issoire's old centre has atmosphere, but for the rest this is an industrial town with the stress on aluminium.
Montferrand Formerly an important wine village, now joined to Clermont-Ferrand. In the heart of Montferrand there are picturesque streets with old half-timbered houses.
Montpeyroux Medieval village with a round defensive tower and a splendid view over the Couze valley.
Parc Naturel Régional des Volcans d'Auvergne This takes in a large part of the Auvergne and is the biggest nature park in France.
Parentignat Village south of Issoire with an attractive 17th-century château.
Puy-de-Dôme A toll road leads to the top of this steep mountain, from where it is said you can see 11 départements. On the mountainside there are the remains of a Gallo-Roman temple to Mercury.
Riom A town rich in history, the former capital of the Auvergne. Old houses, tree-lined boulevards and

▲ The *puys* – dome-shaped volcanic hills – are typical of the Auvergne.

fountains, and the 15th-century church of Notre-Dame-de-Marturet are among its attractions.
Volvic The dark-grey Volvic stone is used for many Auvergne buildings. On a hill not far from Volvic there are the ruins of Château de Tournoël, a feudal stronghold that dominates the surrounding countryside.

WINE ACTIVITIES

St-Pourçain-sur-Sioule organizes a *foire des vins* at the end of February, the election of a Wine Queen in July, and a *fête du vin* in the last weekend in August. Côte Roannaise wines can be tasted during the *foire aux vins et fromages* in Roanne in May. The St-Pourçain fraternity is l'Ordre des Fins Palais de St-Pourçain; Les Compagnons du Bousset d'Auvergne are active in the Auvergne.

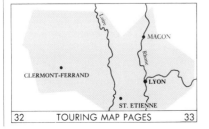

32 TOURING MAP PAGES 33

PRODUCERS OF SPECIAL INTEREST

ST-POURÇAIN

MEILLARD, postcode 03500

Domaine de Bellevue*

LA ROCHE-BRANSAT, postcode 03500

Elie Grosbot

ST-POURÇAIN-SUR-SIOULE, postcode 03500

Cave Coopérative; Guy & Serge Nebout.

SAULCET, postcode 03500

Jean Chérillat; André & Yves Gallas; Joseph Laurent; Ray Père & Fils*.

COTE ROANNAISE

AMBIERLE, postcode 42820

Robert Durier; Marcel Joathan; Maurice Lutz.

RENAISON, postcode 42370

Antoine Chargros*; Claude-Robert Chaucesse*; Robert Sérol.

ST-HAON-LE-VIEUX, postcode 42370

Paul Lapandéry & Fils*; Jean Vagneur-Tachon*.

VILLEMONTAIS, postcode 42370

GIE des Producteurs Vins du Roannais; Auguste Néron.

COTES DU FOREZ

BOEN-SUR-LIGNON, postcode 42130

Georges Bouchand; Cave Coopérative.

COTES D'AUVERGNE

AUBIERE, postcode 63170

Jean-Baptiste Bayle; Jean-Marie Bourcheix.

BOUDES, postcode 63340

Albert Charmensat; Claude Savat.

CHATEAUGAY, postcode 63100

Pierre Lapouge*; Michel & Roland Rougeyron.

CORENT, postcode 63730

Paul Champroux; Louis Chapelle; Michel Montorier; Bertrand Nicoulaud.

LE CREST, postcode 63450

Michel Blanc*

ORCET, postcode 63670

Raymond Roumeuf

VEYRE-MONTON, postcode 63960

Cave Coopérative; Pierre Chevalier.

55

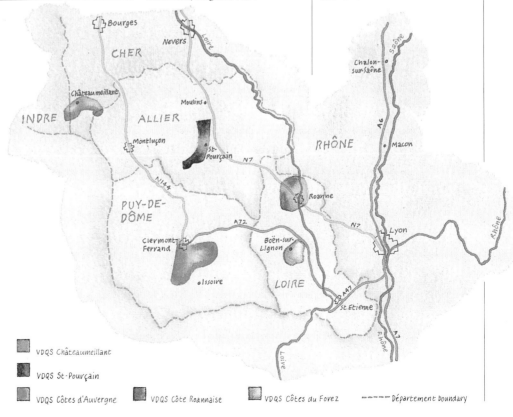

VDQS Châteaumeillant

VDQS St-Pourçain

VDQS Côtes d'Auvergne   VDQS Côte Roannaise   VDQS Côtes du Forez   ----- Département boundary

SOUTHWEST ZONE

The routes of the relatively few roads and the flow of the many rivers spell out the nature of the southwest of France. Hemmed in between the endless peaks and passes of the Massif Central, and to the south the almost unbroken wall of the Pyrenees, it is the corridor between the Atlantic Ocean and the Mediterranean.

Each of its two seas brings benefit to its climate: warmth from the Mediterranean in winter, temperate moist winds from the Bay of Biscay in summer. Frost can occasionally be serious on the French Riviera and south into Italy, but Narbonne and its surrounding countryside rarely suffers badly.

France's two most productive wine regions dominate this corner of the country. Bordeaux clusters around the rivers Garonne and Dordogne and their joint estuary, the broad Gironde. The Languedoc laps from the Mediterranean coastline right up into the foothills of the Cevennes, scarcely breaking at the valley of the Aude before the limestone undulations of the Corbières, which rise towards the Pyrenees into the more dramatic hills and valleys of the Roussillon.

Each of the major rivers draining the centre has its vineyard: Gaillac on the Tarn, Cahors on the Lot, Bergerac on the Dordogne. In the Middle Ages while Bordeaux was establishing its trading dominance, these were called the wines of the Haut-Pays, the high country. Each has a proud tradition.

Both France's famous brandies are grown here, too: cognac to the north of Bordeaux in the calm country of the Charentes, armagnac to the south in a deeply rural land of wood and valley that flows on into the Basque country, a region that attracts a following of those who dote on traditional country food and wine with the more rustic accent of its *terroir*.

VINS DE PAYS

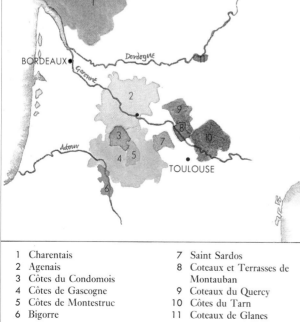

1 Charentais
2 Agenais
3 Côtes du Condomois
4 Côtes de Gascogne
5 Côtes de Montestruc
6 Bigorre
7 Saint Sardos
8 Coteaux et Terrasses de Montauban
9 Coteaux du Quercy
10 Côtes du Tarn
11 Coteaux de Glanes

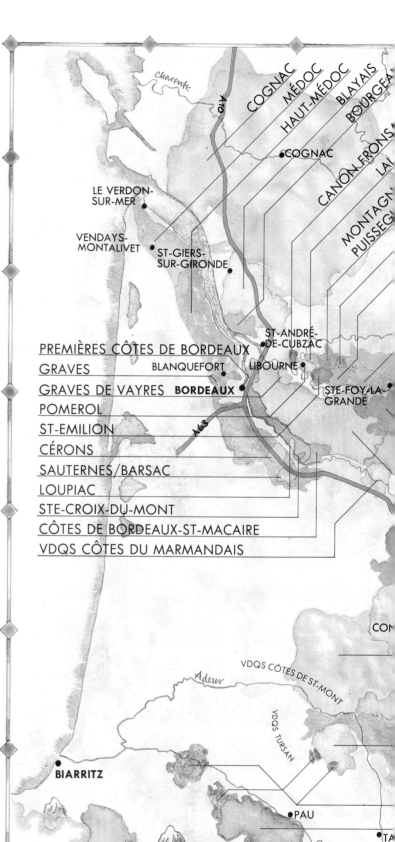

PREMIÈRES CÔTES DE BORDEAUX
GRAVES
GRAVES DE VAYRES
POMEROL
ST-EMILION
CÉRONS
SAUTERNES/BARSAC
LOUPIAC
STE-CROIX-DU-MONT
CÔTES DE BORDEAUX-ST-MACAIRE
VDQS CÔTES DU MARMANDAIS

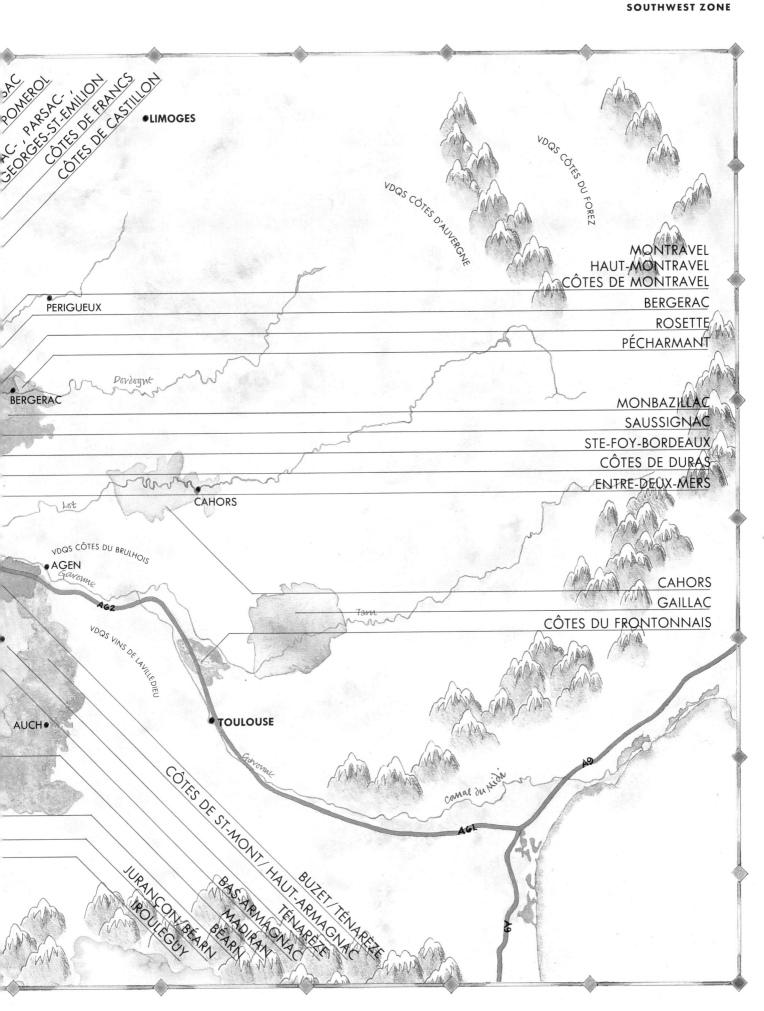

POMEROL
GEORGES-ST-ÉMILION
PARSAC-
CÔTES DE FRANCS
CÔTES DE CASTILLON

●LIMOGES

VDQS CÔTES D'AUVERGNE

VDQS CÔTES DU FOREZ

MONTRAVEL
HAUT-MONTRAVEL
CÔTES DE MONTRAVEL

PERIGUEUX

BERGERAC

ROSETTE

PÉCHARMANT

Dordogne

●BERGERAC

MONBAZILLAC

SAUSSIGNAC

STE-FOY-BORDEAUX

CÔTES DE DURAS

ENTRE-DEUX-MERS

Lot

CAHORS

VDQS CÔTES DU BRULHOIS

●AGEN

Garonne

A62

CAHORS

GAILLAC

Tarn

CÔTES DU FRONTONNAIS

VDQS VINS DE LAVILLEDIEU

●TOULOUSE

Garonne

AUCH●

canal du Midi

A9

A61

CÔTES DE ST-MONT / HAUT-ARMAGNAC

BUZET/TÉNARÈZE

TÉNARÈZE

BAS-ARMAGNAC

MADIRAN

JURANÇON/BÉARN

BÉARN

IROULÉGUY

A9

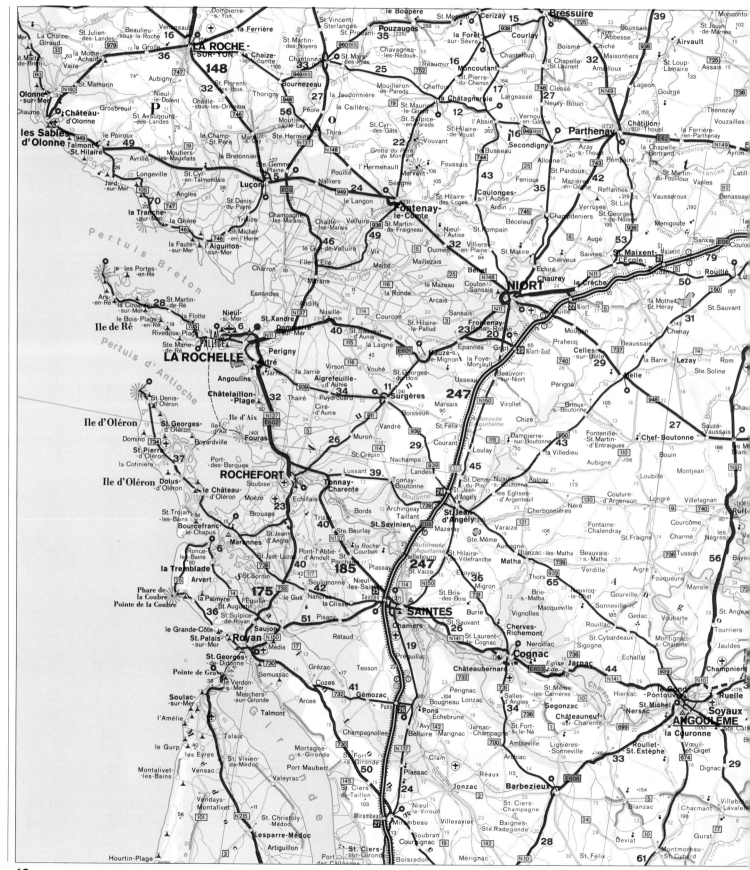

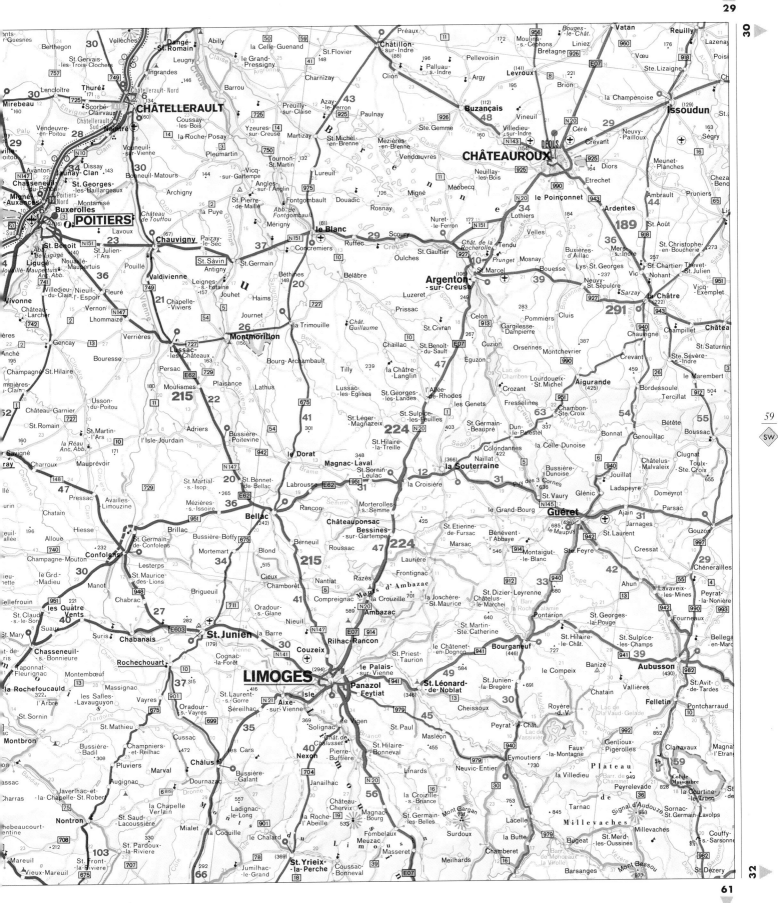

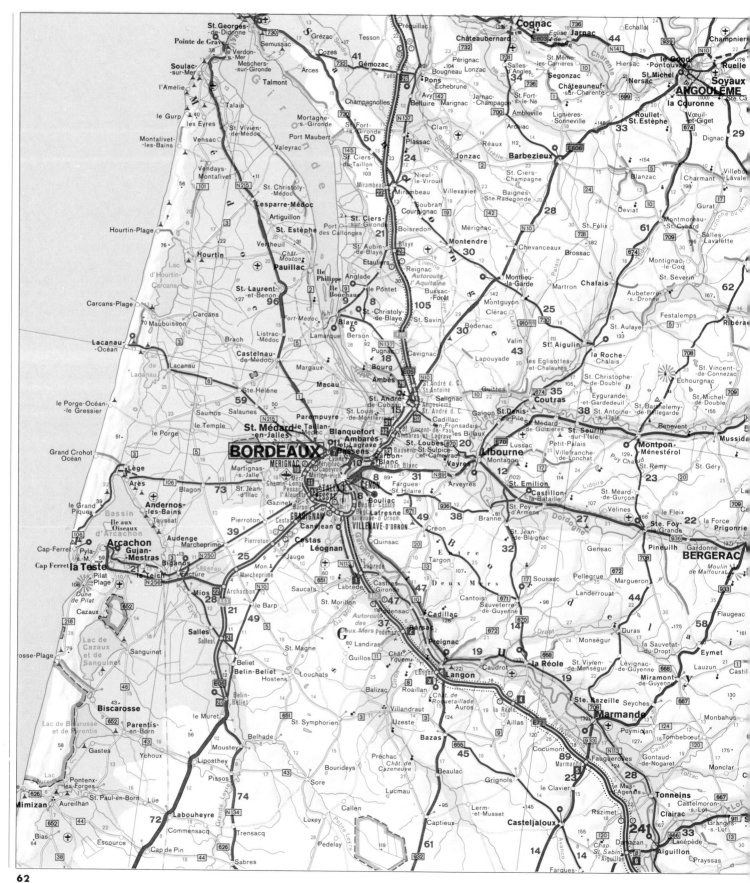

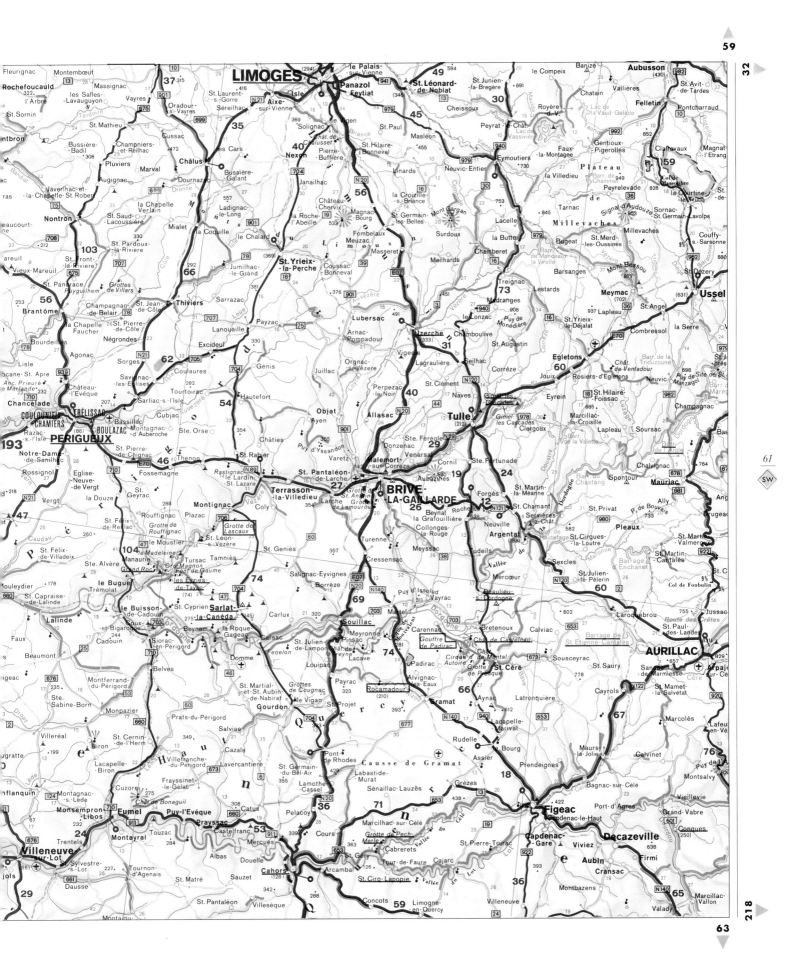

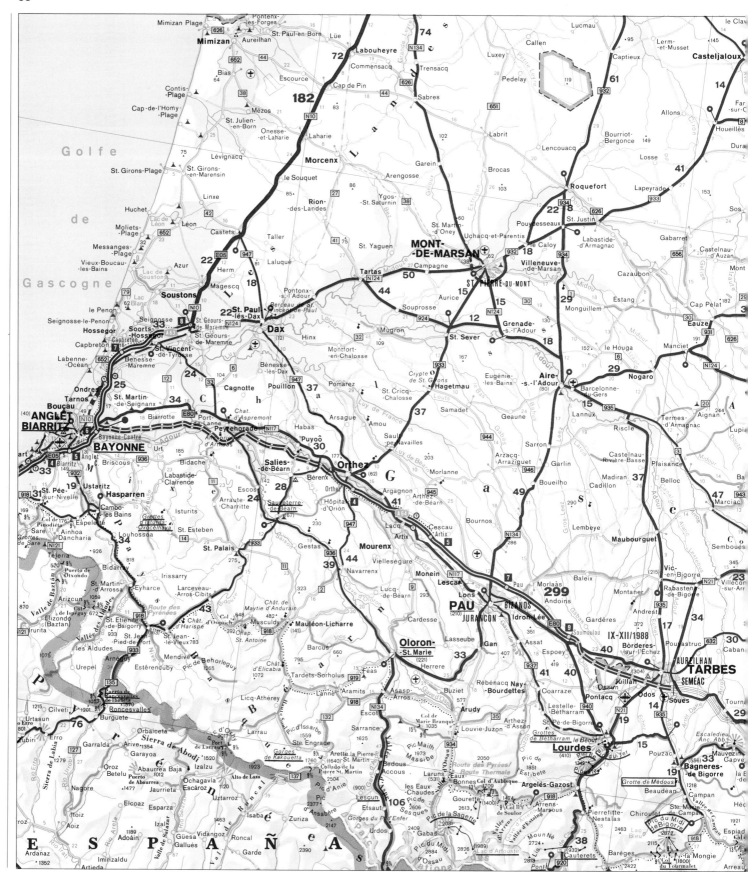

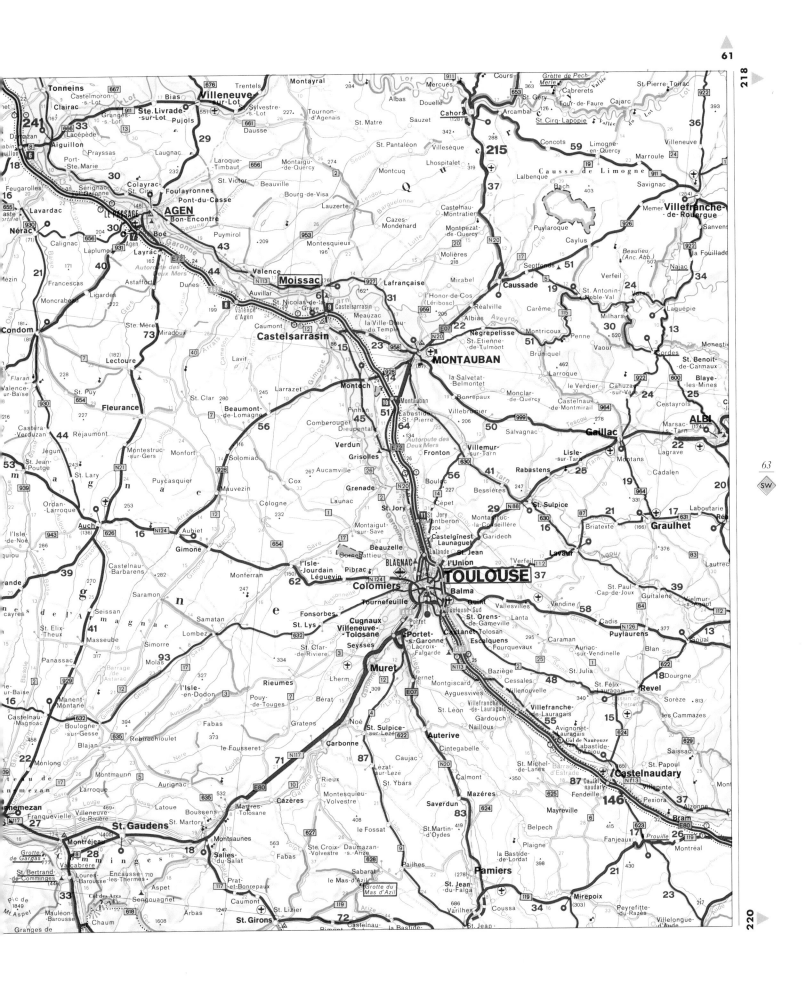

BORDEAUX

The greatest city of wine is also the most handsome: few cities in Europe muster such a gallery of harmonious architecture – squares, terraces and monuments all in grey stone, drawn, it seems, in charcoal by a consummate classicist. Its riverside buildings, although separated today from the river by new quays cluttered with sheds and gantries, remain almost exactly as they appear in eighteenth-century prints, when barrels of wine were loaded in lighters on the beach to be taken out to ships anchored in midstream.

Bordeaux's Grand Théâtre is as fine a classical building as any in France. It is tempting to think of it as a heathen temple to rival the ancient Gothic cathedral. Certainly the age that produced it was known more for commerce than piety: commerce with the Indies, both East and West, and above all the business of making and selling wine.

Most wine towns and cities make hospitality their pride and pleasure. On the face of it Bordeaux is an exception: it is not the friendliest of places to the pilgrims it attracts. Nor is its region oriented to entertaining strangers. Paradoxically, after almost 2,000 years of exporting wine as a way of life, Bordeaux appears aloof to the source of its manifest prosperity. It would rather, you feel, see its visitors taking notes than having fun.

The rather chilling elegance of the city is matched by the vast vineyard of the Médoc to its north. The message of the Médoc seems at first sight to be: come on a serious mission to taste and buy, or remain a mere spectator.

In reality its heart is warm: its doors at least ajar to passing strangers. But a certain tenacity is required to make very much of this great expanse of vines punctuated by more or less pompous mansions: the châteaux whose names are known around the world. A minority are inhabited by their proprietors. Animation arrives once a year, at vintage time; still not, however, in a form that embraces the visitor. The proprietor is busy with his harvest, his wife with catering for the *vendangeurs*, and both with their friends. The Médoc can easily seem like breakfast at Tiffany's: a dream world, behind a pane of glass.

This is far less the feeling of Bordeaux's hinterland to the south and east. To the south the Graves is a comfortably domestic landscape, broken by wood and valley, its villages seemingly less shuttered, its châteaux less formidable. Sauternes, a distinct enclave of concentrated viticulture in the wooded Graves, is a district of handsome houses recalling long-founded prosperity.

East across the River Garonne the region of Entre-Deux-Mers ("Between the Rivers") might be almost anywhere in southwest France. Vines take their place with orchards, maize, woodland and pasture. If there are few sights to turn the head, every bend offers a warm bank for a picnic or a shady corner to rest.

East again, across the Dordogne, the country wears an even friendlier face. The centre of the district that includes St-Emilion, Pomerol, Fronsac and their vine-producing satellites is the market town of Libourne. Libourne is unaffected, cheerfully busy at its centre, timelessly peaceful down on its quays, where ships from northern parts, from England, Holland, Scotland or the Baltic used to tie up among the willows to load barrels of the new season's wine.

The jewel of its region is St-Emilion. One could argue happily for hours about whether St-Emilion or Beaune presents the more perfect picture of an old town that lives for wine. But Beaune, its ramparts once ringed by water, is now encircled by traffic that cuts it off from the surrounding country. St-Emilion could not be more intimately linked to its vines. The old Roman town lies snug in the crook of the vine-covered hill from whose soft stone its buildings are quarried. Its quarries, in turn, are its cellars: a system of galleries that wander under the town and for a considerable distance into the vineyards around. Not only wines but mushrooms, too, are raised in these fragrant caverns.

▶ The vineyards are but one face of Bordeaux. Along the Médoc peninsula, westward towards the sea, comes first a zone of forests, then a landscape of marshy lagoons such as the Etang d'Hourtin, right. Finally you reach the Atlantic beaches, which provide a refuge from the summer heat for the people of Bordeaux.

St-Emilion has both a sense of history and a sense of festival that feel more like Burgundy than Bordeaux. Pomerol, its immediate neighbour, is more like a mini-Médoc: nothing grows except vines; there is nowhere to visit except châteaux – which in Pomerol are rarely more than modest family houses. The wine fanatic will revel in simply reading the litany of famous names on the road signs: learning to put a face, as it were, to what was just a label, and perhaps a flavour, before.

The visitor looking for *agrément*, for the atmosphere of long-settled villages in pretty countryside, will find them in the less famous fringes of the wine district: in Fronsac, just across the River Isle from Libourne, whose deep red wine is still remarkably undervalued and underexploited, and in the cluster of villages north and east of St-Emilion: Montagne, St-Georges, Lussac and Puisseguin, as far as the Côtes de Francs and the Côtes de Castillon, the also-underrated appellations on the boundary of the Gironde département with its beautiful neighbour, the Dordogne.

Equally agreeable is what the French call a *randonnée* (a "ramble") in the small-scale hills and valleys of Bourg and Blaye, downstream along the River Dordogne, facing the Médoc across the wide brown waters of the estuary.

There is little temptation to stay in Bordeaux itself, although many sights for the visitor to enjoy. Most of its old hotels are merely adequate, and most of its modern ones are of the dullest international kind, grouped around a newly developed exhibition centre on drained land around a man-made lake. Biennially, in June, the exhibition centre hosts Vinexpo, the biggest and best of all international wine fairs. It is hard to quarrel with Bordeaux's right to stage it.

Top left: part of the Monument des Girondins in the Esplanade des Quinconces, one of the largest squares in Europe and a monument to the commercial confidence of early 19th-century Bordeaux.
Left: a square in Le Vieux Bordeaux.

Below: traders in the Marché des Capucins in the heart of Bordeaux. The Bordelais take their food as seriously as their wine: regional specialities include *foie gras* and smoked ham, Pauillac lamb and of course *entrecôte* grilled, ideally, over vine prunings.

THE CITY OF BORDEAUX

Bordeaux is the fourth city of France, with a large port, many industries and a major university. Many wine authorities and a large number of merchants have their headquarters here, and various négociants are still based in their traditional haunt, the Quai des Chartrons. The modest 18th-century buildings along the quay give no hint of the often vast cellar complexes that lie behind them.

The heart of Bordeaux is the Place de la Comédie with its splendid Grand Théâtre (below), designed by Victor Louis and completed in 1780. Two shopping streets lead into the square, as well as the grand Allées de Tourny. The Maison du Vin is here, and Europe's largest city square, the Esplanade des Quinconces, is only a few minutes' walk away. On the other side of the Place de la Comédie stretches Le Vieux Bordeaux, the oldest quarter of the city.

Bordeaux has many other sights worth seeing. At first impression formal and even dour, its excitement grows with acquaintance. The most apt description came from Victor Hugo, "Take Versailles, add to it Antwerp and you have Bordeaux."

HOTELS

The Bordeaux postcode is 33000.
Grand Hotel, 2 Place de la Comédie, tel. 56 90 93 44. Opposite the Grand Théâtre. Fine old hotel renovated on the cheap. Most of the rooms are cramped. Class A.
Normandie, 7 Cours du 30-Juillet, tel. 56 52 16 80. Large, traditional hotel. Class B.
Novotel-Bordeaux le Lac, Parc des Expositions, tel. 56 50 99 70. One of the modern hotels in the exhibition area north of the city. Swimming pool and restaurant. Class B.

Royal Médoc, 3 Rue de Sèze, tel. 56 81 72 42. Central, friendly and not too noisy. Much used by wine writers and buyers. Perhaps the best of a disappointing lot. Class B.
Hotel de Sèze, 23 Allées de Tourny, tel. 56 52 65 54. Functional. Class B.

RESTAURANTS

Le Bistrot du Clavel Centre, 7 Rue Montesquieu, tel. 56 51 28 81. Owned by the master chef Francis Garcia. Mainly regional menu. Class B. (M. Garcia is moving his restaurant Clavel, which was by the railway station, into **Le Chapon Fin** adjoining the *bistrot*. Class A/B.)
Le Cellier Bordelais, 30 Quai de la Monnaie, tel. 56 31 30 30. Good cooking and interesting and affordable wines. Class C.
La Chamade, 20 Rue Piliers de Tutelle, tel. 56 48 13 74. Attractive atmosphere and food. A lower-priced lunch menu. Class A/B.
La Ferme St-Michel, 21 Rue des Menuts, tel. 56 91 54 77. Market-fresh ingredients. Class C.
Chez Joël D., 12 Rue Piliers de Tutelle, tel. 56 52 68 21. For oyster lovers. Class C.
Lou Magret, 62 Rue St-Rémi, tel. 56 44 77 94. Good, inexpensive and always busy. Class C.
Le Pavillon des Boulevards, 120 Rue de la Croix-de-Seguey, tel. 56 81 51 02. Venturesome cooking with occasional hints of the Oriental, and a charming courtyard where you can dine in summer. Lower-priced lunch menu. Class A/B.
Ramet, 7 Place Jean-Jaurès, tel.

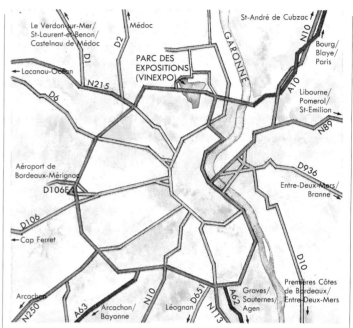

56 44 12 41. Distinctive atmosphere and fine cuisine. Class A/B.
Le Rouzic, 34 Cours du Chapeau Rouge, tel. 56 44 39 11. Inventive menu and a stylish setting. A small Russian restaurant on the first floor, **Le Bolchoi**, serves dinners and suppers. Class B.
La Tupina, 6 Rue de Porte-de-la-Monnaie, tel. 56 91 56 37. The cooking of the French southwest at its best. Class B.

WINE FAIR

Every second year (1989, 1991, etc) the world's biggest wine fair for professionals, Vinexpo, is held in June in the vast Parc des Expositions.

WINE FRATERNITIES

The local fraternities are listed in the chapters on Bordeaux. There are also coordinating associations, the most important of which is l'Académie du Vin de Bordeaux whose members are mainly the owners of prestigious châteaux.

WINE INFORMATION

The Maison du Vin is at 1 Cours du 30-Juillet. For visits to wine districts or individual châteaux you may be referred to the Maison du Tourisme across the street.

▼ Below: all the better red Bordeaux wines are matured in barriques, 225-litre oak casks. The aroma of claret gains in complexity through ageing in wood, and tannin, a preserving agent, is absorbed, adding to that already present naturally in the wine. At the same time the wine develops through the gradual supply of oxygen seeping through the slightly porous wood.
Bottom left: the bars of Bordeaux sometimes offer a surprisingly good range of wines.
Bottom right: samples of the new wines ready for tasting by the blender.

THE 1855 CLASSIFICATION

Of the various wine classifications carried out in the Bordeaux region, that of the Médoc is not only the first and the best known but also the most precise, consisting of 60 Grands Crus Classés (including Haut Brion in Graves) divided into five quality grades. The classification was drawn up in 1855 for the Paris World Exhibition by the *courtiers* (the wine brokers) and was based on the price each wine had commanded over a long period (about 100 years), the wine's reputation and the current situation at the vineyard. There was nothing sensational about the classification, for comparable gradings had been in use among brokers and others for many years, but 130 years on the classification still has value, as is clear from the intensive use made of it.

As well as the classified châteaux, the Grands Crus Classés, the Médoc has a large number of Crus Bourgeois. More than 150 of them have graded themselves – unofficially – via membership of their own syndicate. This has established a classification into Crus Grands Bourgeois Exceptionnels, Crus Grands Bourgeois and Crus Bourgeois. The last official classification of the Crus Bourgeois was in 1932; it is used mainly by properties that are unable, or unwilling, to belong to the Crus Bourgeois syndicate. St-Emilion, Graves and Sauternes have their own classifications, which are discussed in the chapters concerned.

First-Growths (Premiers Crus)
Château Lafite-Rothschild, Pauillac
Château Latour, Pauillac
Château Margaux, Margaux
Château Mouton Rothschild, Pauillac
  (promoted in 1973 to First-Growth)
Château Haut-Brion, Pessac, Graves

Second-Growths (Deuxièmes Crus)
Château Rausan-Ségla, Margaux
Château Rauzan-Gassies, Margaux
Château Léoville-Las-Cases, St-Julien
Château Léoville-Poyferré, St-Julien
Château Léoville-Barton, St-Julien
Château Durfort-Vivens, Margaux
Château Lascombes, Margaux
Château Gruaud-Larose, St-Julien
Château Brane-Cantenac, Cantenac-Margaux
Château Pichon-Longueville Baron, Pauillac
Château Pichon Longueville Comtesse de
  Lalande, Pauillac
Château Ducru-Beaucaillou, St-Julien
Château Cos d'Estournel, St-Estèphe
Château Montrose, St-Estèphe

Third-Growths (Troisièmes Crus)
Château Giscours, Labarde-Margaux
Château Kirwan, Cantenac-Margaux
Château d'Issan, Cantenac-Margaux
Château Lagrange, St-Julien
Château Langoa-Barton, St-Julien
Château Malescot St-Exupéry, Margaux
Château Cantenac Brown, Cantenac-Margaux
Château Palmer, Cantenac-Margaux
Château La Lagune, Ludon
Château Desmirail, Margaux
Château Calon-Ségur, St-Estèphe

Château Ferrière, Margaux
Château Marquis d'Alesme Becker, Margaux
Château Boyd-Cantenac, Cantenac-Margaux

Fourth-Growths (Quatrièmes Crus)
Château St-Pierre, St-Julien
Château Branaire-Ducru, St-Julien
Château Talbot, St-Julien
Château Duhart-Milon-Rothschild, Pauillac
Château Pouget, Cantenac-Margaux
Château La Tour Carnet, St-Laurent
Château Lafon-Rochet, St-Estèphe
Château Beychevelle, St-Julien
Château Prieuré-Lichine, Cantenac-Margaux
Château Marquis-de-Terme, Margaux

Fifth-Growths (Cinquièmes Crus)
Château Pontet-Canet, Pauillac
Château Batailley, Pauillac
Château Grand-Puy-Lacoste, Pauillac
Château Grand-Puy Ducasse, Pauillac
Château Haut-Batailley, Pauillac
Château Lynch-Bages, Pauillac
Château Lynch-Moussas, Pauillac
Château Dauzac, Labarde-Margaux
Château Mouton Baronne Philippe, Pauillac
  (formerly known as Mouton d'Armailhacq)
Château du Tertre, Arsac-Margaux
Château Haut-Bages Libéral, Pauillac
Château Pédesclaux, Pauillac
Château Belgrave, St-Laurent
Château de Camensac, St-Laurent
Château Cos Labory, St-Estèphe
Château Clerc Milon, Pauillac
Château Croizet-Bages, Pauillac
Château Cantemerle, Macau

THE MEDOC

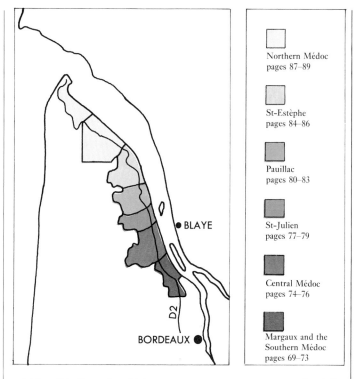

Northern Médoc
pages 87–89

St-Estèphe
pages 84–86

Pauillac
pages 80–83

St-Julien
pages 77–79

Central Médoc
pages 74–76

Margaux and the
Southern Médoc
pages 69–73

▷ The Médoc, as befits its status as one of the world's great wine districts, is portrayed at a large scale in six maps on the following pages. This key map shows the relationship of the communes. The D2, the "Route des Châteaux", runs from south to north, linking them.

Wine growing on a large scale came relatively late to the Médoc, the triangular peninsula to the northwest of the city of Bordeaux. In earlier times this was an inhospitable, thinly populated region, marshy and with mainly poor soil. There was some wine growing in the Middle Ages, but on a modest scale and chiefly around the monasteries, and later the villages of Ludon, Macau, Le Taillan and Blanquefort in the southern Médoc. Until the end of the fifteenth century the wines were drunk locally and in the city of Bordeaux.

In the sixteenth century the vineyards gradually spread northwards, to Margaux and elsewhere. Then, a century later, the great breakthrough came when, under the direction of Dutch engineers, marshes were drained and filled in, bays and inlets reclaimed and coastlines straightened. The Dutch also regulated the courses of the many small streams (*jalles*) that flow through the Médoc and play an important part in draining it. (For a long time the district near Bégadan in the northern Médoc was known as "La Petite Hollande".)

Once the Médoc had been drained the vineyard area grew rapidly. The world began to discover the wines from this new region, and the "new French clarets" won a market in a by now prosperous England. At the end of the seventeenth and the beginning of the eighteenth century the first estate wines appeared. The first name to be noted was that of Haut-Brion, from the Graves district south of Bordeaux, but around 1703 those of Margaux, Lafite and Latour in the Médoc were also being reported. Almost all the wine estates were in the hands of Bordeaux's rich aristocracy who, as profits rose, were not slow to devote more land to vines. Even cornfields, so important to the region, had to make way for vineyards.

Fortune changed in the first half of the nineteenth century, when wars and various political decisions brought the Médoc a long period of depression. Prosperity, once so evident, was proving to be relative. In Bordeaux society it was being said, "There are three ways of ruining yourself: a *danseuse*, a racehorse and an estate in the Médoc. And the last is the quickest and surest!" Despite this and later economic crises, the Médoc has continued to be one of the world's most important regions in setting the standards for red wine. The key word here is finesse: the subtleties that the best Médocs can possess are without equal.

That such stylish, complex wines should be made in this particular region is due to a remarkable interplay of natural factors. The Médoc has a notably mild climate in which extreme temperatures are exceptional. Its situation between two water masses – the Atlantic and the Gironde – contributes considerably to this. The name Médoc itself derives from words meaning "middle land". That it does not have a damp, obviously maritime climate, despite being near the sea, is due to the extensive pinewoods that shelter the wine-growing area from the winds and rains from the west.

The mild climate is complemented by soil that has deep layers of gravel in many places. From the Tertiary period onwards this gravel has been carried down from the Massif Central and the Pyrenees, and its composition is complex and ever changing. The soil itself is generally poor, forcing the vines to push their roots down deep into the subsoil to find nourishment, so the complexity of the soil is reflected in the wine. The high gravel content also has the advantage of making the soil very permeable, resulting in excellent drainage. This is further aided by the fact that many Médoc vineyards are on the low, gently sloping hills: there is a saying that you can always see the Gironde from the best vineyards.

Because of the differences in soil, terrain and situation, each Médoc vineyard produces its own individual wine. Even the differences between wines from neighbouring properties can be surprisingly great. A factor that reinforces these differences is the grape varieties. Every wine grower works with his own proportions of Cabernet Sauvignon, Cabernet Franc and Merlot, which are the main grapes, and Petit Verdot and Malbec which are grown on a small scale.

Wine growing is practised in only a small part of the Médoc peninsula: a relatively narrow strip some 70 to 80 kilometres (43–50 miles) long that follows the Gironde from the first vineyards on the outskirts of Bordeaux almost to the northern tip of the peninsula. Only in one place do the vineyards reach about 12 kilometres (7 miles) inland from the river; usually the distance from the Gironde is less than 5 kilometres (3 miles).

There are eight appellations: Margaux, the largest (it includes the southern Médoc communities Arsac, Cantenac, Labarde and Soussans), Moulis and Listrac (in the central Médoc), St-Julien, Pauillac, St-Estèphe, the Haut-Médoc (which covers wines not included in the previous six) and Médoc (the northern, or Bas Médoc). The classification of 1855 that divided the châteaux of the Médoc into five classes, or Crus Classés, is detailed on page 67.

MARGAUX & THE SOUTHERN MEDOC

The Médoc is a region that every wine lover associates not only with fine wines but with superb châteaux. Nowhere else is there such a concentration of splendid buildings in the service of the vine: the Médoc is the Versailles of wine. Yet as you drive north from the city of Bordeaux you see nothing of any grandeur at first, for the roads lead through interminable suburbs of the ever-expanding city and there is not a vine in sight. Even when you have passed the Bordeaux ring road it is some kilometres before the first vineyard comes into view.

The most interesting route through the Médoc starts at Blanquefort, where you can take either the D2 north or the D210 that runs parallel to it to the east, closer to the Gironde. The D210 is quieter and passes through the peaceful wine villages of Parempuyre, Ludon and Macau as well as by many of the châteaux, including the beautiful d'Agassac. The D2 has the advantage of running closer to such estates as Châteaux Cantemerle and Giscours, and it is easy to turn off for Le Pian-Médoc and Arsac, two wine communities deeper inland. At Labarde the two roads join. You could take one road on your outward journey and the other one back.

The wines of the most southerly villages – Macau, Ludon, Le Pian-Médoc and, closer to Bordeaux, Le Taillon, Parempuyre and Blanquefort – carry the Haut-Médoc appellation. On the flat lands near the river – the *palus* – the wines are simpler and have the appellation Bordeaux or Bordeaux Supérieur, as do the wines from the islands in the Gironde. The farther north you go, the more the vineyards penetrate among the woods and meadows. Directly after the hamlet of Cantenac the landscape opens out, with impressive sweeps of vineyards stretching away on either side of the road. To the left, as soon as you pass Château Prieuré-Lichine, you see a classic example of the gravel plateaux so characteristic of the Médoc. The

hill with its shallow vine-clad slope seems low, but in fact in this flat countryside it is high enough to block your view of Château Brane-Cantenac entirely.

Here you are in the Margaux appellation, which covers some 1,150 hectares (2,850 acres) of vineyards out of the total for the Médoc of almost 11,000 hectares (27,000 acres). Margaux is the biggest of the Médoc appellations, with more Crus Classés – 21 – than any of the others. As well as Margaux itself, the appellation includes Arsac, Cantenac, Labarde and Soussans, a quartet of adjoining communities. The long, low islands in the Gironde form a natural screen against cold winds from the northeast and the microclimate is a little milder than in the rest of the Médoc, which means that the grapes usually ripen eight to ten days earlier. The topsoil is the thinnest in the Médoc but rich in gravel, particularly in the eastern part of the appellation where a number of the delicate and delicious wines so characteristic of Margaux are made. To the west there is more clay and the wines are firmer.

Until late in the seventeenth century Margaux and the surrounding villages were sparsely populated: this was the territory of a few wealthy *seigneurs* who lived in the châteaux of Margaux, d'Issan (in Cantenac) and La Tour de Mons (in Soussans). Châteaux Margaux and d'Issan still stand, but only parts of La Tour de Mons remain.

Today the township of Margaux has a little under 1,400 inhabitants and is more village than town; the other villages of the appellation are little more than hamlets. Almost everyone in Margaux makes his living from wine and most of the châteaux are in a neighbourly cluster around and in the centre of the town, their vineyards divided into small plots that intermingle in the surrounding countryside.

Château Margaux

TRAVEL INFORMATION

Margaux is the only commune in the Médoc to date where you can stay overnight in great comfort and enjoy excellent food, including oysters.

HOTELS

Relais de Margaux, 33460 Margaux, tel. 56 88 38 80. Hotel and restaurant opened in 1985, set in a large park close to Château Margaux and overlooking the river. The rooms are fairly small but modern and comfortable (though the walls are thin). In the restaurant, regional specialities in season include fish in red wine, scallops in Sauternes and Pauillac lamb. Class A.
Le Domaine des Ardillières, 33160 Salaunes, tel. 56 05 20 70. Hotel and restaurant in the middle of pinewoods, with a heated swimming pool and a tennis court. Salaunes is about 20 km (12 miles) west of Margaux on the D105 and N215 via Castelnau-de-Médoc, or you can take the N215 Bordeaux-Lacanau from Bordeaux via St-Médard-en-Jalles. Class B.

RESTAURANTS

Auberge des Criquets, 33290 Blanquefort, tel. 56 35 09 24. Specializes in game but other dishes are also generally of good standard. Friendly service. Eight rooms offer adequate accommodation. Class B.
Auberge le Savoie, 33460 Margaux, tel. 56 88 31 76. Congenial village restaurant with friendly service, a good wine list and both traditional and contemporary dishes. Class C.
Larigaudière, 33460 Soussans, tel. 56 88 74 02. An extension of the wine estate of Château Haut Breton Larigaudière.
Fashionable, and good cooking.
Class B.

PLACES OF INTEREST

Blanquefort South of the village centre, to the right of the D2 as you come from Bordeaux, are the ruins of Château de Duras, a stronghold built in the 13th and 14th centuries and now a historic monument. In Blanquefort itself there is an agricultural and viticultural school with its own vineyard, Château Dillon. The American wine firm Barton & Guestier has its headquarters in Blanquefort.
Macau In summer, drive down to the banks of the Gironde here. There is a charming harbour and you can enjoy fresh *fruits de mer* and a glass of white wine. Shad (*alose*) is the speciality of the local fishermen.
Coast and woodlands Excursions can be made by car, bike or canoe, or on foot or horseback, in and around the pinewoods west of the wine-producing area. A folder showing the various routes is available from the Information Touristique in Bordeaux. To enjoy sun and sand, go to the splendid beaches on the Atlantic coast, or to the two large inland waterways, Etang d'Hourtin and Etang de Lacanau.

WINE ACTIVITIES

The Commanderie du Bontemps de Médoc et des Graves represents the whole of the Médoc and also the Graves district.

WINE INFORMATION

The Maison du Vin in Margaux provides information about visiting the châteaux and you can also buy wine here.

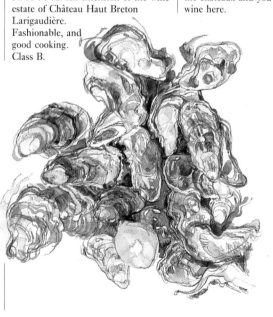

THE CHATEAUX

MARGAUX, postcode 33460
Appellation Margaux

Château Durfort-Vivens 71 B3
2e Grand Cru Classé
A Lucien Lurton estate: the cellars are across the road from the château, on a street corner on the way into Margaux from the south. The actual château is no longer part of the wine estate and is occupied by Bernard Ginestet, the local mayor and son of the former owner of Château Margaux, and his family. The wine is sound rather than fine and demands long keeping.

Château Ferrière 71 B2
3e Grand Cru Classé
A miniature property; the not particularly distinguished wine is made at Château Lascombes.

Château Lascombes 71 B2
2e Grand Cru Classé
Excellently managed and maintained estate, one of the largest in the Médoc, with a rather ungainly Victorian château. The wines are elegant and mature outstandingly well in bottle. They are usually reliable in poor years too. The British brewers Bass Charrington took over in 1971 from Alexis Lichine.

Château Malescot St-Exupéry 71 B3
3e Grand Cru Classé
The comfortable château, dating from 1885, is in the main street in Margaux; the vineyards (typically for Margaux) are scattered and include plots in the northern commune of Soussans. The wine has plenty of colour and tannin, some fruit and a certain refinement; it usually demands years of patience before it begins to become friendly.

Château Margaux * 71 B3
1er Grand Cru Classé
The most impressive château of the Médoc: an avenue lined with tall plane trees leads up to a large country house with the air of a palace. The late André Mentzelopoulos bought Margaux in 1977 and spared neither money nor effort to restore not only the château but also the wine, which had declined in quality, to their former glory. Today his wife and daughters are enthusiastically continuing his work. Château Margaux can be the best red wine of the Médoc: rich, stylish and very concentrated. Tasting it is a privilege. A second label is Pavillon Rouge. A white Bordeaux, Pavillon Blanc du Château Margaux, is also made, from a separate vineyard of Sauvignon Blanc – the Médoc's only top-class white wine.

Château Marquis d'Alesme Becker 71 B3
3e Grand Cru Classé
A neighbour of Malescot St-Exupéry, in the same street in Margaux. The wine is usually very reserved, but since 1979 when a modern *cuvier* and new *chai* were installed it has become more supple and elegant, and more of a true Margaux.

Château Marquis de Terme 71 B3
4e Grand Cru Classé
During the 1980s a great deal has been invested in equipment, cellars and reception rooms. The wine has benefited: it is a pure, firm Margaux with colour, juice and tannin.

Château Rausan-Ségla 71 C3
2e Grand Cru Classé
Older than most well-known Médoc estates, the Rausan vineyards date back to 1661. The property was divided at the time of the French Revolution, a third of it becoming Rauzan (with a "z") Gassies. The château remained with the Ségla portion. For years the wine was not worthy of its second-growth status, but since the early 1980s its quality has been remarkably restored. The owners (since 1960) are British: the Holt firm, of the Lonrho group.

Château Rauzan-Gassies 71 C3
2e Grand Cru Classé
The balance of the old Rausan estate (see above). The wine is an atypical Margaux, rather hard and dour but worth watching.

ALSO IN MARGAUX

Château Canuet 71 B3
Commendable, generally fruity wine; the château is in the middle of Margaux. Changed hands in 1987: future uncertain.

Château La Gurgue * 71 B3
Cru Bourgeois Supérieur
An avenue almost opposite the Maison du Vin in Margaux leads to this completely restored château, where since 1978 remarkably good wines have been made.

Château Labégorce 71 B2
Cru Bourgeois Supérieur
A substantial château, close neighbour of Labégorce-Zédé (they were once part of the same estate), producing supple, rounded, often almost fat wine but somewhat lacking in finesse.

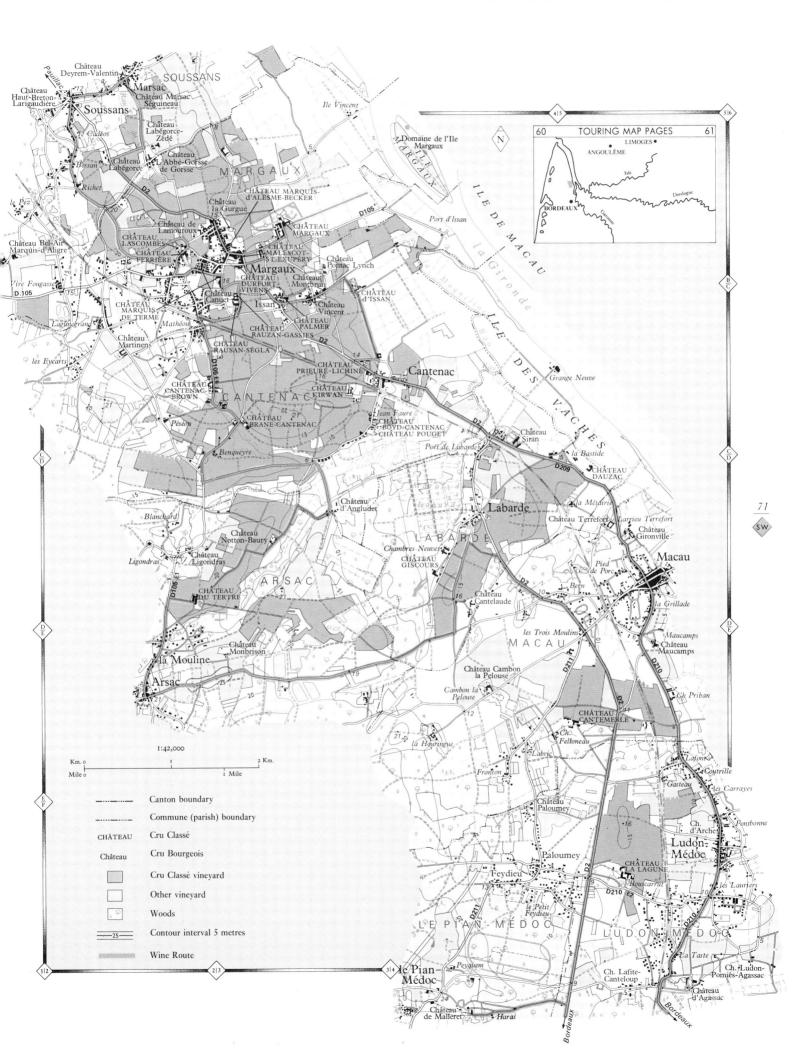

Château
Deyrem-Valentin
SOUSSANS
Marsac
Château
Haut-Breton-
Larigaudière
Château Marsac
Séguineau
Soussans
Château
Labégorce-
Zédé
Château
L'Abbé-Gorsse
de Gorsse
MARGAUX
Château Labégorce
CHÂTEAU MARQUIS-
D'ALESME-BECKER
Château
la Gurgue
Château de
Lamouroux
CHÂTEAU
MARGAUX
Château Bel-Air
Marquis-d'Aligre
CHÂTEAU
LASCOMBES
CHÂTEAU
MALESCOT-
ST-EXUPÉRY
Château
Pontac Lynch
CHÂTEAU
FERRIÈRE
Margaux
CHÂTEAU
DURFORT-
VIVENS
Château
Monbrun
CHÂTEAU
d'ISSAN
Château
Canuet
CHÂTEAU
MARQUIS
DE TERME
Issan
Château
Vincent
CHÂTEAU
PALMER
Château
Martinens
CHÂTEAU
RAUZAN-GASSIES
CHÂTEAU
RAUSAN-SÉGLA
les Eycarts
CHÂTEAU
PRIEURÉ-LICHINE
Cantenac
Grange Neuve
CHÂTEAU
CANTENAC-
BROWN
CHÂTEAU
KIRWAN
CANTENAC
Château
Siran
Château
BRANE-CANTENAC
Jean Faure
CHÂTEAU
BOYD-CANTENAC
CHÂTEAU POUGET
la Bastide
Péséou
Port de Labarde
CHÂTEAU
DAUZAC
Benqueyre
Château
d'Angludet
Labarde
la Métairie
LABARDE
Château Terrefort
Larrieu Terrefort
Château
Notton-Baury
Château
Gironville
Château
Ligondras
Chambres Neuves
CHÂTEAU
GISCOURS
Pied
de Porc
Macau
Blanchard
Ligondras
ARSAC
CHÂTEAU
DU TERTRE
Château
Canteloude
Bern
la Grillade
Château
Monbrison
les Trois Moulins
MACAU
Maucamps
Château
Maucamps
la Mouline
Arsac
Château Cambon
la Pelousé
Cambon la
Pelouse
Ch. Priban
CHÂTEAU
CANTEMERLE
la Houringue
Ch.
Felloneau
Lafon
Coutrille
Labric
les Carrayes
Fronton
Gasteau
Château
Paloumey
Ch.
d'Arche
Fontbonne
Ludon-
Médoc
Paloumey
CHÂTEAU
LA LAGUNE
Feydieu
Bouscarrut
les Lauriers
le Petit
Feydieu
D210
LE PIAN-MÉDOC
LUDON MÉDOC
La Taste
le Pian-
Médoc
Peyquem
Ch. Lafite-
Canteloup
Ch. Ludon-
Pomiés-Agassac
Château
de Malleret
Haras
Château
d'Agassac

1:42,000
Km. 0   1   2 Km.
Mile 0   1 Mile

Canton boundary
Commune (parish) boundary
CHÂTEAU   Cru Classé
Château   Cru Bourgeois
           Cru Classé vineyard
           Other vineyard
           Woods
— 25 —   Contour interval 5 metres
           Wine Route

71
SW

Château Labégorce-Zédé * 71 B2
Cru Bourgeois Supérieur
Luc Thienpont (of the Belgian family who own Vieux Château Certan in Pomerol and other estates) makes a very pure wine full of character, with a pleasing amount of fruit and good ageing potential.

Château Martinens 71 C2
Cru Grand Bourgeois
Partly in Margaux and partly in Cantenac; the château was built, so the annals say, in 1767 by three English sisters called White. The pleasant wine seems to have improved in recent years.

ARSAC, postcode 33460
Appellation Margaux

Château du Tertre * 71 D2
5e Grand Cru Classé
The previously dilapidated building on its low hill has been carefully restored; the wine had already improved. Today this relatively unknown Margaux is one of the most reliably satisfying in the commune.

Also in Arsac: **Château Ligondras,** a robust, old-fashioned wine for long cellaring, and the *cru bourgeois* **Château Monbrison,** where a third of the casks are replaced each year to give the wine a characteristic element of oak.

CANTENAC, postcode 33460
Appellation Margaux

Château Boyd-Cantenac 71 C4
3e Grand Cru Classé
The wine used to be identical to that of Pouget, the adjoining estate with the same owner, but is now vinified and bottled separately. Not a particularly subtle Margaux; it needs time to show its qualities.

Château Brane-Cantenac 71 C3
2e Grand Cru Classé
Large, well-run Lucien Lurton property with vineyards in a prime site on Cantenac's plateau. The wine is likeable but rarely very exciting.

Château Cantenac Brown 71 C3
3e Grand Cru Classé
Imposing structure (it has more than 350 windows) that looks more like an English country house than a château. The wine used to be an old-fashioned Margaux for long maturing but since the second half of the 1970s has become rather more accessible.

Château Desmirail
3e Grand Cru Classé
A low grey building on the left before the crossroads in Cantenac (coming from Bordeaux) serves as the château. The Brane-Cantenac team makes the wine, an elegant Margaux of unmistakable finesse.

Château d'Issan 71 B3
3e Grand Cru Classé
Beautifully restored (by the Cruse family) 17th-century moated castle, one of the most splendid sights in the Médoc. A musical programme is always given in one of the cellars during the annual Bordeaux festival. The wine has consistency, elegance and finesse.

Château Kirwan 71 C3
3e Grand Cru Classé
An 18th-century manor with a beautiful show of flowers in summer. (The château is alongside a small railway embankment and in earlier days the train would stop here to allow guests to alight.) The wine is very reliable with an attractive floral bouquet (to match the garden?).

Château d'Issan

Château Palmer * 71 C3
3e Grand Cru Classé
The picture-book château with its four pointed towers produces splendid, balanced wine with great charm and finesse, obviously far better than its third-growth classification. The château flies British, Dutch and French flags, representing the nationalities of the three owners.

Château Palmer

Château Pouget 71 C4
4e Grand Cru Classé
The château where the wine of Boyd-Cantenac was made until early 1983. Now a new *cuvier* and *chai* across the road from the old cellars (where Boyd-Cantenac is still made) produce sturdy, often rather steely wine with considerable tannin and colour, for long maturing.

Château Prieuré-Lichine 71 C3
4e Grand Cru Classé
Probably the most hospitable Grand Cru in the Médoc: as signs by the roadside indicate, visitors are always welcome. Prieuré-Lichine is a former monastery where Benedictine monks were making wine centuries ago; the property was bought in 1951 by Alexis Lichine who painstakingly extended the vineyard area. The wine is very well made with good balance and enough backbone for ageing. It is also good value for money.

ALSO IN CANTENAC

Château d'Angludet * 71 D3
Cru Bourgeois Supérieur Exceptionnel
The secluded château, set in a peaceful park complete with grazing ponies, is the home of Peter Sichel, the English co-owner of Château Palmer. The wine is of consistently Grand Cru quality, complex and complete.

Château Pontac Lynch 71 B3
Cru Bourgeois
A comparatively modest family estate combining two celebrated Bordeaux names; makes a correct wine.

LABARDE, postcode 33460
Appellation Margaux

Château Dauzac * 71 D5
5e Grand Cru Classé
A totally regenerated vineyard, perfectly equipped, after a long period of decline: the present buildings are alongside the old château which is no longer in use. Since 1978 the wine has become interesting again and seems to be still improving.

Château Giscours * 71 D4
3e Grand Cru Classé
A huge, rambling château and *chais* in a fine park with a lake dug partly to influence the microclimate. Sinewy, concentrated wine with a solid reputation, even in lesser years. The estate has been managed since 1970 by Pierre Tari.

ALSO IN LABARDE

Château Siran * 71 C4
Cru Bourgeois Supérieur
A charming property famous for its

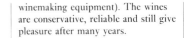

Château Prieuré-Lichine

vintage-time cyclamen as well as its
extremely elegant wine. The owner,
Alain Miailhe, aims to acquire the
status Cru Classé for his wine, which
it certainly deserves. His anti-nuclear
shelter is thoughtfully stocked with
his best vintages.

SOUSSANS, postcode 33460
Appellation Margaux
(See the map of the Central Médoc
on page 75)

Château Paveil de Luze 75 F3
Cru Grand Bourgeois
A more than respectable Médoc
bourgeois, from Baron Geoffroy de
Luze. The château is in the *chartreuse*
(hunting lodge) style typical of the
Médoc – long and low, with two
wings and two square towers.

Château Tayac 75 F3
Cru Bourgeois
Large, modern estate producing
pleasant, mellow wine. (The actual
château, opposite the cellars, is no
longer occupied.)

Château la Tour de Mons * 75 F4
Cru Bourgeois
Soussans is the most northerly of the
five villages entitled to the Margaux
appellation and so small you can go
through it almost without realizing it.
There is a road sign to La Tour de
Mons: a property rich in history,
with the remains of a castle begun in
the 13th century. In good years the
wine is almost opaque; the perfume
and taste develop only after long
cellaring.

BLANQUEFORT, postcode 33290
Appellation Haut-Médoc

Château Dillon
Cru Bourgeois
Pleasant wine, vinified by pupils of
the local Lycée Agricole.

Château Magnol
A mellow, fairly firm Haut-Médoc,
ready for drinking within a few years.
Since 1979 it has been made and sold
by the négociants Barton & Guestier,
whose buildings adjoin the vineyard.

LUDON, postcode 33290
Appellation Haut-Médoc

Château La Lagune 71 F5
3e Grand Cru Classé
The 1730 château was originally a
Carthusian monastery and is a low-
built villa characteristic of the
Bordeaux region. It produces a
particularly reliable wine with fruit,
mellow firmness, a slight spiciness
and the characteristic hint of vanilla
from new oak casks. The estate is
owned by the champagne house
Ayala and meticulously managed.

ALSO IN LUDON

Château d'Agassac * 71 G5
Cru Grand Bourgeois Exceptionnel
A splendidly romantic 13th-century
moated castle; the vineyards of
Ludon spread out in front of it, and
behind it the woods of the Landes
begin. Under the direction of
Philippe Capbern-Gasqueton (of
Calon-Ségur, Capbern and du
Tertre) the estate produces sound,
sturdy wine that benefits from bottle-
ageing.

Château d'Arche 71 F6
Cru Bourgeois Supérieur
The modest château is in the centre
of the village of Ludon, hidden
behind a high wall (it has a pleasant
little museum with antique

Château d'Agassac

winemaking equipment). The wines
are conservative, reliable and still give
pleasure after many years.

MACAU, postcode 33460
Appellation Haut-Médoc

Château Cantemerle * 71 E5
5e Grand Cru Classé
A sleeping-beauty château hidden in
romantic woodlands that flank the
main road; marvellous to visit. Its
wine went through a weak period in
the 1970s but in 1980 the estate was
taken over by a group who, with the
help of the négociants Cordier, totally
renovated the vineyard and cellars.
The quality of the wine is now
exemplary, with concentration, depth
and length.

ALSO IN MACAU

Château Cambon la Pelouse 71 E4
Cru Bourgeois Supérieur
Mild, pleasant wine for early
drinking.

Château Maucamps * 71 E5
Cru Bourgeois
Sound, pure Haut-Médoc with the
elegance of a Margaux. Worth
following, particularly from 1981 on.

PAREMPUYRE, postcode 33290
Appellation Haut-Médoc

Château Pichon
After lying fallow for nearly 60 years,
the vineyard has been replanted and
the large château has also been
restored. The wine is worth
following.

LE-PIAN-MEDOC, postcode 33290
Appellation Haut-Médoc

Château de Malleret 71 G4
Cru Grand Bourgeois
A pleasant family château with
splendid stables – the owner, Count
Bertrand du Vivier, is an enthusiastic
horseman as well as a négociant and
wine maker. The wine is a good,
reasonably firm, balanced Haut-
Médoc.

LE TAILLAN, postcode 33320
Appellation Haut-Médoc

Château du Taillan
Cru Grand Bourgeois
The first important estate as you
approach the Médoc from Bordeaux
(the boundary between the Médoc
and Graves actually crosses it). The
monumental 18th-century château is
beautifully preserved and has a 300-
year-old cellar that has been declared
a historic monument. The wine is
comparatively mellow and supple; a
pleasant white Bordeaux is also made.

73
SW

THE CENTRAL MEDOC

Whereas the neighbouring communes of Margaux and St-Julien shine with their Grands Crus, the light in the Central Médoc is more subdued. There are no great aristocratic châteaux, just comfortably middle-class estates: this is Crus Bourgeois territory. That there is not a single property with a higher classification is to be regretted. Several estates are producing wines that can match the Grands Crus: two convincing examples are Chasse-Spleen and Maucaillou in Moulis-en-Médoc.

The commune of Moulis has its own appellation (the other communes, apart from Listrac, are simply Haut-Médoc). The hamlet itself is little more than one main street and a few houses. Grand Poujeaux, a few kilometres to the northeast, is more important, certainly as far as wine is concerned: grouped in and around Grand Poujeaux are several good estates, many with "Poujeaux" in their name. The name Moulis comes from the French *moulins* – this used to be mainly corn-growing country, with windmills to grind the grain.

Vineyards were first planted in the fifteenth and sixteenth centuries. Most of the fine wines come from the gravel plateau of Poujeaux and the southeast where the gravel is mixed with clay. In the southwest there is gravel and sand, and around Moulis itself there is clay and chalk. These differences in the soil contribute to the various styles of wine in Moulis-en-Médoc. Some mature to the same kind of mellow refinement as St-Juliens; others are firmer and more reserved, or striking for their suppleness, making few demands on your patience.

The other commune of the Central Médoc with its own appellation is Listrac, west and north of Moulis. The appellation used to be simply Listrac, but was changed in 1986 to Listrac-Médoc, allegedly to avoid possible confusion with Lirac in the Rhône. The N215 from Bordeaux, that in summer takes the Bordelais *en masse* to the beaches in the north, runs through the village and alongside the cooperative, where about a third of the local wine is vinified. The village lies at the foot of the highest hill in the Médoc, 43 metres (140 feet) above sea level and topped by a fire tower. This plateau also acts as a watershed, the streams to the east of it flowing into the Gironde, those to the west towards the sea. The subsoil varies: partly gravel from the Pyrenees, partly clay and chalk, and shingle brought down by the river Garonne. Merlot used to be the main grape but on most estates today at least half the vines are Cabernet Sauvignon. This has increased the finesse of the wines, but Listracs in general are fairly virile with plenty of body and a firm structure.

The other communes of the Central Médoc are entitled to the appellation Haut-Médoc. In Avensan and Arcins the wines can sometimes approach those of Margaux in style (the commune of Soussans, in the extreme south, is appellation Margaux). The village of Lamarque – the car ferry to Blaye leaves from here – has rather low-lying land not suitable for producing quality wines. Farther inland, however, there are some flourishing estates, including the splendid Château de Lamarque, a centuries-old castle complete with towers, battlements and courtyard with palms and white doves. The Cussac-Fort-Médoc commune consists of two small hamlets on the D2 (the "Route des Châteaux"). To the left and right of the road the vineyards generally produce classic wines for long maturing.

TRAVEL INFORMATION

There are no culinary high points in the Central Médoc, but it is worth trying the restaurants that specialize in local dishes and of course there are the wines to enjoy.

HOTELS

Hotel de France, 33480 Listrac, tel. 56 58 03 68. Small hotel in the middle of Listrac with neat, clean rooms. Class C.

RESTAURANTS

Le Lion d'Or, 33460 Arcins, tel. 56 58 96 79. Plenty of atmosphere and tasty food. Very popular locally (most tourists drive past). Class C.
Le Relais du Médoc, 33460 Lamarque, tel. 56 58 92 27. Strictly regional cuisine (*escargots bordelaises* are a speciality) and excellent value. A few hotel rooms. Class C.

Cercle Oenologique de Clarke, 33480 Moulis, tel. 56 88 84 29. Run by Château Clarke (in nearby Listrac), open from June to October for lunch and dinner and also for wine tastings. Class B.

PLACES OF INTEREST

Avensan The local church has 15th-century bas-reliefs.
Castelnau-de-Médoc Little hamlet 6 km (4 miles) south of Listrac with an interesting church.
Cussac-Fort-Médoc Fort Médoc, by the Gironde, was built around 1690 by the military architect Vauban. With the citadel at Blaye on the other side of the river and Fort Pâté (on a small island) it formed part of a line of fortifications to defend the Gironde against marauders. The gateway of the fort is ornamented with the royal sun of Louis XIV. Also at Cussac is Château Lanessan with its Musée du Cheval, with a collection of carriages that date back to 1885 and the original 19th-century stables and saddle room.
Lamarque The great feudal Château de Lamarque is a landmark in the Médoc: a splendid battlemented castle with cellars and a chapel from the 11th and 12th centuries. The car ferry across the Gironde to Blaye leaves from the pier at Lamarque.
Listrac The village has a 13th-century Romanesque church with Gothic elements.
Moulis-en-Médoc The Romanesque church has a fortified tower, and there is also an old watermill in the village, the Moulin de Tiquetorte.

WINE INFORMATION

There is no Maison du Vin in the Central Médoc, but enquiries in the larger villages such as Lamarque and Grand Poujeaux about visiting the local châteaux should prove helpful. Visitors are particularly welcome between June and September at Château Clarke, Baron Edmond de Rothschild's spectacular estate in the commune of Listrac.

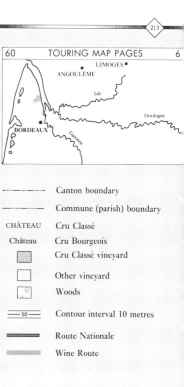

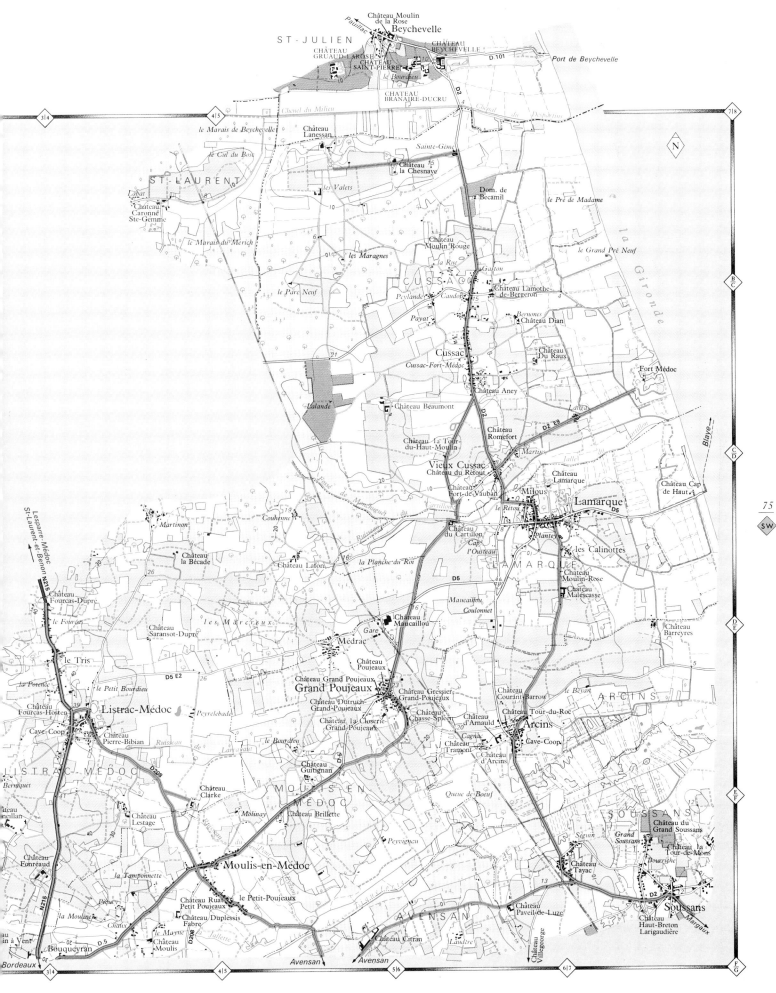

THE CHATEAUX

MOULIS, postcode 33460
Appellation Moulis

Château Chasse-Spleen * 75 E5
Cru Grand Bourgeois Exceptionnel
Indeed an exceptional Moulis that
has repeatedly shown itself to be the
equal of a Grand Cru. The wine is
matured in oak and usually half the
casks are replaced each year. A small
part of the vineyard is in Listrac.

**Château Dutruch Grand
Poujeaux** 75 E5
Cru Grand Bourgeois Exceptionnel
Wine with a good deal of reserve and
tannin, demanding long maturing.

Château Maucaillou * 75 E5
Cru Bourgeois
The name of the estate comes from
an old description of the soil: *mauvais
cailloux*, "bad pebbles", from the
days when it was too gravelly to grow
corn (but proved later, of course, to
be excellent for vines). At blind
tastings the supple, nuanced wine is
hardly distinguishable from a Grand
Cru. The château has a wine museum.

Château Moulin à Vent 74 F3
Cru Grand Bourgeois
Although a third of the vineyard is in
Listrac, all the wine is sold as
Moulis. (The property is on the
boundary of Moulis and Listrac.)
Considerable investment of time and
money by Dominique Hessel since he
bought the estate in 1977 shows in
the competence of the wine.

Château Poujeaux * 75 E5
Cru Grand Bourgeois Exceptionnel
This is the largest estate in Moulis
after Chasse-Spleen and, thanks to
the efforts of the Theil family, the
wine is well enough known to be sold
directly from the château instead of
via the Bordeaux trade. Dark and
long-lived, it usually needs time to
lose its reserve, but patience is richly
rewarded.

Also in Moulis: **Châteaux Biston-
Brillette, Branas Grand Poujeaux***
and **Brillette**.

LISTRAC, postcode 33480
Appellation Listrac-Médoc

Château Clarke * 75 F1
Cru Bourgeois
Since 1973 Baron Edmond de
Rothschild (of the Château Lafite-
Rothschild family) has spent millions
of francs in making this the most
spectacular and technically advanced
estate in Listrac. No other property
has produced, and received, so much
publicity. The wine does not yet have

quite the depth and length to be at
the top in Listrac, but this can only
be a matter of time.

Clos des Demoiselles *
This small estate lies along the D2,
on the vine-clad hill at Listrac.
Brilliant, well-balanced wine of
which, alas, only 2,000 cases a year
are made.

Château Fourcas Dupré * 74 D3
Cru Grand Bourgeois Exceptionnel
A concentrated Listrac of the highest
standard. The vineyard lies about
1 km north of the village centre on
the D2 and has ample parking space
for visitors.

Château Fourcas-Hosten * 75 E3
Cru Grand Bourgeois Exceptionnel
A fine wine with plenty of fruit and
tannin and the class of a Grand Cru.
The château is opposite Listrac's
13th-century church and the splendid
park at the back was designed in 1830
by an Englishman.

Château Lestage * 75 F1
Cru Bourgeois
An imposing château set in a park of
tall old trees, with the same owners
as Château Fonréaud on the other
side of the hill at Listrac. The wine is
an out-and-out Listrac that has
improved in quality since the early
1980s.

Also in Listrac: **Châteaux Cap
Léon Veyrin** (a few rooms above the
chai are rented out to holidaymakers),
Ducluzeau* (belongs to the family
who own Ducru-Beaucaillou in St-
Julien and other estates), **Fonréaud**
and **Peyredon Lagravette*** (a small
family estate near the hamlet of
Médrac).

ARCINS, postcode 33460
Appellation Haut-Médoc

Château d'Arcins 75 E6
Cru Bourgeois
Conspicuous on the D2; the whole
complex has been restored and
enlarged by the Castel family (of
Castelvin tablewine fame). The
Castels have also restored Château
Barreyres, near the river. Their
efforts should make the name of
Arcins better known.

Also in Arcins: **Château Arnauld**,
an elegant, fruity Haut-Médoc.

AVENSAN, postcode 33480
Appellation Haut-Médoc

Château Citran * 75 F3
Cru Grand Bourgeois Exceptionnel
Sound, supple wine that at the

▲ On many Bordeaux estates a small part of the vintage goes into larger than
standard bottles as the wine develops more slowly, and better, in these. The bottles
are much sought after by connoisseurs.

moment seems to lag a little behind
the other *exceptionnels*. The vineyard
is part of a well-wooded estate of
some 400 hectares (990 acres).

Château de Villegeorge *
Cru Bourgeois Supérieur Exceptionnel
A Lucien Lurton (owner of Branc-
Cantenac among other properties)
estate on very gravelly soil, producing
well-rounded wine with plenty of
colour, a long finish and outstanding
ageing potential.

Also in Avensan: **Château Tour
Carelot***.

CUSSAC-FORT-MEDOC,
postcode 33460
Appellation Haut-Médoc

Château Lanessan * 75 B5
Cru Bourgeois Supérieur
Classic, traditionally made, intense
wine that approaches a Grand Cru in
quality. There is also a carriage

museum at the château (see Places of
Interest, Cussac-Fort-Médoc).

Also in Cussac-Fort-Médoc:
Châteaux Beaumont, Lachesnaye
(you pass this château on the way to
Lanessan; it has the same owners)
and **Tour du Haut-Moulin**.

LAMARQUE, postcode 33460
Appellation Haut-Médoc

Château de Lamarque 75 D6
Cru Grand Bourgeois
Generous, firm wine, sometimes
almost velvety after ageing, expertly
produced at this splendid old castle
(see Places of Interest).

Also in Lamarque: **Château
Malescasse**, directed by the owners of
Pontet-Canet in Pauillac and Lafon-
Rochet in St-Estèphe.

ST-JULIEN

A peaceful landscape of meadows, grazing cattle and willows forms the no-man's-land between the vineyards of Cussac-Fort-Médoc to the south and those of St-Julien-Beychevelle. A bridge over a small stream marks the boundary of St-Julien, then the road bends and climbs past Château Beychevelle. A little farther along the D2 stands a gigantic bottle with the painted message "Grand Vin de St-Julien Médoc". It is totally out of place, for this of all communes needs no such publicity: St-Julien wines are among the most celebrated, and most in demand, in the world. If the Médoc was regarded as an art gallery, the St-Julien hall would be hung almost entirely with canvases by the great masters. Grand Crus predominate: there are no fewer than 11, which between them occupy 85 percent of the vineyard area. Nearly all the rest of the St-Julien wines are also of high standard; in quality this is one of the most homogeneous Bordeaux appellations, with almost no lesser wines and only a few middling ones.

Essentially, St-Juliens derive their qualities from the very gravelly soil of two large plateaux. The Beychevelle plateau is bounded on the south by the Jalle du Nord and on the north by a small valley, also with a stream. At the point where the D2 crosses this valley are the Langoa-Barton and Léoville-Barton estates. The second plateau, with the village of St-Julien-Beychevelle at its centre, runs north from the stream. The Ruisseau de Juillac forms the northern boundary and is also the line of demarcation between St-Julien and Pauillac.

The origin of St-Julien probably goes back to the seventh century, but there are few traces left of its early history. The eighteenth century, however, is splendidly represented by a number of châteaux, including Beychevelle, Gruaud-Larose, Langoa Barton, Branaire-Ducru and Lagrange. In the sixteenth century the Beychevelle estate was called Château de Médoc, but this was changed after the Duke of Epernon, Admiral of France, received the property as a marriage portion. Ships on their way into Bordeaux were thereafter instructed to salute the château by lowering

▲ Fishermen's huts stand on rickety piles along the marshy banks of the Gironde, the nets suspended from a pulley.

a sail, as a sign of respect to the admiral, and the relevant order, *baisse voile* (or *bacha velo* in Gascon), became the name of the château. (Or so the story goes.) The Beychevelle label still shows a ship with lowered sail. The château of that time no longer exists; it was replaced in 1757 by a new building in Louis XV style. At the front it looks over a wide flight of steps and a beautiful garden to the distant Gironde; at the back, which can be seen from the road, there is a courtyard with virtuoso flowerbeds.

In this commune dominated by elegant châteaux some enchanting wines are made. They are rounded wines with charm, grace and fruit: usually a little less strong than those of Pauillac and often with the finesse of the most delicate Margaux *crus*.

The commune of St-Julien-Beychevelle has two hamlets of roughly equal size – the former Beychevelle and the original St-Julien. But apart from their wines and their châteaux, these little settlements do not have a great deal to offer the visitor.

Directly west of St-Julien-Beychevelle stretches the commune of St-Laurent-et-Benon. The N215 Bordeaux-Soulac road used to run through St-Laurent but the traffic now bypasses the village. The wines of the commune often show a strong likeness to those of St-Julien and allowing them the same appellation would be justifiable (as has happened, for example, with the wines of Labarde and Arsac, which can be sold as Margaux). Fate, however, has decreed otherwise: St-Laurent is part of the Haut-Médoc appellation. In St-Laurent, too, wine has been made for a long time. Wine from Château La Tour-Carnet – a genuine castle with a moat and a thirteenth-century bastion – was being sold at the beginning of the fifteenth century for almost double the price of the then much-sought-after red Graves.

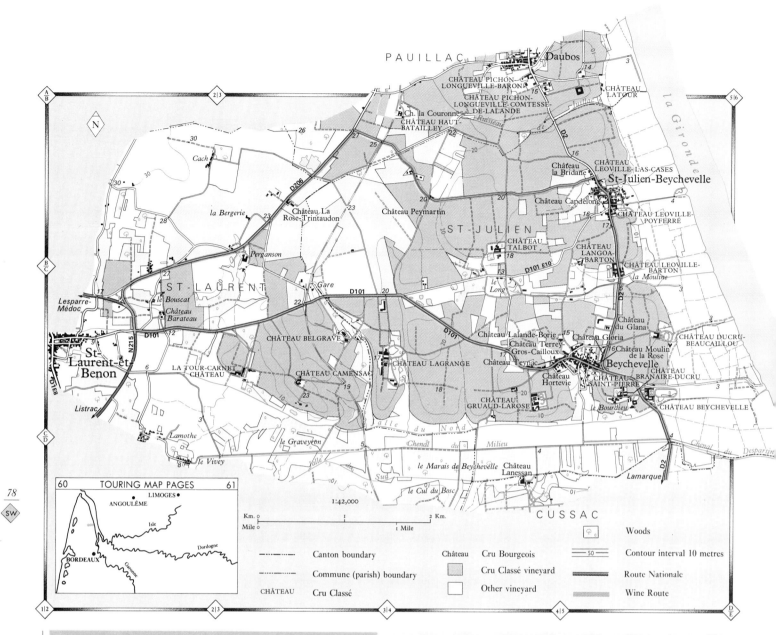

TRAVEL INFORMATION

Although the wines of St-Julien and St-Laurent are served in the world's best restaurants, in the villages themselves you can enjoy them in simple eating houses – or in the châteaux, but this is a rare privilege. There is no hotel in St-Julien-Beychevelle, but it may be possible to stay at one of the two hotel-restaurants in St-Laurent. See also the Travel Information in the chapters on Bordeaux, Margaux and Pauillac.

RESTAURANTS

Bar-Restaurant du Square, 33250 St-Julien-Beychevelle, tel. 56 59 08 26. Country cuisine without frills. Class C.
Hotel-Restaurant Le Lion d'Or, 33112 St-Laurent-et-Benon, tel. 56 59 40 21. Simple and acceptable. Try the regional dishes. Class C.
Hotel-Restaurant de la Renaissance, 33112 St-Laurent-et-

Benon, tel. 56 59 40 29. The *patron* supplies meals to the châteaux (and to pickers). Nourishing, regional fare. Class C.

PLACES OF INTEREST

The villages of St-Julien-Beychevelle and St-Laurent-et-Benon both have an interesting church. Apart from these, just admire the châteaux – and the wines.

WINE INFORMATION

Many properties in St-Julien and throughout the Médoc welcome visitors. Many require an advance appointment (the grander the château, usually the more necessary an appointment). Those open to casual visitors in St-Julien include Beychevelle, Branaire-Ducru and Lagrange. Typically, châteaux are open from 10 to 12 and from 3 to 5, Monday to Friday. Many properties close completely in August.

THE CHATEAUX

ST-JULIEN-BEYCHEVELLE, postcode 33250
Appellation St-Julien

Château Beychevelle * 78 C4
4e Grand Cru Classé
In 1983 a French civil service organization acquired a majority shareholding from the Achille-Fould family and much-needed improvements have been made, including the installation of stainless-steel fermentation tanks. Beychevelle wine has the stamina of a marathon runner and often only shows its real class after many years. The 17th-century château is one of the most beautiful in the Médoc.

Château Branaire-Ducru 78 C4
4e Grand Cru Classé
An alluring perfume of violets and a taste that is gentle yet firm are the most striking characteristics of this consistent St-Julien. The immaculate

château, set well back in its grounds, is opposite Beychevelle.

Château Ducru-Beaucaillou *
78 C4
2e Grand Cru Classé
This château is set majestically against the east (riverside) slope of the more southerly of the St-Julien gravel plateaux. The façade, flanked by two stout Victorian towers, looks towards the Gironde, and a magnificent park enhances the view. Thanks to the effort and expertise of the Borie family, Ducru-Beaucaillou, together with Léoville-las-Cases, is among the top wines of St-Julien – and thus of the whole Médoc. It is a delicious, mouth-filling wine, mellow, stylish, and with sufficient strength for long maturing.

Château Gruaud-Larose 78 C3
2e Grand Cru Classé
Mellow fruit and unmistakable

finesse are the characteristics of this very typical St-Julien. With maturity it becomes almost silky. The large château with its Louis XVI salons, beautiful park and extensive vineyard belongs to the Cordier family, who also own Château Talbot a couple of kilometres to the north.

Château Lagrange 78 C2
3e Grand Cru Classé
Since it was taken over by the Japanese drinks giant Suntory at the end of 1983, almost everything on this big estate has been altered or renovated, from the *cuvier* to the lookout tower. This enormous effort has brought the wine right back up to standard after a long series of mediocre years. The first vintage – in the only moderate year of 1984 – produced an exquisite, satiny wine of great finesse. This is one of the most interesting Médoc châteaux to visit. It may be possible to make an appointment through merchants who import the wine.

Château Langoa Barton 78 B4
3e Grand Cru Classé
One of the gems of the Médoc: a "chartreuse" built above its cellars with a lovely terraced garden behind. This is the only Cru Classé still owned and inhabited by the same family as in 1855 when the Classification was made. The wine is made from the same proportions of grapes (70% Sauvignon, 7% Cabernet Franc, 15% Merlot, 8% Petit Verdot) as Léoville-Barton, and in the same conservative way with the same equipment. Not surprisingly there is a great family resemblance between the two wines, although Léoville is slightly ahead in finesse and complexity.

Château Léoville-Barton 78 C4
2e Grand Cru Classé
The smallest Léoville is owned by the Barton family, who came from Ireland early in the 18th century. The wine is made at Langoa Barton. It is a firmly structured St-Julien, full of character, that should be given a long time to mature; it shows its class even in lesser years.

Château Léoville-las-Cases * 78 B4
2e Grand Cru Classé
After the French revolution, the estate of the Marquis de Léoville was split into three: the present châteaux Léoville-las-Cases (the largest), Léoville-Poyferré and Léoville-Barton. A large part of the vineyard is opposite Château Latour in Pauillac and the winery buildings are in St-Julien itself, on either side of the village street and next to the

Poyferré cellars. Perfectionist management by Michel Delon produces memorable, flawless wine, intense and rich in colour, fragrance and flavour. Even in lesser years its quality usually lives up to high expectations.

Château Léoville-Poyferré 78 B4
2e Grand Cru Classé
Since 1979 there has been great improvement at Poyferré. The owners – the Cuvelier family – have spent a small fortune on total renovation of cellars and plant, and Professor Emile Peynaud (consultant to Léoville-las-Cases and other estates for many years) has been called in to advise. As a result the wine has markedly improved. It has substance and breeding, with body and fruit, and fully justifies its place among the *deuxièmes crus*.

Château St-Pierre 78 C4
4e Grand Cru Classé
In its time St-Pierre has been divided, reunited and then divided again, with different buildings functioning as the château. Since September 1982, however, a good deal of the original vineyard has been reunited with the original château. The man who brought this about was Henri Martin of Château Gloria, who has had the château and surrounding park fully restored – although the château, originally a royal villa, rather unfortunately faces St-Julien's notorious giant bottle. The wine itself is generous and amiable, with an aroma of soft fruits.

Château Talbot 78 B3
4e Grand Cru Classé
With more than 100 hectares (250 acres) of vines, this is the largest property in St-Julien. The name comes from John Talbot, Earl of Shrewsbury, who lodged here in 1453 before departing to die in battle with the French at Castillon. For decades Château Talbot wine has shown its reliability, although Gruaud-Larose, which has the same owners, is consistently finer in ultimate quality.

ALSO IN ST-JULIEN
Châteaux la Bridane (*Cru Bourgeois*); **du Glana** (*Cru Bourgeois Exceptionnel*); **Gloria***; **Hortevie***; **Lalande-Borie*** (*Cru Bourgeois Exceptionnel*) and **Terrey-Gros-Cailloux*** (*Cru Bourgeois*).

ST-LAURENT-ET-BENON, postcode 33112
Appellation Haut-Médoc

Château Belgrave 78 C2
5e Grand Cru Classé
For a considerable time this estate did not deserve its place among the Grand Crus, but a prosperous group of owners since 1979 has invested a good deal in the vineyard and equipment. Their first vintages have been promising.

Château de Camensac * 78 C2
5e Grand Cru Classé
Meaty, lingering Haut-Médoc from an estate that has been lifted out of its neglected state by effort and money. The wine might well obtain a place among the *quatrièmes crus*.

Château Caronne Ste-Gemme 75 B1
Cru Grand Bourgeois Exceptionnel
This isolated château (see the map of the Central Médoc on page 75) can be reached via the N215, just south of St-Laurent. The wine needs long maturing.

Château Larose-Trintaudon 78 B2
Cru Grand Bourgeois
Despite the size of the vineyard – 172 hectares (425 acres), the biggest in the Médoc – the wine is elegant and reliable. The former proprietors (the Forner family, who own Château de Camensac) carried out many renovations before selling the estate in late 1986 to a French insurance company.

Château Langoa-Barton

PAUILLAC

At Pauillac the background changes from rural to urban, for the traveller finds himself in a fairly colourless provincial town of some 6,500 inhabitants, the capital of the Médoc. Most of the streets lead down to the quay where mainly pleasure craft and a few fishing boats tie up. In earlier days large sailing ships and steamers dropped anchor here, for the port is at the limit of the tidal Gironde, between the harbours of Bordeaux or Libourne (on the Dordogne) and the sea. Many ships used to wait for the tide at Pauillac and before the French Revolution their captains were obliged to take a Pauillac pilot on board, together with four seamen, to navigate incoming vessels up the Gironde. It was from here, too, that the Marquis de Lafayette set out in 1777 to join the American rebels, giving up a comfortable life at the court of Versailles.

There are many reminders of this maritime past. Seafaring emblems adorn the fronts of various buildings and a model sailing ship is a feature of the main church. There is also a yacht race every Whitsun.

Wine growing was a relatively late development in Pauillac. Jacques de Ségur was the first to practise it on a large scale and later his son Alexandre, president of the Bordeaux Parlement, was called the *Prince des Vignes* by Louis XV. There was certainly some justification for this title: Alexandre, the Marquis de Ségur, inherited Lafite from his mother, acquired Latour as a marriage portion and owned several other estates, including Calon-Ségur in St-Estèphe.

In the eighteenth century the vigorously expanding wine industry brought Pauillac a golden age. In the second half of that century there were 20 coopers' workshops in the town and a glass factory opened in 1785. The factory has long since disappeared but just to the south of the town centre there is still a district called La Verrerie. It was in Pauillac, too, that sulphur was first added to casks of wine, in the Dutch fashion, to prevent secondary fermentation. Pauillac has remained chiefly a wine community, the development of some transitory industries notwithstanding. The nineteenth-century blast furnaces have vanished and the unlovely oil refinery, opened in 1926, no longer functions.

The roll call of famous Crus Classés makes clear Pauillac's pre-eminence. Latour, Lafite and Mouton, three of the five first-growths of the 1855 classification, are here, and 15 more classed growths, with Rothschild a recurring theme. Their wine is the quintessence of great red Bordeaux: the Médoc of Médocs. In a good Pauillac you find vitality, strength and character; marvellous nuances of blackcurrant, mint, new oak and cedar. Tannin is always present: Pauillac is essentially wine for laying down. It can need 20 years and then last for several decades more.

"Pauillac's soil is rich through being poor", Jean-Michel Cazes of Château Lynch-Bages has said. Poor it certainly is, and meagre, but with a thick layer of gravel rich in iron. Two gravel plateaux of roughly equal size lie north and south of the town, separated by the Chenal du Gaer (and a former railway line). Mouton Rothschild and Pontet-Canet occupy the northern (and higher) plateau; the Bages estates and Grand-Puy-Lacoste the other. There are few châteaux in and around the town; most are spread out over the commune, often around small hamlets such as St-Lambert and Bages south of the town and Le Pouyalet to the north. Pauillac's great estates are less split up than those in, say, Margaux. This is a country-side of broad vineyards under single ownership, surrounding their proprietors' châteaux.

A characteristic of the Médoc is the variation in soil within a single commune and Pauillac is no exception. The result is an exciting and sometimes surprising diversity of wines. In Pauillac the Crus Classés unroll on either side of the main (*départementale*) roads in a band some three kilometres (two miles) wide. Then there is a change in the soil and vines give way to pine woods. Beyond the woods to the west is the commune of St-Sauveur, where some honourable *crus bourgeois* represent the Haut-Médoc appellation.

▶ Looking across the Gironde from Pauillac to the Ile de Patiras, one of the many islands that made navigation up-river to Bordeaux so hazardous in the days when Pauillac was a major port. Today fishing boats replace the men-of-war and merchant fleets, and sheep graze on the salt marshes.

TRAVEL INFORMATION

There are no first-class hotels or restaurants in Pauillac, although improvement is on the way (see Hotels: Château de Cordeillan). To eat or to stay overnight it is better to go farther south, but a speciality to look for here and elsewhere in Bordeaux is *agneau de Pauillac*. Genuine *agneau de Pauillac* is now rare: it is from lambs fed only on the milk of the ewes, which produces very pale meat of incomparable flavour. The lamb you are likely to be served as *agneau de Pauillac*, and certainly a delicacy to be enjoyed, comes from flocks that graze on the salt marshes (prés-salés) down by the river in Pauillac.

HOTELS

Hotel Le Coquille, 33250 Pauillac, tel. 56 59 07 52. On the quay. Do not expect too much. Class C.
Château de Cordeillan, 33250 Pauillac, tel. 56 59 18 92. In the hamlet of Bages, close to Château Lynch-Bages, Pauillac's first quality hotel and restaurant is to open in 1988. It will have 15 comfortable rooms and be managed by a former *sommelier* who also runs the Ecole de Bordeaux, an organization that arranges tastings and excursions, etc., in the area.

RESTAURANTS

La Salamandre, 33250 Pauillac, tel. 56 59 08 68. On the quay, with a bar and tearoom. Herring is a speciality – not a very helpful one if you want to enjoy a glass of Pauillac. The business also goes under the name of Johan. Class C.

PLACES OF INTEREST

No visitor to the Médoc should leave without seeing the splendid wine museum opened by Baron Philippe de Rothschild at Château Mouton Rothschild in 1962: a unique collection, beautifully displayed, that shows how wine and art have been interwoven from early times. The main hall of the museum is a former wine cellar and six smaller rooms open off it. The collection includes Persian beakers from the 9th and 8th centuries BC, pre-Columbian sculptures, Alsace tapestries, Ming vases, Delft pottery, Venetian glasswork and much more. There are also works by modern artists. The museum can only be visited by appointment (tel. 56 59 22 22) and is closed at weekends, on public holidays and during August.

WINE INFORMATION

The Maison du Tourisme et du Vin was reopened in 1986 after being burned down. It used to be at Château Grand-Puy Ducasse but is now in a modern-looking building south of the quay and is open throughout the year. You can ask here for information about visiting the châteaux.

THE PAUILLAC GRANDS CRUS

Château Batailley 83 E3
5e Grand Cru Classé
It is worth visiting this estate to see the park: the trees come from all parts of the world. At harvest time the woodland floor is a carpet of pink cyclamen. Batailley is a respectable Pauillac, not renowned for complexity but with good balance between fruit and tannin.

Château Clerc Milon 83 B4
5e Grand Cru Classé
Since Philippe de Rothschild took over in 1970 the wine has merited attention. A modest house serves as the château.

Château Croizet-Bages 83 D4
5e Grand Cru Classé
Earlier vintages have repeatedly given

great pleasure, but the estate seems to have been going through a difficult period. Even in such great years as 1975, '78 and '82 the wines were below standard.

Château Duhart-Milon-Rothschild 83 B3
4e Grand Cru Classé
The vineyard borders on that of Lafite-Rothschild (with the same owners) and produces a distinguished Pauillac, with recent vintages rather light and pretty. There is a *chai* but no château.

Château Grand-Puy Ducasse *
83 C4
5e Grand Cru Classé
The château is on the quay at Pauillac, some kilometres from the

three scattered plots that make up its vineyard. Considerable investment since 1971 has meant that both production and quality have improved. The wine is sound, with fruit, plenty of colour and more than usual charm. The Maison du Vin used to be here but now has its own building on the quay.

Château Grand-Puy-Lacoste *
83 D3
5e Grand Cru Classé
This estate, in the hands of the Borie family of Ducru-Beaucaillou (St-Julien), produces a meaty Pauillac with plenty of depth and flavour and the class of a *troisième cru*. A little valley beside the château shelters a romantic private garden with hydrangeas bordering a canal.

Château Haut-Bages-Libéral
83 D4
5e Grand Cru Classé
Since 1983 this medium-sized estate has had new owners: the Société Civile, owners of Chasse-Spleen in Moulis and other properties. Serious work has been put in and the wine fully justifies its ranking.

Château Haut-Batailley 83 E3
5e Grand Cru Classé
An unpretentious estate managed by Jean-Eugène Borie of Ducru-Beaucaillou: perhaps why the wine tends more to the amiability of St-Julien than the reserve of Pauillac.

Château Lafite-Rothschild 83 A3
1er Grand Cru Classé
As you drive north from Pauillac,

Lafite-Rothschild is the last château before St-Estèphe. A virile, hearty wine might be expected here, on the very fringe of St-Estèphe – but not so. Lafite has a feminine grace, the subtlety and gentle finesse one would expect more from a St-Julien or a Margaux. Baron Eric de Rothschild took over the management in 1980. Visitors are not able to see inside the spacious 18th-century château but part of the cellars can be visited. Traditional methods are still followed, with fermentation vats of Bosnian oak.

Château Latour 83 E4
1er Grand Cru Classé
The hamlet of St-Lambert used to be part of St-Julien, and a slightly different arrangement of the boundaries would have put Latour in the St-Julien appellation. Despite this, Latour is a thoroughbred Pauillac: concentrated and full of compact power. It can only be described in superlatives, and so can its reliability. Latour produced successful wines even in such notoriously bad years as 1963 and '65. The estate derives its name from a former fortress on the site: the solitary domed tower in the grounds today is not the remains of a medieval fortification but a *pigeonnier*. The actual château is a small, rather middle-class looking Second Empire house surrounded by a little wooded garden. The roomy *chais* lie separately among the vines in a square around a small courtyard, perhaps where the long-destroyed fortress stood. Just as Latour wine contrasts strongly with Lafite, so do the installations: at Latour the wooden fermentation vats had been replaced by stainless-steel tanks by 1964. The year before, the estate had been taken over by English investors, including Lord Cowdray's family interests and Harveys of Bristol.

Château Latour

Château Lynch-Bages * 83 D4
5e Grand Cru Classé
The working buildings dominate the pleasant house here. Both have been completely renovated recently by Jean-Michel Cazes. Lynch-Bages is a complete Pauillac, strong, often with a suggestion of mint in its perfume and an aroma of small red fruits. It is far better than its classification.

Château Lynch-Moussas 83 D2
5e Grand Cru Classé
Since 1969 Emile Castéja, also of Château Batailley, has devoted much money and energy to replanting the vineyard and modernizing the cellars. These efforts are beginning to bear fruit, and as the vines age the wine will undoubtedly gain in depth.

Château Mouton Baronne Philippe * 83 B3
5e Grand Cru Classé
The former Mouton-d'Armailhacq was bought in 1933 by Baron Philippe de Rothschild of Mouton Rothschild, the adjoining estate. The château, actually a half-completed villa, stands beside the Mouton Rothschild drive. The wine is alluring and well balanced, lighter and quicker to develop than the Mouton Rothschild. From 1956 until 1974 the estate was called Mouton Baron Philippe; "Baron" was changed to "Baronne" at the time of the 1975 vintage in honour of the Baron's late wife Pauline.

Château Mouton Rothschild 83 B3
1er Grand Cru Classé
No other Bordeaux estate has had so

much published about it as Mouton Rothschild and no other *propriétaire* has been so much written about as the late Baron Philippe. When the management of Mouton passed to him in 1922 it was more a farm than a château. With great vision and tenacity, the Baron succeeded in making Mouton one of the most respected and most visited wine estates in the world; and this despite the fact that he was also poet, playwright, film and theatre director

Château Lafite-Rothschild

and racing driver. With his American wife Pauline he created a unique wine museum (see Places of Interest) and since 1946 he commissioned a work by a famous artist each year for the Mouton label. The Baron's greatest coup, however, was the promotion of Mouton Rothschild in 1973 from first of the second-growths to its rightful place as a *premier cru* – the only change ever made to the 1855 classification. In character Mouton Rothschild comes closer to Latour than to Lafite: it has a luxurious, concentrated aroma of blackcurrant and cedarwood, plenty of tannin and an aftertaste that lasts in the mouth for minutes. A sumptuous Pauillac, prodigious in every respect.

Château Pédesclaux 83 C4
5e Grand Cru Classé
A carefully made, concentrated and now somewhat soft Pauillac (it used to taste tougher). The vineyard is scattered around the commune.

Château Pichon-Longueville Baron 83 E4
2e Grand Cru Classé
A child asked to draw a château might come up with something like this: an affair of turrets and steep-pitched roofs. It was built in 1851 but has long been unoccupied. The wine is a slender, supple Pauillac with impressions of ripe fruit and noble wood.

Château Pichon-Longueville, Comtesse de Lalande * 83 E4
2e Grand Cru Classé
"The Comtesse" is the larger portion of what was once a single estate. The balance is "the Baron" (see previous entry). Since the second half of the 1970s enormous sums have been invested. The *chai* has been enlarged and in 1980 a new *cuvier* came into use, with stainless-steel fermentation tanks. Today the wines compete with the first-growths in quality.

Château Pontet-Canet * 83 C3
5e Grand Cru Classé
The buildings where the wine is made are enormous. The loft over the *cuvier* can seat 600 (it is often used for receptions) and the high-ceilinged cellar where the casks are stored is almost cathedral-like. After a long period of mediocrity that lasted until well into the 1970s, Pontet-Canet is completely up to the mark again. The wine is dark, intense, with plenty of tannin and fruit that suggests currants: a very typical Pauillac and far superior to its fifth-growth status.

Pauillac *crus bourgeois* include **Colombier-Monpelou, La Couronne*** (*Cru Bourgeois Supérieur Exceptionnel*), **La Fleur Milon, Fonbadet*** (*Cru Bourgeois Supérieur*), **Haut-Bages Monpelou** and **Pibran**. La Rose Pauillac is the well-made brand wine from the local cooperative.

ST-SAUVEUR, postcode 33250
Appellation Haut-Médoc

Château Peyrabon 83 C1
Cru Grand Bourgeois
Queen Victoria once attended a concert here; the ceiling decorations are a reminder. Reliable wine.

Château Ramage La Batisse* 83 B1
Cru Bourgeois
Firm, balanced, award-winning wine.

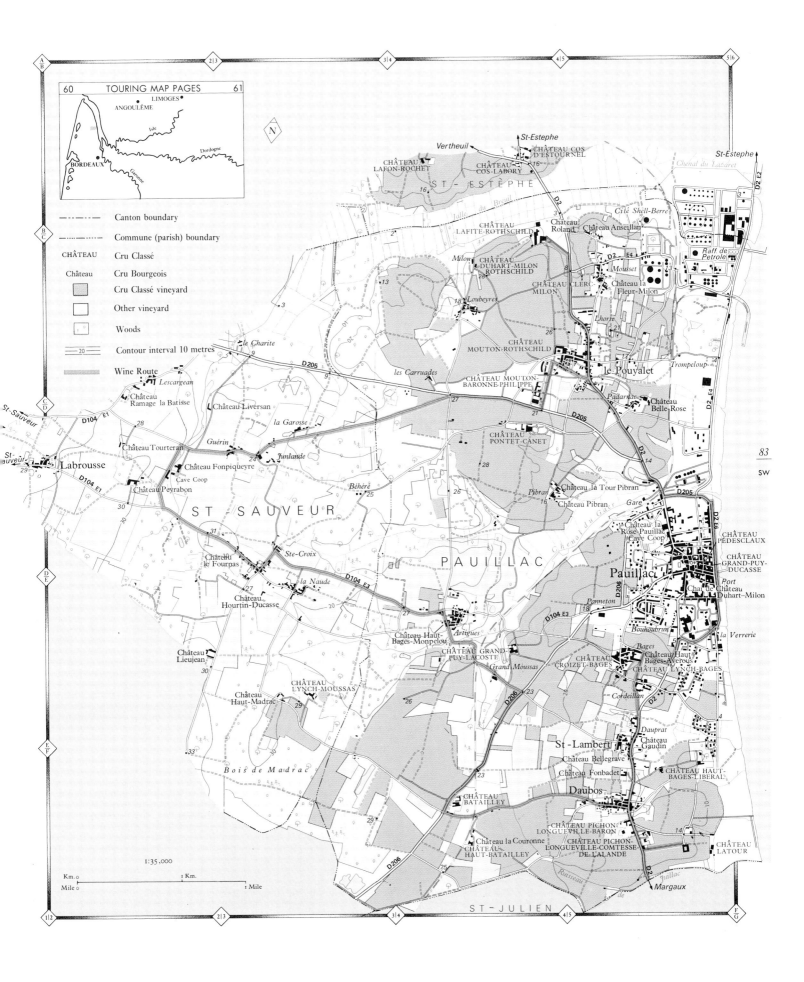

TOURING MAP PAGES

60   61

LIMOGES

ANGOULÊME

Isle

BORDEAUX

Garonne

Dordogne

N

------- Canton boundary

------- Commune (parish) boundary

CHÂTEAU   Cru Classé

Château   Cru Bourgeois

Cru Classé vineyard

Other vineyard

Woods

——20——   Contour interval 10 metres

Wine Route

St-Estephe

Vertheuil

CHÂTEAU COS D'ESTOURNEL

CHÂTEAU LAFON-ROCHET

CHÂTEAU COS-LABORY

St-Estephe

St-Estephe

Chenal du Lazaret

D2 E2

ST-ESTÈPHE

Vallée du Breuil

Cité Shell-Berre

CHÂTEAU LAFITE-ROTHSCHILD

Château Roland

Château Anseillan

Raff de Petrole

CHÂTEAU DUHART-MILON ROTHSCHILD

Milon

D2 E4

Mousset

CHÂTEAU CLERC MILON

Château la Fleur-Milon

Loubeyres

L'horte

le Charite

CHÂTEAU MOUTON-ROTHSCHILD

Trompeloup

Lescargean

D205

les Carruades

le Pouyalet

Château Ramage la Batisse

Château Liversan

CHÂTEAU MOUTON BARONNE-PHILIPPE

Padarnac

Château Belle-Rose

la Garosse

D2 E4

D104 E1

Guérin

CHÂTEAU PONTET-CANET

D205

Château Tourteran

Junlande

83

SW

Château Fonpiqueyre

Cave Coop

Béhéré

Pibran

Château la Tour Pibran

Château Peyrabon

Labrousse

Château Pibran

Gare

D104 E1

ST-SAUVEUR

Château la Rose-Pauillac Cave Coop

CHÂTEAU PÉDESCLAUX

CHÂTEAU GRAND-PUY-DUCASSE

Château le Fournas

Ste-Croix

D104 E3

PAUILLAC

Pauillac

la Naude

Port de Château Duhart-Milon

Château Hourtin-Ducasse

Panneton

la Verrerie

Bouhoubron

Château Haut-Bages-Monpelou

Artigues

Bages

Château Haut-Bages-Averous

Château Lieujean

CHÂTEAU GRAND-PUY-LACOSTE

Grand Moussas

CHÂTEAU CROIZET-BAGES

CHÂTEAU LYNCH-BAGES

CHÂTEAU LYNCH-MOUSSAS

Cordeillan

D2

Château Haut-Madrac

Dauprat

Château Gaudin

St-Lambert

Château Bellegrave

CHÂTEAU HAUT-BAGES-LIBERAL

Bois de Madrac

Château Fonbadet

Daubos

CHÂTEAU BATAILLEY

CHÂTEAU PICHON-LONGUEVILLE-BARON

CHÂTEAU LATOUR

Château la Couronne

CHÂTEAU HAUT-BATAILLEY

CHÂTEAU PICHON-LONGUEVILLE-COMTESSE-DE-LALANDE

D206

Margaux

1:35,000

Km. 0   1 Km.

Mile 0   1 Mile

ST-JULIEN

ST-ESTEPHE

As you drive north along the D2, Château Lafite-Rothschild on its terrace to your left provides the last image of Pauillac. Next comes a meadow of tall poplars around a little stream, called a *jalle* in the Médoc, which marks the boundary of St-Estèphe. The road then bends and climbs to where a surprise awaits the traveller, for suddenly the outline of an Oriental pagoda comes into view. The pagoda, complete with bells, adorns a curious white building, the Grand Cru Classé Château Cos d'Estournel. "Cos" is a leader among the second-growths of Bordeaux: wine of potent character for at least ten years of life.

After this bizarre prelude it hardly comes as a surprise to find the landscape of St-Estèphe different from the rest of the Médoc. After you turn right near Cos d'Estournel into a narrow minor road, the D2E3, a broad undulating plateau opens out, the green of its vineyards interrupted only by a few isolated châteaux.

St-Estèphe is the biggest wine commune of the Médoc, with 1,100 hectares (2,700 acres) under cultivation. A deep bed of gravel extends beneath the often sandy surface soil, especially in the southeast. The stones are sometimes so large, hard and translucent that they can be cut and polished into ornaments. (In the last century one grower had all the gravel removed from his land – and wondered why his wine declined in quality.) Chalk as well as gravel is found around St-Estèphe, particularly in the northeast, and clay is in the subsoil almost everywhere. There is generally a higher proportion of Merlot to Cabernet Sauvignon than farther south – up to 40 percent on some estates.

This is Cru Bourgeois country. There are only five classed growths, led by Cos d'Estournel. The wines are full of colour, vigorous, rather stronger and heartier than those of Pauillac, and as a rule generously provided with tannin. The better ones often demand years of patience: only after long maturing in bottle do their nuances of nose and taste develop, while the tannin discreetly retreats in favour of smoothness and harmony.

The region's history goes back at least to Gallo-Roman times. Until the eighteenth century St-Estèphe was known as St-Estèphe-de-Calon, the *calon* probably derived from a Gaulish term meaning "wood" or "brushwood". (One of the best-known châteaux of the district is Calon-Ségur.) Wine growing began to flourish in the thirteenth century, thanks to the monks of the priory of Notre Dame des Couleys. The buildings of this former religious house still stand: rebuilt in 1662, they now serve as cellars for Château Meyney. When the monks were establishing them-

selves, St-Estèphe itself was a busy port. A new, larger harbour had been created in the twelfth century, where not only merchant ships put in but also the steady traffic of pilgrims on their way to Santiago de Compostela. For many centuries, until 1704, a church, Notre Dame Entre Deux Arcs, stood by the harbour and must have been a conspicuous landmark along the Gironde. Now only a small chapel remains.

St-Estèphe's importance as a port was considerably enhanced in 1469 when Louis XI forbade English captains to sail up the Gironde beyond this point. The result was that for a while the harbour at St-Estèphe replaced that of Bordeaux. There is nothing now to be seen of this proud past. The Port de la Chapelle is no longer important, just a little harbour frequented by fishing boats and yachts. A small modern residential quarter has been built close by.

St-Estèphe is surrounded by a number of villages that belong to the Haut-Médoc appellation. To the north lies St-Seurin-de-Cadourne, which borders on the Médoc district; to the west the partly wooded areas of Vertheuil and Cissac. Gravel is less prevalent here, but outcrops still occur. Generally, too, the countryside is flatter, less undulating. The wines from these neighbouring villages are rather less strong, less rich in tannin than those from St-Estèphe, but their quality can be surprising – a few of the *crus bourgeois* even reach the level of a *cru classé*.

TRAVEL INFORMATION

St-Estèphe itself has no hotels or restaurants and there are few of any quality in the surrounding area – it is the châteaux and their wines that people come here for. It would be wiser to look for food and accommodation elsewhere in the Médoc.

▼ The immaculately maintained Château Meyney – one of the Cordier (the négociants) estates – is a former monastery dating from 1662.

HOTELS

Hotel du Midi, 33250 St-Seurin-de-Cadourne, tel. 56 59 30 49. For anyone who has not been able to find accommodation elsewhere. Totally without atmosphere. There is also a restaurant. Class C.

PLACES OF INTEREST

Cissac Ruins of an old castle, close to the present Château du Breuil.
St-Estèphe The 19th-century church in the village square has a tower that is shaped somewhat like a bottle – a fact that the local wine growers like to point out to their guests.
Vertheuil Romanesque church of the 11th century, rebuilt in the 15th. In summer, exhibitions of work by artists and craftsmen of the region are held in what was the old monastery. (The local château is private property and cannot be visited.)

WINE INFORMATION

The little Maison du Vin of St-Estèphe is on the square facing the church. Information about the region is available here, but of even greater interest is the large range of wines on sale. Art exhibitions are held from time to time, mainly in the summer.

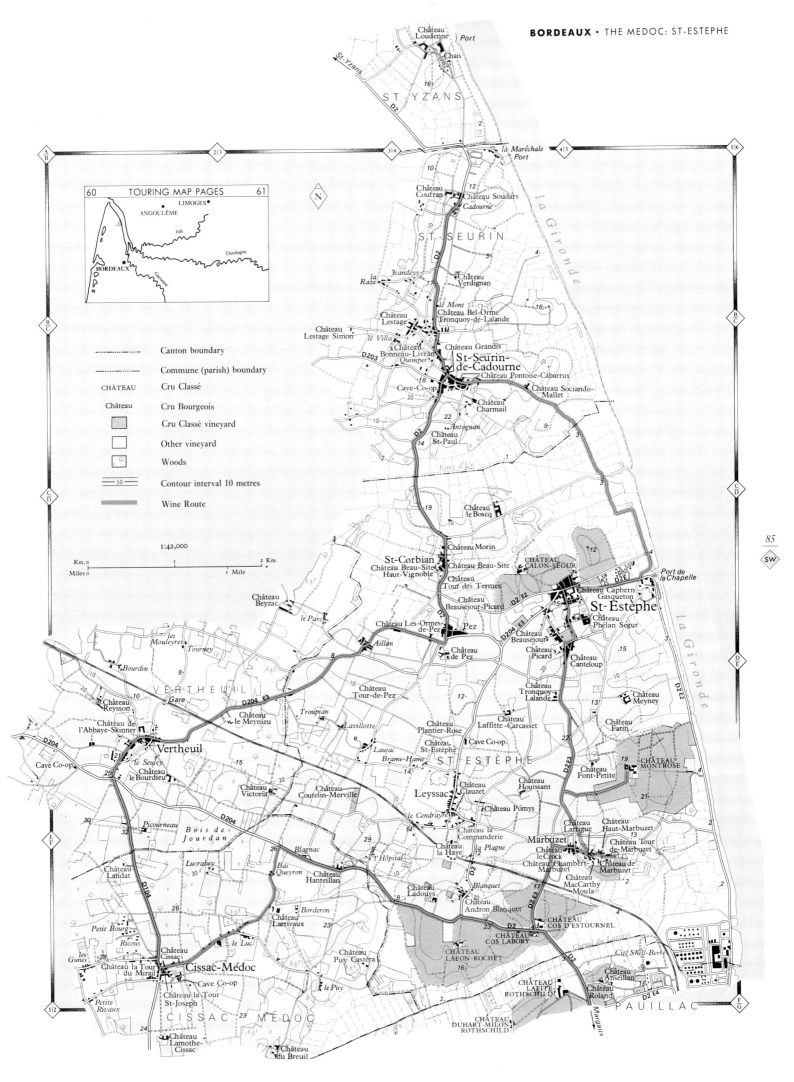

Château Loudenne / Port
Chais
ST-YZANS
D2
la Maréchale Port
10
12
Château Coufran
Château Soudars
Cadourne
ST-SEURIN
D2
4.
3.
Jeandeys
la Raze
17
Château Verdignan
16
le Mont
Château Bel-Orme Tronquoy-de-Lalande
Château Lestage
le Villa
Château Grandis
Château Lestage Simon
10
Château Bonneau-Livran Quimper
D203
St-Seurin-de-Cadourne
Château Pontoise-Cábarrus
Cave-Co-op
20
Château Sociando-Mallet
Château Charmail
22
Antognan
9.
D2
Château St-Paul
14
3
2.
Estey d'Un
1
3
19
Château le Boscq
Chenal de Calon
Château Morin
12
St-Corbian
Château Beau-Site
CHÂTEAU CALON-SÉGUR
4
Château Beau-Site Haut-Vignoble
Château Tour des Termes
Port de la Chapelle
D2 E2
Château Capbern Gasqueton
D2 E
Château Beauséjour-Picard
15
St-Estèphe
Château Beyzac
le Parc
Château Les-Ormes-de-Pez
Pez
D204 E3
Château Beauséjour
Château Phélan Ségur
3
les Mouleyres
Tourney
Aillan
Château de Pez
Château Picard
Château Canteloup
.15
D/E
Bourdin
8.
8
10
Château Tour-de-Pez
Château Tronquoy-Lalande
Château Meyney
13
VERTHEUIL
10
Gare
D204 E3
12.
Laffitte-Carcasset
22
Château Fatin
Château Reysson
20
Château le Meynieu
10
Château Plantier-Rose
Château Laffitte-Carcasset
D2 E3
Château Font-Petite
19
CHÂTEAU MONTROSE
Château de l'Abbaye-Skinner
D204
Troupian
Lavillotte
Château St-Estèphe
Cave Co-op
21
Cave Co-op
Vertheuil
le Seuley
.15
Laujac
Brame-Hame
14
ST-ESTÈPHE
Château le Bourdieu
25
Château Houissant
Château Victoria
20
Château Coutelin-Merville
Château Clauzet
Leyssac
Château Lartigue
Château Haut-Marbuzet
13
30
Picourneau
Bois de Jourdan
D204
29
14
le Cendrayre
Château Pomys
Château la Commanderie
Marbuzet
Château Tour de-Marbuzet
32
Blagnac
26
l'Hôpital
Château la Haye
la Plagne
Château le Crock
Château Chambert-Marbuzet
Château de Marbuzet
Lucrabey
30
Bas Queyron
Château Hanteillan
10
Château MacCarthy Moula
2
Château Landat
Blanquet
17
D104
Borderon
Château Ladouys
CHÂTEAU COS D'ESTOURNEL
Petit Bourg
Château Larrivaux
23
Château Andron Blanquet
20
D2 E3
Ricous
les Gunes
28
23
D2
23
CHÂTEAU COS LABORY
Château Cissac
le Luc
Château Puy Castéra
le Puy
Chenal du Lazaret
Cité Shell-Berre
Château la Tour du Mirail
Cissac-Médoc
Cave Co-op
CHÂTEAU LAFON-ROCHET
16
Château Anseillan
16
D2 E4
Château la Tour St-Joseph
Petite Rivaux
CISSAC MÉDOC
23
2.
Château LAFITE-ROTHSCHILD
Château Roland
D2
Margaux
PAUILLAC
24
Château Lamothe-Cissac
Château du Breuil
CHÂTEAU DUHART-MILON-ROTHSCHILD

TOURING MAP PAGES
60   61
LIMOGES
ANGOULÊME
Isle
Dordogne
BORDEAUX
Garonne
N

- - - - - - Canton boundary
— · — · — Commune (parish) boundary
CHÂTEAU   Cru Classé
Château   Cru Bourgeois
▨   Cru Classé vineyard
▢   Other vineyard
▢   Woods
══50══   Contour interval 10 metres
▬▬▬   Wine Route

1:42,000

Km. 0   1   2 Km.
Miles 0   1 Mile

THE CHATEAUX

ST-ESTEPHE, postcode 33250
Appellation St-Estèphe

Château Calon-Ségur 85 D4
3e Grand Cru Classé
In the 17th century this estate was the property of the rich and powerful Alexandre de Ségur, whose other possessions included Lafite, Latour, Mouton and de Pez. Château Calon was, however, his favourite. The château now belongs to the Capbern-Gasqueton (of Châteaux Capbern-Gasqueton, du Tertre, etc) and Peyrelongue families. The wine is intense, sinewy, a substantial St-Estèphe that lingers in the mouth.

Château Cos d'Estournel * 85 F4
2e Grand Cru Classé
The d'Estournel family had various properties in St-Estèphe in the 17th century, including a vineyard in the hamlet of Caux (the old spelling for Cos). After Gaspard d'Estournel took over the running of the wine properties in 1810, he decided to vinify the Cos wine separately. This "Caux" proved in fact to be better than the other St-Estèphes that Gaspard produced, due largely to the very gravelly slopes on which the vines were planted. Today the Prats family own Cos d'Estournel. Under the management of Bruno Prats the château is perfectly maintained and behind the enclosing walls there are modern installations and a spacious cellar. The wine is excellent: distinguished, with a firm structure and beautiful balance. Normally it needs to age for at least a decade. Almost every vintage is matured in new oak casks. During the summer, visitors are welcomed by a multi-lingual guide.

Château Cos Labory 85 F4
5e Grand Cru Classé
Although the vineyards of Cos Labory and Lafon-Rochet adjoin, they produce totally different wines. Cos Labory is a fairly soft St-Estèphe, accessible quite young, with more suppleness than finesse.

Château Lafon-Rochet 85 F4
4e Grand Cru Classé
In the past, Lafon-Rochet was not only a vineyard but a resting place for pilgrims en route to Santiago de Compostela in Spain. Hence the small chapel that still stands on the estate. The château itself, despite its classical lines, was built in the 1960s. A high percentage of Cabernet grapes makes the wine rather austere and reserved, but it is carefully made and gains in charm with the years.

Château Montrose * 85 E5
2e Grand Cru Classé
Where Cos d'Estournel looks Oriental, Montrose is reminiscent of Alsace. The estate was bought in 1866 by Alsace-born Mathieu Dollfus, who for his time was a very enterprising and enlightened owner. His memory is kept alive by the road signs on the estate: Rue d'Alsace, Rue de Mulhouse, etc. Montrose, the "pink hill" – perhaps so called because it used to be covered with pink-flowering heather – is today under the dynamic management of its owner, Jean-Louis Charmolüe. In 1983, for example, he built an enormous new first-year cellar with the dimensions of an aircraft hangar. Château Montrose wine used to be unapproachably hard in its youth, demanding great patience. Since 1983 it has been rather softer, with more fruit, but colour and tannin are still there in plenty.

ALSO IN ST-ESTEPHE

Château Capbern-Gasqueton 85 D5
Cru Grand Bourgeois Exceptionnel
The château, just behind the church at St-Estèphe, is the home of the Capbern-Gasquetons, owners of Château Calon-Ségur. Sound, traditionally made wine for keeping.

Château Le Crock 85 F4
Cru Grand Bourgeois Exceptionnel
Château surrounded by a large park, in the hamlet of Marbuzet, with the same owners as Léoville-Poyferré in St-Julien. Strong wine rich in tannin, excellent for laying down.

Château Haut-Marbuzet 85 F5
Cru Grand Bourgeois Exceptionnel
A much-visited wine estate in Marbuzet. New casks give the wine a strong flavour of oak; an obvious touch of class.

Château La Haye* 85 F4
Cru Bourgeois Supérieur
Château with rich historical associations: in the 16th century it served as a hunting lodge for Diane de Poitiers and Henry II. Since 1979 it has produced excellent wine. The hospitable owner is André Vincent.

Château de Marbuzet * 85 F5
Cru Grand Bourgeois Exceptionnel
Wine from this small vineyard with its fine Louis XVI château, owned by the Prats family of Cos d'Estournel, is blended with Cos *cuvées* that do not reach Grand Cru standard. Vinified at Cos, it is sold as the Cos second label.

▲ The little wine village of Vertheuil, just to the west of St-Estèphe, is distinguished by the weathered stones of its Romanesque church.

Château Meyney 85 E5
Cru Grand Bourgeois Exceptionnel
A former abbey, perfectly preserved, now a flourishing wine estate making a highly reliable St-Estèphe.

Château Les Ormes-de-Pez * 85 D4
Cru Grand Bourgeois
A very characteristic St-Estèphe of high standard. The equipment was completely modernized in 1981.

Château de Pez * 85 D4
Cru Bourgeois Supérieur
Very reliable estate now generally considered to be on a par with many classed growths. Robert Dousson makes a mouth-filling St-Estèphe needing at least five years to mature.

Other *crus bourgeois* include **Châteaux Houissant***, **Phélan Ségur***, **Pomys*** and **Tronquoy-Lalande**.

CISSAC, postcode 33250
Appellation Haut-Médoc

Crus bourgeois include **Châteaux du Breuil, Cissac*** (a *Cru Grand Bourgeois Exceptionnel*) and **Hanteillan** (well worth a visit: a lot of money has been spent on the restoration of the splendid cellars).

ST-SEURIN-DE-CADOURNE,
postcode 33250
Appellation Haut-Médoc

Châteaux include **Bel-Orme-Tronquoy-de-Lalande** (the small château was designed by the architect of the Grand Théâtre in Bordeaux), **Sociando-Mallet*** and **Verdignan***.

VERTHEUIL, postcode 33250
Appellation Haut-Médoc

Château **Le Bourdieu*** makes a flawless wine; **Château Le Meynieu** is owned by Jacques Pedro, the mayor of the village.

THE NORTHERN MEDOC

This part of the Médoc is, in fact, called Bas-Médoc, "Lower Médoc", because it is downstream on the Gironde. The wine growers, however, would rather not talk of Bas-Médoc; still less does the word Bas appear on labels. This is because "low" or "lower" is hardly the most positive concept to associate with wine, and so the appellation Médoc is used these days for the northern part of the peninsula. The growers are content with this arrangement, but for the relatively uninitiated consumer it is absurdly confusing: it carries the name of the whole district but refers only to its most remote corner.

Be that as it may, after you have passed St-Seurin-de-Cadourne, the last commune of the Haut-Médoc, there is a distinct change in the landscape. It becomes flatter, with more meadowland and fewer vine-clad slopes, and the villages seem smaller and quieter than those farther south. Until early in the seventeenth century this was mainly marshland, desolate and sparsely inhabited. Then the first Dutch engineers, experienced in such matters, arrived to drain the marshes and build dykes. They left their mark: the name of the hamlet By, for example, near Bégadan, is probably of Dutch origin. Dutch influence even extended to the wine. In his *Traité sur les vins du Médoc* of 1845, William Franck describes the wine from Château Livran in St-Germain-d'Esteuil as "eminently Dutch" because of its soft characteristics, and the estate itself is called a *marque hollandaise*. There was also a period when a great deal of corn was grown in the northern Médoc and the district had numerous windmills. These have disappeared, except for one: the splendidly restored mill near Château La Tour Haut-Caussan at Blaignan, still in working order.

Before the draining of the Médoc the hills where the vines now grow formed islands of life and habitation. Roman foundations and mosaics have been discovered beneath the big *cuvier* at Château Laujac in Bégadan, and at St-Yzans the remains of a Roman villa have been excavated. Wine growing did not really make its breakthrough until the nineteenth century: the number of vineyards doubled between 1850 and 1895. One reason for this spurt was the arrival at Château Loudenne of the Gilbey brothers, the London wine and spirits merchants. They bought this estate near the Gironde in 1875 to use as a depot from which they shipped vast quantities of Bordeaux wines to the British market. Here Walter and Alfred Gilbey (and their Grinling and Blyth cousins) built a cellar complex where 16,000 casks and 500,000 bottles could be stored, their own cooperage and a little railway to their dock on the busy river front.

In the nineteenth century more land in the northern Médoc was planted with vines than today, including large parcels of flat, low countryside. After the phylloxera disaster of the late nineteenth century and the subsequent crises in wine production, however, the growers concentrated their efforts on the better, higher land. As in the Haut-Médoc, there are hummocks of gravel outcrops that rise above the surrounding countryside, but they lie farther apart and contain rather heavier clayey soil, often combined with chalk. There are also sandy strips. As a result the wines are generally less fine, less complex than those from the southern Médoc. Often, too, they are more austere, drier and more reserved: the influence of the sea is stronger here, which makes it harder to grow Cabernet Sauvignon successfully. Many Médoc estates therefore plant high percentages of Merlot – 20 to 50 percent is normal, but sometimes 60 percent is encountered. The initial dourness of many Médocs disappears with the years. Like the wines of the Haut-Médoc, they mellow with age – but generally over a shorter period.

Cooperatives play an important part in the Médoc, producing about 40 percent of all the wine. Most work closely with the Uni-Médoc group, which bottles an enormous quantity of wine – a third of all Médoc – at a vast centre at Gaillan. But increasingly it is the individual estates that are giving the appellation a good name and many of today's Médocs are of very high quality.

TRAVEL INFORMATION

This part of the Médoc is thinly populated and off the main tourist route, so there are few hotels or restaurants of importance. Lamb from Queyrac has a good reputation.

HOTELS

Hotel de Paris, 33340 Lesparre, tel. 56 41 00 22. Accommodation without frills. Class C.
Vieux Acacias, 33340 Queyrac, tel. 56 59 80 63. On the D102E a few kilometres north of Lesparre, in the peaceful setting of its own small park. Class B.

RESTAURANTS

La Mare aux Grenouilles, 33340 Lesparre, tel. 56 41 03 46. Rather heavy, almost Flemish cuisine. Caters for a lot of weddings and groups, and full of French families on Sundays. Class B.
Château Loudenne, 33340 St-Yzans-de-Médoc, tel. 56 09 05 03. You can lunch in the **Cuisine des Vendanges** at the beautiful old Gilbey château overlooking the river, but will need to make a reservation at least 48 hours in advance. The price includes a choice of two wines. Class B.
Hotel-Restaurant des Pins, 33780 Soulac-sur-Mer, tel. 56 09 80 01. Try the lamprey or the *confit de canard*

A former beacon, standing on land belonging to Château La Tour de By and dating from 1825, provides a splendid view of the vineyards and the Gironde.

here. There is also an interesting wine list. Soulac is a typical seaside holiday resort at the northern extremity of the D101. Class B.
La Clef des Champs, 33930 Vendays-Montalivet, tel. 56 41 71 11. An eccentric establishment worth a visit. Regional dishes, but the quality can vary. The village of Vendays-Montalivet lies outside the actual wine area, 14 km (9 miles) from Lesparre near the junction of the D101 and D102. Class B.
La Côte d'Argent, 33123 Le Verdon-sur-Mer, tel. 56 09 60 45. Restaurant with a terrace full of flowers. *Fruits de mer* are the speciality. Near the tip of the Médoc peninsula, on the N215. Class B.

PLACES OF INTEREST

Bégadan The church, with its 11th-century apse, is classified as a historic monument.
By At Château La Tour de By, resplendent in the middle of the vineyard, there is an old beacon that was in service until 1860.

Lesparre A busy market town, with good shops, Lesparre acts as a centre for the district. It also has a historic monument: a 14th-century square tower called the Honneur de Lesparre.
St-Yzans-de-Médoc A museum of winemaking equipment at Château Loudenne was destroyed by fire in 1986 but a new collection is being assembled. (See also Restaurants.)
Valeyrac Just north of this village there is a charming little harbour, the Porte de Goulée.

WINE ACTIVITIES

Lesparre holds an annual wine fair at the beginning of August, and St-Yzans-de-Médoc has a *Foire aux Sarments* in mid-June. Wine can be sampled at both events, and food is available.

WINE INFORMATION

The Maison du Médoc in Lesparre, in the Place du Tribunal, provides information concerning wines and tourism. Exhibitions of the work of local craftsmen are also held here.

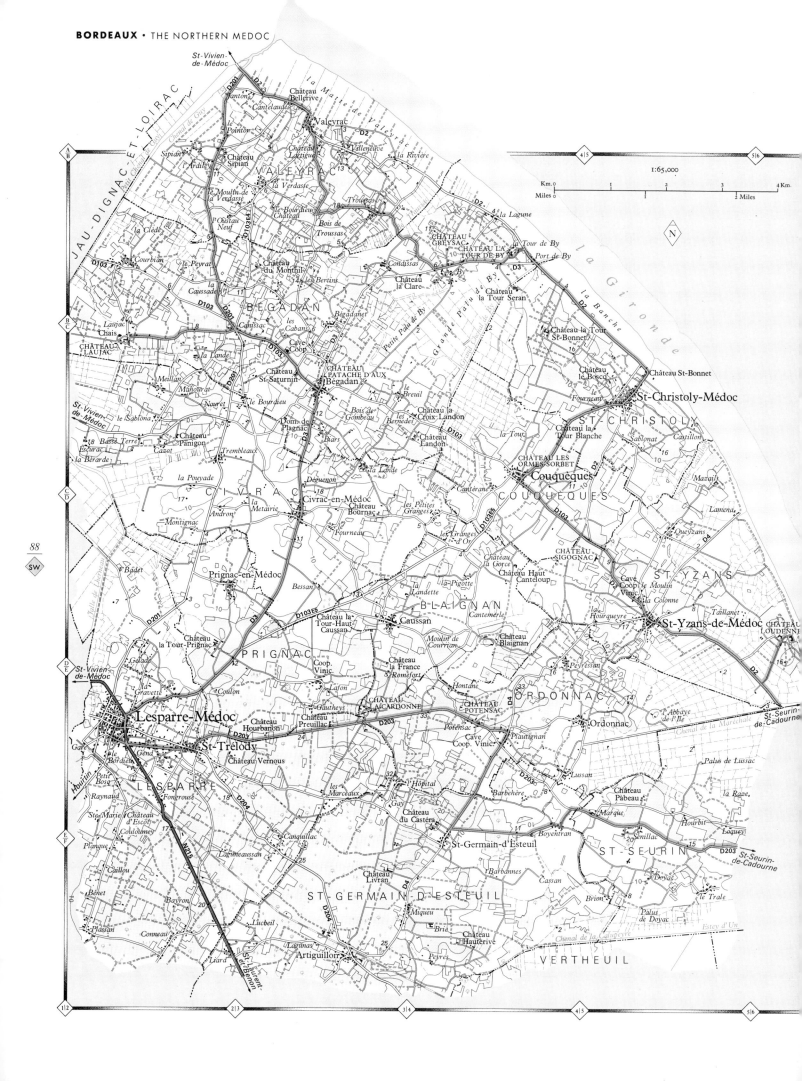

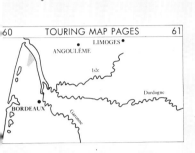

TOURING MAP PAGES

60   61

LIMOGES
ANGOULÊME
Isle
Dordogne
BORDEAUX
Garonne

———— Canton boundary

------- Commune (parish) boundary

CHÂTEAU   Cru Classé

Château   Cru Bourgeois

☐   Vineyards

☐   Woods

—20—   Contour interval 10 metres

———— Route Nationale

———— Wine Route

THE MEDOC CRUS

BEGADAN, postcode 33340

Château Greysac 88 B3
Cru Grand Bourgeois
The graceful grey-white château and its vineyards were bought in 1973 by Baron François de Gunzburg. Much of the wine – a supple, attractive Médoc that develops relatively quickly – is shipped to the US.

Château Laujac 88 C1
Cru Grand Bourgeois
This large château, with an impressive view over park and meadowland, dates from 1810. The cellars are also impressive. The Cruse family make a dark, very traditional wine here with a lot of tannin: a true Médoc, meant for long maturing – 10 years, according to Bernard Cruse.

Château Patache d'Aux 88 C2
Cru Grand Bourgeois
Substantial, mouth-filling wine, less reserved than other Médocs but with the ability to age well. The château is in the centre of Bégadan on the spot where stagecoaches used to stop (there is a stagecoach on the label).

Château La Tour de By * 88 B3
Cru Grand Bourgeois
There are two châteaux at La Tour de By. The smaller and older of the two, Château La Roque de By, dates from the 18th century, the larger one from the 19th (see also Places of Interest). The wine is one of the most successful Médocs.

BLAIGNAN, postcode 33340

Château La Cardonne 88 E2
Cru Grand Bourgeois
Since 1973 this estate has been in the hands of the French Rothschild group, who have made considerable investments in it. The wine is extremely well made and meant for drinking young.

Château La Tour Haut-Caussan * 88 D2
Cru Bourgeois
A modest estate run by the friendly Philippe Courrian, who aims at no less than perfection. As a result the wine is excellent, with elegance backed by wood and tannin. A superior version is called Réserve du Moulin, after the restored windmill that graces the site.

ORDONNAC, postcode 33340

Château Potensac* 88 E3
Cru Grand Bourgeois
A most distinguished Médoc made by the Léoville-las-Cases (St-Julien) Delon team: sinewy, with good colour, the odour of expensive barrels and a strong constitution, and fruit suggesting blackcurrants. The former church at Potensac (a hamlet near Ordonnac) functions as the cellar for the château.

QUEYRAC, postcode 33340

Château Carcanieux *
Cru Bourgeois
A Dutch manager has given the wine from this estate something of a new image, particularly from the 1981 vintage onwards.

ST-GERMAIN-D'ESTEUIL, postcode 33340

Château Castéra 88 E3
Cru Bourgeois
The château, a fine old castle with a drawbridge (the English laid seige to it in the 14th century), is owned by a German company and managed by Alexis Lichine & Co.

Château Livran 88 F2
Cru Bourgeois
A lovely château with a rich history. The wine, unfortunately, no longer justifies its former reputation.

ST-YZANS-DE-MEDOC, postcode 33340

Château Loudenne 88 D6
Cru Grand Bourgeois
The English firm W. & A. Gilbey Ltd. has its French headquarters here, which explains the large (now renovated) Victorian *chais*. The beautiful pale pink château, overlooking the river, has its own gravelly vineyard producing a stylish, balanced Médoc that can mature over a long period. Loudenne also makes a delicious dry white Bordeaux from (unusual for the Médoc) 50% Sauvignon, 50% Sémillon. Visitors are particularly welcome here.

Other châteaux include **La Clare***, **du Monthil** and **St-Saturnin** (Bégadan), **Haut Canteloup** and **Les Ormes Sorbet** (Couqueques), **Pey-Martin*** (Ordonnac), **Le Boscq, La Tour Seran** and **La Tour St-Bonnet** (St-Christoly), **Sigognac** (St-Yzans), **Bellerive** and **Bellevue*** (Valeyrac).

Château Greysac.

BOURG AND BLAYE

In the hierarchy of Bordeaux, Bourg and Blaye come a long way after the Médoc. Nor do they aspire to the heights reached by the great châteaux across the Gironde. But wine was being shipped from here long before wine growing developed in the Médoc, and these are attractive little districts with much to offer the visitor.

To reach Bourg from Bordeaux you can take either the D911 or the autoroute northeast to St-André-de-Cubzac. The D911 is slower as it passes through a number of villages, but it has the advantage of taking you over Eiffel's remarkable bridge across the Dordogne, and in St-André-de-Cubzac the junction with the scenic D669 on to Bourg is easy to find. The Cubzageais wine district around St-André makes a number of good wines under the Bordeaux and Bordeaux Supérieur appellations.

Bourg-sur-Gironde lies opposite the Bec d'Ambès, the spit of land that forms the northern tip of the Entre-Deux-Mers district and the site of a large industrial complex. The Bec has been built up by deposits of silt in the last 300 years; in the seventeenth century Bourg was called Bourg-sur-Mer and faced not the Dordogne but the Gironde. Bourg's strategic importance on its steep riverside hill was recognized by the Romans, and by the English who built a citadel here in 1153. Later, the Château de la Citadelle served as a summer residence for the archbishops of Bordeaux; houses were built around the citadel and down by the river, with long flights of steps linking the two quarters. Despite its illustrious past, Bourg today is little more than a picturesque, sleepy small town.

Bourg's small wine district, the Côtes de Bourg, lies mainly along three valleys parallel with the Dordogne. Châteaux line the river front and vines clothe much of the steep hills – the Côtes de Bourg have been called (with tongue in cheek) "the Switzerland of the Dordogne". The district makes mainly red wines (97 percent) and is right to do so. Côtes de Bourg whites nearly always lack class and personality. The reds, on the other hand, have character. The best are firm, pleasant and reasonably rounded, rustic rather than refined, often with sufficient tannin to mature well. The grapes are Cabernet Sauvignon, Cabernet Franc, Merlot and Malbec. Merlot generally predominates, representing 50–80 percent on many estates. Malbec, which used to be much in vogue, seems to be declining, although some growers still cherish it because in the Bourg microclimate and soil it seems to give its own fragrance to the wine. A certain amount of sparkling wine is also produced: the firm Brouette Petit-Fils makes sparkling Bordeaux in the Caveau du Pain de Sucre – the "Sugarloaf Cellar" – on the outskirts of Bourg-sur-Gironde.

From Bourg to Blaye is just under 15 kilometres (9 miles) and the most pleasant way to get there is by the D669E1, a narrow, romantic road that follows the river until it links up with the D669. In summer the small gardens that line the river are bright with flowers. The little river Brouillon marks the boundary between the two districts.

Blaye, like Bourg, has a Roman origin. In the Middle Ages it was on one of the pilgrim routes to Santiago de Compostela and was a departure point for Crusaders. And like Bourg it has a citadel, built in the late 1600s as part of a defensive line across the Gironde. The citadel, perfectly preserved, is high above Blaye's harbour, with a superb view of the river. Blaye itself is a pleasant little provincial town with some 5,000 inhabitants, a long street full of shops and cafés, and a bustling market on Wednesdays and Saturdays. A car ferry which might have been designed expressly for wine lovers on holiday links Blaye with Lamarque and the Médoc.

The wine-growing district has an area five times that of Bourg. Its northern limit is almost parallel with Lesparre-Médoc, it extends eastwards to the *départementale* boundary with the Charente Maritime, and it is bisected by the A10, the Autoroute l'Aquitaine. Much of the district, however, is unsuitable for vines, and production of appellation contrôlée wine is roughly equal in Bourg and Blaye. Inland is mainly cooperative country. About 85 percent of the wines are red, usually rather more lightweight than those of Bourg: supple, fruity and intended for early drinking. The best, and most frequently encountered, carry the appellation Premières Côtes de Blaye. So, too, with white wines: the more interesting are nearly always Premières Côtes de Blaye; the more run-of-the-mill are Blaye, Blayais or Côtes de Blaye.

TRAVEL INFORMATION

Wine tourism in Bourg and Blaye is relatively undeveloped and it is not a very prosperous region, so the number of good hotels and restaurants is rather limited.

HOTELS

Hotel Bellevue, 33390 Blaye, tel. 57 42 00 36. Country-style hotel in the town of Blaye where you can also eat simple fare. Hotel Class B; restaurant Class C.
Hotel La Citadelle, 33390 Blaye, tel. 57 42 17 10. Modern hotel in Blaye's citadel, with a swimming pool and a panoramic view over the Gironde. Also a restaurant. Class B.
Château La Grange de Luppé, 33390 Blaye, tel. 57 42 80 20. A château in its own park, just over a kilometre north of Blaye along the D255. (Check first: sale of the château in 1987 may mean an uncertain future as a hotel.) Class B.

RESTAURANTS

Le Caneton d'Argent, 33390 Blaye, tel. 57 42 81 00. Small, pleasant eating place with good, fairly contemporary cuisine. Specializes in fish and shellfish. Class C.
Le Rod du Roy, 33710 Bourg, tel. 57 68 30 93. Halfway between the upper and lower parts of Bourg, beneath the Porte de la Mer; do not expect gastronomic masterpieces. Class C.
Le Coq Hardi, 10 Rue de l'Official, 33240 St-André-de-Cubzac, tel. 57 43 02 60. Homely, friendly restaurant. Grilled and regional dishes. Also a hotel. Class C.

PLACES OF INTEREST

CUBZAGEAIS

St-André-de-Cubzac (Where the D669 meets the routes from Bordeaux.) Has a fortified church with a Romanesque apse, and a couple of kilometres north of St-André-de-Cubzac is Château du Bouilh, one of the landmarks of the district and a historic monument. The château was never completed: building began in 1787 under the direction of Victor Louis (who designed the Grand Théâtre in Bordeaux) but was stopped at the outbreak of the French Revolution. The château can be visited, mainly at weekends. Wine is still made there and there are cellars underneath the château.

BOURG

Bayon Has a 12th-century Romanesque church.
Bourg-sur-Gironde From the shaded terrace by the town hall there is a splendid view over the Gironde and the Bec d'Ambès. The Château de la Citadelle has a museum and there is a maze of underground passages.
La Libarde Just north of Bourg; an 11th-century Romanesque crypt.
Magrigne Near Tauriac; has a Templar chapel.
Marmisson Along the D669E towards Blaye; a prehistoric site.
Prignac-et-Marcamps Close to the D669 en route from St-André-de-Cubzac to Bourg are the Pair-non-Pair caves, discovered in 1881, with some 60 prehistoric wall paintings of animals. People were living around Bourg in prehistoric times and the paintings show that they hunted bison, mammoths and wild horses.
Tauriac Splendid, weathered Romanesque church, probably the most beautiful in the district.
Teuillac 9th-century sarcophagi in the church.

BLAYE

Blaye The great citadel of Blaye, almost a kilometre long, was built between 1685 and 1689 on the ruins of the St-Romain church, where Charlemagne is said to have buried his nephew Roland in 778. Within the citadel there is virtually a small village with streets and gardens, the remains of the triangular Château des Rudel and a 17th-century monastery. There is also a hotel (the Hotel La Citadelle, see Hotels), a camping site, a museum of local art and history, and the Tour de l'Aiguillette, a pleasant lookout post.

St-Ciers-
sur-Gironde
St-Androny
Eyrans
Etauliers
Château
le Ménaudat
Château
Latour-Gayet
Château
les Chaumes
Fours
D937
D252
Château
les Alberts
Château
la Salle
St-Seurin
-de-Cursac
Mazion
St-Genès-
de-Blaye
Château
Perenne
Château
Belair
Château
Segonzac
Château
Labrousse
Château
la Garde
les Davids
St-Paul
Château la Carelle
St-Martin-Lacaussade
Château
le Grand
Mazerolle
Château
Charron
Château
le Bédou
Château
les Petits Arnauds
Cars
Château les
Cônes-Sebizeaux
Château
Barbé
Château
l'Escadre
Blaye
Château
Pardaillan
Château
L'oumède
Château Pinet
Lamarque
Château
Gontier
Château
Graulet
Château
St-Germain
Berson
Château
Bellevue
Château de
Beaumont
Château
la Tuilerie
Château
Peyredoulle
Cru
Rousset
Plassac
Château
Gazin
Château
Monconseil
les Arnauds
Château
le Guiraud
Château
Launay
les Grd Bertins
Château
Rousselle
Château
Mendoce
Château
les Heaumes
St-Ciers-
de-Canesse
St-Trojan
Château
Peychaud
Teuillac
Château
les Richards
Château
de Barbe
Château
Coubet
Villeneuve
Château
Bidou
Château
la Graulet
Mombrier
Château
Rivereau
les Androns
Château
Nodoz
Château la Tuilière
de Thau
Samonac
Château
Labrède
Château
Fougas
Château Macau
Château
les Eyquems
Gauriac
Château
Berthou
Château
Rousset
Château
Lamothe
Château
Hourtou
Comps
Château
Blissa
Château
Bel Air
Château
Civrac
Château
Beaulieu
Lansac
Château
Guionne
Château
de la Croix-
Millorit
Château
Falfas
Château
Nodot
Château
de la Grave
Tauriac
Bayon
St-Seurin-de-Bourg
Château
Soucarde
Château
Laurensanne
Château Guerit
Château
Brûle-Secaille
Château
Labarde
Marcamps
Château
Eyquem
Château
Tayac
Château
Caruel
Château
Lalibarde
Château du
Bousquet
Château le
Caillou
la Clotte Blanche
Château
le Moulin Rompu
Bourg
Château
Gros-Moulin
Château
Courpon
Château
Croûte-Charlus
Château
Grand Jour
Château
Christoly
Château
Mille Secousses
Prignac-et-Marcamps
St-André-
de-Cubzac

LA GIRONDE

DORDOGNE

1:88,000

Km. 0   1   2   3   4   5 Km.

Miles 0   1   2   3 Miles

TOURING MAP PAGES
60   61
LIMOGES
ANGOULÊME
Isle
Dordogne
BORDEAUX
Garonne

N

Arrondissement boundary
Canton boundary
Commune (parish) boundary
Vineyards
Woods
Contour interval 10 metres
Route Nationale
Wine Route

Montuzet For a panoramic view over the surrounding countryside, go up the hill from Plassac to Château Bellevue. From here it is a short walk to the Butte de Montuzet and its statue.

Plassac During the summer months, the little museum displays finds from the Gallo-Roman period.

NORTHERN BLAYE

St-Ciers-sur-Gironde On flat land near the Gironde not suitable for vines there is an enormous nuclear reactor that supplies about 8% of France's electricity. Visitors are welcome. In St-Ciers itself there is the greatest possible contrast: a museum of prehistory, open in July and August.

Marcillac Just east of St-Aubin, off the A10 Autoroute l'Aquitaine: a 12th-century church, and a distillery producing *fine bordeaux* (this is, after all, on the fringe of cognac country).

WINE ACTIVITIES

The Connétable de Guyenne wine fraternity, established in 1952, is active in Bourg and Blaye as well as in Entre-Deux-Mers and the Premières Côtes de Bordeaux.

WINE INFORMATION

There are Maisons du Vin in both Bourg (Place de l'Eperon) and in Blaye (on the harbour front, next to the departure point of the Blaye-Lamarque car ferry). In Bourg, ask for the large colourful map on which all the district's châteaux are marked.

THE CHATEAUX

CUBZAGEAIS
Appellations Bordeaux and Bordeaux Supérieur

CUBZAC-LES-PONTS,
postcode 33240

Château de Terrefort-Quancard *
This large property of the Quancard family (wine producers and merchants) demonstrates that pleasant wines can be made in this corner of Bordeaux.

ST-ANDRE-DE-CUBZAC,
postcode 33240

Château du Bouilh
The oldest vineyard in the district (see Places of Interest, St-André-de-Cubzac).

BOURG
Appellations Côtes de Bourg and Bourg

BAYON, postcode 33710

Château Eyquem 91 E3
Beautifully situated by the river. (And a promising name.)
Château Falfas 91 D3
A splendid château in Louis XIII style and a pleasant wine.

BOURG-SUR-GIRONDE,
postcode 33710

Château de la Grave 91 E4
A charming little château making a charming, soft Côtes de Bourg.

Château Beaulieu

Château Tayac 91 E3
The vineyard of this fine château is on the river front and gets the maximum possible sun, and from the château there is a splendid view across the Gironde. The wine is rich in colour and strong in constitution, especially the *Cuvée de Prestige.*

Also in Bourg-sur-Gironde:
Châteaux Caruel*, Le Clos de

Notaire, Croûte Courpon, Croûte Mallard, Dumézil* and Gros Moulin*.

SAMONAC, postcode 33710

Château Beaulieu 91 D4
Idyllically situated in a vine-clad valley, but the quality of the wine fluctuates.

Also in Samonac: **Châteaux du Castenet*, Macay*, Rousset.**

TAURIAC, postcode 33710

Château Le Piat
The showpiece of the excellent cooperative at Tauriac.

Also in Tauriac: **Châteaux Brulesécaille*, Fongalan*, Guerry*** (one of the best wines of the district; a third of the vines are Malbec), and **Haut Macô.**

VILLENEUVE, postcode 33710

Château de Barbe 91 D2
An extensive estate with a spacious château, producing a supple wine.

Château de Mendoce 91 C2
A good Côtes de Bourg from a fine old château that dates largely from the 15th and 16th centuries.

Other châteaux in the Bourg region include **Cantenac Sudre*** at Lansac, **Rousselle** at St-Ciers-de-Canesse and **Peychaud** at Teuillac, all postcode 33710. Ask for details about visiting the châteaux at the Maison du Vin (see Wine Information in the Travel section).

BLAYE
Appellations Premières Côtes de Blaye, Blaye and Côtes de Blaye

In Berson, postcode 33390, **Châteaux Bourdieu** (a red wine to be recommended, particularly the *Cuvée Vignoble de Florimont*) and **Perdoulle***; in Cars, postcode 33390, **Châteaux Crusquet Sabourin*, Gardut Haut-Cluzeau** (fragrant, refreshing white wine from 100% Sauvignon), **Les Rochers** (a vital red Premières Côtes de Blaye) and **Magdeleine-Bouhou***; in Marcillac, postcode 33860, **Château Lardière,** in the far north of Blaye (see Places of Interest), makes a fresh white Côtes de Blaye and also red and white sparkling wine; in St-Androny, postcode 33390, **Château La Tour Gayet;** in St-Genès, postcode 33860, **Châteaux Perenne** and **Ségonzac;** and in St-Martin-de-la-Caussade, postcode 33390, **Château Charron*** flawless red and white wines, among the best that Blaye can offer.

GRAVES

The first Bordeaux vineyards were in the immediate vicinity of the city. Originally their market was mainly local, but this changed after 1152 when Aquitaine came under English rule. Immediately a large new market for Bordeaux wines opened up: England. This proved a powerful stimulus to growing and selling the district's wines and from the twelfth century onwards the vineyards expanded steadily outwards from Bordeaux, the port from where the wines were shipped. Even the archbishop of Bordeaux (later Pope Clement V) established a vineyard of his own in 1300 at Pessac, on the outskirts of Bordeaux: the present Château Pape Clément. In the fourteenth century in particular, wine growing prospered and more and more forest was cut down to make way for vines. Gradually it became apparent that the best wines came from the *terres graveleuses*, the gravelly soils; these were called *vins des graves*, and later simply Graves.

It was these Graves wines that first gave the Bordeaux region its reputation for quality. Even when the Médoc emerged as a wine district, early in the eighteenth century, there was a period when wines from the Médoc or low-lying areas could not be sold or recommended as Graves in the city of Bordeaux. The first Bordeaux wine to be referred to by the name of its estate was from Graves: in 1663 Samuel Pepys, that great *bon vivant*, noted that in the Royal Oak Tavern in London he had drunk "a sort of French wine called Ho Bryan that hath a good and most particular taste that I ever met with" – this pioneer tasting note referred, of course, to Haut-Brion.

Graves remained highly regarded until the middle of the nineteenth century, when it was overshadowed by the Médoc. Many of its vineyards, too, were lost as the city of Bordeaux continued to expand. In 1850 Mérignac had 22 wine estates, compared with just one today. In the same period the number of estates in Pessac fell from 12 to four, and in Talence from 19 to three. Of some 10,000 hectares (24,700 acres) of vineyard in Graves at the end of the nineteenth century, only about 3,200 hectares (7,900 acres) remain. Around 5,000 hectares (12,400 acres) have vanished since 1900: equal to the total area of St-Emilion.

The present Graves area still takes in the city of Bordeaux: Haut Brion and its neighbours La Mission and Les Carmes are actually in the suburbs. Just north of the city the Jalle de Blanquefort marks the boundary between Graves and the Médoc, and southwards the district follows the course of the Garonne to beyond Langon. The whole region is about 55 kilometres (34 miles) in length and nearly 20 kilometres (12 miles) across at its widest point. To the west the pine forests of the Landes form a natural boundary.

Directly south of Bordeaux there are decidedly gravelly soils. These extend over gentle undulations and are well drained by five small streams. The largest and best-known estates are here, including all the *crus classés*. In September 1987, the wines from the northern Graves – almost 900 hectares (2,200 acres) – received their own appellation, Pessac-Léognan. Farther south, beyond Martillac and the little stream Le Soucat, the soil has more sand and clay, and drainage is often more difficult. Vines are less prevalent here: in contrast to the north, there is mixed cultivation with a good deal of forestry. Since the 1960s and '70s, however, the southern Graves has increasingly been producing splendid wines of high quality, such as the red and white Graves from Château de Roquetaillade La Grange in Mazères.

Graves used to produce mainly semi-sweet white wines with the Graves Supérieures appellation. Today about half the wines are red, and the white is usually dry. The grapes for red Graves are the same as those of the Médoc (Cabernet Sauvignon, Cabernet Franc and Merlot) but the wines are quite distinctive: somewhat earthier than the Médocs, a little more supple and with an aroma that can be spicy, smoky or slightly resinous. The English wine writer Maurice Healey once compared the difference between a Médoc and a red Graves to that between a glossy and a mat print of the same photograph. The mat version is just as good as the glossy but less brilliant, its contrasts less marked.

Dry white Graves comes in a variety of styles, from crisp and modern to more traditionally produced and verging on mildness. Semi-sweet Graves Supérieures still exist but their popularity is dwindling. The sweetest white wines come from Cérons, a commune that borders on Barsac and Sauternes (shown on the map on page 94). They are sold under the Cérons appellation, together with those from Illats and Podensac. These wines can approach the richness of a Sauternes but are usually more mellow than opulently sweet. Since 1959 the Graves district has had its own officially approved classification that recognizes Crus Classés for red and white wines from 15 estates.

TRAVEL INFORMATION

The Graves district is easy to visit, using Bordeaux as the departure point – the whole region is shown on the map on page 94. A signposted wine route, the Circuit Touristique des Graves, takes one past many of the world-famous châteaux. Further addresses of hotels and restaurants are in the Sauternes Travel Information.

HOTELS

La Réserve, Avenue Bougailh, 33600 l'Alouette, tel. 56 07 13 28. A luxurious oasis, surrounded by a park, not far from the No. 13 turnoff on the Bordeaux ring road. Also a first-class restaurant using well-prepared local ingredients. Class A.
Relais de Fompeyre, Route de Mont-de-Marsan, 33430 Bazas, tel. 56 25 04 60. A spacious hotel with comfortable modern rooms, a swimming pool and restaurant. Class B.
Hostellerie St-Sauveur, 14 Cours du Général de Gaulle, 33430 Bazas, tel. 56 25 12 18. Somewhat limited facilities but has its own car park. Class C.
La Grappe d'Or 33720 Cérons, tel. 56 27 21 61. Has charm without pretensions; on the D117E. Class B.
Grillobois, 33720 Cérons, tel. 56 27 11 50. On the busy N113.

Roomy, with a simple restaurant and a small wine museum. Class B.
Hotel Le Midi-Modern, Place Général de Gaulle, 33210 Langon, tel. 56 63 06 65. Belongs to a brasserie, which indicates the level. Class C.
Château de Moderis, 33720 Virelade, tel. 56 27 17 78. Reasonably comfortable, congenial provincial hotel. The restaurant is good value. Class C.

RESTAURANTS

Grill Mirambet/Hotel de France, Cours du Général de Gaulle, 33430 Bazas, tel. 56 25 02 37. Busy restaurant with a large open fireplace; grilled meat and fish are a feature. Also a hotel. Class B.
Pascal Le Bistrot, Chemin Salvador Allende, 33610 Canéjan, tel. 56 89 18 57. Rustic style; traditional cuisine. Canéjan is about halfway between Pessac and Léognan, within easy reach of Bordeaux. Class C.
Claude Darrose, 95 Cours Général Leclerc, 33210 Langon, tel. 56 63 00 48. The best restaurant of Graves/Sauternes. Stylish decor and such regional specialities as *salade landaise, foie gras de canard, lamproie au blanc de poireaux* and *agneau de Médoc à l'estragon*, and an extensive wine list. The rooms are pleasant and comfortable. Class A.
La Grangousier (on the D10 to Auros), 33210 Langon, tel. 56 63 30 59. An old manor house with a garden and a terrace. Regional cuisine. Class B.
Hostellerie Lou Pistou, 33650 Martillac, tel. 56 23 71 02. Good value. Class C.
Maeva, 33210 Toulenne (near Langon), tel. 56 62 38 77. A good wine list and regional dishes, including duck. Class B.

PLACES OF INTEREST

Bazas A good base from which to explore the Graves district, about 15 kilometres (9–10 miles) south of Langon down the D932 (see also Hotels and Restaurants). Bazas is a striking little town with a splendid

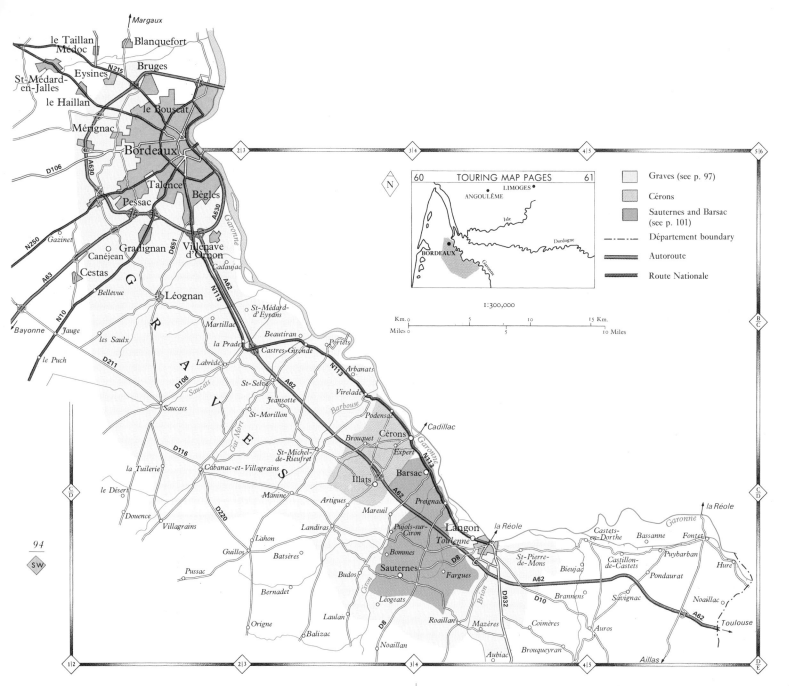

place dominated by the Gothic cathedral of Saint-Jean-Baptiste. Near by is the Jardin de l'Ancien Evêché on the former town walls. At the end of June and the beginning of July a *son et lumière*, with a cast of 400, brings the history of Bazas to life. Bazas also has a big market for calves (usually held on the first Wednesday in the month) and the name of the town has been given to a breed of cattle, the Bazadaise.

Budos This village a few kilometres west of Sauternes (take the D125) has the remains of a 14th-century feudal castle.

Cadaujac Romanesque church. See also Château Bouscaut in Producers.

Cérons and **Illats** Both have interesting churches.

Labrède Château de Labrède, a romantic moated castle, was the birthplace (in 1689) and home of the politician, writer and philosopher Charles de Segondat, Baron de La Brède et de Montesquieu. His library, containing some 7,000 works,

is still intact. In Montesquieu's time the château was exporting wine to England; the estate still produces a modest amount of white wine.

Léognan Has a small, restored Romanesque church.

Mazères One of the most southerly communes of Graves. Its pride is

▷ Right: the splendidly romantic Château de Labrède, complete with moat and 13th-century keep, birthplace and home of the writer and statesman Montesquieu.

▽ Below: music and dancing at the summer wine festival in St-Selve.

Château de Roquetaillade, a massive 14th-century fortress with six enormous round towers, a square keep and impressive vaulted chambers. It was built by a nephew of Pope Clement V and is well worth a visit (and for the wine). Not far away are the ruins of a more primitive 12th- and 13th-century castle, and the beautiful St-Michel chapel with 14th-century paintings.

Podensac The Parc de Chavat has a display of curious statues sculpted between the two World Wars. The firm of Lillet in Podensac makes wine-based apéritifs.

St-Morillon A small village that still looks almost medieval.

Uzeste Has a splendid church built in 1312 to the orders of Pope Clement V (and rebuilt in the 16th century). The papal tomb is here.

Villandraut Small town, ringed by woods, where Bertrand (Pope Clement V) was born. He built the local castle; of what remains, four large towers are particularly striking. Villandraut also has a small regional museum.

Villenave-d'Ornon Has a beautiful church, its nave flanked by two high aisles.

The whole Graves region, enclosing the communes of Sauternes. A detailed map of the Haut Graves — Pessac, Talence, Gradignan, Villenave, Léognan, Cadaujac and Martillac — with their châteaux is on page 97, and of Sauternes, Barsac and Cérons on page 101.

WINE ACTIVITIES

The Commanderie du Bontemps du Médoc et des Graves promotes the wines of both districts. Its headquarters are in Pauillac. Langon holds a *Foire aux Vins* (wine fair) each year at the beginning of September, featuring wines from the Graves and Sauternes districts.

WINE INFORMATION

The Maison des Vins de Graves is at Podensac, just north of Cérons on the N113. As well as providing information about visiting Graves, the Maison has a cellar where wines from the whole district are on sale.

Many of the châteaux welcome visitors, including the great names such as Haut-Brion, Haut-Bailly and de Chevalier. A telephone call or letter beforehand is useful to find out if an advance appointment is necessary and the hours when the château is open to visitors. The most convenient times are usually from 10 to 12 and 3 to 5 on week days, and some châteaux also welcome visitors on Saturday afternoons. Bear in mind that the châteaux are always particularly busy at harvest time, and that many properties close completely in August.

The Maison du Vin at 1 Cours du 30-Juillet in Bordeaux will also be helpful providing information about the individual châteaux. The Union des Crus Classés de Graves has its headquarters at the same address.

THE CRUS CLASSES

Château Bouscaut 97 D5
Cru Classé (red and white)
Splendid 18th-century estate, totally restored in the 1970s with American dollars and since 1980 the property of Lucien Lurton (of Brane-Cantenac in Margaux, Climens in Barsac, etc). Bouscaut white is a fresh, fragrant, clean-tasting Graves; the red is firm, with more fruit and suppleness than formerly.

Château Carbonnieux 97 E4
Cru Classé (red and white)
A famous old estate, taken over by Benedictine monks in 1741 – they managed to export their white wine to the (Muslim) Turkish court as "mineral water" – now run by the Perrin family. Carbonnieux's best wine is still its white Graves: a fresh, fragrant, attractive wine with definite distinction. The red does not quite reach the same standard.

Domaine de Chevalier * 97 F2
Cru Classé (red and white)
This remarkably situated vineyard – in a clearing deep in the woods behind the village of Léognan – produces magnificent white wine that in complexity, length and stamina surpasses almost all the other dry white Bordeaux. It is made with meticulous attention to the smallest details. The red wine is also excellent, tending towards a great Médoc in personality: only after 10 to 20 years does it start to reveal itself. The house itself is small and modest and the word "château" is not used.

Château Couhins 97 D4
Cru Classé (white)
The larger part of the vineyard is the property of INRA, a French agricultural research institute. The white is full and spicy; the red powerful. Various new grape varieties are being experimented with. (See also Château Couhins-Lurton.)

The vines need regular spraying to protect them against fungal diseases, as here at Domaine de la Solitude.

Château Couhins-Lurton *
Cru Classé (white)
Fresh, fruity white from a small plot in the Château Couhins vineyard, bought from the INRA in 1979 by André Lurton. The vineyard (100% Sauvignon) is being extended, and red wines are also planned which will be from new plantings of Cabernet Sauvignon and Merlot.

Château de Fieuzal 97 F3
Cru Classé (red)
The red wine is firm, utterly reliable and very typical of the district – and its quality seems to be improving. Unfortunately not much white wine is produced – it possesses the quality of a Cru Classé. The storage cellars are in Léognan itself, away from the little château.

Château Haut-Bailly * 97 E4
Cru Classé (red)
An unspectacular-looking château making an almost satiny-soft, stylish and very satisfying red Graves. Since 1979, after a short weaker period, the wine has again remained consistent in quality. About a quarter of the vines are more than 40 years old.

Château Haut-Brion 97 A2
1er Grand Cru Classé (1855) and Cru Classé (red)
Haut-Brion was the only Graves estate to be included in the classification of 1855 – and in its top category. The substantial, 16th-century castle used to be beyond the Bordeaux town boundary, but is now surrounded by the suburb of Pessac. The vineyard is in two parts and slopes slightly, on a deep layer of gravel. The red wine from this excellently managed estate is distinguished by a superb balance

between fruity and earthy flavours, a noble, almost mild velvetiness, gentle strength and long aftertaste. The white wine, made only in very small quantities, is also outstanding. Stainless-steel fermentation tanks of the estate's own design were installed as early as 1961. Haut-Brion was bought in 1935 by the American banker Clarence Dillon; the present president is Dillon's granddaughter Joan, the Duchesse de Mouchy.

Château Laville Haut Brion * 97 A3
Cru Classé (white)
Together with that produced by the Domaine de Chevalier, this is the best dry white wine of Bordeaux. The aroma of the Sauvignon (40% of the vines) is still strongly present in this Graves for four to five years. After this, however, the Sémillon (the other 60%) breaks through, giving rise to a concentrated, luxurious, wonderfully nuanced flavour. Since 1983 the modest estate has had the same owner as Haut-Brion.

Château Malartic-Lagravière 97 F3
Cru Classé (red and white)
Modern methods are used to make a traditional red wine with a distinct personality. It usually needs laying down for decades. The white (from 100% Sauvignon grapes) is delightful when young and also after maturing.

Château La Mission Haut Brion * 97 A3
Cru Classé (red)
For years this near neighbour of Haut-Brion was its great rival, but today it is in the hands of the same owner, Domaine Clarence Dillon. La Mission is more sinewy and reserved, darker and earthier than Haut-Brion, and often just as fine. It can mature for decades, its original reserve giving way to warm, deep tones, mysterious and complex.

Château Olivier 97 D3
Cru Classé (red and white)
The château itself is a splendidly medieval moated fortress. The gravelly vineyard produces a fresh, clean white wine and a red that is a little lacking in depth.

Château Pape-Clément * 97 A1
Cru Classé (red)
The wine estate established in 1300 by Archbishop Bertrand de Goth of Bordeaux, later to become Pope Clement V (the label still carries the papal insignia). Today it is owned by Montagne & Cie. The wine is a broad, generous, almost creamy-tasting Graves with a strong constitution, due in part to the traces

of iron in the soil. A white version is less impressive.

Château Smith-Haut-Lafitte 97 E4
Cru Classé (red)
Despite the status of the red wine, the white here is better, particularly since it has been fermented in new casks.

Château La Tour Haut Brion 97 A3
Cru Classé (red)
For a long time the name of this château was used for La Mission Haut Brion's second wine. Today, however, this strong, tannic Graves is once again solely the product of its own vineyard.

Château La Tour Martillac 97 F5
Cru Classé (red and white)
A modest little château with an old tower, the remnant of a 12th-century fort, in the inner courtyard. The red wine is firm, spicy and somewhat austere. The white is a classic dry Graves, improved by bottle-ageing.

ALSO IN GRAVES

ILLATS, postcode 33720
Châteaux d'Archambeau*, d'Ardennes and La Tuilerie*

LANDIRAS, postcode 33720
Château d'Arricaud*

LANGON, postcode 33210
Domaine de Gaillat*

LEOGNAN, postcode 33850
Château Brown 97 D3
Soft, agreeable red Graves.

Château de France 97 F3
Deep, robust red wine. White-wine production is relatively recent.

Château Haut-Bergey 97 E3
Elegant red wine from a beautiful château.

Château Larrivet-Haut-Brion 97 E3
Red and white wines of the second rank, in great demand.

Château La Louvière * 97 E4
It is not only the château that has charm (it was designed by Victor Louis and could be a smaller version of Château Margaux): so do the wines. Both red and white can mature outstandingly well.

MARTILLAC, postcode 33650
Château de Rochemorin * 97 F4
Exquisite red wine with body, wood and tannin. The white is 100% Sauvignon.

Domaine de la Solitude 97 F4
The property of a religious community. The red wine has calibre; the white is softly fresh.

MAZERES, postcode 33210
Château de Roquetaillade La Grange *
Generous, meaty red Graves. The white tends towards gentleness. (See also Places of Interest.)

PESSAC, postcode 33600
Château Les Carmes Haut-Brion
Quite elegant, respectable red-wine neighbour of Haut-Brion.

PODENSAC, postcode 33720
Château de Chantegrive *
A delicious red wine, aged in oak, and a very pure dry white.

PORTETS, postcode 33640

Château Constantin *
An exemplary white Graves. The red also merits attention.

Domaine La Grave *
A rising star with a robust red wine, rich in tannin, and a fresh and charming white. The owner is Danish.

Château Rahoul *
Outstanding, complex white wine and a subtly nuanced red. The status of Cru Classé would not come amiss to either.

PREIGNAC, postcode 33210
Château de Cardaillan
Red wine with tannin and *terroir*, made at Château de Malle (see Sauternes – the vineyard is partly in Graves and partly in Sauternes).

ST-MEDARD-D'EYRANS, postcode 33650
Château de Cruzeau
Estate on deep gravel, replanted when bought by André Lurton in the 1970s. Worth following for both its red and its white.

VILLENAVE D'ORNON, postcode 33140
Château Pontac-Monplaisir *
Mellow, nuanced white wine that can be among the best of all the Graves.

Château La Mission Haut Brion

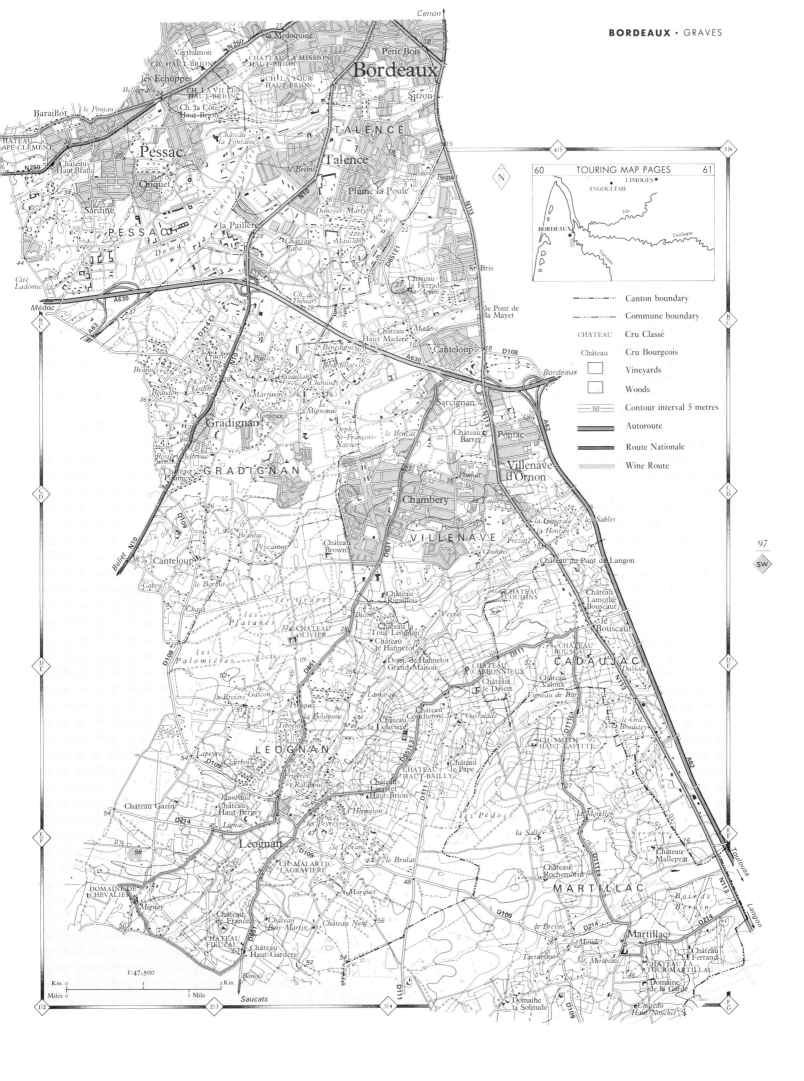

Cenon

la Medoquine

Verthamon
CH. HAUT-BRION
CHÂTEAU LA MISSION
HAUT-BRION
les Echoppes
Bellevre
CH. LA VILLE
HAUT-BRION
CH. LA TOUR
HAUT-BRION
Petit Bois

Bordeaux

Baraillot
le Poujau
Ch. la Côte
Haut-Brion
Suzon

CHÂTEAU
APÉ CLÉMENT
Château
la Fontaine
TALENCE

Pessac
Château
Haut Brana
N250

Chiquet
le Bréuil
Talence
le Béguet

Plume la Poule

Sardine
Dunoyer-Marly
Pacqrit

PESSAC
la Paillère
Maucamp
St Bris

Château
Raba
D651E1

Cité
Ladonne
Providence
Château
la Ferrade
St Agron

Médoc
Ch. de
Thouars

A630
Château
Haut Madère
Madère
Canteloup
D108

A630
Benedigue
Bourdillat

Cité Pradut
le Pailley
Gazaillan
Chouain

Branu
Gazaillan
Martinon
la
Mignoute
Sarcignan
Bordeaux

Decaudon
Cité
Jardin
Monjous
Orph.
St-François-
Xavier
le Brieul
Château
Barret
Pontac

Gradignan
Rosiers Bellevue
Plunjat

Château
Poumey
GRADIGNAN
**Villenave
d'Ornon**

Branlac
Peycamut
la Générale
la Hontan
les Sables

Canteloup
Château
Brown
Chambery
VILLENAVE
la Taille

Catoy
le Barput
Coulins
Château du Pont de Langon

Chaut
les Graves
Château
Rigaillou
CHÂTEAU
COUHINS

les
Platanes
Bicon
Veyrus
Château
Lamothe
Bouscaut

les
Palomières
CHÂTEAU
OLIVIER
Château la
Tour Léognan
le Bouscaut

la Rivière
le Gascon
Château
le Hannetot
Dom. de Hannetot
Grand-Maison
CHÂTEAU
CARBONNIEUX
D111
CHÂTEAU
BOUSCAUT
CADAUJAC

Pireques
la Bouhume
Château
le Désert
Dussole

Tiboeuf
Lamarque
Château
Valoux
Vigneau de Bas

Lapeyre
Château
Coucheroy
l'Oustalade
le Grd.
Broustey

LÉOGNAN
Clairbois
les Sables
Château
la Louvière
CH. SMITH
HAUT-LAFITTE

Frières
Rataboul
CHÂTEAU
HAUT-BAILLY
Château
le Pape

Rambaud
Château
Haut-Bergey
Château
Larrivet
Haut-Brion
Hermiton
les Pédocs

Château Gazin
Lignac
les Peyreyres
la Morelle

Léognan
D109
le Libran
la Salle

CH. MALARTIC-
LAGRAVIÈRE
le Brulat
Château
Malleprat

DOMAINE DE
CHEVALIER
Marquet
Château
Rochemorin
MARTILLAC

Mignoy
Bois de
Bernin

Château
de France
Château
Bois-Martin
Château Neuf
le Breyra

CHÂTEAU
FIEUZAL
Château
Haut-Gardère
Mondet
Tartaussat
Mirebeau
Martillac
Château
Ferrand

Bonus
Saucats
Domaine
la Solitude
CHÂTEAU LA
TOUR MARTILLAC
Domaine
de la Garde
Château
Haut-Nouchet

TOURING MAP PAGES
60   61
LIMOGES
ANGOULÊME
BORDEAUX
Isle
Dordogne
Garonne
N

Canton boundary
Commune boundary
CHÂTEAU   Cru Classé
Château   Cru Bourgeois
Vineyards
Woods
50   Contour interval 5 metres
Autoroute
Route Nationale
Wine Route

1:47,500

Km.
Miles   1 Mile

97
SW

SAUTERNES

The Sauternes district is a small enclave in Graves, about 40 kilometres (25 miles) southeast of Bordeaux (the map on page 94 makes its situation clear). The Autoroute des Deux Mers, the A62, crosses it and also partially delimits it, and so does the little river Ciron that flows into the Garonne here.

Sauternes has been a white-wine area for hundreds of years. In the sixteenth and seventeenth centuries the wines were sweet, heavy Muscats to compete with the then-fashionable Muscadels from Spain, but gradually the Muscat grapes were replaced by local varieties better suited to the climate and soil, and the wines changed to a more individual style. The growers noticed that picking the grapes late produced a richer, sweeter wine, but the practice was too costly to be applied on a large scale and most Sauternes were drier than they are today. Nevertheless, when Thomas Jefferson, American ambassador and later president, visited Yquem in 1787 he described Sauternes as one of the best white wines of France (after champagne and Hermitage Blanc), ordered wine from Yquem and introduced it to his friend George Washington.

The first half of the nineteenth century saw an increasing number of strong, sweet Sauternes. They did not, however, bring in much money. This changed with the 1847 vintage at Yquem. By chance the grapes were picked exceptionally late and were affected far more than usual by *pourriture noble* ("noble rot"), producing wine so different from the customary style that the château decided not to put it on sale. Twelve years later the Russian Archduke Constantine was at Yquem, tasted the '47 and

was so delighted that he offered a small fortune for it: 20,000 gold francs for one *tonneau* (the equivalent of 100 cases). The Russian court subsequently made this style of Sauternes so popular that not only Yquem but other estates began to make it. A statue of Constantine would not be out of place in Sauternes.

The secret of Sauternes lies not so much in the grape varieties (mainly Sémillon, supplemented by Sauvignon and sometimes a little Muscadelle) or in the soil (gravel in many places, often mixed with clay) but in the microclimate. In autumn, cold water from the river Ciron flowing into the warmer water of the Garonne brings about a morning mist that wreathes the vineyards until the sun breaks through in the early afternoon. The alternation between damp and warmth produces ideal conditions for *Botrytis cinerea*, the beneficent bacteria that cause *pourriture noble* in the grapes. As the grapes rot and shrivel on the vine much of their moisture is lost, leaving the remaining juice concentrated, intensely sweet and rich in glycerine. A certain amount of acid is also lost, and the natural scent of the grapes is changed into the *rôti* aroma so characteristic of genuine Sauternes – somewhat reminiscent of cooked plums.

"Noble rot" can occur only if the grapes are at optimum ripeness. This is why the harvest is much later in Sauternes than in the rest of Bordeaux – with all the risks involved. The district has a milder, somewhat drier climate than the surrounding areas, but autumn rains can still spoil an entire vintage. Nor are all the grapes affected by noble rot, or not at the same time. Except in exceptional years, the pickers must work through the

TRAVEL INFORMATION

In the local restaurants you can discover how excellent Sauternes is as an apéritif and during the meal itself, as well as being a superb dessert wine. More hotels and restaurants within easy reach of Sauternes are described in the chapter on Graves, page 93.

HOTELS

Château de Commarque, 33210 Sauternes, tel. 56 63 65 94. Charming hotel with extensive grounds including a vineyard, swimming pool, restaurant (Basque cuisine, fish) and spacious rooms around a courtyard. British owners. Class B.

RESTAURANTS

Restaurant du Cap, 33210 Preignac, tel. 56 63 27 38. Mainly regional dishes and a delightful view over the Garonne. Class B.
Le Sauternais, 33210 Sauternes, tel. 56 63 67 13. In a former annex of Château Guiraud. Interesting wines can be ordered by the glass. Class B.
Les Vignes, 33210 Sauternes, tel. 56 63 60 06. Inn next to the church serving regional dishes such as *entrecôte bordelaise*, without trimmings but with love. Try the *tarte aux poires*, an excellent partner for a Sauternes. Wines are served by the glass as well as by the bottle and half-bottle. Class C.

WINE ROUTE

The *Circuit du Sauternais* is a signposted route that takes you, via

pleasant country roads, through the vineyards and past many of the châteaux (the route is shown on the map on page 101). Many of the châteaux or their cellars can be visited; ask at the Maison du Vin and look for *Vente directe* (direct sales) on roadside signs.

PLACES OF INTEREST

Barsac The oldest wine-village in the region. The Romans introduced wine-growing to Barsac and the remains of a Roman villa have been found alongside the church. The church itself has elements from the 16th, 17th and 18th centuries. Two marks high up on the wall near the main door indicate the height the water reached in the floods of 1770 and 1930 when the river Garonne burst its banks.
Sauternes A small but charming village; partly Romanesque church.

WINE ACTIVITIES

The Commanderie du Bontemps de Sauternes-Barsac organizes a Fête du Vin Nouveau each September/October in Barsac. The September wine fair at Langon in Graves also features wines from Sauternes.

WINE INFORMATION

The modest Maison du Vin is in the Place de la Mairie, Sauternes. In Barsac, near the church, the Office Viticole de Sauternes et Barsac is mainly a sales counter for the region's wines and also sells its own wines under the Terre Noble label.

vineyard several times, picking the grapes from their bunches one by one as the rotting process becomes complete. In addition, the yield is low – the grapes have, after all, lost moisture. The legal maximum is 25 hectolitres per hectare, but in practice this is rarely reached. At Yquem the average is only nine hectolitres, the equivalent of one glass of wine per vine.

A good Sauternes is a feast for all the senses: its glowing gold tinged with green, its luxurious perfume with overtones of ripe apricots, honey and nuts, its rich, intense, sweet yet vital taste. It goes excellently with fresh fruit (pears, strawberries, peaches) and desserts (but not chocolate). Lighter Sauternes can be enjoyed as an apéritif, with hors d'oeuvres (*foie gras* is a classic partner in Bordeaux) and with some main courses (such as *canard aux peches*).

The roughly 2,000 hectares (4,900 acres) of Sauternes is divided among five communes. The most northerly, and the flattest, is Barsac. The wines here are usually more elegant, less sumptuous, than elsewhere in the district, often with a sublime balance between sweetness and *fraîcheur*. They can be sold as Sauternes or as Barsac. Preignac, like Barsac, lies close to the Garonne but is not quite so flat. Farther inland the landscape becomes almost hilly: in Sauternes, Bommes and Fargues, many vineyard slopes rise to quite respectable heights.

Sauternes were the only white wines to be included in the 1855 classification, but to an even greater extent than in the Médoc the classification appears to have only a relative value: to make a very good Sauternes, human qualities are at least as important as those of nature.

SAUTERNES CHATEAUX

SAUTERNES, postcode 33210

Château Filhot 101 F3
2e Cru Classé
Large estate on the southern boundary of Sauternes with a particularly fine château and park. Not a sumptuous Sauternes but delicate and finely structured wine with plenty of fruit.

Château Guiraud 101 F3
1er Cru Classé
Under the direction of Canadian owner Hamilton Narby, this estate started a new lease of life in 1981. Improvements include selective picking and the use of at least 50% new casks. An attractive dry white Bordeaux, "G", is also made, and a red Bordeaux Supérieur. The château welcomes visitors and there is a restaurant (see Travel Information).

Château Raymond-Lafon *
101 E3
Although its "château" is no castle, this is usually a splendid wine with the quality of a Premier Cru. It is made with exceptional care and expertise by the owner, Pierre Meslier, who also manages Yquem.

Château d'Yquem 101 E3
1er Grand Cru Classé
Literally in a class of its own as the sole Premier Grand Cru in the 1855 classification. For more than two centuries Yquem, with its superb château, has belonged to the de Lur Saluces family. The present owner, Count Alexandre de Lur Saluces, like his predecessors, spares neither cost nor effort to make the wine as perfect as possible. Harvesting might begin in mid-October (Yquem is always one of the last harvests in the district) and continue until the end of November or into December. The wine is fermented in new oak casks and then matured for at least three years. In the same extravagantly expensive way the estate produces a dry white called "Y" (Ygrec).

BARSAC, postcode 33720
Appellation Barsac or Sauternes

Château Climens 101 C3
1er Cru Classé
The Climens vineyard lies on a low hill and produces one of the richest Barsacs. The wine often manages to be of surprising quality in poorer years such as 1964 and '72.

Château Coutet 101 B3
1er Cru Classé
One of the most influential estates of Barsac. In the very best years a small amount of wine is selected for the "Cuvée Madame", which approaches the class of Yquem. The present château is near a 13th-century tower, a reminder that the history of Coutet goes back to the Middle Ages.

Château Doisy-Daëne 101 B3
2e Cru Classé
Technically one of the most progressive estates of the district. The wine is made solely from Sémillon grapes and vinified and matured in stainless-steel tanks and oak casks. The trio of Doisy châteaux were originally one estate that was divided and sold in the 19th century.

Château Doisy-Dubroca 101 B3
2e Cru Classé
A tiny vineyard attached to Climens, where the wine is made.

Château Doisy-Védrines 101 C3
2e Cru Classé
The largest of the three Doisy estates, with the original 16th-century château and *chais*.

Château Gravas * 101 B3
One of the best of the Barsac *bourgeois*. The 16th-century château and its vineyards are in the heart of the Barsac appellation, between the Premiers Crus Climens and Coutet.

Château Nairac * 101 A4
2e Cru Classé
Bought in 1972 by American winemaker Tom Heeter and totally renovated. It produces a distinguished Sauternes that can usually be kept for a decade or more.

PREIGNAC, postcode 33210
Appellation Sauternes

Château Gilette * 101 C5
The wine here is aged for at least 20 years in underground tanks before being bottled. This unique method produces sumptuous, warm-gold wines of tremendous vitality. A younger version is sold as Château Les Justices.

Château de Malle 101 D5
2e Cru Classé
The showplace of Sauternes: Malle alone would justify a visit to the region. The château, flanked by

◀ A blaze of poppies among the vines in early June. In autumn, when the grapes are ripe, mists alternating with the warmth of the sun will induce the "noble rot" that in a good year results in the rich, sweet wines for which Sauternes is famous.

pepperpot towers, is the only historic monument in Sauternes; it dates from the 17th century and can be visited from Easter to mid-October. A splendid collection of furniture and *objets d'art* has been brought together in its rooms and the Italian-style garden is filled with statuary. The wine has almost the delicacy of a Barsac. The estate also makes a dry white wine (Chevalier de Malle) and a red Graves – the vineyard extends into Graves (see Château du Cardaillan, Graves).

Château St-Amand * 101 B4
The owner, a friendly and experienced local grower, aims to make a Sauternes of *cru* standard and succeeds. Part of the vintage is sold as Château de la Chartreuse.

Château Suduiraut * 101 D4
1er Cru Classé
A splendid estate with a 17th-century château and a park designed by Le Nôtre, the landscape architect who created the gardens of Versailles. Since the 1975 vintage the wine has been among the most opulent and impressive of the whole district.

BOMMES, postcode 33210
Appellation Sauternes

Château Clos Haut-Peyraguey
101 E3
1er Cru Classé
A small estate, separated from Lafaurie-Peyraguey when the original Peyraguey estate was split up in 1878. Produces a fairly light Sauternes.

Château Lafaurie-Peyraguey
101 E3
1er Cru Classé
One of the oldest Sauternes châteaux, part 13th-century fortress and almost as spectacular as Yquem. The wine has gained in richness and quality since the second half of the 1970s. The estate is a Cordier property.

Château Rabaud-Promis 101 E3
1er Cru Classé
The larger portion of what was originally one estate, Château Rabaud (the balance is Château Sigalas-Rabaud). The château was built by Victor Louis, architect of the Grand Théâtre in Bordeaux, but a fine view is its only claim to grandeur today. After a long period of neglect, the wine is seriously improving.

Château de Rayne-Vigneau
101 E3
1er Cru Classé
Large estate celebrated in the late 1800s and early 1900s for the semi-precious stones found among the gravel in the vineyard; some of them are displayed in the *chai*. The wine

has been through a very weak period but since 1982 has been up to standard again. A dry wine is called Rayne Sec.

Château Sigalas-Rabaud 101 E3
1er Cru Classé
The wine here is not aged in casks but spends two years in tanks. Once bottled, it demands patience: it is often ten years before it shows its true richness and finesse.

Château La Tour Blanche 101 E2
1er Cru Classé
The estate where the German wine grower Focke experimented with late harvesting from 1836. Today it is owned by the Ministry of Agriculture and is a school of viticulture. The

wine has lacked great class but has recently improved.

FARGUES, postcode 33210
Appellation Sauternes

Château de Fargues * 101 F5
Estate with romantic old castle ruins, owned by the de Lur Saluces of Yquem. A brilliant Sauternes, lighter than Yquem but certainly worth a place among the Crus Classés.

Château Rieussec * 101 E4
1er Cru Classé
Generally the wine that comes closest to Yquem – and the two estates are neighbours, superbly situated on the highest hills in the district. Rieussec is an impressive Sauternes, often reminiscent of ripe peaches or

apricots. A dry white Rieussec is called "R". In 1985 the French Rothschilds (of Lafite-Rothschild, etc.) acquired a majority of the shares. There is no actual "château" but a rambling collection of various buildings, with a prominent ivy-covered lookout tower.

Other châteaux include the 2e Crus Classés d'**Arche**, **Lamothe** and **Lamothe Guignard** (Sauternes); **Broustet**, **Caillou** and **Suau** (Barsac); and **Romer du Hayot** (Preignac). In Preignac you will also find **Château Bastor-Lamontagne**, which plans to establish an international school for *sommeliers* (wine waiters), and châteaux **Haut-Bergeron*** and **de Veyres***.

▽ Below: the peaceful landscape of Preignac, where woods and fields of maize mingle with the vines.
Bottom left: the golden glow of Sauternes in the cellars of Clos Haut-Peyraguey.
Bottom right: pigeon shooting is a favourite pastime in this part of France. Villagers train live decoys to attract wild birds (*palombes*) migrating between northern Europe, where they spend the summer, and Spain where they winter.

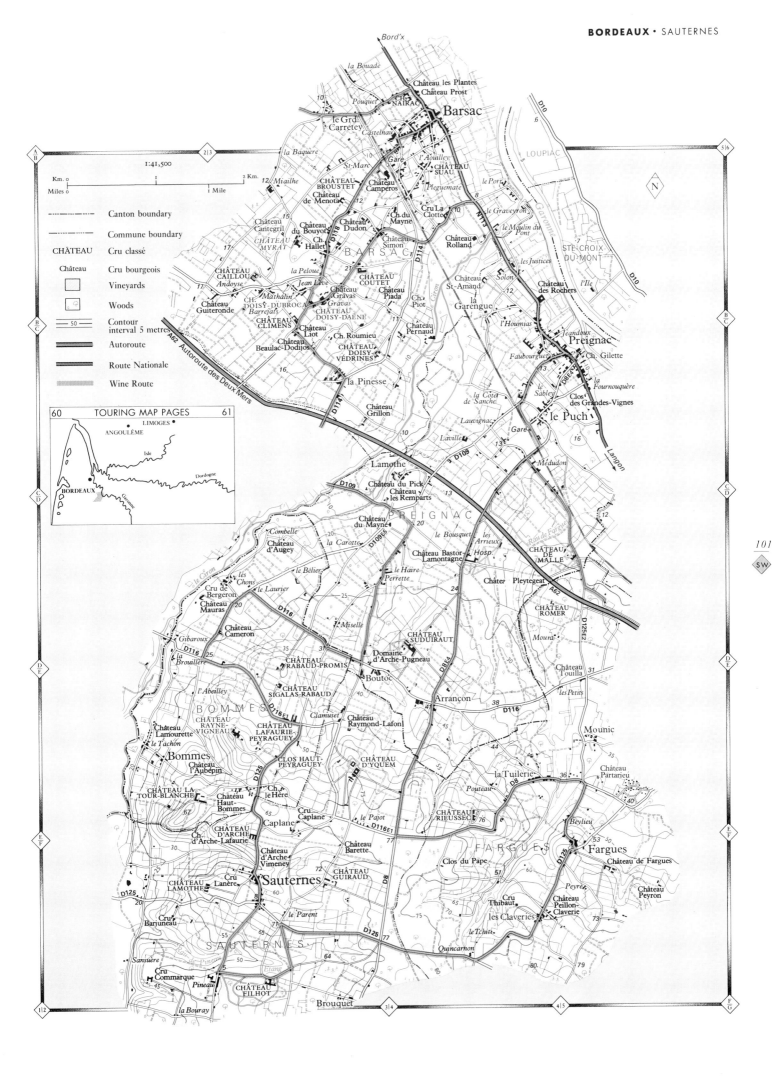

Bord'x

la Bouade

Château les Plantes
Château Prost

NAIRAC

Pouquet

10

le Grd
Carretey

Barsac

LOUPIAC

D 10

6

Castelnau

la Baquere

St-Marc

Gare

l'Aouilley

CHÂTEAU
SUAU

le Port

STE-CROIX-
DU-MONT

l'Ile

Miaille

CHÂTEAU
BROUSTET

Château
Camperos

Pleguemate

le Graveyron

le Moulin du
Pont

Château
de Menota

Ch. du
Mayne

Cru La
Clotte

les Justices

Château
des Rochers

Château
Cantegril

Château
du Bouyot

Château
Dudon

Château
Rolland

CHÂTEAU
MYRAT

Ch.
Hallet

BARSAC

Château
Simon

Solon

Jeandoux

Preignac

CHÂTEAU
CAILLOU

la Peloue

Château
St-Amand

Château
St-Amand

la
Garengue

l'Houmias

Ch. Gilette

Andoyse

Jean Lève

Château
Gravas

CHÂTEAU
COUTET

Château
Piada

Ch.
Piot

Faubourguet

Ch.
DOISY-DUBROCA

Mathalin

Gravas

l'Houmias

le
Sabley

la
Fournouquère

Château
Guiteronde

Barrejats

CHÂTEAU
DOISY-DAËNE

Château
Pernaud

Lauvignac

Clos
des Grandes-Vignes

CHÂTEAU
CLIMENS

Château
Liot

Ch. Roumieu

le Puch

Château
Beaulac-Dodijos

CHÂTEAU
DOISY-
VÉDRINES

Gare

16

la Pinesse

Château
Grillon

Laville

10

Lamothe

D 109

13

PREIGNAC

Médudon

Château du Pick
Château
les Remparts

12

D 109

Château
du Mayne

20

le Bousquet

les
Arrieux

Ruu de Fargue

CHÂTEAU
DE MALLE

Combelle

la Carotte

D 109

Château Bastor-
Lamontagne

Hosp.

Château
d'Augey

le Bélier

le Haire
Perrette

Château
Pleytegeat

les Chons

Cru de
Bergeron

le Laurier

25

24

CHÂTEAU
ROMER

Moura

Château
Mauras

Miselle

CHÂTEAU
SUDUIRAUT

Château
Cameron

Gibaroux

Domaine
d'Archie-Pugneau

Château
Touilla

31

D 116

la
Brouillère

CHÂTEAU
RABAUD-PROMIS

Boutoc

les Petits

l'Abeilley

Arrançon

38

CHÂTEAU
SIGALAS-RABAUD

Clamuset

Château
Raymond-Lafon

D 116

Mounic

BOMMES

CHÂTEAU
RAYNE-
VIGNEAU

CHÂTEAU
LAFAURIE-
PEYRAGUEY

Château
Partarieu

Château
Lamourette

le Tachon

CLOS HAUT-
PEYRAGUEY

CHÂTEAU
D'YQUEM

la Tuilerie

Bommes

Château
l'Aubépin

D 125

Pouteau

CHÂTEAU LA
TOUR-BLANCHE

Château
Haut-
Bommes

Ch.
le Hère

CHÂTEAU
RIEUSSEC

Béylieu

Cru
Caplane

le Pajot

Caplane

D 116 E1

CHÂTEAU
D'ARCHE

Château
Barette

FARGUES

Fargues

Ch.
d'Arche-Lafaurie

Château de Fargues

Château
d'Arche-
Vimeney

Clos du Pape

Peyre

CHÂTEAU
LAMOTHE

CHÂTEAU
GUIRAUD

Château
Peyron

Cru
Lanère

Sauternes

Cru
Thibaut

Château
Peillon-
Claverie

Cru
Barjuneau

le Parent

les Claveries

le Tchitt

SAUTERNES

Quincarnon

Sansuère

Etang

Cru
Commarque

Pineau

CHÂTEAU
FILHOT

Brouquet

la Bouray

BETWEEN THE RIVERS

Between the Dordogne, the Garonne and the département's eastern boundary stretches the biggest wine district of Bordeaux. This splendidly typical wedge of French countryside extends some 80 kilometres (50 miles) southeast of Bordeaux and is about 30 kilometres (19 miles) across at its broadest point. What is impressive is not just its size but its rich history, the splendour of its churches, monasteries, forts and castles, mementos of a turbulent past. (This was a frontier district in the wars between the French and the English, hence the large number of forts and fortified – *bastide* – towns.) Today it is a pastoral countryside of many small rivers, hills and valleys, with ever-changing distant views over woods, pastures and fields of maize, tobacco and other crops. There are also vineyards in plenty.

This "land of the two rivers" is made up of several districts, with Entre-Deux-Mers by far the most important in area and scale. For decades the wine was of little interest, semi-sweet and dull. Today the Entre-Deux-Mers name is used only for dry white wines whose quality has improved rapidly since the 1970s, due partly to better winemaking and considerable investment in modern equipment. Sixteen cooperatives dominate the scene for both white and red wines (with further cooperatives in the border districts). The large private estates should not, however, be underestimated: increasingly they are producing wines that are well worth exploring. Some estates, such as André Lurton's Château Bonnet in Grézillac, mature a proportion of their red wines in wood, and the whites are cold-fermented. Cabernet Sauvignon, Cabernet Franc and Merlot are used for the red wines, with Merlot the most common; Sémillon, Sauvignon and Muscadelle for the white.

Haut-Benauge is a small subdistrict of Entre-Deux-Mers, made up of nine villages between Targon and Cadillac. You will not come across many Haut-Benauge wines – they represent less than five percent of the Entre-Deux-Mers production – but the district is also a great supplier of red wines which are sold as Bordeaux or Bordeaux Supérieur. Château Toutigeac at Targon is a well-known estate that uses the Entre-Deux-Mers Haut-Benauge sub-appellation for its white wine, made exclusively from Sémillon.

The narrow, hilly stretch where Entre-Deux-Mers comes to the right bank of the Garonne is called the Premières Côtes de Bordeaux. It is about 60 kilometres (37 miles) long and 4 to 5 kilometres (2–3 miles) wide in most places. Vines were grown on the clay and limestone slopes in Roman times, and during the Middle Ages it was wines from this district, together with those from Graves, that established Bordeaux's reputation as a wine producer. That Premières Côtes de Bordeaux is not very well known today is largely because until the 1960s few of the wines were estate-bottled, but were blended into anonymity by the négociants. In addition the white wines – about a fifth of the vintage – are semi-sweet, as the appellation specifies more than four grams per litre of residual sugar. This means there is little interest in them in the world market. The red wines, however, deserve attention. Like Fronsac, the Premières Côtes de Bordeaux is a district with a future. The best red wines come from the northern half of the Côtes; white is dominant in the south. A fully sweet version of Premières Côtes de Bordeaux is called Cadillac.

In the adjoining enclaves of Loupiac and Ste-Croix-du-Mont, facing Sauternes across the Garonne, the white wines are rich, almost liqueur

Left: Thursday is market day at La Réole, a picturesque old town on the Garonne. Everything from shoes to sweets is on sale, and the local farmers come into town for shopping and gossip. Nearly every town and village in this part of France has such a weekly market.

Below: in Entre-Deux-Mers the word "château" can mean anything from a small cottage to a genuine castle, but Château Le Grand Verdus at Sadirac is a true 16th-century fortified "gentilhommière", or manor house.

like, the Ste-Croix-du-Mont being the slightly sweeter of the two. Neither, however, matches the sumptuousness of Sauternes, and *pourriture noble* ("noble rot") occurs less often here. This is also apparent from the higher yield permitted: not 25 hectolitres per hectare as in Sauternes, but 40. Château Loubens produces one of the best wines of Ste-Croix-du-Mont, matured in deep cellars hewn out of rock. Loubens also makes a dry white Bordeaux (Fleuron Blanc) and some red. The château itself was once a fort. Château de Tastes at Ste-Croix-du-Mont is a medieval castle, built by the English, high above the Garonne with a spectacular view across the river to Sauternes and Graves. The château makes very little of its own wine today, but other wines of the district can be sampled on the terrace below the castle. Loupiac and Ste-Croix-du-Mont are not solely dessert wines. Locally they are preferred as apéritifs or as partners to carefully chosen hors d'oeuvres or main courses.

Farther south, around St-Macaire, are the ten communes of Côtes de Bordeaux-St-Macaire. Most of the wine made here is sold as Bordeaux or Bordeaux Supérieur; just a small quantity of white wine goes out into the world under the district name.

Another little-mentioned appellation is Ste-Foy-Bordeaux, in the far northeastern corner, named after the old town of Ste-Foy-la-Grande, where a busy *départementale* road crosses the Dordogne. The wines are mainly white and semi-sweet. Down the Dordogne to the west, almost opposite Libourne, is the small wine district of Graves de Vayres, the last of the between-the-rivers appellations. A cooperative and various estates make simple red wines and white wines which used to be semi-sweet but increasingly now are dry, following the trend of the rest of the region.

TRAVEL INFORMATION

Comfortable places to stay are limited, but there is compensation in the number of restaurants where you can lunch or dine.

HOTELS

Hotel de France, 33420 Branne, tel. 57 84 50 06. Country hotel on the banks of the Dordogne. The plumbing is somewhat limited. Restaurant. Class B.
Hotel St-Martin, 33550 Langoiran, tel. 56 67 02 67. Simple; situated by the river. Restaurant. Class C.
Le Grand Hotel, 33580 Monségur, tel. 56 61 60 28. Family hotel. Authentic regional food served in the quite large dining room. Hotel Class C; restaurant Class B.
Grand Hotel, 117 Rue de République, 33220 Ste-Foy-la-Grande, tel. 57 46 00 08. Old hotel that has kept its character despite modernization. In the centre of town. Restaurant. Class B.
Hostellerie St-Pierre, 33490 Verdelais, tel. 56 62 02 03. Rooms without private showers or toilets. Restaurant. Class C.

RESTAURANTS

Auberge du Marais, 33270 Bouliac, tel. 56 20 52 17. Seasonally based cuisine. Servings are generous, and so are the agreeably priced lunch menus through the week. Class B.
Le St-James, 33270 Bouliac, tel. 56 20 52 19. One of the best restaurants of the Gironde, only a few kilometres south of Bordeaux along the D10. Chef and owner Jean-Marie Amat excels at inventive dishes of the highest standard. The duck, in particular, is excellent and the Pauillac lamb with garlic. The wine, too, is worth a detour. Class A.
Auberge André, 33880 Cambes, tel. 56 21 31 08. Congenial riverside restaurant furnished in country style, with a talented young chef. Class B.
Le Prévôt, 33670 Créon, tel. 56 23 08 08. Village restaurant with an excellent reputation. Regional cuisine includes *foie gras* and *filets d'oie à l'oseille*. Class B.
A la Varenne, 33880 Esconac, tel. 56 21 31 15. By the Garonne (between Quinsac and Cambes) with a park and terrace. Regional cuisine. Rooms. Class B.
La Fontine, 33190 Fontet, tel. 56 61 11 81. A large farm, just south of La Réole on the D9. Friendly service and tasty food. Class C.
La Belvédère, 33890 Juillac, tel. 57 40 40 33. Restaurant and terrace with a pleasant view over a bend of the Dordogne. (Juillac is between Pujols and Gensac.) Good cooking at

moderate prices. *Quenelles de brochet* are a speciality. Class C.
Le Commerce, 33450 Montussan, tel. 56 72 96 72. Rather unfortunately alongside the busy N89, but the cooking is talented. A few hotel rooms. Class B.
Hostellerie Robinson, 33360 Quinsac, tel. 56 21 31 09. A trusted address, right on the River Garonne. Dishes are strictly regional. Try the Clairet (rosé) from the local cooperative. Class B.
Hotel du Centre, 33190 La Réole, tel. 56 61 02 64. The oysters are excellent. Also a hotel. Class C.
Café des Arts, 33490 St-Macaire, tel. 56 63 07 40. Duck often features on the menu. Also a hotel. Class C.
Auberge du Lion d'Or, 33760 Targon, tel. 56 23 90 23. Popular, serving mainly local dishes. Class C.
Le Vatel, 33870 Vayres, tel. 57 74 80 79. Locally based cuisine and dishes from the grill. Class B.

WINE ACTIVITIES

The region has several *foires aux vins* (wine fairs): in La Réole (beginning of June); Sauveterre-de-Guyenne (last week in July); Ste-Croix-du-Mont (end of July, beginning of August); and Créon (first week in November).

The Connétable de Guyenne (wine fraternity) is active on behalf of the Premières Côtes de Bordeaux and Entre-Deux-Mers. Ste-Croix-du-Mont and Loupiac also have their own fraternities: the Commanderie du Bontemps de Ste-Croix-du-Mont and Les Compagnons de Loupiac.

WINE INFORMATION

There is a Maison du Vin in the Château des Ducs d'Epernon at Cadillac where you can go for information and to taste and buy wine. Ste-Croix-du-Mont has its own tasting cellar, near Château de Tastes. Opposite Beychac-et-Cailleau, along the N9 Bordeaux-Libourne road, is the Maison de Qualité, housing the bodies that watch over the quality of Bordeaux and Bordeaux Supérieur. It also has a tasting room and information office.

WINE ROUTE

To discover the many aspects of this large region, including most of the wine districts, try the following route (shown on the map on page 105). It starts and ends in Bordeaux and will comfortably fill a whole day.

Take the D10 south out of Bordeaux, following the east bank of the Garonne. In Floirac, the first village off to the left, there is an observatory that is open to visitors, and a little farther along the D10 is Bouliac, a great magnet for gastronomes (see Restaurants).

Continuing along the D10 through the Premières Côtes de Bordeaux you come to Langoiran, with the remains of a splendid fortress and 13th-century keep, and a few kilometres north, on the D13, is the Parc de la Peyruche, which has caves and a zoo.

Leave the D13 here and take the D20 north into the rolling countryside of the interior of Entre-Deux-Mers. In St-Genès-de-Lombaud the church apparently stands on the site of a Roman dwelling, and farther along the D20 is Créon, the capital of Entre-Deux-Mers. Turn right at Créon, on to the D671, and it is only a few kilometres to La Sauve, with the magnificent ruins of a Benedictine monastery and a church. Follow the D671 to the intersection with the D11 and then go south to Targon. Entre-Deux-Mers is rich in Romanesque churches and one of them is to be found in this wine village.

The D11 follows a winding, picturesque route south to Cadillac. This little town along the Garonne still has part of its 14th-century walls and two fortified towers. The most impressive sight, however, is the 17th-century Château des Ducs d'Epernon, built to the orders of Jean-Louis de Nogaret de Lavalette (the same Admiral who built Château Beychevelle).

The route continues along the D10

southwards to the peaceful village of Loupiac, where there have been excavations of Gallo-Roman sites and the Romanesque church has been declared a historic monument. (It is also typical of Loupiac that there is a vineyard in front of the church.)

In Ste-Croix-du-Mont the road climbs to a shaded viewing point overlooking the Garonne and the Sauternes district. You can visit caves here cut out of a thick layer of chalk originally formed from myriad oyster shells. A regional broadcasting station has been set up in the nearby Château de Tastes but some wine is still made (see page 103).

Via the D117 or the D10 you can drive on to Verdelais, an old pilgrim destination. Above the high altar of the 17th-century basilica of Notre Dame there is a 14th-century wooden carving of the Virgin Mary. A road beside the church leads up to the local cemetery where the painter Henri de Toulouse-Lautrec is buried. He lived at Château Malromé in St-André-du-Bois, a few kilometres to the north; the meticulously maintained château can be visited.

The next stop is St-Macaire, a medieval village on a cliff overlooking the Garonne. There is much to see: beautiful old houses, defensive walls and gateways, a partly 13th-century church and, for stamp enthusiasts, the Aquitaine postal musuem. Near the Benauge gate is the Maison du Pays, an information centre.

Take the N113 eastwards and you come to La Réole, and a few hundred

metres past La Réole, along the N113, you can turn off for the Signal du Mirail, a splendid viewing point. From here you can pick up the D129 west to the D668 and follow this to Monségur, a town founded by the Romans.

From Monségur the route continues north for a few kilometres in the direction of Bordepaille. Turn off left before this hamlet on to the D21E and follow this narrow road to the picturesque fortified village of Castelmoron-d'Albret. Only 4 hectares (10 acres) in area, it is the smallest commune in France.

Farther west is Sauveterre-de-Guyenne, a town founded in the 13th century; four gates remain from the original fortifications, and the central square with its four arcades is worth visiting. From here drive south for a few kilometres and then by the D131 and D11E west to Castelviel. The

Romanesque church on the hill has a marvellous porch; one of the carvings shows a vine being pruned.

North along the winding D123 is Blasimon, with a fine Romanesque monastery, and northwest along the D127E is Rauzan, with the old Château de Duras and, on the far side of the valley, a 12th-century church. West to the D936 and then north on the D20 you come to Château du Grand-Puch, a splendid little 14th-century fortified castle.

Continuing on the D20 to Goudon, then past the N89 and on to the D242 brings you to the last stop – Vayres. The monumental castle is a great attraction. Its gardens and terraces reach down to the river, and there is a huge *colombier* which can hold 2,600 pigeons.

From Vayres, return to the N89 and it is only some 20 kilometres (12 miles) back to Bordeaux.

PRODUCERS OF SPECIAL INTEREST

ENTRE-DEUX-MERS
Appellations Entre-Deux-Mers (white), Bordeaux and Bordeaux Supérieur

BAURECH, postcode 33880
Château de Beau Rivage Laguens*

BEYCHAC-ET-CAILLEAU, postcode 33750, 105 A2
Château Lesparre*

BONNETAN, postcode 33370, 105 B2
Château les Gauthiers*

CADILLAC, postcode 33410, 105 C3
Château David La Closière*

GENSAC, postcode 33890, 105 B5
Château Courson*

GREZILLAC, postcode 33420, 105 B3
Châteaux Bonnet*; de Bouchet; Reynier.

GUILLAC, postcode 33420, 105 B3
Château Canet*

LANGOIRAN, postcode 33550, 105 C3
Domaine de Cazères; Château Laurétan.

LUGASSON, postcode 33119
Château Turon La Croix*

MASSUGAS, postcode 33790, 105 B5
Château Pailhas

ROMAGNE, postcode 33760, 105 B3
Château La Rose St-Germain

ST-ANTOINE-DU-QUEYRET, postcode 33790, 105 B5
Château Queyret-Pouillac

ST-MARTIAL, postcode 33490, 105 C4
Château Courtey*

ST-QUENTIN-DE-BARON, postcode 33750, 105 B3
Château de Sours*

SALLEBOEUF, postcode 33370, 105 B2
Château Lafite Monteil*

LA SAUVE, postcode 33670, 105 B3
Château Thieuley*

SOUSSAC, postcode 33790, 105 C5
Châteaux La Croix du Moulin; Launay*; Moulin de Launay*.

▼ The lower Dordogne, here a sizeable river, bounds Entre-Deux-Mers to the north. The low riverside hills provide idyllic views across to the Libournais.

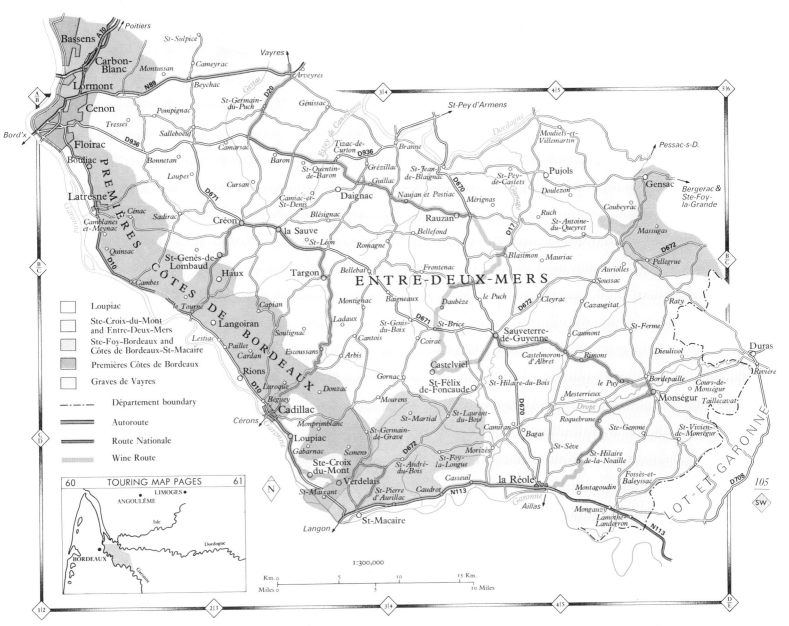

TARGON, postcode 33760, 105 C3

Château Toutigeac*

VERAC, postcode 33240

Château La Mongie*

VERDELAIS, postcode 33490, 105 D3

Château Pomirol du Pin

PREMIERES COTES DE BORDEAUX
Appellations Premières Côtes de Bordeaux, Cadillac, Bordeaux and Bordeaux Supérieur

BEGUEY, postcode 33410, 105 C3

Château Reynon*

CADILLAC, postcode 33410, 105 C3

Château Fayau

CAMBES, postcode 33880, 105 C2

Château Melin*

CAMBLANES, postcode 33360, 105 B2

Château Brethous

CAPIAN, postcode 33550, 105 C3

Château du Grand Mouëys

CENAC, postcode 33360, 105 B2

Domaine de la Meulière*;
Château Rauzé-Lafargue.

DONZAC, postcode 33410, 105 C3

Domaine du Pin Franc

GABARNAC, postcode 33410, 105 D3

Château Marcelin Laffitte

HAUX, postcode 33550, 105 C3

Château Anniche

LANGOIRAN, postcode 33550, 105 C3

Châteaux du Biac; Lezongars; Tanesse.

PAILLET, postcode 33550, 105 C3

Château de Paillet-Quancard

QUINSAC, postcode 33360, 105 B2

Domaine de Chastelet*; Château Péconnet*.

RIONS, postcode 33410, 105 C3

Château Carsin

ST-GERMAIN-DE-GRAVE, postcode 33490, 105 D3

Château Génisson

ST-MAIXANT, postcode 33490, 105 D3

Château Labatut

TABANAC, postcode 33550, 105 B2

Châteaux la Clyde*; Renon.

VILLENAVE-DE-RIONS, postcode 33550

Château Fauchey

COTES DE BORDEAUX-ST-MACAIRE

CAUDROT, postcode 33490, 105 D4

Domaine de Majoureau

ST-ANDRE-DE-BOIS, postcode 33490, 105 D4

Château la Serre

GRAVES DE VAYRES, postcode 33870

Châteaux Bacchus; Bel-Air; Bussac*; Pichon-Bellevue; Pontète Bellegrave.

LOUPIAC, postcode 33410, 105 D3

Château de Cros; Clos Jean; Châteaux de Loupiac (Gaudiet); Mazarin; de Ricaud*; du Vieux Moulin.

STE-CROIX-DU-MONT, postcode 33410

Châteaux Coullac; La Grave; Lamarque; Loubens*; Lousteau-Vieil*; du Mont; La Rame; de Tastes.

STE-FOY-BORDEAUX

PINEUILH, postcode 33220

Châteaux les Mangons; le Pré de la Lande.

ST-EMILION

The very name St-Emilion seems to melt on the tongue – warm, mellow and resonant, it suits the place and the wine. Both owe their character to thousands of years of development. Scratch the surface of the soil between the rows of vines and you may find a reindeer bone, a prehistoric stone axe, a Bronze Age arrowhead or a fragment of Roman pottery.

It was the Romans who laid the real foundations of the St-Emilion wine industry, bringing their own vines which they grafted on to the native ones. That was the beginning of a tradition that has continued unbroken to the present day. Today's growers still plant most of the vines, as the Romans did, in rows 1.33 metres (4 feet 3 inches) apart. Only in places has the width been increased to accommodate modern machinery.

The town is named after a holy man known as Aemilianus or Emilion who settled here in the eighth century and gathered around him a group of followers. Later the Franciscans and Dominicans established monasteries here, and the town came under a dual administration shared between a clerical chapter and a secular body known as the Jurade, instituted by King John of England and France in 1199. The Jurade played a key role in the development of viticulture in the area and remains in existence today as probably the oldest body of its kind in France. It continues to regulate the local wine industry and promote its produce, and performs impressive ceremonies in which its members wear striking red robes.

The area of the St-Emilion appellation covers eight communes and a part of Libourne (there are also five "satellite" communes, see pages 116–117). It is one of the most intensively cultivated areas in the Bordeaux region, comprising 5,200 hectares (some 12,800 acres) of vineyards owned by just over 1,000 proprietors. The average estate is therefore comparatively small and it is easy to lose your way among the little lanes and the patchwork of vineyards.

The district is roughly divided into four geological zones. The *côtes* is a limestone plateau and its slopes around the town of St-Emilion. The *plaine*, at the foot of the plateau to the south towards the river Dordogne, is sandy with gravel in some places. This flat countryside was the last to be planted with vines, mainly between the two World Wars. The *plateau des sables*, to the west and north of St-Emilion, is very sandy, as is clear from the name; and the *graves*, just 60 hectares (148 acres) in the west, adjoining Pomerol, has deep layers of gravel. The best – and usually the strongest – wines come from the limestone plateau and the gravelly areas.

In general the wines of St-Emilion are fuller, softer, fruitier, less astringent and more easy to enjoy than those of the Médoc. They are also slightly more alcoholic. This is partly because of the richer soil and partly because a different balance of grape varieties is grown. There is less of the rather austere Cabernet Sauvignon and more Merlot and Cabernet Franc. Consequently, many people find that St-Emilion wines are a good first step in learning to appreciate the world of claret.

The classification of St-Emilion is a law unto itself. The Bordeaux classification of 1855 (which concentrated on the Médoc) ignored it altogether. Not until a century later, in 1954, did St-Emilion set up a system of four appellations, in ascending order: St-Emilion, St-Emilion Grand Cru, St-Emilion Grand Cru Classé and St-Emilion Premier Grand Cru Classé. A reclassification in 1984 reduced these to two appellations: St-Emilion for the basic wines of the region and St-Emilion Grand Cru for the 90 best vineyards. However, provided they meet certain requirements, Grand Cru proprietors can still use the designations Grand Cru Classé or Premier Grand Cru Classé, even though these no longer count as appellations. Premiers Grands Crus Classés are also rated A (Châteaux Ausone and Cheval Blanc) and B (the rest).

It is certainly worth sampling a wide spectrum of St-Emilion wines. Those lower down the scale are often agreeable surprises. And the area from which they come is one of timeless beauty, where traditions are jealously guarded.

▶ The town of St-Emilion, constrained for centuries within its walls, is a unique jumble of ancient buildings and unexpected gardens. Little has changed here for hundreds of years.

TRAVEL INFORMATION

A St-Emilion speciality is a kind of macaroon: crunchy cakes made from finely ground almonds, sugar and white of egg, on sale at local cake shops and remarkably good with the wines of the district. Michel Poupin in Rue Guadet also sells chocolates with vinous themes, such as vine branches (*sarments des vignes*) – not recommended with the wine.

HOTELS

Auberge de la Commanderie, Rue des Cordeliers, 33330 St-Emilion, tel. 57 24 70 19. Middle-range hotel with a simple, brasserie-style restaurant. Class B.

Hostellerie de Plaisance, Place du Clocher, 33330 St-Emilion, tel. 57 24 72 32. Beautifully situated on the square next to the belfrey tower and above the *Eglise monolithe*. The comfortable rooms are named after wine estates and the restaurant is the best in town. Hotel class A, restaurant class B.

Logis des Remparts, Rue Guadet, 33330 St-Emilion, tel. 57 24 70 43. Well-furnished rooms with every comfort. Own car park, Class A.

RESTAURANTS

Logis de la Cadène, Rue de la Cadène, 33330 St-Emilion, tel. 57 24 71 40. Excellent place for lunch (it has a covered terrace) and reasonable prices. Family cooking, fairly rich, with regional dishes. Class C.

Cloître des Cordeliers Not a restaurant, but you can sit in the open air here among the ruins of the 14th-century cloisters and enjoy a glass of Clos des Cordeliers sparkling wine. This is a favourite place for visitors, especially on Sunday afternoons, often with a box of macaroons on the table. There are also underground wine cellars that can be visited.

Emiliano, Place Cap du Pont, 33330 St-Emilion, tel. 57 24 44 64. Local dishes as well as pizzas and a fine view over the town. Class C.

Goullée Francis, Rue Guadet, 33330 St-Emilion, tel. 57 24 70 49. Elegant decor and often very fine dishes (such as *soupe de foie gras*). Class B.

Chez Germaine, Place du Clocher, 33330 St-Emilion, tel. 57 24 70 88. Traditional dishes based on local ingredients. Class B.

Auberge de la Monolithe, Place du Marché, 33330 St-Emilion, tel. 57 24 47 77. Attractively situated: dinner is served outside in fine weather. One of the specialities is *aiguillettes de canard*. Class B.

THE TOWN OF ST-EMILION

To an eye surveying the town from any of its many vantage points, nothing breaks the delicate harmony of St-Emilion, clustered on its hillside, tier upon tier of old stone houses with red-tiled roofs, the sunlight forming age-old patterns of shadow on eaves and cloisters, archways and winding cobbled streets. It is reassuring to know that the whole town, shadows and all, is an ancient monument. These days such fragile beauty has to be protected by law.

The visitor finds it hard to imagine the violent history this tranquil little town has been through. Founded in the 11th century, it came under English rule in the 12th. It changed hands many times during the Hundred Years War of 1337–1453, and was the scene of many battles during the 16th-century Wars of Religion and again during the French Revolution. Between fights, the town was an important resting place on the great medieval pilgrim route to Santiago de Compostela in northwest Spain.

Today pilgrims of another kind flock to St-Emilion, drawn by the wine and the beauty of the place. Leave your car in one of the six car parks: in an afternoon's walk you can easily cover all the main sites.

St-Emilion's most memorable monument is the *Eglise monolithe* (Monolithic Church), entered from the Place du Marché. It was carved out of the limestone of the hill by Benedictine monks in the 11th and 12th centuries and is the largest chamber-cave of its kind in Europe. During the Revolution it was stripped of its adornments and turned into a saltpetre store, which ruined most of the frescos. It was reconsecrated in 1837 and is used now only on ceremonial occasions, such as when members of the Jurade meet there in their scarlet robes. The subterranean church is an impressive but rather gloomy and forbidding place, smelling of dampness and mould.

Near the Monolithic Church is the small medieval Trinity Chapel, beneath which is the underground cavern that Emilion used as his hermitage. It contains the saint's stone bed, his altar and water supply from a spring. The less reverent of the local guides will tell you that young women complaining of infertility would go to the holy man for help and would invariably give birth nine months later.

Directly above the Monolithic Church, in the Place du Clocher, is the belfrey tower of the church, as though thrusting up from the cave below. From this square there is a fine view over the town and the surrounding vineyards.

Other religious buildings include the ruined Franciscan friary in the eastern part of the town, the Jacobin monastery, now the cellars of a château, and the splendid 12th-century Collegiate Church with its rich Romanesque façade. Of the 13th-century Dominican monastery nothing remains but a single high wall (outside the Porte Bourgeoise to the north).

Towering over the southern part of the town is the Château du Roy in the Venelle du Château du Roy. This castle was probably built in the 13th century in the time of Henry III of England and is the only Romanesque *donjon* (fortress) in the Gironde. Also in the Romanesque style is the ruined Cardinal's Palace near the Porte Bourgeoise, former residence of the first dean of St-Emilion, Cardinal de St-Luce.

One of the town's most romantic touches is the stone archway called the Porte de la Cadène, a few steps away from La Commanderie, one of the oldest dwellings of the city and former residence of the garrison's officers.

A vivid reminder of the French Revolution is the grotto where deputies of the Gironde hid for several months to escape the Terror.

The town is still encircled by stretches of the medieval ramparts but there remains only one of the old fortified gates, the eastern Porte Brunet. Just to the south of it is one of the watchtowers, the Tour du Guetteur.

The local museum in the Logis de Malet contains artefacts, documents and displays that give an overall view of the remarkably varied history of St-Emilion.

OTHER PLACES OF INTEREST

St-Christophe-des-Bardes One of the oldest castles of the district, Château Laroque, is here. It was largely rebuilt in the 18th century but the keep is medieval. The local church with its rather worn carvings is a historic monument.

Below: the limestone quarried to build St-Emilion has left galleries that extend beneath the town and are used by the châteaux to mature their wine. By far the largest of these galleries are at Château Villemaurine.

Bottom: the Rue de la Cadène, typical of St-Emilion's steep cobbled streets. On the left is one of the best-known local restaurants, the Logis de Cadène, and on the right a shop selling an interesting mixture of antiques and macaroons, the crunchy little almond cakes that are a speciality of the town.

St-Hippolyte Beneath Château de Ferrand, a wine estate, there is a maze of underground passages, probably prehistoric, and a spring. The partly 14th-century village church stands on a hill that dominates the surrounding countryside.

St-Martin This little hamlet lies just west of St-Emilion and consists mainly of wine-producing châteaux (Château Canon, for example, is here). The church is Romanesque.

St-Sulpice-de-Faleyrens North of St-Sulpice, near the little river harbour of Pierrefitte, is the best-preserved prehistoric menhir of the département. More than 5,000 years old, the stone is 5 metres (17 ft) high and 3 metres (10 ft) wide, and is in the shape of a hand. The church of St-Sulpice dates from the 11th century. A number of French monarchs, including Henry of Navarre, stayed at the nearby Château Lescours.

WINE ACTIVITIES

La Jurade de St-Emilion was set up in 1199 as a governing body for the town and its wine. The fraternity was revived in 1948. At the end of September it proclaims the *ban des vendanges* from the roof of the Château du Roy, after which the grape harvest may begin. In mid-June a "new wine" festival is organized.

WINE INFORMATION

St-Emilion's Maison du Vin is in the former Maison de l'Abbé, one of the buildings of the Cloître de la Collégiale. For information about wine and visits to the châteaux you can also ask at the Office du Tourisme round the corner.

During the summer, wine information is also provided at the Pavillon d'Accueil at St-Etienne-de-Lisse and the Pavillon du Vin at St-Pey-d'Armens.

Arvouet
la Chichonne

CHÂTEAU L'EVANGILE

CHÂTEAU LA CONSEILLANTE

Château Croque Michotte

la Croix Chante-Caille

le Jura

Château Corbin

MONTAGNE

Ch. Grand Corbin Despagne

Château Carrie

Maison Neuve

Montagne

ST-GEORGES

POMEROL

Ch. Corbin Michotte

Château la Dominique

Château de Grand-Corbin

Château Jean-Faure

Toulifaut

Château la Tour du Pin Figeac

CH. CHEVAL BLANC

Château Ripeau

Jean Voisin

Chasteau

Vachon

Château la Tour-Figeac

la Grange Neuve

CHÂTEAU FIGEAC

Petit Montlabert

Fortin

Château Chauvin

Clos Grand Faurie

Château Trimoulet

Sarrensot

Bézineau

Château Montlabert

la Croix Figeac

Petit Figeac

la Rose

Château Dassault

Merissac

Château du Tailhas

Château Grand Barrail-Lamarzelle-Figeac

Château la Marzelle

le Fougueyrat

Bellevue

D243

Médé

Magnan

Château Yon-Figeac

Château Laroze

Ch. Clos des Jacobins

Pourret

Balau

Château Fonroque

Ch. Cap-de-Mourlin

Château Larmande

Peyraud

Château Petit Faurie de Soutard

Château Faurie-de-Soutard

Berthonneau

Château Cadet-Piola

Château Soutard

Château Mauvezin

Château Haut-Sarpe

Jacquemeau

Château Grand-Mayne

Ch. Franc Mayne

Ch. Grand Pontet

Château Pontet Clauzure

Cadet-Bon

Ch. Guadet St-Julien

Balestard-la-Tonnelle

Château Sansonnet

Château Couspaude

le Rivalon

Bord

Château Coutet

Château Trois Moulins

Ch. la Carte et le Chatelet

CLOS FOURTET

St-Martin

Château Villemaurine

Couvent des Jacobins

Château la Serre

CHÂTEAU TROTTE-VIEILLE

Gaubert

Barrail

Château Bellevue

Ch. Beau Séjour Bécot

CHÂTEAU BEAUSÉJOUR DUFFAU LAGAROSSE

Château l'Angélus

Mazerat

Fonrazade

Château Matras

Château Curé-Bon la Madeleine

St-Emilion

Ch. Chapelle Madeleine

CHÂTEAU CANON

Ch. la Clotte

St-Christophe

la Barde

Mondotte

Château la Pelleterie

Royland

Château Cadet

Château Magdelaine

Ch. Grandes Murailles

CH. AUSONE

Ch. Moulin St-Georges

Ch. Troplong-Mondot

Pin de Fleur

TOURING MAP PAGES

LIMOGES
ANGOULÊME
Isle
Dordogne
BORDEAUX
Garonne

CHÂTEAU LA GAFFELIÈRE

Château Fonplégade

Château Dassay Tertre-Daugay

Château BELAIR

St-Georges

Château St-Georges Côte Pavie

CHÂTEAU PAVIE

Ch. Pavie-Decesse

les Carrières

ST-LAURENT

Goudeau

Château l'Arrosée

Cave Coop

Château Pavie-Macquin

Château Larcis Ducasse

Château Bellefont-Belcier

St-Laurent-des-Combes

Château Canon-la-Gaffelière

l'Arsu

Gueyrot

Canton boundary

Commune (parish) boundary

CHÂTEAU Premier Grand Cru Classé (1985)

Château Leading Grand Cru Classé

Château Other Grand Cru Classé

Wine Route

Vineyards

Woods

Contour interval 5 metres

1:34,250

THE CHATEAUX

ST-EMILION, postcode 33330
Premiers Grands Crus Classés

Château Ausone 109 E4
The showplace of the Côtes and one of the two Premiers Grands Crus Classés A (the other is Cheval-Blanc). The estate, named after the Roman consul and poet Ausonius, is on the edge of St-Emilion's limestone plateau commanding long views of other vineyards and the valley of the Dordogne. Its penetratingly perfumed wines can rival the great Médocs in style and finesse.

Château Beauséjour 109 D4
A pretty property on the west-facing Côtes. The traditionally made, concentrated wine has a lot of tannin and a refinement that demands patience: a wine for laying down.

Château Belair 109 E4
Close to Château Ausone and owned by Madame Helyett Dubois-Challon, co-owner of Ausone. The wine is among the best of the Côtes, with a beautiful aroma of oak as a prelude to its silky substance.

Château Canon 109 D4
A most distinguished, sturdy wine from a partly walled vineyard on St-Emilion's limestone plateau. It is made in the traditional way for long cellaring.

Château Cheval Blanc 109 B2
Premier Grand Cru Classé A (with Château Ausone). The vineyard of this charming white château is close to the Pomerol boundary and has a

109
SW

lot of gravel in its soil. The wine has luxury and refinement, strength and subtlety. Great vintages are legendary; unsurpassed even among the first-growths of the Médoc.

Château Figeac 109 C2
The dignified château has a long history; the estate once included what is now Cheval Blanc as well as other properties. The surrounding vineyard on low gravel hills is 70% Cabernet (half Sauvignon, a high proportion for St-Emilion) and the wine has a velvety softness and great allure. It can be drunk early but is also capable of long maturing.

Clos Fourtet 109 D4
One of the most interesting estates to visit, with extensive cellars hewn from the rock, almost opposite the Eglise Collégiale. Since the early 1970s Fourtet has increased in stature from a rather dour wine to a true Côtes classic.

Château La Gaffelière 109 E4
A supple, meaty St-Emilion matures in the cellars opposite the large Gothic château. The wine has become reliable again since the start of the 1980s; the 1982 was among the best of the whole district.

Château Magdelaine 109 E4
The interest here lies in the wine rather than the property. Magdelaine is hard to equal for flawless quality and a complete and generous taste with a style of its own. The vineyard is 80% Merlot. The estate belongs to Jean-Pierre Moueix, a Libourne négociant firm which also owns Châteaux Fonroque and Moulin du Cadet, and the greater share of Château Pétrus in Pomerol.

Château Pavie 109 E4
The château and its large vineyard lie on the southwest slope of St-Emilion's plateau; its cellars are hewn out of the limestone slope and the roots of vines growing 8 metres (some 26 ft) farther up the hill penetrate the cellar ceiling. Pavie produces stylish, supple, fragrant wine that matures excellently in bottle.

Château Trotte Vieille 109 D5
A quite sturdy, pleasant St-Emilion but lacking refinement.

ALSO IN ST-EMILION

Château l'Angélus * 109 D3
Grand Cru Classé
A big and business-like farm whose wine has been stored in new casks since the vintage of 1979 and as a result has gained significantly in depth.

Château l'Annonciation *
A rounded wine with a good aftertaste; very successful for an ordinary St-Emilion.

Château l'Arrosée * 109 E4
Grand Cru Classé
A strong, generous wine of *premier cru* standard. The vineyard is on the southwest slope of the limestone plateau.

Château Balestard-la-Tonnelle 109 D5
Grand Cru Classé
A very old estate – a verse from the 15th-century poet François Villon, reproduced on the label, refers to "the divine nectar . . . of Balestard". The wine today is full, vital and reliable. An old stone tower on the estate has been restored and is used for receptions.

Château Barberousse
A St-Emilion plain and simple that since 1981 has stood out from the crowd.

Château Beau-Séjour Bécot * 109 D4
Grand Cru Classé
In 1984 this estate was deprived of its Premier Grand Cru Classé status for reasons that can only be termed dubious. The wine is still of excellent standard. The château stands high on the plateau of St-Emilion and has fine underground cellars cut into the limestone.

Château Berliquet 109 E4
Grand Cru Classé
A substantial house in a pleasant garden, whose wine is well made under the direction of the local cooperative.

Château Cadet-Piola * 109 D4
Grand Cru Classé
A generous wine, better than its status.

Couvent des Jacobins * 109 D4
Grand Cru Classé
Established in a former 13th-century monastery, with splendid rock cellars. Excellent wine.

Château Curé Bon La Madeleine * 109 E4
Grand Cru Classé
Intense, formidable wine, usually from grapes at optimum ripeness.

Château La Fleur *
Grand Cru
A distinguished wine that deserves Grand Cru Classé status.

Château Fonplégade * 109 E4
Grand Cru Classé
A distinguished château producing a firmly structured, stylish wine, often undervalued.

Château Franc Grâce-Dieu *
Grand Cru Classé
Fine, well-bred wine made by the owners of Premier Grand Cru Classé Château Canon.

Château La Grâce Dieu Les Menuts *
Grand Cru
A substantial Grand Cru, with depth.

Château Guadet-St-Julien 109 D4
Grand Cru Classé
The ancient cellars are full of atmosphere – they date from the 5th century. The wine has abundant tannin and needs time to develop.

Château Haut-Sarpe 109 D5
Grand Cru Classé
One of the most beautiful châteaux of St-Emilion, inspired by the Trianons at Versailles and set in a spacious park. The wine is well rounded and enjoys a good reputation in France.

Château Larmande * 109 C4
Grand Cru Classé
A rising star: the wines from this well-managed estate are steadily improving.

Château Monbousquet 111 C3
Grand Cru
An almost velvety Grand Cru listed by many good French restaurants.

Château Puy-Razac *
Grand Cru
An exemplary St-Emilion, with style.

Château Rolland-Maillet *
A meaty, complex wine with plenty of colour, of Grand Cru standard.

Château La Tour du Pin Figeac 109 B2
Grand Cru Classé
Firm, somewhat earthy St-Emilion

The belfrey tower of the *Eglise monolithe* (the Monolithic Church). The church itself is subterranean, carved out of the limestone of the hill.

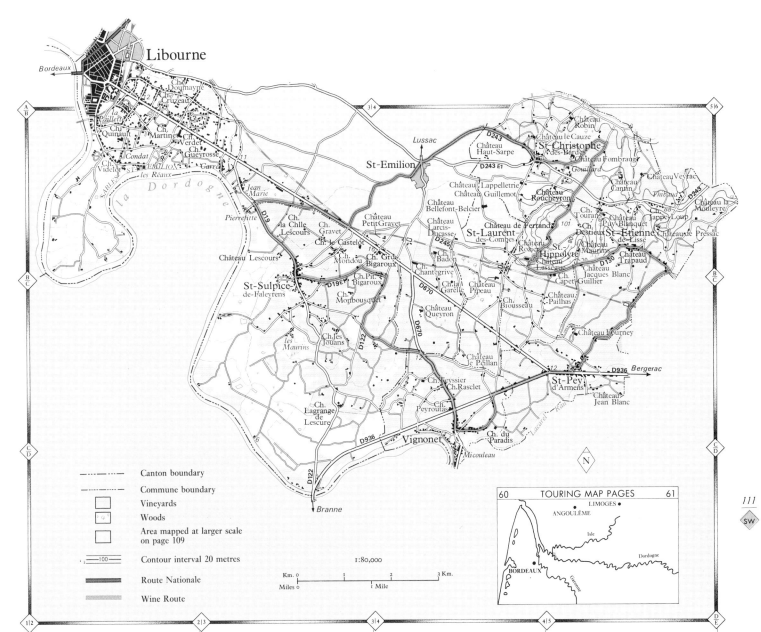

Libourne

Bordeaux

St-Emilion

Lussac

St-Christophe-des-Bardes

St-Laurent-des-Combes

St-Hippolyte

St-Etienne-de-Lisse

St-Sulpice-de-Faleyrens

St-Pey d'Armens

Vignonet

Branne

Bergerac

Canton boundary

Commune boundary

Vineyards

Woods

Area mapped at larger scale on page 109

Contour interval 20 metres

1:80,000

Route Nationale

Wine Route

Km. 0   1   2   3 Km.
Miles 0   1 Mile

TOURING MAP PAGES
60   61
LIMOGES
ANGOULÊME
Isle
Dordogne
BORDEAUX
Garonne

111

SW

from the Moueix family (there is a second estate of this name with different owners).

Château Villemaurine * 109 D4
Grand Cru Classé
The splendid cellars here host banquets as well as wine. Since the early 1980s the deep-coloured wine has again been of impressive quality.

Other Grands Crus Classés in St-Emilion include **Châteaux Bellevue, Bergat, Canon-la-Gaffelière, Cap de Mourlin, Clos des Jacobins** (under the wing of the Cordier establishment), **La Clotte, Corbin and Corbin Michotte, Croque-Michotte, la Dominique, Faurie de Souchard, Fonroque, Franc-Mayne, Grand Barrail Lamarzelle Figeac**, a number of other estates with the prefix **Grand** (-Corbin, -Corbin-Despagne, -Mayne and -Pontet), **Larcis-Ducasse, Laroze, Matras, Mauvezin, Pavie Decesse** and **Pavie Macquin, Petit-Faurie-de-Soutard, St-Georges** (Côte

Pavie), **La Serre, Soutard, Tertre Daugay, la Tour Figeac, Trimoulet, Troplong Mondot** and **Yon-Figeac**.

ST-CHRISTOPHE-DES-BARDES, postcode 33330

This commune to the east of St-Emilion includes the Grand Cru Classé **Château Dassault** (map page 109 C5) and the Grands Crus **Fombrauge*** 111 B5 (Danish owned), **Lapelleterie** 109 D5 and 111 B4, **Laroque, Puyblanquet Carrille*** (a lively, deep-coloured wine that lingers beautifully) and **Quentin**.

ST-ETIENNE-DE-LISSE, postcode 33330

The easternmost of the four eastern villages, well placed at the foot of the limestone scarp. The Grands Crus include **Châteaux Gaillard de la Gorce, Puy-Blanquet** 111 B5 and **Tourans** 111 B5.

ST-HIPPOLYTE, postcode 33330

A little to the west of St-Etienne, also at the foot of the limestone slope, with the Grands Crus **Châteaux de Ferrand** 111 B5, **Franc Pipeau, Gaillard*** (often a very successful wine: stylish, generous and concentrated), **Monlot-Capet** and **Domaine de la Vieille Eglise**.

ST-LAURENT-DES-COMBES, postcode 33330

Just outside the commune of St-Emilion to the east, on the limestone Côtes. Includes the Grands Crus **Châteaux Béard, Belille-Mondotte, de Candale*** (a pure wine with good taste and wood), **La Croizille** and **Le Tertre Roteboeuf*** (a wine of Grand Cru Classé level).

ST-PEY-D'ARMENS, postcode 33330

Château Bonnet* here is an excellent, firmly constituted Grand Cru from a family that has owned the estate for six generations.

ST-SULPICE-DE-FALEYRENS, postcode 33330

St-Sulpice is to the southeast of St-Emilion, down on the *plaine*. The Grands Crus include **Châteaux Bigaroux, La Chapelle-Lescours** 111 B3, **Flouquet, Grand-Pey-Lescours, Gravet*** 111 B3 (repeatedly, and deservedly, an award-winning wine with fruit, tannin and vitality) and **Lescours** 111 B3.

St-Etienne-de-Lisse and St-Pey-d'Armens both have centres that provide information about local wines and châteaux: see Wine Information in the Travel Information section, page 108.

POMEROL

The little district of Pomerol fans out from the port of Libourne on the north bank of the Dordogne, bisected by the busy N89 that links Bordeaux with Périgueux. To the east its vineyards merge with those of St-Emilion; to the west, across the D910 and the River Isle, lies Fronsac. If, as is probable, "Pomerol" derives from *pomarium*, Latin for "orchard", it may once have been a market garden for Libourne, but now the only fruit it grows is the grape.

There is no actual village called Pomerol: the commune is made up of a number of small hamlets – Catusseau, Cloquet, Grand- and Petit-Moulinet, Maillet, Pignon, René – each with the name Pomerol preceding its own. Administratively and socially the commune is based on Pomerol-Centre, which can be pinpointed on the rural landscape by the steeple of its church. The church, built in 1898, replaced one built in the twelfth century by the Knights of St. John (the Hospitallers), later known as the Knights of Malta, who gave help and shelter to travellers at the time of the Crusades. Pomerol was on one of the pilgrim routes to Santiago de Compostela in northwest Spain: there are still stone signposts marked with the Maltese cross at several places (near Châteaux Beauregard, Moulinet and La Commanderie, for example), and at a crossroads near the hamlet of Pignon a weathered column marks the old route. It is also probable that the Knights stimulated vinegrowing in Pomerol, if only to have wine for Mass and to use as a medicine. This is why the local wine fraternity was given the name La Confrérie des Hospitaliers, and its members have a Maltese cross on their robes.

Pomerol's vineyards, introduced by the Romans, were destroyed during the Hundred Years War. They were gradually restored during the fifteenth and sixteenth centuries, but for several hundred years the district was regarded in wine terms – if considered at all – as part of St-Emilion. It did not acquire an identity of its own until 1923, confirmed by an appellation contrôlée in 1936. Today the demand for Pomerol so exceeds supply that the prices paid for the better wines can equal those of renowned Médoc Crus Classés.

Pomerol itself has no classification system, mainly because the more important growers do not particularly want one. Nevertheless, there is justification for distinguishing an élite group of estates: the most interesting are marked on the following pages with an asterisk. The leading estates, after Pétrus, are generally considered to be (in no particular order) Trotanoy, Vieux Château Certan and Certan (De May de Certan), La Conseillante, l'Evangile, La Fleur-Pétrus, Lafleur-Gazin, Petit Village and Latour à Pomerol.

The centre of Pomerol is a plateau some 35 metres (115 feet) high with an abundance of clay. Here strong, generous, richly coloured wines are produced, with Château Pétrus supreme. Around the plateau there is a fairly narrow belt consisting of gravel, clay and sand: the wines grown here are robust, intense, but often less rounded and luxurious than those from the plateau. To the west the land is flatter and the soil sandier, resulting in relatively light, supple wines. In many places there is a hard, compact layer of iron-bearing sandstone in the subsoil and it is this *crasse de fer* that is said to give Pomerols their sometimes truffle-like aroma. A good Pomerol, however, will have other elements: of cocoa, blackberry and violets, roasted almonds and liquorice, and oak.

Most Pomerols are more accessible, warmer, more charming and less reserved than wines from most of the other districts of Bordeaux (although they can also mature well). Merlot, the grape that thrives on clay and loamy soils, contributes greatly to this and accounts for three-quarters of the vines.

The typical Pomerol "château" is comfortable rather than grand, set tranquilly among its vines. There are some 180 growers, so in this small district most of the estates are small, averaging around ten hectares (25 acres), with many only a mere hectare or two. Château Pétrus has only 11.4 hectares (28 acres); by far the largest property is Château de Sales with 47.5 hectares (117 acres).

▲ The parish church of Pomerol stands sentinel at the centre of this scattered commune of small hamlets and tranquil farms.

TRAVEL INFORMATION

Pomerol has no hotels or restaurants, so Libourne is the place to go. (See also the Travel Information in the chapters on St-Emilion and Fronsac.)

HOTELS

Hotel Backgammon, 16 Quai de l'Isle, 33500 Libourne, tel. 57 74 06 06. The rooms are acceptable but the restaurant is relatively expensive. Class B.
Hotel de la Gare, 43 Rue Chanzy, 33500 Libourne, tel. 57 51 06 86. A simple, decent place to sleep. Also has a restaurant. Class C.
Hotel Loubat, 32 Rue Chanzy, 33500 Libourne, tel. 57 51 17 58. The best-known hotel in Libourne, near the station. The rooms have been modernized and the restaurant, Les Trois Toques, serves carefully prepared local dishes (*entrecôte*

libournaise, lampreys, etc), and a range of Pomerol wines. Class B.
Hotel Le Petit Duc, 22 Place Decazes, 33500 Libourne, tel. 57 51 03 39. Modern, friendly hotel. Class B.
Hotel Climat de France, Port du Nouguey, 33500 Arveyres, tel. 57 51 41 41. Modern hotel, with restaurant, opened at the beginning of the 1980s. Across the river from Libourne, opposite the Quai du Priourat. Class B.

RESTAURANTS

L'Etrier, 21 Place Decazes, 33500 Libourne, tel. 57 51 13 59. A rather elegant establishment with prices to match, but the cooking is good and the wine list tempting. Class B. For something cheaper, you could go to the grill next door. Class C.

Le Landais, 15 Rue des Treilles, 33500 Libourne, tel. 57 74 07 40. No-frills restaurant belonging to the same owners as Hotel Loubat round the corner. The oysters, *coq au vin* and duck are good. Meals are served out of doors in summer. Class C.

PLACES OF INTEREST

Apart from its wine and a few reminders of the Order of St. John, Pomerol does not have much to offer the visitor. In Libourne, however, there are a number of attractions.

The town of Libourne (just under 25,000 inhabitants) was founded in the 13th century by the Englishman Roger de Leyburn, who built a fortified settlement where an earlier stronghold had probably stood. In 1270 Libourne was given its municipal charter. The old town walls have been replaced by quays and embankments lined with plane trees; most of Libourne's wine merchants are concentrated on the Quai du Priourat, and behind their offices there are cellar complexes that are often very extensive.

Coming from Bordeaux, you enter Libourne by way of a long 19th-century bridge. (Heavy through traffic is diverted around the old centre of the town.) In the heart of the town is the Place Abel Surchamp, a large square surrounded by old houses, arcades and the 15th-century town hall. The town hall has a museum of archaeology and art, including paintings by René Princeteau who taught Toulouse-Lautrec. Three days a week the square comes to life when the market is held. Where the little river Isle flows past the quays in the town centre and into the Dordogne is the Tour du Grand-Port, one of two fortified towers remaining from the original town walls. It used to command the entrance to the harbour.

WINE ACTIVITIES

La Confrérie des Hospitaliers de Pomerol was founded in 1968 and named after the Order that built a hospital in Pomerol in 1298.

WINE INFORMATION

There is no Maison du Vin in Pomerol, but details about the wines and the châteaux should be available from the tourist information offices in Libourne and also in Bordeaux (see page 66). It is also worth making enquiries at the larger hotels or restaurants in Libourne, such as the Hotel Loubat. Many of the châteaux welcome visitors (with advance warning), including Beauregard, La Conseillante, La Croix de Gay, Nenin, La Pointe, De Sales and Vieux Château Certan.

▼ There is more to Bordeaux than the great estates: on the smaller properties, tradition — and traditional ways — live on.

PRODUCERS OF SPECIAL INTEREST

POMEROL, postcode 33500

Château Beauregard 115 D4
One of the few grand châteaux in
Pomerol, complete with moat, towers
and impressive stairway. It dates
from the 17th century. (A replica was
built for the Guggenheims on Long
Island, New York, in the 1920s.) The
wine is an elegant Pomerol with good
balance.

Château Le Bon Pasteur *
A characteristic, generous Pomerol of
high quality. The modest estate, in
the northeast corner of the district, is
managed by a locally well-known
oenologist.

Château Bourgneuf-Vayron
115 C3
Dark, firmly structured wine but
somewhat lacking finesse. It is not
wood-aged.

Château La Cabanne 115 C4
Pleasant, supple wine with a distinct
oak aroma. It often has a good
amount of colour and matures well.

**Château Certan (De May de
Certan)** * 115 C5
A small estate opposite Vieux
Château Certan (they were once one
estate) with modern equipment,
making wine with style and strength.

Château Certan-Giraud 115 C5
Strong but not particularly refined
wine.

Château Clinet 115 C4
A quarter of the vines here are
Cabernet Sauvignon, an unusually
high proportion for Pomerol. The
wine therefore has something of
Pauillac about it, sombre and rather
hard. It demands long cellaring.

Château La Commanderie 115 D4
Modern-equipped estate making a
well-bred, reliable wine.

Château La Conseillante * 115 D5
Estate on the St-Emilion-Pomerol
boundary that has belonged
to the same family for more
than a century. The wine is
one of the finest of the
district, with a delicate
perfume and firm yet silky
taste of great distinction.

Château La Croix 115 D4
A fairly sturdy Pomerol that can age
well but lacks real class. A small
museum at the château houses items
connected with the old pilgrim route
to Santiago de Compostela.

Château La Croix de Gay *
115 C5
A noble Pomerol with subtle nuances.
A *supérieure* selection from a small
plot is sold as Château La Fleur de
Gay and can match the best in the
district.

Clos de l'Eglise 115 C4
Exquisite, not particularly broad
Pomerol that usually demands years
of patience.

Château l'Eglise-Clinet * 115 C4
Very vital, stylish wine with a creamy
roundness, tannin and a beautiful
balance.

Château l'Enclos 115 B3
Very sound, reasonably generous
wine with an unmistakable charm; it
needs ageing. L'Enclos proves what
can be achieved on the flat, sandy
land in the west of Pomerol – the
secluded estate is in the hamlet of
Grand-Moulinet, on the west side of
the Libourne-Périgueux road.

Château l'Evangile * 115 C5
The vineyard borders on Château
Pétrus and produces a splendid,
stylish Pomerol, characterized by an
impression of violets in the perfume.

Château Feytit-Clinet 115 C4
Juicy, meaty, attractive wine.

Château La Fleur-Pétrus * 115 C5
The château is striking for its egg-
yellow shutters; the wine is a
distinguished Pomerol with more
subtlety than most, but tastes softer
and less fat. It should be allowed to
mature. The stylish flag on the label
looks as if it could belong to a
shipping line.

Château Le Gay 115 C5
Wine with softness and tannin but
not a striking personality.

Château Gazin 115 C5
A reasonably firm Pomerol that in
good years can be concentrated and
fruity. Normally, however, it is
simply pleasant, correct and slightly
dull. With 20 hectares Gazin is
among the larger Pomerol estates.

Château Gombaude-Guillot
115 C3
A full, sometimes almost luxurious
wine that is not aged in wood.

**Château la Grave Trigant de
Boisset** * 115 B4
Balance, refinement and a good deal
of tannin mark this consistent wine,
from 90% Merlot.

Château Lafleur 115 C5
Initially very reserved, with colour
and strength, Lafleur develops
beautifully in bottle.

Château Lafleur-Gazin * 115 C5
A carefully made, generous wine with
fruit and noble wood.

Château Lafleur du Roy 115 D4
Fairly fresh, slender, classically made
wine, from the mayor's estate.

Château Lagrange 115 C4
In terms of class and complexity,
Lagrange just misses the top group of
Pomerols but is better than average.

Château Latour à Pomerol *
115 B4
An almost corpulent, very generous
Pomerol with a lot of soft tannin and
ripe fruit.

Château Mazeyres 115 C2
Sound but not very exciting wine.

Château Moulinet 115 B3
A rounded wine with reasonable
tannin and a sometimes earthy aroma.

Château Nenin 115 D3
One of the bigger Pomerol estates, its
handsome château set in a large park.
The compact, deep-coloured wine has
less meat, depth or charm than its
reputation might lead you to expect,
but it usually develops well in bottle.

Château Petit Village * 115 D4
Excellent wine that is anything but
petit. The owners are Domaines Prats
(of Cos d'Estournel in St-Estèphe
and other properties).

Château Pétrus * 115 C5
Pétrus, for all its fame, will
disappoint anyone who is looking for
a grand château – until you taste the
wine. Pétrus is the Pomerol of
Pomerols: a dark, exceptionally
intense wine that overwhelms the
senses with its authoritative power.
Its unique class puts its price beyond
the reach of ordinary mortals: it is
three times the price of the Médoc
first-growths. The estate (the vines
are 95% Merlot) belongs to Mme
Lacoste and Jean-Pierre Moueix (of
the Libourne firm of the same name).
A Moueix team looks after the
vineyard and makes the wine. Other
Moueix properties in Pomerol include
Feytit-Clinet, La Fleur-Pétrus, La
Grave Trigant de Boisset, Lagrange,
Latour à Pomerol and Trotanoy.

Château Plince 115 D3
A relatively unknown Pomerol that
deserves following; its quality has
made great strides since the second
half of the 1970s.

Château La Pointe 115 C3
An extensive estate just outside
Libourne, where two
roads from Pomerol
join at the Libourne
boundary – hence the
name La Pointe. The
château itself looks out
over a magnificent park
with stately old trees.
If conditions are right,
La Pointe produces
colourful, sinewy but not
particularly refined
wines for laying down.

Clos René 115 C3
Sound, serious Pomerol.

Château Lapointe

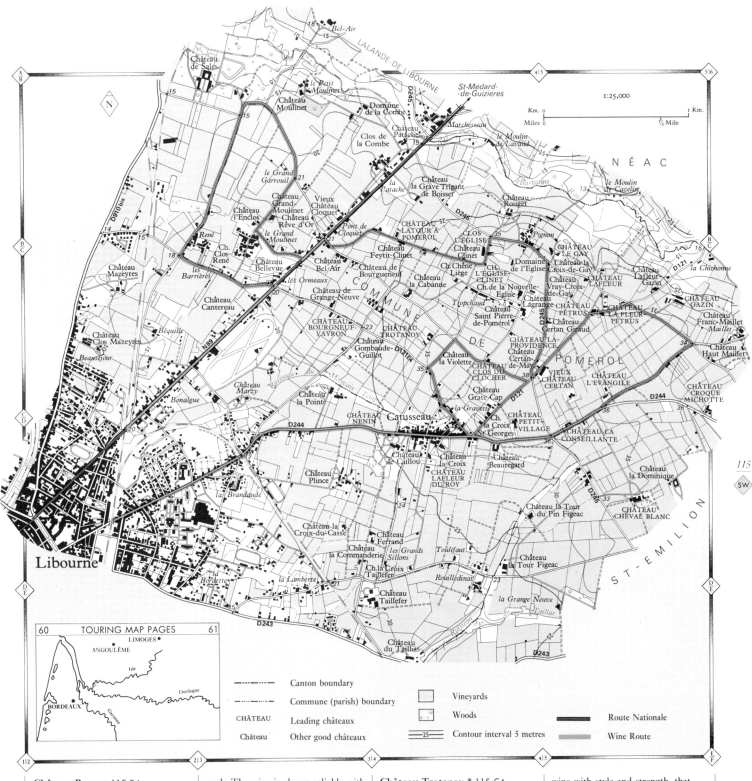

1:25,000

Km. 0   1 Km.
Miles 0   ½ Mile

115

TOURING MAP PAGES   60   61

LIMOGES
ANGOULÊME
Isle
BORDEAUX
Dordogne
Garonne

- – – – – – – Canton boundary
- – – – – – – Commune (parish) boundary
- CHÂTEAU   Leading châteaux
- Château   Other good châteaux
- Vineyards
- Woods
- —25— Contour interval 5 metres
- Route Nationale
- Wine Route

Château Rouget 115 B4
The ivy-covered country house, built in 1750, is one of the oldest châteaux in Pomerol. Winemaking here is conservative, producing wine intended for laying down for a couple of decades. The initial hardness is due partly to two-thirds of the vines being Cabernets.

Château de Sales 115 B3
Pomerol's biggest estate with an impressive château set in an extensive park. The wine is always reliable with style, structure, a certain elegance and a fine perfume.

Château du Tailhas 115 E4
Broad, rounded wine made with modern equipment, reliable even in lesser years.

Château Taillefer 115 E4
A somewhat rustic wine that benefits from ageing. The aftertaste can be quite dry.

Château Trotanoy * 115 C4
A Moueix estate on Pomerol's central plateau: the wine is decidedly more grand than the château, a pleasant country house. Trotanoy is an extraordinarily distinguished wine with plenty of colour, concentration and strength. If Pétrus is the emperor of Pomerol, Trotanoy is the king.

Vieux Château Certan * 115 C5
The Belgian owners (the Thienpont family) produce a flawless, charming wine with style and strength, that gains in fragrance and complexity with the years. The bottle is easily recognized by its pink cap.

Château La Violette * 115 C4
A Pomerol with grace, a perfume of violets and a nice finish.

Château Vray Croix de Gay *
115 C5
The age of many of the vines makes this a good Pomerol, with depth.

THE SATELLITES
OF ST-EMILION AND POMEROL

Beyond the river Barbanne, the northern boundary of St-Emilion and Pomerol, lie the so-called satellites. The villages of Lussac, Montagne, Parsac, Puisseguin and St-Georges each constitute an appellation whose wines can be sold under the name of the commune coupled with that of St-Emilion. To the west are the satellites of Pomerol: the communes of Lalande and Néac, most of whose wines carry the appellation Lalande-de-Pomerol.

On this north side of the river, small hills and charming valleys replace the well-ordered rows of vines of St-Emilion's central plateau. There are woods and meadows as well as vineyards, small villages, winding roads and modest châteaux. The visitors who throng St-Emilion at weekends do not disturb the stillness here.

By far the most important appellation is Montagne-St-Emilion. The wines are often earthier and more robust than St-Emilions but can be of surprising quality – and often reasonably priced. As well as the wines from Montagne, most of those from Parsac and St-Georges are also sold under the Montagne-St-Emilion appellation. The most important exception is Château St-Georges, the splendid estate that dominates the surrounding countryside and produces wine with at least the distinction of a St-Emilion *grand cru*. It proudly carries the St-Georges-St-Emilion appellation.

The wines of Lussac often seem a little fuller and more rounded than those of Montagne. Almost half the harvest is processed by the cooperative in Puisseguin, a commune that itself makes many agreeable wines, rounded and with charm.

Like Pomerol, the commune of Lalande has many small properties: of some 230 growers, about 50 cultivate less than a hectare. The wines, too, show a family likeness with those of Pomerol but have just a little less generosity, strength and appeal. The village of Lalande-de-Libourne used to be called Lalande-de-Pomerol; the name was changed in 1978 for administrative reasons, but the appellation remains Lalande-de-Pomerol. The producers of Néac are entitled to sell their wine either as Néac or as Lalande-de-Pomerol.

▼ The outlying districts of St-Emilion and Pomerol, the "satellites", contribute many sound bottles to the world's wine lists.

TRAVEL INFORMATION

These rural villages have little to offer in the way of hotels and restaurants; see instead places to eat and stay in St-Emilion, Pomerol and, for restaurants, Fronsac.

RESTAURANTS

Restaurant de l'Aérodrome, 33500 Les Artigues-de-Lussac, tel. 57 24 31 44. By the local airfield, close to the N89. A speciality is *rôti de lotte au basilic*. The wine list has a generous selection including St-Emilions. Class B.

PLACES OF INTEREST

Cornemps Hamlet northeast of Lussac with a monastery where Henry of Navarre once stayed.
Lalande-de-Libourne Well-preserved 12th-century church with an open belfry.
Lussac The church has a bas-relief with harvest scenes, and just west of the village is the Picampeau menhir (sometimes called the Pierre des Martyrs because it was used as a sacrificial stone).
Montagne A 12th-century Romanesque church with a ribbed dome, and the Eco-Musée de Montagne, next to the Maison du Vin, has displays concerning rural life in times past. On a hilltop near the village are the five mills of Calong, a reminder that corn used to be grown here. Also close to Montagne is the Château des Tours, with 72 hectares (178 acres) of vineyards and an imposing 14th-century château.
Petit-Palais Attractive 12th-century church with two 16th-century belfries. The village is northwest of Lussac along the D21.
St-Georges High on the hill, overlooking its sweep of vines, is Château St-Georges, built in 1770 on medieval foundations by Victor Louis (of the Grand Théâtre in Bordeaux). Neither the château nor its wine should be missed. The cellar entrance bears the motto *vini templum* ("temple of wine").

WINE ACTIVITIES

The wine fraternity Les Baillis de Lalande-de-Pomerol has been active since 1984. The Montagne fraternity, Les Vignerons de Montagne de St-Emilion, is three years older. The Echevins de Lussac-St-Emilion was created in 1986.

WINE INFORMATION

There are Maisons du Vin in Lussac, Montagne and Puisseguin.

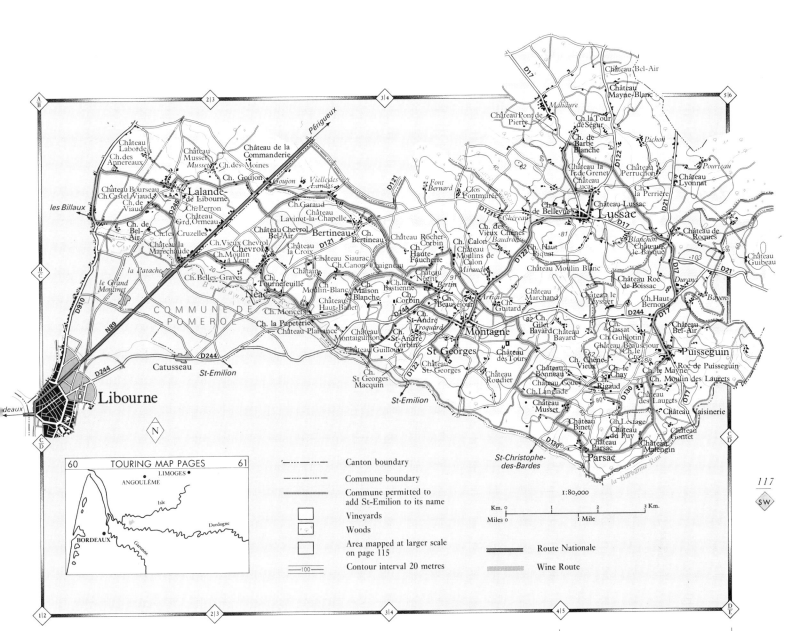

PRODUCERS OF SPECIAL INTEREST

LUSSAC, postcode 33570
Appellation Lussac-St-Emilion

Château de Barbe-Blanche * 117 B5
Château Bel-Air 117 A5
Château Bois-Tiffray (bottled by the cooperative)
Château Chambeau
Château du Courlat
Château La France de Roques
Château de la Grenière
Château Lion-Perruchon
Château Lucas 117 B5
Château de Lussac 117 B5
Château Lyonnat 117 B5
Château Milon
Château St-Pierre
Château de Tabuteau
Château Vieux-Busquet
Château les Vieux-Chênes 117 B4
Château Vieux-Fournay

MONTAGNE, postcode 33570
Appellation Montagne-St-Emilion

Château Baudron
Château Calon 117 B4
Château Corbin 117 B4
Château Coucy
Château La Croix de Mouchet
Château La Fleur Musset *
Château Laroze-Bayard
Château Maison Blanche * 117 C3
Château Négrit 117 C4
Château La Papeterie 117 C3
Château Rocher Corbin 117 B4
Château Roudier * 117 C4
Château des Tours 117 C4
Vieux Château Négrit
Vieux Château Saint André *
117 C4

PARSAC, postcode 33570
Appellation Montagne-St-Emilion or Parsac-St-Emilion

Château Parsac 117 D5

Château Plaisance 117 C3
Château du Puy 117 C5

PUISSEGUIN, postcode 33570
Appellation Puisseguin-St-Emilion

Château Beaulieu *
Château Durand-Laplagne
Château Guibeau 117 B6
Château des Laurets * 117 C5
Château de Roques 117 B5
Château du Roy (bottled by the cooperative)
Château Soleil

ST-GEORGES, postcode 33570
Appellation St-Georges-St-Emilion or Montagne-St-Emilion

Château Calon
Château Cap d'Or *
Château Macquin St-Georges 117 C4
Château St-Georges * 117 C4

LALANDE-DE-LIBOURNE,
postcode 33500
Appellation Lalande-de-Pomerol

Château de Bel-Air * 117 B2

Château Bourseau 117 B2
Château de la Commanderie 117 B3
Château de l'Evêché
Château Grand Ormeau * 117 B3
Château Graves des Annereaux * 117 B2
Château La Maréchaude
Clos des Moines * 117 B3
Château Tour Colombier

NEAC, postcode 33500
Appellations Lalande-de-Pomerol or Néac

Château Belles-Graves 117 B3
Château Canon Chaigneau 117 B3
Château Chatain-Pineau
Château la Fleur St-Georges
Château Haut-Chaigneau
Château les Hauts-Conseillants
Château Moulin à Vent * 117 B3
Château Siaurac 117 B3
Château Les Templiers *
Château Treytins
Château Vieux Chevrol * 117 B3
Château Yveline

FRONSAC

The river Isle, meandering in its broad valley, forms the boundary between Pomerol and Fronsac. The two districts are very different. Pomerol is a gently undulating plateau; Fronsac a tangle of small hills and valleys. The most important of the hills is the Tertre de Fronsac, which commands the surrounding countryside and provides a superb view of the Dordogne. The Gauls and then the Romans fortified it, and Charlemagne built a stronghold in 769 which for centuries did service for military purposes and as a residence for often tyrannical lords.

The castle's most notorious inhabitant was d'Argilemont, a *seigneur* who took great delight in sinking any passing ship that did not immediately heave to when he fired a shot across its bows. In 1620 d'Argilemont was arrested on the orders of Louis XIII and ended on the scaffold. Three years later the castle was dismantled and nothing now remains of it, nor of the later Italianate palace built on the hill by the Duc de Richelieu (grand-nephew of the famous cardinal and a military commander) – for *fêtes galantes*, it is said. The name of the local wine fraternity, Les Gentilshommes du Duché de Fronsac, established in the late 1960s, is a reminder of this period. Today the Tertre de Fronsac is crowned by a pavilion, or lodge, built in the last century by a wealthy Libourne family. It is private property.

Grapes have been grown in Fronsac since very early times. Until the eighteenth century the wines were more highly valued than those of St-Emilion. It was only during the first half of the nineteenth century that St-Emilion began to outstrip Fronsac in reputation, although the first edition of *Bordeaux et Ses Vins*, which appeared in 1850, described Fronsac as one of the communes "where the best wines of the Libourne *arrondissement* are harvested". But from disasters such as the phylloxera and economic depressions, Fronsac has made a less energetic recovery than St-Emilion and Pomerol, and the name of Fronsac remained virtually forgotten until the 1960s.

The renewal of interest since then has been justified by the better wines. Their characteristics are a strong, deep colour, plenty of power, a hearty finesse, a slightly bitter undertone and long life. These qualities are found particularly in the wines from the sub-district of Canon Fronsac, the southern, hilliest parts of the communes of St-Michel-de-Fronsac and Fronsac. The subsoil here contains a good deal of lime beneath a thin top layer with clay and sand. Most of the vines are red, mainly Merlot and Cabernet.

The Fronsac appellation embraces all or parts of seven communes and the wines vary considerably. The comparatively homogeneous standard of Pomerol is not achieved here: alongside some distinguished wines there are also light, not very interesting ones. Experts agree, however, that of all the lesser-known appellations in Bordeaux, those of Canon Fronsac and Fronsac are strong candidates for a reputation at world level.

Whether this opportunity will be taken is up to the winemakers. In area the Fronsac district, with some 1,000 hectares (2,400 acres) of vines, is larger than Pomerol, so the quantity produced is adequate for achieving an international name. A stimulus in this direction has already been given by the distinguished firm of Jean-Pierre Moueix of Libourne, which took over three leading châteaux in the 1970s and 1980s: Canon, Canon de Brem and La Dauphine.

Fronsac is worth visiting not only for its wines but also for its landscape and its architecture. The châteaux display a great variety of styles. Some, such as Château de la Rivière, are genuine castles. Others, such as Canon in St-Michel-de-Fronsac, are comfortable mid-nineteenth-century country villas, built by prosperous merchants from Libourne.

TRAVEL INFORMATION

Attractive though it is, the district is not yet equipped for tourism; see hotels and restaurants in St-Emilion and Pomerol.

RESTAURANTS

Clo-Luc, 33133 Galgon, tel. 57 84 36 16. Beside the D18 into Galgon from the south. (Parts of the village just come within the Fronsac appellation.) A speciality is *gigoton* (leg of lamb) *au vieux Bordeaux*. Class C.

Auberge de l'Isle, 33230 Sablons-de-Guîtres, tel. 57 69 22 58. Sablons is a hamlet off the D910 to the north of Libourne, beyond St-Denis-de-Pile. At the Auberge you can eat out of doors, on a shaded terrace, in fine weather. The cooking is good: fish dishes, *escalope de foie gras aux pommes*, roast breast of duck and reasonable prices attract a faithful clientele. Class C.

PLACES OF INTEREST

Asques Picturesque river village with view across the Dordogne.
Cadillac-en-Fronsadais 19th-century chapel and Ste-Ruffine fountain.

This commune is outside the Fronsac appellation: Château de Cadillac, an impressive 12th-century fortress, produces red and white wines under the Bordeaux Supérieur and Bordeaux appellations.
Fronsac The ancient centre of the district, eclipsed in the 13th century by Libourne. The Romanesque church is a historic monument. There are also many lovely old houses, some dating from the 17th century.
St-Aignan The remains of a Gallo-Roman villa have been found here; the church is Romanesque.
St-Genès-de-Fronsac An 11th-century church, restored in the 16th century.
Vérac The church is 12th century, and a tower near the village was a cornmill until 1776. Lovers of cheese should make a point of visiting the dairy next to the 18th-century Château de Pommiers.

WINE INFORMATION

Les Gentilshommes du Duché de Fronsac have functioned since 1969. The Maison du Vin is in the village of Fronsac.

PRODUCERS OF SPECIAL INTEREST

FRONSAC, postcode 33126
Appellation Canon-Fronsac

Château Canon *: A minuscule, historic estate that has belonged to Christian Moueix (director of J–P Moueix of Libourne) since 1971. If Fronsac had a first-growth, this would be it. (See also Château Canon, St-Michel-de-Fronsac.) **Château Canon de Brem** * 119 C3 Another J–P Moueix property. Very fine, long-lived wine. **Château Coustolle** 119 C3; **Château La Fleur Cailleau; Château Haut-Panet; Château Junayme** 119 C3; **Château La Marche-Canon; Château Moulin Pey-Labrie** * 119 C3: Consistently well-made wine. **Château Toumalin** 119 C3.

ST-MICHEL-DE-FRONSAC, postcode 33145
Appellation Canon-Fronsac

Château Canon * 119 C2: Confusingly there are two Châteaux Canon, one in Fronsac (see above), the other in St-Michel-de-Fronsac. The St-Michel Canon is the property of the Horeau family and the birthplace of a strong, typically full-flavoured Fronsac that takes 10 years or more before it is ready to drink. The steeply sloping vineyard has many old vines. **Château Cassagne Haut-Canon; Château La Fleur Canon; Château Haut-Mazeris;** **Château Lariveau; Château Mazeris** 119 C3; **Château Mazeris-Bellevue; Château Vray Canon Boyer** * 119 C2: One of the best wines of its commune, tangy and unready for at least five years.

FRONSAC, postcode 33126
Appellation Fronsac

Château La Croix-Gandineau; Château de la Dauphine * 119 C3: A pretty château by the river, belonging to J–P Moueix. Exemplary Fronsac with plenty of flavour, a long finish and beautiful balance. **Château La Grave; Château Pontus** 119 C3; **Château La Valade** 119 C3.

GALGON, postcode 33133
Appellation Fronsac

Château Mayne-Vieil

LA RIVIERE, postcode 33145
Appellation Fronsac

Château de la Rivière * 119 B2: The showpiece of the whole district: a 13th-century castle flanked by two square towers and built against a wooded slope looking out over the valley of the Dordogne. Some distance behind the castle are the eccentric, almost Wagnerian rock cellars where the wine is aged. The wine is one of the most formidable of Fronsac: full of colour, meaty and with plenty of tannin. In blind tastings it has repeatedly held its own against great wines from both St-Emilion and the Médoc.

SAILLANS, postcode 33141
Appellation Fronsac

Château du Carillon; Château Dalem; Château Moulin Haut-Laroque; Château Villars *.

ST-AIGNAN, postcode 33126
Appellation Fronsac

Château Hauchat; Château Haut-Ferrand; Château Tasta; Château des Tonnelles; Vieux Château Vincent.

Fronsac, with the Dordogne and Entre-Deux-Mers in the distance.

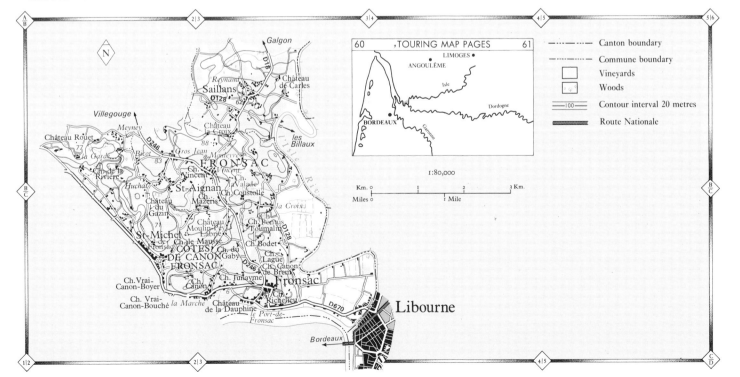

119

SW

COTES DE CASTILLON AND COTES DE FRANCS

Immediately to the east of St-Emilion and its satellite communes of Parsac, Puisseguin and Lussac are nine villages entitled to the appellation Bordeaux Supérieur Côtes de Castillon. Near the Dordogne the landscape is fairly flat, but farther north it becomes hilly and very pretty. The vineyards are usually more than 50 percent Merlot, with Cabernet Franc the second variety. In this they follow the example of St-Emilion, but there is no great similarity between the wines of Côtes de Castillon and St-Emilion; at most they could be compared with the wines from the satellite communes, although they are less rounded. Côtes de Castillon wines must contain a minimum 11 percent alcohol, a half percent more than the ordinary Bordeaux Supérieurs.

The district derives its name from Castillon-la-Bataille, an unmemorable little town on the Dordogne. It was here on 17 June 1453 that a decisive battle was fought between the English and the French: the battle that parted Aquitane from England after 300 years. In it the English commander Talbot, an old fighter in his 80s, lost the battle and his life.

To the north of Côtes de Castillon lies the small, little-known district of Bordeaux Côtes de Francs: three communes and part of the Salles-de-Castillon commune (the other part of this village comes within the Côtes de Castillon). There was a Frankish settlement here in early times, commemorated by the hamlet of Francs.

Côtes de Francs is a green and peaceful district with hills everywhere, including the highest in the entire Gironde département. The soil with its clay and limestone lends itself well to wine growing, and the microclimate is perhaps the warmest and driest in all Bordeaux. Some of the growers still have the "St-Emilion" stamps for their casks: Côtes de Francs used to belong to that district but the adjustment of the appellations in the 1920s put an end to this arrangement and a rather wretched period began. Many vineyards were dug up or planted with inferior grape varieties. Since the beginning of the 1980s, however, great interest has been shown in the Côtes, thanks to the efforts of the Belgian Thienpont family who own two leading and influential estates, Puygueraud and La Claverie. And in 1985 two St-Emilion families (joint owners of Cheval Blanc and l'Angélus) bought the run-down Château de Francs with the aim of creating a first-class vineyard there.

TRAVEL INFORMATION

The Côtes are not richly endowed with hotels or restaurants; see instead the chapters on St-Emilion, Entre-Deux-Mers and Bergerac.

HOTEL

La Bonne Auberge, 33350 Castillon-la-Bataille, tel. 57 40 11 56. Reasonable comfort at reasonable prices, and a restaurant that serves mainly regional dishes. Hotel class C; restaurant Class B.

RESTAURANT

Chez Régis, 33350 Ste-Terre, tel. 57 47 16 21. You can lunch or dine here quite inexpensively. *Friture d'anguilles* (fried eel) is a speciality. Simple accommodation is also available. Class C.

PLACES OF INTEREST

Belvès-de-Castillon In July and August the battle between the English and the French is re-created on open ground next to the 15th-century Château de Castegens. The colourful spectacle starts at 10.30 in the evening, with some 600 people in costume taking part.

Castillon-la-Bataille Little river town where in 1453 the historic battle was fought that finally returned Aquitane to the French. In 1953 Castillon commemorated the 500th anniversary of the event by adding "la Bataille" to its name. To the east of the village there is a simple memorial to John Talbot, Earl of Shrewsbury, who led the English in the battle. The local church dates from the 18th century, and the *mairie* is in what used to be a hospital.

Champ de la Hire In the Côtes de Francs district, between St-Cibard and Salles-de-Castillon. A hill here was fortified by the French during the Hundred Years War.

Francs The Château de Francs could be partly 12th century, but most of the buildings date from the 14th and 17th centuries. A fine gateway gives access to this wine estate.

Gardegan Has a 12th-century church.

Monbadon A 14th-century feudal castle crowns one of the hills.

St-Cibard Has a 13th-century church.

Ste-Colombe Provides a panoramic view of the surrounding countryside. The church dates from the 11th and 12th centuries.

St-Genès-de-Castillon Has a beautiful 15th-century house.

St-Magne-de-Castillon The church is 11th to 12th century.

Salles-de-Castillon There is a menhir (ancient stone) and a Romanesque church.

Tayac The remains of a Gallic settlement were found near this hamlet in the Côtes de Francs in the 19th century. The church is Romanesque.

WINE ACTIVITIES

The annual *foire aux vins* at Castillon-la-Bataille is usually held in the second half of July.

WINE INFORMATION

There is a Maison du Vin in Castillon-la-Bataille which will provide information about the wines and the châteaux of the district.

▼ Castillon-la-Bataille: a promenade leads down to the Dordogne, and beside the river there are the remains of old defensive walls and a large iron gate.

PRODUCERS OF SPECIAL INTEREST

COTES DE CASTILLON

BELVES-DE-CASTILLON,
postcode 33350

Château Bel-Air, 121 C3; Château de Prade 121 C3.

GARDEGAN, postcode 33350

Château Pitray 121 C3: The splendid château is worth a visit. Château La Fourquerie 121 C3.

STE-COLOMBE, postcode 33350

Château Thibaud-Bellevue 121 C2

ST-MAGNE-DE-CASTILLON,
postcode 33350

Château Moulin Rouge 121 D2; Château Rocher Bellevue 121 C2.

ST-PHILIPPE-D'AIGUILHE,
postcode 33350

Château d'Aiguilhe 121 C3: An isolated estate (follow the blue signposts) rich in history. Parts of the château date from the 14th and 15th centuries.

SALLES-DE-CASTILLON,
postcode 33350

Château de Belcier 121 B3; Château de Clotte 121 B3.

COTES DE FRANCS

FRANCS, postcode 33570

Château de Francs* 121 B3

ST-CIBARD, postcode 33570

Château La Claverie 121 B3: The first harvest was in 1985 and already impressive. The estate belongs to the Thienpont family, who also own Château Puygueraud. **Château Puygueraud*** 121 B3: The undisputed star of the Côtes de Francs (and the surrounding area). The wine is deep coloured with a firm structure and plenty of tannin and oak. It matures for four to six months in casks (half of them new) and is not filtered.

TOURING MAP PAGES 60 61

LIMOGES
ANGOULÊME
Isle
BORDEAUX
Garonne
Dordogne

N

1:100,000

Km. 0   1   2   3   4 Km.
Miles 0   1   2 Miles

—·—·— Département boundary

——— Canton boundary

- - - - Commune boundary

▬▬▬ A.C. Côtes de Castillon

▬▬▬ A.C. Côtes de Francs

▢ Vineyards

▢ Woods

—100— Contour interval 20 metres

▬▬ Wine route

COGNAC

The only area in the world where cognac may legally be made lies directly north of the Bordeaux region and takes in the whole of the Charente-Maritime département, a large part of Charente and two enclaves in Dordogne (to the southeast) and Deux-Sèvres (to the north). It may also be produced on a few offshore islands. The landscape is a harmonious one of gently sloping hills with fields and small woods, peaceful villages and isolated, often walled farms. Hazy sunlight makes colours more mellow, contours less sharp, and across the region flows the languid grey Charente. Haste seems absent here, despite the executive jets owned by some of the cognac houses: not for nothing have the inhabitants been given the nickname *cagouillards*, after the small *cagouille* snails of the region.

Various remains – including the arena at Saintes, which could hold 20,000 people – show that the Romans were here in considerable numbers. They probably introduced wine growing, but for many centuries wine was made only for local consumption. The first, and the most important, export was salt, from which Cognac derived its prosperity from the eleventh century on. It was not until the second half of the seventeenth century that a lively trade in wine arose. This was due to the Dutch, newly independent, who imported great quantities of wine for distilling. Their *brandewijn* ("burnt wine") gave us our word "brandy". Later they increasingly left the wines to be distilled in their region of origin. At first this *eau-de-vie* was drunk with water, but eventually the qualities of pure, wood-aged cognac were more and more appreciated. In the seventeenth and eighteenth centuries it began to enjoy a worldwide reputation; the nineteenth century saw the rise of many of the great cognac houses and of the sale of cognac in the bottle.

The name and origin of cognac were given legal protection in 1909 when the boundaries of its production area were laid down. Official recognition of the zones that make up the district followed nearly 30 years later. These lie in concentric circles around Cognac itself. The heart is the chalky area of Grande Champagne, which is surrounded in succession by Petite Champagne, Borderies, Fins Bois, Bons Bois and Bois Ordinaires. The proportion of chalk in the soil decreases successively through these zones – and with it the quality of the cognacs produced. To achieve a balanced and consistent quality, most houses use cognacs from different zones and of various ages. Fine Champagne, a special appellation, is a blend of Grande Champagne (at least 50 percent) and Petite Champagne.

The age of a cognac is indicated by a range of legally protected terms. For three-star cognac (or VS) the minimum age of the youngest brandy used is 30 months. For VSOP (Very Superior Old Pale), VO and Réserve this minimum is raised to four and a half years, and to six years for XO, Vieille Réserve, Napoleon, VVSOP, Royal, etc. In practice, conscientious cognac firms maintain much stricter norms. For example, the youngest brandy from the house of Delamain, its Pale and Dry, is on average 20 years old.

The basis for cognac is a thin, acidic white wine from the Ugni Blanc (known here as St-Emilion), the grape that accounts for 95 percent of the vineyard area. This is distilled twice in a special still, or alembic. At this stage the colourless liquid – very alcoholic at around 70 percent – is not yet a cognac. Only a quarter of the eventual quality is present; the rest comes from the oak of the maturing casks (Limousin), the quality of the cellar in which it is aged and the length of time it is kept there. During its time in cask the alcohol content gradually decreases, while every year 3 to 4 percent of the volume is lost by evaporation. This "angel's share" means an annual loss for the whole district of 22 million bottles. The normal drinking strength of around 40 percent alcohol is achieved by diluting the distillate, usually with distilled water, but some firms mix the distilled water with a little very old cognac.

Not all the wine of the Cognac region passes through the stills. Partly in order to soak up the surplus of grapes, the wines of the Charente have been given Vins de Pays status. A more enterprising attempt is Pineau des Charentes, a mixture of unfermented grape juice and brandy, which must spend a year in wood and be between 16 and 22 percent alcohol. It is pleasant cold as an apéritif.

The coast of the Charente-Maritime and the islands just offshore attract many tourists in summer and are liberally provided with hotels and restaurants. There are also many inland places (see below) where it is pleasant to stay. Gastronomic specialities include oysters, especially those of Marennes and Oléron; mussels (try the *mouclade*); snails (called *cagouilles* here); and the region's butter.

HOTELS

Hotel François 1er, 3 Place François 1er, 16100 Cognac, tel. 45 32 07 18. Very central. Class B.
Mapotel Le Valois, 34 Rue du 14-Juillet, 16100 Cognac, tel. 45 82 76 00. Businesslike comfort. Class B.
Le Moderne, Rue Elysée-Mousnier, 16100 Cognac, tel. 45 82 19 53. Quite modern, in fact. Class B.
Hotel de l'Orangerie, 16200 Jarnac, tel. 45 81 13 72. Small and pleasantly situated on the riverside. Class B.
Le Logis de Beaulieu, 16100 St-Laurent-de-Cognac, tel. 45 82 30 50. Peacefully situated, classically furnished hotel. The restaurant has a fairly conservative menu (including *mouclade*) and a choice of more than 100 cognacs. Class B.
Les Bosquets, Route de Rochefort, 17100 Saintes, tel. 46 74 04 47. Set in the middle of woods. There is also a restaurant. Class B.

RESTAURANTS

La Ribaudière, 16200 Bourg-Charente, tel. 45 81 30 54. By the river; has a terrace. Uncomplicated regional cuisine and a good wine list. Class C.
Le Relais, 17120 Boutenac-Touvent, tel. 46 90 63 06. Traditional. Class C.
Le Coq d'Or, 33 Place François 1er, 16100 Cognac, tel. 45 82 07 51. Excellent for oysters. Class B.
La Halle aux Vins, 7 Place François 1er, 16100 Cognac, tel. 45 32 07 51. Honest country dishes such as *mouclade* and *choucroute*, and regional wines. Class C.
Les Pigeons Blancs, 10 Rue Jules-Brisson, 16100 Cognac, tel. 45 82 16 36. Good cooking based on produce fresh from the market. Try the *foie gras de canard au Pineau* and *sole aux essences de Cognac*. Also a hotel. Class B.
Le Relais du Bois St-Georges, Rue de Royan, Cours Genêt, 17100 Saintes, tel. 46 93 50 99. Inventive menu and a country atmosphere. Also a luxury hotel with an indoor pool, a large park and a lake, 1 km from the autoroute.

Domaine de Fleurac, 16200 Fleurac, tel. 45 81 78 22. Light-hearted cuisine, and a tasting room where a selection of cognacs can be sampled. Also a good hotel. Tranquil situation in a park. Class B.
Restaurant du Château, 16200 Jarnac, tel. 45 81 07 17. Regional dishes including snails (*cagouilles*). Class C.
Le Vieux Logis, 17500 Jonzac, tel. 46 48 15 11. Many dishes made with Pineau des Charentes (grape juice with cognac); good helpings. Garden and terrace. Class C.
Grottes de Matata, 17120 Meschers-sur-Gironde, tel. 46 02 70 02. In one of the local caves (see Places of Interest), with a large terrace. Try the dishes with oysters or fresh fish. Class C.
Auberge Pontoise, 17800 Pons, tel. 46 94 00 99. Plenty of atmosphere. Oysters (*huîtres chaudes au beurre*

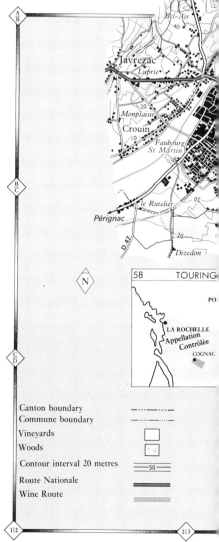

rouge) and duck (*magret de canard*) are among the specialities. Also a hotel. Class B.

Mancini, Rue des Messagiers, 17100 Saintes, tel. 46 93 06 61. Famous establishment with good cuisine (including *canard aux pêches fraîches*). The hotel is more rural than its central situation implies. Class B.

l'Auberge, 17350 St-Savinien, tel. 46 90 20 79. Mainly regionally based cooking. Class C.

Le Soubise, 17780 Soubise, tel. 46 84 93 36. Excellent restaurant, with hotel. Restaurant class A; hotel class B.

PLACES OF INTEREST

Aulnay Superb 12th-century church with a wealth of sculpture.

Bourg-Charente Romanesque church. The liqueur firm of Marnier-Lapostolle ("Grand Marnier") is here, in the Château de Bourg.

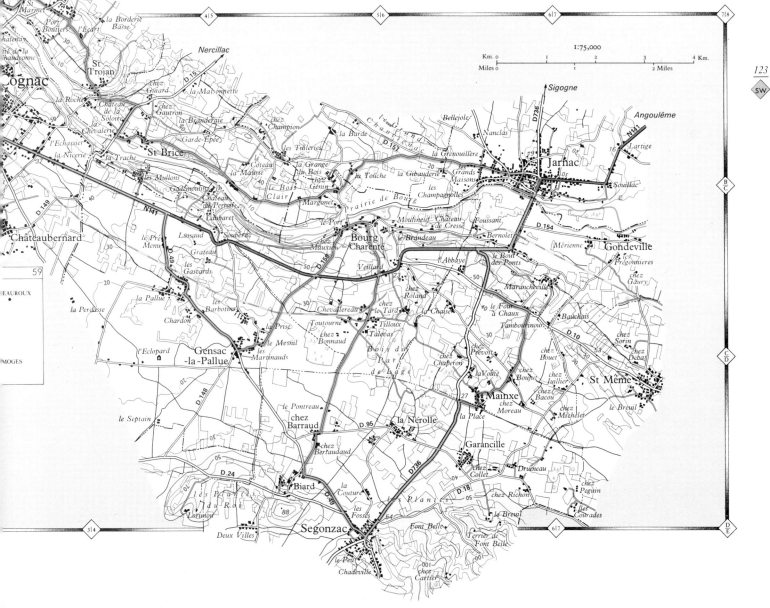

Grey houses with shutters characterize part of Cognac, and roofs are blackened by the fungus that lives on the fumes of the cognac lost to the air during ageing.

Brouage A former harbour with 17th-century walls and seven bastions, built by the military architect Vauban.

Châteauneuf-sur-Charente The bell tower of Bassac abbey is a landmark in the region. The abbey was founded in 1002 but rebuilt in later centuries.

Cognac Many of the well-known cognac houses have their warehouses here. The black fungus on the roofs and walls arises from the evaporation of cognac, stored here in casks by the thousand: the fungus lives on the fumes. The most famous building of the locality is the Château des Valois, also known as Château de Cognac, where King Francis I was born in 1492. The château belongs to the cognac firm of Otard. Visitors can see a vaulted prison chamber (with inscriptions made by British prisoners of war at the end of the 18th century) and there is also a *son et lumière*. Near the château stands the Porte St-Jacques, with its two thick, round towers, where pilgrims to Santiago de Compostela could lodge. Also in Cognac: the part-12th-century church of Saint-Léger has a painting from 1629 by Jacques Blanchard, and the Musée de Cognac has a wine press that dates back to 1760. Rest and shade can be found in the large François 1er park by the river on the northern outskirts of the town.

Crazannes The present Château de Crazannes dates from the 15th century, but it stands on the site of an 11th-century structure, of which the chapel remains.

Le Douhet The bishops of Saintes built the rather austere château here. Beneath it is an 11th-century hall.

Fenioux Next to the partly Romanesque church is the Lanterne des Morts, a funerary tower that can be climbed from inside by a spiral stairway.

Jonzac A 12th- and 13th-century castle (three French kings stayed there at various times).

Marennes Famous for its oysters (there is a diorama of oyster culture).

Meschers-sur-Gironde Prehistoric caves; there is a pleasant restaurant in one of them (see Restaurants).

Pons Medieval town built on a hill; exhibitions are held in the enormous castle keep, built in 1187.

Port d'Envaux The Château de Pauloy is an excellent example of Louis XV architecture; it also includes parts of an older castle. It has a fine dining hall and a dovecot that dates back to 1620.

Rochefort-sur-Mer A former naval town, now a resort. The house of the writer Pierre Loti is its most remarkable sight; among other things it has a Turkish salon. The old ropeyard beside the harbour is now a museum. Rochefort also has a maritime museum with beautiful models of ships, and a Musée des Beaux-Arts.

Royan Devastated in World War II; now a harbour and holiday resort, with the remarkable 20th-century church of Notre-Dame.

St-Cybardeau "Les Bouchauds" is a Gallo-Roman theatre from the 1st century AD; it can seat nearly 10,000 people.

St-Jean-d'Angély A former halt for pilgrims, with half-timbered houses of the 15th and 16th centuries.

St-Fort-le-Né Beside the D44 is one of the region's prehistoric stone dolmens.

St-Porchaire Just north of this village is Château de la Roche Courbon, which the writer Pierre Loti (see Rochefort-sur-Mer above) called "Sleeping Beauty's castle". The 15th-century château contains furniture and paintings and is surrounded by a charming garden. Prehistoric caves nearby can be visited.

Saintes An interesting town with examples of Roman and Romanesque art. The Germanicus arch (by the river Charente) was built by the Romans, and the Roman arena could hold 20,000 people. The Romanesque church of Sainte-Eutrope has a large crypt; the Abbaye aux Dames, with its church of Sainte-Marie is partly 12th, partly 16th century. Saintes also has three museums: archaeology, art and regional history.

WINE ACTIVITIES

The Confrérie du Franc Pineau was established in 1982. Pineau des Charentes is an apéritif made from the juice of white or black grapes and cognac. A *fête des vendanges* is held every year in Cognac, around grape harvest time.

WINE INFORMATION

A number of the cognac houses are happy to show visitors around. Information concerning such visits can be obtained from the Office de Tourisme, Place J.-Monnet, Cognac.

PRODUCERS OF SPECIAL INTEREST

AMBLEVILLE, postcode 16300

d'Ambleville*, De la Voûte*

ANGEAC, postcode 16120

Domaine de Lasdoux

BOURG-CHARENTE, postcode 16200

Cartais-Lanaure

CHÂTEAUNEUF-SUR-CHARENTE, postcode 16120

J.R. Brillet

CLAIX-BLANSAN, postcode 16440

Domaine de Chez Maillard

COGNAC, postcode 16100

Camus, Léopold Gourmel*, A. Hardy, Hennessy, Gaston Delagrange, Martell, Otard, Rémy Martin*

JARNAC, postcode 16200

Courvoisier, Delamain*, Hine

JUILLAC-LE-COQ, postcode 16131

Fillioux Fils*

MOSNAC, postcode 16120

Jean & Dominique Philippon Known for their Très Vieille Réserve and Pineau des Charentes.

ROUILLAC, postcode 16170

Bisquit

ST-DIZANT-DU-GUA, postcode 17240

Château de Beaulon* Noted in particular for its excellent varieties of Pineau des Charentes.

SEGONZAC, postcode 16130

Beau, Frapin, Gourry de Chaudeville

VERDILLE, postcode 16140

Domaine de Guignefolle

▽ The casks so essential for ageing cognac are still largely made by hand.

BERGERAC

The Dordogne might have been expressly designed to attract visitors. It is rich in prehistory – the caves at Lascaux and Les Eyzies-de-Tayac are suitably world famous – and well endowed with impressive châteaux, old fortified villages and medieval strongholds. The countryside ranges from gently undulating green landscapes of orchards and fields of wheat and maize to large stretches where nature is still unspoiled, with dark forests, steep ravines and swift-flowing rivers. Little wonder that the Dordogne – often called Périgord, after the former provincial name – draws crowds of tourists every year.

Winegrowing is concentrated around the town of Bergerac, in the southeast of the département. There has always been fierce competition with Bordeaux; for centuries Bordeaux's merchants tried to exclude the wines of the "hinterland". As Bordeaux was the only port from which the wines could be shipped, one ploy was to stipulate a smaller cask for Bergerac wines because duty was payable not on the quantity of wine exported but on the number of casks. Despite such obstacles, the wines of Bergerac were exported in large quantities. In the seventeenth and eighteenth centuries Holland was the biggest market, taking about half of every vintage.

The wines of that time were mainly white and sweet, a style that has markedly declined in popularity in the second half of this century. Many growers have therefore turned increasingly to red wine: at present, red wine represents about half of production. The grapes used are those of Bordeaux: the two Cabernets, Merlot and some Malbec. Most of the wines are lighter than the average claret from Bordeaux and leave few memorable impressions, but a few growers succeed in making more full-bodied wines which can also have depth and finesse. The best red wines come from the little district of Pécharmant, just northeast of Bergerac; but the Bergerac appellation, and the generally somewhat stronger Côtes de Bergerac, can also produce good reds.

Among the white wines, the drier styles are gaining ground. In particular, those made solely from Sauvignon grapes are often as good as similar wines from Bordeaux. Bergerac Sec is made mainly from Sémillon, Sauvignon and Muscadelle, as is Montravel. Production of semi-sweet white wines is declining. There are five appellations: Côtes de Bergerac, Saussignac (the best quality), Côtes de Montravel, Haut-Montravel and Rosette (which has all but disappeared).

Dominating the sweet white wines is Monbazillac. The district lies due south of Bergerac, up the slopes and along the first hills flanking the Dordogne valley. There is also a village of Monbazillac. The name is apparently derived from Mont Bazailhac, which probably meant "Mountain of Fire" or "Mountain of Gold". Vineyards had already been planted here in the eleventh century and the fame of Monbazillac wine even reached Rome. In the sixteenth century two pilgrims, mentioning the name Monbazillac, are said to have heard the pope mutter "vinum bonum" (good wine). Later, French ambassadors served Monbazillac as a "wine of peace", and Talleyrand introduced it at the Congress of Vienna.

Despite its almost legendary reputation, the demand for Monbazillac declined so dramatically after World War II that the appellation almost disappeared. Only through measures taken in the 1970s, such as limiting the production per hectare, was the quality rescued and Monbazillac made a hesitant comeback. The local cooperative, which is now responsible for the wine of Château Monbazillac, played a key role in this revival.

A good Monbazillac is akin to Sauternes. The grape varieties are the same: Sémillon, Sauvignon and Muscadelle; and harvesting is left as late as possible to take advantage of overripeness and "noble rot". But in luxury, sweetness and concentration, Monbazillac is no longer a rival to the best Sauternes; and the *rôti* aroma so characteristic of genuine Sauternes is much less distinct. Most Monbazillacs are therefore not rich enough to accompany sweet desserts. On the other hand they taste delicious with *foie gras* (one of the Dordogne's most celebrated specialities), with fish or poultry served with a sweet sauce, with nuts (in the Dordogne, walnuts), with not-too-sweet cake or – in the French manner – chilled, as an apéritif. They also often have a formidable capacity to mature in bottle.

Bergerac, on the Dordogne, merits a visit for its picturesque streets as well as for its three museums – including a museum of wine – and for the Maison du Vin with its old vaulted cellars.

TRAVEL INFORMATION

The Dordogne has two supreme specialities: *foie gras* and truffles. Dishes containing them are listed on many menus, and goose and duck are also used in all kinds of recipes. The district is also famous for its walnuts, used for making superb oil and liqueurs, and – more recently – for its strawberries.

HOTELS

Hotel de Bordeaux, 38 Place Gambetta, 24100 Bergerac, tel. 53 57 12 83. Family-run provincial hotel; in fine weather you can eat in the garden or on the terrace. Class B.
Hotel La Flambée, Route de Périgueux, 24100 Bergerac, tel. 53 57 52 33. Comfortable country hotel with a large park, swimming pool and restaurant. Class B.

Hotel de la France, 18 Place Gambetta, 24100 Bergerac, tel. 53 57 11 61. Modern furniture and fittings. Class B.
Château Mounet-Sully, Route de Mussidan, 24100 Bergerac, tel. 53 57 04 21. About 2 km from Bergerac; a genuine château with modern rooms. Class B.
Hotel du Château, 24150 Lalinde, tel. 53 61 01 82. A small château by the river, with terrace. Regional cuisine. *Demi-pension* is obligatory in season. Class B.
La Forge, 24150 Lalinde, tel. 53 24 92 24. Comparatively new hotel and restaurant. Lalinde is about 20 km (12½ miles) west of Bergerac on the river Dordogne. Class B.
Relais de la Diligence, 24240 Monbazillac, tel. 53 58 30 48. Small

hotel near the D933 to Eymet, with a fine view over the Dordogne valley. Restaurant. Class B.

Manoir Le Grand Vignoble, 24140 St-Julien-de-Crempse, tel. 53 57 92 44. Luxurious complex about 12 km (7½ miles) north of Bergerac, on the D107, with a large park and a swimming pool. Hotel class A; restaurant class B.

Relais de Saussignac, 24240 Saussignac, tel. 53 27 92 08. Friendly village hotel, surrounded by vineyards. Fully adequate, if sometimes slightly noisy, rooms and strictly regional cuisine. Hotel class B; restaurant class C.

RESTAURANTS

Le Cyrano, 2 Boulevard Montaigne, 24100 Bergerac, tel. 53 57 02 76. Bergerac's best restaurant with distinctive regional cuisine. There is usually a choice of three menus and a good selection of local wines. Class B.

La Grappe d'Or, 24240 Monbazillac, tel. 53 28 27 67. In the hamlet of La Peyrat: from Bergerac take the D933 to Eymet and turn right at the first hill. Regional cooking in a somewhat rustic setting. Class B.

Château de Monbazillac, 24240 Monbazillac, tel. 53 58 38 93. Visitors to the château can eat in the restaurant here. Sustaining regional dishes. Class C.

La Closerie St-Jacques, 24240 Monbazillac, tel. 53 58 37 77. Small restaurant; fresh fish and *escalope de foie de canard* are specialities. Economy lunch menu on weekdays. Class B.

Auberge Lou Peyrol, 24510 St-Marcel-du-Perigord, tel. 53 61 04 78. St-Marcel is some 20 km (12½ miles) from Bergerac on the D32, through extremely beautiful countryside. A friendly restaurant and regional dishes. Meals are served on the terrace in fine weather. Class C.

La Vieille Grange, 24520 St-Nexans, tel. 53 24 32 21. Stylish farm restaurant in the hamlet of La Petite Forêt, on the D19 to St-Nexans (still marked St-Naixent on the map). A peaceful place for a splendid meal. Class B.

PLACES OF INTEREST

Bergerac Bustling provincial town with an atmospheric old centre where there is a museum of wine and inland waterways, an interesting museum of tobacco (with local history department), and a museum of religious art. The town hall is a former convent dating from the 18th century. The Maison du Vin faces the little harbour.

Carsac-de-Curson Ruins of a feudal castle and a Romanesque church.

Les Eyzies-de-Tayac A visit to this village makes a most interesting day trip: there are world-famous prehistoric caves and also the French national museum of prehistory. If you follow the little river Vézère northwards, 25 km (15½ miles) on you reach Montignac where there is a replica of the Lascaux cave with its renowned animal paintings, Lascaux itself being shut for conservation reasons.

Le Fleix There is a large cooperative in the village and a street of ancient houses, the Rue des Canons.

Lalinde A former fortified village.

Lamothe-Montravel There used to be many coopers' shops here. A tower, the remains of the old archbishop's palace, is used as the *mairie*.

Lanquais The large Château de Lanquais, surrounded by woods, was built between the 14th and 16th centuries. Inside there is period furniture.

Malfourat South of Bergarac and the highest point of the locality, with a superb view of the surrounding countryside. A restored windmill allows you to climb still higher.

Monbazillac Château de Monbazillac is the showpiece of the region, a handsome 16th-century fortress that now functions as a museum. You can buy Château de Monbazillac wine at the entrance: it is a good idea to take advantage of this, for the wine is sold almost nowhere else.

Montastruc Château de Montastruc, rebuilt in classical style.

Montcaret Gallo-Roman excavations, with a splendid mosaic.

Montpeyroux Château de Montecoulon and the adjoining church are worth visiting.

Montréal Castle from the 11th–16th centuries and the remarkable Sainte-Epine chapel.

St-Michel-de-Montaigne The essayist Montaigne was born at Château Michel de Montaigne in 1533. The Tour de la Librairie where he wrote is still intact, but the rest of the château was destroyed by fire in 1885 and subsequently rebuilt. It is owned by the Mähler-Besse négociant family of Bordeaux, co-owners of Château Palmer. Wine is still made at the château.

Saussignac Wine village with Château de Saussignac, a vast building surrounded by cedars 200 years old, best viewed from the west side. It is gradually being restored.

Vélines The wine capital of the Montravel district. The church is a historic monument.

WINE ACTIVITIES

In Sigoulès the *foire aux vins* normally takes place in the third weekend in July; at Cénac (a village south of Sarlat-la-Canéda) there is a wine fair during the second weekend in August.

Le Consulat de la Vinée de Bergerac has been in existence since 1954, modelled on a similar association of 700 years ago.

WINE INFORMATION

Bergerac's Maison du Vin merits a visit not only for the information you can obtain and the wines you can sample, but also for its location: in the Cloître des Récollets, a 17th- and 18th-century monastery in the heart of the old town. In the wine districts there is a signposted *route des vins*.

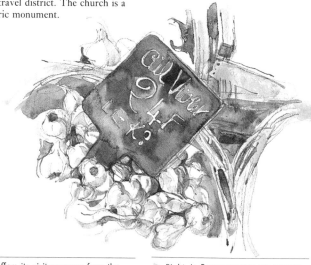

Bergerac, in the heart of the lush Dordogne, offers its visitors game from the countryside and fish and shellfish from the nearby Atlantic. The region glories in its truffles, its geese and ducks — and its garlic. Preserved goose meat (*confit*) and *magret de canard* (duck breast) are also specialities.

Right: In Bergerac you can savour the peace and quiet of the French countryside even in summer. The green spaces gently absorb the many tourists.

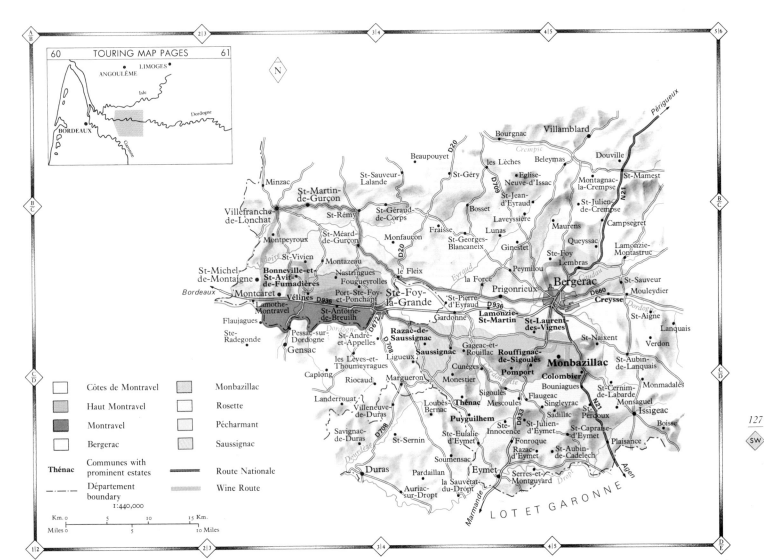

PRODUCERS OF SPECIAL INTEREST

BERGERAC/PECHARMANT,
postcode 24100, 127 C5

Chartreuse de Peyrelevade,
Domaine du Haut-Pécharmant

BONNEVILLE, postcode 24230, 127 C3

Château du Bloy

COLOMBIER, postcode 24560, 127 D5

Château La Jaubertie*

CREYSSE, postcode 24100, 127 C5

Château de Tiregand*

LE FLEIX, postcode 24130, 127 C4

Domaine de la Vaure Run by the
local cooperative.

FOUGEYROLLES, postcode 33220,
127 C3

Château Bonnières, Château de
Masburel

LAMONZIE-ST-MARTIN,
postcode 24130, 127 C4

Domaine Constant

MONBAZILLAC, postcode 24240,
127 C5

Château La Borderie, Cave
Coopérative, Château
Monbazillac*, Château Poulvère,
Château Theulet, Château du
Treuil de Nailhac*, Vieux
Vignoble du Repaire*

MONTPEYROUX, postcode 24610,
127 C3

Domaine de Fonfrède

POMPORT, postcode 24240, 127 C4

Château La Brie (via the Cave
Coopérative), Château du Chayne,
Château Le Fagé, Château Pion
(via the Cave Coopérative), Château
Septy (via the Cave Coopérative)

RAZAC-DE-SAUSSIGNAC,
postcode 24240, 127 C4

Château Court-Les-Mûts*

ROUFFIGNAC, postcode 24240,
127 C4

Château Le Caillou

ST-LAURENT-DES-VIGNES,
postcode 24100, 127 C4

Domaine Theylet Marsalet,
UNIDOR

ST-MEARD-DE-GURCON,
postcode 24160, 127 C3

Domaine du Gouyat*

ST-MICHEL-DE-MONTAIGNE,
postcode 24230, 127 C3

Château Michel de Montaigne*

SIGOULES, postcode 24240, 127 D4

Coopérative, Château Le Mayne

THENAC, postcode 24240, 127 D4

Château Caillevet, Château de
Panisseau*, Château Thénac

LOT-ET-GARONNE

The green landscape, mild climate and soft light of Lot-et-Garonne once put Stendhal in mind of Tuscany. There are indeed landscapes in this département, which largely corresponds with ancient Agenais, which are reminiscent of Italy. The scenery is varied: in the east it is hilly and a large part of the west is woodland, with in between the broad flat valley of the Garonne, fed by its many tributaries including the Lot. These streams, flowing down from the Massif Central, have brought a good deal of fertile soil down to Lot-et-Garonne, ideal for growing fruit and vegetables.

Because the Garonne valley forms the most convenient corridor, the region has always provided an important link between the Atlantic and the Mediterranean and it has a rich history, with many old towns and villages, castles and churches. The history of its wine, though, is brief. Only since the 1970s have four districts acquired an as yet modest renown. From north to south they are the Côtes de Duras, Côtes du Marmandais, Buzet and the Côtes du Brulhois.

The Côtes de Duras takes its name from the little hill town of Duras, which is just short of the Gironde département boundary – and the Bordeaux appellation. Its wines therefore show a strong resemblance to those of Bordeaux, the more so since the same grape varieties are used. The most interesting Côtes de Duras is the white wine made from Sauvignon. This can be fresh, fragrant, with sound balance, and was pioneered by the Duras cooperative. The cooperative also makes a fruity, supple style of red for drinking earlier than the average Bordeaux.

The town of Marmande is about 20 kilometres (12½ miles) south of Duras, on the Garonne. Here wine growing takes place on both sides of the broad valley. More than 95 percent of production comes from two cooperatives; the better of the two is at Cocumont, which has modern equipment and experiments continuously with new grape varieties. Almost all Côtes du Marmandais wine is red. Up to now it has mostly been a fairly light, reasonably supple wine, rather lacking in personality and intended for everyday consumption.

At Buzet (formerly the Côtes de Buzet) a single cooperative processes some 95 percent of the harvest from the scattered vineyards, using modern methods and then maturing the red wine in oak in the traditional way. All the casks – more than 5,000 – are made by the cooperative's own cooper. Buzet's red wine is closely related to that of Bordeaux, but is rather more accessible and has a little less finesse. Thanks to the sound quality and very reasonable prices of its wine, the area of vineyard in this extensive district of 27 communes has increased steadily and continuing growth is forecast. (The vineyards intermingle with those of Armagnac, as the map makes clear. Much of the appellation is also in the Haut-Armagnac zone, and a portion overlaps with one of the other Armagnac districts, Ténarèze). The standard of the wine, too, has been improving, particularly since the cooperative has been vinifying wines from some of the member châteaux separately, according to grape variety. Château de Gueyze is usually very successful. The top wine is Baron d'Ardeuil (formerly Cuvée Napoléon) from selected grapes from the best vineyards in the district.

Like Buzet, the Côtes du Brulhois lie on the south bank of the Garonne, around the valley of the Gers and not far from Agen. The Goulens-en-Brulhois cooperative dominates production. The wines, mainly red, are fresh, simple and drunk mainly in the region itself.

TRAVEL INFORMATION

Marmande is renowned for its tomatoes, but asparagus, peaches, plums, melons and other fruit and vegetables are also grown. Agen is famed for its prunes which, like its fresh plums, appear in many recipes.

HOTELS

Atlantic Hotel, 133 Avenue Jean-Jaurès, 47000 Agen, tel. 53 96 16 56. A modern business hotel: not much atmosphere but well equipped. Class B.
Résidence des Jacobins, Place des Jacobins, 47000 Agen, tel. 53 47 03 31. Despite its central position, a quiet hotel with atmosphere. Class B.
Hotel Le Quercy, Rue de la Grande-Horloge, 47000 Agen, tel. 53 66 35 49. Pleasant family business where great care is taken with the cooking. Hotel class B; restaurant class C.
Hotel de la Tour, 47220 Astaffort, tel. 53 67 11 96. Small, quiet, pleasant hotel, with a park and a restaurant. The village is south of Agen. Class C.
Savary, 47120 Baleyssagues, tel. 53 83 77 82. Small, very peacefully situated and hospitable hotel with a pool and a view from the terrace. In the evening you can dine beside a medieval fireplace. The village is just west of Duras. Class B.

Hostellerie des Ducs, 47120 Duras, tel. 53 83 74 58. Comfortable, with a good restaurant. Class B.
Le Capricorne, Route d'Agen, 47200 Marmande, tel. 53 64 16 14. Modern-style hotel and restaurant with garden and pool. Class B.
Auberge de Guyenne, 19 Rue Martignac, 47200 Marmande, tel. 53 64 01 77. Peaceful hotel with restaurant. Class C.

RESTAURANTS

l'Absinthe, 29bis Rue Voltaire, 47000 Agen, tel. 53 66 16 94. Convivial bistro with lunchtime *plats du jour* and specialities such as *tarte aux poireaux* (leeks) and turbot. Class B.
Le Voltaire, 36 Rue Voltaire, 47000 Agen, tel. 53 47 27 01. A good bistro, in a 16th-century building. Menu includes *magret de canard au cassis*. Class B.
Les Cygnes, Route de Villeneuve, 47190 Aiguillon, tel. 53 79 60 02. Attractive place to stay at and to dine, with a garden and terrace. Class B.
La Table de Cœur, 47240 Bon-Encontre, tel. 53 96 10 73. Excellent restaurant in a little place east of Agen. Charming interior with flowers and imaginative dishes, such as salmon with crayfish. Class A.
La Corne d'Or, 47450 Colayrac-St-Cirq, tel. 53 47 02 76. A few kilometres west of Agen, by the Garonne. Classical and contemporary

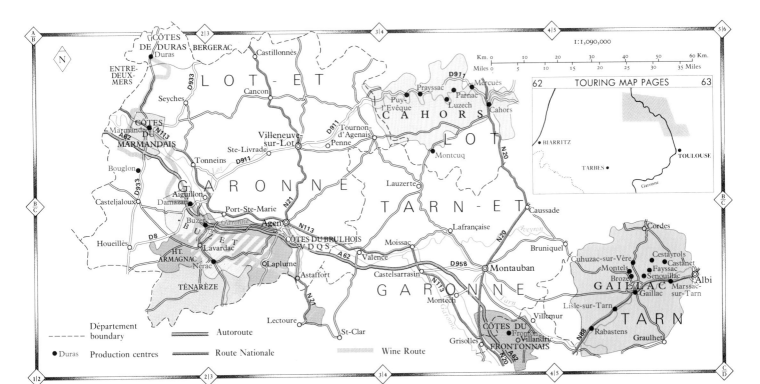

Département boundary | **Autoroute**

●Duras **Production centres** | **Route Nationale** | **Wine Route**

cuisine. Also a hotel. Class B.
Auberge du Château, 47120 Duras,
tel. 53 83 70 58. Simple, honest
regional dishes; also a hotel. Class C.
Auberge des Quatre Vents, 47190
Lagarrigue (east of Aiguillon), tel.
53 79 62 18. Situated high above the
hamlet, with a fine view. Large
terrace. Try the salads; also agreeable
local wines. Class C.
La Chaumière d'Albert, Route de
Nérac, 47230 Laverdac, tel.
53 65 51 75. Generous helpings of
regional dishes at agreeable prices.
Large garden and also a terrace.
Class C.
Auberge du Moulin d'Ané, 47200
Virazeil, tel. 53 20 18 25. In an old
mill; serves both grills and more
sophisticated dishes. The village is
just east of Marmande. Class B.

PLACES OF INTEREST

Agen The Quartier des Cornières,
the old district by the cathedral of St
Capras, is picturesque and full of
atmosphere. The Musée Municipale
des Beaux-Arts has paintings by
Goya and a Greek marble Venus.
Damazan The "town of a hundred
towers".
Duras The local château dates from
the 14th century and is now a
museum, with many wine exhibits. It
gives a panoramic view over the
Dropt valley. Duras itself has several
old buildings, including a 13th-
century gate with a clock.
Marmande Church of Notre-Dame
(part 13th century) with a view from
its cloisters.
Le Mas d'Agenais Village of Roman

origin. In the 12th-century church
(ask the priest for the key) there is an
early Rembrandt, "The Crucifixion".
In front of the church are 16th-
century wooden market halls.
Monteton Hill village in the Duras
area with a splendid view: in good
weather you can see 13 village church
towers.
Nérac Well-known little town south
of Buzet, with a Renaissance château,
partly destroyed in 1793, which is
now a museum. Beside the Garonne
is the old quarter of Petit-Nérac.
Vianne Still largely ringed by its
13th century defensive walls. The
church is pure Romanesque.
Xaintrailles A partly 15th-century
castle in the middle of the village.
Ponton de Xaintrailles, Joan of Arc's
companion, was born here.

WINE ACTIVITIES

There is usually a *foire aux vins* in
Duras in the second half of July. In
Buzet the Confrérie du Vin de Buzet
is active.

WINE INFORMATION

Not many tourists go to see the
smaller wine growers of Lot-et-
Garonne so visitors are usually very
welcome. The cooperatives, too, are
pleased to have you taste their wines
and you can also buy bottles from
them.

PRODUCERS OF SPECIAL INTEREST

COTES DU BRULHOIS, 129 C3

GOULENS-EN-BRULHOIS,
postcode 47390

Cave Coopérative

BUZET, 129 C2

AMBRUS, postcode 47160

Château de Padère*

BUZET SUR BAISE, postcode 47610

Cave Coopérative*

COTES DE DURAS, 129 A2

DURAS, postcode 47120

Cave Coopérative*

ESCLOTTES, postcode 47120

Domaine de Ferrant*, Jean
Paquier, Château Les Savignattes

LANDERROUAT, postcode 37390

Cave Coopérative

ST-COLOMBE, postcode 47120

Domaine des Cours*

ST-JEAN-DE-DURAS, postcode 47120

Domaine de Durand

COTES DU MARMANDAIS, 129 B2

BEAUPUY, postcode 47200

Cave Coopérative

COCUMONT, postcode 47250

Cave Coopérative

ST-MICHEL-DE-LAPUJADE,
postcode 33190

Domaine des Geais*

CAHORS

The ancient town of Cahors, founded by the Gauls, occupies a spectacular site in a loop of the river Lot. Cahors used to be not only an important trading place but also one of Europe's banking centres, making loans in the thirteenth century to kings and even to the pope. It also had a university for some 400 years, founded in 1332 by Pope John XII who was born in the town and had Cahors wine delivered to his palace at Avignon. By this time the district's winemaking tradition was already old: documents suggest that Cahors wine has been made since at least the seventh century.

For hundreds of years the wine enjoyed such an excellent reputation that King Francis I tried to imitate it at Fontainebleau, using vines imported from the region. In the mid-nineteenth century the Lot département – of which Cahors is the capital – had nearly 60,000 hectares (148,000 acres) of vineyards. After this a decline set in. Plant diseases and economic problems caused an enormous reduction in both quantity and quality, and many growers gave up. As far as wine was concerned, Cahors simply disappeared.

Recovery did not begin until after World War II and was due largely to the energetic cooperative at Parnac. At first the cooperative, set up in 1947, could only check further decline, but the great frost of 1956 forced a change of direction. At the urging of the cooperative the devastated vineyards were largely replanted with Auxerrois (the Cahors name for Malbec, also known, confusingly, as Cot). This grape variety thrives on the rugged limestone plateaux, the *causses*, found on either side of the Lot. The sand and gravel terraces of the Lot valley are also excellent for growing Auxerrois.

The new plantings brought about marked improvement in the quality of the wines and in 1971 Cahors was given its appellation contrôlée.

Almost half the growers are affiliated to the Parnac cooperative, but there are also many flourishing individual estates. These produce the best wines. The classic Cahors is dark red, almost opaque. The "black wines" of Cahors were legendary; and today a number of growers are consciously striving to achieve this deep hue. A good, classic Cahors is also distinguished by an intense taste rich in tannin. The Auxerrois – a legal minumum of 70 percent of the grapes must be of this variety – gives a basically austere, reserved wine. This is why it is often given more roundness by the addition of a proportion of Merlot.

As well as the traditional "black" Cahors that demands patience, the district is also producing lighter wines, less concentrated and less full of character, which can readily be drunk after a couple of years or so.

▼ The Lot is one of the most deeply rural districts of France. Less well known and thus quieter than the Dordogne to the north, it repays a leisurely visit.

TRAVEL INFORMATION

The truffles and *foie gras* of Cahors are famous and feature a good deal in the restaurants. A market for both is held on Saturdays in the town of Cahors from the beginning of November to the end of March. *Ecrevisses* (freshwater crayfish) also appear on a number of menus.

HOTELS

Hotel de la Bourse, 7 Place Tousseau, 46000 Cahors, tel. 65 35 17 78. Fairly old place with its own restaurant. Class C.
Hotel de l'Escargot, 5 Boulevard Gambetta, 46000 Cahors, tel. 65 35 07 66. Simple and decent. Class C.
France, 252 Avenue Jean-Jaurès, 46000 Cahors, tel. 65 35 16 76. Somewhat colourless but comfortable modern hotel, not far from the station. Class B.
Terminus, 5 Avenue Charles-de-Freycinet, 46000 Cahors, tel. 65 35 24 50. Provincial hotel; the excellent restaurant is separate (see Le Balandre below). Class B.
Wilson, 72 Rue Président-Wilson, 46000 Cahors, tel. 65 35 41 80. A luxurious middle-of-the-range modern hotel. Class B.
Relais des Champs, 46140 Caillac, tel. 65 30 92 35. A hotel complex to which **Chez Nadal** also belongs, surrounded by vineyards. The Relais has rooms with small kitchens; Chez Nadal (*demi-pension* is obligatory in season) has a good regional restaurant. Class A/B.
Château de Mercuès, 46090 Mercuès, tel. 65 20 00 01. A château hotel high up on a rock, with a park and swimming pool. Very expensive. The restaurant serves *oeufs brouillés*

aux truffes and other delicious dishes.

The same owner, a wine grower (Château de Haute-Serre in Cieurac), also has the neighbouring **Les Cèdres** hotel where prices are a little lower and the facilities slightly simpler – but both establishments are class A.
Hotel Bellevue, Place de la Truffière, 46700 Puy-l'Evêque, tel. 65 21 30 70. A good view and dependable country cooking. Class B.
Moulin de la Source Bleue, 46700 Touzac, tel. 65 36 52 01. In a 14th-century watermill; also a restaurant. Class B.

RESTAURANTS

Le Balandre, 5 Avenue Charles-de-Freycinet, 46000 Cahors, tel. 65 35 01 97. Connected to the Terminus hotel; the style is *fin de siècle*, the cooking talented and contemporary. Class B.
Le Fénelon, 4 Place Imbert, 46000 Cahors, tel. 65 35 32 38. Nostalgic restaurant in the centre of the old town. Try the fresh fish and the quail. Class C.
Restaurant de la Préfecture, 22 Rue de la Préfecture, 46000 Cahors, tel. 65 35 12 54. Many regular customers, thanks to the excellent value. Class C.
La Taverne, 1 Rue J.B. Delpech, 46000 Cahors, tel. 65 35 28 66. Strictly regional: the *truffe en croustade* here is famous. Extensive wine list. Class B.
Marco, 46000 Lamagdelaine, tel. 65 35 30 64. One of the best restaurants of the region, in a remarkable vaulted dining hall. A very good selection of wines. Class B.
Le Gindreau, 46150 St-Médard, tel. 65 36 22 27. A dependable inn 15 km (9½ miles) from Cahors, just off the D911. A speciality is *foie gras de canard chaud aux cèpes*. Class B.

PLACES OF INTEREST

Château de Bonaguil A stronghold of enormous dimensions – one of the largest in France. The partly ruined structure dates back to the 13th century.
Cabrerets This village lies outside the actual wine district, about 30 km (19 miles) east of Cahors, but it has the prehistoric Pech-Merle cave in which human handprints as well as wall paintings of animals can be seen.
Cahors The town is full of history and splendid old buildings – ask at the Office de Tourisme at 12 Boulevard Clemenceau for a plan of the town showing the main points of interest. There is also a pleasant walk up to the viewpoint on Mont St-Cyr,

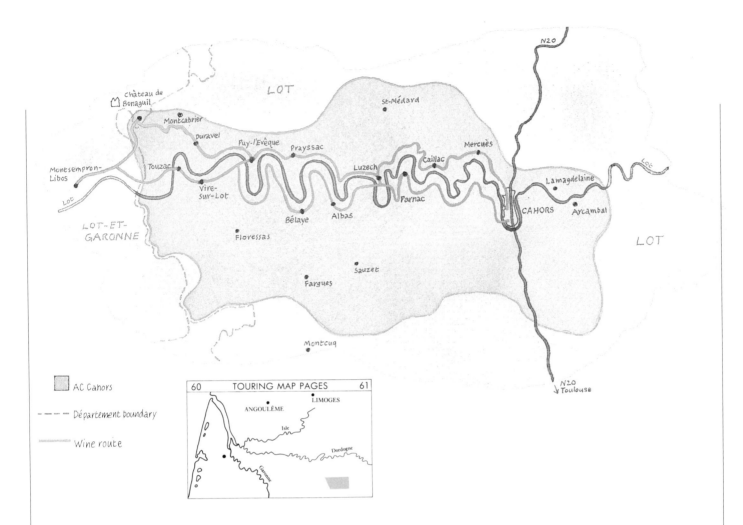

AC Cahors

---- Département boundary

Wine route

| 60 | TOURING MAP PAGES | 61 |

the hill directly to the south of Cahors.

Luzech This village set in a bend in the Lot has a museum of prehistory and of the Gallo-Roman period, with many objects excavated locally. The keep of a feudal castle is a landmark. Near Luzech is the 17th-century Château de Caix, which belongs to the Danish royal family.

Martignac A hamlet north of Puy-l'Evêque. The church has 16th-century frescos.

◁ Left: The Pont Valentre, Cahors.

▽ Below: View of the oldest part of Cahors, from Mont St-Cyr.

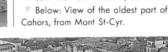

Montcabrier This village was fortified in the 13th century and has a fine church.

Puy-l'Evêque An important wine community, formerly a fortified town: the central tower gives a view over the surrounding district and the old houses in the centre.

Sauzet A truffle market is held here on Thursdays from December to March.

WINE ACTIVITIES

Vire-sur-Lot celebrates the Fête des Vins de Cahors at the end of July. The region's fraternity is La Confrérie du Vin de Cahors.

WINE INFORMATION

In Cahors, which is not overrun by tourists, the wine growers are generally happy to welcome visitors. The cooperative at Parnac is also well worth a visit.

PRODUCERS OF SPECIAL INTEREST

ALBAS, postcode 46140

Prieuré de Cénac*: Impressive wine bottled by Rigal & Fils at Château de St-Didier-Parnac in Parnac.

BAGAT-EN-QUERCY, postcode 46800

Domaine de Quattre

BOVILA-FARGUES, postcode 46800

Domaine de Bovila

CIEURAC, postcode 46003

Château de Haute-Serre: The owner also has Château de Mercuès, the luxury hotel and restaurant.

DOUELLE, postcode 46140

Domaine du Pic

FLORESSAS, postcode 46700

Château de Chambert*

PARNAC, postcode 46140

Cave Coopérative, Château de St-Didier-Parnac*

PRAYSSAC, postcode 46220

André Bouloumie, Métairie Grande du Théron

PUY-L'EVEQUE, postcode 46700

Clos des Batuts, Domaine de la Caminade, Château du Cayron*, Clos La Coutale, Clos du Gamot, Domaine de la Pineraie, Clos Triguedina*

GAILLAC

To the west of the lovely town of Albi, the capital of the Tarn département, lies Gaillac, one of the largest and most productive wine districts of southwest France. It takes in at least 73 communes, and vines have probably been grown here for almost 20 centuries. The district takes its name from the little town on the right bank of the river Tarn where Benedictine monks became established in the tenth century. As elsewhere in France, viticulture flourished under their care. Gaillac wines were already being exported in the twelfth century, and from the fourteenth century their authenticity was guaranteed by the cock (from the town's coat of arms) branded on the barrels. This was why Gaillac wines were long known as *vins du coq*.

For a variety of reasons Gaillac winemaking was in serious decline from the mid-nineteenth to the mid-twentieth century. One cause was the dwindling demand for sweet wine, in which Gaillac had specialized. But during the 1960s with some energetic producers (including cooperatives) in the lead, a start was made planting black grapes, mostly of strictly local varieties, for the production of red and rosé wines. At its best, the red is a fairly rustic wine with a pleasant perfume, a full-flavoured taste, hints of fruit and a good deal of tannin, but there are also lighter wines including some *vins de primeur*: Gaillac red comes in many styles. This is true to an even greater extent of the white wines. There are four main categories: dry; semi-sweet; sweet (with Gaillac Premières Côtes as a superior version, from eight communes); and *perlé* (slightly sparkling). In addition the district produces two types of (fully) sparkling wine – a dry wine made by the *méthode champenoise* and a semi-sweet *méthode gaillaçoise* (in which fermentation is interrupted and then continues in bottle). As every producer makes his own versions of the various kinds, the resulting picture is too complex for convenient survey. This may be why exports have been slow. Locally, however, the wines are drunk with great enthusiasm. The better restaurants in particular often carry an exciting selection.

Directly west of Gaillac, between Montauban and Toulouse, is a relatively young appellation, the Côtes du Frontonnais. The district was given its appellation contrôlée in 1975 – although as early as 1119 a papal document was full of praise for wine from the "Négret", known today as the Négrette. This local grape needs plenty of sun and is vulnerable to rain, so it thrives in the sunny, dry climate that characterizes the Côtes. A cooperative is active in the district as well as a large number of small growers (a second cooperative, at Villaudric, has had to close because of financial problems). The bulk of the red wines can be drunk early and are characterized by soft fruitiness, but there are also wines for laying down, with more colour, strength and tannin. If the wine comes from specified communes, "Fronton" or "Villaudric" can be added to the label. The district takes its name from the old village of Fronton, recognizable from a long way off by the square redbrick tower of its church.

Northwest of the Côtes du Frontonnais is the small wine district of Lavilledieu. The Négrette is planted here, too, with other mainly local varieties. The cooperative at La Ville-Dieu-du-Temple controls production. Red Lavilledieu wine comes somewhere between a simple Bordeaux and a Côtes du Rhône and is restricted to the area around nearby Montauban.

Also of local importance but unknown elsewhere are the wines from the Aveyron département, which has three tiny districts among its mountains, valleys and ravines. The Marcillac district lies northwest of the old town of Rodez; Estaing and Entraygues-et-du-Fel, farther north, can only be reached by way of extraordinarily narrow twisting roads over hills or through river valleys. With some 150 hectares (370 acres) Marcillac is the biggest of the districts; Estaing and Entraygues-et-du-Fel together have only one seventh of this area. The wines are mainly red and generally rather rough: they go well with the rugged natural beauty of Aveyron – and with the Roquefort cheese made in this département.

Right and top of page 133: In the mountainous region north of Gaillac, the river Aveyron, a tributary of the Tarn, flows through the département of that name, between lovely wooded banks as well as wild ravines.

TRAVEL INFORMATION

This part of the French southwest is famed for its *cassoulet*, a rich meat and bean stew for which there are various recipes. *Foie gras* and *confits* also appear regularly on menus, and in the markets the stalls are piled high with the vegetables and fruit of the region.

HOTELS

AVEYRON

La Truyère, 12140 Entraygues-sur-Truyère, tel. 65 44 51 10. The river Truyère is close by. Garden terrace and restaurant. Class B.
Aux Armes d'Estaing, 12190 Estaing, tel. 65 44 70 02. Typical provincial hotel. Class C.

FRONTONNAIS

Villa Les Pins, 31340 Vacquiers, tel. 61 84 96 04. Peaceful, in the middle of woods. Comfortable rooms, good restaurant. Class B.

GAILLAC

Le Vieux Cordes, Rue Voltaire, 81170 Cordes, tel. 63 56 00 12. In a centuries-old building; has the same owner as the restaurant Le Grand Ecuyer in the same street. Class B.
La Réserve, 81000 Fonvialane, tel. 63 60 79 79. Prestige hotel beautifully situated a few kilometres outside Albi, on the D606 to Cordes. Swimming pool. The restaurant is recommended. Class A.
l'Occitan, 81600 Gaillac, tel. 63 57 11 52. Adequate but not very large hotel. Class B.
Auberge des Bartes, 81600 Técou, tel. 63 33 02 43. Simple place to stay at and to eat in, southeast of Gaillac. Class C.

RESTAURANTS

AVEYRON

Restaurant La Gare, 12330 Nuces, tel. 65 72 60 20. Modern restaurant some 5 km (3 miles) west of Marcillac-Vallon. Also a hotel. The cooking is good and you can buy regional products here. Class B.

FRONTONNAIS AND LAVILLEDIEU

La Feuilleraie Lacourtensourt 31140 Aucamville, tel. 61 70 16 01.

Noted for its service, cooking and agreeably priced menus. Class C.
Le St-Porquier, 82700 St-Porquier, tel. 63 64 76 55. Has a terrace – and marvellous *cassoulet*. Class C.
Auberge de la Braise, 31340 Villematier, tel. 61 35 35 64. Menu includes *cassoulet* and grills. Covered terrace. Class B.

La Ferme de Bernadou, 31340 Villemur-sur-Tarn, tel. 61 09 02 38. A country inn with pleasant local wines. Class B.

GAILLAC

Hostellerie St-Antoine/Mapotel, Rue St-Antonin, 81000 Albi, tel. 63 54 04 04. Stylish, with an indoor garden. Also a comfortable hotel. Restaurant class B; hotel class A.
Le Grand Ecuyer, Rue Voltaire, 81170 Cordes, tel. 63 56 01 03. Almost worth a detour just for its desserts. Other dishes are also delicious and the wine list offers a rich choice. Class A.
La Taverne de Mordagne, Rue St-Michel, 81170 Cordes, tel. 63 56 13 64. For a cheap lunch. Class C.
Hostellerie du Parc, Route de St-Antonin, 81170 Cordes, tel. 63 56 02 59. Excellently prepared dishes with a local accent, such as *lapin aux choux*. Also a hotel, surrounded by a park. Class B.
Le Vieux Cordes, Rue de la République, 81170 Cordes, tel. 63 56 00 12. Restaurant and hotel, with a garden. One of the specialities is *foie gras de Gaillac*. Class B.
Le Vigneron, 81600 Gaillac, tel. 63 57 07 20. On the N88, just out of

the town in a westerly direction. Good value. Class C.
Francis Cardaillac/Le Tilbury, 81150 Marssac-sur-Tarn, tel. 63 55 41 90. One of the best restaurants of the region, by the river Tarn, with a swimming pool and also a *vinothèque* where local wines are served. Class B.
Hostellerie du Pré-Vert, 81800 Rabastens-sur-Tarn, tel. 63 33 70 51. Also a hotel, in an 18th-century building with a garden and terrace. Restaurant class C; hotel class B.
Auberge de St-Caprais, 81800 St-Caprais, tel. 63 33 83 32. A roomy inn just north of Rabastens, on the D18. Choose regional dishes such as *confit de canard*. Class C.

PLACES OF INTEREST

AVEYRON

Entraygues-sur-Truyère Delightful village between the river Truyère and the Lot, where the rare red Vin d'Entraygues-et-du-Fel is made.
Estaign Picturesque old village on the river Lot, around a granite outcrop on which stands an imposing 15th- to 16th-century castle. Nearby are the spectacular Gorges du Lot.
Marcillac-Vallon A fortified village and the centre of Marcillac wine production. Aveyron's only cooperative is here.

FRONTONNAIS

Fronton The church, with houses clustered around it, has a decorated vaulted roof.
Grisolles Museum of regional art and costume.

GAILLAC

Albi Just outside the wine area but well worth visiting. Near the imposing cathedral is the house where the painter Henri de Toulouse-Lautrec was born: a unique collection

of his works is exhibited in the old Palais de la Berbie.
Castelnau-de-Montmirail Romantic part 15th-century castle, the Château du Cayla.
Cordes Medieval hill village and one of the greatest attractions in this part of France. It dates from 1222 and has been splendidly restored. The church tower gives a fine view.
Gaillac Has the church of St-Michel (11th to 13th century); the Parc de Foncaud, laid out by Le Nôtre (of Versailles fame); and a wine museum (in the Tour Pierre de Brens).
Labastide-de-Lévis A 12th-century fortified town, or *bastide*.
Lisle-sur-Tarn Also once fortified, as can be seen from the central square. There are also fine old half-timbered houses, and a museum with local archaeological finds and art.
Rabastens-sur-Tarn The castle of St-Céry has a monumental 14th-century entrance and the kitchen also dates from this time. Cardinal Richelieu once lived here.
St-Lieux-les-Lavaur During the tourist season, and every weekend, a steam train runs from this village south of Rabastens.

WINE ACTIVITIES

Gaillac's Cocagne des Vins attracts thousands of visitors: for two days the wines of the region can be sampled in abundance. The festival takes place on the last weekend before 15 August. Other wine festivals are the *fêtes du vin* at Lisle-sur-Tarn (the Sunday nearest to 14 July) and Amarens (end of August).

The wine fraternities are l'Ordre de la Dive Bouteille de Gaillac and La Commanderie des Maîtres Vignerons du Frontonnais.

WINE INFORMATION

The Maison de la Vigne et du Vin is at the Abbaye St-Michel, Gaillac.

133
◆SW◆

PRODUCERS OF SPECIAL INTEREST

AVEYRON

ENTRAYGUES-SUR-TRUYERE, postcode 12140
Jean-Marc Viguier
ESTAING, postcode 12190
Pierre Rieu
MARCILLAC-VALLON, postcode 12330
Cave Coopérative

FRONTONNAIS & LAVILLEDIEU

CAMPSAS, postcode 82370
Domaine Bois d'Huguet
FRONTON, postcode 31620
Domaine de Bel-Air*, Château Bellevue La Forêt, Cave Coopérative, Domaine de Laurou

VILLAUDRIC, postcode 31620
Domaine de la Colombière*
LA VILLE-DIEU-DU-TEMPLE, postcode 82290
Cave Coopérative

GAILLAC

BRENS, postcode 81600
Domaine de Pialentou
CAHUZAC-SUR-VERE, postcode 81140
Jean Cros* (also Château Larroze).
CASTANET, postcode 81150
Domaine de Labarthe*
CASTELNAU-DE-MONTMIRAIL, postcode 81140
Domaine de Roucou-Cantemerle, Robert Plageoles

CORDES, postcode 81170
Château de Frauseilles
DONNAZAC, postcode 81170
Mas d'Aurel
GAILLAC, postcode 81600
Jacques Auque*, GAEC de Boissel-Rhodes Names used include Château de Rhodes and René Rieux. Domaine Très-Cantoux*
LABASTIDE-DE-LEVIS, postcode 81150
Cave Coopérative
LAGRAVE, postcode 81150
Domaine de Balagès
LISLE-SUR-TARN, postcode 81310
Domaine Clément Termes, Domaine de Mazou

ARMAGNAC

After cognac, armagnac is France's second great spirit. It is also probably France's oldest distillate of wine: a document of 1411 in the Musée de l'Armagnac at Condom shows that wine was already being distilled in Gascony at that time, centuries earlier than in Cognac, although this *eau-de-vie* may have been only for medicinal purposes.

Armagnac comes from a considerable part of the former province of Gascony: a few hundred hectares are in the départements of Landes and Lot-et-Garonne, but some 90 percent of the vineyard area is in Gers. This is a beautiful rural region not yet discovered by mass tourism. Its friendly landscape, often bathed in a soft, seemingly filtered light, is threaded by small rivers and streams and has an abundance of ancient towns, villages and hamlets. It is also a region of cellars and kitchens. Gascon cuisine is one of the richest in France: *foie gras*, goose and duck are served in all kinds of ways and in exuberant quantities. It is said that the Gers département has more geese and ducks than people – a million in all. The hearty local cooking has given rise, with admirable logic, to the *trou gascon*, the glass of young white armagnac taken halfway through a meal to clear the way for the courses still to come.

The area entitled to the appellation armagnac was defined in 1905 and divided into three zones, each with its own distinctive characteristics. The most westerly is Bas-Armagnac, also known as Armagnac Noir because of its dark oak forests. The landscape here is relatively flat and the soil mainly clay and sand. Sixteen communes are included in the (unofficial) zone of Grand Bas-Armagnac, which for connoisseurs represents the pinnacle of armagnacs, fine and subtle.

The central district is Ténarèze, which from early times has functioned as a corridor between the Pyrenees and Bordeaux. Its capital, the market town of Condom, is one of the main centres of the armagnac trade (the other main centres are Eauze in Bas-Armagnac and Auch, on the river Gers, in Haut-Armagnac). Ténarèze is a gently rolling countryside of orchards as well as vines, of wooded hills and fields of maize and sunflowers. The soil is chalk and clay, producing full-flavoured armagnac with plenty of character.

In the eastern district, Haut-Armagnac (also called Armagnac Blanc), the armagnacs lack the character and quality of those from the other districts. The soil is mainly chalk, well suited to vines, but the wines are soft and better for drinking than distilling. Much of what is distilled is for liqueurs. This is the largest district in Armagnac, most of it in the département of Gers, with steep hills in the south where it borders the Hautes-Pyrenees.

The main grapes of Armagnac are the Folle Blanche (known here, appropriately, as Picpoule, or "lip stinger"), Ugni Blanc, Colombard and Baco Blanc – all varieties that produce wines low in alcohol, high in acidity and ideal for distilling. Production of armagnac is, in fact, steadily decreasing. In 1976 the region had some 21,500 hectares (53,100 acres) of vineyards; a decade later this had shrunk to just under 13,000 hectares (32,100 acres).

An important difference between cognac and armagnac lies in the method of distillation. For cognac the thin, light white wine is distilled twice. Armagnac has its own alembic, or distilling vessel, in which the wine is heated twice but distilled only once. As a result, pure armagnac has less alcohol than cognac (between 53 and 63 percent, as against cognac's 70 percent), but possesses more of the elements of perfume and flavour. It is also drier, since sugar is not normally added.

Under the influence of Cognac houses that have acquired interests in Armagnac, distilling vessels from Cognac are being seen more and more in the district. In addition, the local dark, hard oak in which armagnac traditionally matured has become scarce, and increasingly wood from other areas is being used. Some armagnacs are thus growing closer to cognac in style.

Whereas production of cognac is dominated by large firms, the armagnac houses are on a smaller scale and many producers market their spirit directly. This means that the diversity of styles between producers, and from vintage to vintage (armagnac, unlike cognac, can indicate its year of vintage on the label) is enormous, and fascinating to explore.

Top: Condom, on the river Baïse, is the main town of Ténarèze.
Above: The ancient village of Labastide d'Armagnac.

TRAVEL INFORMATION

The many restaurants keep mainly to the regional cuisine, with *foie gras*, goose and duck in abundance.

HOTELS

Le Relais de Gascogne, 5 Avenue de la Marne, 32000 Auch, tel. 62 05 26 81. Solid and quite modern; also a restaurant. Class B.
Auberge de Guinlet, 32800 Guinlet, tel. 62 09 85 99. North of Eauze, on the D43. Park, swimming pool and restaurant; *demi-pension* is obligatory in season. Class B.
Many restaurants are combined with hotels (see below).

RESTAURANTS

Hotel de France, Place de la Libération, 32000 Auch, tel. 62 05 00 44. Central, very comfortable hotel with a restaurant where Gascon cuisine is splendidly represented. The *foie gras* is excellent and so is the *lou magret* (breast of duck). Owner and chef is André Daguin. Restaurant class B; hotel class A. Regional products are on sale at a shop here and there are separate restaurants for simpler meals. Class C.
Claude Laffitte, 38 Rue Dessoles, 32000 Auch, tel. 62 05 04 18. Good cooking without fuss. Class B.
Le Florida, 32410 Castéra-Verduzan, tel. 62 68 13 22. Congenial inn and hotel, in a small spa town. Class C.
La Table des Cordeliers, Rue des Cordeliers, 32100 Condom, tel. 62 28 03 68. Uniquely situated in a 14th-century chapel. Contemporary cuisine. Also a modern hotel. Class B.
Restaurant de l'Armagnac, 32800 Eauze, tel. 62 09 88 11. Pleasant and convivial. Class C.
Le Moulin du Pouy, 32800 Eauze, tel. 62 09 82 58. A good place to eat out of doors. Regional cooking. Class C.
La Patte d'Oie, 32340 Flamarens, tel. 62 28 66 28. In the country, opened in 1985. Regional cooking. Class C.
Le Fleurance, 32500 Fleurance, tel. 62 06 07 70. Regional wines and cooking (and generous helpings). Pleasant hotel. Class B.
Château Larroque, 32200 Gimont, tel. 62 67 77 44. Luxurious château hotel; *demi-pension* obligatory in season. Try the *soufflé au foie gras*, and visit the colourful local market on Sunday. Restaurant class B; hotel class A.
Auberge de Gascogne, 32300 l'Isle-de-Noé, tel. 62 64 17 05. Very moderately priced food and wines. Class C.

Le Relais d'Armagnac, 32110 Luppé-Violles, tel. 62 09 04 54. Traditional regional cooking. Also a hotel. Class B.
La Rapière, 32120 Mauvezin, tel. 62 06 80 08. Charming, busy address; menu includes *confit de canard*. Class C.
Hotel des Pyrénées, 32300 Mirande, tel. 62 66 51 16. Hotel and restaurant; local dishes and fish are prepared with great care. Restaurant class C; hotel class B.
La Gare, 32250 Montréal-du-Gers, tel. 62 28 43 37. A former railway station where one platform has been made into a terrace. Fish specialities and regional dishes. Class C.
Chez Simone, 32250 Montréal-du-Gers, tel. 62 28 44 40. Traditional, with game in season. Class C.
Le Relais de Cardeneau, 32450 Ste-Christie, tel. 62 65 51 80. Traditional cooking and local wines. Class B.
La Ferme de Flaran, 32310 Valence-sur-Baïse, tel. 62 28 58 22. Ideal for lunch after visiting the abbey. The hotel has a swimming pool. Class B.
Le Relais des Postes, 32190 Vic-Fezensac, tel. 62 06 44 22. Provincial hotel with regionally based cuisine. Book very early if you want to attend the local (bloodless) bullfights at Whitsun. Class C.

PLACES OF INTEREST

Auch The biggest town of the region, its old centre perched on a hill overlooking the river. The cathedral of Ste-Marie has superb choir stalls and 16th-century stained-glass windows. 232 steps link the Quai de Gers with the Place Salinis and its tall Tour d'Armagnac, and a statue of d'Artagnan commemorates the famous Gascon musketeer whose adventures were immortalized by Alexandre Dumas.
Castelnau-Barbarens Village encircling its church. There is a fine viewpoint at the D349 and D626 intersection.
Condom Gothic cathedral and a museum with armagnac as its theme.
Fourcès Fortified village, one of the rare circular *bastides*. The central square is surrounded by houses and a wooden gallery. Also a Gothic bridge and a 15th-century castle.
Gimont A bustling market town with a 13th-century fortified church.
Labastide d'Armagnac Viticultural museum at Château Garreau.
Mauvezin An octagonal tower, winding streets, a covered market and, for the strong, a garlic festival on the third Monday in August.

Montréal-du-Gers One of the first, and finest, *bastides* in Gascony.
St-Puy Château Monluc makes Pousse Rapière, a potent liqueur, and sparkling white wine.
Samatan The national *Foire aux Foies Gras* takes place here during the fourth weekend in August.
Seviac A luxurious Gallo-Roman villa with colourful mosaics.
Termes d'Armagnac Exhibitions are held in the historic castle keep. One hall is devoted to wine.
Valence-sur-Baïse The 12th-century Cistercian abbey functions as a cultural centre for Gers.

WINE ACTIVITIES

A market for Armagnac is held on most Thursdays in the centre of Auch. The *foire aux eaux-de-vie d'Armagnac* is at end May – beginning June.

WINE INFORMATION

At the end of 1986 the Maison du Floc de Gascogne was opened in Eauze to provide information about this Armagnac speciality: white or red must mixed with Armagnac, comparable to Pineau des Charentes..

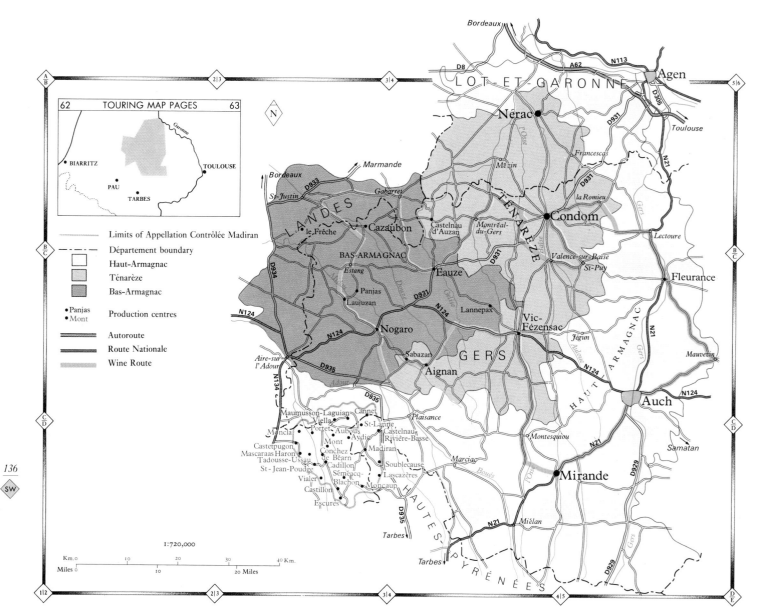

Today, the vineyards in the green and peaceful Armagnac landscape produce not only thin white wines for distilling but also an increasing quantity of Vins de Pays. The most successful are made in the modern manner, with low-temperature fermentation, usually with the Colombard grape as their basis, and possess plenty of aroma as well as a refreshing taste. They are sold mainly as Vins de Pays des Côtes de Gascogne.

PRODUCERS OF SPECIAL INTEREST

AIGNAN-EN-ARMAGNAC, postcode 32290, 136 C4

Sempé

ARTHES-D'ARMAGNAC, postcode 40190

Domaine de Jouanda*

CASTELNAU D'AUZAN, postcode 32800, 136 B4

Compagnie des Grands Armagnacs

CAZENEUVE, postcode 32800

Domaine de Sans*

CONDOM, postcode 32100, 136 B4

Janneau, Etablissements Papelorey, Château Pomès-Péberère*, Jacques Ryst

EAUZE, postcode 32800, 136 C4

Domaine du Tariquet: A remarkable white Vin de Pays.

LABASTIDE-D'ARMAGNAC, postcode 40240

Domaine Boignères*, Laberdolive*, Domaine Martine Lafitte*

LAUJUZAN, postcode 32110, 136 C3

Domaine Le Basque*, Armagnac Samalens*

MONTREAL-DU-GERS, postcode 32250, 136 B4

Ste-Fermière du Château de Maillac

NOGARO, postcode 32110, 136 C3

Dartigalonhue & Fils

ROQUEFORT, postcode 32390

Francis Darroze*

VIC-FEZENSAC, postcode 32190, 136 C4

Trépout*

THE PYRENEES

▲ The western Pyrenees, among the most spectacular and romantic mountains in France, rise up above the vineyards of Irouleguy. Monks in the 15th century planted the first vines here in the foothills. Irouleguy is one of the smallest and most isolated of the French vineyards.

Some of the least-known wine districts of France lie in the foothills of the western Pyrenees. The most northerly is the Côtes de St-Mont, which takes in part of Armagnac. Then come Madiran, Tursan, Béarn, Jurançon and, deep into Basque country, Irouleguy. Most of the grape varieties are strictly local. The Tannat is the main black grape: according to tradition it was brought here from Bordeaux by monks in the eleventh century; white varieties have unusual names such as Arrufiac, Gros Manseng, Petit Manseng and Courbu. More familiar varieties are also present, including the classic quartet Cabernet Sauvignon, Cabernet Franc, Sauvignon and Sémillon.

Several of the small districts have been on the verge of disaster and been saved at the last moment by the efforts of a few dynamic and expert winemakers. Madiran, for example, had only 6 hectares (15 acres) of vineyard left in 1953; Jurançon, too, was in danger of disappearing altogether as a source of wine at that time. Today, however, the wines of the Pyrenees are steadily gaining recognition in France and beyond.

Côtes de St-Mont is the most recent as well as the northernmost appellation. It received VDQS (vin délimité de qualité supérieure) status in 1981; the appellation contrôlée will not be long in coming now. Yet viticulture has long been practised in this extensive district of nearly 50 communes. The Romans probably planted the first vines, and from 1050 vineyards were cultivated by monks from the abbey of St-Mont. In the nineteenth century wine was the most important source of income.

The decline following the arrival of the phylloxera in the 1870s was not made good until after World War II and the emergence of three cooperatives. Since 1976 they have worked closely together under the name of Union de Producteurs Plaimont. The headquarters in St-Mont,

in the cooperative there, has very modern equipment and bottles about two-thirds of all Côtes de St-Mont wine. Some of the red wine is matured in barrel; the white wines are fresh and pure.

On the southern boundary of Côtes de St-Mont is Madiran, a district that used to be called Vic-Bilh. As early as the sixteenth century Madiran wines were being exported via Bayonne as far as Finland and Russia. One reason for a decline in this century was the virtual disappearance of the essential Tannat grape. Not until the 1970s was the technique mastered of reproducing this variety on a sufficient scale. For many years the Crouseilles cooperative was the only producer of Madiran wine, but today a number of private estates are also flourishing. Two other cooperatives (including the cooperative of St-Mont) also make Madiran. Classic Madiran is a deep but lively red with a dark taste full of tannin. It needs a good five years of bottle age, but the reward is wine of singular silky fluidity; no country boy this, but a courtier of character. Fruit can also be present, particularly cherries and currants. The district also makes a modest amount of white wine: Pacherenc du Vic-Bilh. Usually this is a softly fresh, dry wine with a somewhat exotic fragrance, but in sunny years some producers make a fairly sweet variant.

To the west of Madiran lies Tursan, a district that produces red, white and rosé wines of VDQS level, almost all processed by the cooperative at Geaune. In the course of the 1980s the wines have improved considerably. The reds are supple, with some fruit and a firm colour; the whites are fresh and juicy. Further improvement is on the way through experiments with Sauvignon Blanc and other grapes.

The Béarn appellation, spread over three départements, is also dominated by a cooperative: at Bellocq, a village northeast of Orthez.

Béarn's speciality is a dry, slightly fruity, very agreeable rosé. The wine made from Cabernet can be a particularly delicious thirst quencher. There are also red and white Béarns.

Just south of the spa town of Pau is Jurançon, one of the most beautiful wine districts in the whole of France. It is made up of steep hills that run parallel to the Pyrenees and are luxuriantly covered with trees, the intense green of which gives way in autumn to gold-brown tints – often still lit by a radiantly shining sun. The wines from this little paradise are white. Classic Jurançon is made from overripe grapes, preferably affected by *pourriture noble*, concentrated, sweet, dense and memorable. It is less rich than Sauternes and acids are noticeably present. The wine, which is strong and can be long matured, combines better with hors d'oeuvres and main courses than with rich desserts. Since 1975 there has also been a dry variant, Jurançon Sec, which should share at least some of the strong character of the old-style wine.

Irouleguy is an isolated district not far from the Spanish frontier and the mountain chain of the Pyrenees. It is, moreover, a very small district, covering a total of less than 150 hectares (370 acres). The character of Irouleguy red goes well with the rather rugged landscape and the strong Basque cuisine. The white (which is rare) and rosé are less interesting. The St-Etienne-de-Baïgorry cooperative used to have the monopoly, but the distiller and wine merchant Etienne Brana has recently established the first private estate. Its vines will be yielding fruit in 1989.

TRAVEL INFORMATION

Specialities of the Pyrenees include salmon, trout, mountain game, duck and pigeon; and Bayonne ham.

HOTELS

Climat de France, 40320 Eugénie-les-Bains, tel. 58 51 14 14. For anyone who wants to eat at Michel Guérard's (see below) but finds staying there too expensive. Class B.
Hostellerie de Canastel, Avenue Rausky, 64110 Jurançon, tel. 59 06 13 40. On the road to Oloron-Ste-Marie. Own park, swimming pool and restaurant. Class B.
Mapotel Continental, 2 Rue Maréchal-Foch, 64000 Pau, tel. 59 27 69 31. Large, distinguished hotel. Excellent fish dishes in the Le Conti restaurant. Class A.
Montpensier, 36 Rue Montpensier, 64000 Pau, tel. 59 27 42 72. Renovated; quite central. Class B.
Hotel Paris, 80 Rue Emile-Ganot, 64000 Pau, 59 27 34 39. Central but comparatively peaceful. Class B.
Roncevaux 25 Rue Louis-Barthou, 64000 Pau, tel. 59 27 08 44. A comfortable place, behind Boulevard des Pyrénées. Class B.
Hotel Arcé, 64430 St-Etienne-de-Baïgorry, tel. 59 37 40 14. One of the most pleasant places to stay in the region, with a riverside terrace and a restaurant, Le Trinquet, serving fresh trout, Pyrenean lamb, *marcassin*, etc. Class B.
Le Beau Manoir, 64110 Uzos, tel. 59 06 17 30. From Jurançon take the D209 south. Peaceful setting with a park, swimming pool and restaurant. Class B.

RESTAURANTS

Chez l'Ahumat, 40800 Aire-sur-l'Adour, tel. 58 71 82 61. Traditional regional cooking. Also a hotel. *Demi-pension* in summer. Class C.
Le Commerce, 40800 Aire-sur-l'Adour, tel. 58 71 60 06. Regional dishes such as *jambon à l'Armagnac* are served around an old hearth. Hotel rooms overlooking the street are noisy. Class B.
Auberge Labarthe, 64290 Bosdarros, tel. 59 21 72 03. Traditional and popular. Class C.
Michel Guérard/Les Prés et les Sources d'Eugénie, 40320 Eugénie-les-Bains, tel. 58 51 19 01. A place of pilgrimage for gastronomes, with an impressive wine list. Also luxurious hotel rooms. Class A.
Le Tucq, 64290 Gan, tel. 59 21 61 26. Relaxed, with hunting trophies on the wall. Class C.
Hotel de France, 40320 Geaune, tel. 58 44 51 18. Drink red Tursan here with *filet de boeuf à la Tursane*. Also a hotel. Class C.
Chez Ruffet, 3 Avenue Charles-Touzet, 64110 Jurançon, tel. 59 06 25 13. Try the fresh salmon and enjoy a Jurançon wine with it. Class B.
Auberge St-Loup, 64300 Orthez, tel. 59 69 15 40. Good cooking. Class B.
Patrick Jourdan, 14 Rue Latapie, 64000 Pau, tel. 59 27 68 70. Excellent wines. Class B.
Chez Pierre, 16 Rue Louis-Barthou, 64000 Pau, tel. 59 27 76 86. Expensive but excellent. Class A.

La Ripa-Alta, 32160 Plaisance-du-Gers, tel. 62 69 30 43. Friendly restaurant with hotel on the village square. Fine selection of armagnacs, some very old. Class B.
La Paix, 32400 Riscle, tel. 62 69 70 14. Recommended for its duck dishes and regional wines. A fairly quiet hotel. Class C.
Les Pyrénées, 64220 St-Jean-de-Port, tel. 59 37 01 01. The best restaurant of the district (try the salmon). Also a hotel. Class B.
Domaine de Bassibé, 32400 Ségos, tel. 62 09 46 71. Small, luxurious hotel and restaurant. Restaurant class B; hotel class A.

PLACES OF INTEREST

Bellocq The local cooperative is the biggest producer of Béarn wines.
Geaune The centre for Tursan wines.
Oloron-Ste-Marie The church of Ste-Croix has a porch of Pyrenean marble, with sculptures of a vineyard worker and salmon fishers.
Orthez Pleasant market town with an old (13th-century) fortified bridge.
Pau Here (so the story goes) the lips of King Henry IV were rubbed at birth with garlic and Jurançon wine. He was born in the château at Pau, a gracious palace that now contains two museums. To the west of the château is the ancient Parc National and to the east the Boulevard des Pyrénées, with breathtaking view of the nearby and often snow-capped mountains. The boulevard leads to Parc Beaumont, the most beautiful in Pau.
St-Jean-Pied-de Port A much-used halt for traffic to and from Spain, dominated by a 15th-century citadel. Pilgrims used to pass through here in great numbers: the scallop shell, emblem of Santiago de Compostela, is still much in evidence.
Salies-de-Béarn A spa with many 17th-century houses. Salt from Salies is essential to authentic Bayonne ham, which is cured in Orthez and Sauveterre-de-Béarn.
Vieille-Tursan Panoramic views.

WINE ACTIVITIES

A *fête des vins* is held in Madiran in mid-August and another around mid-December in Aire-sur-l'Adour. The splendid exhibition *Vins et Fruits* is organized at Monein (in Jurançon) on the first Sunday of August. There are three fraternities: the Viguerie Royale de Jurançon; the Viguerie Royale de Madiran; and the Commanderie des Chevaliers du Tursan.

WINE INFORMATION

A Maison du Vin opened in the town of Monein in the Jurançon in 1987. The cooperatives are also good places to taste and buy the local wines.

Orchards and woods mingle with the vines in the hilly, luxuriant landscape of the Jurançon. Warm, misty autumn mornings encourage the "noble rot" which creates the classic sweet white wines of this beautiful district.

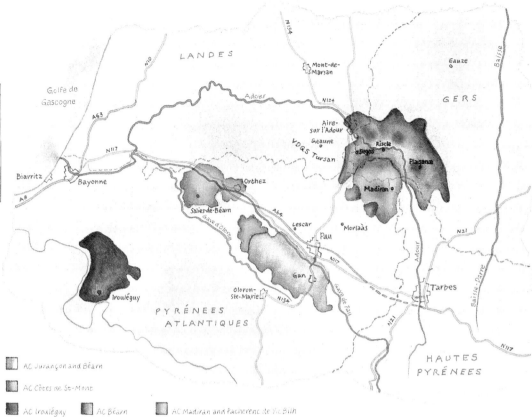

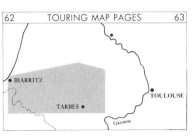

TOURING MAP PAGES 62 63

- AC Jurançon and Béarn
- AC Côtes de St-Mont
- AC Irouléguy
- AC Béarn
- AC Madiran and Pacherenc de Vic-Bilh
- ---- Département boundary

PRODUCERS OF SPECIAL INTEREST

BEARN

BELLOCQ, postcode 64270

Cave Coopérative* Notable especially for its Cabernet rosé.

LA CHAPELLE DE ROUSSE, postcode 64110

Cru Lamouroux*

COTES DE ST-MONT

AURENSAN, postcode 32400

Domaine de la Bergalesse

ST-MONT, postcode 32400

Union de Producteurs Plaimont* This organization also bottles the white and red Vin de Pays des Côtes de Gascogne from master chef Michel Guérard's Domaine du Meunier.

IROULEGUY

ST-ETIENNE-DE-BAIGORRY, postcode 64430

Cave Coopérative

ST-JEAN-PIED-DE-PORT, postcode 64220

Etienne Brana The first vintage will be in 1989.

JURANCON

GAN, postcode 64290

Cave Coopérative*, Château Jolies*, Domaine Moudinat

LAHOURCADE, postcode 64150

Alfred Barrère*

LASSEUBE, postcode 64290

Domaine Guirouilh

MONEIN, postcode 64360

Domaine Bru-Baché*, Clos Castéra, Domaine Cahaupé, Raymond Gaillot*, Vincent Labasse, Clos Uroulat

ST-FAUST, postcode 64110

Domaine Lasserre

MADIRAN

AURIONS-IDERNES, postcode 64350

Domaine de Crampilh

AYDIE, postcode 64330

Domaine Damiens, Vignobles Laplace*

CANNET, postcode 32400

Jacques Achilli, Domaine de Fitère

CORBERES-ABERES, postcode 64350

Château Peyros

CROUSEILLES, postcode 64350

Cave Coopérative* Notable for its Château de Gayon and Rôt du Roy in particular; also the biggest producer of Pacherenc du Vic-Bilh.

GARLIN, postcode 64330

Domaine de Diusse

LASSERRE, postcode 64350

Domaine de la Motte

MADIRAN, postcode 65700

Château de Perron

MAUMUSSON, postcode 32400

Domaine Barréjat*, Domaine Bousacassé Some of the best Madiran; also Pacherenc du Vic-Bilh. Domaine Labranche-Laffont, Château Montus*, Domaine de Teston Also Pacherenc du Vic-Bilh.

ST LANNE, postcode 65700

Domaine Maumus/Cru du Paradis

ST-MONT, postcode 32400

Cave Coopérative

TURSAN

GEAUNE, postcode 40320

Cave Coopérative

VIEILLE-TURSAN, postcode 40320

Domaine de la Castèle

139

SW

NORTHEAST ZONE

The country lying between Paris and the German border is so deeply associated with wars and battles that the names of its rivers ring sombrely even today. It comes as a surprise to find Reims, the capital of Champagne, right in the heart of this troubled land. But champagne is overwhelmingly the most important product of this quarter of vineyard France.

Three-quarters of the Champagne vineyards are clustered along the valley of the Marne, north of it to Reims and south beyond Epernay. The remaining quarter, much less famous but also well worth visiting, lies around the town of Bar-sur-Aube – a halfway stop on the road to Chablis.

All the considerable wines in this northeastern section are white with the exception of the burgundies of the Côte d'Or, which intrude here as if from a more southern world.

Southernmost are Sancerre and Pouilly on the upper Loire. Chablis is the northern outpost of Burgundy, along with its neighbour St-Bris the only remnant of a former vast wine region, centred on Auxerre, which supplied Paris with its everyday wine.

In the extreme east, Alsace lies between the Vosges and the Rhine, sheltered by its mountain range from cloud-laden westerlies, and regularly clocking up more hours of sunshine than anywhere else in France. The contrast in landscape and outline between the neighbours Champagne and Alsace could hardly be more complete.

Oddly, winegrowing on the French upper reaches of the Moselle is merely tentative. It is not until Luxembourg that the riverbanks are dressed in vines, and not until Trier (in French Trèves) that its wine becomes a matter of importance.

The northern limit of winegrowing crosses this map in a line from Orléans, passing just east of Paris, to reach the Moselle in Germany. It is one of the paradoxes of the vine that the closer, in general, to this limit, the finer the quality of the resulting wine.

VINS DE PAYS

1 Coteaux du Cher et de l'Arnon
2 Coteaux Charitois
3 Franche-Comté

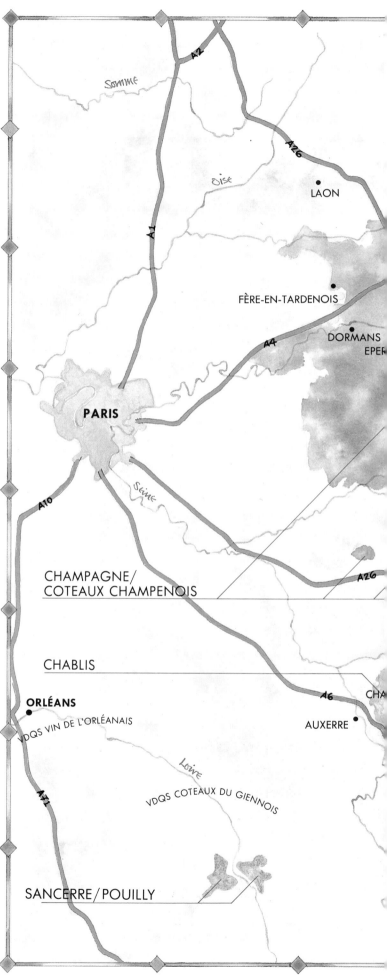

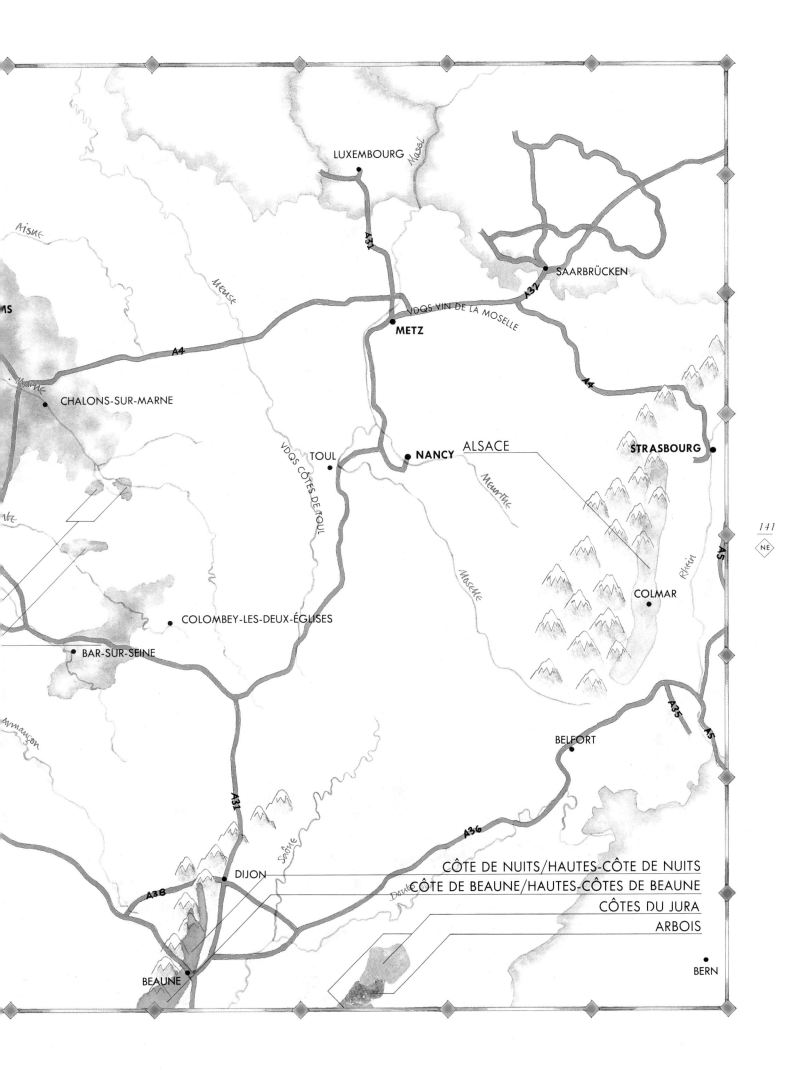

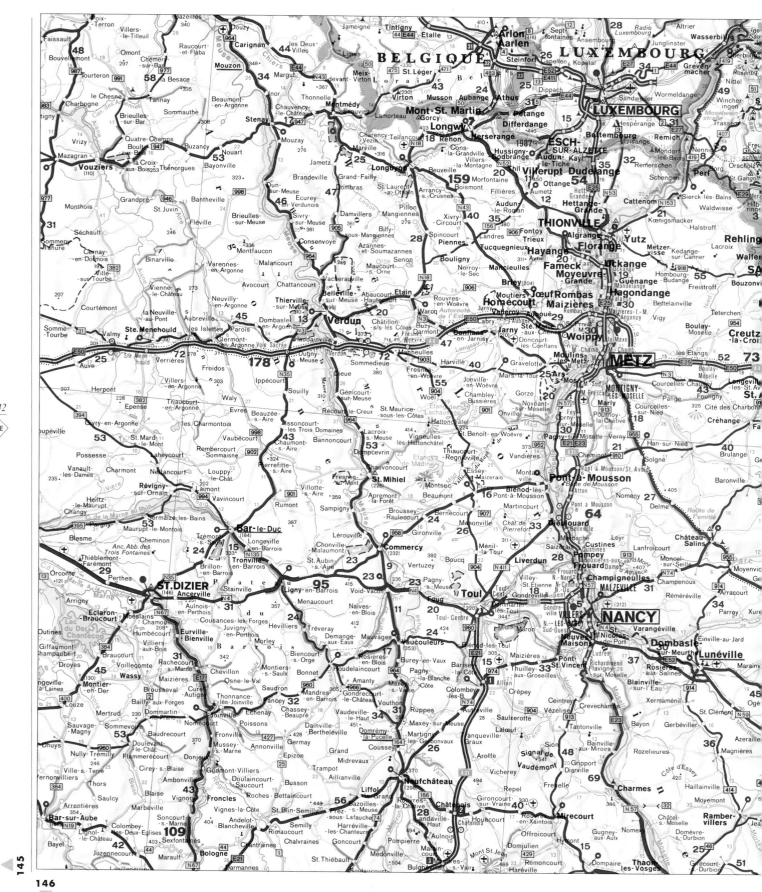

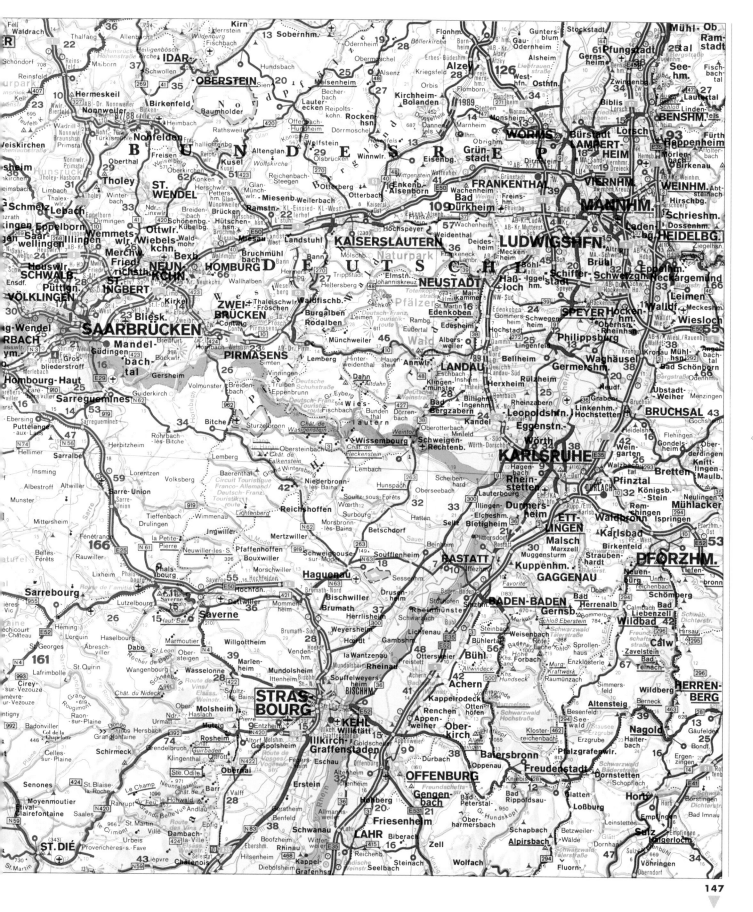

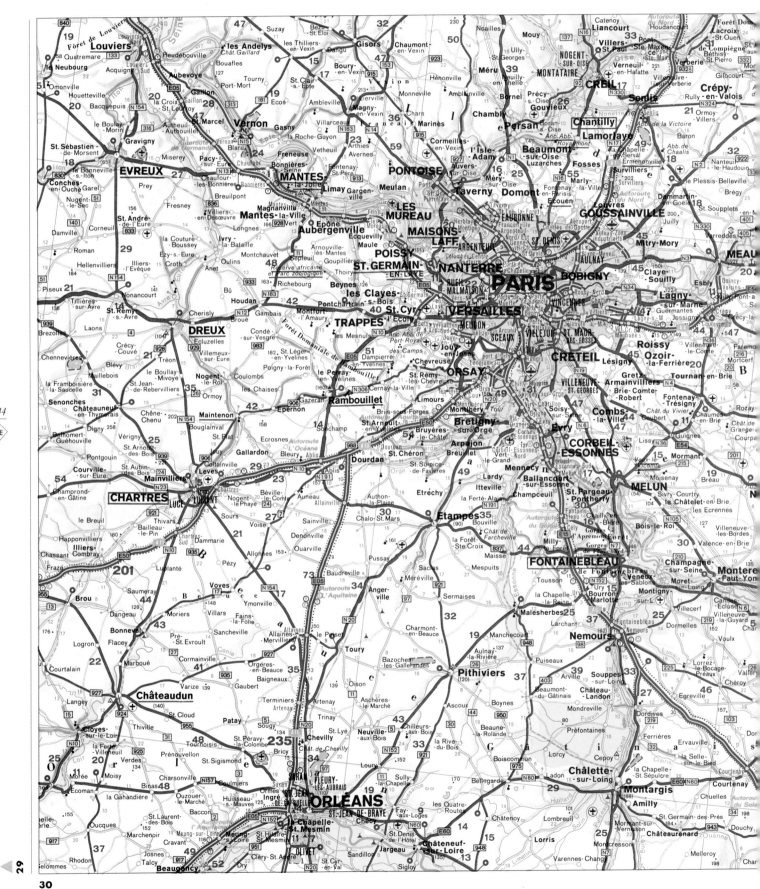

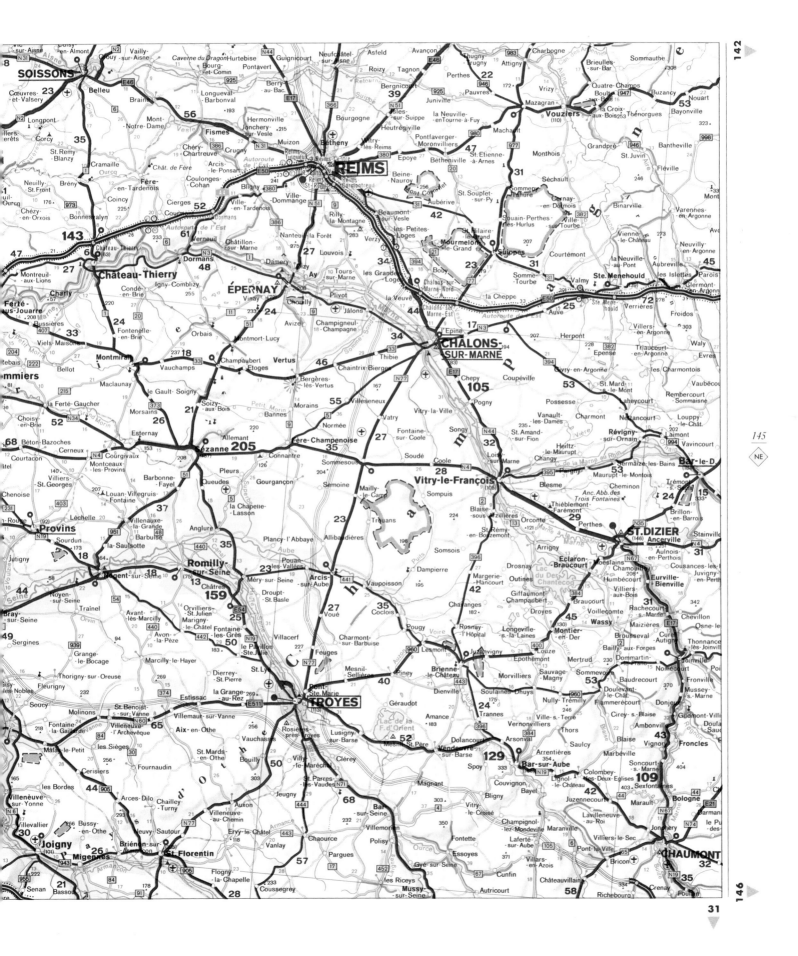

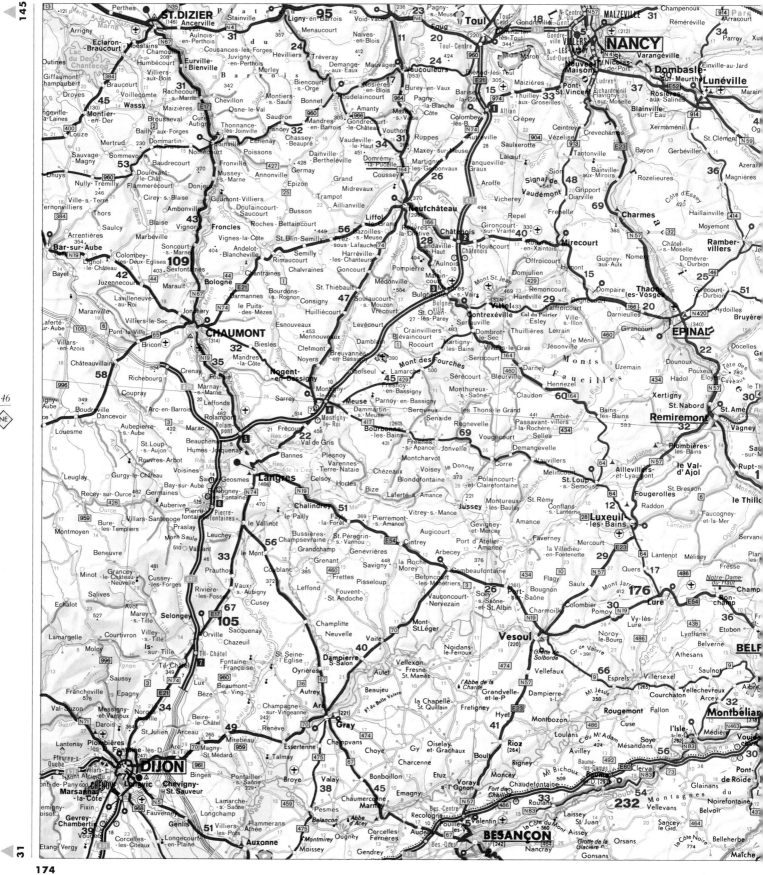

CHAMPAGNE

Given the festive image of champagne one might expect its homeland to be a landscape full of flowers, among joyful folk with a history of happiness. The reality, however, is not at all like this. *La Champagne*, birthplace of *le champagne*, is the most northerly of the great wine regions of France. The average annual temperature is only 10°C (50°F) – just one degree above the minimum at which the grape will ripen – and there is thus no question of an exuberant, flower-strewn paradise. Moreover, the people work hard and are of a very businesslike disposition. How else could the annual sales have exceeded 200 million bottles of champagne in 1986? In their attitude the Champenois seem closer to the people of Bordeaux than to the neighbouring Burgundians; it is noticeable that a great deal of Bordeaux wine is served in Champagne – and vice versa. The history of Champagne has been far from happy. It is ironic that joyful, elegant champagne should come from a region that has been ravaged time and again by wars, from the bloody battle between Attila the Hun and the Romans to the two world conflicts of our century.

Yet Champagne is well worth a visit. The landscape, though open, is certainly not monotonous: the north side of the Marne valley offers some surprising distant views; the villages on the slopes of the Montagne de Reims have charm; and in early autumn a diffuse light lends the red and gold vineyards a romantic air. The people of the Champagne give convincing demonstrations of their hospitality: many cellars are open to visitors and every year hundreds of thousands of people are shown around. Visitors receive literature, and often a glass of champagne, and all of it free. The history of the region has had its brighter moments. Practically all the kings of France were crowned in its capital, Reims. The creation of champagne can also be considered as an historic high point – although this was more a gradual process than a single discovery.

Certain individuals contributed greatly to the perfecting of the process by which champagne is made. One of them was the monk Dom Pierre Pérignon (1638–1715), cellarmaster at the abbey of Hautvilliers. He devised the concept of the *cuvée*, the careful blending of wines from different grapes and vineyards in which the whole proved to be more than the sum of the parts. Dom Pérignon's method is still used by all the champagne firms; it is the *cuvée* that determines the house style and the class of a champagne. There are many other sparkling wines made according to the *méthode champenoise*, yet a good champagne is a unique wine with unequlled qualities. The explanation lies in Champagne's chalk subsoil, which can go down hundreds of feet in places. This same substratum provides ideal storage cellars for millions of bottles of champagne: beneath Reims, Epernay and other places are more than 250 kilometres (over 150 miles) of underground passages. The grapes, too, contribute a good deal to the particular character of champagne – the black Pinot Noir and Pinot Meunier and the white Chardonnay. The quality of these grapes is partly determined by the commune they come from. There are 17 Grands Crus, villages that produce the highest possible quality, rated at 100 percent. Then there are some 40 Premiers Crus, with a quality rating of 90 to 99 percent, followed by the communes with a lower classification. Grape prices are related to these ratings.

The black grapes are vinified as if they were white. They are quickly pressed and fermented without their skins, which would impart colour to wine, so that even champagnes made solely from Pinot Noir are white. After fermentation and the blending of the *cuvée* the wine is bottled and induced to ferment again. This is done by adding yeast and sugar. During this second fermentation carbon dioxide is produced and trapped in the wine under great pressure: this is what causes the sparkle. A side-effect of this fermentation in bottle is the formation of sediment, which has to be removed. In the classic method the bottles are placed on slanting racks (*pupitres*), cork downwards, at an angle of 45 degrees. Then every day for two or three months the bottles are shaken, turned and moved nearer to the

Left and far left: formal and pastoral in Champagne. The orangery at Moët & Chandon's Epernay headquarters is a copy of that at Versailles. By contrast, the river Marne nearby.
Below: on the Montagne de Reims.

TRAVEL INFORMATION

The Champagne region has a good reputation for hospitality, its restaurants and hotels benefitting from the custom of the grand and prosperous champagne houses, and from its location at a crossroads of north–south and east–west routes. There are many good if expensive restaurants at which you can test the fervent contention of the champagne producers that their wine goes with any kind of food.

HOTELS

La Maison du Champagne, 51400 Beaumont-sur-Vesle, tel. 26 61 62 45. Small, simple, spotless hotel in a village southeast of Reims, with restaurant. The plumbing varies. Class B/C.
Royal Champagne, 51160 Champillon-Bellevue, tel. 26 51 11 51. Beautifully placed with a fine view of the Marne valley. Totally renovated rooms. The cooking can be very good. Class A.
Les Berceaux, 13 Rue des Berceaux, 51200 Epernay, tel. 26 55 28 84. The amenities at this old hotel have been improved in recent years. The cooking is fairly traditional (e.g. *escargots au Champagne*). Les Berceaux runs a bar in the same street selling wines by the glass. Class B.
Le Champagne, 30 Rue Eugène-Mercier, 51200 Epernay, tel. 26 55 30 22. Functional comfort. Class B.
Aux Armes de Champagne, 51460 l'Epine, tel. 26 68 10 43. Tastefully furnished rooms, good cooking, and a view of the basilica. Class B/C.
Hostellerie du Château, 02130 Fère-en-Tardenois, tel. 23 82 21 13. Luxurious château hotel (16th-century) nearly 50 km (30 miles) west of Reims. Glorious position in a park. Good standard of cooking. Class A.
Hotel de la Paix, 9 Rue Buirette, 51100 Reims, tel. 26 40 04 08. Within walking distance of the cathedral and with functional rooms and a swimming pool, this is one of the better places in Reims. Front rooms are far from peaceful. Class B.
La Briqueterie, 51200 Vinay, tel. 26 54 11 22. Just a few kilometres south of Epernay, this is an ideal place to stay for the wine region. Modern comfort, gardens – and peace and quiet. The cooking is talented. Class A/B.
Cheval Blanc Sept-Saulx, 51400 Mourmelon-le-Grand, tel. 26 61 60 27. Country inn by a stream just east of the Châlons road. Comfortable rooms: very good food. Class A/B.

RESTAURANTS

Many of the region's restaurants serve dishes of a finesse for which champagne makes an excellent partner (and in which champagne sometimes features as an ingredient). There are, however, regional specialities of a simpler kind. One of the best known is *potée champenoise*, a thick, nourishing soup containing stewed meat and vegetables. It is customarily served to the grape pickers, as well as to visitors to the champagne firms during the harvest. In the same category are *andouillettes* (a type of sausage), hams from Reims and Oger, *pieds de cochon* or *mouton* (pigs' or sheeps' trotters, sometimes stuffed), and *tarte aux raisins* (grape tart – also a harvest dish).

Hotel d'Angleterre, 19 Place Monseigneur-Tissier, 5100 Châlons-sur-Marne, tel. 26 68 21 51. Very good restaurant near the cathedral; also a hotel. Class B.
Le Relais de Cherville, 51150 Cherville, tel. 26 69 52 76. Fine establishment halfway between Epernay and Châlons. Opened in 1980 by a member of the Trouillard family, of the champagne firm. Specialities include *foie gras* and *rognons de veau à l'estragon*. Class B.
La Table Sourdet, 51700 Dormans, tel. 26 58 20 57. The Sourdet family enjoys a good local reputation as caterers and restaurateurs. Class B.
Jean Burin, 10 Place Mendès-France, 51200 Epernay, tel. 26 51 66 69. Regional dishes in a *fin de siècle* setting; e.g. oysters in champagne. Class C.
Le Chapon Fin, 2 Place Mendès-France, 51200 Epernay, tel. 26 55 40 03. Growers often eat here. Unpretentious dishes. Also a hotel. Class C.
Le Mesnil, 51190 Le Mesnil-sur-Oger, tel. 26 57 95 57. Fish specialities and a wide choice of wine in the heart of the Côte des Blancs. Class B.
Auberge du Grand Cerf, 51500 Montchenot, tel. 26 97 60 07. Inn on the Reims-Epernay road where guests are received with friendliness and style. Seasonally orientated fine cuisine and an extensive cellar, a garden and terrace. Class B.
Le Chardonnay, 184 Avenue d'Epernay, 51100 Reims, tel. 26 06 08 60. Elegant, well-maintained restaurant (it was formerly Gérard Boyer's Chaumière; he is now at Les Crayères). The cooking is of a good standard. Garden. Class B.
Les Crayères, 64 Boulevard Henri-Vasnier, 51100 Reims, tel. 26 82 80 80. Eating here is an experience. Not only is the cooking, under the direction of Gérard Boyer, sublime, but the whole ambience is magnificent: a very finely appointed

perpendicular – until they are standing on their heads with the deposit on the underside of the cork. Their necks are then dipped into an ice-cold brine bath, the bottles are opened, the plug of frozen deposit shoots out and the bottles are immediately topped up with a mixture of, usually, champagne and cane sugar. This gives the champagne its desired mildness; even an average *brut* is never absolutely dry.

Nowadays the *remuage* (the turning, shaking and tilting of the bottles) is carried out by mechanical means in many of the firms – although some of them, conscious that tradition is more picturesque, do not yet let their visitors see this.

Many small details influence the quality of champagne. One of the most important is the period of rest the wine is given after its second fermentation. One year is prescribed for the ordinary kinds, but all the great houses make three years the rule, for the longer the wine matures, the finer, and more persistent, the bubbles, the mellower and more harmonious the taste.

The champagne trade is dominated by the big "houses". Most of these firms have no vineyards, or too small an area to meet their needs. They therefore buy their grapes from more than 14,000 growers. A number of growers do make their own champagnes; most of which are drunk in France itself. The range of champagnes produced by a large firm may include a standard non-vintage (often in *brut* and *demi-sec* versions); a vintage, or *millésimé* champagne; a blanc de blancs (made from white grapes only); a rosé (usually a champagne to which some still red wine has been added); and a *cuvée de prestige* (a superior, always expensive wine, the firm's best). Less common types are crémant (with half the carbon dioxide pressure and therefore more gently sparkling); an absolutely dry wine, or one that is very nearly so (known as *brut de brut*, *brut sauvage*, *brut zéro*, etc); Coteaux Champenois (still white or red wine from the Champagne region); and ratafia (grape juice with added alcohol).

small château in a beautiful park with a view over Reims. The hotel rooms are tastefully done. Class A.

Le Florence, 43 Boulevard Foch, 51100 Reims, tel. 26 88 12 70. Elegantly furnished old building; the service has style, the food finesse. Class A/B.

Foch, 37 Boulevard Foch, 51100 Reims, tel. 26 47 48 22. Very pleasant, reliable restaurant; great care is taken with the cooking and the reception is friendly. Class B.

Le Vigneron, Place Paul-Jamot, 51100 Reims, tel. 26 47 00 71. With its old posters, vast selection of regional wines and strictly regional cooking (*potée champenoise, canard au ratafia*), this place is pure Champagne. Class B.

Le Relais de Sillery, 51500 Sillery, tel. 26 49 10 11. Congenial place to lunch, in a wine commune. Class B.

l'Assiette Champenoise, 40 Avenue Paul-Vaillant-Couturier, 51430 Tinqueux, tel. 26 49 34 94. In summer 1987 this restaurant moved from Châlons-sur-Vesle to this southwest suburb of Reims. Great care is taken over the cuisine. Class B.

La Touraine Champenoise, 51150 Tours-sur-Marne, tel. 26 48 91 93. Charming inn by a canal, with rooms. Straightforward, simple meals. Restaurant class C; hotel class B/C.

▶ Right: Champagne's wide views and windy days are reflected in the complexion of a vineyard worker.
▼ Below: near Bouzy on the southern slopes of the Montagne de Reims.

THE CHAMPAGNE TOWNS

REIMS

Cellars, churches and art are the triple attractions in Reims. The great champagne houses (see producers) welcome visitors. The centre is dominated by Notre-Dame, one of the great cathedrals of the world. It dates from the 13th and 14th centuries; the towers were completed in the 15th. All had to be restored, however, after the bombardment of World War I when the roof was entirely destroyed. The richly decorated Gothic west front is of an exceptional quality and inside there is an impressive organ and brilliant stained-glass windows (some designed by Chagall). Nearly all the kings of France were crowned here.

Beside the cathedral is the Palais

du Tau containing a museum of sculpture (monumental works from the cathedral) and religious art. Also near the cathedral is one of France's richest art museums, the Musée St-Denis (tapestries, paintings by the French masters, etc.). The 11th- and 12th-century basilica of St-Rémi looks austere from outside, but grand within and is well worth a visit, as is the Musée St-Rémi beside it (10 tapestries of the life of St Rémi, archaeological finds). The history of Reims comes to life through engravings (including some Dürers), paintings, sculptures and furniture in the Musée Hôtel Le Vergeur (36 Place du Forum – where there are remains of the Roman forum). Mention should also be made of the chapel of Nôtre-Dame de la Paix, decorated by the painter Léonard

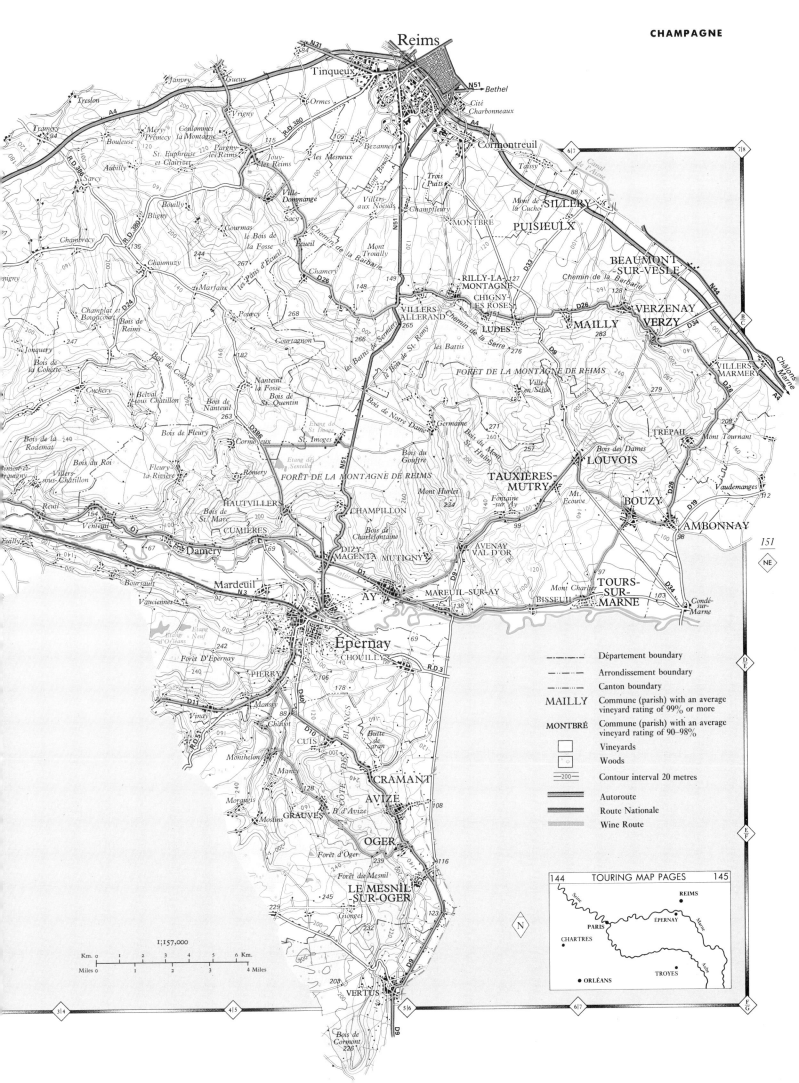

Foujita (33 Rue Champ-de-Mars); the former Jesuit college (furniture, religious art, library, planetarium – 1 Place Museaux); the Porte Mars (Roman triumphal arch, just north of the centre); the Salle de la Reddition (where the German surrender was signed on 7 May 1945 – 12 Rue Franklin-Roosevelt); and the Musée de l'Automobile Française (84 Avenue Georges-Clemenceau).

EPERNAY

Underground Epernay, with its dozens of miles of wine cellars, is visited by many thousands of people every year. But above ground, too, this bustling town (population about 30,000 – less than one sixth that of Reims) has a number of attractions. Foremost is the Musée Municipal, in the Avenue de Champagne, opposite Perrier-Jouët. It consists of three museums: the Musée du Vin de Champagne (implements, glasses, bottles, a diorama, etc.); the Musée des Beaux-Arts (fine arts); and the Musée de Préhistoire et d'Archéologie Régional. At the end of the same avenue the Champagne firm of Mercier has set up a museum for old wine presses – it has about 40 of them. Between the Avenue de Champagne and the river Marne are the cellars belonging to de Castellane, signposted by a quite remarkable water tower. This Tour de Castellane contains a wine museum with labels, posters, etc., and can be climbed.

PLACES OF INTEREST

Avenay-Val-d'Or Church with a front in Flamboyant Gothic style.
Avize Fine church with a Romanesque porch.
Ay The Musée Champenois here shows how wine growing and making have evolved. The Gothic church has a richly decorated front. Not far away is the house where Henri IV, "Lord of Ay", had a wine press (11 Rue St-Vincent).
Boursault Above this village – after which a cheese is named – stands the château the Widow Clicquot had built in 1842. It belongs today to a local grower.
Châlons-sur-Marne Old, half-timbered houses and churches reward visitors. The oldest church is the St-Jean (12th-century); the biggest the cathedral of St-Etienne (Gothic, with fine windows); the most sonorous the church of Notre-Dame-en-Vaux (a 56-bell carillon). Many fine medieval sculptures are displayed in the Musée de Notre-Dame-en-Vaux. The Musée Garinet/Musée Goethe-Schiller (3 Rue Louis-Pasteur) commemorate the battle of Valmy and the two writers. Archaeology and painting is exhibited in the Musée Municipal (Place

Godart). There is also a Musée d'Histoire Militaire (68 Rue Léon-Bourgeois). A park and an "English" garden lie beside the Marne.
Châtillon-sur-Marne Birthplace of Pope Urban II (1042). There is a colossal statue to him: you can climb up inside it. There are also the remains of a feudal castle.
La Cheppe Outside this village (which is northeast of Châlons) lies the valley where the army of Attila the Hun camped in AD 451 just before its decisive encounter with the allied armies of the Romans and the Franks. A million men were engaged in the battle at Champs Catalauniques, of whom a fifth perished. The Romans won, but only just.
Cramant A huge bottle stands at the entrance to this Chardonnay-growing village. A few miles to the north is the Château de Saran, where Moët & Chandon entertains its VIP visitors.
Cuis 12th-century church.
Cumières Terrace with one of the best views of the Marne valley and its vineyards.
Damery Strikingly beautiful 13th- to 16th-century church.
Dormans Badly hit in both world wars, but painstakingly rebuilt. Besides its partly 13th-century church and a 17th-century château Dormans has the Chapelle de la Reconnaissance, which Marshal Foch had built to commemorate the fighting along the Marne. The chapel is on high ground with a fine view.
l'Epine The 15th-century basilica of Notre-Dame is built in Flamboyant Gothic style. Old farming and wine-growing implements can be seen in the Musée Agricole de la Bertauge.
Germaine Museum of forestry.
Grauves In the church a statue of the Madonna stands on an old wine press.
Hautvillers Buildings of the former Benedictine abbey (founded 650) where Dom Pérignon worked have been made into a museum by Moët & Chandon. It has a replica of Dom Pérignon's cell and laboratory. He is buried in the church, as is Dom Ruinart. The museum can only be visited by prior arrangement with Moët & Chandon. Hautvillers itself is

characterized by its many wrought-iron tradesmen's signs.
Louvois In front of the château, which is not open to visitors, and was once much bigger than it is now, there is a park by Le Nôtre. The village has a 12th-century church.
Mareuil-sur-Ay Romanesque church and the château of Montebello, after which a champagne was named.
Le Mesnil-sur-Oger Romanesque church.
Puisieulx On the RN44 is the Fort de la Pompelle, which contains a museum devoted to World War I and the history of the fort itself.

Rilly-la-Montagne Lively wine village. In the church the choir stalls are carved with amusing figures engaged in wine-growing tasks.
Sacy Church of St-Rémi (12th-century).
Vertus Old houses and an interesting Romanesque and Gothic church built over natural springs. Remains of defensive walls.
Verzenay One of the rare old windmills of Champagne stands here. It belongs to Heidsieck Monopole and is used by the firm for dinners and receptions.
Verzy Not far from this village are the Faux de Verzy, fantastically contorted beeches with parasol-shaped crowns. Some are more than 500 years old. Also near by is the highest point of the Montagne de Reims, where the Mont-Sinaï observatory has been set up.
Ville-Dommange The 15th-century chapel of St-Lié is close to the village and there is a fine view of the countryside.

WINE ACTIVITES

Wine fairs are held only in the Aube département (see the Aube chapter).

Apart from the festivities around St Vincent's day (22 January) the only other ones worth mentioning are the Heures Champenoises, which Bouzy organizes at the end of May.

The region has the following, in order of seniority: l'Ordre des Coteaux de Champagne; l'Ordre des Pieds de Vigne Champenois; and La Confrérie des Echevins de Bouzy.

WINE INFORMATION

Champagne's *comité interprofessionnel*, the CIVC, at 5 Rue Henri-Martin, Epernay, has some of the most comprehensive reference material of any such body.

The champagne firms are on the whole welcoming to visitors, and many offer guided tours, literature – and samples. Tours usually take place between 10 a.m. and 12 noon, and 2 p.m. and 4 p.m. Companies often suspend these visits during August.

▷ Right: bottles *en pupitre*, with a *remueur* displaying the sediment in the neck of a bottle by means of a light.
▽ Below: the house of Krug is one of the few firms to ferment all its wines in small oak casks, seen here in their premises in Reims.

PRODUCERS OF SPECIAL INTEREST

AVIZE, postcode 51190, 151 E5

Bricout & Koch; Union Champagne: Gigantic modern cooperative with brands including Pierre Vauson, St. Gall and St. Michel.

AY, postcode 51160, 151 D5

Ayala & Co*: Serious, traditional firm of modest size. It also owns the Montebello brand and Château La Lagune in the Médoc. Has a very attractive Blanc de Blancs. **Bollinger*:** One of the great names of Champagne, a quality-minded family firm. Its own excellent vineyards supply 70% of the grapes. In perfume and taste Bollinger wines have distinction and breadth. RD (recently disgorged) is a vintage champagne that has spent 7 to 10 years resting on its sediment, with a resulting richness and subtlety. **Raoul Collet:** An energetic cooperative. **Deutz & Geldermann*:** Dynamic small firm with some 40 hectares (100 acres) of vineyards and an energetic policy of diversification. It has subsidiaries in the Rhône valley, Touraine and California. Vintage champagnes are the speciality. **Gosset*:** For many generations the Gosset family has been making and selling its wines in Ay. The firm is proud of being the oldest in Champagne (founded 1584).

Makes good vintage champagnes and an excellent rosé. Owns 10 hectares (25 acres) of land. **Henri Goutorbe; Ivernel*:** Stylish wines with a fine *mousse*.

BOUZY, postcode 51150, 151 D7

Paul Bara; Barancourt: About 90% of the champagne is made from grapes from the firm's own vineyards – about 45 hectares (110 acres), roughly half of this in Aube. Strong champagnes that age well. **Georges Vesselle; Jean Vesselle.**

CHALONS-SUR-MARNE, postcode 51000, 151 C8

Joseph Perrier*: A firm with a growing name for quality. The wines

have an elegant firmness. About a third of the grapes comes from its own 20 hectares (50 acres) of vineyard. Star of the range is the Cuvée Cent Cinquantenaire.

CHIGNY-LES-ROSES, postcode 51500, 151 B6

Cattier

CHOUILLY, postcode 51200, 151 E5

Centre Vinicole de la Champagne: Cooperative with brands including Nicolas Feuillatte; **R. & L. Legras*:** Carefully made wines almost exclusively from white grapes. Famous Parisian restaurants buy their house champagnes here.

The Legras family owns 22 hectares (55 acres) of vineyards.

CRAMANT, postcode 51200, 151 E5

Bonnaire-Bouquemont; Pertois-Lebrun.

CUMIÈRES, postcode 51200, 151 D5

René Geoffroy

DIZY, postcode 51200, 151 D5

Jacquesson & Fils Delicate, exquisite Blanc de Blancs, but also wines of lesser level.

EPERNAY, postcode 51200, 151 D5

Boizel; De Castellane: Laurent Perrier bought a minority shareholding in 1984. Not great, but sound, reliable champagnes. Also a liqueur producer. **A. Charbaut & Fils; Alfred Gratien*:** Small firm

that uses traditional methods. The vintage champagnes in particular are excellent. Has the same owners as Gratien & Meyer in Saumur. **Mercier:** Firm that puts great emphasis on the French market and has about 210 productive hectares (520 acres). The champagnes are of decent quality and quite mild in taste. Visitors are driven around the cellars in electric carts. Mercier belongs to the Moët-Hennessy group (see next entry). **Moët & Chandon*:** With an annual production of 18 million bottles, about 485 hectares (1,200 acres) of vineyard and 28 km (more than 17 miles) of cellars this is

by far the biggest firm in the Champagne region. The quality of its wines varies from plain good (the non-vintage *brut*) to excellent (the Dom Pérignon *cuvée de prestige*). With Hennessy, the cognac firm, Moët & Chandon formed the powerful Moët-Hennessy group, which also owns Mercier and Ruinart, as well as wine interests in California, and has close connections with Veuve Clicquot and Christian Dior. **Oudinot:** Firm run by two brothers of the Trouillard family. Its 65 hectares (160 acres) meet almost all its grape requirements. Other brands: Jeanmaire, Beaumet. **Perrier-Jouët*:** The property of the Canadian Seagram concern, like Heidsieck Monopole and Mumm. Its champagnes have great vitality, the best being the vintage rosé, Blason de France (white and rosé) and Belle Epoque (white and rosé, in a splendidly decorated art nouveau bottle). **Pol Roger*:** Very conscientious family firm that produces exquisite, classic champagnes of a consistently high standard. The rosé and the white Chardonnay are among the best of their kind. About 70 hectares (more than 170 acres) of its own vineyards provide around a third of the grapes required. **De Venoge:** After various take-overs, this firm has been rejuvenated and is worth following.

LUDES, postcode 51500, 151 C6

Canard-Duchêne: Belongs to Veuve Clicquot of Reims. **Victor Canard.**

MAILLY-CHAMPAGNE, postcode 51500, 151 C6

Cave Coopérative.

LE MESNIL-SUR-OGER, postcode 51190, 151 F6

Guy Charlemagne; Launois Père & Fils*; Salon*: Only wines from white grapes and of superior vintages are marketed by this small, prestigious firm. They benefit greatly from maturing in bottle. The firm, which belongs to the Pernod-Ricard group, owns just 1 hectare (about 2½ acres) of land. **Julien Tarin.**

OGER, postcode 51190, 151 F5

F. Bonnet & Fils*: Family firm with 22 hectares (55 acres) of vineyard in the Côte des Blancs (providing two thirds of their needs). Elegant, mildly fresh champagnes, the vintage Blanc de Blancs being the best.

MAREUIL-SUR-AY, postcode 51160, 151 D6

Billecart-Salmon*: A cool, slow fermentation gives the champagnes from this small house a light, fresh style, yet they also have sufficient backbone to mature. **Philipponat**: Belongs to Gosset of Ay. Very correct wines, the best being the Clos des Goisses.

REIMS, postcode 51100, 151 A6

Besserat de Bellefon (RN51, Murigny): Very modern firm, part of the Pernod-Ricard group. It has about 10 hectares (25 acres) of vineyards. The best wines are the Crémant des Moines rosé and the B de B (*cuvée de prestige*). **Charles Heidsieck*** (3 Place des Droits-de-l'Homme)*: Classic, long-lived wines with a fine *mousse*, fruit and *fraîcheur*. The firm has modern equipment and since 1985 it has belonged to Rémy-Martin (as does Krug). The founder, Charles-Camille Heidsieck, was the inspiration for the song "Champagne Charlie". **Heidsieck & Co Monopole** (83 Rue Coquebert)*: Although this firm takes the second part of its name from its best-known brand, Dry Monopole, the quality of this non-vintage *brut* seems to vary. The vintage has more class, and *cuvée de prestige* Diamant Bleu is better still. About 110 hectares (270 acres) provide for around a third of requirements. Belongs to Seagram. **Henriot** (12 Rue du Temple)*: After expanding strongly, this family firm was taken over in 1985 by Veuve Clicquot-Ponsardin. The champagnes are made from 40% or more white grapes, which makes them relatively light and fresh, with good fruit. The vintage ones are distinctly the best. The grapes come from the 110 hectares (272 acres) still owned by the Henriot family. **Jacquart** (5 Rue de Champ): A very dynamic cooperative (Coopérative Régional des Vins de Champagne) which has had considerable success with its Jacquart brand both at home and abroad. On the facade of its cellar premises (6 Rue de Champ) are the famous mosaics that depict the making of champagne. **Krug** (5 Rue Coquebert)*: At this small firm (maximum sales of 500,000 bottles a year) you encounter total perfection. The Krug family attends to every detail; no concessions are made. All the wine here still ferments in small oak casks. In terms of class and price all Krug champagnes belong to the *cuvée de prestige* category: the brilliant, complex and very dry Grande Cuvée, the slightly stronger Vintage, the fragrant, elegant rosé and the very rare Clos du Mesnil, a single-vineyard Blanc de Blancs of

extraordinary finesse. The house forms part of the Rémy-Martin group and owns 15.5 hectares (38½ acres) of vineyard. **Lanson Père & Fils** (12 Boulevard Lundy)*: This firm is especially well known for its non-vintage Black Label, a very reliable, fragrant, fruity champagne with a softly fresh taste. But the vintage wines, including two *cuvées de prestige*, are also distinguished examples of their kind. Lanson has 210 hectares

▼ The solid virtues of Bollinger are echoed in the architecture of their headquarters in Ay. The building houses offices and reception rooms. Cellars lie below.

(520 acres) of vineyards. Since 1983 it has belonged to the BSN food and drinks concern. Lanson's second brand is Massé. **Abel Lepitre** (2–4 Avenue Général-Giraud): Like George Goulet, Henry Goulet, St-Marceaux and other brands, Abel Lepitre is part of Les Grands Champagnes de Reims. Abel Lepitre's speciality is the vintage Crémant Blanc de Blancs. **G. H. Mumm & Co** (29 Rue du Champ-de-Mars)*: This large firm, which belongs to Seagram, has the non-vintage Cordon Rouge as its best-selling wine. This is a gently bubbling, almost mild and very commercial *brut*. The quality level rises appreciably with the Crémant de Crémant, the vintage rosé and the René Lalou *cuvée de prestige*. About

one fifth of production originates from its own 225 hectares (550 acres) of vineyard. **Bruno Paillard** (Rue Jacques-Maritain)*: Young firm, founded in 1981, that sells both grapes and made wines. In both cases selection is stringent: hence the very good *brut*, the vintage wines so full of character, and the delightful Crémant Blanc de Blancs. **Piper-Heidsieck** (51 Boulevard Henri-Vasnier)*: A technically and commercially progressive firm with interests in Touraine, California, India and elsewhere. The style of its wines is light and fresh. Among the best wines are the totally dry Brut Sauvage, made up from various years; the *cuvée de prestige* Florens-Louis; and the refined Rare (the 1976 was blended from 12 Grands Crus of the time). **Pommery & Greno** (5 Place Général-Giraud)*: The buildings and cellars of this firm (which belongs to the BSN group, like Lanson) are among the most striking in Reims. Pommery & Greno has more than 320 hectares (790 acres) of vineyard, providing almost half of its needs. After a temporary falling off the firm now makes dry, almost airy champagnes of good to very good quality. In 1985 Louise Pommery, a

cuvée de prestige of considerable grace, was launched. **Louis Roederer** (21 Boulevard Lundy)*: This family concern obtains about 80% of its grapes from its own 185 hectares (nearly 460 acres). It produces its champagnes with extraordinary care and a great feeling for tradition. Most of the wines have a mellow maturity and a firm structure. At the top come the luxurious, harmonious Cristal and the Cristal rosé with all its flavour; and the robust vintage and the subtly coloured vintage rosé are exquisite wines. **Ruinart Père & Fils** (4 Rue de Crayère)*: Ruinart's modern buildings house the oldest champagne firm in Reims and stand over chalk cellars that have been declared a historic monument. The house style is light and fresh wines. There are two *cuvées de prestige*: Dom Ruinart Blanc de Blancs and Dom Ruinart rosé, both vintage. The firm is part of the Moët-Hennessy group and owns 15 hectares (37 acres) of vineyard. **Taittinger** (9 Place St-Niçaise)*: The high Chardonnay content in Taittinger's wines shows in an elegance of style. About half of production is provided for by this family firm's 250 hectares (nearly 620 acres). Among the most distinguished of the Taittinger champagnes are the totally dry Brut Absolu, the Collection vintage and the sublime Comtes de Champagne Blanc de Blancs. The Taittinger family owns the Irroy brand. **Veuve Clicquot-Ponsardin** (12 Rue du Temple)*: This firm is distinguished by its classic, utterly reliable, meticulously made wines. Stars are the vintage rosé and the Grande Dame *cuvée de prestige*. The firm derives its name from Nicole-Barbe Ponsardin who was widowed in 1805 at 27 and continued her husband's business with great energy. The house owns 280 hectares (690 acres) of vineyards and a wide spread of business interests. In Champagne itself it owns Canard-Duchêne and Henriot, was taken over in turn in 1986 by Louis Vuitton, and is now closely connected with Moët-Hennessy.

TOURS-SUR-MARNE, postcode 51150, 151 D7

Laurent Perrier*: Thanks to its pure, exhilarating, expertly made wines this house has experienced a tremendous growth since World War II. It is now one of the most important in the region. The grapes come from about 500 hectares (1,235 acres) under contract and the firm itself owns a further 80 hectares (nearly 200 acres). Among its best wines are the mature, finely sparkling Ultra Brut; the rosé; and the stylish Cuvée Grand Siècle.

THE AUBE

Visitors to Champagne concentrate on Reims and Epernay and the countryside around. All this is in the Marne département, the heart of Champagne. Yet a good proportion of the grapes – a quarter at present, and even more in future – is grown outside the Marne département. The Aube in particular has a large area of champagne vineyards: about 5,000 hectares (12,350 acres) – out of the total for Champagne of around 26,000 hectares (64,250 acres). This is expected to increase by 2,000 hectares (nearly 5,000 acres) by the turn of the century. The Aube vineyards lie southwest of Troyes, not far from the border with the Côte d'Or département (and, therefore, Burgundy). They stretch between, and beyond, the towns of Bar-sur-Aube and Bar-sur-Seine. The underlying rock here is limestone, but more like that of Chablis than of Reims. The climate has more extremes of temperature than does the Marne, with periods of sometimes quite heavy frost. Growers here fear both late spring frosts and those of early autumn, which can severely harm the vintage. In this the area resembles Burgundy.

Pinot Noir vines account for 80 percent of those planted in this hilly, wooded country. The champagnes made here therefore have a rather more pronounced taste, are relatively firmer in structure and softer than those from the more northerly areas, and tend to a pale straw yellow in colour. A large part of the grape harvest is processed by the Reims and Epernay houses, some of which have land of their own in the Aube. However, there are also local cooperatives and individual growers who make and sell their own champagnes. With the recent rise in the sales of champagne worldwide, the Aube has been in a strong position as supplies of Marne wines have become short.

The rarest Aube wine is Rosé des Riceys, a dark, dry, still rosé with a distinctive aroma (people talk of gooseberries, mint and chocolate) and an average annual production of only 10,000 to 12,000 bottles. It is made from Pinot Noir grapes in an appellation which covers the commune of Les Riceys, which consists of three hamlets.

Not many tourists as yet follow the Aube wine route, but this will change with the opening of the A26. This autoroute will link Reims and Dijon, pass close to Troyes and right through the Aube wine district.

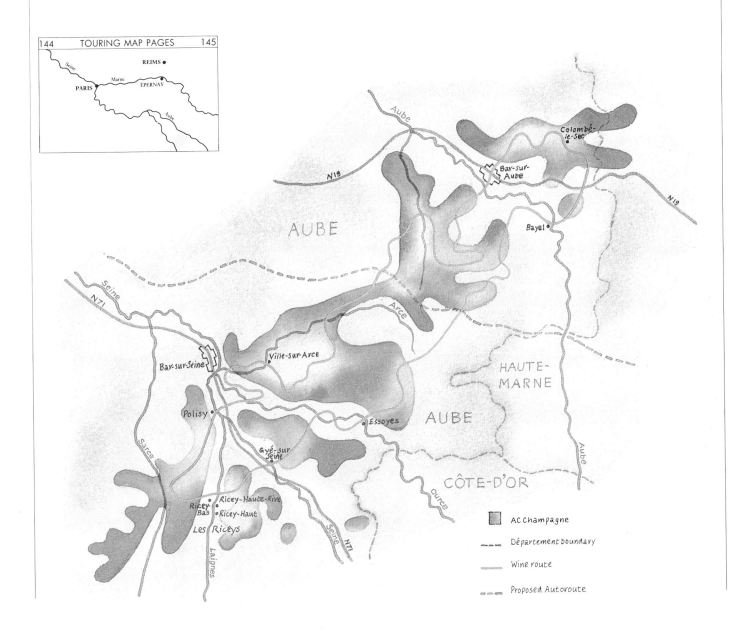

TRAVEL INFORMATION

Rural, remote (at least until the autoroute is finished) and green, the Aube rewards explorers.

HOTELS

Le Commerce, 38 Rue Nationale, 10200 Bar-sur-Aube, tel. 25 27 08 76. In the heart of the little town. Good rooms, conservative cooking. Hotel class B; restaurant class C.
Barsequanais, 6 Avenue Général-Leclerc, 10110 Bar-sur-Seine, tel. 25 29 82 75. Quiet situation; simple rooms. Restaurant. Class C.
Grand Hotel, 4 Avenue Maréchal-Joffre, 10000 Troyes, tel. 25 79 90 90. A hundred rooms with modern comfort and four restaurants, opposite the railway station. Class B.

RESTAURANTS

La Croix Blanche, 7 Avenue Louis-Pasteur, 10500 Brienne-le-Château, tel. 25 92 80 27. Peaceful hotel and restaurant with garden and terrace. Classic dishes. Class C.
Hôtellerie de la Seine, 10110 Polisot, tel. 25 38 54 41. Recommended by wine growers. Regional food. Also a hotel. Restaurant class C; hotel class B.
La Valentino, Cour de la Rencontre, 10000 Troyes, tel. 25 73 14 14. Enjoyable food, with the stress on fish, and interesting wines. In the centre of the town, yet with a garden. Class B.

PLACES OF INTEREST

Bar-sur-Aube This small town is the centre of the Aube champagne business. Its most intriguing monument, a chapel on the bridge, was sadly destroyed in the fighting of 1940. The chapel commemorated the incident in 1440 when the Bastard of Bourbon, who had rebelled against the Crown, was sewn up in a sack and thrown into the river on the orders of King Charles VII. The 12th- to 14th-century church of St-Pierre is surrounded by unusual wooden galleries. Just south of the town the Ste-Germaine hill offers a panoramic view and there is a chapel shaded by ancient trees. In summer wine can be tasted at a chalet on the RN19 east of the town.
Bar-sur-Seine This little town between cliffs and the river has half-timbered houses, the Tour de l'Horloge, the only remains of a castle, and is the seat of the biggest wine cooperative in the Aube.
Bayel Large glassworks (guided tours available) and a partly 12th-century church with interesting statuary.
Brienne-le-Château This town is about 25 km (15½ miles) northwest of

Bar-sur-Aube, at the foot of a castle. The little town is worth visiting for a wooden hall that dates from 1270 (with a vast roof and beautiful wood carving) and its museums, dedicated to Napoleon, international aeronautics and farm and vineyard implements (the last being open only on Friday and Sunday afternoons).
Clairvaux The ancient abbey was founded in 1115 by St Bernard. After the revolution it became a prison, which housed the Russian anarchist Prince Kropotkin in the 1880s.
Colombé-le-Sec A wine cooperative, a gigantic cellar dating from 1154 and a 12th-century church.
Colombey-les-Deux-Eglises From 1933 Général Charles de Gaulle had an estate in this village (east of Bar-sur-Aube and just outside the wine district). The statesman died here in 1970 and is buried in the churchyard. He is commemorated by a large cross of Lorraine on a hill that rises to about 400 m (1,300 ft).
Essoyes One of the prettiest villages on the wine route. There is here a Maison de la Vigne et du Vin, a small museum (a sculpture made from 300 bottles among the exhibits) and the graves of the painter Pierre-Auguste

Renoir, his wife and their two sons.
Gyé-sur-Seine Remains of a 14th-century castle, a tree of liberty of 1792 and a partly 12th-century church.
Neuville-sur-Seine There is a wine cooperative here and on a hilltop a modern sculpture of Notre-Dame-des-Vignes.
Polisy The château by the river has a 16th-century floor of enamelled tiles.
Les Riceys The three hamlets of Les Riceys are due south of Bar-sur-Seine. Ricey-Bas has a Gothic and Renaissance church, and a castle, the oldest parts of which date from 1088. An impressive avenue of plane trees leads up to the castle, which is private property and not open to visitors. Ricey-Haut has a 16th-century church with an elegant nave. At Ricey-Haut-Rive, as in the other two Riceys, the church has been declared a historic monument.
Troyes This former capital of Champagne lies on the river Seine and the Haute-Seine canal. The old centre is resplendent with the cathedral of St-Pierre-et-St-Paul (Gothic, with a single tower which you can ascend); the extraordinarily beautiful basilica of St-Urbain (a

▼ Bar-sur-Aube gains much of its quiet charm from the river whose banks it lines. The Aube is a tributary of the Seine. The Aube vineyards lie between the two.

Gothic masterpiece, with a statue of the Madonna with Grapes to the right of the choir); the 12th-century church of St-Martin, the town's oldest; and many half-timbered houses. There are also various museums to visit, among them the Musée des Beaux-Arts (to the left of the cathedral, in a former monastery: fine arts, prehistory, natural history and a huge library); the Musée d'Art Moderne (to the right of the cathedral, with Braque, Derain, Dufy, La Fresnaye in the collection); the Hôtel-Dieu-le-Comte with its dispensary (Quai des Comtes-de-Champagne); and the Musée Historique de Troyes et Champagne (4 Rue de Vauluisant: painting and sculpture).

Ville-sur-Arce A fine view here out over the vineyards. Also the home of a large cooperative.

WINE ACTIVITIES

The Foire de Champagne takes place in Troyes in the second week of June. Bar-sur-Aube runs its Foire aux Vins de Champagne in the second weekend in September.

The wine growers of Aube have had their own fraternity since 1975, La Commanderie de Saulte-Bouchon Champenoise.

PRODUCERS OF SPECIAL INTEREST

BAR-SUR-SEINE, postcode 10110

Union Auboise des Producteurs de Vin de Champagne: Energetic group of cooperatives processing the larger part of the grape harvest from more than 700 growers. Léonce d'Albe, Abel Jeannin, Maurice Leroy and Paul de Richebourg are its brands.

CELLES-SUR-OUZE, postcode 10110

Marcel Vezien.

RICEY-BAS, LES RICEYS, postcode 10340

Horiot Père & Fils: Champagne and Rosé des Riceys.

RICEY-HAUT, LES RICEYS, postcode 10340

Alexandre Bonnet*: Modern equipment, a sizeable vineyard – 25 hectares (62 acres) – and an emphasis on quality put this estate among the leaders in Aube. As well as various champagnes, Rosé de Riceys is also produced.

Morel Père & Fils: exclusively Rosé de Riceys.

URVILLE, postcode 10200

Drappier.

▲ Top: In the Aube, cornfields elbow in among the vines. There is none of the monoculture of the Montagne de Reims or the Côte des Blancs.
Above: winegrower's cottage at Val Perdu.

ALSACE

A lsace has a markedly different appearance to the other French wine regions. It was German for some seven centuries and has, despite the frequent wars, kept many of its ancient buildings. The wine towns and villages of Alsace often have the romantic, almost fairytale charm that was so characteristic of the Central Europe of old. In the wine communities here you see striking half-timbered houses, beautifully ornamented Renaissance buildings, lovely wells and fountains, imposing churches and old gateways. And most of the towns and villages are set in splendid countryside. They lie between or on the slopes of outliers of the Vosges, which are covered with green vineyards and dark woods. This range runs parallel with the Rhine and shelters Alsace from rain-laden west winds: Colmar, where in the long summers many houses are decked with colourful displays of flowers, is one of the driest, sunniest towns in France.

There are other ways too in which Alsace emphasizes its own identity. Among themselves the locals speak a language incomprehensible to outsiders – not quite German, certainly not French. The region has its own traditions and costume – and a cuisine that combines German amplitude with French finesse. The Alsatians themselves are very proud of their province. The better bookshops of Strasbourg and Colmar sell dozens of works, large and small, about Alsace.

Alsace wines also have a personality of their own. From grapes that are usually the same as those grown just to the east in Germany totally different wines are produced: absolutely dry, firm and aromatic. The Alsatian wines are named, quite simply, after their grape varieties. The numerous appellations and classifications of, for example, Bordeaux and Burgundy, do not occur here. Even mention of the vineyard is the exception rather than the rule. Only 25 vineyards are entitled to Grand Cru status, which therefore appears on their labels. This number will be increased in the coming years; the next selection of 22 vineyards has

▲ Vines in Alsace are usually trained on posts and wires, as here above Riquewihr. The wooded hills of the Vosges crowd the western horizon.

already been made. But even then Grands Crus will represent at most nine or ten percent of the total vineyard area. The requirements laid down for Grand Cru wines are of course more stringent than those for the ordinary kinds. They can only be made from superior grape varieties (Riesling, Gewürztraminer, Tokay – Pinot Gris, Muscat); and the legally permitted yield per hectare is nearly a third lower than for straightforward AC Alsace. Besides these Grands Crus a few other vineyards of great repute have their names on labels: the Kaefferkopf at Ammerschwihr and the Gaensbroennel at Barr are two examples. All Alsace wines, of whatever level, must be bottled in the region.

Even in this northerly region, a sunny autumn can produce grapes with such a high concentration of sugar that the wines retain a natural sweetness after fermentation. Wines of this type are called Vendange Tardive (late-harvested). For wine with an even higher sugar content the term Sélection des Grains Nobles is used. Sometimes grapes of this rare and expensive category have undergone a measure of *pourriture noble* (noble rot). This is discussed in the Sauternes chapter.

The most widely planted and finest grape variety in Alsace is the Riesling. It gives distinctly dry wines that can vary in style from fresh, open and elegant to supple, firm and aromatic. The soil type is very influential here. Rieslings from light soils can be drunk young; those from the limestone often require some years' patience. The Alsatians themselves are proud of this wine. They say "anyone who knows his Riesling knows Alsace; and anyone who loves Alsace loves Riesling."

A second very characteristic wine is the Gewürztraminer. Nearly as much is planted as of the Riesling. As the name indicates (Gewürz is German for "spice") this wine has a spicy aroma. Sometimes this can be so sultry and overpowering that the dry taste comes almost as a surprise. Because of its natural strength a good Gewürztraminer can mature excellently. In Alsace the classic type of this wine is served at the end of a meal; it combines perfectly with the Munster cheese of the region. The lighter kinds of Gewürztraminer can readily be served during a dinner.

The third great grape of Alsace is the Pinot Gris; it is prone to problems in the vineyard and therefore not much planted. Locally the Pinot Gris is still stubbornly called the Tokay d'Alsace, despite an EEC ruling in 1980 prohibiting the name (it was thought possible to confuse it with Hungary's Tokay). A typical Tokay d'Alsace wine has a firm, even thick, structure and an intriguing, almost elusive scent and taste. Sometimes you can detect a slight smokiness to it, sometimes a hint of nuts or honey. It was because of this exotic, mysterious character that the wine acquired the sobriquet "Sultan". A thirst-quencher it is not.

Alsace is one of those rare wine regions where Muscat grapes make a dry wine. A Muscat from Alsace has an ingratiating aroma of fruit and is light enough to be served as an apéritif. Unfortunately, not a great deal of this delightful wine is made. Because of their delicacy Muscat grapes are planted on only about three percent of the available area.

The Pinot Blanc is a rather complicated wine. As a rule it has not only the Pinot Blanc variety as its basis but also the Auxerrois Blanc. However, there are also pure Pinot Blanc and pure Auxerrois wines. The custom is to sell the latter category as Klevner or Clevner, or sometimes as Auxerrois. Producers such as Blanck in Kientzheim, Josmeyer in Wintzenheim, Rolly-Gassman in Rorschwihr, Louis Hauller in Dambach-la-Ville and Kuehn in Ammerschwihr prove that Pinot Blanc, Klevner and Auxerrois can be exceptionally pleasant, mildly fresh and lightly aromatic wines with a lively taste. The amount of Pinot Blanc and Auxerrois planted is on the increase and is already approaching the Gewürztraminer level. One of the reasons is the frost-resistant qualities of the Auxerrois in particular. Another is the increasing popularity of sparkling wines (which are as a rule made mainly from Pinot Blanc). In 1979 half a million bottles of Crémant d'Alsace were produced; less than ten years later the figure was 13 million.

The Sylvaner is the fourth Alsace grape to produce a large volume of wine, along with the Riesling, Gewürztraminer and Pinot Blanc. Together these varieties account for about 80 percent of the vines. Sylvaner wine is fresh and uncomplicated, often with an agreeable juiciness. Part of the Sylvaner harvest is blended with other grapes, including the similarly simple Chasselas and Knipperlé, to make Edelzwicker, an everyday wine that mostly comes in litre bottles.

The rarest Alsace wine is called Klevener de Heiligenstein. Its area of origin is Heiligenstein and a few neighbouring communes, its grape the Savagnin Rosé. This variety shows an affinity with both the Savagnin Blanc of the Jura and the Gewürztraminer. Its wine is not a great one but certainly notable, with a distinctive, mild aroma and a fresh finish.

White wines are the true vocation of Alsace, but nevertheless some six percent of the available area is planted with the black Pinot Noir. Practically the whole of the harvest used to be made into rosé, but today a growing number of producers are going to great trouble to make a proper red wine. A few of the most successful are aged in small oak barrels.

The vineyards of Alsace lie in a narrow band, interrupted in only a few places, about 110 kilometres (70 miles) long. It stretches through the départements of Haut- and Bas-Rhin and is provided with a splendid, clearly signposted wine route. In quality terms Haut-Rhin holds most of the aces, but excellent wines are also produced in some of the Bas-Rhin communes (such as Andlau).

Right in the north of the region there is a small wine-producing area separated from the rest. The cooperative at Cléebourg, not far from the border town of Wissembourg, has the monopoly here. Cooperatives also play an important part in the main wine areas. The roughly 12,600 hectares (just over 31,000 acres) of Alsace vineyards are worked by about 9,200 growers, so that the average holding is less than one and a half hectares (3¾ acres). Many growers therefore belong to cooperatives or sell their grapes to négociants; individual estates are responsible for processing and selling about one third of the vintage.

TRAVEL INFORMATION

The people of Alsace enjoy the good things the earth offers – and their many visitors are only too pleased to follow their example. Alsace is therefore richly provided with restaurants. The simplest type is called a *winstub*, where for a modest price regional fare and regional wines are served. But there are also plenty of luxurious establishments with two or three Michelin stars.

The cuisine of Alsace features numerous specialities. Among the best known are *pâté de foie gras* (goose-liver pâté); *tarte à l'oignon*; *tarte flambée* or *flammekueche* (a kind of crisp pizza); trout; *baeckeoffe* (variously spelled – a stew with beef, pork and mutton in it); *choucroute* (a sauerkraut dish, usually richly garnished); *schiefala* (smoked shoulder of pork, generally with horseradish sauce); game recipes; the well-flavoured Munster cheese; and *kugelhopf* (a sort of dry sponge ring).

Relais du Vignoble, 68420 Gueberschwihr, tel. 89 49 22 22. Comparatively new hotel, quietly placed about 10 km (6 miles) south of Colmar. The owner makes wine. Restaurant. Hotel class B; restaurant class C.

La Clairière, 68150 Ribeauvillé, tel. 89 71 80 80. Country house surrounded by trees, halfway between Guémar and Illhaeusern. The place for visitors to Auberge de l'Ill to stay overnight. Class A.

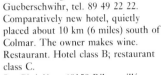

HOTELS

l'Arbre Vert, 68770 Ammerschwihr, tel. 89 47 12 23. Village hotel with country cooking. *Kugelhopf* on Sunday evenings. *Demi-pension* obligatory in the season. Class B.

Hotel Kastelberg, 67140 Andlau, tel. 88 08 97 83. Fairly large hotel in a half-timbered building. The modernized rooms have a rustic chic. Has restaurant. Class B.

Château d'Andlau, 67140 Barr, tel. 88 08 96 78. Peacefully situated just outside the town on the D854. Class B/C.

St-Martin, 38 Grand' Rue, 68000 Colmar, tel. 89 24 11 51. Decent small hotel (a dozen rooms) in the centre of town. Class B.

Terminus-Bristol, 7 Place de la Gare, 68000 Colmar, tel. 89 41 10 10. The best hotel in the place. The restaurant Le Rendez-vous de la Chasse is also excellent; game and contemporary-style regional dishes are served. Hotel class A; restaurant class A.

Au Raisin d'Or, 67650 Dambach-la-Ville, tel. 88 92 48 66. Pleasant small hotel owned by a wine grower. Restaurant. Class B/C.

Hotel au Moulin, 68420 Herrlisheim-près-Colmar, tel. 89 49 31 20. Architect husband and wife have converted this old mill south of Colmar into a comfortable, quiet hotel. Class B.

Arnold, 67140 Itterswiller, tel. 88 85 50 58. Pleasant hotel with a modern (more luxurious) annexe. Some of the rooms have a beautiful view. Also a convivial, genuinely Alsatian restaurant (*baeckeoffe*, *choucroute*, etc). Hotel class A/B; restaurant class B.

l'Abbaye d'Alspach, 68240 Kientzheim, tel. 89 47 16 00. Fairly small but neat rooms in an old building. Simple meals are served. Hotel class B; restaurant class C.

A la Verte Vallée, 68140 Munster, tel. 89 77 15 15. Modern comfort. Also a restaurant. Class B.

Hostellerie St-Barnabé, 68530 Murbach, tel. 89 76 92 15. Chalet-like hotel in a valley west of Guebwiller. Has restaurant. Class B.

Le Parc, 67210 Obernai, tel 88 95 50 08. A truly Alsatian setting and good value for money. The restaurant is very popular locally, especially for Sunday lunch. Try the farmhouse Munster cheese and the *eaux-de-vie*. *Demi-pension* obligatory in the season. Hotel class A/B; restaurant class B.

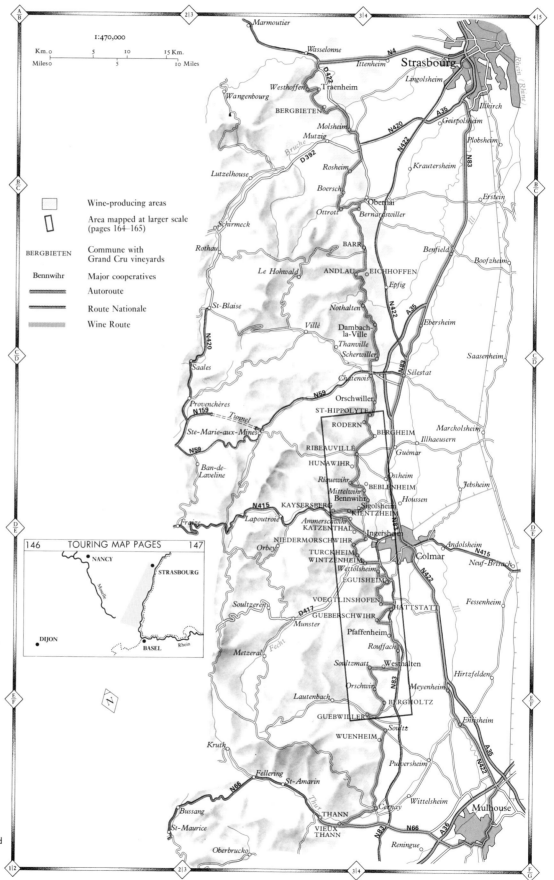

1:470,000

Km. 0 — 5 — 10 — 15 Km.
Miles 0 — 5 — 10 Miles

Wine-producing areas

Area mapped at larger scale
(pages 164–165)

BERGBIETEN   Commune with
Grand Cru vineyards

Bennwihr   Major cooperatives

Autoroute

Route Nationale

Wine Route

160
NE

TOURING MAP PAGES
146   147

NANCY

STRASBOURG

DIJON

BASEL

Rhein

▶ The full extent of the Alsace
vineyard. One small area, not on this
map, lies in the extreme north near
Wissembourg, on the border with
Germany. The heart of the area,
enclosed here by a red line, is mapped
at a larger scale on pages 164 and
165.

Hostellerie des Seigneurs de Ribeaupierre, 68150 Ribeauvillé, tel. 89 73 70 31. Handsomely furnished small hotel in a 17th-century building. Class A/B.

Hotel la Tour, 68150 Ribeauvillé, tel. 89 73 72 73. Functional hotel owned by a wine-growing family. Has a *winstub*. Hotel class B; restaurant class C.

Le Riquewihr, 68340 Riquewihr, tel. 89 47 83 13. Set among the vineyards. Generally spacious rooms, with rustic-style furnishings and variable plumbing. Class B.

Château d'Isenbourg, 68250 Rouffach, tel. 89 49 63 53. Beautiful position high above the little town. Luxurious rooms in the château and an annexe. Park and swimming pool. Meals can be expensive. Class A.

Hotel Hannong, 15 Rue du 22-Novembre, 67000 Strasbourg, tel. 88 32 16 22. Central, businesslike, but decorated with 18th-century porcelain and old paintings. Around the corner (9 Rue Hannong) the hotel runs Le Wyn' Bar (simple restaurant and wine bar). Hotel class A; restaurant class C.

Hilton International, Avenue Herrenschmidt, 67000 Strasbourg, tel. 88 37 10 10. Large, somewhat austere rooms with a view. La Maison du Boeuf is the justifiably renowned restaurant (attractive lunch menu). Simpler and cheaper eating in Le Jardin brasserie. Hotel class A; restaurant class B.

Monopole-Métropole, 16 Rue Kuen, 67000 Strasbourg, tel. 88 32 11 94. Congenial, friendly place to stay with an Alsace atmosphere. Class A/B.

Hotel des Rohan, 17 Rue Maroquin, 67000 Strasbourg, tel. 88 32 85 11. Near the cathedral in the old centre. Small but comfortable rooms. Class A/B.

Au Riesling, 68340 Zellenberg, tel. 89 47 85 85. Modern hotel on the wine route, with a view across the plain towards the Rhine. Belongs to a wine-growing family. Restaurant. Class B.

RESTAURANTS

Aux Armes de France, 68770 Ammerschwihr, tel. 89 47 10 12. This restaurant enjoys great fame. A splendid wine list, classic cuisine with modern elements (the *foie gras* is fantastic) and sometimes rather offhand service. Has rooms. Class A/B.

Au Boeuf Rouge, 67140 Andlau, tel. 88 08 96 26. Spacious dining room with beams and antlers. Many fish specialities and game dishes. *Winstub* on the first floor. Class B.

Winstub du Sommelier, 68750 Bergheim, tel. 89 73 69 99. Carefully prepared regional dishes, expertly chosen wines. Class B.

Au Fer Rouge, 52 Grand' Rue, 68000 Colmar, tel. 89 41 37 24. A happy contrast: very modern cooking in a fine old building. Class B.

Schillinger, 16 Rue Stanislas, 68000 Colmar, tel. 89 41 43 17. Excellent, stylish place. Ask to be shown the wine cellar. Class B.

Le Caveau d'Eguisheim, 68420 Eguisheim, tel. 89 41 08 89. Strictly regional: renowned for its *choucroute*. Class B.

Auberge de l'Ill, 68150 Illhaeusern, tel. 89 71 83 23. This restaurant's cooking, wine list and interior can only be described in superlatives. The Haeberlin family has made it one of the best and most beautiful eating places in France. Despite continual revision the menu always retains some of the establishment's classic dishes, such as *foie gras* and *saumon soufflé*. Class A.

A l'Arbre Vert, 68240 Kayserberg, tel. 89 47 11 51. Always busy, but with a relaxed atmosphere. Trout and, in season, asparagus and game. Also a hotel (across the square). Restaurant class C; hotel class B.

Chambard, 68240 Kaysersberg, tel. 89 47 10 17. Excellent cooking (fine sauces, fish, classic dishes) and an extensive wine list. The service can sometimes be a little distant. Comfortable, quiet hotel rooms. Restaurant class A/B; hotel class A.

Auberge St-Martin, 67600 Kintzheim, tel. 88 82 04 78. The speciality is *tarte flambée*. Class C.

Auberge du Kochersberg, 67490 Landersheim, tel. 88 69 91 58. You can only take lunch here after 1.00 pm; before this the large restaurant functions as a works "canteen" for Adidas. The cooking is of a high standard and in cellars in the rock there are tens of thousands of bottles of wine. These can also be enjoyed in the wine bar/*winstub*. Class B.

Auberge Bouton d'Or, 68650 Lapoutroie, tel. 89 47 50 95. Simple, convivial restaurant where the Munster cheese is fresh and delightful. Class C.

Hostellerie du Cerf, 67520 Marlenheim, tel. 88 87 73 73. Family concern that grows some of its own fruit and herbs. The cuisine is both traditional and fashionable, with many fish specialities. Has good hotel rooms around the charming inner courtyard. Restaurant class A; hotel class B.

Winstub Gilg, 67140 Mittelbergheim, tel. 88 08 91 37. *Pâté en brioche*, *baeckeoffe*, *choucroute* and more contemporary dishes. The setting is rural. Has rooms. Class B.

Auberge les Amandiers, 68630 Mittelwihr, tel. 89 47 89 89. Dark, traditional interior and regional dishes. Class B.

Beau Site, 67530 Ottrott, tel. 88 95 80 61. Reliable, hospitable hotel and restaurant where the regional dishes in particular are splendid. Class B.

Zum Pfifferhüs, 68150 Ribeauvillé, tel. 89 73 62 28. An authentic *winstub* (*choucroute*, for example). An excellent reputation. Class C.

Le Clos St-Vincent, 68150 Ribeauvillé, tel. 89 73 67 65. Glorious situation, high above the little town among the vineyards. Painstaking cuisine and a luxurious hotel. Restaurant class B; hotel class A.

Hotel des Vosges, 68150 Ribeauvillé, tel. 89 73 61 39. Talented cooking here (*foie gras*, fish dishes) and an ample wine list. Stylish interior. Restaurant class A/B.

Auberge du Schoenenbourg, 68340 Riquewihr, tel. 89 47 92 28. Just outside the town walls. Fresh ingredients are prepared in an honest yet inventive way. The nearby modern Le Schoenenbourg hotel is under the same management (tel. 89 47 83 13). Class B.

Le Moulin du Kaegy, 68440 Steinbrunn-le-Bas, tel. 89 81 30 34. This restaurant to the south of Mulhouse occupies an old mill. The cooking is sublime, from the marvellous *foie gras* to the astonishing desserts. Class B.

l'Ami Schutz, 1 Ponts-Couverts, 67000 Strasbourg, tel. 88 32 76 98. Regional cuisine in a regional ambience in the middle of the Petite France quarter. Class C.

A l'Arbre de Vie, 14 Rue Paul-Janet, 67000 Strasbourg, tel. 88 35 58 40. Small place specializing in rediscovered regional dishes. Class B.

Buerehiesel, 4 Parc d l'Orangerie, 67000 Strasbourg, tel. 88 61 62 24. Old farmhouse in a beautiful city park. Cooking with finesse and an Oriental touch. Class B.

▽ Below: Riquewihr is a town of flowers and old buildings. The fountain reflects a purveyor of *charcuterie* providing the local pork specialities.
Bottom: the roofs of Kaysersberg, a village tucked into a valley in the Vosges. Its most noted vineyard is the superbly sited, south-facing Grand Cru Schlossberg.

161
NE

Le Crocodile, 10 Rue de l'Outre, 67000 Strasbourg, tel. 88 32 13 02. The city's best restaurant: dishes that are culinary masterpieces and large 19th-century paintings. Attractive lunch menu. Class A/B.

Maison Kammerzell, 16 Place de la Cathédrale, 67000 Strasbourg, tel. 88 43 42 14. Splendid building, an historic monument. Cooking is traditional downstairs, contemporary on the two floors above. There is also a *winstub* with richly decorated walls. Class B.

Chez Yvonne/S'Burjerstuewel, 10 Rue du Sanglier, 67000 Strasbourg, tel. 88 32 84 15. Famous *winstub* where regional dishes (such as *choucroute*) are served generously and with a smile. Dinner only. Class B.

Hotel des Vosges, 68230 Turckheim, tel. 89 27 02 37. By one of the old town gates. Good regional cuisine (e.g. asparagus, *choucroute*). Also rooms. Class B.

Auberge du Père Floranc, 68920 Wettolsheim, tel. 89 41 39 14. Rather austere from outside, but once inside you eat well (*tourte de cailles*, fish, etc). Also hotel and park. Class B.

Au Bon Coin, 68000 Wintzenheim, tel. 89 27 48 04. Honest simplicity. Class C.

Ange, Rue de la République, 67160 Wissembourg, tel. 88 94 12 11. Restaurant, in a 16th-century building, with the best reputation in this most northerly town in Alsace. Regional dishes on the menu. A few rooms. Class C.

PLACES OF INTEREST

Ammerschwihr Although the lovely 16th-century wine village of Ammerschwihr was laid waste in the battles of 1944 it has retained much charm. An old gate and a trio of towers remained intact. In the church there is a large wooden figure of Christ dating from 1606. A winding uphill road takes you to Les Trois-Epis (viewing point with a number of hotels and restaurants).

Andlau The abbey of Ste-Richarde was founded in 880 and rebuilt in 1049. It is worth a visit for the abbey church alone, with its 30 m (98 ft) long frieze full of curious animal figures.

Avolsheim Isolated in a field on the southeast side of this village stands the Dompeter church with its fortified churchyard. This 11th-century monument is the oldest church in Alsace.

Barr Small wine town with a maze of little winding streets. The tower of the St-Martin church is Romanesque below and Gothic above. The town hall, with an old fountain in front of it, dates from the 17th century. The Musée de la Folie Marco displays Alsace furniture, pewter and pottery.

Bergheim The atmospheric old centre is partly surrounded by walls with three towers. The sandstone church has frescoes. A footpath (*sentier viticole*) has been marked out through the vineyards.

Boersch *Hôtel de ville* dating from 1578, fine well from 1617, picturesque houses and three medieval gates.

Châtenois The wide main street flanked by old houses is almost like a square. The church tower is Romanesque and has four turrets. Inside the church there are 16th-century bas-reliefs. The *hôtel de ville* is late 15th century.

Colmar The centre of Colmar has many notable places of interest. Among them are the Maison Pfister (1537, with a remarkable wooden gallery); the Maison des Têtes (1608 – a façade decorated with heads); the Ancienne Douane (1480); and the cathedral of St-Martin (13th to 14th century) – to the left of the choir there is the beautiful Schongauer painting of the Madonna in the Rose Garden. One of the most-visited museums in France, the Musée Unterlinden (1 Rue Unterlinden), is housed in a 13th-century former Dominican monastery. As well as its magnificent collection of medieval and Renaissance art it has an interesting section devoted to wine. The Musée Bartholdi (30 Rue des Marchands) contains not only reminders of the sculptor Bartholdi, creator of the Statue of Liberty, but is also Colmar's historical museum.

Dambach-la-Ville The largest wine commune of Bas-Rhin. Within its walls with their three gates there is a lovely historic centre with half-timbered houses. Above the village, among the vineyards, the St-Sebastien chapel was built six centuries ago (it has a carved wooden Baroque altar and a Virgin in Alsace costume). A wine walk encircles Dambach-la-Ville.

Eguisheim Photogenic wine village. The walk around its centre through the Rue des Remparts is one of the prettiest in the Alsace. In the middle of the village stands the Château d'Eguisheim. The octagonal outer wall is 8th century but the château itself (birthplace of Pope Leon IX) was extensively rebuilt in 1894.

Epfig The 11th-century Ste-Marguerite chapel stands beside the churchyard. There is a wine walk.

Gueberschwihr There is a beautiful Romanesque tower beside the 19th-century church.

Guebwiller Both the industry and the wine-growing activities of this town are dominated by Schlumberger (see producers). Local history, medieval art and ceramics are displayed in the Musée du Florival, which occupies a former church. Still functioning as churches are St-Léger (12th century, with two belltowers and ladders left behind by 15th-century besiegers) and Notre-Dame (18th century). The town hall dates from 1514.

Haut-Koenigsbourg The fortress of Haut-Koenigsbourg is perched like an eagle's eyrie on a mountain top. The whole imposing structure was built at the beginning of this century, commissioned by Kaiser Wilhelm II (Alsace was German from 1870 to 1918). Every year it is visited by hundreds of thousands of tourists.

Hunawihr This village has a striking 14th- to 16th-century fortified church, surrounded by a thick, hexagonal wall. There are frescoes on the church walls and the hands of the clock are ornamented with bunches of grapes. Outside the village there is a centre for breeding and reintroducing storks, a bird much loved in Alsace.

Kaysersberg A jewel of a place with half-timbered and Renaissance houses. In addition the town hall, the church (a 1518 altarpiece), the two-storey St-Michel chapel, the Oberhof chapel (with a 15th-century figure of Christ with a bunch of grapes) and the fortified bridge over the Weiss make a visit to this small town very rewarding. Two steep paths take you up to the castle ruins above the town for the view. Albert Schweitzer was born in Kaysersberg in 1875. He is commemorated in the house where he was born and in a museum.

Kientzheim The local château belongs to La Confrérie St-Etienne. This wine fraternity organizes festivities here and it also houses the Musée du Vignoble et des Vins d'Alsace. This is open from July to the end of September and its contents include a replica of an old wine cellar, wine-making implements, a 1716 wine press, flasks, glasses and costumes.

Kintzheim La Volerie des Aigles near the château ruins puts on displays with birds of prey. Higher up the mountain is La Montagne des Singes, where 300 monkeys wander freely through woodland. On the east side of the village a small amusement park has been opened.

Lapoutroie A distillery museum with displays of apparatus and a collection of French liqueurs from the 1920s.

Marlenheim A wine walk.

Mittelbergheim Wine village set on a hill, with narrow streets, 16th- and 17th-century houses and a partly 12th-century church tower.

Molsheim On the first floor of the most beautiful building here, the Metzig (Butchers' Guildhouse) of 1525, there is a history museum. Molsheim has a large 17th-century church and the town is also a place of pilgrimage for Bugatti owners, for this is where cars of this legendary marque were made.

Mont Ste-Odile Every year many pilgrims and tourists come here to the convent that Saint Odile founded in the 7th century. The convent church, the chapel with the tomb of Saint Odile, the cloisters with their frescoes and the viewing terrace are among the highlights of a visit.

Mulhouse A town with many museums and therefore ideal for a rainy day. Europe's biggest car collection is in the Musée National de l'Automobile (192 Avenue de Colmar). Mulhouse also has the finest railway museum of continental Europe, with next to it a fire service museum (2 Rue Alfred-de-Glehn). The Maison de la Céramique (25 Rue José-Hofer); the Musée des Impression sur Etoffes (vast collection of printed fabrics from all over the world, at 3 Rue des Bonnes-Gens); the Musée des Beaux-Arts (4 Place Guillaume-Tell); the Musée Historique (in the 16th-century town hall, Place de la Réunion); and the Musée de la Chapelle St-Jean (Grand' Rue). The zoo is laid out in a park with rare trees.

Mutzig Better known for its beer than for its wine. The town's museum, which features a large collection of firearms, is in the Château des Rohan.

Niedermorschwihr The 13th-century church tower has a spiral steeple and the town hall an unusual roofed outside wooden staircase.

Obermorschwihr A gilded statue of the Virgin watches over the village fountain. The church has a unique half-timbered tower.

Obernai The Place du Marché is ringed by attractive buildings, among them the 16th-century town hall, the 13th- to 15th-century Tour de la Chapelle and the 16th-century Halle aux Blés (also the museum). There is a wine walk.

Pfaffenheim Deep grooves in the wall of the church show where the farmers used to beat the Devil out of their billhooks every evening. There is a wine walk.

Ribeauvillé Very pretty small town with many half-timbered houses and other old buildings. The 18th-century town hall contains a museum of goblets and gold- and silversmith's work. Of the three ruined castles the St-Ulrich is the biggest and most beautiful. France's first wine cooperative was founded in this town in 1895.

Riquewihr What St-Emilion is to Bordeaux, Riquewihr is to Alsace. Masses of visitors throng this village, which has been declared a historic monument in its entirety, especially at weekends. Riquewihr (the name derives from Old High German words meaning "rich village" is one big museum, with marvellous houses, 90% of them dating from before 1640. Shops, tasting rooms, wine firms and restaurants all contribute to the atmosphere. Riquewihr also has a museum of history (in the Dolder, a half-timbered tower of 1291); and the museum in the Tour des Voleurs (prison and torture chamber).

Rosheim The 12th-century Heidenhüss, the oldest house in Alsace, stands here. Three gates and the Romanesque church of St-Pierre-et-St-Paul are also worth noting. Between mid-July and mid-August a steam train runs to Ottrott.

Rott Village in the north of Alsace, near Wissembourg, with a fortified churchyard.

Rouffach Around the large Place de la République stand the large, cathedral-like church of Notre-Dame-de-l'Assomption (Romanesque and early Gothic); a corn exchange with stepped gables (15th to 16th century), a former town hall (16th to 17th century) and the Tour des Sorcières ("Witches' Tower", 13th to 15th century).

Scherwiller A wine walk.

Sélestat A unique 15th- to 16th-century humanist library here is not far from the Gothic church of St-Georges.

Sigolsheim There was fearful fighting here during World War II; war graves are movingly laid out on a wide hill above the vineyards. The village church has a Romanesque porch.

Strasbourg University and music city, a Rhine port and the seat of the Council of Europe. The old city centre clusters around the cathedral of Notre-Dame, which was begun in the 12th century and completed in the 15th. Inside there hangs an astronomical clock with a 16th-century mechanism; the rest is 19th-century. The most charming quarter of Strasbourg is La Petite France, with half-timbered houses and canals. Beside the cathedral stands the early 18th-century Château des Rohan, with three museums: the Musée des Beaux-Arts (many still-lifes); the Musée des Arts Décoratifs (a notable collection of porcelain); and the Musée Archéologique (prehistoric and Gallo-Roman finds). Wine is dealt with in the Musée Alsacien (23 Quai St-Nicolas); the Musée Historique (3 Place de la Grande-Boucherie) displays a three-dimensional map of Strasbourg of 1727; and the Musée d'Art Moderne (1 Rue du Vieux-Marché-aux-Poissons) is devoted to painting since the Impressionists. Religious art and a 17th-century doll's house are to be seen in the Musée de l'Œuvre Notre-Dame (beside the cathedral). The beautiful Orangerie park was designed by Le Nôtre in 1692. Strasbourg is also the town where the *marseillaise* was sung for the first time (see the plaque at 4 Place Broglie) and where Gutenberg invented printing between 1434 and 1444. His statue in the square named after him bears the text of the American Declaration of Independence.

Thann The church of St-Thiébaut is in Flamboyant Gothic style and is a masterpiece of its kind. Thann also has a museum of history and a 13th- to 15th-century Witches' Tower.

Traenheim A wine walk.

Turckheim Half-timbered houses, three 14th-century town gates and a wine walk. Every summer evening at 10.00 pm a nightwatchman goes around the little town, complete with halberd and lantern, singing to the inhabitants.

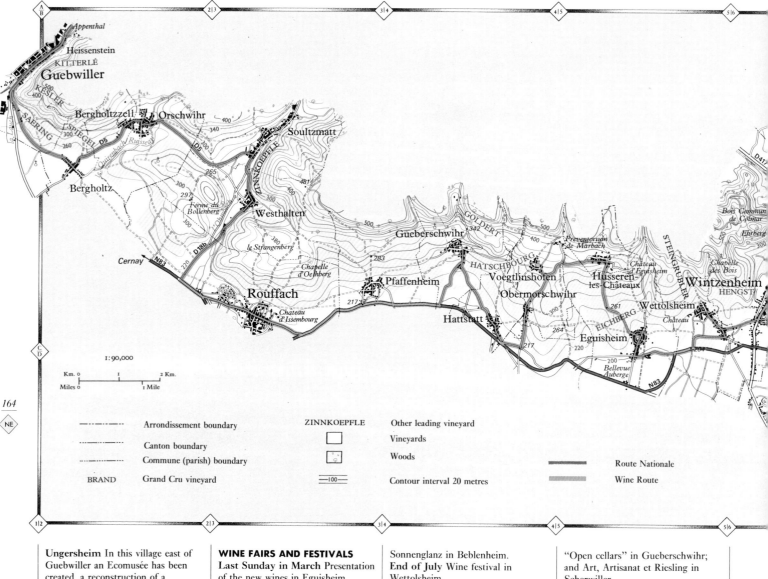

Map legend

—————	Arrondissement boundary
—·—·—	Canton boundary
—··—··—	Commune (parish) boundary
BRAND	Grand Cru vineyard
ZINNKOEPFLE ☐	Other leading vineyard / Vineyards
☐	Woods
—100—	Contour interval 20 metres
████	Route Nationale
▓▓▓▓	Wine Route

1:90,000

Km. 0   1   2 Km.
Miles 0   1 Mile

Ungersheim In this village east of Guebwiller an Ecomusée has been created, a reconstruction of a traditional Haut-Rhin village, with 20 half-timbered farmhouses.

Wissembourg The most northerly town in Alsace. After Strasbourg Cathedral, the church of St-Pierre-et-St-Paul is the most important Gothic structure in the region. The town centre has old buildings and canals. The Musée Westercamp displays weapons, uniforms and furniture.

WINE FAIRS AND FESTIVALS

Last Sunday in March Presentation of the new wines in Eguisheim.

End of April Ammerschwihr wine fair.

1 May Molsheim wine fair.

Last weekend in May Dorlisheim wine festival.

Ascension Day *Foire aux vins* in Guebwiller.

Saturday nearest to 25 May Fête de St-Urbain in Kintzheim.

First Saturday in July "Open cellars" in Dambach-la-Ville.

First weekend in July Fête du Crémant in Orschwihr.

First Sunday in July Nothalten wine fair.

14 July Barr wine fair.

Sunday after 14 July Fête des Guinguettes d'Europe in Husseren-les-Châteaux.

Third weekend in July Fête du Pinot Noir in Rodern.

Last weekend but one in July Wine fair in Ribeauvillé, Fête du Riesling in Riquewihr, Fête du

Sonnenglanz in Beblenheim.

End of July Wine festival in Wettolsheim.

Last weekend in July Wine festivals in Kientzheim and Mittelbergheim.

First weekend in August Wine festivals in Turckheim and Westhalten.

First Sunday in August Fête du Gewürztraminer in Bergheim, Fête des Amandiers in Mittelwihr.

First two weeks in August The great Foire Régionale des Vins d'Alsace in Colmar.

Second weekend in August Wine festival in Bennwihr, Fête du Kaefferkopf in Ammerschwihr.

Second Sunday in August Fête du Klevener in Heiligenstein.

14 and 15 August Fête des Vins de France in Dambach-la-Ville.

15 August Mariage de l'Ami Fritz in Marlenheim; "open cellars" in Orschwiller.

Weekend nearest to 15 August Mini wine fair in Obernai.

Last weekend but one in August

"Open cellars" in Gueberschwihr; and Art, Artisanat et Riesling in Scherwiller.

Last weekend in August Open day at the Turckheim cooperative.

Last Sunday in August Fête des Vignerons in Eguisheim.

First Sunday in September Fête des Ménétriers (minstrels) in Ribeauvillé.

Early September Fête du Riesling in Wolxheim.

Last weekend in September Wine festivals in Dahlenheim and Wuenheim.

First two weeks in October Grape harvest festivals in Barr, Hunawihr, Itterswiller, Katzenthal, Molsheim, Niedermorschwihr, Rosheim and elsewhere.

Third Sunday in October Grape harvest festivals in Marlenheim and Obernai.

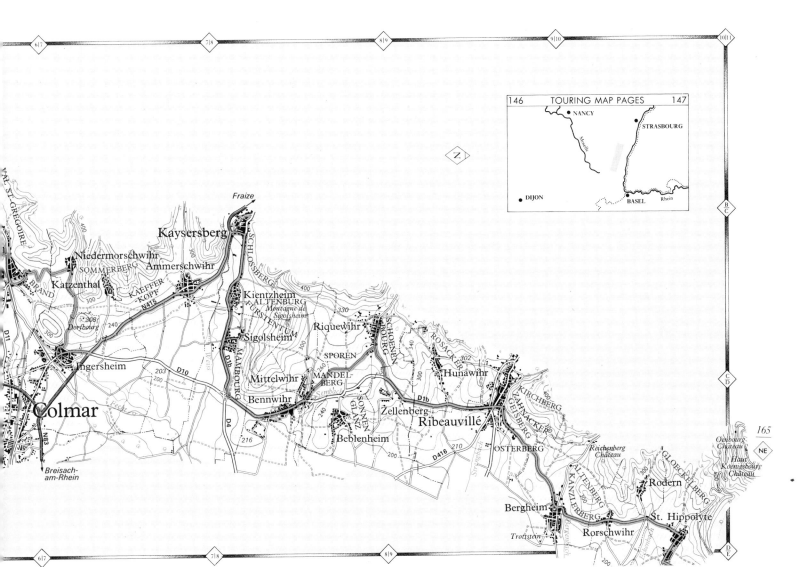

WINE ACTIVITIES

The very energetic wine fraternity for the whole of Alsace is La Confrérie St-Etienne, which owns the Château de Kientzheim. In addition there are La Confrérie des Hospitaliers du Haut-Andlau (Andlau); La Confrérie des Rieslinger (Scherwiller); La Confrérie des Rois-Mages (Ribeauvillé); and La Confrérie St-Sébastien (Bergheim).

WINE INFORMATION

The Maison du Vin d'Alsace (12 Avenue de la Foire aux Vins) is in a modern commercial district on the north side of Colmar. It has very good documentation.

▲ Looking east into storm-clouds over the wide, flat Rhine Valley from above the vineyards near Riquewihr. The houses in Alsace, even the modern ones, display the steep pitched roof so characteristic of the area. The vineyards here are all on the east-facing slopes of the Vosges.

PRODUCERS OF SPECIAL INTEREST

AMMERSCHWIHR, postcode 68770, 160 D3, 165 C7

J. B. Adam; Straightforward wines from this négociant; **Henri Ehrhart; Jérôme Geschickt & Fils***: Gewürztraminer Kaefferkopf, etc; **H. & J. Heitzmann; Kuehn***: Quality firm with old, vaulted cellars, a modest estate of its own and very pure wines (including the nuanced Riesling Kaefferkopf). The Ingersheim cooperative has a majority shareholding; **André & Pierre Mercklé***: Riesling and Gewürztraminer Kaefferkopf, also wood-aged Pinot Noir; **J. Schaetzel; René Schneider; Sick-Dreyer***: Family estate producing excellent wines, including Riesling, Gewürztraminer Kaefferkopf and Tokay.

ANDLAU, postcode 67140, 160 C3

André Gresser*: Estate run by the energetic Rémy Gresser, with notable wines that include various Grands Crus; **Marc Kreydenweiss/ Domaine Fernand Gresser***: Exceptionally expert and committed winemaker whose labels artistically convey the style of each vintage. His wife runs a wine shop and négociant concern under the name Catherine Lacoste.

BARR, postcode 67140, 160 C3

Klipfel: Firm that produces attractive estate wines and a Riesling Primeur. Large tasting room with old wine presses. **Alsace Willm:** This concern belongs to the Eguisheim cooperative. Good Riesling Kirchberg, Sylvaner and Gewürztraminer Clos Gaensbroennel. **Ch. Wantz:** Négociant whose wines include Klevener de Heiligenstein.

BEBLENHEIM, postcode 68980, 160 D4, 165 D8

Bott-Geyl: Small family firm with steadily improving wines. Worth following; **Cave Coopérative.**

BENNWIHR, postcode 68630, 160 D4, 165 D8

Cave Coopérative: Large concern with its own regional restaurant, Chez Hansi, on the site.

BERGHEIM, postcode 68750, 160 D4, 165 D9

Marcel Deiss*: Property run on modern lines (Gewürztraminer and Riesling Altenberg); **Louis Freyburger & Fils; Lorentz:** This firm, which operates under two names (Gustave Lorentz, Jérôme Lorentz) has made a good deal of progress in quality in recent years. About 30 hectares (74 acres) of its own land. Fine Riesling and Gewürztraminer Altenberg.

BERGHOLTZ, postcode 68500, 160 F4, 164 C2

Jean-Pierre Dirler*: Very natural wines of high quality: Sylvaner Vieilles Vignes, Rieslings from the Kessler and the Spiegel.

CLEEBOURG, postcode 67160

Cave Coopérative.

COLMAR, postcode 68000, 160 E4, 165 D6

Robert Schoffit (27 Rue des Aubépines)

DAHLENHEIM, postcode 67310

Jean-Pierre Bechtold*; **André Pfister.**

DAMBACH-LA-VILLE, postcode 67650, 160 C4

Maison Louis Gisselbrecht; Willy Gisselbrecht & Fils: Good firm with wines that regularly win awards (Sylvaner, Pinot Blanc, Riesling, Gewürztraminer); **J. Hauller & Fils:** Formerly coopers, now négociants; **Louis Hauller***: Klevner and Gewürztraminer of class; **Hubert Metz; Jean Maurer.**

EGUISHEIM, postcode 68420, 160 E4, 164 C5

Léon Beyer*: Committed family concern with an excellent name. Big supplier to high-class restaurants. Usually firm wines for drinking with meals, among them broad Gewürztraminers and powerful Tokays; **Cave Cooperative:** The largest wine concern in Alsace and the most visited (about 100,000 people a year). The cooperatives at Dambach-la-Ville and Wuenheim are associated with it, as is Alsace Willm. A big range of wines, including good special *cuvées* and about a half of all Crémant d'Alsace. Distillates and delicatessen complete the selection. **Paul Ginglinger; Bruno Sorg***: Rieslings Pfersigberg and Florimont and Gewürztraminer; **Antoine Stoffel.**

EPFIG, postcode 67680

Patrick Beyer; Domaine Ostertag*: Sylvaner, Riesling Munchberg, Tokay.

GUEBERSCHWIHR, postcode 68420, 160 E4, 164 C4

Maurice Schueller.

GUEBWILLER, postcode 68500, 160 F4, 164, B1

Domaines Viticoles Schlumberger*: With 135 hectares (334 acres) the largest estate in Alsace. Most of the vines grow on terraces up the steep hillsides. They give rich, rounded, powerful wines. The best come from the Grands Crus Kitterlé, Kessler and Saering.

HEILIGENSTEIN, postcode 67140

Jean Heywang*: Klevener de Heiligenstein, Gewürztraminer Kirchberg; **Gilbert Hutt & Fils.**

HUNAWIHR, postcode 68150, 160 D3, 165 C9

Cave Coopérative; Frédéric Mallo & Fils*: Riesling Rosacker; Mittnacht Frères.

HUSSEREN-LES-CHATEAUX, postcode 68420, 164 C5

Kuentz-Bas*: One of the very best firms in the region, with splendid, balanced wines. The Rieslings in particular are brilliant. This family concern sells the vintage from its own vineyards as "Cuvée personnelle".

KAYSERSBERG, postcode 68240, 160 D3, 165 C8

Domaine Dietrich*; Faller Frères/Domaine Weinbach*: From not quite 25 hectares (62 acres) Mme Colette Faller produces a range of exceptional lively and vivid wines; **Thomann-Saltzmann.**

KATZENTHAL, postcode 68230, 160 E3, 165 C7

Jean-Paul Ecklé.

KIENTZHEIM, postcode 68240, 160 D3, 165 C8

Blanck/Domaine des Comtes de Lupfen*: The Blanck family takes great care to match grape variety and soil type. The wines are then vinified with the greatest possible care. Sound, very pure and utterly reliable wines are the result. Buying for the négociant firm of Blanck Frères is also very expert. **Cave Coopérative.**

MARLENHEIM, postcode 67250

Laugel: Very dynamic négociant: Mosbach.

▼ Below: vines rise above the roof tiles in a recurring Alsace pattern.
Below right: Colmar offers its many visitors some superb old buildings.

MITTELBERGHEIM, postcode 67140

E. Boeckel: Négociant and wine grower working in the traditional way; Armand Gilg & Fils; A. Seltz & Fils*: The "Réserve" and "Réserve Particulière" from this family concern are excellent. Sylvaner Zotzenberg is a speciality.

MITTELWIHR, postcode 68630, 160 D3, 165 D8

Frédéric Berger; Alfred Burghoffer Père & Fils; Preiss-Henny*: Delightful estate wines, such as the Riesling and Gewürztraminer Mandelberg; J. Siegler Père & Fils; Patrick Schaller*: Property with very successful Crémant d'Alsace, Muscat and Riesling.

NIEDERMORSCHWIHR, postcode 68230, 160 E3, 165 C7

Albert Boxler & Fils*: The best estate hereabouts; Marcel Mullenbach*: Muscat, Riesling, Tokay, Gewürztraminer.

NOTHALTEN, postcode 67680, 160 C3

Madame Julien Meyer & Fils.

OBERMORSCHWIHR, postcode 68420, 164 C4

Stempfel.

OBERNAI, postcode 67210, 160 C4

Domaine du Clos Ste-Odile.

OHRSCHWIHR, postcode 68500, 160 E4

Lucien Albrecht; Paul Reinhart.

ORSCHWILLER, postcode 67600, 160 D4

Louis Siffert & Fils.

PFAFFENHEIM, postcode 68250, 160 E4, 164 C3

Cave Coopérative: Thanks to a talented cellarmaster this has become one of the best cooperatives in Alsace; Pierre Frick & Fils; Joseph Rieflé & Fils.

RIBEAUVILLE, postcode 68150, 160 D3, 165 D9

Bott Frères; Cave Coopérative; Robert Faller & Fils; Henri Fuchs & Fils; André Kientzler*: Family holding where with great integrity and expertise a range of excellent wines is made; Metz Frères; Jean Sipp*: Large estate of 20 hectares (49 acres). Its wines are of very good quality across the whole range. Louis Sipp: Négociant of average standard. F.E. Trimbach*: This house has acquired fame in Europe, and even more particularly in America, with its fragrant, pure, often austere wines full of character. Some come from its own land (e.g. the Riesling Clos Ste-Hune and the Gewürztraminer Cuvée des Seigneurs de Ribeaupierre).

RIQUEWIHR, postcode 68340, 160 D3, 165 C8

Jean-Jacques Baumann; Dopff & Irion: After a period of financial trouble this large export firm was restructured. Dopff & Irion remained in charge and the 30 hectares (74 acres) of vineyards was retained. This is where the best wines originate, such as the Riesling Les Murailles, the Gewürztraminer Les Sorcières, the Tokay Les Marquisards and the Muscat les Amandiers; Dopff "au Moulin": A firm with big vineyards – 75 hectares (185 acres) – and a range of divergent qualities. At the top come the estate wines (Riesling

▲ Strasbourg, the capital of Alsace, is a large modern city with an old centre. The city is at the confluence of the Rhine and the Ill. It is a major river port, and the many canals and basins give the centre a distinctly watery air, especially in the old Petite France quarter and around the cathedral.

Schoenenbourg, Gewürztraminer Eichberg) and various Crémants; **Hugel & Fils***: Family firm famous for its ubiquitous exports. Among the leaders in Alsace. The Hugels have been involved in wine since 1639. The house style is one of full, supple, rounded wines, less dry than those from many other firms. A two-year stock is held. The simplest qualities comprise branded wines; at the top come wines from late-picked grapes (with the designations Vendange Tardive and Sélection des Grains Nobles; **Preiss-Zimmer**; Clear-tasting, dry wines are the hallmark of this firm; **René Schmidt.**

RODERN, postcode 68590, 160 D3, 165 D10

Koeberlé-Kreyer; Charles Koehly & Fils*: Christian Koehly makes fine, stylish wines from, for example, the Grand Cru Gloeckelberg.

RORSCHWIHR, postcode 68590, 165 D10

Rolly-Gassmann*: Aromatic,

sometimes almost luxurious wines (Auxerrois, Tokay, Gewürztraminer).

ROUFFACH, postcode 68250, 160 E4, 164 C3

Clément Bannwarth & Fils; Muré/Clos St. Landelin.

SIGOLSHEIM, postcode 68240, 160 D3, 165 C8

Cave Coopérative; Maison Ringenbach-Moser; Pierre Sparr & Ses Fils: Firm with wines that taste powerful rather than fine.

SOULTZMATT, postcode 68570, 160 E4, 164 B3

Kandmann-Ostholt; Paul Kubler*.

TRAENHEIM, postcode 67310, 160 B3
Frédéric Mochel.

TURCKHEIM, postcode 68230, 160 E3, 165 C6

Cave Coopérative*: The wines from this cooperative can match those from the best estates. The wood-aged

Pinot Noir Cuvée à l'Ancienne is extraordinary and white wines are produced from the Grands Crus Brand, Hengst and Sommerberg and elsewhere; **Armand Hurst***; **Charles Schleret***: Year after year this grower manages to surprise with his excellent wines.

VOEGTLINSHOFFEN,
postcode 68420, 160 E4, 164 C4

Gérard Hartmann & Fils; Joseph Cattin & Ses Fils: Specialities of this firm are the Muscat, Tokay, and Gewürztraminer from Hatschbourg.

WESTHALTEN, postcode 68111, 160 E4, 164 C3

Cave Coopérative; A. Heim*: A négociant with clear-tasting, fresh wines. Recommended are the Pinot Clos du Strangenberg, the Riesling Les Eglantiers and the Crémant.

WETTOLSHEIM, postcode 68000, 160 E4, 164 C5

A. Gaschy – F. Brucker: One of the biggest négociants.

WINTZENHEIM, postcode 68000, 160 E3, 164 C6

Josmeyer & Fils*: Under the direction of Jean Meyer the wines from this firm have continued to improve. Delicious Pinot Blanc, Pinot Auxerrois, Riesling Hengst, Gewürztraminer Hengst; **Domaine Zind-Humbrecht***: Léonard Humbrecht believes firmly in the individuality of soil and microclimate, and bases his choice of grape variety on them. He was also the first in Alsace to adopt low-temperature fermentation. His efforts to replant the Rangen vineyard in Thann are worthy of praise. The Zind-Humbrecht wines have a good deal of personality and often require time.

ZELLENBERG, postcode 68340, 165 D9

J. Becker: The many wines that have won awards witness to the fact that this old, small family concern is run with dedication and skill.

LORRAINE

The four départements of Lorraine are between Alsace and Champagne. Until late in the last century thousands of hectares of vineyard were cultivated, but these fell into a decline in the first years of the century and today only a few dozen remain. They are divided between two small VDQS districts: Côtes de Toul and Vins de Moselle. Together they produce some 4,000 hectolitres (44,400 cases) a year. More than 90 percent of production is concentrated in Côtes de Toul. This district takes its name from the fortified town of Toul, west of Nancy. The vineyards lie to the north and the southwest of Toul; there is even a small wine route signposted. For centuries the bishops of Toul dominated wine growing here. Thus a wine village like Lucey has hardly any cellars: all the grapes used to be transported to Toul. The Côtes de Toul speciality is Vin Gris, a rosé wine usually made from Gamay. This light, fresh-tasting wine is good for serving with a *quiche lorraine*. Côtes de Toul reds can also be pleasant, particularly if they have been made from ripe Pinot Noir grapes. The whites are often too acidic.

The Vins de Moselle zone is extensive, divided into three zones. The most northerly of these lies near the West German-Luxembourg border, the southern one near Vic-sur-Seille, to the east of Nancy. The district's tiny production is, however, concentrated mainly to the south of Metz. The wines do not amount to a great deal. They are simple, light and fresh, the Vin Gris being the most pleasant.

PRODUCERS

COTES DE TOUL

BRULEY, postcode 54200

Gabriel Demange; Michel Laroppe; Fernand Poirson.

BULLIGNY, postcode 54170

Yves Masson; Claude Vosgien; Michel Vosgien.

LUCEY, postcode 54200

Lelièvre Frères/GAEC des Coteaux Toulois

VINS DE MOSELLE

LAQUENEXY, postcode 57530

Centre d'Exploitation Fruitière.

VEZON, postcode 57420

Gabriel et Georges Gaspard; Jean Gaspard.

Food is taken seriously in Alsace-Lorraine. The region has a fine concentration of rosette-bedecked restaurants.

Lorraine's yellow Mirabelle plums sometimes appear in recipes and are made into the famous fruit brandy.

HOTELS

Hotel de l'Europe, 35 Avenue Victor-Hugo, 54200 Toul, tel. 83 43 00 10. Simple, adequate provincial hotel. Class B.

RESTAURANTS

La Belle Epoque, 31 Avenue Victor-Hugo, 54200 Toul, tel. 83 43 23 71. The ambience of this small restaurant matches its name. Many fish specialities. Class B.
Le Dauphin, Route de Villey-St-Etienne, 54200 Toul, tel. 83 43 13 46. This is not the place to visit for its location (an industrial estate 5 km from the centre) or for its appearance (modern and rather lacking in atmosphere). The cooking, however, is highly inventive. Class B.

TRAVEL INFORMATION

PLACES OF INTEREST

Blénod-les-Toul The local church is unusual in being in the courtyard of a former castle. Just south of the village is the 16th- to 18th-century Château de Tumejus.
Metz An industrial town badly damaged in World War II. Well worth seeing are the Gothic cathedral of St-Etienne with its beautiful windows, the 13th- to 16th-century fortified Porte des Allemands and the Musée d'Art et d'Histoire (2 Rue du Haut-Poireu).
Nancy University and industrial town with a strikingly beautiful Baroque centre. The buildings around the Place Stanislas are particularly splendid. The former ducal palace, the church and monastery of the Cordeliers (Franciscans) and the Porte de la Graffe serve as museums.
Toul This once important town lies on the Moselle, which makes a sharp bend here. 17th-century walls surround the centre of Toul, interrupted by four gateways. Toul suffered greatly in World War II, but fortunately it has been possible to restore the former cathedral of St-Etienne. Its façade in Flamboyant Gothic was completed in 1496 and is flanked by two 65 m (213 ft) octagonal towers. There are Renaissance chapels on either side of its splendid nave and the cloisters have galleries on three sides (13th- and 14th-century). The cloisters of the church of St-Gengoult are even more beautiful. Toul has a number of old houses, in particular in the Rue du Général-Gengoult.

WINE ACTIVITIES

Côtes de Toul has its own wine fraternity, Les Compagnons de la Capucine.

EASTERN ZONE

The spinal column of eastern France is the valley of the Sâone, joined from the east first by the river Doubs, then at Lyon by the Rhône, flowing from its Alpine glaciers through Lake Geneva.

Mountains force all France's north-south traffic into the Rhône valley: the importance of this ancient highway at least partly explains the extent and quality of the vineyards that line it, from the Côte d'Or of Burgundy, centred on Beaune, to the more scattered vineyards of the region of Mercurey near Châlon-sur-Sâone, to the crescendo of concentration through the country of Mâcon to the huge spread of the Beaujolais.

Lyon also has its own "Coteaux" of vines before the Rhône valley narrows, and whole hills give way to narrow, laborious terraces in the region of the northern Rhône around Tournon. The fluid openness of the Beaujolais gives way to the deep concentration of Côte Rôtie and Hermitage.

Compared with this central core of great appellations, the remaining vineyards of the eastern sector are almost desultory. What they contribute is not an important mass of wine, but some of the most distinct and charming local characters of France.

The Jura, small producer though it is, offers its unique "yellow" wines, as well as mellow reds and close-to-Burgundian whites.

The scattered vineyards of Savoie, reaching up towards the ski slopes, make white wines of lovely prickling freshness, and vigorous reds from the rare Mondeuse.

Recently the few wine districts in the mountains west of Lyon have been undergoing a revival: the Côtes du Forez and the Côte Roannaise (helped by one of France's most famous restaurants) are no longer unknown. St-Pourçain remains a remnant of a once-famous monastic vineyard that has held on down through the centuries. Curious wine lovers on their travels are bringing this little district, too, back to at least a modest prosperity.

VINS DE PAYS

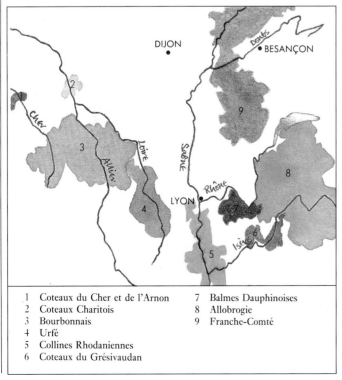

 1 Coteaux du Cher et de l'Arnon
 2 Coteaux Charitois
 3 Bourbonnais
 4 Urfé
 5 Collines Rhodaniennes
 6 Coteaux du Grésivaudan
 7 Balmes Dauphinoises
 8 Allobrogie
 9 Franche-Comté

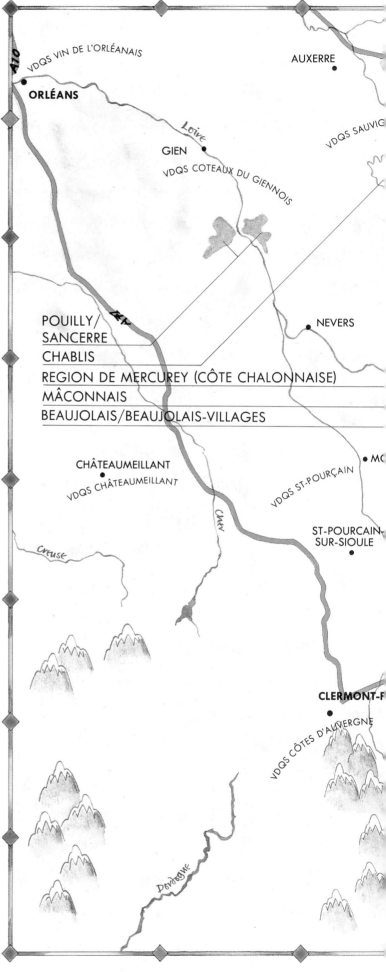

VDQS VIN DE L'ORLÉANAIS

AUXERRE

ORLÉANS

GIEN

VDQS SAUVIG

VDQS COTEAUX DU GIENNOIS

NEVERS

POUILLY/SANCERRE
CHABLIS
REGION DE MERCUREY (CÔTE CHALONNAISE)
MÂCONNAIS
BEAUJOLAIS/BEAUJOLAIS-VILLAGES

CHÂTEAUMEILLANT
VDQS CHÂTEAUMEILLANT

MO

VDQS ST-POURÇAIN

ST-POURÇAIN-SUR-SIOULE

CLERMONT-F

VDQS CÔTES D'AUVERGNE

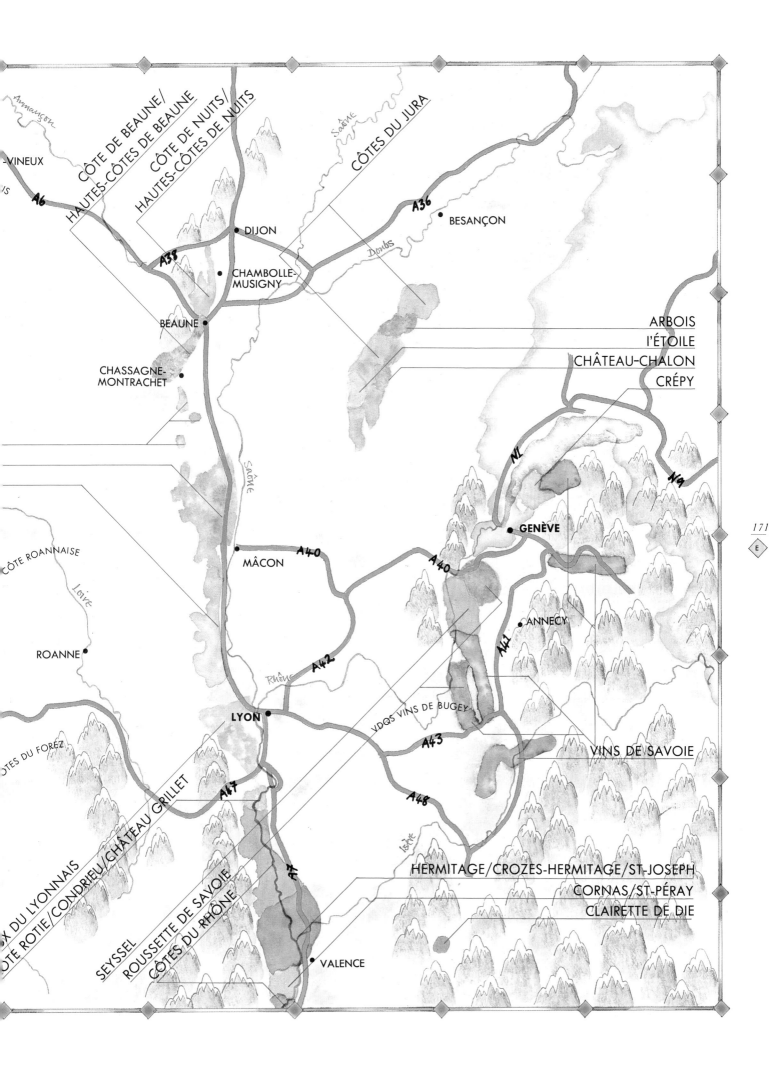

CÔTE DE BEAUNE/
HAUTES-CÔTES DE BEAUNE

CÔTE DE NUITS/
HAUTES-CÔTES DE NUITS

CÔTES DU JURA

-VINEUX

A6

A36

BESANÇON

Annançon

Saône

Doubs

A38

DIJON

CHAMBOLLE-
MUSIGNY

BEAUNE

CHASSAGNE-
MONTRACHET

Saône

ARBOIS

l'ÉTOILE

CHÂTEAU–CHALON

CRÉPY

N1

N9

GENÈVE

CÔTE ROANNAISE

Loire

A40

MÂCON

A40

ANNECY

A41

ROANNE

A42

Rhône

LYON

VDQS VINS DE BUGEY

VINS DE SAVOIE

A43

ÔTES DU FORÉZ

A48

X DU LYONNAIS

TE ROTIE/CONDRIEU/CHÂTEAU GRILLET

A47

A7

SEYSSEL

ROUSSETTE DE SAVOIE

CÔTES DU RHÔNE

Isère

HERMITAGE/CROZES-HERMITAGE/ST-JOSEPH

CORNAS/ST-PÉRAY

CLAIRETTE DE DIE

VALENCE

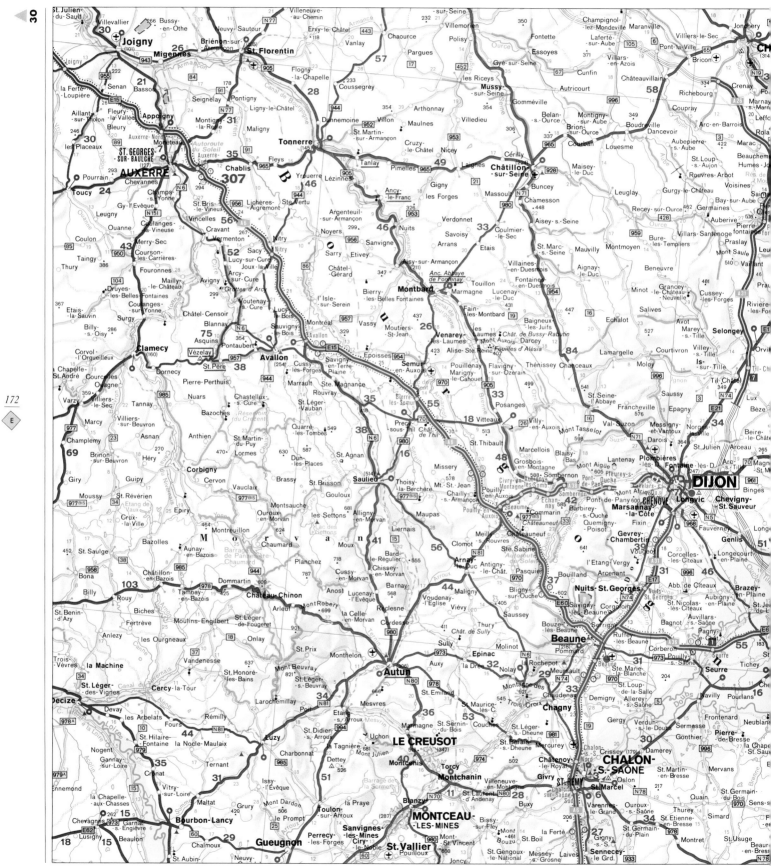

172

E

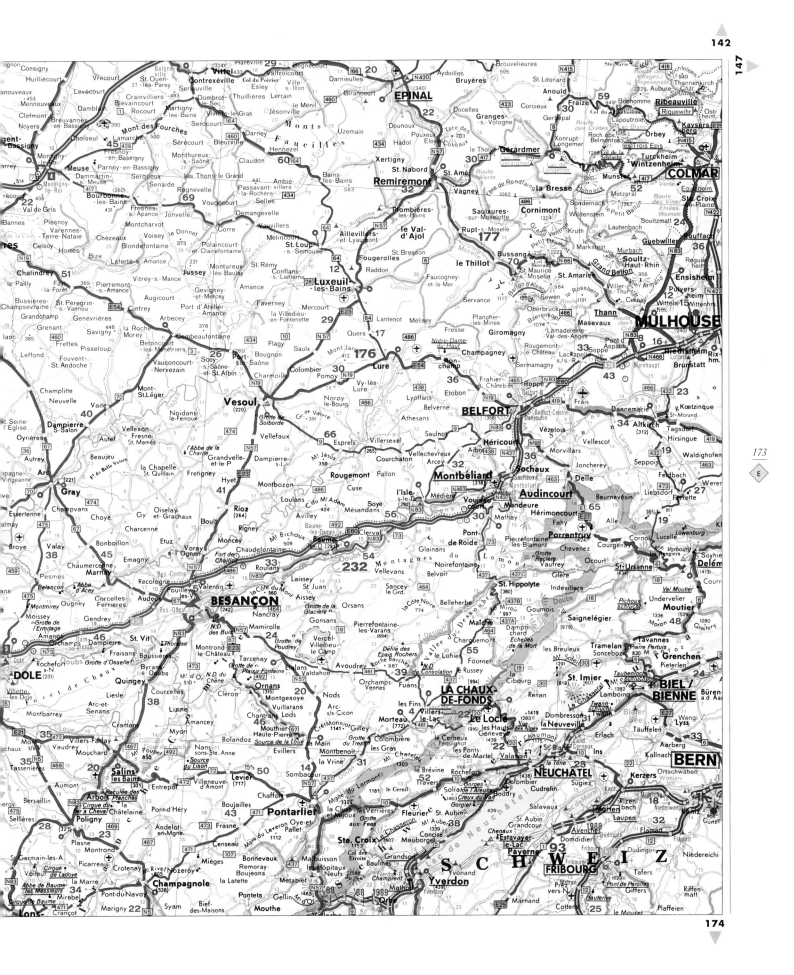

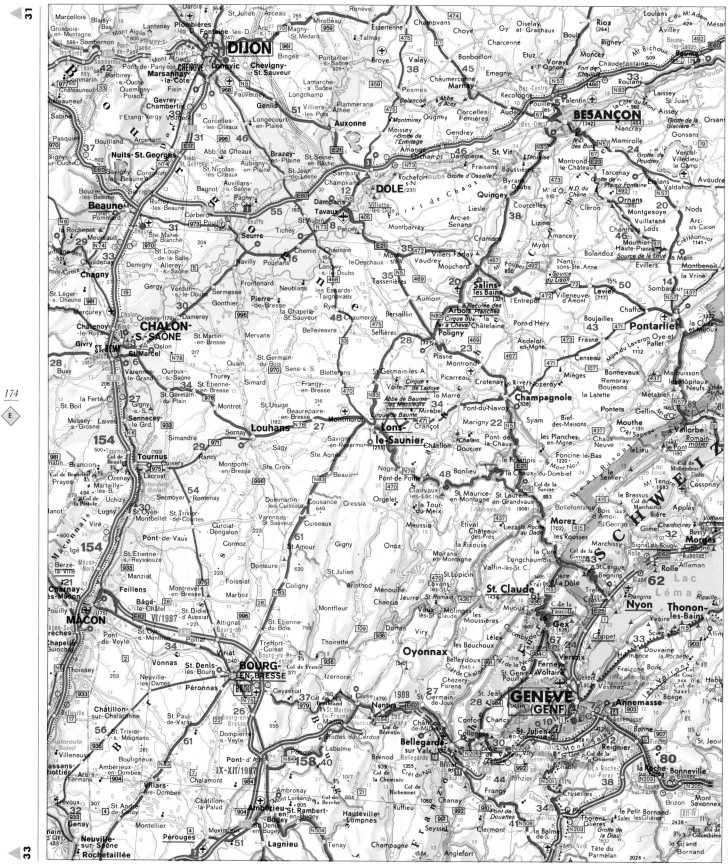

174

E

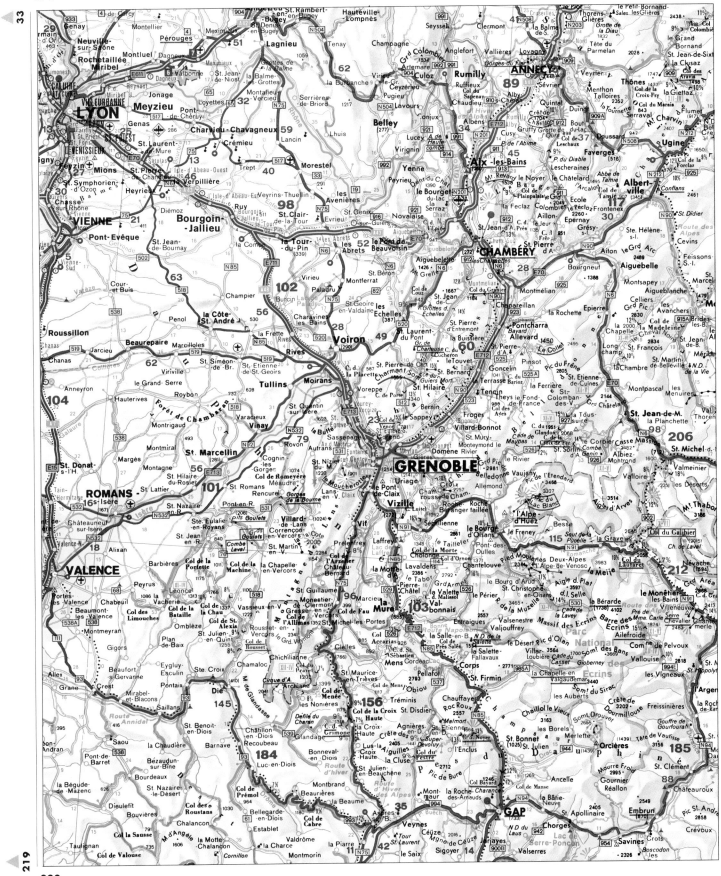

BURGUNDY

It is perfectly possible to pass through Burgundy and not to know that you have been in wine country at all – let alone in the most renowned of all the regions of France. The Paris–Lyon autoroute sails disdainfully from the hills of the Morvan over the vines of Beaune, then plunges on south following the plain of the Saône, the hills where the vineyards are concentrated scarcely noticeable on the western horizon.

"Concentrated" is a relative term. There is little of the monoculture of the Médoc, or of the Midi, in Burgundy. In the Beaujolais, hill after hill is covered with vines, and yet the accidents of the landscapes, its villages, copses, streams, sudden escarpments and long views eastward towards the Alps give it a rural character. There is usually room for a meadow, or a hen run, and in the higher hills deep woods of oak and chestnut.

Concentration is more evident on the Côte d'Or, but only along a narrow front: the Côte is a simple ridge sheltering a belt of vines rarely more than a mile wide. Elsewhere in the ancient province vines are concealed down byways in a countryside that seems set on satisfying all the senses.

The formal capital of Burgundy is Dijon, but its wine capital is Beaune. Beaune is the logical lodging place for a serious survey of the region, halfway between Chablis to the north and Villefranche, the heart of Beaujolais, to the south. The ancient ramparts of the town, still encircling it, have protected the centre of Beaune from the hideous trivialization which has wrecked so many ancient city centres. There is still a distinct sense of pilgrimage in visiting the cloistered Hôtel-Dieu, the hospital-cum-convent better known as the Hospices de Beaune. Five hundred years of routinely caring for the old and the sick, with the wine in the cellars below paying all the bills, makes it a unique monument to practical piety – or perhaps appropriate atonement.

Beaune is a town so hollow with cellars that it would not be surprising to be told that you can cross it from end to end without seeing daylight. You can also circumnavigate it, or nearly, in the above-ground cellars that occupy the ramparts of the bastions with their immensely thick stone walls.

Beaune has the great advantage that all its attractions are within a short walk from any of its numerous little hotels – or its one hostelry with grander pretensions, the Hôtel de la Poste. If it has no famous restaurant, it is still serious about food and expects its visitors to be the same. The third Sunday in November is Beaune's annual moment of glory: the public auction of the new vintage wines from the vineyards of the Hospices, held not in the Hospices but in the more humdrum town hall across the street. To be involved in the auction, to taste the raw young wines in the Hospices' cellars (for which you need an invitation) and to bid for them in the strange *auction la chandalle* – a piece of jiggery-pokery particularly French – is a privilege for which merchants, restaurateurs and amateurs come from all over the world. The weekend is referred to as Les Trois Glorieuses ("Three Glorious Days") because the Chevaliers de Tastevin hold a banquet at the Château de Vougeot the night before the auction, and the citizens of Meursault hold a gargantuan bottle party the day after.

This is Burgundy's set piece, its centrepiece, but it is only the ceremonial part of the story.

The workaday side can be observed in a thousand cellars, most small and rather cramped, workshops rather than Médoc-style set-piece *chais*. It can be seen in the vineyards, where many thousands of people, men and women, labour amid their vines. This is a countryside of smallholders, proprietors owning a hectare or two, often in ten or more tiny, separated patches in as many vineyards. To own ten hectares in Burgundy is to be a major figure in your village. In Bordeaux, such a holding would push a château well down the local pecking order.

Burgundy's close-focus scale is the product of history, of inheritance laws, of tradition. The same factors are at work all over France, yet here they combine with a certain quirky individuality of character to split everything, vineyards and ownership, into a thousand varying fragments. Buying and understanding burgundy is thus a process fraught with complication. Names matter as much as geography, more perhaps. Reputations, of growers and négociants, rise and fall and must be followed.

Some people get the best out of a tricky vintage, others make mistakes when rot, or over-ripening, makes winemaking more than usually difficult.

There are more than 100 distinct appellations in Burgundy. Most of them are concentrated in the Côte d'Or, the central strip of vineyards between Dijon and Santenay. Here each field is judged, weighed in the scales by the authorities, and accorded a rank. Chablis follows the same system for its isolated northern vineyard. Farther south, things are simpler. Beaujolais singles out nine "crus", the Mâconnais a few named villages. Growers right across the region can use the AoCs Bourgogne, Bourgogne Grand Ordinaire, Passe-Tout-Grains and Bourgogne Aligoté, the so-called regional appellations. These take in lesser land in the Côte d'Or villages as well as outlying vineyards and areas such as the Mâconnais. Regional appellations form a relatively small, and declining, portion of the Burgundy whole.

Luckily, the grapes of Burgundy are simple to grasp. Pinot Noir makes all the great red wine, Chardonnay all the great white. Gamay has a special place as the grape of Beaujolais, and Aligoté makes white wine of character in a few places. A few hectares of Pinot Blanc go towards Bourgogne Blanc, and in the Yonne the rare César and Tressot make red wines. The one outsider to break this Burgundian solidarity is the Sauvignon Blanc, grown around St-Bris in the Yonne to make small amounts of a wine which owes more to the Loire than to the Côte d'Or: from St-Bris, Sancerre is closer than Beaune.

Subtlety reasserts itself in the bewildering variety of environmental factors which influence wine in the Côte d'Or. Perhaps this hillside does possess attributes not found elsewhere. Or perhaps the fame of its wine has led people to look particularly hard for subtle nuances of site, soil and slope. The environment is there, and the wines are undoubtedly great. The connection, the cause and effect, is what is hard to disentangle. The Côte faces east and a little south, with many small variations caused by side valleys and outlying slopes. The slope provides shelter from wet west winds, and beneficial exposure to the morning sun. It lifts the vines above the cold fogs of the plains, above the frosts which form as the cold night air flows downhill.

Beneath the wooded and vine-clad surface, the Côte is basically a limestone shelf, the edge of a great plateau which slopes away to the west. The scarp slope, which is what the Côte technically is, displays the various rock strata of the plateau like layers in a cake. Erosion has mingled the surface soils and complicated the picture, but the combination of limestone beneath and a topsoil stemming from eroded marlstone occurs again and again in the best vineyard sites. It may be that the geology is dominant and the microclimate secondary. It is more likely that both form a pattern with other factors such as the (crucial) choice of the exact clone of vine, the method of pruning employed, the age of the vines, to make up a balance of quality which cannot be duplicated. And truly, great burgundy alone among the great French wines has no competition, from within the borders of France or in the world at large.

When all the data has been sifted and all the *crus* tasted, wine remains only a part of the Burgundian whole. This ancient province, once a proud and rich nation, has as many art treasures as any part of France. The monks of the great abbeys such as Cluny were early winemakers as well as protectors of learning and religion. Burgundy is a noted centre of gastronomy, inheriting a tradition begun by Duke Phillip the Bold who made a great octagonal kitchen a centrepiece of his palace in Dijon. This remarkable room can still be seen, a monument to a court which considered hospitality as important as politics, forming an apt part of the great Musée des Beaux Arts which shelters a wonderful collection of Burgundian art.

◁ The village of St-Romain lies at the head of a valley which pierces the slope of the Côte d'Or. In the distance are the vineyards of Auxey-Duresses and Meursault, and beyond, the fertile Saône valley.

▽ Below left: Gevrey-Chambertin. Below: the little river Serein at Chablis.

CHABLIS

▶ Right: the gentle landscape of the Chablis country, with the vineyards punctuating the woods. Much of the land has been replanted in the last two decades after having reverted to forest in the years of Chablis' decline.

▽ Chichée, below, is a village in the Serein valley.

Of the five districts of Burgundy, Chablis is the most northerly and the most isolated, lying almost as far north of Beaune as it is southeast of Paris. In 1477 Chablis was absorbed into the then-independent Duchy of Burgundy. But for this historical accident, the district might have been joined to Champagne. The Champagne vineyards of the Aube are closer to Chablis than is the heart of Burgundy, the Côte d'Or; and the Chablis climate is broadly similar to that of Champagne. There is a good deal of limestone in both areas and the Chardonnay, the only grape variety grown in Chablis (where it is known as the Beaunois), is also widely planted in Champagne. History, however, has made Chablis Burgundian, and its wines mainly still.

The history of wine in Chablis goes back at least to Roman times. It was, however, the monks who first seriously developed wine growing, with the abbey of Pontigny, 15 kilometres (9 miles) from Chablis, in the forefront. The position of Chablis also stimulated viticulture: Paris is not far away and used to be accessible via the waterways. The casks had only to be carted to Auxerre and from there they could be shipped down the Yonne and the Seine to the capital. Wine brought prosperity to Chablis. In the early fifteenth century, for example, the little place was rich enough to build a defensive wall and moat. The most striking remains of this fortification are the towers of the Porte Noël, which was the south gate. At the end of the fifteenth century Chablis had at least 4,000 inhabitants, considerably more than the 2,400 or so today.

The period of prosperity came to an end through a series of disasters that hit the region in the nineteenth century. Around 1886 the dreaded oidium disease appeared and the phylloxera parasite came not long afterwards. The railway between Paris and the south of France enabled low-priced Midi wines to flood the market, destroying the Chablis trade. Then World War I exacted its sad toll of manpower – and claimed the horses, too. After a short revival in the late 1920s the world economic crisis set in, to be followed by World War II. The result of these and other factors was the reduction of the vineyards of Chablis and the surrounding countryside to a fraction of their original extent. In the nineteenth century the Yonne département had 40,000 hectares (nearly 99,000 acres) of vineyard, but less than 1,000 hectares (2,470 acres) by the 1950s.

Chablis has survived all these reverses, and even expanded again, because its wine is unique. In colour it is pale, often with a faint hint of green. The taste is very dry, mineral-cool, and despite the obvious acidity often soft and even fruity. The soil – clay, with a lot of limestone in the best vineyards – is an important influence on the particular personality of Chablis. The soil of the better vineyards has a high lime content. The thick underlying stratum of limestone is composed of the fossils of countless billions of shellfish, principally *Ostrea virgula*, a small oyster with a comma-shaped shell. This chalky clay is called the Kimmeridgian, after the spot on the English coast where it is also found.

But quality alone could not have made the Chablis comeback possible. Until the 1960s wine growing in Chablis was an extremely risky business because of the danger of night frosts. The district often has to contend with

TRAVEL INFORMATION

As in many other wine districts, the cuisine in Chablis takes on a local accent because of the regional wines used in them. The restaurants in Chablis also often serve snails, crayfish and *andouillettes* (small tripe sausages); and the splendid ham from nearby Morvan frequently appears on the menus.

HOTELS

Hostellerie des Clos, 89800 Chablis, tel. 86 42 10 63. This hotel and restaurant opened in 1986. The rooms are comfortable and modern. In the restaurant, a la carte dishes are expensive and variable in quality, so keep to the menus. Hotel class B; restaurant class A.
l'Etoile, 89800 Chablis, tel. 86 42 10 50. A country hotel lacking character and offering limited comfort. The cooking is not bad, but by no means remarkable. However the wine list is interesting. Class B/C.
Le Relais St-Vincent, 89144 Ligny-le-Châtel, tel. 86 47 53 38. About 10km (6 miles) from Chablis. Small, quiet hotel (provides a good choice for breakfast). Hotel class B; restaurant class C.
l'Abbaye St-Michel, 89700 Tonnerre, tel. 86 55 05 99. About 15 km (9½ miles) from Chablis. Very luxurious hotel and restaurant with a medieval interior, a view over a river valley and a meticulous cuisine. Hotel class A; restaurant class A.
Hotel du Centre, 89700 Tonnerre, tel. 86 55 10 56. Almost opposite the Ancien Hôpital. Class C.

RESTAURANTS

Au Vrai Chablis, 89800 Chablis, tel. 86 42 11 43. Simple and dependable, on the market square. Class C.
Auberge du Bief, 89144 Ligny-le-Châtel, tel. 86 47 84 56. About 10 km (6 miles) from Chablis. Good cooking and an agreeable atmosphere. Very popular with locals. Class B.
Le St-Bris, 89350 St-Bris-le-Vineux, tel. 86 53 84 56. About 18 km (11 miles) from Chablis. You can enjoy a good-value menu and local wines either inside the old building or out on the terrace. Class C.
La Petite Auberge, 89290 Vaux, tel. 86 53 80 08. About 25 km (15½ miles) from Chablis. Here a talented chef

from Paris surprises guests with dishes of refinement. The inn is furnished in rustic fashion and stands beside the Yonne. Class B.

WINE ROUTE

Chablis does not have a signposted wine route as such, but this short journey provides a good introduction to the district. Start in Chablis itself. Cross the bridge to the east bank of the Serein and take the D91 along the river bank, heading north. The best vineyards of the district rise up on your right, the Grands Crus, their territory ending at the junction with the D216. Continue north on the D91. The long stretch of vineyard that next appears on the right-hand side is the Premier Cru of Fourchaume. In the village of Maligny the château is worth a visit. This was once a feudal castle, one of the few to be built not on a hill but in a valley. The 12th-century structure was rebuilt in the 18th century and is now in a sorry state. Fortunately, however, it is being patiently restored by a wine grower, Jean Durup. The kitchen is vast, the salons contain interesting collections, and centuries-old trees grow in the park that runs right down to the Serein.

Leave Maligny on the D35 to the west, crossing the river and pausing in Villy, a hamlet whose church has a Romanesque porch. Return to the junction with the D131 and continue south to La Chapelle-Vaupelteigne. This is a classic wine village with a

frosts late in spring – and sometimes even in September, when the grapes can be frozen. It was only when effective countermeasures were devised that growers succeeded in making their estates viable again. At first the cold was banished by means of stoves amid the vines, and later by burning flares. Today the growers mostly spray a water mist over the vines (the water freezes, but the plants do not). Despite all this the frost can sometimes occur so severely that even the most modern techniques cannot help. This is what happened in February 1985.

Frost protection meant it was worth replanting long-abandoned land. The total vineyard area in the 20 communes of the appellation has increased from around 500 hectares (1,480 acres) in the early 1960s to around 2,000 hectares (4,940 acres) today. In addition the average yield per hectare has increased.

Wine legislation distinguishes four categories of Chablis. At the top is Chablis Grand Cru, from one of the seven vineyards on slopes directly north and east of the village, on the opposite bank of the little river Serein. The 100 hectares (250 acres) of Grand Cru are split between seven vineyards: Blanchots, Les Clos, Valmur, Grenouilles, Vaudésir, Les Preuses and Bougros. A good Chablis Grand Cru offers an intensity of taste, with much strength and character; as a rule its subtleties only develop properly after a few years in bottle. Premier Cru wines are usually lighter and less pronounced in character – but nonetheless wines of very marked identity. They come from some 580 hectares (1,430 acres) divided among 30 vineyards. Premier Cru Chablis may be sold either with the

names of individual vineyards, or those of groups of fields. The latter is generally the case, so in practice only a relatively small number of names are in use. In alphabetical order, together with the number of vineyards that have the right to use the name in question, they are (since 1987): Les Beauregards (2), Beauroy (3), Berdiot (1), Chaume de Talvat (1), Fourchaume (5), Les Fourneaux (3), Cote de Jouan (1), Côte de Léchet (1), Mont de Milieu (1), Montée de Tonnerre (4), Montmains (3), Vaillons (8), Côte de Vaubarousse (1), Vaucoupin (1), Vaudevey (2), Vauligneau (1) and Vosgros (2). Most of the land, around 1,200 hectares (2,960 acres), produces straightforward Chablis. Its quality can vary greatly, from fruity and pure to flat and aggressive. The simplest wine of the district, from outlying vineyards, is called Petit Chablis. It often requires an effort to discover in it the Chablis characteristics.

Chablis is not the only wine district in the département of the Yonne. About 18 kilometres (11 miles) southwest is the village of St-Bris-le-Vineux where a quite different type of white wine is produced. This has as its basis not the Chardonnay grape but the Sauvignon of the Loire Valley. Sauvignon-de-St-Bris is a fragrant, fresh thirst-quencher worthy of attention. The St-Bris district also makes quantities of worthwhile Bourgogne Aligoté.

Appealing red and rosé wines are the speciality of the charming villages of Irancy and Coulanges-la-Vineuse, a little to the south. Production of these mostly light wines is very limited and most is drunk locally: one more reason to visit Burgundy's most northerly district.

few dozen growers. The church dates from the 12th and 13th centuries.

In the next village, Poinchy, take the turning west to Milly on the D965. In the medieval chapel there you can see a fine sculpture of a kneeling monk. The local château dates from the same period. Milly lies at the foot of the Premier Cru vineyard Côte de Léchet. Walk up through the vineyard for a splendid view out over Chablis. The route ends by returning to Chablis via Poinchy.

PLACES OF INTEREST

Unfortunately the centre of Chablis was largely destroyed by shelling in 1940. Nevertheless some old streets, such as the Rue des Moulins, remain and are flanked by old wine growers' houses. Some houses have cellars dating from the 13th century. In the middle of Chablis stands the church of St-Martin, its doors covered with wrought-iron work and containing a diversity of religious art treasures. Just outside the village is the 12th-century church of St-Pierre, which is classified as a historic monument. The Maison du Vigne et du Vin provides information about the region, and several shops sell wines and *andouillettes*. Footpaths by the river Serein provide a pleasant place to stroll.

PLACES OF INTEREST IN THE REGION

Auxerre A town of churches. The cathedral was built between the 13th and 16th centuries on the site of its Romanesque predecessor, the 11th-century crypt of which still remains. The single, 68 m (223 ft) tower can be climbed. In the old centre of the town there are half-timbered houses and the splendid Tour d'Horloge, a gateway with a large clock that shows the movements of the sun and moon.
Irancy Charming wine village, nestling idyllically in a valley with vineyards and cherry trees.
Ligny-le-Châtel Remains of the defensive walls, houses from the 13th to the 16th centuries and a 12th-century church.
Noyers A beautifully preserved little medieval walled town about 25 km (15½ miles) southeast of Chablis on the Serein. Many wine cellars open onto its narrow streets.
Pontigny The magnificent 12th- and 13th-century monastery church is one of the most remarkable examples of Cistercian architecture in Burgundy. The monks of Pontigny were making wine in the Middle Ages.
St-Bris-le-Vineux A large firm in the hamlet of Bailly makes sparkling wines. It possesses an immense "wine cathedral", a cellar hewn out of a

limestone quarry where a million bottles are stored. Stone from here was used for the Panthéon in Paris. The village also has an interesting partly-13th century church.
Tanlay The château of Tanlay, 8 km (5 miles) east of Tonnerre, dates mainly from the 17th century and is one of the most sumptuous of the Burgundian Renaissance.
Tonnerre The old hospital here was built at the end of the 13th century; it has an imposing roof and an oak-panelled hall 80 m (262 ft) long.

WINE ACTIVITIES

The Fête du Sauvignon takes place in St-Bris-le-Vineux during the weekend preceding 11 November. The Fête du Chablis is held on the fourth Sunday in November.

The Piliers Chablisiens were founded in 1960; the Confrérie des Trois Ceps (for St-Bris-le-Vineux, Irancy, etc.) in 1965.

PRODUCERS OF SPECIAL INTEREST

CHABLIS, postcode 89800, 181 E4

Cave Coopérative La Chablisienne, René & Vincent Dauvissat*, Jean-Paul Droin*, Domaine Laroche*: premises worth a visit, Domaine de la Maladière (William Fèvre)*, Domaine des Malantes (formerly Domaine Rottiers-Clotilde), Louis Michel & Fils*, J. Moreau & Fils (merchants), Domaine Pinson*, François & Jean-Marie Raveneau*, A. Régnard & Fils (merchants)*, Simonnet-Febvre (merchants), Domaine de Vauroux, Domaine Robert Vocoret & Ses Fils*.

BEINES, postcode 89800

Alain Geoffroy

LA CHAPELLE-VAUPELTEIGNE, postcode 89800, 181 C3

GAEC de Chantemerle*

FLEYS, postcode 89800, 181 E6

André Philippon

FONTENAY, postcode 89800

GAEC du Colombier

LIGNORELLES, postcode 89800, 181 B1

Roland Lavantureux

MALIGNY, postcode 89800, 181 B3

Domaine de l'Eglantière (Jean Durup)*

MILLY, postcode 89800, 181 E3

Domaine des Courtis, Domaine Jean Defaix.

POINCHY, postcode 89800, 181 D3

Gérard Tremblay (Domaine des Iles)

PREHY, postcode 89800

Domaine des Maronniers, Domaine Ste-Claire.

OTHER WINES OF THE YONNE

COULANGES-LA-VINEUSE, postcode 89580

Raymond Dupuis*, GAEC du Clos du Roi.

IRANCY, postcode 89290

Léon Bienvenue*, Bernard Cantin*, Robert Colinot, Roger Delaloge*, Jean Podor.

ST-BRIS-LE-VINEUX, postcode 89530

Caves de Bailly* (in Bailly), Bersan & Fils*, Robert & Philippe Defrance*, Hugues Goisot*, Domaine des Remparts*, Luc Sorin*.

The limestone soil of Chablis shows clearly in this vineyard near Fleys. The underlying Kimmeridgian strata also occurs at Sancerre in the Loire.

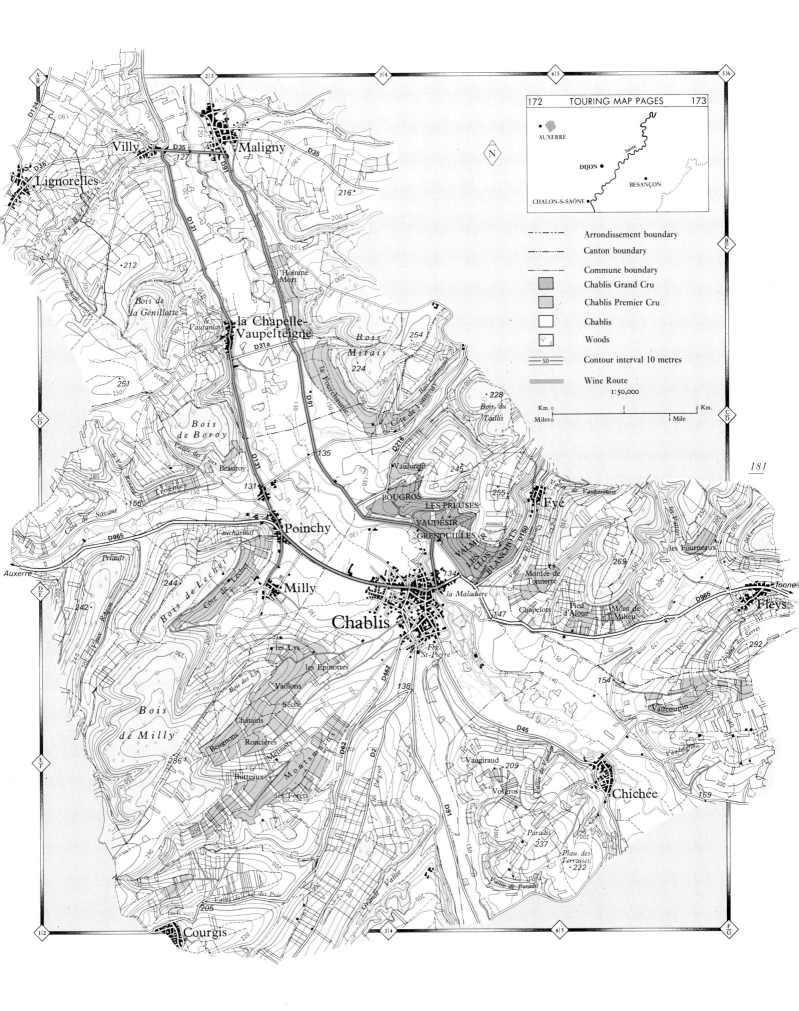

N

Arrondissement boundary

Canton boundary

Commune boundary

Chablis Grand Cru

Chablis Premier Cru

Chablis

Woods

50 Contour interval 10 metres

Wine Route
1:50,000

Km. 0   1   2 Km.
Miles 0   1 Mile

181

Villy

Maligny

Lignorelles

l'Homme Mort

Bois de la Génillotte

la Chapelle-Vaupelteigne

Bois Mitais

Côte de Fontenay

Bois du Taillis

Bois de Boroy

Vaulorent

Beauroy

BOUGROS

LES PREUSES

Fyé

Tróémie

VAUDÉSIR

GRENOUILLES

les Fourneaux

Poinchy

VALMUR

LES CLOS

BLANCHOTS

Vauchariot

Montée de Tonnerre

Milly

Côte de Léchet

Bois de Léchet

Chablis

la Maladière

Chapelots

Pied d'Aloue

Mont de Milieu

Fleys

Tonne

Auxerre

Priault

Fbg St-Pierre

les Lys

les Epinottes

Vaillons

Séche

Vaucoupin

Chatains

Bois des Lys

Bois de Milly

Beugnons

Roncières

Mélinots

Vaugiraud

Vosgros

Chichée

Butteaux

Montsars

les Forêts

Paradis

Plau. des Terrasses

Courgis

Vallée de Paradis

THE CÔTE D'OR

The heart of Burgundy is the Côte d'Or, a long, irregular hillside that starts just south of Dijon and ends 50 kilometres (31 miles) to the southwest at Santenay. The wine villages and their vineyards lie along Route Nationale 74 that links Dijon with Chagny. Only at a few places, such as the marble quarries of Comblanchien and Corgoloin, do vines disappear from view. For centuries now the best vineyards have been on the sunny, east-facing slopes below a wooded escarpment that protects them from rain-bearing winds from the west. The soil on these slopes differs with every commune – and often even with every vineyard. This diversity is further intensified by the fragmentation of Burgundian wine properties. There are very few large consolidated vineyards belonging to a single owner. The growers here mostly cultivate a number of small plots scattered over various ancient fields. The result is that most wine growers make small amounts of a range of diverse wines. The quantities are often so minute that it would make no sense for the grower to nurture, bottle and market the wine himself. This is why the shippers play such an important part: they buy small consignments of wine of the appellations they want and then blend them to produce a marketable amount. However these merchants, the *négociants-éleveurs*, by no means have a monopoly, for a substantial minority of growers do sell their own wines in the bottle, and with considerable success.

Another result of the fragmented vineyard holdings is the enormous variation in the wine produced by a single vineyard in the same year, simply because every plot owner makes a different burgundy. In the Côte d'Or, therefore, it is at least as important to know the reputation of a wine's maker as the name and possibly the classification of the vineyard. A "village" wine bearing just the name of its commune, but from a quality-conscious, expert grower, may be better than a Premier Cru from a slipshod estate.

The wines of the Côte d'Or are officially divided into four classes. The top category is Grand Cru, which applies to 30 individual vineyards, including Chambertin, Musigny, Clos Vougeot and Montrachet. The wines they produce are sold under their own names, with no mention of the commune where the Grand Cru vineyard is situated.

The next class is Premier Cru, which includes over 300 of the best sites along the whole Côte d'Or. Wines in this class are always sold with the name of the relevant commune, followed by that of the vineyard – or simply by the words "Premier (or 1er) Cru" if the wine comes from more than one vineyard.

The third class comprises village appellations (Gevrey-Chambertin etc.). Wines in this category may be sold with their vineyard names providing these are printed on the label in smaller type than that of their commune. The Côte de Nuits-Villages and Côte de Beaune-Villages appellations also come in this category: they are used by two groups of lesser-known communes.

The fourth category applies to the regional wines – Bourgogne, Bourgogne Aligoté, etc. These wines often come from the flatter land to the east of Route Nationale 74. A superior version within this classification comes from the Hautes-Côtes, the hilly hinterland to the west of the Côte d'Or. Wines produced there are entitled to the appellations Bourgogne Hautes-Côtes de Nuits or Bourgogne Hautes-Côtes de Beaune. Prices in the actual Côte d'Or are so high that the Hautes-Côtes wines are a welcome chance to drink real burgundy as more than a very occasional treat.

The Côte d'Or itself is divided into two. The southern part is called the Côte de Beaune, the northern the Côte de Nuits. The boundary comes at Corgoloin, about halfway between Beaune and Nuits-St-Georges, and is marked by a sign on the roadside. All the great white wines of the Côte d'Or are produced in the Côte de Beaune, together with many good reds. In the Côte de Nuits the emphasis is on red and whites are a rarity.

▶ The Côte d'Or is mapped in detail on the following pages, working from south to north. Here, more so than anywhere else in France, geographical detail matters. Therefore the maps show individual vineyards and the category to which they belong.

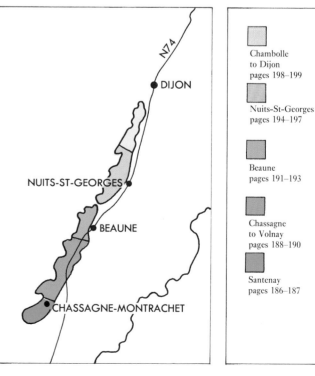

Chambolle to Dijon
pages 198–199

Nuits-St-Georges
pages 194–197

Beaune
pages 191–193

Chassagne to Volnay
pages 188–190

Santenay
pages 186–187

N74

DIJON

NUITS-ST-GEORGES

BEAUNE

CHASSAGNE-MONTRACHET

△ Above: harvest-time twilight in the Côte de Beaune.
▽ Below: the city of Beaune is a honeycomb of cellars.

◁ The centrepiece of the village of Aloxe-Corton, at the foot of the hill of Corton, is Château Corton-André. This beautiful manor-house roofed with multi-coloured tiles belongs to the firm La Reine Pédauque.

TRAVEL INFORMATION

Two busy routes to the south converge in the Côte d'Or, one from Paris and one from the northeast (Germany, the Benelux countries and Scandinavia). Travellers have used these routes for many centuries. Thus Beaune has a tradition of hospitality and numerous hotels and restaurants, often serving regional dishes. These include *escargots*; *jambon persillé* (ham in a jelly made with white wine and parsley); eggs or fish *en meurette* (in a red wine sauce); *pauchouse* or *pochouse* (a casserole of freshwater fish); *écrevisses* (crayfish); *coq au vin*; *bœuf bourguignon* (with red wine, onions, mushrooms and pieces of bacon); and *fondue bourguignonne* (meat fondue). Blackcurrants are often used in sauces and desserts. For hotels and restaurants see also Côte de Nuits and Chalonnais (pages 195; 200).

HOTELS

Hotel Clarion, 21420 Aloxe-Corton, tel. 80 26 46 70. Small hotel with a good reputation. Rooms are furnished in styles from the 1930s to 1950s. Chassagne marble in the bathrooms and lounge. Class A.
Belle Epoque, 15 Faubourg Bretonnière, 21200 Beaune, tel. 80 24 66 15. Opened Easter 1986. Rooms and apartments. Class A.
Hotel Bellevue, 5 Route de Seurre, 21200 Beaune, tel. 80 22 26 95. Simple, but the rooms are clean. Restaurant. Class C.
Bourgogne, Avenue Général-de-Gaulle, 21200 Beaune, tel. 80 22 22 00. Modern, with restaurant. Class B.
Hostellerie de Bretonnière, 43 Faubourg Bretonnière, 21200 Beaune,

tel. 80 22 15 77. A decent place to stay, built around an inner car park with a simple garden. Class B.

Le Cep, 27 Rue Maufoux, 21200 Beaune, tel. 80 22 35 48. Stylish, luxurious rooms. Extensions planned include a restaurant. Class A.

La Closerie, 61 Route de Pommard, 21200 Beaune, tel. 80 22 15 07. Functional comfort. Much used by wine merhants and their business customers. Class B.

Hotel Le Grillon, 21 Route de Seurre, 21200 Beaune, tel. 80 22 44 25. Peaceful position just outside the centre. Attempts are sometimes made in the tourist season to make room bookings conditional on eating in the mediocre restaurant. Class B.

Hotel Henry II, 12–14 Faubourg de Nicolas, 21200 Beaune, tel. 80 22 83 84. Comparatively new, but in a historic building. Attractive rooms. Class A/B.

Hotel de la Poste, Boulevard Clemenceau, 21200 Beaune, tel. 80 22 08 11. On the bypass road, near traffic lights, so for preference choose a room at the rear. Breakfast is excellent and you can eat very well in the elegant restaurant. Among the specialities are crayfish, *tartare de saumon* and *civet de lotte aux pâtes fraîches*. Large wine list. Class A.

Samotel, Route de Pommard, 21200 Beaune, tel. 80 22 35 55. Perfectly adequate rooms overlooking the vineyards, but try to avoid the restaurant. Class B.

Hotel du Parc, 21200 Levernais, tel. 80 22 22 51. A few kilometres from Beaune, east of the autoroute. Rooms at the front are quiet. Limited plumbing. Class B.

l'Ouvrée, 21420 Savigny-lès-Beaune, tel. 80 21 51 52. A pleasant place to sleep and eat. *Demi-pension* is obligatory in the season. Class B.

RESTAURANTS

La Cremaillière, 21190 Auxey-Duresses, tel. 80 21 22 60. In some ways this place was more pleasant when it was less formal (and the prices lower). However, the cooking is still good. Class B.

Alain Billard/Dame Tartine, 3 Rue Nicolas Rolin, 21200 Beaune, tel. 80 22 64 20. Small restaurant where the cooking is creative. Helpings of the cheapest set meal can be very small. Class B.

Au Bon Accueil, La Montagne, 21200 Beaune, tel. 80 22 08 80. This is where the French eat, on the Montagne de Beaune. Strictly regional cuisine, low prices. Initiates call it "Chez Nono". You eat outside in summer. Take the D970 out of Beaune and turn right and up the hill. Class C.

Le Bistrot Bourguignon, 8 Rue Monge, 21200 Beaune, tel. 80 22 23 24. Wines by the glass and by the bottle, with pâtés, salads, cheeses and other light dishes. Class C.

Central Hotel, 2 Rue Victor-Millot, 21200 Beaune, tel. 80 24 77 24. Both dining rooms are always full of people attracted here by the reasonable prices and the reliable cooking. Class B.

Hostellerie de l'Ecusson, Place Malmédy, 21200 Beaune, tel. 80 22 83 08. The cheapest set meal here offers good value for money and the more extensive ones are also satisfactory. Delicious *jambon persillé*. Quite a lengthy wine list. Class B.

Ermitage de Corton, Route de Dijon, 21200 Beaune, tel. 80 22 05 28. North of Beaune on the N74. The interior has the grandeur of a small palace. The cuisine, including *filet de Saint-Pierre au basilic*, is excellent. Also a luxurious hotel. Class A.

Jacques Lainé, 10–12 Boulevard Foch, 21200 Beaune, tel. 80 24 76 10. Old, dignified town house. Great care is taken with the cuisine. Marvellous lamb. Has own car park and terrace. Class B.

Grand Café de Lyon, 36 Place Carnot, 21200 Beaune, tel. 80 22 23 00. The place to meet in Beaune for a glass and a chat. Class C.

Rôtisserie de la Paix, 47 Faubourg Madeleine, 21200 Beaune, tel. 80 22 33 33. Tucked away in an alley. Very talented cooking here (including *raviolis de langoustines aux truffes* and *fricassé de pigeon au vinaigre*). Good-value set menus. Class B.

Au P'tit Pressoir, 15 Place Fleury, 21200 Beaune, tel. 80 22 07 31. Simple, genial place to eat. Choose onc of the set menus. Class C.

Le Relais de Saulx, 6 Rue Louis-Véry, 21200 Beaune, tel. 80 22 01 35. Renowned locally. Small dining room, with tiled floor and beams. Besides à la carte specialities, such as *feuilleté de bar en Crémant de Bourgogne* and *volaille de Bresse farcie*, there are attractive set menus. Booking essential. Class B.

Auberge St-Vincent, Place de la Halle, 21200 Beaune, tel. 80 22 42 34. Rustic, with uncomfortable chairs, but the food is good and not too expensive (the menu can include *magret de canard au baies de cassis*, etc). Class B.

Hostellerie du Vieux Moulin, 21420 Bouilland, tel. 80 21 51 16. Hotel with some charm, the lower-priced set menus are often more attractive than the dearer ones.

Large, rather expensive wine list. Class A/B.

Le Bareuzai, Route de Dijon, 21200 Chorey-lès-Beaune, tel. 80 22 02 90. Looks like a furniture shop from outside, but inside it has atmosphere. Acceptable quality at acceptable prices. Class B.

Hotel du Chevreuil, 21190 Meursault, tel. 80 21 23 25. Nothing special, but enjoyable *escargots* and hot pâté. Hotel accommodation. Class B.

Le Relais de la Diligence, 21190 Meursault, tel. 80 21 21 32. Not in the village itself but some distance east of the *route nationale*. Good traditional cooking. Class C.

Le Montrachet, 21190 Puligny-Montrachet, tel. 80 21 30 06. This restaurant is worth a detour. The cooking is excellent and the cellar has a choice selection of local and regional wines. Also a hotel. Class B.

Le Moulin d'Hauterive, 71350 St-Gervaise-en-Vallière, tel. 85 91 55 56. Outside the wine district, southeast of Beaune. A small hotel peacefully situated by a river. The cooking is recommended. *Demi-pension* obligatory in the season. Restaurant class B; hotel class A.

Au Petit Truc, 21200 Vignolles, tel. 80 22 01 70. A tiny place in a village east of Beaune. Country dishes of quality (*poulet au vinaigre*, for example). Class A.

Auberge des Vignes, Nationale 74, 21190 Volnay, tel. 80 22 24 48. Rustic interior, with tiles and wooden chairs. An expert chef produces good-value set menus (dishes include *la caille rôti à la grume de raisin*). Estate names appear on the wine list – which is less common than you might think in Burgundy. Class C.

PLACES OF INTEREST: CÔTE DE BEAUNE

Alôxe-Corton The 15th-century Château Corton-André belongs to a wine company. Tastings available.

Auxey-Duresses The 14th–15th century church shelters a 16th century triptych.

Beaune See the description of the town on page 192.

Ladoix-Serrigny The chapel of Notre-Dame-du-Chemin (12th-century) was for centuries a place of pilgrimage. Serrigny has an 18th-century château.

Meursault The cellars of the Château de Meursault are impressive and well worth a visit. A permanent wine-tasting is laid out in the crypt-like vaults. The splendidly restored 15th- to 19th-century building now houses a wine firm. The Boisseaux family (of Patriarche Père & Fils), who own the château, sometimes arrange exhibitions of paintings on

the theme of wine. The Paulée de Meursault takes place here every year in the *cuverie*. Meursault also has a fine town hall and the Gothic church of St-Nicolas.

Nolay Picturesque village with half-timbered houses and a 14th-century market hall.

La Rochepot Dominated by its 15th-century château with polychrome roof, which has a splendid dining hall and a terrace offering a fine view. In the village itself there is a 12th-century Benedictine church.

St-Romain A wine village in two parts, upper and lower. A signposted footpath takes you to the site of a medieval castle. Archaeological finds are displayed in the *mairie* from July to September.

Santenay At the beginning of the 13th century one of the first Gothic churches of the region, St-Jean-de-Narosse was built here at the foot of the Mont de Sène. The Mont, 521 m (1,709 ft) high, has a viewing point. Santenay's castle, the Château Philippe-le-Hardi, is in good condition and has a 14th-century keep and large cellars. It belongs to a

wine grower. Santenay also has medicinal springs and a rather staid casino.

Savigny-lès-Beaune There is a motor museum in the local château. Note, too, the proverbs carved over various doorways in the village.

Volnay The 14th-century church has been carefully restored. A 16th-century chapel stands near the N73 and the village is dominated by the century-old statue of Notre-Dame-des-Vignes.

WINE ACTIVITIES

France's best-known wine fraternity is undoubtedly La Confrérie des Chevaliers du Tastevin, which promotes the wines of the Côte d'Or in an intelligent and exuberant fashion. The "Knights" are owners of the Château de Vougeot, where several times a year banquets and enthronements are organized. In addition there are wine tastings twice a year: wines that pass the panel are distinguished by the epithet *tasteviné* and are given a special numbered label. Savigny-lès-Beaune has its own fraternity, La Cousinerie de Bourgogne.

WINE AUCTIONS

The world's greatest charity auction is held annually in Beaune, at which wines from the vineyards of the Hospices de Beaune come under the hammer. Over the centuries the charitable hospital has been donated plots in fine Côte d'Or vineyards. With the world's press looking on, burgundies, still young and in the cask, are sold at extremely high prices, the proceeds going to run the large modern hospital that lurks behind the medieval building. The auction takes place on the third Sunday in November and is the climax of three days of festival, Les Trois Glorieuses. Wine tasting and banquets are organized on the preceding Saturday and Beaune is decorated with flowers. On the following Monday Meursault celebrates its Paulée, in the Château de Meursault. This is a big lunch party to which every grower takes bottles from his own cellar.

Nuits-St-Georges also has an auction, at the Hospices de Nuits, held on Palm Sunday. On this day, and on the Saturday before, hundreds of Côte d'Or wines can be tasted in the local *salle des fêtes*.

WINE FESTIVALS

On the Saturday after 22 January every year the villages take it in turns to celebrate the Saint-Vincent Tournant in which this patron saint of wine growers is honoured by delegations from the whole district. Despite the winter cold this is usually a warming occasion, not least because the wine flows so liberally.

On the Friday before Palm Sunday Morey-St-Denis puts its wines on show in the *salle des fêtes* there; and visitors are welcome in the cellars. The occasion is called the Carrefour de Dionysos.

Interest in the Paulée de Meursault is so great that every year many would-be participants have to be disappointed. So a second event of exactly the same kind has been created, the Banée de Meursault, held at the beginning of September. On the day after there is a big tasting of local wines, the Trinquée de Meursault.

WINE INFORMATION

The CIB in Beaune (Rue Henri Dunant) supplies useful documents and will give information to visitors.

◀ Far left: the wide vineyards north of Beaune belie the Côte's hilly reputation. Left: an autumn afternoon near Nuits-St-Georges, looking west towards the wooded hills which shield the vineyards from rain-bearing winds.

185

E

SANTENAY AND ITS SURROUNDINGS

The only vineyards that belong to the Côte d'Or wine district, but do not come within the département of that name, lie just to the west and southwest of Santenay. Cheilly-lès-Maranges, Dezize-lès-Maranges and Sampigny-lès-Maranges are politically in the Saône-et-Loire département while their wines are entitled to the Côte de Beaune-Villages appellation. The properties there are mainly small and the terrain is very hilly in places. These villages have few visitors even during the busiest weeks of the tourist season. The wines made here are mostly quite light in taste, but they can be pleasant. Most of the local growers also have land in Santenay, the Hautes-Côtes de Beaune or elsewhere, so that their cellars may contain some vinous surprises. Of the three Maranges communes Cheilly-lès-Maranges is the most productive, Sampigny-lès-Maranges the smallest.

The village of Santenay is known not only for its wine but also for its waters: medicinal springs were discovered here in Roman times and they are still being exploited. Under an idiosyncratic French law, casinos are allowed only in spas – and so Santenay has its gambling palace. It is partly because of the waters that Santenay (formerly known as Santenay-lès-Bains) has quite a concentration of second homes belonging to people who visit the place frequently. The village consists of an upper and a lower section (Santenay Haut and Bas), with a band of vineyards 1 kilometre (1,100 yards) wide between them. The underlying geology of this part of the Côte is very complex. Faults break up the smooth sequence of strata. Consequently the soil in Santenay is very varied so that different styles of wine emerge, most of it red. According to a local saying, the best vineyards lie "east of the belfry" – and it is there that most of the Premiers Crus are found, including Les Gravières, La Comme and Clos de Tavannes. Les Gravières with its heavy, stony soil is the best-known, while Clos de Tavannes, on the border with Chassagne, has a name for solid, reserved wines. La Comme, a big vineyard farther up the slope, has lighter soil and corresponding wine.

Red Santenay is a rather reserved kind of burgundy, firm of structure and modest in finesse and complexity. The better wines, however, can mature into fine bottles. Some of the whites can be amazingly good, examples being the Clos des Gravières from the firm of Prosper Maufoux, which is based in Santenay. Wines from Remigny, a village southeast of Santenay, are sold under the Santenay appellation.

▷ Right: cellar entrances in Chambolle-Musigny, the village that produces the finest and most delicate wines of the Côte de Nuits.
▷ Far right: Burgundian growers prefer to taste wine from a *tastevin*, a shallow silver tasting cup that reflects the light in dim cellars. The wine fraternity of the Côte d'Or is called La Confrérie des Chevaliers du Tastevin.

186

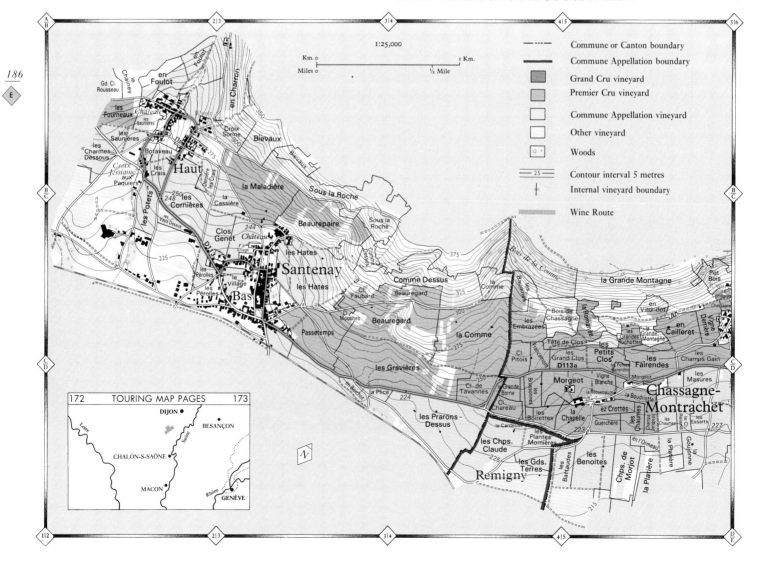

PRODUCERS OF SPECIAL INTEREST

SANTENAY AND SURROUNDINGS AND HAUTES-CÔTES DE BEAUNE

CHEILLY-LES-MARANGES, postcode 71150

Domaine Paul Chevrot, Yvon & Chantal Contat-Grange, René Martin, Domaine du Château de Mercey*, Manoir de Mercey/ Domaine Gérard Berger-Rive & Fils.

DEZIZE-LES-MARANGES, postcode 71150

Domaine B. Bachelet & Ses Fils*: more than 15 different wines. There is a second cellar in Chassagne-Montrachet. Maurice Charleux.

ECHEVRONNE, postcode 21420

Jean Féry, Domaine Lucien Jacob*.

MELOISEY, postcode 21190

Guillemard Dupont & Ses Fils* This estate is associated with André Guillemard-Pothier. Mazilly Père & Fils, Parigot Père & Fils.

▼ Casks are the common denominator of Côte d'Or cellars, since all the region's great red and white wines are subjected to wood-ageing.

NANTOUX, postcode 21190

François Charles*, Jean Joliot & Fils.

NOLAY, postcode 21340

Domaine des Vignes des Demoiselles

REMIGNY, postcode 71150, 186 F4

Château de Remigny

SANTENAY, postcode 21590, 186 E3

Adrien Belland, Domaine Joseph Belland*, Château de la Charrière, Michel Clair, Domaine Fleurot-Larose: based at the Château du Passe-Temps with its impressive cellars. Correct wines. Jessiaume Père & Fils, Domaine Lequin-Roussot*, Prosper Maufoux: an important wine firm.
Jean Moreau*, Mestre Père & Fils*: has good Premiers Crus from Santenay. Château Philippe-le-Hardi, Domaine Prieur-Brunet.

SAMPIGNY-LES-MARANGES, postcode 71150

Joseph Martin, Maurice Prieur.

FROM CHASSAGNE TO VOLNAY

The modest village of Chassagne, grouped around a few winding streets, glories at the presence within its boundaries of almost half of the great vineyard of Montrachet. This field of about 8 hectares (20 acres) produces the greatest of all white burgundies, a majestic wine with a splendid concentration in both its rich perfume and its noble, complex taste. Nearly half of Le Montrachet, surrounded by a low wall and marked by a number of stone gateways, lies in Chassagne. The village also has a share in the Grand Cru Bâtard-Montrachet, the birthplace of similarly brilliant white wines. One very small Grand Cru lies wholly within Chassagne-Montrachet. Criots-Bâtard-Montrachet has an average annual production of only 70 hectolitres – 5,000 bottles of wine. Besides these Grands Crus the Premiers Crus from this commune can also be of impressive depth and distinction. Chassagne-Montrachet produces considerably more red than white wine. The red wines do not in general reach the exalted level of the whites, though they can give a good deal of pleasure. In style they vary from richly coloured and firm to light red and smooth-drinking.

In Puligny-Montrachet, the next village to the north, white wine predominates. In this unremarkable, rather dull village beautiful white burgundies are created, including those from the Grands Crus Le Montrachet, Bâtard-Montrachet, Bienvenues-Bâtard-Montrachet, Chevalier-Montrachet and about ten Premiers Crus. The best wines from Puligny are marked by an aroma that suggests honey and is dominated by fruit – peaches, apricots – and a subtle, stylish taste that can be somewhat racier, with more juicy acidity and more sinew than Meursault wines.

In the valley that leads up into the hills behind Chassagne and Puligny is the village of St-Aubin and its associated hamlet of Gamay. Production here has greatly increased through the 1970s and '80s, thanks to new plantings. White St-Aubin can be a quite delicious – and still reasonably priced – burgundy, always rounded and occasionally showing some finesse. The red is usually more rustic in character. The best-known vineyard is the Premier Cru Les Frionnes, which produces both red and white wines.

Whereas in many Burgundy villages it can take a good deal of effort to find particular growers, so anonymous are their premises, many in Meursault have put up signboards on their house fronts: they adorn practically every building in the long street leading in from Puligny. This is typical of Meursault, for this is one of the most energetic of the Côte d'Or wine communities, as the annual Paulée de Meursault and other events (see page 184) bear witness. This is a village where it is relatively easy to buy direct from the growers. Levels of commercialism vary. At some cellars it is hard to taste without making a commitment to buy.

The wine here is principally white. Meursault has no Grands Crus but does have some very renowned Premiers Crus. The best known of these are Charmes, Genevrières and Perrières, which are situated on the south side of the village, by the boundary with Puligny-Montrachet. The classic style of Meursault has an almost buttery taste, due to its high natural glycerine content. It can also contain notes of fruit, nuts and toasted bread.

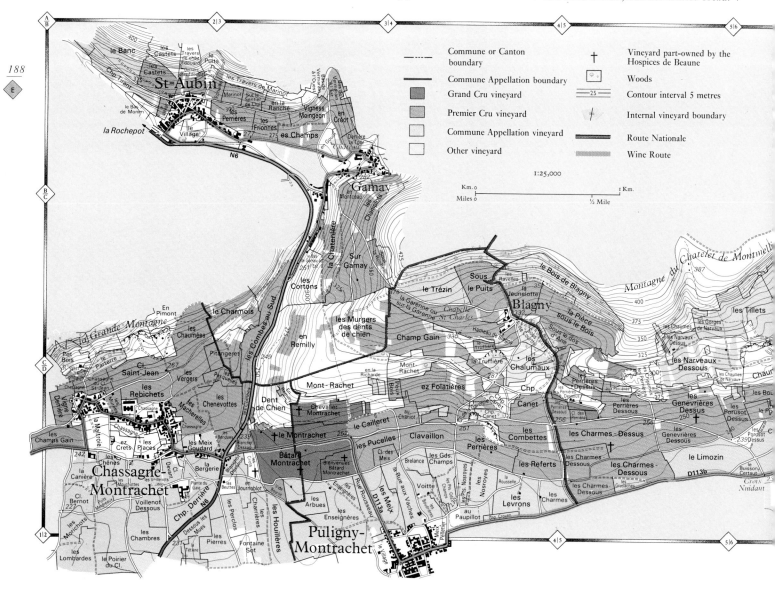

Commune or Canton boundary

Commune Appellation boundary

Grand Cru vineyard

Premier Cru vineyard

Commune Appellation vineyard

Other vineyard

Vineyard part-owned by the Hospices de Beaune

Woods

Contour interval 5 metres

Internal vineyard boundary

Route Nationale

Wine Route

1:25,000

A good Meursault is a wine for laying down and even after decades can still surprise with its great vitality. There is also red Meursault – a wine that is seldom convincing; the best kind is in fact sold under the name of Volnay-Santenots, not as Meursault.

If you drive west from Meursault, up the valley, the village of Auxey-Duresses is soon reached. The red wines here are often rather dour and are mainly sold as Côte de Beaune-Villages. The whites have more charm and quality, but less is made: red outnumbers white by two to one. The red wines come from the west- and southwest- facing vineyards adjoining Volnay, while the whites predominantly come from the other side of the valley, closer to Meursault.

White wine of some interest is also made in St-Romain, a hamlet divided into a higher and a lower part and reached from Auxey-Duresses by way of a narrow, winding road. Both the red and the white St-Romains are fairly light wines, but very attractive none the less. The reds have a cherry-like flavour with earthy notes, the whites are fruity and fresh.

Monthelie borders on Auxey-Duresses, Meursault and Volnay. The wines from this small village, built on a hill, most resemble those from Volnay. You often find a similar grace in them, but in a more slender form. The best vineyards are the Premiers Crus les Champs Fulliot and Sur la Velle, both of which border on Volnay. At the other end of the commune, Monthelie can claim part of the Premier Cru les Duresses, which it shares with Auxey. White Monthelie is rather rare.

The wines of Volnay, a village that nestles against a hill where the dukes of Burgundy had a castle, are among the finest reds of the Côte d'Or. Centuries ago they were greatly liked by the French kings; and Camille Rodier wrote that they were striking for their elegance, their soft taste, their perfect balance and their delicate bouquet. However, not all the local growers make this gracious kind of wine today: there are also Volnays that are quite hard and rich in tannin. Among the best fields are the Premiers Crus of Clos de la Bousse d'Or, Caillerets, Champans, Clos des Chênes, Clos des Ducs and Fremiets.

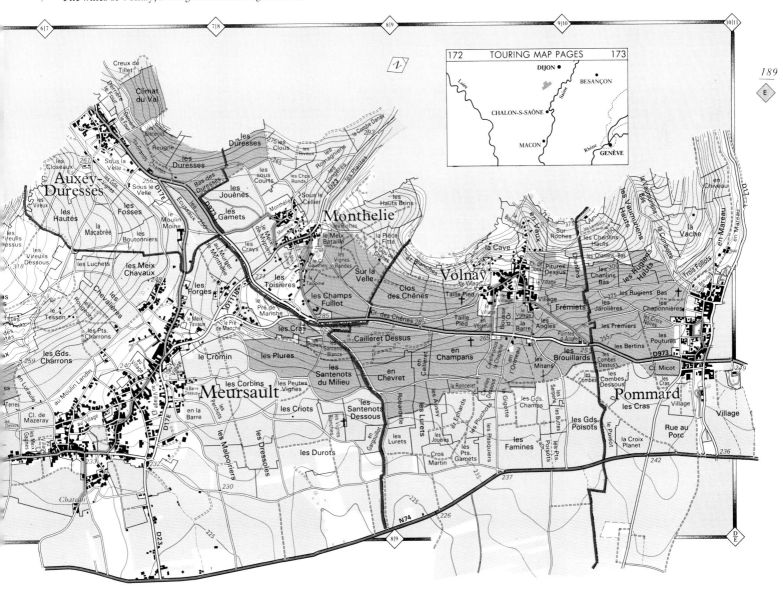

INTERESTING PRODUCERS IN THE COTE DE BEAUNE

Producers are listed under the village in which they are based. Most own land in more than one commune.

ALOXE-CORTON, postcode 21420, 193 C9

Maurice Chapuis, Max Quenot Fils & Meuneveaux, Caves de la Reine Pédauque: large wine firm that operates under various names and owns the beautiful Château Corton-André. **Domaine Daniel Senard*, Domaine Michel Voarick*.**

AUXEY-DURESSES, postcode 21190, 189 B7

Jean-Pierre Diconne, Domaine André & Bernard Labry: in the hamlet of Melin. **Henri Latour*, Leroy*:** fine expensive burgundies mainly of mature vintages. **Michel Prunier*, Roger Prunier, Roy Frères.**

BEAUNE, postcode 21200, 192 D5

Domaine Besancenot-Mathouillet*, Albert Bichot: very large wine-exporting firm with numerous brand names. The best burgundies are those from the Domaine du Clos Frantin (Vosne-Romanée) and the Domaine Long-Depaquit (Chablis). **Bouchard Aîné & Fils:** firm of average quality with a fair amount of land in Mercurey. **Bouchard Père & Fils*:** very conscientious firm with more than 80 ha (198 acres) of its own vineyards. Harmonious wines full of character. HQ in the Château de Beaune in the town ramparts – a fascinating visit. **J. Calvet & Cie, Domaine Cauvard Père & Fils*, Champy Père & Cie:** small firm, old-fashioned in style. **Chanson Père & Fils:** good white and light-coloured red wines which can develop over a long period. Almost 45 ha (111 acres) of vineyard. Cellars in the town ramparts. **Coron Père & Fils:** reliable small wine firm. **Joseph Drouhin*:** stylish, subtle burgundies with backbone. The firm's own estate covers some 60 ha (148 acres), about 36 ha (89 acres) in Chablis. **Les Caves des Hautes-Côtes** (cooperative), **Domaine des Hospices de Beaune*:** the wines from this charitable estate are auctioned on the third Sunday in November. **Jaboulet-Vercherre; Louis Jadot:** balanced white and red burgundies with style and strength: top class. **Jaffelin:** subsidiary of

Joseph Drouhin, with quite a few attractive wines. **Louis Latour*:** excellent firm with about 43 ha (106 acres) of vineyard. **Lycée Agricole & Viticole, P. de Marcilly Frères, Albert Morot, Patriarche Père & Fils:** firm that puts the emphasis on volume – but also with some particularly fine wines, such as that from the Château de Meursault. Their splendid cellars stay hospitably open. **Domaine des Pierres Blanches*, Remoissenet Père & Fils:** introvert small firm with good wines, especially very good whites. **Domaine des Terregelesses***

CHASSAGNE-MONTRACHET, postcode 21190, 186 F5, 188 D2

Pierre Amiot, **Domaine Bachelet-Ramonet Père & Fils*, Ch. Bader-Mimeur, Blain-Gagnard*, Georges Déléger*, Jean-Noël Gagnard*,** Gagnard-Delagrange*, René Lamy, **Domaine Duc de Magenta:** since 1987 controlled by Louis Jadot. Bernard Moreau, **Bernard Morey*, Jean-Marc Morey*, Marc Morey*, Michel Niellon*,** Paul Pillot, Jean & Fernand Pillot, **Domaine Ramonet*:** magnificent white Grands Crus and Premiers Crus, as well as some delightful reds.

CHOREY-LES-BEAUNE, postcode 21200

Domaine Jacques Germain: based at the Château de Chorey. **Domaine Maillard Père & Fils, Tollot-Beaut & Fils*:** harmonious wines with finesse in Corton and neighbouring vineyards.

LADOIX-SERRIGNY, postcode 21550

Capitain-Gagnerot, Chevalier Père & Fils, Edmond Cornu, Domaine Michel Mallard & Fils, **Prince Florent de Mérode*,** Domaine André Nudant & Fils, Gaston & Pierre Ravaut.

MEURSAULT, postcode 21190, 189 D7

Robert Ampeau & Fils*: about 15 different whites plus red wines of exquisite quality. **Raymond Ballot-Millot Père & Fils*:** includes Veuve Ch. Dancer-Lochardet and Ballot & Dancer. Domaine de Blagny, **Pierre Boillot*,** Hubert Bouzereau-Gruyère, A. Buisson-Battault*, **Jean-François Coche-Dury*, Domaine des Comtes Lafon*,** Domaine Darnat, Domaine Gabriel Fournier,

Château Génot-Boulanger, **Henri Germain*, Maison Jean Germain*:** wine merchants, specializing in white wine. **Domaine Albert Grivault, Patrick Javillier, François Jobard*, Domaine Latour-Giraud*, Domaine Joseph Matrot, Château de Meursault*:** the showpiece of the village, worth a visit for its cellars as well as its wines. **Michelot-Buisson*:** four other Michelot names are also used. **Raymond Millot & Fils*, Patrick Millot-Battault, Domaine René Monnier*, Domaine Jean Monnier & Fils*, Pierre Morey*,** Pierre Perrin-Ponsot, Pitoiset-Urena*, **Domaine Jacques Prieur*, Domaine Rougeot, Domaine Guy Roulot*.**

MONTHELIE, postcode 21190, 189 C8

Xavier Bouzerand*, Marcel & Louis Deschamps, Potinet-Ampeau, **Eric de Suremain*:** of the Château de Monthelie.

PERNAND-VERGELESSES, postcode 21420, 193 A9

Domaine Bonneau du Martray*: a top producer of Corton-Charlemagne. Denis Père & Fils, **Domaine P. Dubreuil-Fontaine Père & Fils*:** famous property with fragrant wines. Domaine Laleure-Piot, Gabriel Muskovac, Domaine Pavelot, **Domaine Rapet Père & Fils*.**

POMMARD, postcode 21630, 189 C10, 192 C2

Comte Armand*, Domaine Billard-Gonnet*, **Domaine de Madame Bernard de Courcel*, Domaine Michel Gaunoux*,** Domaine Lahaye Père & Fils, **Domaine Lejeune*,** Domaine Mussy, **Domaine Parent*,** Jean-Luc Joillot-Porcheray, **Château de Pommard*:** very good, very expensive wines. Pothier-Rieusset*, René Virely-Arcelain, Bernard Virely-Rougeot.

PULIGNY-MONTRACHET, postcode 21190, 188 E4

Louis Carillon & Fils *, Domaine Jean Chartron*, Domaine Henri Clerc & Fils*, Domaine Leflaive*: reckoned by many the best white-wine estate of the Côte d'Or: stylish, sensual wines of the very highest standard. **Olivier Leflaive Frères*** a négociant firm started in 1985. Veuve Henri Moroni, **Domaine Jean Pascal &**

Fils, Paul Pernot & Fils, **Domaine Etienne Sauzet*.**

ST-AUBIN, postcode 21190, 188 B2

Jean-Claude Bachelet, Raoul Clerget: sound firm with about 16 ha (40 acres). **Marc Colin, Hubert Lamy, Larue, Domaine Roux Père & Fils*,** Gérard Thomas.

ST-ROMAIN, postcode 21190

Alain Gras, Taupenot Père & Fils, **Domaine René Thévenin-Monthelie & Fils:** likeable, pure, white and red wines.

SAVIGNY-LES-BEAUNE, postcode 21420, 193 A7

Simon Bize & Fils*: pure wines with good bouquet. Bonnot-Lamblot, Capron-Manieux*, Lucien Camus-Bruchon, **Domaine Chandon de Briailles*:** the little 18th-century château with its garden and statuary is a historic monument. Charming, quite concentrated wines. **Maurice Ecard & Fils,** Maurice & Jean-Michel Giboulet, Girard-Vollot & Fils, Pierre Guillemot: another name used is Anne-Marie Guillemot. **Domaine Antonin Guyon*:** wine estate of nearly 50 ha (124 acres) that produces subtle, carefully nurtured burgundies. **Parigot & Richard:** producer of sparkling wines. Pavelot-Glantenay, **Domaine du Prieuré, Henri de Villamont:** large firm with various brands.

VOLNAY, postcode 21190, 189 C9

Domaine Marquis d'Angerville*: almost satiny Volnays of the highest quality. **Bitouzet-Prieur, Domaine Henri Boillot*:** substantial red and white wines. Almost 20 different bottlings. Domaine Yvon Clerget, Bernard Glantenay, **Domaine Michel Lafarge*,** Hubert de Montille, **Domaine de la Pousse d'Or*:** A beautifully-situated manor house and garden. Premiers Crus of the top level with grace, here and in Santenay. **Joseph Voillot.**

AROUND BEAUNE

▼ Below: the city of Beaune, ancient capital of the Côte d'Or.
Bottom: the village of Pernand-Vergelesses, and the little chapel above it, lie at the head of a narrow valley which cuts into the western slope of the Corton hill.

ommard does not make much impact as a village, with its spireless church, spacious tree-shaded square and its narrow streets. Close as it is to Volnay, the wines are quite different. Finesse gives way to substance. If the wines of Volnay can be described as feminine and gracious, those of Pommard are masculine and robust. The best vineyard is the Premier Cru Les Rugiens, where the reddish soil contains iron. Les Epenots also produces great Pommards, as do various less well-known Premiers Crus. And Château de Pommard with its walled, 20 hectare (49 acre) vineyard proves that a Pommard of *village* level can be impressive. This château attracts visitors by various means, who can then pay to visit the cellars, where wine can be bought. The prices are high, however. Great care is needed when choosing a Pommard, as quite a few are of disappointing quality.

Wine production in Beaune is largely dominated by the shippers: Bouchard Père & Fils by itself vinifies about half of all the wine produced by this commune. But in addition to this very big firm Beaune numbers dozens of *négociants-éleveurs* of varying degrees of importance. Some concerns belong to families that have lived in the area for centuries.

On the Montagne de Beaune, a modest ridge northwest of the town, are the most famous of the Premiers Crus, among them Grèves (with its Vigne de l'Enfant Jésus), Cent Vignes, Marconnets, Bressandes and Teurons. A number of Premiers Crus in the southern half of the Beaune appellation also produce beautiful wines. Clos des Mouches and Vignes Franches, for example, enjoy an excellent reputation. The great majority of the wine from Beaune is red, although the white should by no means be underestimated. Drouhin's white Clos des Mouches, for example, is consistently among the very fine white wines of the Côte d'Or.

To the east of the N74 linking Beaune with Dijon are the flat vineyards of Chorey-lès-Beaune, a modest village where the most interesting building is the château, which belongs to a wine grower. Nearly all the Chorey wines are red and may use the commune name or Côte de Beaune-Villages. They can have much charm and be good value.

West from the *route nationale*, vines cover a broad plateau, then clothe both sides of a narrowing valley to Savigny-lès-Beaune. Savigny is both a dormitory village for nearby Beaune and an important wine community in its own right. The soil here varies considerably and the – chiefly red – wines may be firm or rather more "supple". On a stone near the local château (which is also a museum) are chiselled the words, "The wines of Savigny are nourishing, theological and drive away depression."

The countryside to the northeast of Beaune is dominated by the broad, flat-topped hill of Corton. The wooded summit reaches to almost 390 metres (1,280 feet) above sea level. On its slopes are more than 200 hectares (494 acres) of vineyards, nearly all with Grand Cru status. A small part of the Corton hill comes within the commune of Pernand-Vergelesses, a little village of steep and winding streets. Of the Pernand-Vergelesses wines the whites have the most to offer, with the Grand Cru Corton-Charlemagne (which it shares with Aloxe-Corton) in the lead. The reds are often powerful and develop well in bottle.

By far the biggest share of the Corton hill belongs to Aloxe-Corton, a hamlet built where two Roman roads crossed. This is the only commune in the Côte de Beaune where the Grand Cru vineyards outnumber Premiers Crus and other categories combined. The strongly structured, luxurious Corton-Charlemagne is among the world's greatest white wines. Red Corton is a deep-red, often beefy burgundy capable of great style and depth. To reach their best, both Corton-Charlemagne and Corton often need to mature in bottle for seven to eight years. The most important owner on the Corton hill is Louis Latour, a firm that has 9 hectares (22 acres) of Corton-Charlemagne and 17 hectares (42 acres) of Corton (most of Latour's Corton is sold as Château Corton Grancey).

The third commune with a share in the Corton hill is Ladoix-Serrigny, which produces small quantities of the Corton-Charlemagne and Corton Grands Crus. A few other plots are entitled to the appellation Aloxe-Corton Premier Cru, but there is also a Ladoix appellation for red and white wines. These can be very respectable and reasonable in price. The Ladoix wines can also be sold as Côte de Beaune-Villages.

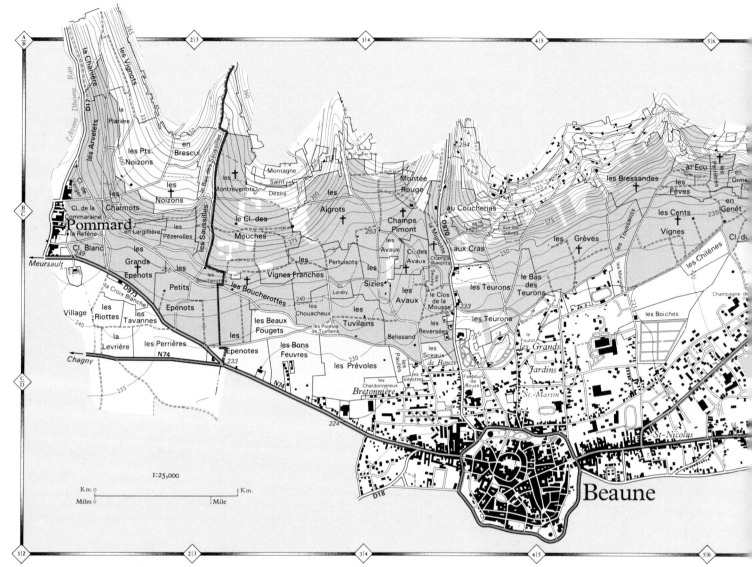

1:25,000

Km.o   Km.
Miles o   Mile

TRAVEL INFORMATION: BEAUNE

In Beaune, capital of Burgundy, art and wine are closely intertwined. Under the beautifully preserved centre of the old town stretches a maze of wine cellars; above ground there are dozens of wine firms and wine shops. The best and most pleasant way of getting to know Beaune is to take a walk through the heart of the town. This walk begins in the central square, Place Carnot, where there is (not always ample) parking space. Leave the square, walking north along the Rue Carnot, the most important shopping street. On the corner of this street and Place Carnot there is an excellent wine shop, Denis Perret. Follow Rue Carnot to Place Monge, which is dominated by its 14th-century belfry, a tall tower with a remarkable wooden roof. Now turn right into Rue des Tonneliers (Street of Coopers) with its many dignified 18th-century houses.

At the end of the street turn left and then straight away left again into Rue Rousseau-Deslandes. No. 10 is one of the most remarkable buildings in Beaune, the former Hôtel de Cîteaux, dating from the end of the 12th century. Continue by turning right into Rue de Lorraine. On the corner stands the Hospice de la Charité, with its chapel and court.

Follow the Rue de Lorraine, then turn right along a small side street to the Hôtel de Ville, in a former Ursuline convent of the 17th century.

Now turn back towards Rue de Lorraine. At the end of the street, on your right, stands the most beautiful of Beaune's town gates, the Porte St-Nicolas. Near this gate are the Chapelle de l'Oratoire, where art exhibitions are sometimes held, and the cellars of the firm of La Reine Pédauque, which attract many

visitors. Continue the walk by turning left and follow part of the old town walls. The round Bastion des Filles (or de l'Oratoire)

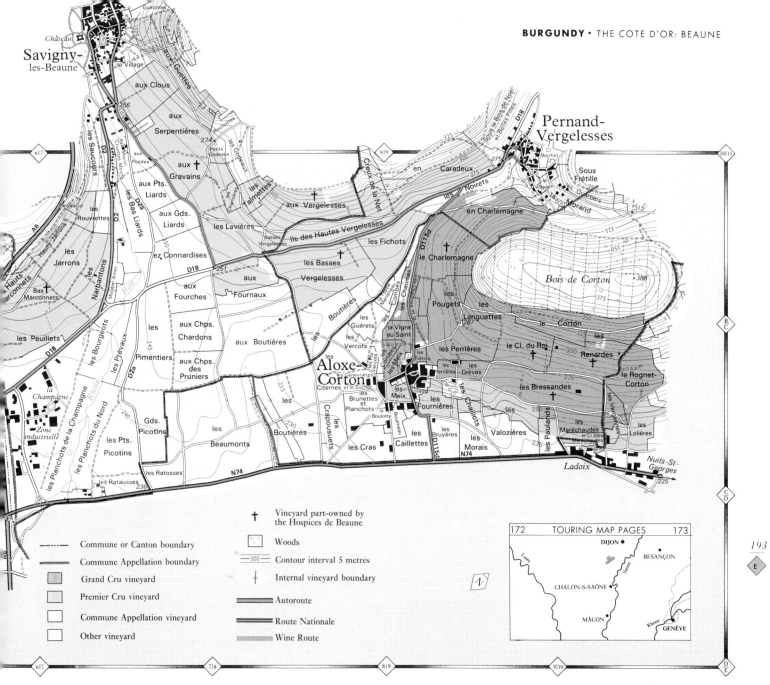

Savigny-les-Beaune

Pernand-Vergelesses

Aloxe-Corton

Bois de Corton

Ladoix

Nuits-St-Georges

Legend:

✝ Vineyard part-owned by the Hospices de Beaune

▫ Woods

═300═ Contour interval 5 metres

✝ Internal vineyard boundary

---·---·--- Commune or Canton boundary

————— Commune Appellation boundary

▦ Grand Cru vineyard

▨ Premier Cru vineyard

▢ Commune Appellation vineyard

▢ Other vineyard

═══ Autoroute

═══ Route Nationale

═══ Wine Route

TOURING MAP PAGES 172 | 173

DIJON • BESANÇON • CHALON-S-SAÔNE • MÂCON • GENÈVE

193

E

on the corner of Boulevard Foch now serves as an above-ground wine cellar for Chanson Père & Fils. Now turn left back into the old town on Rue Paul Chanson, also called Rue du Collège. On the right-hand side is the entrance to Patriarche Père & Fils, whose cellars deserve a visit. You pay a small charge, which goes to charity. An extensive range of wines can be tasted in these cellars.

Turn right, walking south along Rue Gandelot to the basilica of Notre-Dame. Despite much alteration and rebuilding this church still has clear traces of Burgundian Romanesque architecture. From April to November marvellous wall tapestries depicting the 'Life of the Virgin' are displayed.

It is only a minute's walk from here to the Musée du Vin de Bourgogne, one of France's most exciting wine museums, tucked away to the south of Notre-Dame. The museum houses a rich collection of objects and works of art connected

with wine. It is housed in the former 15th- and 16th-century residence of the dukes of Burgundy.

Via the narrow Rue d'Enfer (with the offices of the firm of Joseph Drouhin at No. 7) you come to

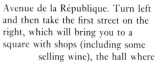

Avenue de la République. Turn left and then take the first street on the right, which will bring you to a square with shops (including some selling wine), the hall where the Hospices de Beaune auction is held (see page 176), the Office du

Tourisme and, the climax of this tour, the Hôtel-Dieu. This charitable hospital was completed in 1451 and constitutes a magnificent example of Flemish Burgundian architecture. It was built to the order of Nicolas Rolin, chancellor to Duke Philippe le Bon and was in use as an old people's home until 1971. The main buildings, which are now a museum – a modern hospital has been built – have a colourful mosaic of enamelled roof tiles, a paved inner courtyard with old wells, a high-roofed hall for the sick with places for 28 beds, an enormous kitchen, a dispensary, a second courtyard with the statues of Nicolas Rolin and his wife, Guigone de Salins, together with an exhibition of tapestries, furniture and the sublime altarpiece by Rogier van der Weyden, *The Last Judgement* (1443), commissioned by the Hospice and one of the transcendental masterpieces of Flemish art. It alone justifies a visit to Beaune. The walk ends back at Place Carnot.

AROUND NUITS-ST-GEORGES

North of Beaune, beyond the village of Ladoix on the slopes of the Corton hill, comes a relatively low-key passage in the Côte d'Or litany. Three villages between Ladoix and Nuits-St-Georges all make wine, but their names are little known.

These three southernmost villages of the Côte de Nuits form part of the Côte de Nuits-Villages appellation. In the best vineyard in Corgoloin, the walled Clos des Langres, there is a board that marks the boundary between the Côte de Beaune and the Côte de Nuits. Comblanchien, the next village, is dominated by quarries rather than vineyards. The pinkish stone sawn from the hillside here (you can watch the process) looks very like marble when polished. It was used, for example, for the Opéra in Paris. The wines of Prémeaux-Prissey are sometimes sold under the Côte de Nuits-Villages appellation, but most of the vineyards are entitled to the Nuits-St-Georges Premier Cru and Nuits-St-Georges appellations.

Nuits-St-Georges is a major centre of the Burgundian wine business and a number of important négociants have their headquarters in the little town. Nuits has a long history – Gallo-Roman remains have been found nearby – but in appearance Nuits-St-Georges is more utilitarian than Beaune. There are hardly any beautiful buildings, and a continuous stream of heavy traffic trundles noisily through the centre.

The commune has no Grand Cru vineyards, but a good number of Premiers Crus. Many of them have considerable reputation, including Les Vaucrains, Les Perrières, Les Pruliers, Les Porrets – and the field from which the commune takes the second part of its name, Les St-Georges. The mainly red wines of Nuits-St-Georges are characteristically tannic, sinewy and dour. Sometimes they have an elusive, wild aroma that suggests bitter fruit or smoky oakwood. This classic style of Nuits-St-Georges demands patience. The commune also produces lighter wines which are ready sooner.

Going north you come to Vosne-Romanée, an undistinguished-looking village that produces a number of Burgundy's most outstanding wines. Within its boundaries are no fewer than five Grands Crus. The most famous is La Romanée-Conti, whose wine has an almost exotic perfume and a satiny, richly nuanced taste that seems to go on for ever. The vineyard, which is distinguished by its gravelly red soil and a simple stone cross, is the exclusive property of the Domaine de la Romanée-Conti. The same estate also owns all of the Grand Cru La Tâche, together with plots in Le Richebourg and La Romanée-St-Vivant. With less than a hectare, the remaining Grand Cru, La Romanée, constitutes the smallest appellation in France. Its wine is sold exclusively by Bouchard Père & Fils. In general the wines of Vosne-Romanée are striking for the velvety finesse of their taste, natural balance and a resounding ring to their flavour which proclaims them classics. Besides its Grands Crus this commune also has various Premiers Crus of repute, including La Grande Rue, Les Beaumonts, Les Suchots and Malconsorts.

East of the N74 lies the village of Flagey-Echézeaux, which does not have a commune appellation. It possesses two Grands Crus, Echézeaux and Grands Echézeaux. These are both to the west of the *route nationale* – the good side, between Vosne-Romanée and Vougeot. The character of the wines made here is akin to that of the better Vosne-Romanées. As a rule, therefore, Echézeaux and Grands Echézeaux are reckoned to be Vosne-Romanées, particularly since the other Flagey-Echézeaux wines go out into the world labelled as Vosne-Romanée or Vosne Romanée Premier Cru.

Vougeot, a tiny little place, enjoys worldwide fame for the Clos de Vougeot vineyard, surrounded by a stone wall and covering about 50 hectares (124 acres). Once monastic property, Vougeot's history as a single vineyard spans 700 years. It was the monks who in the sixteenth century built the Château de Vougeot, an austere-looking edifice among the vines. In 1944 it was bought by La Confrérie des Chevaliers du Tastevin, who organize great banquets and celebrations there several times a year. The château is also a museum, with exhibits including enormous wooden wine presses.

The land inside the Vougeot walls belongs to some 70 different growers who have on average less than a hectare each. Given this great fragmentation – and the resultant diversity of wines – the Clos de Vougeot could be regarded as representing Burgundy in miniature. It is essential that you select your wine according to the reputation of its producer. The words Clos de Vougeot alone are not enough. At its best the Grand Cru is an extraordinarily satisfying, strong and meaty wine; but some can disappoint. Among Vougeot's Premiers Crus and village wines that deserve mention is Clos Blanc de Vougeot, a white Premier Cru.

▲ Above left: "Bordeaux mixture", a concoction of copper sulphate, slaked lime and water, is used to protect the vines against disease. These stakes, which will be used to support the vines, are tinted bright blue by it.
Above right: Vosne-Romanée may call itself "the central pearl in the Burgundian necklace", thanks to some eminent Grands Crus, but its charm is still rural rather than sophisticated. Grower Robert Sirugue, whose venerable house is shown, makes an excellent Grands-Echézeaux.
▶ Right: Vines lap up to the garden walls on the outskirts of Nuits-St-Georges.

TRAVEL INFORMATION

See also the hotels and restaurants listed under the Travel Information on pages 182–183.

HOTELS

Hotel Les Grands Crus, 21220 Gevrey-Chambertin, tel. 80 34 34 15. Comfortable hotel built in 1976 in a quiet position near the local château. Stylish rooms and a garden. Class B.
Hostellerie La Gentilhommière, 21700 Nuits-St-Georges, tel. 80 61 12 06. A spacious old building in a peaceful setting west of Nuits, on the road to Meuilley. Good traditional food. Class B.

RESTAURANTS

Chez Jeanette, 21220 Fixin, tel. 80 52 45 49. Rustic décor and traditional cuisine, plus a simple hotel. Class C.
Balvay, 21640 Flagey-Echézeaux, tel. 80 62 88 10. Very popular with local wine growers because of its well-prepared regional dishes. Class C.
Rôtisserie du Chambertin, 21200 Gevrey-Chambertin, tel. 80 34 33 20. In a luxuriously converted 18th-century cellar. *Escargots* and *coq au vin* cooked with finesse. Class A.
Les Millésimes, 21200 Gevrey-Chambertin, tel. 80 51 84 24. Family concern with a friendly welcome. The dining room is a vaulted cellar. Classic, fairly rich dishes. Class B.

Maison des Hautes-Côtes, 21700 Marey-lès-Fussey, tel. 80 62 91 29. Southwest of Nuits on the D115. Wines from the Hautes-Côtes are served with honest regional dishes. Class C.
Les Gourmets, 21160 Marsannay-la-Côte, tel. 80 52 16 32. Full of atmosphere, with interesting paintings on the walls. Good-value set menus served here during the week. Reliable. Class B.
La Côte d'Or, 1 Rue Thurot, 21700 Nuits-St-Georges, tel. 80 61 06 10. Perhaps the best restaurant in the Côte d'Or. Skilled cooking (*les escargots de Bourgogne en cocotte lutée, le rognon de veau aux morilles,* beautiful desserts) and friendly service. Large wine list. Also rooms. Class A.
La Ferme de Rolle, Hameau de Rolle, 21200 Ternant, tel. 80 61 40 10. On the D35 beyond Villars-Fontaine. A convivial place to eat, enthusiastically run in an old farmhouse. Regional cuisine with, for example, *agneau en meurette, lapin à la moutarde,* grills, and an interesting cheese board. Class C.
La Toute Petite Auberge, 21700 Vosne-Romanée, tel. 80 61 02 03. Indeed small, but with a loyal clientele. On the N74. Try the *bœuf bourguignon*. Class C.
Les Gastronomes, 21640 Vougeot, tel. 80 62 85 10. Regional, fairly classic dishes. Fine wine list. Opened in 1983. Class B.

PLACES OF INTEREST

Arcenant (West of Nuits-St-Georges.) Fortified 13th-century monastery.
Bévy Artistic and cultural centre of the Hautes-Côtes.
Brochon Neo-Renaissance château that now serves as a school.
Chambolle-Musigny A 16th-century church with a separate tower and an ancient hollow lime tree in the churchyard. Also a triumphal arch erected for Henri IV.
Chenôve (just south of Dijon.) In the steep village street visit the place where two mighty, centuries-old wine presses stand.
Collonges-lès-Bévy (Hautes-Côtes.) A Roman encampment, a Romanesque church and a 17th-century château.
Corgoloin The 18th-century Château de Cussigny forms a well-preserved whole.
Curtil-Vergy (Hautes-Côtes.) Ruins of 9th-century St-Vivant abbey.
l'Etang-Vergy (NW of Nuits.) Walls of a fortress dismantled in 1609.
Fixin In the Parc Noiset there is a

museum dedicated to Napoleon and the monumental statue *Reveil de Napoleon* which the Dijon-born sculptor François Rude carved in 1846. Here, too, is the grave of Noiset himself, a former captain of the Imperial Guard.
Gevrey-Chambertin The 10th-century castle, restored by monks from Cluny in the 13th century, has vaulted wine cellars. The church dates from the 13th–15th centuries.
Gilly-lès-Cîteaux (E of Nuits.) Cultural centre in a former residence of the abbots of Cîteaux.
Marey-lès-Fussey (Southwest of Nuits-St-Georges.) An 11th-century church, remains of the abbey of Lieu-Dieu des Champs and the Maison des Hautes-Côtes (wine-tasting room and restaurant).
Nuits-St-Georges Finds from the Gallo-Roman excavations at Les Bolards are on show in the 17th-century bell tower. The church of St-Symphorien is late Romanesque.
Ternant (Northwest of Nuits-St-Georges.) Château dating from 1670. To the west towards Rolle there are two fine dolmens dating from 2000 BC.
Villers-la-Faye (West of Comblanchien.) Church dating from the 11th century and a 15th-century château.
Vougeot For every lover of Burgundy the Château de Vougeot, with its monumental kitchen and 14th-century presses, is an obligatory stop.

WINE ACTIVITIES

The Hospice de Nuits auction is held each spring on the Sunday before Palm Sunday. A major winetasting takes place in Nuits on the Saturday and Sunday.

WINE INFORMATION

Consult the Syndicat d'Initiative in the rue Sonays, tel. 80 61 22 47.

PRODUCERS OF SPECIAL INTEREST

Producers are listed under the village in which they are based. Most own land in more than one commune.

HAUTES-COTES DE NUITS

ARCENANT, postcode 21700
Alain Verdet

CURTIL-VERGY, postcode 21220
Yves Chaley*

MAGNY-LES-VILLERS, postcode 21700
Claude Cornu; Jayer-Gilles*: his Echézeaux is impressive; **Henri Naudin-Ferrand***: the white wines in particular are delicious.

MAREY-LES-FUSSEY, postcode 21700
Simon Fils; Domaine Thévenot-Le-Brun & Fils*: one of the largest properties in the Hautes-Côtes; white grapes grown include Pinot Blanc and Pinot Beurot as well as Chardonnay.

VILLARS-FONTAINE, postcode 21700
Domaine Bernard Hudelot-Verdel

VILLERS-LA-FAYE, postcode 21700
Domaine Marcel & Bernard Fribourg

COTES DE NUITS

CHAMBOLLE-MUSIGNY, postcode 21220, 198 B3
Gaston Barthod-Noëllat; Domaine Bertheau; Daniel Moine-Hudelot*: Grands and Premiers Crus full of character; **Domaine Jacques-Frédéric Mugnier**: important Le Musigny owner; **Domaine G. Roumier**: splendid property with memorable wines; **Hervé Roumier***; **Servelle-Tachot; Domaine Comte Georges de Vogüé***: this estate has the largest holding in Le Musigny; the Musigny Cuvée Vieilles Vignes represents the very peak of finesse.

COMBLANCHIEN, postcode 21700
André Chopin & Fils

CORGOLOIN, postcode 21700
Paul Reitz: small-scale wine merchant and broker.

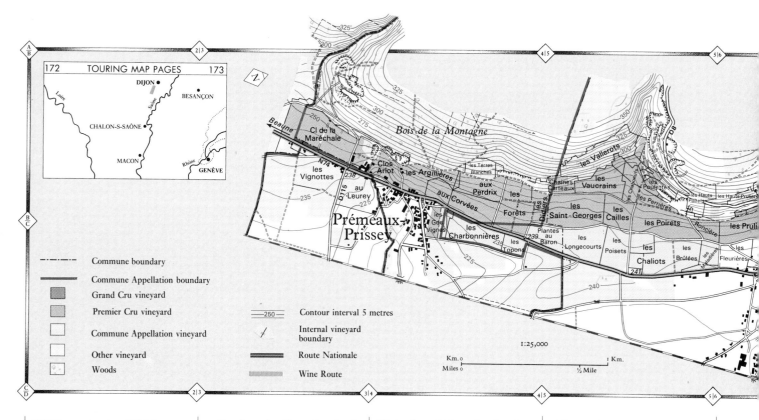

FIXIN, postcode 21200, 199 B8

Vincent & Denis Berthaut;
Jacques Durand-Roblot*; Philippe
Joliet*: sole owner of the Clos de la
Perrière; Domaine Pierre Gelin*:
sinewy Grands and Premiers Crus
from Fixin and Gevrey-Chambertin.

FLAGEY-ECHEZEAUX,
postcode 21640

Cocquard-Loison-Fleurot

GEVREY-CHAMBERTIN,
postcode 21200, 199 B7

Domaine Bachelet*; Philippe
Batacchi*; Lucien Boillot & Fils;
Pierre Bourée Fils: small wine firm
with durable burgundies; Alain
Burguet*: sound, balanced village
wine; Camus Père & Fils*: an
impressive range of Grands Crus;
Domaine Pierre Damoy*: biggest
owner in Chambertin Clos de Bèze;
Domaine Drouhin-Laroze*: light,
fragrant, pure and vital wines;
Geantet-Pansiot*; Laurent
Goillot-Bernollin; Frédéric
Humbert; Philippe Leclerc*;
Domaine René Leclerc; Henri
Magnien*: small estate that never has
enough wine to meet demand;
Domaine Maume*; Naigeon-
Chauveau: reliable firm; Domaine
Pernot-Fourrier*; Domaine Les
Perrières*; Domaine Henri
Rebourseau; Philippe Rossignol*;
Joseph Roty*: an extraordinarily
painstaking wine grower; Domaine
Armand Rousseau Père & Fils: a
great reputation – but variable in

quality; Domaine Tortochot; Louis
Trapet Père & Fils; G. Vachet-
Rousseau; Domaine des Varoilles*:
a rich palette of red wines, including
the Clos des Varoilles, a local Premier
Cru; André Ziltener Père & Fils:
Swiss wine firm.

GILLY-LES-CITEAUX, postcode 26140

Bernard Munier

MARSANNAY-LA-COTE,
postcode 21160

André Bart; René Bouvier: one of
the few growers with land in
Chenôve; Domaine Philippe
Charlopin-Parizot*; Bruno Clair;
Domaine Clair-Daü*: an excellent
estate that since 1986 has belonged to
the firm of Louis Jadot; Cave
Coopérative; Domaine Huguenot
Père & Fils.

MOREY-ST-DENIS, postcode 21200,
198 C4

Domaine Pierre Amiot & Fils*:
firm, elegant wines with softness and
depth; Domaine Arlaud Père &
Fils*: classic red burgundies, among
them four Grands Crus; Bryczek
Père & Fils*: expressive,
concentrated wines; Domaine
Dujac*: Morey-St-Denis at its best,
from Grand Cru to village wine; the
estate also has land in other villages;
Domaine Robert Groffier;
Domaine des Lambrays*: owner of
all except a quarter of a hectare of
Clos des Lambrays (a Grand Cru
since 1981); Georges Lignier &

Fils*: a large, high-quality domaine;
Hubert Lignier*; Michel
Magnien*: charming, unfiltered
wines; Henri Perrot-Minot;
Domaine Ponsot*: intense red
wines, and a rare white Morey-St-
Denis; Jean Raphet & Fils;
Domaine Louis Rémy; Domaine
B. Serveau & Fils*; Clos de Tart*:
this whole Grand Cru is the property
of the firm of Mommessin, based in
the Mâconnais; J. Taupenot-
Merme*: distinguished red wines
from an estate with modern
equipment; J. Truchot-Martin.

NUITS-ST-GEORGES,
postcode 21700, 197 C6

Marcel Bocquenet*; Jean Claude
Boisset: one of the largest wine firms

of Burgundy, partly due to its take-
over of such houses as Lionel
J. Bruck, Pierre Ponnelle, Thomas-
Bassot and Charles Viénot; various
brand names; F. Chauvenet:
energetic firm with moderate wines
and a 50% interest in Louis Max;
Jean Chauvenet*: faultless estate
wines; Robert Chevillon*: one of
the best estates of Nuits-St-Georges,
consistently good; Dufouleur Père &
Fils: wines distributed by this firm
include those of Domaine Guy
Dufouleur and various Domaine
Liger-Belair wines; Joseph
Faiveley*: has more than 100 hectares
(247 acres) of its own vineyards and
its generous, firmly structured wines
are some of Burgundy's best; those
from the Côte de Nuits and

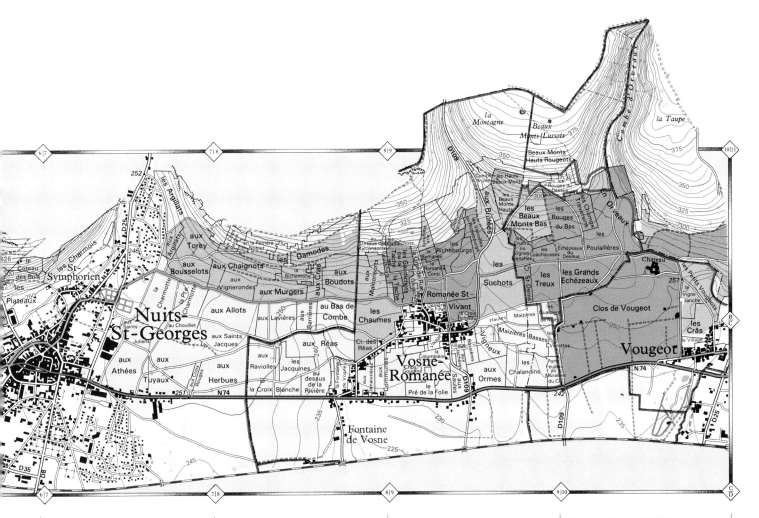

Mercurey in particular invite attention; **Geisweiler & Fils**: has 70 hectares (173 acres) in the Hautes-Côtes; **Domaine Henri Gouges***: fruity red wines with finesse from Nuits, as well as a rare white, La Perrière; **Hospices de Nuits***: wines from this charity, a smaller version of the Beaune hospice, are auctioned two weeks before Easter; **Labouré-Roi***: fairly small firm with carefully made red and white wines; **Alain Michelot***: specialist in Premiers Crus from Nuits; **Moillard**: the average quality from this large firm has improved appreciably; **Henri Remoriquet**.

PREMEAUX-PRISSEY, postcode 21700, 196 B4

Robert Dubois & Fils; Domaine Machard de Gramont*: a considerable estate producing more than 20 different wines, mainly red; **Domaine des Perdrix; Domaine Daniel Rion & Fils***: fruity, fragrant wines.

VOSNE-ROMANEE, postcode 21700, 197 C9
Robert Arnoux*: the Grands Crus

and Premiers Crus in particular are alluring; **Jacques Cacheux-Blée & Fils; Domaine René Engel; Forey Père & Fils; Domaine François Gerbet; Jean Grivot***: balanced wines with personality; the Clos de Vougeot and Echézeaux are sublime; **Jean Gros***: in all categories, from Hautes-Côtes to Grand Cru, the wines here have allure; **Domaine Gros Frère & Sœur; Henri Jayer***: talented winemaker who matures most of his wines in new casks; **Jacqueline Jayer***; **Domaine Lamarche***: La Grande Rue is the great speciality here; **Domaine Méo-Camuzet; Mongeard-Mugneret***: aristocratic burgundies rich in fruit; **Georges Mugneret***: also operates as A. Mugneret-Gibourg; **Gérard & René Mugneret***: sound red wines, including Les Suchots; **Domaine Charles Noëllat; A. Pernin-Rossin; Domaine de la Romanée-Conti***: the most famous of Burgundy's wine estates; almost 90% of the 30 hectares (74 acres) is made up of Grands Crus: La Romanée-Conti, La Tâche, Richebourg, Romanée-St-Vivant, Grands Echézeaux, Echézeaux, Montrachet and Bâtard-Montrachet (an invitation to visit is very difficult to acquire although occasional groups are admitted); **Robert Sirugue**.

VOUGEOT, postcode 21640, 197 C10, 198 C2

Domaine Bertagna*: since being taken over by a German grower the quality has greatly improved;

Georges Clerget*; **Michel Clerget***; **Alain Hudelot-Noëllat***: mouth-filling and at the same time fine wines; **Domaine Jean Grivot***: has nearly 2 hectares in the Clos (a relatively large holding) and makes fine, characterful wines; **Domaine Jean Gros***: Vosne-Romanée grower with a small plot in the Clos; **Domaine Mongeard-Mugneret***: one of half or dozen or so local concerns carrying the name Mugneret (see Vosne-Romanée). This one has some fine Vougeot land. **Domaine des Varoilles***: see Gevrey-Chambertin. Vougeot which needs time in bottle. **Château de la Tour**.

FROM CHAMBOLLE TO DIJON

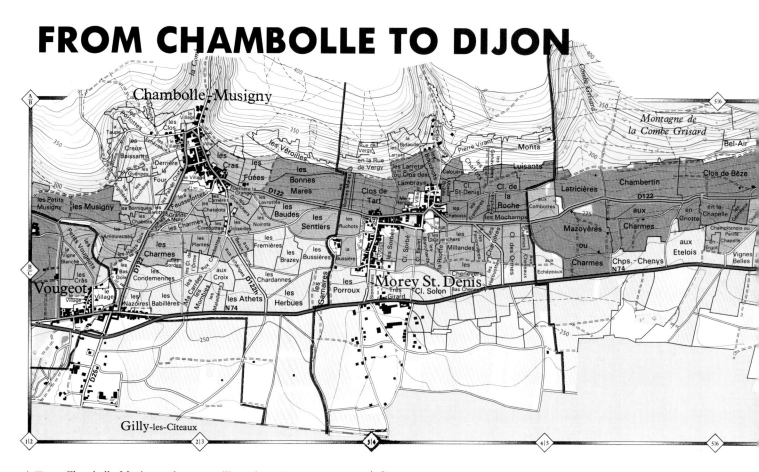

In Chambolle-Musigny, the next village from Vougeot, the soil becomes lighter as clay gives way to limestone. As a result the wines are the finest and most delicate of the whole Côte de Nuits. The Grand Cru Le Musigny offers the utmost in finesse. This wine was poetically described by Gaston Roupnel as being "of silk and lace"; and its perfume put him in mind of the scents of "a damp garden, a rose and a violet covered in morning dew". A white Musigny is also produced but this does not reach the class of the red. The other Grand Cru here is Bonnes Mares (a small part of which belongs to the neighbouring commune of Morey-St-Denis). This field gives a rather more rounded wine, with more reserve when young than Le Musigny. With the years, however, this great burgundy also becomes delicate and soft. That Chambolle-Musigny's Premiers Crus can also have charm and allure is shown by such names as Les Amoureuses and Les Charmes. The village of Chambolle is certainly worth a quiet stroll for its atmosphere of rather reticent prosperity.

The wines of Morey-St-Denis hold the middle ground between the elegant burgundies of Chambolle-Musigny and the powerful products of Gevrey-Chambertin. In the Côte de Nuits choir they are the tenors, not sopranos or baritones. Wines of all categories here can taste marvellous. The average quality is high and you often detect a soft taste of fruit. The Grands Crus are Clos de la Roche (from where the firmest wines come); Clos St-Denis (characteristically soft yet substantial wines); Clos de Tart (the exclusive property of the firm of Mommessin); and Clos des Lambrays (only promoted to Grand Cru in 1981). The Premier Cru Monts Luisants produces an attractive white wine.

Gevrey-Chambertin is by far the biggest wine commune of the Côte de Nuits. The village centre lies a few hundred metres west of the *route nationale*, but there is also a sizable settlement around the main road. The quality of the wines produced here varies a good deal, because wine from a considerable area of flat land east of the N74 comes under the appellation Gevrey-Chambertin (see map). The Grands Crus, however, have a very good reputation, with Chambertin and Chambertin Clos de Bèze to the fore. Both fields – of about the same size – yield formidable, strong burgundies that need long ageing in bottle to reach their best. Six other Grands Crus can add the name of Chambertin to their own: Chapelle-Chambertin, Charmes-Chambertin (more wine than from the other five together), Griotte-Chambertin, Latricières-Chambertin, Mazis-

Chambertin and Ruchottes-Chambertin. Clos St-Jacques is one of the very best Premiers Crus.

Brochon is the next village north. Seemingly as well-placed as Gevrey, it nevertheless has no commune appellation of its own. The southern vineyards are entitled to the Gevrey-Chambertin name, but the rest of Brochon's land has to use the Côte de Nuits-Villages appellation.

Fixin's growers are free to sell their wine either under the name of the commune or as Côte de Nuits-Villages. Fixin is a charming village with a beautiful church, a museum dedicated to Napoleon set in a park, and a number of good vineyards. The wines have a little less lustre than those of Gevrey-Chambertin, but they are akin to them. They usually have lots of colour and are firm in structure. Clos du Chapitre and Clos de la Perrière are regarded as the best Premiers Crus.

You reach Marsannay-la-Côte, the northernmost wine commune, by way of Couchey. Both communes can produce the rosé of Marsannay, an excellent dry wine made from the Pinot Noir grape. The innovative grower Joseph Clair first made this rosé in 1919. There are also red and white burgundies with the name of Marsannay, but both lack the charm of the rosé.

From Marsannay-la-Côte the suburbs extend without a break to Dijon. In the last century there were some 3,000 hectares (7,400 acres) of vineyard around this growing town, but these have almost all disappeared. Only Chenôve still has a few productive plots left, the best known of them being the Clos du Roy. These vineyards are entitled to the Marsannay appellation.

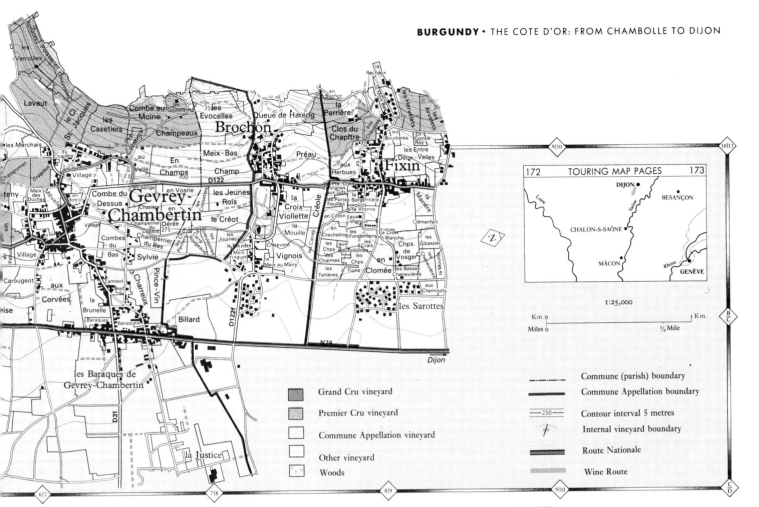

TOURING MAP PAGES

172   173

1:25,000

Km. 0 _____ Km.
Miles 0 _____ ½ Mile

Grand Cru vineyard

Premier Cru vineyard

Commune Appellation vineyard

Other vineyard

Woods

Commune (parish) boundary

Commune Appellation boundary

Contour interval 5 metres

Internal vineyard boundary

Route Nationale

Wine Route

◀ Left: In the year 1257, the inhabitants of Gevrey received permission from the abbey of Cluny to enlarge the small local stronghold to true castle size. This château still exists, although it was almost destroyed by a fire in 1976. Under the building are huge vaulted medieval cellars.

▼ Below far left: Growers sometimes display their pride in their Grands Crus in the Côte d'Or by building formal entrance gates to their plot. Here M. Rémy proclaimed his ownership of a portion of Latricières in Chambertin. Beyond is the Montagne de la Combe Grisard. The picture was taken from the D122.

Below left: Burgundy is used to visitors: in many villages, tourists are invited to taste and (by heavy-hinted inference) buy wines.

THE CHALONNAIS

South across the valley from Santenay, where the Côte d'Or comes to an end, another belt of vines begins. This district takes its name from the town of Chalon to the east, but its northern anchorpoint is the somewhat dreary town of Chagny (which does, however, have the one three-star restaurant of the Côte d'Or region). The countryside of the Côte Chalonnaise is less regular than the Côte d'Or: the escarpment is more broken up by valleys, and other crops interrupt the vines. It is leafy, sleepy country.

Five communes here have their own appellations, and in addition much wine is made under the regional appellations as straightforward red and white burgundy. The Chalonnais also makes a considerable amount of sparkling wine. The smallest and most northerly of the commune appellations is Bouzeron, where the Bourgogne Aligoté reaches such a high standard that since 1979 its sale with the name of the village added has been permitted. As you go south the next district is Rully, where a lot of new planting has been carried out since the 1970s. Red Rully is often a fairly modest, light wine, although there are also estates that make surprisingly substantial, strong-coloured kinds. White Rully nearly always merits attention, however, not least because of the reasonable prices asked for it. It can taste cool and juicy at the same time, with an attractive perfume and a slightly fruity aroma. A number of producers of sparkling wines are based in Rully, including the leading and influential firm of André Delorme. The Crémant de Bourgogne appellation is worth looking out for. Most of the wines that are "champagned" in Rully do not come from the local vineyards but from other Chalonnais communes; and estates in the Côte d'Or also have their sparkling wines made here (then sell them under their own labels).

The best-known Chalonnais village is Mercurey, where 95 percent of the vintage consists of red wine. A number of Côte d'Or firms and estates have considerable holdings in Mercurey (a village of not much more than one long street) and in various of the surrounding hamlets. Among them are Château Philippe-le-Hardi of Santenay with 75 hectares (185 acres); Faiveley of Nuits-St-Georges with nearly 60 hectares (148 acres); Bouchard Aîné of Beaune with more than 20 hectares (50 acres); and Château Genot-Boulanger of Meursault with almost 13 hectares (32 acres). A good deal of the local wine is therefore handled outside the district. Red Mercurey is usually a firm, good-tasting wine that seldom conveys either finesse or exuberance, but can have fruit, tannin and suppleness. White Mercurey does not always satisfy as it sometimes lacks breeding and vitality.

The little village of Givry lies due west of Chalon-sur-Saône and is growing as commuters move in. Fortunately, however, the best vineyards have been protected from the continuing threat of urbanization. Givry was once the wine centre of the Chalonnais, not least because the French court and nobility drank so much of the local wine. Henri IV in particular liked Givry, a fact that is still commemorated on many labels. Today Givry makes a lot less wine than Mercurey. In Givry, too, the emphasis is on red: an often strong, rounded wine that benefits from bottle-age. The best of the whites can be subtly nuanced and fruity.

The last of the Chalonnais appellations is Montagny, named after a small hillside village. The district also takes in the communes of Buxy, Jully-lès-Buxy and St-Vallerin. Montagny's wine is exclusively white; it is often firm, slightly nutty in taste and somewhat less lively than white Rully. A curious rule allows all Montagny of 11.5 percent or stronger to be sold as Montagny Premier Cru.

▼ The vineyards of Givry are devoted almost entirely to red wine.

TRAVEL INFORMATION

See also the chapters on the Côte d'Or and the Mâconnais.

HOTELS

Hostellerie du Château de Bellecroix, 71150 Chagny, tel. 85 87 13 86. Quietly situated south of the town, just beside the N6. The rooms are comfortable and the cooking very good. Hotel class A; restaurant class B.
Auberge du Camp Romain, 71150 Chassey-le-Camp, tel. 85 87 09 91. In a tranquil and beautiful setting with a fine view. Rooms simple but snug. Restaurant closed in winter. Class B.
Le Dracy, 71640 Dracy-le-Fort, tel. 85 41 55 88. Functional, modern place to stay the night about halfway between Givry and Chalon-sur-Saône, with restaurant. Class B.

RESTAURANTS

Lameloise, Place d'Armes, 71150 Chagny, tel. 85 87 08 85. Excellent, famous and expensive restaurant where regional ingredients are prepared with great finesse. Splendid wine list. Also a hotel, with stylish rooms. Class A.
Hotel de Paris, 6 Route de Beaune, 71150 Chagny, tel. 85 87 08 38. Quite decent cooking. Rooms. Class C.
Auberge des Fontaines, 71150 Fontaines, tel. 85 43 07 35. Hotel and restaurant with local dishes and wines. Class C.

La Halle, 71640 Givry, tel. 85 44 32 45. Mainly Burgundian fare. Also a hotel. Class C.
Les Templiers de Mercure, 71640 Mercurey, tel. 85 45 23 63. Restaurant in classical style over a wine-tasting room. Class B.
Hostellerie du Val d'Or, 71640 Mercurey, tel. 85 47 13 70. Carefully run village inn with cuisine showing increasing finesse and an excellent wine list. Frogs' legs and duck in wine are among the specialities. Also a hotel. Class B.
Auberge du Moulin de la Chapelle, 71940 Messey-sur-Grosne, tel. 85 44 00 58. Large, worthwhile restaurant by a river. Also a simple hotel. Class C.
Le Commerce, 71150 Rully, tel. 85 87 20 09. *Escargots, coq au vin* and other traditional dishes. Also a hotel. Class C.

PLACES OF INTEREST

Buxy Parts of the old town walls still stand, as do two fortified towers. Houses from the 15th century and a Romanesque church.
Chalon-sur-Saône Once a great wine port: tens of thousands of Roman amphorae have been found in the river during dredging work. From the Tour du Doyenné, on an island in the Saône, you have a good view over the old town centre.
Givry Many 18th-century buildings.

Mercurey Touches, just south of Mercurey, has a 12th-century church. **Rully** Outside the village stands the Château de Rully, a 13th- to 16th-century castle with its own vineyard.

WINE ACTIVITIES

Chagny's *foire des vins* is held for a few days around 15 August.

La Confrérie des Vignerons de la Chanteflûté acts on behalf of Mercurey and the other wines of the district. It does this not only by means of *chapitres* and a *Paulée* (in November, following the example of Meursault), but also by picking out the best wines. Twice a year a *Chanteflûtage* or tasting chooses wines good enough to be sold with a numbered "Chante Flûté" label.

WINE INFORMATION

The Maison des Vins de la Côte Chalonnaise, where you can taste the wines, is in the Promenade Ste-Marie, 71100 Chalon-sur-Saône, tel. 85 41 64 00.

PRODUCERS OF SPECIAL INTEREST

BOUZERON, postcode 71150, 201 A3

Chanzy Frères/Domaine de l'Hermitage*: wines that have often won awards, among them Aligoté from Bouzeron and white and red wines from Rully and Mercurey; **A. & P. de Villaine***: aromatic, softly fruity wines from a grower who is joint owner of the Domaine de la Romanée-Conti.

BUXY, postcode 71390, 201 F3

Cave Coopérative*: well-equipped concern that has as its specialities Montagny Premier Cru, Bourgogne Aligoté and a Bourgogne Pinot Noir matured in small casks.

CHAGNY, postcode 71150

Domaine de la Folie*: considerable estate with excellent white and red wines; **André l'Héritier**.

FONTAINES, postcode 71150

Emile Chandesais: négociant with in particular good red regional wines.

GIVRY, postcode 71640, 201 D3

Lumpp Frères*: fine wines from expert makers; **Domaine Ragot**; **Clos Salomon***: after a bad spell, the red Givry from this property is again fully up to standard; **Domaine Thénard***: the biggest property in Givry, also with Grand Cru plots in the Côte d'Or.

JAMBLES, postcode 71640, 201 D2

René Bourgeon: Givry and regional wines.

JULLY-LES-BUXY, postcode 71390, 201 F2

Pierre Bernollin*: splendid Montagny and Crémant de Bourgogne.

MERCUREY, postcode 71640, 201 B3

Domaine Bordeaux-Montrieux; Luc Brintet & Frédéric Charles; Domaine du Château de Chamilly; Jeannin-Naltet Père & Fils; Michel Juillot*: beautiful red and white Mercureys from one of the biggest private estates here; **Yves de Launay/Domaine du Meix-Foulot; Domaine de la Monette***: firmly structured red Mercurey; the owner is Paul Jean Granger; **Jean Maréchal; Louis Menand Père & Fils; Antonin Rodet**: dynamic négociant, increasingly quality-orientated, with almost 25 hectares (62 acres) of land; among the best wines are the red and white Mercureys from the firm's own Château de Chamirey; **Domaine Fabien & Louis Saier**: joint owners of the Domaine des Lambrays in Morey-St-Denis; **Domaine de Suremain***: complex, noble red Mercureys.

MONTAGNY, postcode 71390, 201 F2

Château de la Saule*: Montagny wines of the highest standard; **Veuve Steinmaier & Fils**.

PONCEY, postcode 71640, 201 F3

Propriété Desvignes: Givry Clos du Vernoy is the best wine.

RULLY, postcode 71150, 201 B3

Jean-Claude Brelière*: juicy white Rully Les Margotey and a steadily improving red; **Michel Briday; Domaine du Chapitre/Madame H. Niepce; André Delorme/ Domaine de la Renarde***: superior sparkling wines that are excellent alternatives to champagne; the firm's own Domaine de la Renarde – almost 60 hectares (148 acres) – produces fairly light wines of which the white Rullys and the Aligoté from Bouzeron are the best; **Château de Rully**: farmed by Antonin Rodet.

ST-DESERT, postcode 71390, 201 E3

Michel Goubard

ST-VALLERIN, postcode 71390

Jean Vachet*: distinguished, quite generous Montagnys, and good red burgundies.

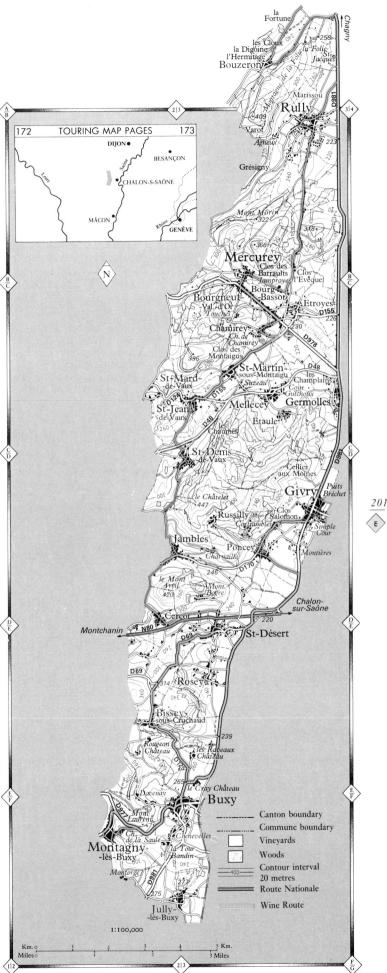

TOURING MAP PAGES 172 173

DIJON
BESANÇON
CHALON-S-SAONE
MÂCON
GENÈVE

Canton boundary
Commune boundary
Vineyards
Woods
Contour interval
20 metres
Route Nationale
Wine Route

1:100,000

Km. 0   1   2   3   4   5 Km.
Miles 0   3 Miles

THE MACONNAIS

The transition from the region known as Chalonnais to the region of Mâcon, the Mâconnais, is imperceptible. The landscape remains agricultural, with other crops as well as wine growing. But as you continue south a small ridge rises up, followed by broad hills with wooded tops. In this district, too, come the first hints of the Mediterranean south: houses with Provençal-looking roofs and a mild climate that ripens the grapes just a little earlier than in the Chalonnais. The Mâconnais takes its name from Mâcon, a bridge town on the river Saône. The Romans made wine here, but it was the monks who, from the eleventh and twelfth centuries, made viticulture flourish. The town of Cluny, where the Benedictines had their headquarters, is in the Mâconnais. Very characteristic of the district, and scattered in villages and hamlets all across it, are the Romanesque churches.

After being of merely local fame for many centuries, the wines of Mâcon became known at the French court in the 1600s. According to tradition, this was due thanks to an enterprising grower, Claude Brosse, who travelled to Paris with two casks of his wine, braving bad roads and highwaymen.

The Mâconnais wine country is shaped like a bunch of grapes: broad at the top, narrow at the bottom and with whimsically configured boundaries. Most of the wine – about 90 percent – comes from cooperatives. The white wines are the more important, both in terms of quality and quantity, whereas in the past it was the reds that dominated. Today the Chardonnay is grown in roughly two-thirds of the vineyards. The biggest appellation is Mâcon-Villages, or Mâcon followed by a commune name. Other white wines, produced in much smaller quantities, are Mâcon and Mâcon Supérieur (one percent more alcohol). Mâcon and Mâcon Supérieur are also appellations for red wines, with most coming into the Supérieur category. The basic grape for red Mâcon is Gamay, which in general gives a somewhat thinner, less fruity wine here than in the Beaujolais. There are exceptions, however: various cooperatives and estates make red Mâcon that approach the level of a Beaujolais *cru*. The Mâconnais is also a great supplier of regional wines, including red and white burgundy, Bourgogne Passe-Tout-Grains and the sparkling Crémant de Bourgogne.

The best wines of the area come from down in its southern tip, from three small, adjoining appellations, and are exclusively white. The birthplace of Pouilly-Fuissé is marked by the cliffs of Solutré and Vergisson, which rise like ship's bows above a sea of waving vines. Pouilly-Fuissé can be looked on as Mâcon-Villages in the superlative. At its best – for not all is good by any means – it is a gold-green burgundy with a pleasant, gently fruity and often floral perfume and a mouth-filling, juicy taste, frequently with a suggestion of nuts and, again, fruit (sometimes peaches).

Unfortunately Pouilly-Fuissé has become very expensive. You pay less for Pouilly-Vinzelles, a close relative, usually with a somewhat lighter structure. Pouilly-Vinzelles' production (with which is included the wines of Pouilly-Loché) amounts to less than 10 percent of the volume of Pouilly-Fuissé. The St-Véran district produces significantly more – nearly half the volume of Pouilly-Fuissé. The St-Véran appellation was created in 1971 out of land in eight communes which had formerly supplied Mâcon-Villages or white Beaujolais. It was years before St-Véran received recognition but today there is no problem selling the wine. Its structure is more slender and its taste fresher than Pouilly-Fuissé. If the name of the vineyard is given on the label then the wine must have at least 12 percent alcohol – which brings it closer in style to its famous neighbour. The appellation St-Véran includes the village of St-Vérand, a fertile source of confusion.

▶ Mâcon, the industrious capital of the Mâconnais, lies along the Saône and is linked to the east bank by the St-Laurent bridge. This dates from the 14th century and offers a view of the oldest part of the town.

TRAVEL INFORMATION

In essence the gastronomy of the Mâconnais is still fully Burgundian – but with, if possible, an even greater supply of splendid ingredients, including chickens from nearby Bresse and beef from the Charolais. For additional recommendations see the Chalonnais and Beaujolais chapters.

HOTELS

Château de Fleurville, 71260 Fleurville, tel. 85 33 12 17. About 15 km (9½ miles) north of Mâcon. A pleasant place to stay – an old building surrounded by a park. With restaurant. Class B.
Château d'Igé, 71960 Igé, tel. 85 33 33 99. Small 13th-century castle with excellent rooms and a medieval ambience. The cuisine tends to be classical. Hotel class A; restaurant class B.
Mapotel Bellevue, 416 Quai Lamartine, 71000 Mâcon, tel. 85 38 05 07. Comfortable hotel with a good restaurant. Class B.
Frantel, 26 Rue de Coubertin, 71000 Mâcon, tel. 85 38 28 06. Modern comfort. There are always fresh-from-the-market dishes on the restaurant menu. Class B.
Hotel de Genève, 1 Rue Bigonnet, 71000 Mâcon, tel. 85 38 18 10. Not far from the station, a functional sort of hotel, with a restaurant. Class B.
Terminus, 91 Rue Victor-Hugo, 71000 Mâcon, tel. 85 39 17 11. Quite tastefully decorated rooms with soundproofed windows. With restaurant. Class B.
Relais de Solutré, 71960 Solutré, tel. 85 35 80 81. Quiet situation, near vineyards. Has restaurant. Hotel class B; restaurant class C.

RESTAURANTS

Relais Lamartine, 71960 Bussières, tel. 85 36 64 71. Regional dishes, including *andouillette au vin blanc* and roast chicken, etc. Class C.
Hotel Le Moderne, Le Pont de l'Etang, 71250 Cluny, tel. 85 59 05 65. Food of quality (*charolais au jus de truffe,* for example) and good value. Also a hotel. *Demi-pension* obligatory in summer. Class B.
Relais du Mâconnais, 71960 La Croix-Blanche, tel. 85 36 60 72. Near Sologny. The cooking is creative and light. Also a hotel. Class B.
Le Fleurville, 71260 Fleurville, tel. 85 33 10 65. Traditional, straightforward cuisine. Also a cheap hotel. Class C.
Relais du Beaujolais-Mâconnais, 71570 Leynes, tel. 85 35 11 29. Simple, regional dishes. The restaurant faces the charming square at Leynes, one of the villages of St-Véran. Class C.
Caveau St-Pierre, 71260 Lugny, tel. 85 33 20 27. Wine-tasting room with

a simple restaurant, open from March
to the end of October. Panorama.
Class C.

Auberge Bressane, 114 Rue du 28-
Juin, 71000 Mâcon, tel. 85 38 07 42.
A very famous place. Specialities
include *feuilleté d'escargots à la crème
d'ail, matelote d'anguille au Mâcon
rouge.* Class B.

Maison Mâconnaise des Vins,
Avenue de Lattre-de-Tassigny, 7100
Mâcon, tel. 85 38 36 70. (See also
Wine Information.) A simple,
spacious restaurant (onion soup, ham
on the bone, *choucroute*, cheeses, etc).
Class C.

Au Rocher de Cancale, 393 Quai
Jean-Jaurès, 71000 Mâcon,
tel. 85 38 07 50. Good-value,
carefully prepared set meals with
usually at least one fish dish. Class C.

Auberge de la Grange du Bois,
71960 Solutré, tel. 85 37 80 78. Very
rustic. Class C.

PLACES OF INTEREST

Azé Prehistoric caves with an
associated museum (only open in the
season).

Berzé-la-Ville The Romanesque
chapel of the Château des Moines has
wall paintings from the 12th century,
rather Byzantine in style.

Berzé-le-Châtel Large feudal
stronghold, once the seat of the first
barony of the Mâconnais.

Bray Roman walls and an 11th-
century church.

Burgy Romanesque church (11th-
century) on the hill above the village.

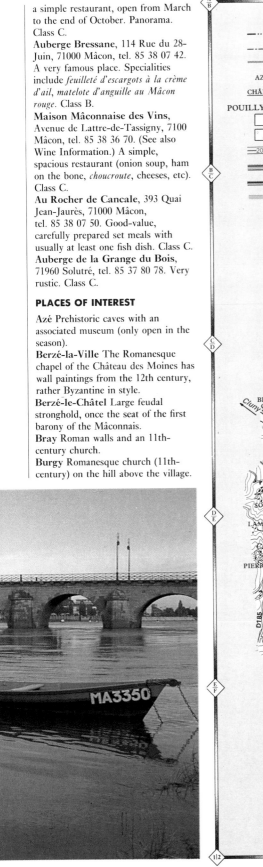

203

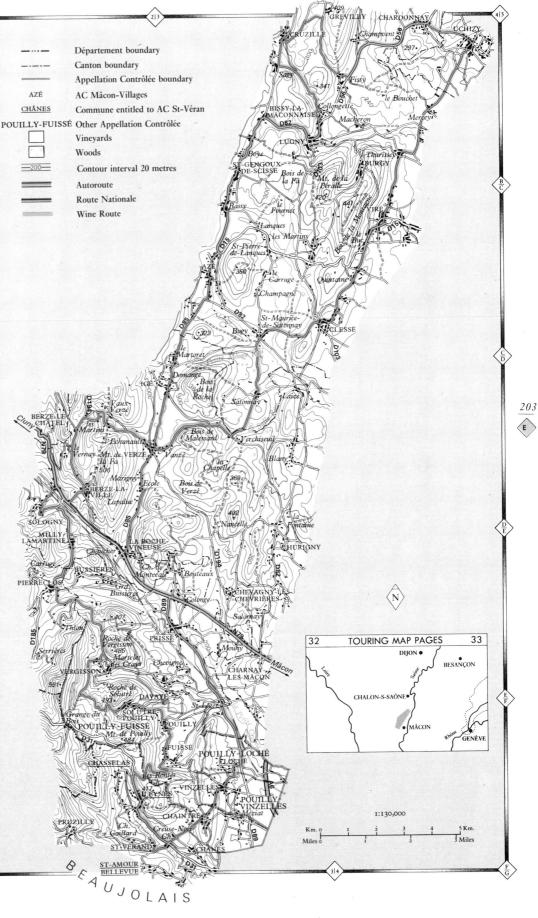

Bussières Beside the 12th-century church lies the grave of Father Dumont, the inspiration for the poet Lamartine's *Jocelyn*.

Chaintré A 15th-century château.

Chardonnay Dolmen and a 16th-century château.

Chasselas Church of the 12th century and a château of the 15th.

Clessé The 11th-century church with its octagonal tower has Lombardic elements.

Cluny In 910 an abbey was founded here that two centuries later was to have some 2,000 Benedictine daughter houses throughout Europe. Until the building of St Peter's in Rome, the church at Cluny was

Europe's biggest. It had seven towers, was 30 m (98 ft) high and 187 m (614 ft) long. Only the south wing remains. There is a model of the original building in the Musée Ochier. Cluny town has many old houses and monuments, remains of its walls and a second museum (early sculpture).

Cruzille-en-Mâconnais Museum devoted to some 30 agricultural crafts and occupations (with about 35,000 items).

Farges-lès-Mâcon Small Mediterranean Romanesque church from the beginning of the 11th century.

Fuissé A 12th-century church.

Grévilly Romanesque church (12th-century).

Igé Wine museum and tasting room in a Romanesque chapel.

Leynes A 12th-century church.

Loché A church of the 12 century and, by way of contrast, a station for the high-speed TGV Paris–Lyon train, which has brought the Beaujolais into day-trip range from Paris.

Lugny Remains of a castle.

Mâcon The writer, poet and politician Alphonse Prat de Lamartine was born in 1790 in this commercial and industrial town with its long riverside quay. There is a museum dedicated to him (21 Rue Sigrogne), and a Circuit Lamartine

can be followed around the town. In the Musée des Ursulines (5 Rue des Ursulines) prehistoric finds and art of many periods is exhibited. The Hôtel-Dieu (Cours Moreau) has a dispensary with, for example, earthenware from the time of Louis XV.

Milly-Lamartine The house where Lamartine (see Mâcon) lived as a child. The church is 12th-century.

Pierreclos A 15th-century castle.

Prissé Château de Montceau (13th-century).

La Roche Vineuse A 12th-century bell tower, remains of a feudal stronghold, an African village ("Au Bout du Monde") and a view over the Charolais country.

St-Gengoux-de-Scissé Old houses and an 11th-century church.

St-Vérand Ancient village with a Romanesque church. A 16th-century wine press stands in the wine-tasting room here.

Sologny An 11th-century church.

Solutré Situated near the foot of a high limestone cliff, where the fossilized bones of tens of thousands of horses have been found – they were driven over the cliff by prehistoric hunters. There is a small museum of prehistory in the village.

Tournus A fine old abbey and the church of St-Philibert – plus a well-reputed restaurant, Greuz.

Uchizy Beautiful 12th-century church with frescoes and a five-storey tower.

Vergisson Has a cliff like the one at Solutré and also a menhir.

Verzé A 12th-century chapel.

Vinzelles Feudal fort; Romanesque church.

Viré Small wine museum.

WINE ROUTE

In 1986 the Route des Vins Mâconnais-Beaujolais was opened; 450 km (280 miles) long, it leads the traveller criss-cross through the two districts by means of a thousand or so signposts. Information about the route is supplied in the Cellier-Expo at Crèches-sur-Saône, a village just south of Mâcon on the N6.

WINE ACTIVITIES

Lugny holds its Foire des Vins du Haut-Mâconnais during the weekend of Palm Sunday. Another wine fair takes place in Mâcon (about 10 days around 20 May).

WINE INFORMATION

The Maison Mâconnaise des Vins in Mâcon (Avenue de Lattre-de-Tassigny, tel 85 38 36 70) supplies information, sells wine and also has a simple restaurant.

PRODUCERS OF SPECIAL INTEREST

BRAY, postcode 71250

Henri Lafarge*: sound, fairly broad red and white wines.

CHAINTRE, postcode 71570, 203 F3

Domaine des Granges; Cave Coopérative*: the biggest producer of Pouilly-Fuissé; **Roger Duboeuf & Fils*:** white wines, including Pouilly-Fuissé and white Beaujolais, with a lot of charm; **Domaine Mathias.**

CHARNAY-LES-MACON, postcode 71000, 203 E3

Auvigue-Burrier-Revel: small firm specializing in white wines; **Cave Coopérative; Mommessin:** important merchant house with consistent, correct wines; the better ones come from its own region and the Beaujolais. The Mommessin family also owns the Clos de Tart in Morey-St-Denis; **Trénel Fils*:** firm, substantial wines from the Beaujolais and Mâconnais; also excellent fruit liqueurs. A family business.

CHASSELAS, postcode 71570, 203 F2

Domaine des Pierres Rouges

CLESSE, postcode 71260, 203 C3

Cave Coopérative

DAVAYE, postcode 71960, 203 E2

Henry-Lucius Gregoire*: successful St-Vérans and an enjoyable Crémant de Bourgogne; **Lycée Agricole de Mâcon-Davaye; Maurice Martin.**

▼ Berzé-le-Châtel in the Mâconnais. The hilly, wooded countryside is rich in historical intrest. Not far to the northeast is the abbey of Cluny, founded in the year 910.

FUISSE, postcode 71960, 203 F2

Château de Beauregard*: Jacques Burrier ferments and ages his Pouilly-Fuissés (one ordinary and one special *cuvée*) and his St-Véran in casks; **Louis Curveux*:** small-scale, quality-conscious wine grower; **Domaine Corsin; J. A. Ferret; Château Fuissé*:** the unofficial 'first growth' of Pouilly Fuissé. Large property with excellent white and red wines, including the glorious Pouilly-Fuissé Vieilles Vignes; **Roger Luquet; Gilles Noblet*:** very good, subtly nuanced Pouilly-Fuissé.

IGE, postcode 71960

Cave Coopérative

LEVIGNY, postcode 71850

Domaine Maciat-Poncet*: juicy white wines made in the modern way. The village is near Charnay-lès-Mâcon.

LEYNES, postcode 71570, 203 F2

Château des Correaux; Georges Chagny/Domaine de la Maison.

VINZELLES, postcode 71145, 203 F3

Cave Coopérative*: an active and well-regarded concern which produces almost 90% of all Pouilly-Vinzelles (and Pouilly-Loché).

VIRE, postcode 71260, 203 C4

Domaine André Bonhomme*: pure, firm Mâcon-Viré; **Cave Coopérative*:** soundly run cooperative; its Mâcon-Viré is supplied to Piat, among others; **Domaine de Roally*:** limited production, high quality; **Château de Viré:** highly competent winemaking.

BEAUJOLAIS AND LYONNAIS

▲ A hill of vines near Fleurie. Beaujolais is a vinous monoculture broken only by woods and granite hills. Here in the north of the region, the Cru villages such as Fleurie produce the most sought-after wines.

More than half the Burgundian vineyards are in Beaujolais, making the district by far the largest of the region. It is also the most beautiful. It is made up of a long sequence of granite hills, the spurs of a chain of wooded mountains that rise to heights of from 700 metres (2,300 feet) to more than 1,000 metres (3,300 feet). These hills act as a shield against westerly winds so that a mild climate prevails. Winding, often narrow roads traverse the district, past green hills, through quiet valleys and dreaming villages. In a timeless, romantic way the Beaujolais symbolizes the French countryside. With good reason Gabriel Chevallier chose Vaux-en-Beaujolais as the model for his *Clochemerle*, the comic novel of rural life that has appeared in many languages.

The grape variety Gamay Noir à Jus Blanc (to give it its full title) thrives in the sandy, stony or schistous soils of the district. Helped by the climate, these soils give the wines a rounded quality and depth of taste that elsewhere is seldom reached with Gamay. Yet the world has come to know the Beaujolais not through its best wines, its Crus, but through its simplest: the fruity, fresh Beaujolais Primeur or Nouveau that begins its brief triumphal progress on the third Thursday of every November. Commercially, Beaujolais Primeur is a tremendous success – with the result that at present it represents about half of all Beaujolais production.

Ordinary Beaujolais comes on the market roughly a month after the Primeur and is mainly grown in the southern part of the district. A better version can be sold as Beaujolais-Villages or as Beaujolais with the commune name added. The legislators have selected 39 communes for this category, most of them in the northern half of the district. Beaujolais-Villages is usually a rather fuller, more satisfying wine than straightforward Beaujolais.

The best wine of the district consists of a number of Crus. These wines come from villages or groups of villages in the north of the Beaujolais: part of the St-Amour Cru in fact lies within the Mâconnais. In character St-Amour is fairly reserved, although fruit, charm and suppleness are nearly always perceptible. Like all the Crus it has to contain at least 10.5 percent alcohol – 11 percent if the name of the vineyard appears on the label. The next Cru to the south is Juliénas. At its best this is a firm wine, with a rich colour and sufficient staying power to mature for a few years.

The communes of Juliénas and Chénas are separated from each other by a wooded hill (Chénas is derived from *chêne*, "oak tree"). Two-thirds of the appellation area of the Chénas Cru, the smallest of the district, lie within the commune of La Chapelle-de-Guinchay. Most of the wines from the commune of Chénas itself are sold (confusingly) as Moulin-à-Vent. Chénas is closely akin to its neighbour Moulin-à-Vent: substance and strength are its characteristics.

There is no Moulin-à-Vent commune. The Cru wines with this name come from Romanèche-Thorins (where a number of merchant houses are established) and from part of Chénas. The appellation Moulin-à-Vent was created in 1936 and took its name from the only windmill still in existence in the Beaujolais. This stands northwest of Romanèche-Thorins, is at least 300 years old and has been declared a historic monument. Beside it there is a wine-tasting room. Moulin-à-Vent is the Cru with the greatest reputation, thanks to a robust structure, broad taste, tannin, and a perfume that often needs a few years to develop. When several sorts of Beaujolais accompany a meal, Moulin-à-Vent is nearly always served last.

In Fleurie the masculine power of Moulin-à-Vent gives way to feminine elegance. Its "playful" character and fresh fruitiness have created a great demand for this Cru – and the attractive name has also helped. A famous restaurant draws visitors to the pleasant village itself.

Chiroubles is farthest to the west and has the highest situation. Here the southeast-facing vineyards with granite-based soils give a light, tender

Beaujolais that usually tastes best within a year after it is made.

The fields of the Morgon Cru lie within the commune of Villié-Morgon. Underlying schistous rock gives an often substantial, generous Beaujolais with (so locals would have you believe) "the fruit of a Beaujolais, the meat of a burgundy". The classic Morgon has a hint of wild cherries in its taste and there is frequently a substantial core of alcohol present. But there are lighter wines as well. Two well-known vineyards whose names appear on labels are Charmes and Le Py (so called after Mont du Py, a former volcano).

Brouilly is the Cru with the biggest yield. Its appellation is made up of parts of the communes of Cercié, Charentay, Odenas, Quincié, St-Etienne-la-Varenne and St-Lager. Differences in the soil and the large number of producers mean that there are many styles of Brouilly. Firmness and fruitiness are the most prevalent properties. In the middle of the Brouilly country rises an abrupt 483-metre (1,585-foot) hill, Mont Brouilly. This extinct volcano has vineyards on its blue granite slopes and the summit is covered with trees. The hillside wines carry the appellation Côte de Brouilly. Often they have a mouth-filling taste with considerable alcohol (the flanks of the hill receive the optimum sun) and at the same time a refined perfume in which you can sometimes detect violets and raspberries. A good Côte de Brouilly needs to be kept for some years.

It looks as if the nine existing Crus will be joined in the foreseeable future by a tenth, Regnié. This wine will come from Regnié-Durette, the commune west of Morgon and Brouilly, Regnié shows a particular resemblance to Brouilly wine.

Although the Beaujolais is essentially a red-wine district, a modest amount of white is produced mostly in the far north. In quality it is often comparable to St-Véran or Mâcon-Villages: it is a wine that certainly has merit.

The dominion of the Gamay grape does not end at the southern boundary of the Beaujolais. Here begins the Coteaux du Lyonnais, a broad district that makes only a very limited amount of wine. It acquired the status of appellation contrôlée in 1984. Around 1900 there were more vineyards in the hills west of Lyon than in the Beaujolais, but various circumstances brought about a decline. The better wines of the Lyonnais are very similar to those of the Beaujolais, except perhaps that their taste is rather less rounded. Their average standard is continuing to improve, thanks to a number of well-educated, very quality-conscious growers, and production is gradually increasing. There may well come a time when it will seem only logical to join the Coteaux du Lyonnais to the Beaujolais – but who would be bold enough to predict that the French legislators will see things this way?

▼ The smaller growers in the Beaujolais cannot afford their own bottling plant. In the spring, mobile bottling units move from cellar to cellar, often operating in the open air.

Partly because of the proximity of Lyon and other towns, many restaurants, at all levels, thrive in this district. They range from simple village inns to veritable palaces with three Michelin stars. Among the traditional specialities are various kinds of charcuterie (*andouillette*, *cervelas*, *Jésus de Lyon*, *rosette de Lyon*, *saucisse*), *friture* (freshwater fish fried in butter), dishes with *écrevisses* (freshwater crayfish), poultry from Bresse and beef from the Charolais. The dish that appears most frequently is *coq au vin*, prepared in every Beaujolais village with the local wine.

The places described below are in geographical order, from north to south.

HOTELS

Hotel des Vignes, 69840 Juliénas, tel. 74 04 43 70. Fairly modern. Tranquillity assured. Class B.

Les Maritonnes, 71570 Romanèche-Thorins, tel. 85 35 51 70. Good hotel with a garden, swimming pool and a renowned restaurant (*andouillette au vin blanc, poulet de Bresse au Beaujolais*, Charolais beef, *soufflé glacé*). Class B.

Hotel des Grands Vins, 69820 Fleurie, tel. 74 69 81 43. Opened in 1985. Swimming pool. Class B.

Anne de Beaujeu, 69430 Beaujeu, tel. 74 04 87 58. Small, quiet hotel with regional restaurant (*coq au vin*, etc). Class C.

Château de Pizay, 69430 Pizay, tel. 74 66 51 41. Splendid château-hotel complex, between Pizay and Villié-Morgon. It has apartments, a swimming pool, a park and a good restaurant. Class A.

Le Rivage, 01090 Montmerle-sur-Saône, tel. 74 69 33 92. Situated close to the east bank of the Saône. Quite modern, with an above-average restaurant. Class B.

Hotel-St-Romain, 69480 Anse, tel. 74 67 01 12. A pleasant place to stay in a large old building. Classic dishes and more inventive ones, such as *salade tiède d'escargots poêlés aux lardons*. Hotel class B; restaurant C.

RESTAURANTS

Georges Blanc, 01540 Vonnas, tel. 74 50 00 10. In the centre of the village of Vonnas, southeast of Mâcon, is one of the best restaurants in France. In warm, elegant surroundings you can enjoy *crêpe parmentière au saumon, volaille de Bresse à la crème, agneau mariné rôti à la fleur de sel* and splendid wines. There is also a luxurious hotel. Class A.

Auberge du Paradis, 71570 St-Amour, tel. 85 37 10 26. Country cooking. Class C.

Le Coq au Vin, 69840 Juliénas, tel. 74 04 41 98. Named after its speciality. Generous helpings. Also a hotel. Class C.

Chez la Rose/La Petite Auberge, 69840 Juliénas, tel. 74 04 41 20. Regional cuisine. Also rooms. Class C.

Daniel Robin, 69840 Chénas, tel. 85 36 72 67. Recommended for a quality lunch of regional fare (*andouillette de Chénas*). Shady terrace. Class B.

La Poularde, 71570 Pontaneveaux, tel. 85 36 72 41. Country cooking, reasonable prices. Class C.

La Maison Blanche, N6, 71570 Romanèche-Thorins, tel. 85 35 50 53. Short on atmosphere, but the food is good. Class C.

Auberge Le Cep, 69820 Fleurie, tel. 74 04 10 77. Capable and inventive dishes, but not cheap. Class A.

Restaurant des Sports, 69820 Fleurie, tel. 74 04 12 69. For tasty *coq au vin*, etc. Class C.

Au Chapon Fin, 01140 Thoissey, tel. 74 04 04 74. Functional hotel and a fairly traditional cuisine. Good wine list. Restaurant class B; hotel class A/B.

Le Relais des Caveaux, 69910 Villié-Morgon, tel. 74 02 21 77. Regional cuisine. Class C.

La Maison des Beaujolais, N6, 69220 St-Jean-d'Ardières, tel. 74 66 16 46. Very good-value regional set menus. The Maison is also a wine information centre. Class C.

Le Relais Beaujolais, 69220 Cercié, tel. 74 66 19 51. Traditional restaurant. Fine selection of Brouilly wines. Class C.

Le Beaujolais, 40 Rue Maréchal-Foch, 69220 Belleville, tel. 74 66 05 31. Fairly conservative, regionally orientated and carefully prepared cuisine. Also a hotel. Class C.

Christian Mabeau, 69460 Odenas, tel. 74 03 41 79. Small, good-value restaurant. Class C.

Castel de Valrose, 01090 Montmerle-sur-Saône, tel. 74 69 30 52. Classic cuisine at this quiet hotel and restaurant on the east bank of the Saône. Class B.

Le Beaujolais, 69830 Blaceret, tel. 74 67 54 75. Café and restaurant; strictly regional. Class C.

Hostellerie St-Vincent, 69460 Salles-Arbuissonnas, tel. 74 67 55 50. Plenty of atmosphere, an owner who knows his wine and full-flavoured, often spicy dishes. Also a hotel with park and swimming pool. Class B.

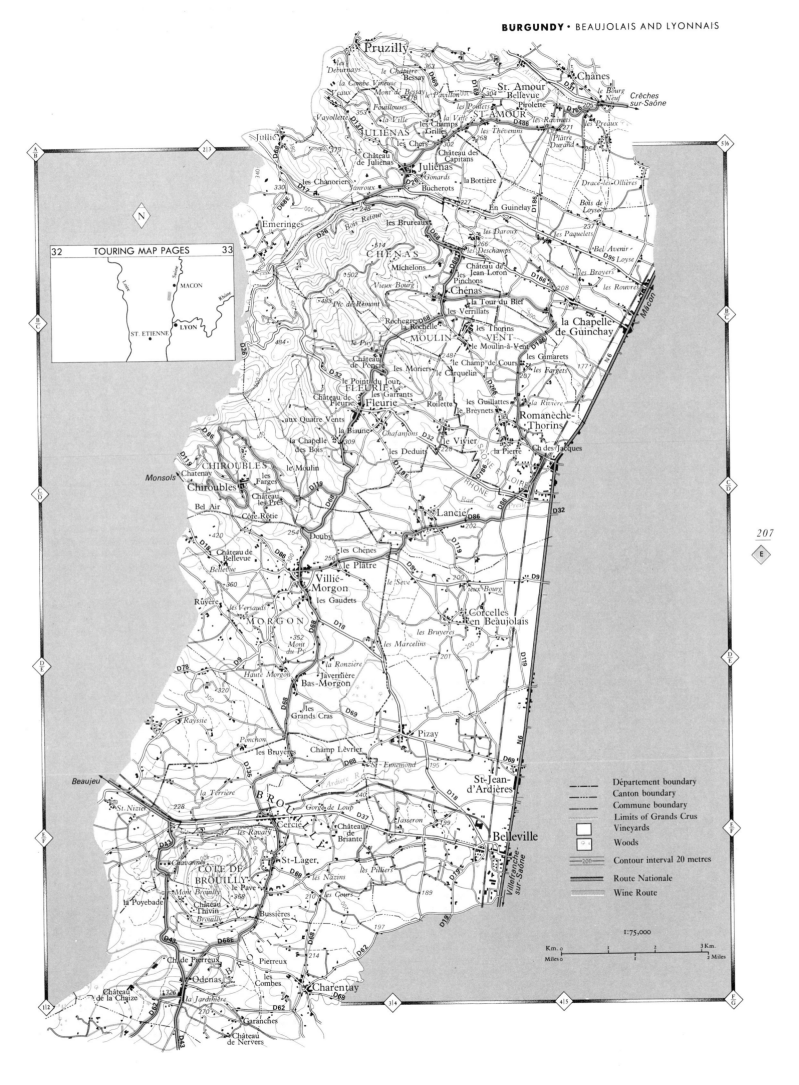

207

E

TOURING MAP PAGES

32   33

MACON

ST. ETIENNE   LYON

Pruzilly
les Deburnays
le Chapitre   Bessay
la Combe Vineuse
Veaux   Mont de Bessay
Pavillon
les Poulets
353
Fouillouses

Chânes
le Bourg Neuf
Crèches-sur-Saône

St. Amour
Bellevue   Pirolette
ST-AMOUR
les Ravinets
205

Vayollette
375   la Ville
les Champs
Grilles
271
les Thévenins
Plâtre
Durand
264

Jullié
Château
de Juliénas
JULIÉNAS
les Chers
Château des
Capitans
268

227

Drace-les-Ollières

Juliénas
Gonards
la Bottière
En Guinelay
237

les Chanoriers
Bûcherots
Janroux

Bois de
Loyse

Emeringes
les Brureaux
les Daroux
266
les Paquelets
Bel Avenir   Loyse

Bois-Retour
514
les Deschamps
Château de
Jean Loron
les Broyers

CHÉNAS
Michelons
les Pinchons
Chénas
les Rouvres
208

Vieux Bourg
502
Pic du Rémont
483
la Tour du Bief
les Verrillats
la Chapelle
de Guinchay

Rochegrès
la Rochelle
les Thorins
MOULIN-A-VENT
le Moulin-à-Vent
les Gimarets
177

le Puy
484
248
le Champ de Cours
les Fargets
207

Château
de Poncié
les Moriers
le Carquelin

FLEURIE
le Point du Jour
les Garrants
la Roilette
les Guillattes
la Rivière
Romanèche-Thorins

Château de
Fleurie   Fleurie
le Breynets

aux Quatre Vents
la Biaune
Chafanjons
le Vivier
Ch des Jacques

CHIROUBLES
la Chapelle
des Bois
309
les Deduits
228
la Pierre

Monsols
Chatenay
les Farges
le Moulin

Chiroubles
Château
les Prés

Bel Air
Côte-Rôtie
254
Douby
les Chênes
Lancié
202
D86

Château de
Bellevue
420
256
le Plâtre
les Chênes

Bellevue
360
Villié-Morgon
le Seve
Vieux Bourg
200

Ruyère
les Versauds
les Gaudets

MORGON
352
Mont du Py
les Bruyeres
Corcelles
en Beaujolais

D78
Haute Morgon
la Ronzière
les Marcelins
201

Javernière
Bas-Morgon

320
les Grands Cras

Rayssie
Ponchon
Pizay

les Bruyeres
Champ Lèvrier
St-Emmemond
195

Beaujeu
St. Jean-
d'Ardières

la Térrière
St-Niziér
228
Gorge de Loup
240
Jasseron
99
Belleville

BROUILLY
Cercié
Château
de Briante

les Ravaty
St-Lager
les Nazins
les Pilliers

Chavannes
CÔTE DE
BROUILLY
le Pave
les Gours
189

Mont Brouilly
368
Château
Thivin
Brouilly

la Poyebade
Bussières
197

Ch. de Pierreux
Pierreux
les Combes

Odenas
BROUILLY
214

Château
de la Chaize
326
la Jardinière
270
Charentay

Garanches
Château
de Nervers

Département boundary
Canton boundary
Commune boundary
Limits of Grands Crus
Vineyards
Woods
Contour interval 20 metres
Route Nationale
Wine Route

1:75,000

Km. 0   1   2   3 Km.
Miles 0   1   2 Miles

Jean Fouillet, 01480 Jassans-Riottier, tel. 74 67 91 94. On the east bank of the Saône. Jean Fouillet cooks in the contemporary manner. Meals are served in the garden in fine weather. Class B.

La Terrasse du Beaujolais, Buisante, 69840 Pommiers, tel. 74 65 05 27. *Specialités beaujolaises.* Class C.

La Vieille Auberge, 69620 Oingt, tel. 74 71 21 14. Rustic décor, decent quality. Class C.

l'Espérance, 69260 Theizé, tel. 74 71 22 26. Sturdy cooking (*entrecôte Charolais*) and a view. Class C.

Le Vieux Moulin, 49380 Alix, tel. 78 43 91 66. Honest, carefully prepared dishes. Has terrace. Class C.

Les Maronniers, 69830 Lozanne, tel. 78 43 70 15. At the southern tip of the Beaujolais. Good but rather pricey restaurant. Class B.

Paul Bocuse, 69660 Collonges-au-Mont d'Or, tel. 78 22 01 40. World-famous restaurant where you can eat in both the classical and the contemporary style (*soupe aux truffes, volaille de Bresse en vessie, loup farci à la mousse de homard,* etc). Bocuse is a travelling ambassador for French gastronomy – and for himself. Collonges is north of Lyon, on the west bank of the Saône. Class A.

Hotel San Be, 69210 Sain-Bel, tel. 74 01 24 05. Talented, creative chef. Class C.

Auberge de la Brévenne, 69690 Bessenay, tel. 74 70 80 01. Simple place with a few rooms. Try the *poulet aux morilles.* Class C.

Le Gigandon, 5 Avenue Charles-de-Gaulle, 69620 Charbonnières-les-Bains, tel. 78 87 15 51. Traditional cuisine in a spa town. Class B.

It would be impossible to list all the good restaurants in Lyon, so here are two names only, at two different levels, both under the supervision of the same chef.

Léon de Lyon, 1 Rue Pleney, 69001 Lyon, tel. 78 28 11 33. Very atmospheric interior and serves perfectly prepared local specialities at very reasonable prices. Class B.

Le Bistrot de Lyon, 64 Rue Mercière, 69002 Lyon, tel. 78 37 00 62. Pleasant Art Deco furnishings, regional specialities, agreeable prices. Open until after midnight. Class C.

Auberge Labeye, 69440 Taluyers, tel. 78 48 73 06. Pleasant place to eat in the southern Coteaux du Lyonnais, northeast of Mornant. Class C.

PLACES OF INTEREST

The Beaujolais is a big area, so this list is divided into a northern and a southern half, the river Nizerand, which flows into the Saône at Villefranche, being the boundary.

NORTHERN BEAUJOLAIS

Beaujeu Former capital of the Beaujolais. Displays in the Musée Audin include an 11th-century bas-relief, old interiors and dolls. Local *objets d'art* are on show in the Maison du Pays, near the St-Nicolas church (1130). Country walks signposted.

Corcelles-en-Beaujolais Intact 15th-century castle that is also a wine estate. Utrillo stayed here a number of times and also painted it.

Fleurie The view from the chapel above the village is worth the drive.

Juliénas The Château de Juliénas, which in parts is 14th century, has fine 18th-century cellars still used for storing wine.

Odenas Château de la Chaize is a historic monument. The *cuvier* and the immense cellar can be visited.

Quincié The Château de Varennes dates from the 15th century.

Romanèche-Thorins The windmill is at least 300 years old, and gives its name to the Moulin-à-Vent Cru. Next to it is a wine-tasting room.

St-Amour Beautiful Romanesque figure of Christ in the church.

St-Georges-de-Reneins The 12th-century church in this village is one of the most beautiful in the Beaujolais. There is a charming little port on the Saône (Porte-Rivière).

Salles-Arbuissonnas An attractive village with a glorious square with lime trees, an 11th- and 12th-century church, 12th-century cloisters and a monumental gate.

Vaux-en-Beaujolais Large wine commune. The picturesque village served as the model for *Clochemerle,* the comic novel by Gabriel Chevallier.

SOUTHERN BEAUJOLAIS

This district is known as the *pierres dorées* ("gilded stones") because many of its houses, churches and châteaux are built in an ochre-coloured stone. There are two signposted *Circuits des Pierres Dorées* tourist routes.

Anse Gallo-Roman mosaics are displayed in the 12th- and 13th-century Château de Tours (formerly the town hall). On the east bank of the Saône is Château de St-Bernard, where the artists André Utten, Suzanne Valadon and Maurice Utrillo lived between 1923 and 1935.

Bagnols Village near Le Bois-d'Oingt with old buildings and a 15th-century château.

Bully Nicely restored 15th-century castle and an old village centre.

Charnay Feudal stronghold, Romanesque church.

Châtillon-d'Azergues A large, partly restored 12th-century castle rises above the village. Its chapel has wall paintings.

Lacenas Village near Villefranche.

The *cuvage* at Château Montauzon consists of an enormous hall above a vaulted cellar. Here the Compagnons du Beaujolais hold their fraternal meetings.

Lachassagne Village near Anse, with a beautiful view.

Oingt Medieval, with a fortified church.

Ternand On a hill near the Azergues. Formerly fortified, and the summer residence of the archbishops of Lyon. Houses from the 14th and 15th centuries. There are frescoes in the crypt of the 15th-century church.

Villefranche-sur-Saône Take time to look at a number of old buildings in Rue National: between Nos. 476 and 834 on one side of the street, and between 375 and 793 on the other. The church of Notre-Dame-des-Marais has a late-Gothic front.

LYONNAIS

l'Arbresle Parts of the old fortifications (gatehouse, two towers, keep) and old houses, including one that belonged to Jacques Coeur (1395–1456).

Eveux The Couvent de la Tourette is by Le Corbusier.

Lyon It would be impossible to list here all the places of interest in Lyon, France's second city. It certainly merits a visit for its old centre and numerous museums at least. Detailed information can be obtained from the Syndicat d'Initiative, Place Bellecourt (on the peninsula between the Rhône and the Saône).

Millery The most important wine village of the southern Lyonnais, situated high above the Rhône valley.

Mornant Gothic church with beautiful wood carving. North of the village stands the only surviving arch of a Roman aqueduct.

Riverie Medieval village southwest of Mornant. An artists' colony.

Savigny West of Sain-Bel. Old abbey.

Soucien-en-Jarrest Remains of a Roman aqueduct over the Pilat east of the village, which is situated to the north of Mornant.

WINE TASTINGS

Like every wine district, the Beaujolais has many cellars where visitors are welcome. What is exceptional is the large number of village *caveaux de dégustation,* usually run by the wine growers of the commune. They attract many customers, particularly at weekends. The complete list follows, in alphabetical order.

Beaujeu Le Temple de Bacchus, variable opening times.

Châtillon-d'Azergues Le Pavillon des Pierres Dorées, open weekends.

Chénas Caveau du Cru Chénas, run by the cooperative. Daily mid-July to mid-October, weekends only at other times.

Chiroubles The Terrasse de Chiroubles stands high above the village. Open afternoons in the season.

Cogny Le Caveau des Voûtes, variable opening times

Fleurie Le Caveau de Dégustation des Viticulteurs, open daily.

Gleizé Le Caveau de Gleizé, in the cooperative, open afternoons at weekends and public holidays.

Juliénas Le Cellier de la Vieille Eglise, open daily. The cooperative has a wine-tasting room in the 17th-century Château du Bois de la Salle.

Jullié Caveau de Jullié, open Sundays.

Leynes Le Relais Beaujolais-Mâconnais, mainly a simple restaurant (see the Mâconnais chapter). Closed Wednesdays.

Pommiers La Terrasse des Beaujolais, above the village at the Notre-Dame-de-Buissante chapel. Also a restaurant. Closed Wednesdays in winter.

Regnié-Durette Le Caveau des Deux-Clochers, weekend afternoons from Easter to mid-September.

Romanèche-Thorins Le Caveau de l'Union des Viticulteurs du Moulin-à-Vent, by the N6, also serves simple

dishes. A second tasting room, Le
Caveau du Moulin-à-Vent, is by the
famous windmill; closed Tuesdays.
St-Amour Le Caveau du Cru St-
Amour, variable opening times.
St-Jean-d'Ardières La Maison des
Beaujolais, on the N6, represents the
whole district. Also a restaurant.
Closed Wednesday evenings and
Thursdays.
St-Jean-des-Vignes Le Refuge des
Pierres Dorées, open Sundays and
public holidays.
St-Lager Le Cuvage des Brouilly,
open daily except Tuesday morning.
St-Vérand Le Caveau de l'Union des
Viticulteurs de St-Vérand, variable
opening times.
Salles-Arbuissonnas La Tassée du
Chapitre is open weekends and public
holidays, May to October.
Vaux-en-Beaujolais Le Caveau de
Clochemerle, variable opening times.
Villié-Morgon Le Caveau des
Morgon, variable opening times.

WINE ACTIVITIES

One of the greatest joys of the
Beaujolais is to visit a grower at
harvest-time when a fragrant must is
fermenting in the vats. The workers
permit themselves (with a degree of
caution) to try the half-made wine.
The name for this sweet, perfumed,
heady drink is "paradis".

More formal events, such as big
tastings, fairs and banquets, occur on
nearly every autumn weekend. The
declaration of the *primeur* wines
(third Thursday in November) and
the Hospice de Beaujeu auction
(second Sunday in December) are
highlights. For more details see
pages 11–13.

There are also three wine
fraternities active in the Beaujolais:
Les Compagnons du Beaujolais (the
whole district); La Confrérie des
Gosiers Secs (mainly operating in
Vaux-en-Beaujolais); and La
Confrérie des Grapilleurs des Pierres
Dorées (southern Beaujolais).

WINE INFORMATION

The very energetic Union
Interprofessionelle des Vins du
Beaujolais, 210 Boulevard Vermorel,
69400 Villefranche-sur-Saône,
embraces all the official bodies
relating to Beaujolais wine. In
addition there is a Maison des
Beaujolais, on the N6 between St-
Jean-d'Ardières and Belleville-sur-
Saône, where information can be
obtained and which has a restaurant
(see Restaurants).

▷ Shade is welcome here in summer.
The blue granite of Mont Brouilly is
used to build these sturdy homes.

PRODUCERS OF SPECIAL INTEREST

BEAUJOLAIS AND BEAUJOLAIS-VILLAGES

BELLEVILLE, postcode 69220, 207 F4

Pierre Ferraud & Fils: company with solid wines of variable quality; Robert Sarrau/Caves de l'Ardière: Beaujolais Crus are a speciality.

BLACE, postcode 69460

Paul Gauthier

BLACERET, postcode 69460

Gobet: a reliable négociant.

LE BREUIL, postcode 69620

Jean-Marc Charmet*: family estate making excellent red and white wines.

CHATILLON-D'AZERGUES, postcode 69380

Les Vins Mathelin*: small, very reliable family firm; pure, fruity wines.

JARNIOUX, postcode 69640

Château de Boisfranc

LANCIE, postcode 69220, 207 D4

Paul Sapin: firm wines.

LANTIGNIE, postcode 69430

Château du Basty

PIZAY, postcode 69220, 207 E4

Château de Pizay*: hotel with its own vineyard which produces good wines (including a white Beaujolais and a Morgon).

PONTANEVAUX, postcode 71570

Paul Beaudet: fruity, firm red wines; family firm dating from 1869; Loron & Fils: bulk wines and delicious Crus full of character; Thorin: the Beaujolais and Mâconnais wines exclusive to this négociant are very successful.

REGNIE-DURETTE, postcode 69430

Desplace Frères/Dom. du Crêt des Bruyères*: wines that often win awards; Jean & Yves Durand; Domaine de la Gérarde*; Joël Rochette; Château de la Tour Bourdon.

ST-ETIENNE-DES-OULLIERES, postcode 69460

Domaine des Grandes Bruyères

ST-JEAN-D'ARDIERES, postcode 69220, 207 E4

Vins Dessalle*: energetic quality firm; Vins Fessy: small but serious.

SALLES-ARBUISSONNAS, postcode 69460

René & Christian Miolane*: good Beaujolais-Villages.

VILLEFRANCHE-SUR-SAONE, postcode 69400

Jacques Dépagneux: négociant whose best wine is the Mâcon-Viré Clos du Chapitre.

THE CRUS

CERCIE, postcode 69220, 207 E3
Brouilly and Côte de Brouilly

Jean Lathuilière*: much-commended Brouilly Pisse Vieille; Domaine Ruet*: substantial, fruity and bottled early.

LA CHAPELLE-DE-GUINCHAY, postcode 71570, 207 C5

Partly in the Chénas appellation

Château Bonnet*: Pierre Perrachon's best wine is the Chénas; Hubert Lapierre*: wines that win awards with nearly every vintage.

CHENAS, postcode 69840, 207 B4
Appellation Chénas

Domaine des Brureaux: belongs to the local restaurateur Daniel Robin; Cave Coopérative; Domaine Champagnon*; Amédée Degrange.

CHIROUBLES, postcode 69115, 207 C3
Appellation Chiroubles

Domaine Bouillard; Domaine Cheysson-les-Fargues*: typically elegant Chiroubles; Bernard Méziat; Alain Passot*; Château de Raousset; Francis Tomatis & Fils*: supplies top French restaurants.

FLEURIE, postcode 69820, 207 C3
Appellation Fleurie

Domaine Bernard*: excellent Fleurie; René Berrod/Les Roches du Vivier; Cave Coopérative; Michel Chignard*; Domaine de la Grand Cour*; Château des Labourons; Quinson: négociant; variable quality; Michel Tribolet.

JULIENAS, postcode 69840, 207 B4
Appellation Juliénas

Domaine de la Boittière; Cave Coopérative; Château de Juliénas*: the biggest local producer; Raymond & Michel Tête*: the best of Juliénas; good even in lesser years.

ODENAS, postcode 69460, 207 F2
Brouilly and Côte de Brouilly

Château de la Chaize: impressive château with above-average wines;

Touring map pages 32–33 For location map see page 207

Alain Bernillon; Bernard Champier*: strong, juicy Côte de Brouilly; Guy Cotton; Claudius Guérin*: top-class Côte de Brouilly; Château de Pierreux; Château Thivin*: wines from both Crus.

QUINCIE, postcode 69430
Brouilly and Côte de Brouilly

Cellier des Samsons: up-to-date firm that bottles and markets a large part of the production from 10 cooperatives; Claudius Geoffray.

ROMANECHE-THORINS, postcode 71570, 207 C4
Appellation Moulin-à-Vent

Domaine de la Bruyère*: concentrated, strong Moulin-à-Vent; Chanut Frères: somewhat rustic, mostly correct wines; Georges Duboeuf*: successful company that despite its scale has managed to maintain a high average quality; many wines are marketed under their estate names; Château des Jacques*: pure, fine wines, including a white Beaujolais (Grand Clos de Loyse); Jacky Janodet; Jean Mortet; Château du Moulin-à-Vent*: large estate where the wines are aged in small casks; Michel Gaidon: various wines, led by the Moulin-à-Vent Château Portier.

ST-AMOUR, postcode 71570, 207 A4
Appellation St-Amour

Domaine des Ducs*: absolutely sound, delicious wines; Raymond Durand; Domaine de la Cave Lamartine*: charming St-Amours; Francis Saillant; Georges Trichard*: a property of repute.

ST-ETIENNE-LA-VARENNE, postcode 69830
Appellation Brouilly

Domaine du Levant; G. F. A. de Combiaty*: small estate; Dominique Piron is the owner; Albert Sothier; Château des Tours: large estate, very reliable.

ST-LAGER, postcode 69220, 207 F3
Brouilly and Côte de Brouilly

Alain Bernillon; l'Ecluse/Lucien & Robert Verger*: exquisite Côte de Brouilly; Pasquier-Desvignes.

VILLIE-MORGON, postcode 69110, 207 D3
Appellation Morgon

Domaine de la Chanaise*: aromatic wines, supple and not too heavy; Louis Claude Desvignes; Georges Passot*: the owner lives here but makes an excellent Chiroubles (and a Fleurie); Domaine des Pillets; Domaine Savoye*: meaty Morgon Côte du Py, often with an aroma suggesting cherries; Domaine de Ruyère.

AC Beaujolais

AC Lyonnais

---- Département boundary

—— Wine route

JURA

▶ L'Etoile, the peaceful hamlet which, together with two other communes, is the birthplace of the rare, mostly white Jura wine l'Etoile. When made from Chardonnay, l'Etoile white can stand comparison with minor white burgundies. The red wine is of less interest.

About halfway between Beaune and Geneva lies Arbois, the wine centre of the Jura area. Viticulture here is rooted in the distant past: Roman amphorae have been found in the neighbourhood. The vineyards of the Jura (this is also the name of the département) are concentrated in a strip about 10 kilometres (6 miles) wide that begins north of Arbois and ends south of Lons-le-Saunier. The meticulously cultivated vineyards stand out in contrast to the large areas of the countryside around, where untamed nature prevails. About a third of the département is forest, interspersed with lakes and rugged rock formations.

The vineyards of the Jura declined greatly in the first half of this century. In the nineteenth century the Jura had some 18,500 hectares (nearly 46,000 acres), compared with about 1,500 hectares (3,700 acres) now. Just before World War II the area growing vines was even smaller: roughly 500 hectares (1,235 acres). It was the grower and merchant Henri Maire who in the 1950s and '60s stimulated expansion in the Jura and won recognition for its wines.

The Jura has a number of indigenous grape varieties found nowhere else in France. One of them is the black Poulsard, which gives a fairly delicate wine without much colour. This is often mixed with wine from the Trousseau, a grape that gives more strength and colour. The Savagnin is noticeable among the white grapes. This is related to the Gewürztraminer and is used, for example, for the striking *vin jaune*. Grapes from nearby Burgundy, including Pinot Noir, Chardonnay and Pinot Blanc, are also used.

Arbois is the biggest appellation of the Jura. About half of all the region's vineyards are around Arbois. Most of them are on gently sloping hillsides. Lime and gravel are prevalent in the soil, and so is clay. A Jura characteristic is the wide range of wines that the majority of the producers make: in Arbois most of the growers make whites, rosés and reds, and often a sparkling wine and a *vin jaune* as well. The still wines are nearly always light and may be either traditional (i.e. wood-aged and fairly dour) or more contemporary (no wood ageing and with fruit and freshness in the taste). In general the white Arbois wines are better than the reds. The white sparkling wines can also be attractive.

Vin jaune is the great speciality of the Jura. By law this wine, made exclusively from the Savagnin, must be matured for at least six years in oak casks. These casks are never completely filled – and must not be topped up. If nature collaborates, a wrinkled film of yeast cells grows on the surface of the wine, resembling the *flor del vino* that gives sherry its distinctive nutty aroma. After six years, *vin jaune* is still fully vital: the layer of yeast cells absorbs oxygen and thus protect the wine from oxidation. Once bottled – a special 62-centilitre bottle called a *clavelin* is used – a *vin jaune* can last for decades. The wine is very similar to fino sherry, but in an unfortified form. Locally it tastes splendid with *coq* or *poulet au vin jaune*, as well as with the Comté cheese of the region. A superior version of *vin jaune* comes from the hill village of Château-Chalon and a few adjoining communes. The little district of Château-Chalon is about 25 kilometres (15 miles) south of Arbois and forms an enclave in the Côtes du Jura appellation.

The Côtes du Jura wines resemble those of Arbois – but are a little lighter. Another small district within the Côtes du Jura is l'Etoile, where fresh, still and sparkling white wines of good quality are made, as well as the *vin jaune*.

The rarest Jura wine (at one time virtually extinct) is *vin de paille*, made from bunches of grapes that have been laid out to dry; this causes the fruit to lose moisture and its sugar content to increase. The grapes used to be dried on straw (*paille* in French), but nowadays they are placed in small boxes in well-ventilated rooms. A *vin de paille* has a mild but at the same time fresh and lively taste, an aroma of nuts and figs, and at least 14.5 percent alcohol. Production is very limited: *vin de paille* is usually marketed in half-bottles.

TRAVEL INFORMATION

The peaceful woods and hills of the Jura reward a visit. Pike, trout and other freshwater fish frequently appear on menus in the Jura, as do chicken with *vin jaune* and local game.

HOTELS

Hotel de Paris, 9 Rue de l'Hôtel-de-Ville, 39600 Arbois, tel. 84 66 05 67. A provincial hotel offering good food and regional wines. Try *poularde au Vin Jaune* with a *vin jaune* or Château-Chalon wine. Class B.

Hostellerie des Monts de Vaux, 39800 Barretaine, tel. 84 37 12 50. Southeast of Poligny. Good restaurant (*demi-pension* obligatory in season). Hotel class A; restaurant B.

Hotel du Cheval Rouge, 47 Rue Lecourbe, 39570 Lons-le-Saunier, tel. 84 47 20 44. Run by the same family for four generations. Plumbing in the rooms is less reliable than the cooking. Class B.

Le Moulin de la Mère Michelle, 39600 Les Planches-en-Arbois, tel. 84 66 08 17. Modernized hotel with restaurant in a peaceful old mill. Trout is a speciality. Hotel class B; restaurant C.

Hotel de Paris, 39800 Poligny, tel. 84 37 13 87. There is a congenial hotel behind the rough stone frontage, with swimming pool and a restaurant with a regional bias. Hotel class B; restaurant class C.

Hostellerie St-Germain, 39210 St-Germain-les-Arlay, tel. 84 44 60 91. Simple, quiet hotel in the heart of the Côtes du Jura. Garden, terrace, and an atmospheric old restaurant. Hotel class B; restaurant class C.

RESTAURANTS

La Finette, 22 Avenue Pasteur, 39600 Arbois, tel. 84 66 06 78. Country-style dishes, such as fondue, omelettes, sausage, etc. Class C.

Auberge de Chavannes, 39570 Courlans, tel. 84 47 05 52. Good cooking: they like to combine chicken from Bresse with white l'Etoile; also good fish. There is a garden. Class B.

PLACES OF INTEREST

Arbois This hard-working provincial town, plagued by heavy traffic, was the home of Louis Pasteur (1822–95). The parental home of this greatest of French scientists is now a museum; and a few kilometres to the north, on the N83, is the little vineyard that used to belong to him. Today it is farmed by Henri Maire. The town also has a Musée de la Vigne et du Vin in the basement of the town hall.

Arlay The Château d'Arlay, built in classical style in the 17th century, was originally a monastery. It was rebuilt in 1774 and renovated in 1830. The present Château d'Arlay is a museum and also one of the biggest and best wine estates of the Jura.

Baume-les-Messieurs This village lies at a point where three valleys converge – one of them the imposing Cirque de Baume, a canyon with steep rock walls and caves. In the village there is an old abbey with a craft museum and a church with art treasures.

Château-Chalon (see page 212) The walls of a former castle are still standing. The church of St-Pierre dates from the 10th century. At the end of July and the beginning of August a *son et lumière* depicts the conquest of the region by Louis XIV.

l'Etoile The hill above the village is well worth climbing for the panorama. On this hill stands the Château de l'Etoile, the most important local wine estate.

Lons-le-Saunier The crypt of the church of St-Désiré dates from the 11th century. The Rue de Commerce has arcades full of atmosphere. The kitchen and dispensary of the 18th-century hospital are also worth visiting. The way into the old centre is by the Tour d'Horloge.

Le Pin A village just north of Lons-le-Saunier with a feudal castle. Its massive keep offers a splendid panoramic view.

Poligny Old town full of treasures.

The cooperative occupies a fine Gothic church, the vats fitting in neatly between the columns.

WINE ACTIVITIES

The Fête des Vins d'Arbois is celebrated around the middle of July. At the end of July the Foire des Vins du Sud-Revermont is held in

Maynal. And during the first Sunday of September Arbois holds its Fête du Biou. Wine growers carry an enormous made-up bunch of grapes through the streets to the church of St-Just. Jura has two wine fraternities:

the Commanderie des Nobles Vins du Jura and the Pairie des Vins d'Arbois, led by Henri Maire.

WINE INFORMATION

The local Société de Viticulture is at BP 396, Avenue du 44 RI, 39016 Lons-le-Saunier. Tel. 84 24 21 07.

PRODUCERS OF SPECIAL INTEREST

ARBOIS, postcode 39600, 212 B3

Fruitière Vinicole d'Arbois; Henri Maire*: no one has done more for the restoration of Jura as a wine district than Henri Maire. Under his energetic leadership the largest estate and the largest merchant house of the region has been created (with more *vin jaune* and Château-Chalon in its cellars than any other firm). Henri Maire actively promotes Jura wine.

Domaine de la Pinte; Jacques Tissot: not to be confused with other Tissots; the address is 39 Rue de Courcelles.

LONS-LE-SAUNIER, postcode 39570, 212 D2

Lycée Agricole du Jura

MENETRU-LE-VIGNOBLE, postcode 39210, 212 C2

Jean-Claude Peltier*: Château-Chalon of an excellent standard.

MONTIGNY-LES-ARSURES, postcode 39600, 212 B3

Lucien Aviet; Roger et Frédéric Lornet; Jacques Puffeney; Rolet Père & Fils*: one of the biggest and most modern estates of the district.

ARLAY, postcode 39140, 212 D2

Château d'Arlay*: a fine property with excellent wines. The red Côtes du Jura resembles an elegant light burgundy; the rosé is called Corail and the white is about 90% Chardonnay; **Christian Bourdy.**

CHATEAU-CHALON, postcode 39210, 212 D2

Jean Macle*: excellent Château-Chalon.

DOMBLANS, postcode 39210, 212 C2

Domaine de la Muyre

l'ETOILE, postcode 39570, 212 D2

Cave Coopérative; Château d'Etoile*: the biggest producer in the Etoile district. Good quality – the white l'Etoile for example (98% Chardonnay); **Domaine de Montbourgeau/Jean Gros.**

NEVY-SUR-SEILLE, postcode 39210

Jean-Marc Courbet

POLIGNY, postcode 39800, 212 C3

Bernard Badoz; Christian Dupuis; GAEC Reverchon.

PUPILLIN, postcode 39600, 212 C3

Cave Coopérative; Désiré Petit & Fils*: wines that regularly win awards.

ROTALIER, postcode 39190

Guy Boudet; Château Gréa/Pierre de Boissieu.

LE VERNOIS, postcode 39210, 212 D2

GAEC Clavelin

VOITEUR, postcode 39210, 212 D2

Marius Perron*: top-quality Château-Chalon.

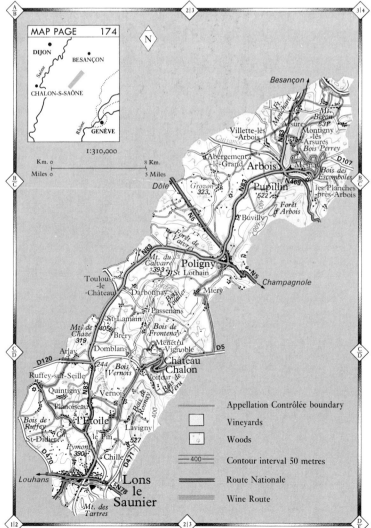

SAVOIE

The wine district of Savoie consists of a number of isolated small areas scattered like islands across four départements. Most of the vineyards are in Savoie and Haute-Savoie; Ain and Isère also produce a little Savoie wine. The distance between the most northerly areas (by Lake Geneva) and the most southerly (below Chambéry, near Ste-Marie-d'Alloix) is more than 100 kilometres (over 60 miles). The closeness of the Alps affects the whole zone. The landscape is mountainous and well-watered. Savoie also has some vast lakes, including the Lac du Bourget, the biggest in France. White wines are the speciality. They taste light, fresh and pure: you are drinking bottled mountain air. The crowds of tourists who visit the region in summer and winter soon discover that Savoie white wines combine perfectly with the many kinds of freshwater fish caught here, as they do with the various local cheeses. Not to mention a mountain thirst.

For a district that has only 1,500 hectares (3,700 acres) of vineyards the number of different wines is very great. There are two main groups: Vin de Savoie and Roussette de Savoie, which can both come from a specific Cru. There are fifteen Crus for Vin de Savoie and four for Roussette. The laws also distinguish district wines.

An example of a district wine is Crépy, from a hill 5 kilometres (3 miles) from Lake Geneva. The Crépy appellation had almost disappeared but was rescued through the efforts of Léon Mercier of Douvaine and his son Louis. This exclusively white wine is made from the Chasselas grape (often called Fendant in Switzerland). The better kinds of Crépy, like the better Muscadets, are bottled *sur lie*, making them very slightly sparkling from the trapped carbon dioxide.

Seyssel wine takes its name from the town of Seyssel, which is divided by the river Rhône so that the western part is in Haute-Savoie and the eastern in Ain. Still white wine, dry and firm, and also delicate sparkling wines of a high standard are made here. The Roussette (or Altesse), said to

Domaine de la Violette, a property in the Cru Abymes, amid the mountain scenery of the southern Savoie.

be identical to the Hungarian Furmint, is the only grape permitted for the still wines. Roussette is widely planted in the Savoie: its wines are sold under the appellation Roussette de Savoie. Those from the Crus of Frangy (11 villages north of Seyssel) and Marestel (on the west bank of the Lac du Bourget) enjoy the best reputation.

The white Jacquère is the grape most used for the most important appellation, that of Vin de Savoie. This variety does well on both lime and gravel; it gives perfectly refreshing, crisply dry wines. However, white Vin de Savoie can also come from other grape varieties such as the Roussanne (which also grows in the Rhône valley and is sometimes called the Bergeron in Savoie); the Grignet (the Savagnin of the Jura); and Chasselas and Chardonnay. The best Crus for white Vin de Savoie are, from north to south, Ripaille, Marignan (both grown in the Crépy neighbourhood and related to it), Ayze (aromatic and slightly *pétillant*, from the Bonneville area), Apremont, Abymes, Chignin and Montmélian (the last four lie to the south of Chambéry).

Although Savoie is largely devoted to white wine, the reds should not go untasted. The black Mondeuse, a grape rich in tannin and colour, makes excellent country wines; they have an exceptionally lively taste, full of character. Nothing is better after skiing. The Mondeuse grape does well in Frangy, Chignin and Arbin. Pleasant Gamay wines are also made; the best come from Chautagne, halfway between Seyssel and Aix-les-Bains.

Another wine district, Vin du Bugey (VDQS), to the west of Savoie, has only 250 hectares (620 acres) under vines. The range is varied but the Chardonnay is much the best. This wine is lighter and fresher than burgundy, but a good drink nevertheless. As in Savoie there are various Crus in Bugey. The most noteworthy is Cerdon, with its sparkling rosé.

TRAVEL INFORMATION

Savoie is skiing country, and many visitors come to the summer resorts on the lakes and mountains. The lakes and streams provide freshwater fish: bass, trout, salmon trout, pike, char, and crayfish are frequently served. Other specialities are poultry from Bresse, *fondue savoyarde*, *raclette*, *charcuterie* and walnuts from Grenoble. The hotels and restaurants listed below cover the whole district, from north to south.

HOTELS

Hostellerie Château de Coudrée, 74140 Douvaine, tel. 50 72 62 33. In a medieval castle by Lake Geneva. Stylish rooms, a park, heated swimming pool and restaurant. Class A.

Hotel de la Couronne, 74140 Douvaine, tel. 50 94 10 62. Enjoys a good reputation locally for its cuisine. Class B.

Hotel Bellevue, 74130 Ayse, tel. 50 97 20 83. The rooms with their balconies offer a fine view, which compensates for a certain lack of atmosphere within. Peaceful position; restaurant; *demi-pension* obligatory in season. Class C.

Hotel du Rhône, 01420 Seyssel, tel. 50 59 20 30. On the west bank of the Rhône. A traditional hotel with limited plumbing and traditional if not always sparkling cuisine. The dining room is congenial. Class B.

Lille, Le Grand Port, 73100 Aix-les-Bains, tel. 79 35 04 22. Quietly placed near the lakeside harbour. The restaurant with its regional cuisine has a faithful local clientele. Class B.

Les Princes, 4 Rue de Boigne, 73000 Chambéry, tel. 79 33 45 36. Sound-proofed rooms with modern comfort. Good restaurant serving many fish dishes. Class B.

Château de Challes, 73190 Challes-les-Eaux, tel. 79 85 24 15. Spa south of Chambéry. Château hotel quietly placed in its own park, with a swimming pool. Restaurant. Class B.

Château de Trivier, 73190 Challes-les-Eaux, tel. 79 85 07 27. Hotel in tranquil setting in a château. Spacious, somewhat rustic rooms where the plumbing can provide amusement. Park and restaurant. Class B.

RESTAURANTS

Auberge de la Porte d'Yvoire, 74140 Yvoire, tel. 50 72 80 12. Try the fresh bass and explore the cellar with exciting, sometimes rare Savoie wines. Class C.

Auberge Gourmande, 74140 Massogny, tel. 50 94 16 97. Large premises, decorated with paintings. Careful cuisine with country dishes. Attractive set menus. Many regional wines. Class C.

Hotel Sapeur, Place de l'Hôtel-de-Ville, 74130 Bonneville, tel. 50 97 20 68. Enjoy *grillades* and regional dishes in the Grill La Vivandière in the basement. The hotel is functional. Class B.

Rôtisserie du Fier, 74190 Seyssel, tel. 50 59 21 64. Conservative, solid cooking (*volaille de Bresse au Seyssel*). In the eastern half of Seyssel. Class C.

Château de Collonges, 73310 Ruffieux, tel. 79 54 27 38. Small château with good, fairly conservative cuisine. Also a small luxurious hotel. Beautiful park. *Demi-pension* obligatory in season. Restaurant class B; hotel class A.

Colombié, 73310 Chindrieux, tel. 79 54 20 13. Quiet inn. Fish on the menu. Class C.

Le Bateau Ivre, 73370 Le Bourget-du-Lac, tel. 79 25 02 60. In a 17th-century salt store by the lake. Menu has sophisticated dishes alongside more traditional ones. Good wine list. Class A/B.

Roubatcheff, 6 Rue du Théâtre, 73000 Chambéry, tel. 79 33 24 91. As well as French dishes there are also some with a Russian accent. Good selection of Savoie wines. One of the best restaurants in the town. Class B.

Le Chignerain, 73800 Chignin, tel. 79 28 10 01. Village restaurant in one of the best wine communes (fondues, *faux filet chignerain*). This is the place to drink reds. Class C.

Les Cinq Voûtes, 73800 Montmélian, tel. 79 84 05 78. Old vaulted dining room. *Côte de boeuf à la Mondeuse* is a speciality. Class B.

PLACES OF INTEREST

Aix-les-Bains The medicinal springs beside Lac du Bourget have been known since Roman times. The Gallo-Roman baths can still be seen beneath the present ones.

Belley This town in the Bugey has the remains of Gallo-Roman fortifications and a medieval centre. In one of the houses (62 Grande-Rue) Anthelme Brillat-Savarin was born in 1755. His collected meditations on eating and good living (*La Physiologie du Gout*, 1825), are still read and appreciated today. Other sights are the cathedral of St-Jean with its 15th-century choir and the former bishop's palace.

Le-Bourget-du-Lac In this former seat of the House of Savoy there is a restored 13th-century monastery church with some beautiful carving. Beside it there are 15th-century cloisters and a park in Italian style.

Bonneville A museum of the Resistance is to be found in this town in the Arve valley. Just east of Bonneville the rare, slightly *pétillant* white wines of the Ayze Cru are grown.

Chambéry Although parts of this town were destroyed during World War II and in 1946, many old buildings remain, among them the Château des Ducs de Savoie, built in the 13th and 15th centuries, and restored and extended in the 19th. The interior of the Ste-Chapelle is painted with *trompe-l'oeil*. Until 1578 the Saint Suaire – the Holy Shroud, or so it was claimed – was kept here. It is now in Italy.

Southeast of the town is Les Charmettes, the house where the writer and philosopher Jean-Jacques Rousseau lived from 1736 to 1742 and which he immortalized in his *Confessions*. He also wrote in praise of Savoie wines.

In the centre of Chambéry there are old houses, in Rue Croix d'Or, for example, and covered alleyways. The Fontaine des Eléphants is undoubtedly the most photographed monument. The Gothic cathedral of St-François-de-Sales (15th and 16th century) was once a chapel.

Culoz Bugey village where Henri Dunant, founder of the International Red Cross, was born. The Château de Montvéran is near the village and wine is produced high up on the slopes.

Hautecombe This abbey projects into the Lac du Bourget, on its west bank near Ontex. It was founded in this isolated spot in 1125 and contains the tombs of princes of Savoy.

Thonons-les-Bains Spa on Lake Geneva with some interesting churches (the basilica of St-François-de-Sales and the church of St-Hippolyte, for example) and the local museum for the Chablais. Just to the north is Château de Ripaille, the former hunting castle of the Savoy court. The kitchen dates from the 15th century, when the castle was built. Near by is a vineyard that produces the rare Cru of Ripaille.

Yvoire Picturesque medieval village on Lake Geneva. As well as old houses it has a 14th-century castle, remains of defensive walls and two fortified gates.

WINE ACTIVITIES

In the first or second week of May the Salon des Vins is held in Annecy. The Savoie fraternity is called the Compagnie du Sarto.

PRODUCERS OF SPECIAL INTEREST

NORTHERN SAVOIE

AYSE, postcode 74130, 215 B3
Mainly Ayze
(Confusingly, the town is Ayse but the wine is Ayze)

Bernard Cailler; Jean-Marie & Justin Gantin; Louis & Paul Gantin.

BALLAISON, postcode 74140, 215 B3
Appellation Crépy

Goy*: fairly large family estate. The Crépy is bottled *sur lie.*

CHENS-SUR-LEMAN, postcode 74140

Fichard*: one of the wines made by this firm is Château de Ripaille, sole representative of the Ripaille Cru.

LA COTE D'HYOT, postcode 74130

Michel Ménétrey*: the speciality is Ayze.

DOUVAINE, postcode 74140, 215 B4
Appellation Crépy

Mercier*: the Mercier family are the biggest owners of land here and are also merchants; the Crépy is of flawless quality; **François Rossiaud.**

LOISIN, postcode 74140
Appellation Crépy

Jean & Jacques Métral*: the Crépy has won medals.

MARIGNIER, postcode 73130
Mainly Ayze

Marcel Fert

MARIN, postcode 74200

Claude Delalex*: producer of the very rare Marin, a white wine of character made mostly from the Chasselas grape.

SCIEZ, postcode 74140, 215 B3

Caves de la Tour Marignan*: only Bernard Canelli-Suchet handles the Marignan Cru on a commercial basis.

THONON-LES-BAINS,
postcode 74200, 215 A3

Château de Ripaille*: worth a visit for its rare white wine, which is made and sold by Fichard in Chens-sur-Léman.

BETWEEN FRANGY AND CHAMBERY

AIX-LES-BAINS, postcode 73100

Cavaillé SA*: firm specializing in estate wines from the Savoie (88 Avenue du Petit-Port).

CHEVIGNEUX, postcode 73310

Fernand Ducruet: for Gamay de Chautagne among other wines.

CORBONOD, postcode 01420, 215 B2

Mollex*: splendid Seyssel wines from its own vineyards (Clos de la Péclette among them) and good wines from other producers.

JONGIEUX, postcode 73170, 215 C2

Three good producers of Roussette-Marestel are: Noël Dupasquier; Edmond Jacquin; Henri Jeandet/Château de la Marre.

PLANAZ, postcode 74270

GAEC Les Aricoques/Jean-Paul Neyroud*: excellent Roussette from the Frangy Cru.

RUFFIEUX, postcode 73310, 215 C2

Cave Coopérative: makes Gamay de Chautagne.

ST-ALBAN LEYSSE, postcode 73230

Château Monterminod: the château rises above a very steep vineyard that produces a Roussette of the Monterminod Cru and other wines.

SEYSSEL, postcode 01420, 215 B2

Varichon & Clerc*: négociant with outstanding sparkling Seyssel wines (such as Diners and Royal Seyssel).

SOUTH OF CHAMBERY

APREMONT, postcode 73190, 215 C2

Coopérative Le Vigneron Savoyard: small establishment with good Apremont and Abymes.

ARBIN, postcode 73800, 215 C2

Louis Magnin: a sturdy Mondeuse.

CHIGNIN, postcode 73800, 215 C2

François Cartier; GAEC Le Cellier des Tours/Les Fils René Quenard; Lucien Gonnet; André Quenard & Fils*: excellent whites and very successful reds; **Raymond Quenard***.

CRUET, postcode 73800, 215 C2

Cave Coopérative

LES MARCHES, postcode 73800

Gaston Maurin; Domaine de la Violette/Daniel Fustinoni: small estate with a delicious Abymes.

MONTMELIAN, postcode 73800, 215 C2

Cave Coopérative

ST-ANDRE-LES-MARCHES,
postcode 73800

Pierre Boniface/Domaine des Rocailles*: pure, juicy, excellent Apremont; Jean-Claude Perret:

tasting room here and a small museum.

BUGEY

CULOZ, postcode 01350

Cellier de Bel-Air*: high-altitude vineyard that produces an exquisite Chardonnay.

FLAXIEU, postcode 01350

Camille Crussy

GROSLEE, postcode 01680

Duport Frères

MAGNIEU, postcode 01300

Raymond Vallet

MARIGNIEU, postcode 01300

Maxime Angelot

MERIGNAT, postcode 01450

Philippe Balivet: source of the classic Rosé de Cerdon.

VOGNES, postcode 01350

Caveau Bugiste; Eugène Monin & Fils*: a greatly respected family estate with an extensive range; the fragrant Chardonnay is usually bottled *sur lie.*

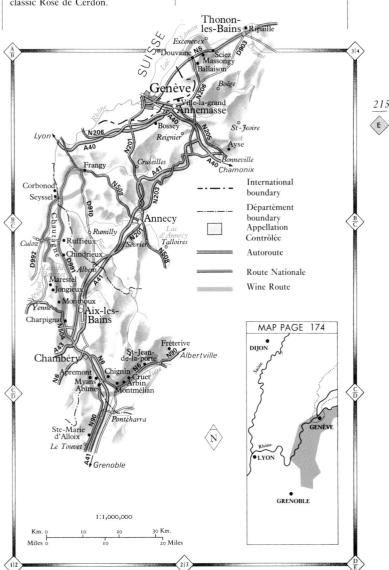

SOUTHEAST ZONE

Travellers coming down the Rhône valley have a difficult decision to make. Turn left after Avignon for Provence, or right for the Languedoc. Or indeed stay in the rich Rhône valley itself, with its splendid concentration of Roman cities.

Whether it was the Phoenicians or the Greeks who first brought wine to France, this is where they landed, and where French wine was born. It is the Midi.

The département of the Hérault has more vines than any other in France. It is the land of low-strength vin ordinaire, grown on fertile land with low-quality vines in a perpetual state of overproduction. Its hill-vineyards rise both physically and metaphysically above this level. Today, new planting has already produced good wines, many of them appellation contrôlée.

Towards the Pyrenees, south of the Aude, Corbières and Roussillon make red wines of notable character. Perhaps the least-expected product of this region, though, is the sparkling Blanquette de Limoux from the country near the museum-city of Carcassonne. France has few better bargains.

It was only 25 years ago that most of the coast between Perpignan and the Rhône was a waste of malarial lagoons. Now modernistic resorts and marinas bring a huge holiday population. Two extraordinary vineyard areas lie right on the sea here: the limestone massif of La Clape at the mouth of the Aude, and the beach-vineyards of Listel near the Camargue.

The one true classic vineyard of the region is Châteauneuf-du-Pape at its very centre. North in the narrowing Rhône valley lies the Côtes du Rhône – lovely touring country, especially to the northeast towards the Dents du Midi and Vaison-la-Romaine.

But Aix-en-Provence also has a widening circle of excellent wine estates. The wine road, indeed, winds right through Provence, and today new plantings and new techniques make this as much a region to explore as any in the south of France.

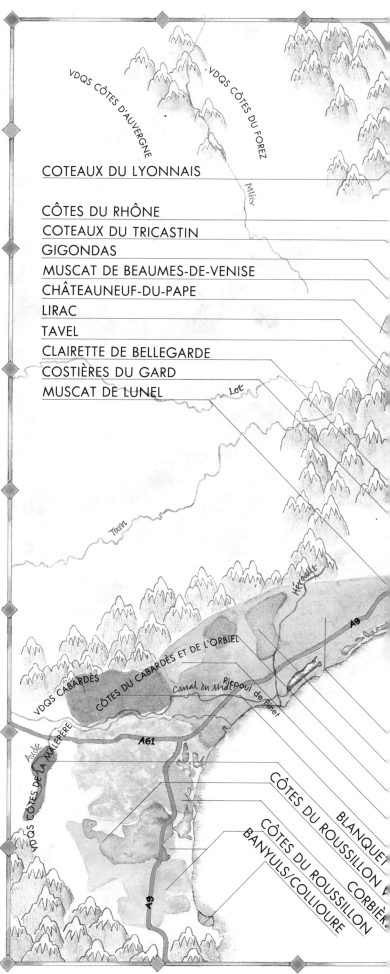

COTEAUX DU LYONNAIS

CÔTES DU RHÔNE
COTEAUX DU TRICASTIN
GIGONDAS
MUSCAT DE BEAUMES-DE-VENISE
CHÂTEAUNEUF-DU-PAPE
LIRAC
TAVEL
CLAIRETTE DE BELLEGARDE
COSTIÈRES DU GARD
MUSCAT DE LUNEL

VDQS CÔTES D'AUVERGNE

VDQS CÔTES DU FOREZ

VDQS CABARDÈS

CÔTES DU CABARDÈS ET DE L'ORBIEL

VDQS CÔTES DE LA MALEPÈRE

BLANQUET

CÔTES DU ROUSSILLON

CORBIÈ

CÔTES DU ROUSSILLON

BANYULS/COLLIOURE

VINS DE PAYS

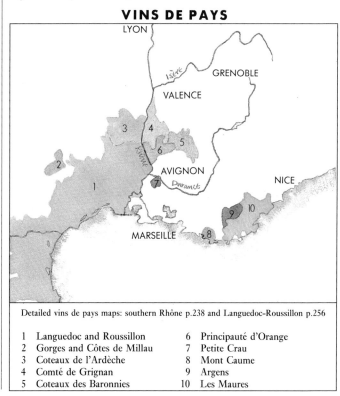

Detailed vins de pays maps: southern Rhône p.238 and Languedoc-Roussillon p.256

1 Languedoc and Roussillon	6 Principauté d'Orange
2 Gorges and Côtes de Millau	7 Petite Crau
3 Coteaux de l'Ardèche	8 Mont Caume
4 Comté de Grignan	9 Argens
5 Coteaux des Baronnies	10 Les Maures

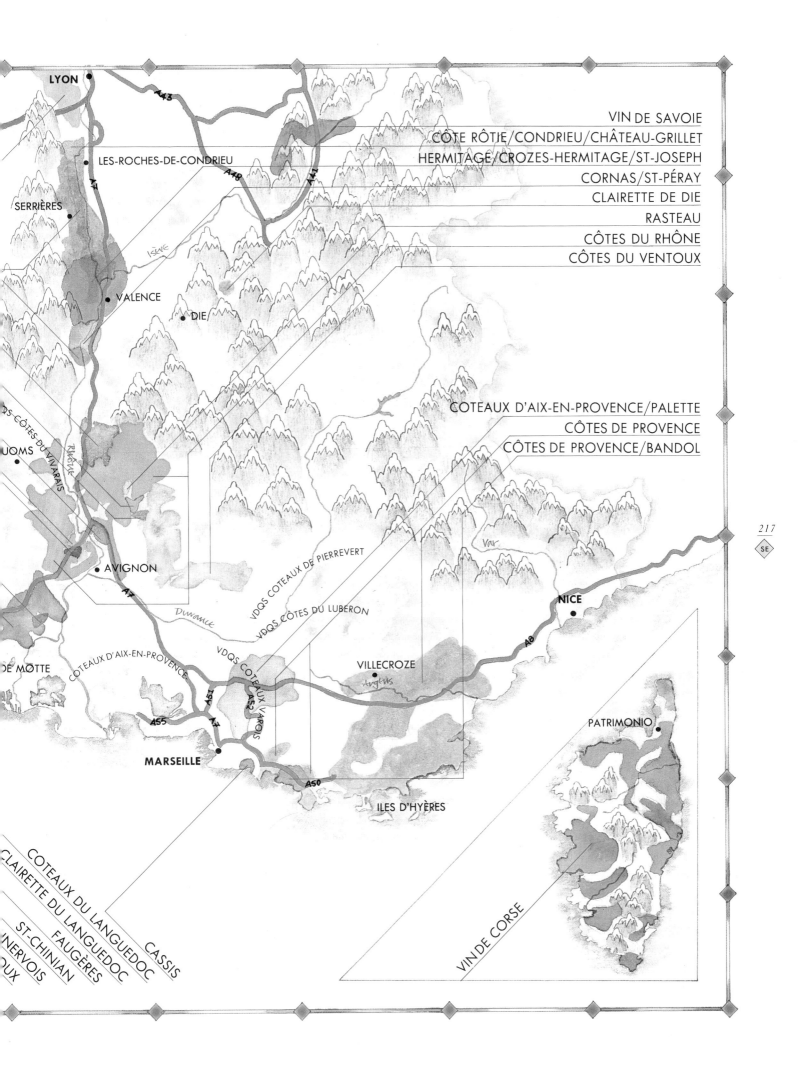

LYON

A43

VIN DE SAVOIE

CÔTE RÔTIE/CONDRIEU/CHÂTEAU-GRILLET

LES-ROCHES-DE-CONDRIEU

A48

HERMITAGE/CROZES-HERMITAGE/ST-JOSEPH

A7

CORNAS/ST-PÉRAY

SERRIÈRES

CLAIRETTE DE DIE

RASTEAU

CÔTES DU RHÔNE

Isère

CÔTES DU VENTOUX

VALENCE

DIE

QS CÔTES DU VIVARAIS

COTEAUX D'AIX-EN-PROVENCE/PALETTE

CÔTES DE PROVENCE

UOMS

CÔTES DE PROVENCE/BANDOL

Rhône

217

SE

Var

VDQS COTEAUX DE PIERREVERT

AVIGNON

A7

NICE

Durance

A8

VDQS CÔTES DU LUBERON

DE MOTTE

COTEAUX D'AIX-EN-PROVENCE

VDQS COTEAUX VAROIS

VILLECROZE

Argens

PATRIMONIO

A52

A51

A55

A7

A50

MARSEILLE

ILES D'HYÈRES

COTEAUX DU LANGUEDOC

CLAIRETTE DU LANGUEDOC

FAUGÈRES

CASSIS

ST-CHINIAN

NERVOIS

UX

VIN DE CORSE

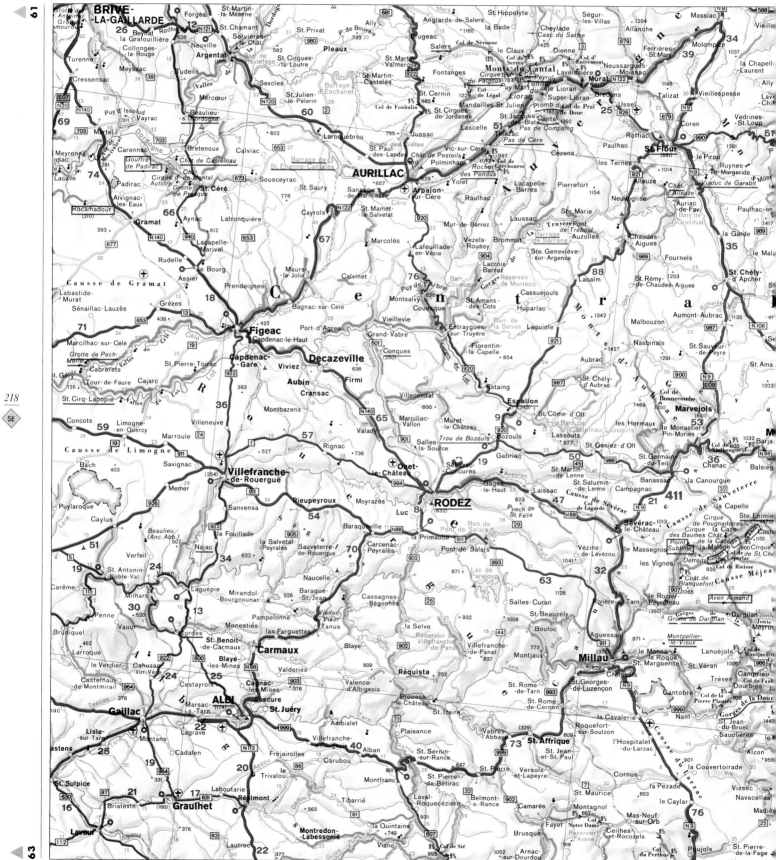

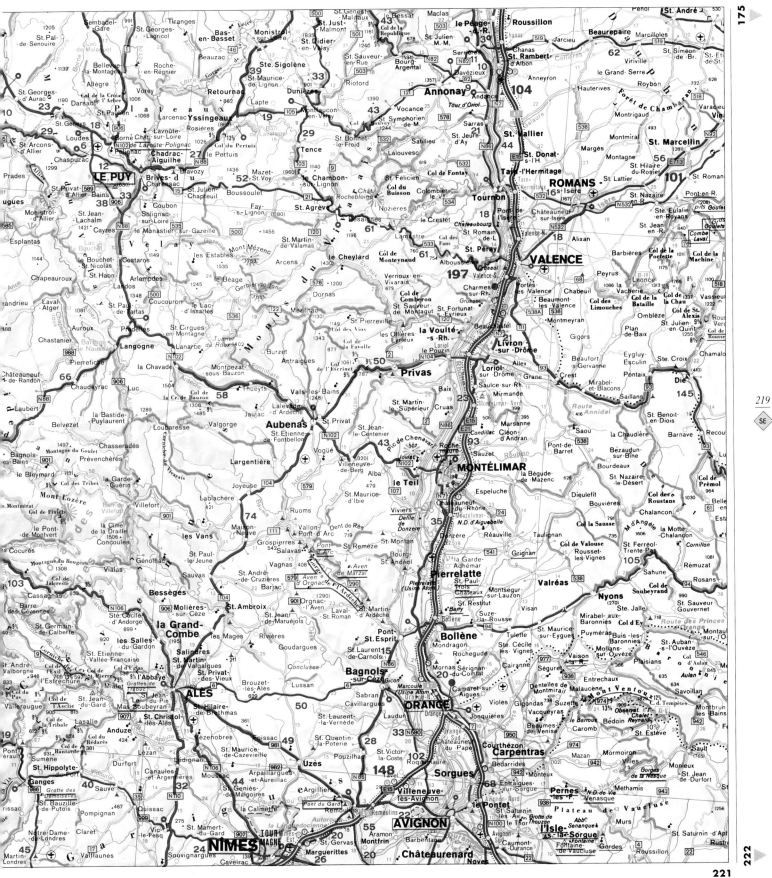

Golfe du Lion
Gulf of Lions

Mittelmeer

diterranean Sea

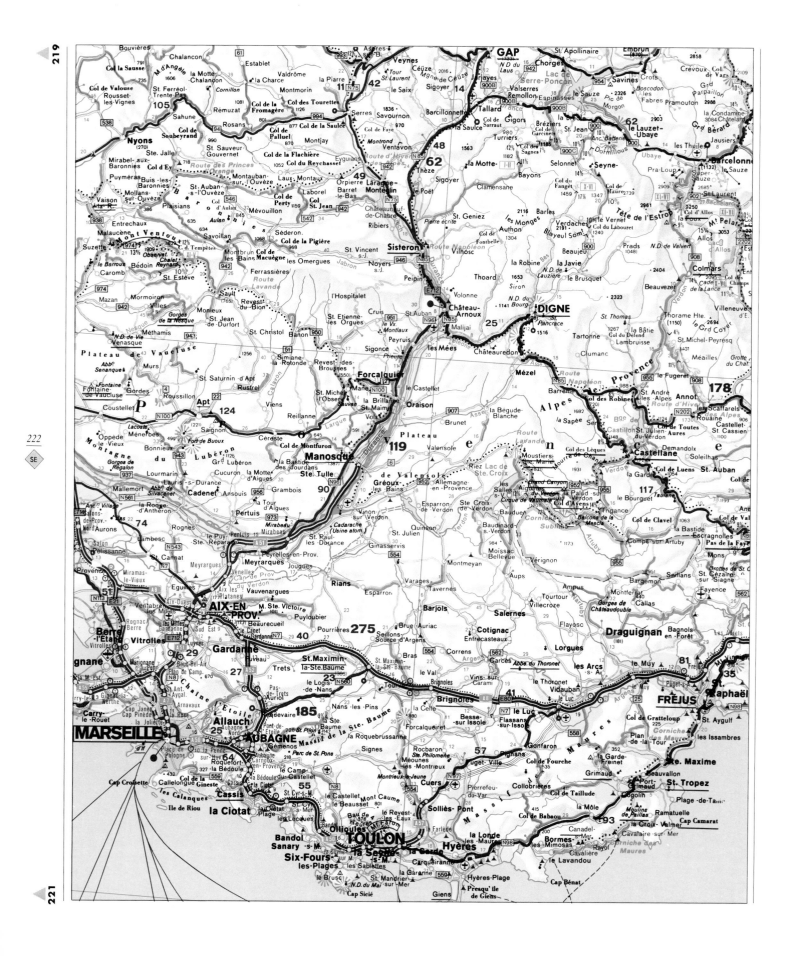

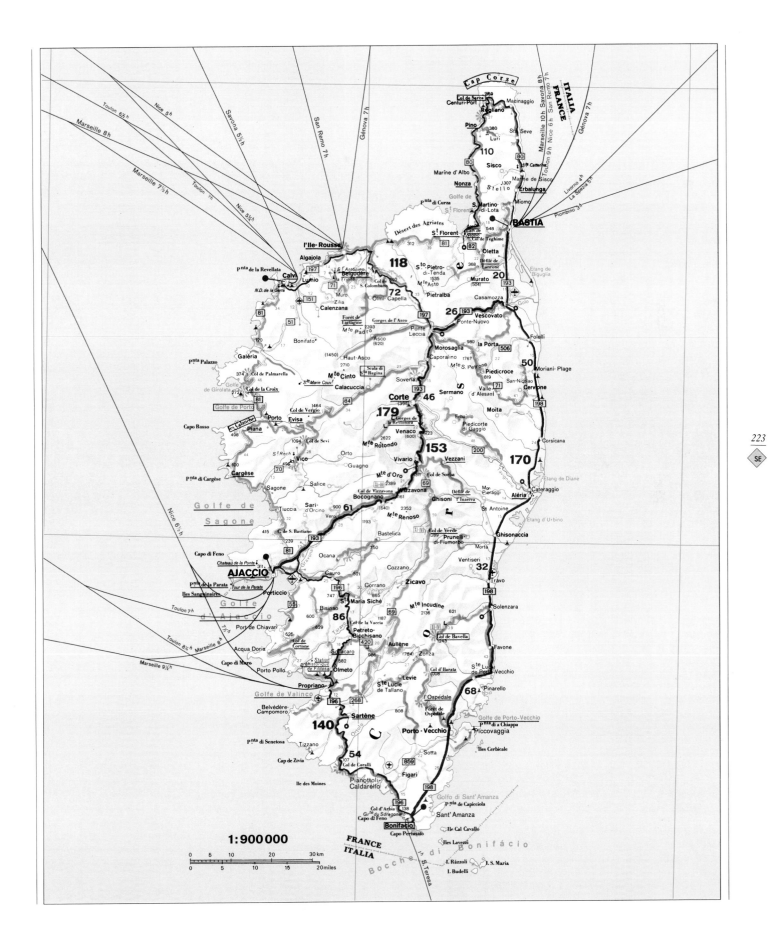

1:900 000

0 5 10   20   30 km

0   5   10   15   20 miles

THE RHONE VALLEY

Sun, rocky hillsides and old towns with Roman-tiled roofs epitomize the Rhône valley.

▶ Right: Grignan, a village high up in the Coteaux du Tricastin; part of the castle that overlooks the village is now a museum.

Below right: west of the Rhône the new vineyards of the Ardèche lie amid wooded hills. Even the classic Chardonnay and Cabernet Sauvignon grapes give remarkably good wine here.

▼ Below: one of the best wines of the central Rhône is produced at Cornas. Charlemagne is said to have tasted wine from here, and documents dating back to the 9th century mention the wine of Cornatico or Cornatis.

The Rhône, in its narrow valley between the mountains of the Massif Central and the foothills of the Alps, is one of the great natural arteries to and from northern Europe and the Mediterranean. Today, hundreds of thousands of tourists and other travellers pass through the valley every year on the Autoroute du Soleil, the A7.

There is nothing new in this mass traffic. Three and a half thousand years ago the Ligurians migrated this way from Italy. They were followed by the Celts, the Phoenicians and the Greeks. It was the Greeks who founded what is now the city of Marseille at the river's mouth and, it is presumed, brought the vine to the Rhône valley (although there are historians who claim that the Syrah grape dates back further still and is of Phoenician origin). It was the Romans who started wine growing on a large scale here – as the many amphorae, mosaics with wine motifs and figures of Bacchus bear witness. The Romans reached Vienne, in the north of the valley, in 121 BC – a full two generations before Julius Caesar completed the conquest of the rest of Gaul. Impressive evidence of Roman activity in the region can be seen in a magnificent museum at Lyon, the Musée de la Civilisation Gallo-Romaine.

After the Romans departed it was hundreds of years before wine growing became important again. The resurgence began in the ninth century and was due to the establishment of monasteries and churches. Since then the significance of the Rhône area as a supplier of wine has continued to increase. In this century the arrival of the tractor has contributed greatly to this growth: around 1950 the area had some 16,000 hectares (nearly 40,000 acres) of vineyards; today there are more than 60,000 hectares (150,000 acres), including the vineyards of neighbouring Ardèche. This makes the Rhône valley the biggest French region after Bordeaux and the Languedoc for the production of quality wine.

The vineyards stretch from near Vienne to just below Avignon, some 200 kilometres (125 miles) to the south. In places, too, the vineyards fan out to east or west – along the valley of the Drôme, for example, where Clairette de Die is produced, and on the flanks of Mont Ventoux, where Côtes du Ventoux originates. In the north the valley is relatively narrow and the vines are often grown on small terraces on steep slopes with schistous soil, where the maximum possible sun is guaranteed. Farther south the valley becomes steadily wider, with broad plateaux between the generally low hills. Here the dark screens of cypresses around the houses and fields form a striking picture: these are to break the force of the mistral, the hard, cold, dry wind that blows out of the northwest and can reach a speed of 100 kilometres (60 miles) an hour. As many a holiday maker has experienced, the mistral, which usually blows violently for days on end, can be felt right down to the Provençal coast.

Just as the Loire valley grows mainly white wine, so red is the speciality of the Rhône. White wine represents only a small percentage of the total but shows great diversity, from dry and still to distinctly sweet, and various styles of sparkling wines. Rhône reds also offer something for every taste. The range covers everything from cheap and easy everyday wines to complex, costly kinds that need to age for decades.

For the wine lover – and for the traveller – the Rhône valley is a horn of plenty, as the following pages show.

TRAVEL INFORMATION

Through the centuries, the Rhône valley's role has been as a route for travellers, and the business of catering for them has spurred the region to heights of hotel keeping and gastronomy.

Before the railways, boats were an important means of transport, and the chain of river ports where they stopped for food and rest still dominates the cuisine of the valley.

Lyon, not far to the north, is perhaps the gastronomic heart of France, and a compulsory stop for anyone on a culinary pilgrimage. A remarkable string of restaurants, a veritable daisy-chain of Michelin stars, links the city with the south via the Rhône valley. Valence has a starred restaurant of legendary excellence. Les Baux, at the southern end of the valley, has another. Avignon, Condrieu, Châteauneuf and a dozen other places offer almost equal degrees of temptation.

Lyon has a distinctly "northern" cuisine, with an emphasis on charcuterie, although the Lyon culinary tradition is also for refined and gracious dishes. Provence, into which the valley merges in the south, emphasizes olive oil, herbs and fish – an almost classical repertoire recalling the province's Roman origins.

SPECIALITIES OF THE REGION

Although in some communes (such as Châteauneuf-du-Pape and Vacqueyras) almost all the land that can be cultivated is planted with vines, large areas of this sunny valley are used for growing vegetables and fruit. This is especially true of the fertile valley floor. Among other produce the area grows potatoes, artichokes, asparagus, cabbages, lettuce, tomatoes (Carpentras is an important centre) and onions; apricots, apples, raspberries, cherries, melons (including the small, fragrant ones from Cavaillon), pears, peaches, plums, blackcurrants and other fruit. The local restaurants take full advantage.

Olives are another speciality, notably those from Nyons where there is an olive festival and an olive fraternity. As elsewhere in the south of France they make *tapenade* ("the poor man's caviare"), a black purée of olives, anchovies, tuna and capers.

Mention should also be made of nuts (including almonds, used for the nougat of Montélimar), birds (a well-known pâté is made from thrushes), freshwater fish, crayfish and honey. Many herbs grow wild here and perfume the food, as they do in the countryside.

HOTELS AND RESTAURANTS

See the Travel Information sections in the chapters on the Northern, Central and Southern Rhône, and Châteauneuf-du-Pape.

WINE INFORMATION

The Maison du Tourisme et du Vin for the Rhône valley is in the heart of the ancient papal city of Avignon in the southern Rhône (41 Cours Jean-Jaurès). Quite a lot of interesting material is available, including maps of the wine routes that can be taken in various parts of the valley. Enquire, too, at local Syndicats d'Initiative about travelling in the Rhône.

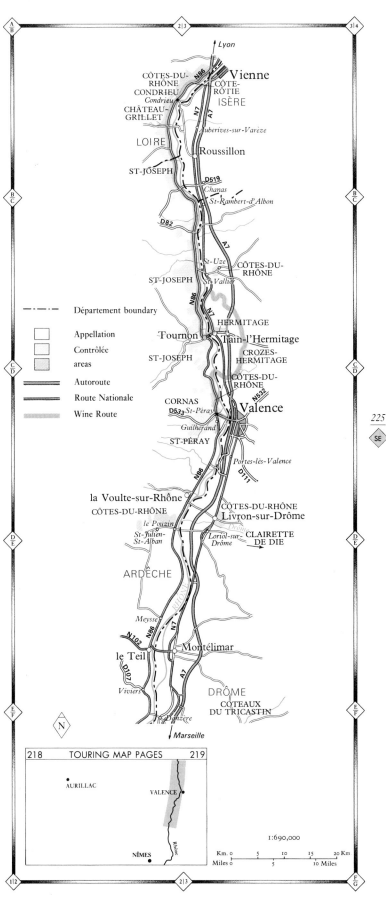

THE NORTHERN RHONE

The Romans cultivated vines in the northern Rhône valley, but they were not the first. There have probably been vineyards on the slopes of Côte Rôtie for 24 centuries: the district could almost be regarded as a museum. See it, and it is immediately understandable why grapes have been grown here for so long, for the hills that rise above Ampuis and two neighbouring villages are not only very steep but also face southeast. They are perfect suntraps, earning the name Côte Rôtie – the "roasted slope". The angle of the slopes is a precipitous 65 degrees in places, and the vines are mainly planted in small terraces.

At the heart of the Côte Rôtie are two slopes, the Côte Brune and the Côte Blonde. There are some splendid legends about the origin of the names, most of them referring to the colour of the hair of two sisters who are supposed to have inherited the hillsides. The reality is much more prosaic. The Côte Brune (the more northerly) has dark brown soil with iron in it; the Côte Blonde has lighter-coloured soil, with more chalk. You can taste the difference in their wines: those from the Côte Brune are usually leaner, less buxom than wines from the Côte Blonde. Some growers vinify and bottle the wines from the two slopes separately, but generally they are mixed.

The grape variety of the Côte Rôtie is the Syrah, which gives a dark red, fragrant wine: concentrated, fruity and tannic at the same time. The addition of, at most, 20 percent of the white Viognier grape is permitted in the Côte Rôtie district to make the wine softer and more supple, but in practice this maximum is never reached. Most growers use only three or four percent and some have no Viognier at all. It is only since the 1960s that Côte Rôtie has been recognized as one of the greatest Rhône wines.

Before that it was sometimes served as a cheap, everyday wine in local cafés and restaurants.

A good Côte Rôtie combines strength and finesse. It also needs long maturing: often a decade or more. Only then does it unlock its enchanting perfume of violets and other flowers, and often raspberries. Unfortunately, however, not all Côte Rôtie wine is of a high standard, for in 1966 it was decided to extend the little appellation by some 20 hectares (50 acres), most of it up on plateaus above the actual slopes. Their wine cannot reproduce the qualities of the "roasted slope".

Côte Rôtie may have a total of only around 110 hectares (270 acres) but Condrieu, the next district immediately south, has even less – some 20 hectares (50 acres). The steep slopes and terraces of Condrieu produce the Rhône's most exclusive treasure: white wine from the Viognier. This rare variety gives a sparse crop and is subject to rot and the disease called *coulure* (which greatly reduces the yield per vine). That it manages to do so well in Condrieu is due to the microclimate: the wind blows nearly all the time, so there is no still or stagnant air to encourage fungus diseases. Condrieu's wine is soft and elusively spicy, smelling, some say, of May blossom. Very young and fresh it is seductively sweet: impossible to resist (but never cheap).

In the Condrieu district and just south of the village of Vérin lies a vineyard with its own appellation: Château Grillet. It covers only three hectares (7½ acres) and is, after La Romanée in Burgundy, the smallest appellation in France. The château and its vines are in a natural amphitheatre that traps the warmth of the sun; here the Viognier grape gives wine very like Condrieu but traditionally made for ageing.

TRAVEL INFORMATION

The places included here are outside the larger towns. See also the travel infomation in the chapter on the Central Rhône.

HOTELS

Domaine de Clairefontaine, 38121 Chonas-l'Amballan, tel. 74 58 81 52. Hotel with generally spacious rooms and surrounded by a park. The plumbing varies. Also a restaurant. Class B.
La Marais de St-Jean, 38121 Chonas-l'Amballan, tel. 74 58 83 28. Small hotel and restaurant, quietly situated, in an old building that has been restored. Good, sometimes venturesome cuisine. Hotel class A; restaurant class B.

RESTAURANTS

Alain Charles, 42410 Chavanay, tel. 77 87 23 02. Regional cuisine that includes *pâté chaud de canard aux truffes.* Chavanay is a village in the Condrieu district. Class B.

Beau Rivage, 69420 Condrieu, tel. 74 59 52 24. Overlooking the Rhône. Also a hotel. Classic cuisine of high standard (*matalote d'anguille,* for example) and an extensive wine list. The rooms and public areas are full of antiques. The perfect place to drink Condrieu. Class A/B.
Hotel Bellevue, 38370 Les Roches-de-Condrieu, tel. 74 56 41 42. The functional-looking hotel offers not only a view of Condrieu and its vineyards but a splendid vista of the Rhône. Meticulous, fairly conservative cuisine and good wine. Class B.

La Diligence, 42410 St-Pierre-de-Boeuf, tel. 74 87 12 19. Reliable restaurant with reasonable prices. An extensive wine list. Class C.

PLACES OF INTEREST

Ampuis It is well worth the effort to drive up one of the narrow, winding roads of the Côte Brune or the Côte Blonde; this will give you a fine impression of the terracing of the vineyards in this district and a panoramic view across Ampuis and the Rhône valley. Ampuis is also famous for its apricots.
Condrieu In the old town centre there is the striking 16th-century Maison de la Gabelle, where the salt tax used to be collected. Its grey stone front is decorated with medallions. Near Condrieu are the ruins of a castle with a tower called La Tour Garon. Drive through Condrieu and up the vine-covered slopes and you will be rewarded with a fine view over the Rhône valley. A river tournament is held at Condrieu every year on the first Sunday in August.
Malleval This commune belongs to the Condrieu district; it has 16th-century houses as well as the remains of an old castle. West of Malleval there is a ravine with a waterfall.
St-Romain-en-Gal Important Gallo-Roman excavations here since

◄ Château Grillet, in its sunbaked bowl of vines, is an appellation and an estate. The wine is made of Viognier, the rare white grape of the northern Rhône, and is consequently expensive.

the late 1960s have uncovered, among other things, a number of splendid mosaics.

Vienne Although no wine is made here (it is the centre of a fruit-growing area), Vienne is worth a detour for its monuments and museums. Vienne's Roman past is kept alive by, for example, one of the biggest amphitheatres of the empire; the temple of Augustus and Livia (1st century); the many exhibits assembled in the Musée Lapidaire (established in one of the oldest churches in France, built in the 4th century); and the 23m (75½ft) high "pyramid" on the site of a former arena. Near this monument, which resembles an obelisk, is the legendary La Pyramide restaurant (very expensive and no longer fully deserving its reputation). The arcaded cathedral of St-Maurice (12th- to 15th-century) has richly painted ceilings and near the church of St-André-le-Bas there is a square Roman tower and also 12th-century cloisters. The terrace here gives a view of the river. Vienne was once

strategically important as a crossing of the Rhône.

Vienne's Musée des Beaux-Arts et d'Archéologie has a considerable collection of art from various periods. Religious art objects, including sarcophagi, are in the Musée d'Art Chrétien.

WINE ACTIVITIES

At Chavenay a *marché aux vins* ("wine market") is usually organized at the end of November.

The wine fraternity for Côte Rôtie and Condrieu is l'Ordre de St-Romain.

WINE INFORMATION

The very extensive Rhône valley has one centre for wine information: the Maison du Tourisme et du Vin at 41 Cours Jean-Jaurès, Avignon, in the southern Rhone. Local Syndicats d'Initiative can also be very helpful, and so are friendly hotel keepers.

PRODUCERS OF SPECIAL INTEREST

AMPUIS, postcode 69420, 227 B3
Appellation Côte Rôtie

Bernard Burgaud: Established in the hamlet of Champin, northwest of Ampuis. **Emile Champet; Gentaz-Dervieux; Guigal*:** Very traditional, quality-minded négociants and also growers with small plots on both the Côte Brune and the Côte Blonde. The wines from these, La Landonne and La Mouline respectively, are of extraordinary quality. Guigal, a family firm, took over Vidal-Fleury (see below) in the early 1980s. **Robert Jasmin*:** Small producer of sinewy yet fine wines. They are never filtered. **Vidal-Fleury*:** The biggest owner of land on the Côte Brune and Côte Blonde – 8 hectares (20 acres) – and also a merchant house. It now belongs to Guigal. The pure Côte Blonde from its own estate is called Châtillonne and is delicious.

CHAVANAY, postcode 42410, 227 C2
Appellation Condrieu

De Bosseyt/Chol & Fils*: Excellent balanced Côte Rôtie. The red St-Joseph is also successful. **Antoine Guilleron.**

CONDRIEU, postcode 69420, 225 B2, 227 B2

Jean Pinchon*: Fragrant, charming Condrieu. Unfortunately there is very little of it. **Château du Rozay*:** Situated on a plateau northwest of Condrieu. Pure, elegant wine.

Georges Vernay & Fils*: By far the biggest wine estate in Condrieu with a tasting and sales room on the N86, which runs through the little town. The wines are of immaculate quality.

LIMONY, postcode 07340, 227 E4
Appellation Condrieu

Pierre Dumazet

LE VERENAY, postcode 69420, 227 A4
Appellation Côte Rôtie

Albert Dervieux*: Reliable estate producing various styles of Côte Rôtie. The best is the La Garde, a Côte Blonde, followed by the pure Côte Brune.

VERIN, postcode 42410, 227 B2

Château Grillet*, 227 C2: This château, built on medieval foundations, has belonged to the Neyret-Gachet family since 1830 but is not permanently occupied. With its tiers of terraced vines it lies in a sheltered amphitheatre overlooking the river. The white wine, sold in slender brown bottles, has its own appellation and is usually at its best after five to six years. It is rare and (over) expensive.

Map legend:

1:104,000

Km. 0 1 2 3 4 5 Km.
Miles 0 1 2 3 Miles

TOURING MAP PAGES 32 33

MACON
ST. ETIENNE · LYON

N

Département boundary
Commune (parish) boundary
Limit of Appellation
— 200 Contour interval 20 metres
Autoroute
Route Nationale

Appellation Condrieu and Côte Rôtie
Appellation St-Joseph
Woods
Wine Route

THE CENTRAL RHONE

Follow the Rhône southwards from Condrieu and you come to the very extensive vineyards of St-Joseph, which stretch for some 55 kilometres (30 miles) along the west bank of the river (see the map of the Rhône valley on page 225). Until 1969 the St-Joseph appellation consisted of half a dozen communes in the neighbourhood of Tournon, but then its area was extended to take in 20 more villages. As a result the district now covers every sort of soil and slope. The original nucleus was granite hills with sand, clay and chalk, but since the expansion flatter land – without the helpful granite – has been brought into cultivation. Consequently the wines lack consistency.

St-Joseph wine is mainly red. It is made – like the red wines of Côte Rôtie and Hermitage – solely from the Syrah grape but never achieves the class and depth of it illustrious neighbours. Much of it is distinctly rustic and only a few growers succeed in making wines with charm and style. The same is true of the very small amount of white St-Joseph wine that is made.

Just a few kilometres off latitude 45°N a massive obstacle on the east bank forces the Rhône to change course: the grey granite rock of the Hermitage, at the foot of which lies the little town of Tain-l'Hermitage. On the south-facing slopes of the hill is one of the oldest vineyards in France. Historians believe that vines were planted here by the Phoenicians in the 4th century BC, and it is certain that the Romans cultivated the hill. The name Hermitage apparently derives from the retirement plans of a Crusader, Henri Gaspard de Sterimberg, in 1224. The little chapel he used is still there and is the property of the Hermitage growers and négociants Paul Jaboulet Aîné.

Vines are planted on 126 hectares (310 acres) of the steep, irregularly shaped southern flank of the hill. The slope receives sunshine in abundance – and the granite holds in the warmth. Rot is rarely a problem because rainwater soon drains away in the porous soil and the mistral, which blows often, keeps the vines dry. Even in wet years Hermitage usually delivers wines of quality. Black Syrah grapes are grown on about three-quarters of the slope. The remainder is planted with the white varieties Marsanne and Roussanne. These not only produce white Hermitage but can also be used, up to a maximum 15 percent, in the red wines. Red Hermitage is one of the world's strongest-flavoured wines: dark in colour, broad and sinewy in taste, rich in tannin and with an aftertaste that lingers for minutes on end. It can take decades for a red Hermitage to be absolutely ready for drinking. White Hermitage, too, can be impressive – and can age well. The best possess an almost exotic perfume of spices, summer flowers and flint, as well as a broad, powerful taste with sometimes surprisingly delicate nuances.

The vineyards of Crozes-Hermitage lie in a broad band around the rock of Hermitage. The district takes in 11 communes and its production is increasing steadily. The grape varieties are identical to those of Hermitage, but the wines never reach the same nobility: they are lighter, more supple, less deep. They also vary much more in quality, although the better red and white wines of Crozes-Hermitage do offer good value for money.

One of the most underrated wines of the Rhône valley is Cornas, from the village and district of that name, about 6 kilometres (some 4 miles) northwest of Valence. Good Cornas – a red wine made solely from the Syrah grape – can regale the senses with its intensely red colour, a perfume of small red fruits, sometimes a hint of bitter chocolate, and a virile, substantial taste rich in extract and with a considerable dose of tannin. At first there can also be a soft acidity, but this goes with the years. The wine derives its class from the sheltered, sloping vineyards, where terracing is often necessary, from the underlying granite and limestone, and from a relatively dry and warm microclimate. The name Cornas is from a Celtic word meaning "burned earth".

In the south, the vineyards of Cornas border on those of St-Péray, where only white wines are produced. Most are sparkling, and have long been so: in 1877 Richard Wagner had 100 bottles of sparkling St-Péray dispatched posthaste to Bayreuth, where he was composing his opera *Parsifal*. Today St-Péray's production of sparkling wine is much smaller than it used to be; increased competition is to blame. Compared with other French sparkling wines, those of St-Péray seem fat and flabby. In fact, still

▲ Top: the landscape of the Crozes-Hermitage vineyards, which stretch north from the Hermitage hill above Tain-l'Hermitage. The village is Crozes-Hermitage. Above: looking southwest from the Hermitage hill vineyards to Tain and the old bridge-town of Tournon across the river.

St-Péray is frequently more attractive, with sufficient acidity, a certain softness and reasonable fruit in a wine that should be enjoyed young.

Below Valence the river Drôme flows into the Rhône, and if you follow the Drôme valley east you come to the appellation Clairette de Die. There are two styles of sparkling Clairette de Die. "Tradition" is made from a minimum 50 percent of Muscat grapes (in practice it is 75 to 100 percent) by the *méthode dioise*: the wine is bottled before it has fully fermented, producing carbon dioxide that remains trapped in the wine in the form of bubbles. Nothing at all is added to the wine. This traditional Clairette de Die (Muscat de Die would have been a better name) is very pure, rather mild and slightly sparkling; it is generally an excellent wine. The other style is made from at least 75 percent Clairette grapes by the *méthode champenoise*. As a rule it is not the equal of the traditional Clairette de Die in quality or personality. Production is centred on the town of Die, where a large regional cooperative has its headquarters. Southeast of Die is the village of Châtillon-en-Diois where simple, still wines are made.

The Drôme valley is much narrower than that of the Rhône, at least to the east of Crest. It is also more beautiful, with mighty mountains, wooded hillsides, bright yellow broom in spring and ancient villages. The Romans established themselves here and made wine: in AD 77 the historian Pliny the Elder was describing the wine of Dea Augusta (the modern Die) as the best naturally sweet wine of the empire. It was probably already being made from Muscat grapes.

TRAVEL INFORMATION

The hotels and restaurants are arranged to run from north to south.

HOTELS

Schaeffer, 07340 Serrières, tel. 75 34 00 07. Old hotel, revitalized by a young couple. Friendly reception and pleasant restaurant. Class C.

Hotel du Commerce, 69 Avenue Jean-Jaurès, 26600 Tain-l'Hermitage, tel. 75 08 65 00. Comfortable hotel with garden and restaurant, the Pintadeau de la Drôme. Class B.

Hotel des Deux Coteaux, 81 Rue Joseph Péala, 26600 Tain-l'Hermitage, tel. 75 08 33 01. Well-run, not far from the riverside. Class B.

l'Abricotine, 26600 Mercurol, tel. 75 08 42 00. Small quiet modern villa-hotel in a Crozes-Hermitage village. Restaurant. Class B.

Hotel du Château, 07300 Tournon, tel. 75 08 60 22. A place to note, with large rooms and an adequate restaurant. Class B.

Le Manoir, 07300 Tournon, tel. 75 08 20 31. Small, quiet hotel on the road to Lamastre, with swimming pool. Class C.

Château du Besset, 07130 St-Romain-de Lerps, tel. 75 58 52 22. Splendid hotel surrounded by a vast park; the owner has made each room a small work of art. There is a swimming pool and the cuisine is of a good standard. Class A.

Hotel Les Bains, 07130 St-Péray, tel. 75 40 30 13. Quiet provincial hotel with its own grounds. The rooms vary in comfort. Hotel class B; restaurant class C.

Hotel St-Domingue, 26150 Die, tel. 75 22 03 08. Unpretentious holiday hotel. Restaurant with regional cooking. Class C.

RESTAURANTS

Terminus, 26240 St-Vallier, tel. 75 23 01 12. Attractive set menus and many local wines. Also a hotel. Class B.

Hotel Les Voyageurs, 26240 St-Vallier, tel. 75 23 04 42. Traditional cooking. Also a hotel. (Better than it looks from the outside.) Class C.

Restaurant Reynaud, 82 Avenue Président-Roosevelt, 26600 Tain-l'Hermitage, tel. 75 07 22 10. Contemporary cuisine and an ample wine list. The best place to eat in the district, with a terrace overlooking the river. Class B.

La Grappe d'Or, 13 Avenue Jean-Jaurès, 26600 Tain-l'Hermitage, tel. 75 08 28 52. Congenial and usually full. Class C.

Chabran, 26600 Pont-de-l'Isère, tel. 74 84 60 09. Excellent restaurant with a splendid wine list. Also a hotel. Class A.

Restaurant Ollier, 07130 Cornas, tel. 75 40 32 17. Inn in a wine village; country dishes such as *estouffade de boeuf au Cornas*. Class C.

Pic, 15 Avenue Félix-Faure, 26000 Valence, tel. 75 43 23 19. One of the most welcoming three-star restaurants in France. The cuisine is excellent and so is the selection of Rhône wines. Also a few luxury hotel rooms. Class A.

La Vieille Auberge, 07800 Charmes-sur-Rhône, tel. 74 60 80 10. High up in a village on the west bank of the river. Sound, traditional cooking. Class B.

Giffon, 26400 Grane, tel. 75 62 60 64. Hospitable restaurant on the road to Die. Class B.

La Porte de Montségur, 26400 Crest, tel. 75 25 41 48. On the north bank of the Drôme and on the east side of the village. Fine cooking based on fresh ingredients. Shaded terrace. Class B.

La Petite Auberge, 13 Avenue Sadi-Carnot, 26150 Die, tel. 75 22 05 91. Good value and generous helpings. Also a hotel. Class C.

PLACES OF INTEREST

Crest The castle that dominates Crest is one of France's tallest. East of Crest the Drôme valley narrows and the Clairette de Die appellation begins.

Die A town of Roman origin, as shown by the St-Marcel gate and exhibits in the Musée d'Histoire et d'Archéologie.

Mauves The wine of Mauves is mentioned in Victor Hugo's *Les Misérables*. The commune now belongs to the St-Joseph appellation: the latter name is taken from a hill of vineyards north of the village, marked by a large hoarding put up by the Chapoutier firm.

St-Péray The extensive ruins of Château de Crussol, a fortress mentioned in the 10th century, are near the wine-village of St-Péray – you can walk there in half an hour and there are splendid views. Below the ruins there is another castle, Château de Beauregard, still intact and in private hands.

St-Vallier-sur-Rhône From various points on both the east and west banks of the river here there are fine views over the Défilé de St-Vallier, a beautiful part of the Rhône valley. Near the village is the Château of Diane de Poitiers, with its garden designed by the famous Le Nôtre (of Versailles).

Serrières In a former church a pleasant museum is devoted to the Rhône inland waterway system and its boatmen.

Serves In 1642, when Louis XIII was crossing the Rhône here, he and his retinue paused on a large flat rock in the river. The king was given Hermitage to drink, and the rock has been called La Table du Roi ever since. There is also a ruined castle at Serves (and another one across the river at Arras).

Tain-l'Hermitage You can drive up to the top of the Hermitage hill and then walk to the hermit's chapel, which is a historic monument. The view from here of Tain, Tournon and the river valley is particularly beautiful. In Tain there is a granite *taurobole* from 184 BC, an altar where bulls were sacrificed.

Tournon From the terrace of the 15th-16th century castle there is a fine view of Tain and the Hermitage, and inside the castle a small museum is devoted to the Rhône. Tournon has the oldest *lycée* in France, founded in 1536. In the tourist season a steam train departs for Lamastre every morning: the journey lasts for four hours and runs through the romantic Doux valley.

Valence A town with about 70,000 inhabitants. A university was founded here in 1452 and François Rabelais was one of its students. At 57 Grande-Rue the Maison des Têtes, a house dating from 1532, has sculptured heads in medallions on its façade. The cathedral of St-Apollinaire is Romanesque in origin, but was extensively rebuilt in the 17th century.

WINE ACTIVITIES

A great market for Rhône wines is held in St-Péray at the beginning of September. In Cornas a local *marché aux vins* is usually arranged in December.

La Confrérie des Chevaliers de la Syrah et Roussette acts for the wines of Cornas, Hermitage, St-Joseph and St-Péray. The Crozes-Hermitage district has its own fraternity, La Confrérie de Crozes-Hermitage.

◀ In the Rhône the flavour of the Midi is strong, expressed in stone buildings and widows' costume.

PRODUCERS OF SPECIAL INTEREST

BARSAC, postcode 26150
Appellation Clairette de Die

Claude-Marcel Achard; Jean-Claude Vincent

BEAUMONT-MONTEUX,
postcode 26600
Appellation Crozes-Hermitage

Cave des Clairmonts

CHANOS-CURSON, postcode 26600

Domaine des Entrefaux*: Wood-aged red and a white Crozes-Hermitage. Domaine Pradelle.

CORNAS, postcode 07130, 225 D2

Guy de Barjac*: Small property making a much-respected Cornas. Auguste Clape*: The best of Cornas: brilliant, concentrated, long-living. Marcel Juge; Robert Michel*: Unfiltered, unclarified wine, one from a slope (strong), the other from lower ground (rather lighter). Alain Vogue*: Balanced, deep-red wine. Noël Verset: Wine with depth.

DIE, postcode 26150
Appellation Clairette de Die

Cave Coopérative*: Up-to-date winery producing about three quarters of all Clairette de Die.

EROME, postcode 26600
Appellation Crozes-Hermitage

Robert Roussett*: Firm, classic wines.

GERVANS, postcode 26600
Appellation Crozes-Hermitage

Jules Fayolle & ses Fils; Raymond Roure*: His red Les Picaudières is concentrated and demands patience.

MAUVES, postcode 07300
Appellation St-Joseph

Gérard Chave*: Among the best red and white Hermitage. Pierre Gonon; Bernard Gripa*: Exemplary red and white wines. Marsanne Frères.

SAILLANS, postcode 26340
Appellation Clairette de Die

Jean-Claude Raspail*: Makes an extraordinarily successful *méthode champenoise*, an exception to the rule.

ST-DESIRAT-CHAMPAGNE,
postcode 07340
Appellation St-Joseph

Cave Coopérative

ST-PERAY, postcode 07130, 225 D3

Jean-François Chaboud*: Produces good sparkling and still white wines. Cotte-Vergne Fils; Pierre Darona; Milliand Frères; Jean Teysseire.

SERVES, postcode 26600
Appellation Crozes-Hermitage

Albert Bégot

STE-CROIX, postcode 26150
Appellation Clairette de Die

Domaine Achard-Vincent

TAIN-L'HERMITAGE, postcode 26600, 225 C3, 230 C2

Cave Coopérative; M. Chapoutier*: Sound, very traditional firm with a large area of vineyards, including 30 hectares (74 acres) of Hermitage. Paul Jaboulet Aîné*: Important family firm producing wines of high quality and character. Henri Sorrel.*

TOURNON, postcode 07300, 225 C3, 230 C2
Appellation St-Joseph

Delas Frères: Firm owned by Deutz of Champagne. The best wines come from its own vineyards (including Condrieu, Hermitage). Jean-Louis Grippat*: Superior red and white St-Joseph and Hermitage.

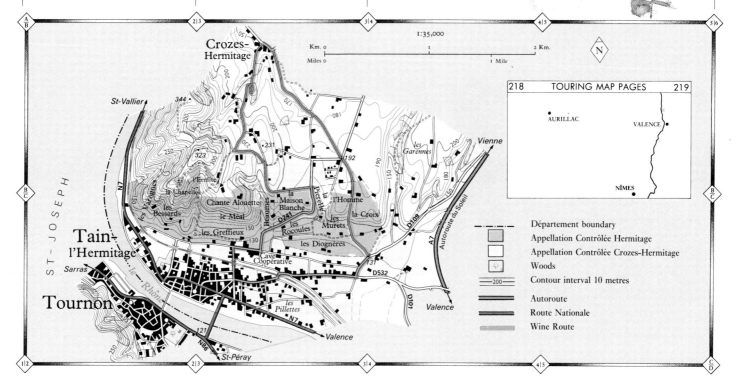

	Département boundary
	Appellation Contrôlée Hermitage
	Appellation Contrôlée Crozes-Hermitage
	Woods
200	Contour interval 10 metres
	Autoroute
	Route Nationale
	Wine Route

THE SOUTHERN RHONE

The wine map of the Rhône valley has roughly the shape of a carafe – narrow at the top, broad at the bottom. Thus the southern part produces by far the most wine. Following the river south on its route to the sea, after the town of Montélimar, the Coteaux du Tricastin is the first wine district you come to. It lies east of the river, between Donzère (where there is a mighty dam) and Bollène.

Viticulture expanded and prospered here in the 1960s when French repatriates from Algeria turned vast areas of unreclaimed land into vineyards. The landscape, with its low hills and wide plateaux, has many places where the soil resembles that of Châteauneuf-du-Pape, with a similar covering of smooth, round stones that absorb the warmth of the sun during the day and radiate it to the vines at night. As well as its wine and the fruit and vegetables it grows, Tricastin is an important source of truffles and many *chênes truffiers* (the oaks near which the truffles are found) are to be seen. It is not easy to distinguish the wines of Coteaux du Tricastin – mainly red – from those bearing the appellation Côtes du Rhône. As a rule they are supple, slightly fruity and reasonably full-bodied.

To the east and the south, the Coteaux du Tricastin district shades almost imperceptibly into the vast Côtes du Rhône appellation. This embraces more than 100 communes in six different départements: Ardèche, Drôme, Gard, Loire, Rhône and Vaucluse. Of these, Vaucluse produces far and away the most wine (about half), then come Gard and Drôme. In recent years, Côtes du Rhône production has increased tremendously and now comes from more than 40,000 hectares (nearly 99,000 acres) of vineyards. The average quality has improved, too, thanks to better winemaking techniques, among other factors. The great bulk of the wines are red and the average Côtes du Rhône is quite likely to come from a cooperative, to cost little and to be a pleasant, everyday drink.

As well as this "standard" Côtes du Rhône, wines of more exciting quality are being made. On many estates growers have been striving – successfully – to make Côtes du Rhône wines with character, and since 1953 the French legislators have distinguished communes in the Côtes du Rhône area where superior wines are produced. This category has grown to 65 villages with nearly 5,000 hectares (12,400 acres) of vineyard. The wines either carry the appellation Côtes du Rhône-Villages or are sold as Côtes du Rhône with the village name added. Seventeen villages qualify. In Drôme: Rochegude, Rousset-les-Vignes, St-Maurice-sur-Eygues, St-Pantaléon-les-Vignes and Vinsobres; in Gard: Chusclan, Laudun, St-Gervais; in Vaucluse: Beaumes-de-Venise, Cairanne, Rasteau, Roaix, Sablet, Séguret, Valréas, Vacqueyras and Visan.

Some of these villages deserve an appellation of their own, particularly Vacqueyras where the wines have the clean "attack" that means quality, and can also show finesse. Their fragrance and taste often suggest spices, spring flowers and soft fruit. Chusclan, too, deserves promotion, thanks to an exemplary cooperative that controls all the production. As well as the red wine (various *cuvées*), the rosé is very successful and the white well above average. Rasteau and Sablet are two other villages producing wine of above-average quality.

Two of the leading "villages" of the Côtes du Rhône, Beaumes-de-Venise and Rasteau, have a notable speciality in addition to their ordinary wines: Vin Doux Naturel. "VDN" has alcohol added during fermentation, stopping the fermentation and leaving unfermented "natural" sugar. In Beaumes-de-Venise only Muscat grapes are used for VDN wine. A good Muscat de Beaumes-de-Venise has a marvellous aroma of fresh, juicy fruit, especially apricots and peaches. The wine from Rasteau is quite different. It is nearly always made solely from the black Grenache grape and in two versions. The more common version is the orange-brown *doré*, made from the juice of the Grenache fermented without the skins. The *rouge*, fermented with the skins, is regarded by the experts as the better and more authentic version.

Between Rasteau and Beaumes-de-Venise lies a range of mountains called the Dentelles de Montmirail, whose ragged outline does indeed suggest lace to the fanciful. In Roman times Iocunditas ("happy town") was built at their foot, and "Iocunditas" has become Gigondas. For nearly 20 years Gigondas was grouped with the Côtes du Rhône-Villages, but in 1971 it was given its own appellation contrôlée. The wine is perhaps the most powerful of the whole Rhône valley. Partly because of the high proportion of Grenache, a natural alcoholic strength of 13 to 14 percent is normal. Gigondas has a warming, full-bodied taste you can almost chew on. A local producer once compared the wine to a "charging rhinoceros".

East of Gigondas stretches the Côtes du Ventoux, a large wine district that received appellation contrôlée status in 1973. It takes its name from "the giant of Provence", the 1,912-metre (6,273-foot) high Mont Ventoux. Production is largely in the hands of cooperatives: less than one percent of the 4,000 or so growers do their own winemaking. The better Côtes du Ventoux wines are red with a firm, spicy, substantial taste that conveys impressions of sun-baked fruit. Most of the wines, however, are easy-drinking and quite light, resembling those from the Coteaux du Tricastin.

The most famous name on the west bank of the Rhône is Tavel, where Tavel rosé is made. "Tavel 1er Rosé de France" is written in large letters on the roof of the local cooperative (but nowhere else). Tavel can be made in two ways from no fewer than nine grape varieties. In the better and more usual of the two methods, the grapeskins soak for a few hours in the juice to colour it. The other method, also designed to produce colour, is to press the grapes very firmly. The better Tavels are characterized by a solid, often somewhat fat taste with 12.5 to 13 percent alcohol, a modest amount of fruit, a mild freshness and a peppery-spicy tinge.

Tavel never really possesses complexity or finesse and the quality varies greatly according to the producer. It is usually at its best within two to three years of being made.

The Tavel district is bordered to the north by that of Lirac. Red is the most important wine here (although about a third of the production is rosé). Red Lirac from certain estates can surprise with its lightness and delicacy, suggesting cherries, currants, plums, strawberries. A grower has called red Lirac "the Margaux of the Rhône valley" – and with reason. The rosés are nearly always more delicate, fresher and fruitier than those from Tavel. A small amount of white wine is also produced: it can occasionally be very successful but usually lacks breeding and sufficient acidity to make it refreshing. The Lirac appellation takes in Roquemaure, St-Geniès-de-Comolas and St-Laurent-des-Arbres, as well as Lirac itself.

Although the vineyards of the Côtes du Vivarais do not belong officially to the Rhône region, they lie close enough to be included in a survey of the southern Rhône. The district forms an untidy circle around the river Ardèche, which flows into the Rhône at Pont-St-Esprit. The grape varieties are comparable to those of the Côtes du Rhône and so, in fact, are the wines.

The best quality wine comes from three *crus*, Orgnac, St-Montant and St-Remèze, comprising groups of communes. Cooperatives dominate production, but in contrast to cooperatives in some of the other French wine districts these are very progressive establishments. Together they have set up a modern bottling and marketing concern and are experimenting intensively with superior grape varieties. These trials have already resulted in remarkably good Vins de Pays from plantings of Chardonnay and Cabernet Sauvignon.

The map on page 232 shows the whole of the southern Rhône, including districts that are discussed in the chapters that follow. Châteauneuf-du-Pape is on pages 239–241; Coteaux des Baux-de-Provence (now promoted from VDQS to AC and called Coteaux d'Aix-en-Provence-les-Baux) and Côtes du Lubéron (a candidate for early promotion) are in the chapter on Provence (pages 242–249); the districts around Nîmes in the chapter on the Languedoc (pages 250–258). The Vins de Pays of the southern Rhône are on page 238.

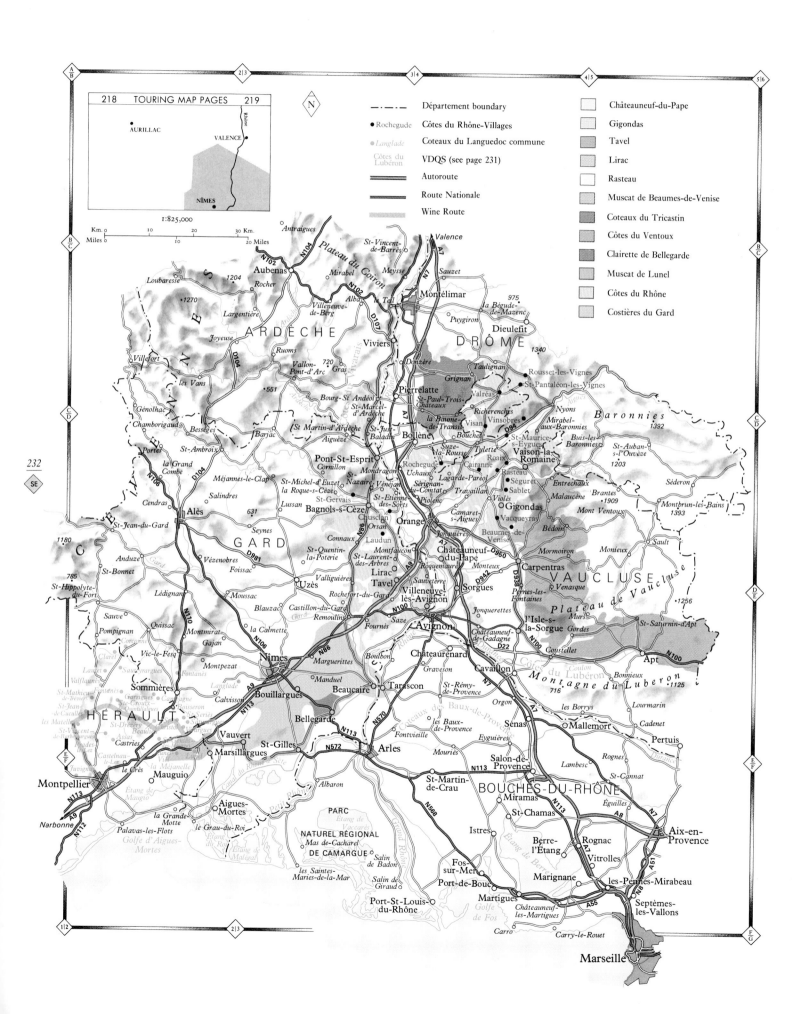

▲ The fantastically shaped Dentelles de Montmirail are a prominent feature in the southern Rhône. Their steep walls attract mountaineers.

TRAVEL INFORMATION

Because of its sunny climate and natural beauty, the southern Rhône region is very popular with tourists. The addresses given here, more or less in geographical order from north to south and on either side of the river, represent only a small selection of what is available.

HOTELS

Hotel Sévigné, 26230 Grignan, tel. 74 46 50 97. Budget hotel with plumbing that varies from room to room. Class B/C.

Savel, 01720 Ruoms, tel. 75 39 60 02. Standard hotel in a park. The restaurant has a good wine list. Class C.

La Picholine, 26110 Nyons, tel. 75 26 06 21. Quiet setting, with a swimming pool and a restaurant. Hotel class B; restaurant class C.

Relais de Château, 26130 Suze-la-Rousse, tel. 75 04 87 07. Modern, with swimming pool and restaurant. Class B.

Château de Rochegude, 26790 Rochegude, tel. 75 04 81 88. A castle with 12th-century origins (Roman relics have also been excavated including a figure of Bacchus). Great comfort, good cooking, a large park, a swimming pool and undergound cellars. Class A.

Burrhuss, 84110 Vaison-la-Romaine, tel. 90 36 00 11. Fairly modern hotel in the centre of town. Attentive service. Also a restaurant. Class B.

Hostellerie Le Beffroi, 844110 Vaison-la-Romaine, tel. 90 36 04 71. In the old part of town, and the best place to stay and to eat. *Demi-pension* is obligatory in season. Class A/B.

La Bellerive, 84110 Rasteau, tel. 90 46 10 20. Modern hotel surrounded by vineyards. Swimming pool and restaurant. Hotel class B; restaurant class C.

Domaine de Cabasse, 84110 Séguret, tel. 90 36 91 12. Friendly hotel that is part of a wine estate. Good restaurant; swimming pool. *Demi-pension* is obligatory in season. Hotel class B; restaurant class C.

Le Manoir, 84420 Mornas, tel. 90 37 00 79. Meticulous rooms and a restaurant below the ruins of an old castle. Class B.

Château de Coulorgues, Route d'Avignon, 30200 Bagnols-sur-Cèze, tel. 66 89 52 78. Small château surrounded by a park, with a restaurant and swimming pool. Class B.

Les Florets, 84190 Gigondas, tel. 90 65 85 01. Very peaceful setting in the countryside, with a large terrace and a restaurant. Hotel class B; restaurant class C.

Hotel Arène, Place de Langes, 84100 Orange, tel. 90 34 10 95. A quiet hotel, despite its central situation (and an easy walk to the great Roman theatre). Class B.

Fiacre, 153 Rue Vigne, 84200 Carpentras, tel. 90 63 03 15. An 18th-century building in the heart of the town. Quiet. Class B.

Univers, Place Aristide-Briand, 84200 Carpentras, tel. 90 63 00 05. Businessman's hotel with a solid reputation. Restaurant. Class B.

Château de Cubières, 30150 Roquemaure, tel. 66 50 29 33. Château-hotel with additional chalets in the surrounding park. Restaurant. Class B.

La Genestière, 84170 Monteux, tel. 90 62 27 04. Hotel, romantically surrounded by trees, with comfortable rooms. Traditional restaurant. Swimming pool. Class B.

l'Atelier, 5 Rue de la Foire, 30400 Villeneuve-lès-Avignon, tel. 90 25 01 84. Comfortable hotel in the old centre of the town. Class B.

La Magnaneraie, 37 Rue Champ-de-Bataille, 30400 Villeneuve-lès-Avignon, tel. 90 25 11 11. Large rooms with modern comforts in a delightful old manor. Restaurant (*feuilleté aux truffes du Ventoux*), swimming pool and garden. Hotel class A; restaurant class B.

Les Frênes, 84140 Montfavet, tel. 90 31 17 93. Luxurious, quietly situated hotel in an eastern suburb of Avignon, with park. Good restaurant. Hotel class A; restaurant class B.

RESTAURANTS

Le Manoir du Raveyron, 07150 Vallon-Pont-d'Arc, tel. 75 88 03 59. Shaded by trees and a pleasant place for lunch in the Ardèche. Traditional cooking. Class C.

Ferme Champ-Rond, 84600 Valréas, tel. 90 37 31 68. Charming old farmstead where you can enjoy modern interpretations of classic dishes. Class B.

Le Petit Caveau, 26110 Nyons, tel. 75 26 20 21. In the old part of town but quite modern *cuisine*. Class C.

Le Prieuré, 26110 Vinsobres, tel. 75 27 63 32. Country inn (*coq au vin*, etc). Class C.

Les Troubadours, 84820 Visan, tel. 90 41 92 55. In the cellar of a château; conservative, strictly regional menu. Class C.

Le Relais, 84290 Ste-Cécile-les-Vignes, tel. 90 30 84 39. Very congenial restaurant that maintains a high standard. Class B.

La Beaugravière, 84430 Mondragon, tel. 90 30 13 40. A long wine list, with many old vintages at very reasonable prices. The food is also good (*saumon au Châteauneuf-du-Pape*). All this makes you forget the rather mediocre location and lack of atmosphere. Also a hotel. Class C.

St-Hubert. 84340 Entrechaux, tel. 90 36 07 05. Ideal place to lunch when visiting nearby Vaison-la-Romaine (see Places of Interest), with an inviting shady terrace and quite good-value, fine regional cuisine. Class C.

Le Table du Comtat, 84110 Séguret, tel. 90 46 91 49. In a picturesque wine village with a superb view of the surrounding countryside, excellent cooking and many wines of the region: what more could one want? Also a hotel, with swimming pool. Class B.

Le Mas du Belier, 30200 La Roque-sur-Cèze, tel. 66 82 78 73. Good cheap restaurant at the bottom end of the village (northwest of Bagnols-sur-Cèze). The Sautadet waterfall close by is worth seeing. Class C.

Le Mas de Bouvan, 84150 Violès, tel. 90 70 84 08. Carefully prepared regional dishes (such as *lapin au Côtes du Rhône*). Class C.

l'Oustau de Baumo, 84190, Beaumes-de-Venise, tel. 90 62 95 19. Country dishes, including *cotelette de porc au Muscat de Beaumes-de-Venise*, and a terrace. Class C.

Les Géraniums, Le Barroux, 84330 Caromb, tel. 90 62 41 08. Generous helpings of Provençal dishes. It is also a hotel with 10 modern and 12 older rooms, and a shaded terrace. In all respects, good value for money. Restaurant class C; hotel class B/C.

l'Oustau d'Anaïs, 84410 Bédoin, tel. 90 65 67 43. Good country food at the foot of Mont Ventoux (pâté with onion compôte; roast lamb). Class C.

Restaurant des Halles, Rue Gallone, 84200 Carpentras, tel. 90 63 24 11. Authentic regional cooking, very reasonably priced. Class C.

l'Orangerie, 26 Rue Duplessis, 84200 Carpentras, tel. 90 67 27 23. Not very striking from the outside, but inside you find cooking of a high order and many expertly chosen regional wines. There is a garden. Class C.

Le Saule Pleurier, Quartier Beauregard, 84170 Monteux, tel. 90 61 01 35. Good cooking and a terrace. Class B.

Auberge de Tavel, 30126 Tavel, tel. 66 50 03 41. A brilliant wine list and appropriate dishes. Also a hotel, with swimming pool. Class B.

Hostellerie du Seigneur, 30126 Tavel, tel. 66 50 04 26. In the middle of the village. Agreeably priced wines and set menus. Also a hotel. Class C.

Auberge de Cassagne, 84130 Le Pontet, tel. 90 31 04 18. Very good restaurant in a luxury hotel near Avignon. Regional dishes; swimming pool. *Demi-pension* is obligatory in season. Restaurant class B; hotel class A.

Hiély-Lucullus, 5 Rue de la République, 84000 Avignon, tel. 90 82 56 01. Renowned restaurant with a wide range of classic and more contemporary dishes. You are unlikely to be disappointed. Class B.

Brunel, 46 Rue de la Balance, 84000 Avignon, tel. 90 85 24 83. Inventive, light cuisine (*ravioli de palourdes au safran*), splendid desserts. Class A.

La Fourchette, 17 Rue Racine, 84000 Avignon, tel. 90 82 56 01. A favourite place with the locals; the cooking has a regional accent. Good value. Class C.

Le Vernet, 58 Rue Joseph-Vernet, 84000 Avignon, tel. 90 86 64 53. A large garden outside; romantic paintings inside; market-fresh ingredients. Class C.

Les Trois Clefs, 26 Rue des Trois-Faucons, 84000 Avignon, tel. 90 86 51 53. Good cooking in a distinctive setting. Class B.

Le Bistrot d'Avignon, 1 Place Jean-Vilar, 84000 Avignon, tel. 90 88 06 45. Close to the papal palace. About 50 different Rhône wines are served by the glass. Class C.

l'Ermitage Meissonnier, 30400 Les Angles, tel. 90 25 41 68. The food is much more exciting than the setting, and there is an extensive selection of wines. It is also a hotel. Class B.

David, 84220 Roussillon, tel. 90 05 60 13. In the Côtes du Ventoux: Provençal cooking, an interesting wine list and a fine view. Class C.

Le Val des Fées, 84220 Roussillon, tel. 90 75 64 99. Small restaurant with enthusiastic cooking. Class B.

PLACES OF INTEREST

Avignon The most important building in this busy town is the papal palace, the Palais des Papes. In fact there are two palaces, both built in the first half of the 14th century. The Palais Vieux looks sober, almost severe: the Palais Nouveau is more decorative. Enormous halls, long corridors and the many chapels show

how impressive the papal court here must have been; works of art include paintings, frescos and tapestries. Beside the palace stands the cathedral of Notre-Dame-des-Doms (12th century, later rebuilt) with the tomb of Pope John XXII, and behind the cathedral is the Rocher des Doms, with a garden and a fine view over the Rhône.

The Pont St-Bénézet ("Sur le pont d'Avignon"), half crosses the river. Only four of the original 22 arches remain (the river used to be much wider than it is today). On one of the

arches there is a small chapel. Avignon is amply provided with museums. The Musée Calvet (65 Rue Joseph-Vernet) is one of the richest of southern France, with exhibits from prehistory and Greek antiquity, examples of the ironsmiths' craft and 16th- to 20th-century paintings (including two Utrillos). Beside it is the Musée Requin, devoted to the natural history of the region. Opposite the Palais des Papes is the Petit Palais, now a museum with some 300 canvases and sculptures. Sculpture, including (appropriately) a torso of Bacchus, has also been collected in the Musée Lapidaire (in a former Jesuit chapel at 27 Rue de la République). The Musée Théodore-Aubale displays the printers' craft (7 Place St-Pierre) and the Musée Vouland 18th-century furniture (17 rue Victor-Hugo). Two beautiful churches are St-Didier and St-Pierre.

Beaumes-de-Venise Apart from its wine, the village has the remains of a medieval bastion, various caves (including the Ambrosi), and a prehistoric burial chamber. The charming little chapel of Notre-Dame-d'Aubune, just outside the village, has a Romanesque belfry.

Bouchet The huge firm of Cellier des Dauphins ages its Côtes du Rhône and Côtes du Rhône-Villages in a former abbey here.

Cairanne The walls and gates of old fortifications are still partly standing. Next to the local cooperative is the 1962 chapel of Notre-Dame-de-la-Vigne, a memorial to the years of German Occupation, with remarkable modern stained-glass windows.

Caromb In the St-Marc cooperative growers have assembled reminders of rural life as it used to be.

Carpentras Busy provincial holiday town but the Arc de Triomphe dates from Roman times, the synagogue from the 14th century, the Palais de Justice from the 17th and the Hôtel-Dieu, with its dispensary, from the 18th. The Musée de Poésie, founded in 1976, is unique in France. Works by the 18th-century local portrait painter Joseph-Siffrein Duplessis are exhibited in the Musée Duplessis; a museum of regional history and art is in the same building. Period rooms are the attraction at the Musée Sobirats. The 15th-century church of St-Siffrein has a collection of religious art.

Fontaine-de-Vaucluse A tourist spot: the "fountain" is a spring at the foot of a cliff. The walk there is very pretty. A museum is devoted to the 14th-century Italian poet Petrarch, who climbed Mont Ventoux – the first recorded mountaineer. A tall column in the village is a monument to him. The Musée des Restrictions commemorates the Occupation years. There is a *son et lumière* in summer.

Gigondas Attractive wine-village at the foot of the Dentelles du Montmirail, with the remains of old fortifications, and carved wooden figures in the church, in front of which is a terrace with a fine view. There is a tasting room in the village where wines from some 30 producers can be sampled.

Gordes Straggling hill village that was "rescued" by artists. It has two museums, one for archaeology and the Vasaléry for modern art.

Grignan The imposing castle above the village became famous through the letters of the Marquise de Sévigné, whose daughter and son-in-law lived there. The castle contains the Musée Faure-Cabrol (tapestries and furniture). In summer, recitals are given on the 17th-century organ in the church of St-Sauveur.

Mornas Above the village there are the remains of what was once the strongest fortification in the Rhône valley. Mornas itself has a Romanesque chapel.

Nyons Town noted for wine, olives, jam and truffles, with a pleasant old quarter, the Quartier des Forts. There is a small museum of archaeology in the Tour Sarrazaine and 16th- and 17th-century paintings in the St-Vincent church.

▲ Gigondas is a respected appellation for red wine of better than Côtes du Rhône-Villages standards. The village (above) has a tasting room for local wines.

Orange In Roman times this town had some 100,000 inhabitants, many more than today. The Roman theatre is the finest to have survived from the ancient world: it has perfect acoustics (it is still used in summer) and an impressive statue of the Emperor Augustus. Beside it are the remains of a Roman temple and a gymnasium, and behind the theatre a road leads up to a park and castle ruins. On the northern side of the town stands a large Roman triumphal arch with reliefs depicting Caesar's victories. The municipal museum (near the theatre) has many reminders of both the Romans and the princes of Orange-Nassau.

Orgnac-l'Aven Immense caves with stalactites and stalagmites.

Rasteau On the road to Roaix there is the Domaine de Beaurenard with a Musée du Vigneron.

Richerenches Village surrounded by walls and towers where the powerful *commanderie* of the Knights Templars was established in the 12th century. The village also has a truffle market.

Roussas Old Tricastin village with a château.

Rousset-les-Vignes At the foot of a 800m (2,625ft) mountain. There is a 16th-century château.

Roussillon Built on hilltops in the Côtes du Ventoux district. Many artists live here: the ochre deposits near by are quarried for the yellowish pigment used in paints (demonstrated in a small museum here). There is a fine view from the Castrum.

Sablet Built step-wise up a hill, with the remains of old fortifications – walls, towers and gates. There is a small church on the hilltop. (Don't forget to try the wine.)

St-Gervais Has an atmospheric old town centre. A temple of Jupiter is believed to have stood where the church is today.

St-Laurent-des-Arbres Old towers and a 13th-century fortified church.

St-Paul-Trois-Châteaux The cathedral has a splendid west front, and a municipal museum is devoted to the early history of the region. There are also the remains of defensive walls. The town has never had three châteaux: "Trois Châteaux" is a corruption of "Tricastin".

St-Restitut The biggest natural cave-cellar in France (the property of the Cellier des Dauphins, bottlers and négociants).

Séguret An almost perfect medieval village perched on a hillside. It has been declared a historic monument.

Suze-la-Rousse A wine university was set up here in 1977 in the thoroughly restored château, a former hunting lodge of the princes of Orange. Activities will cover the whole of the French wine world. Exhibitions on wine themes are regularly held, and all Rhône wines are tasted here before being granted their appellations.

Le Thor The Thouzon cave, with stalactites and stalagmites, is a few kilometres north of this village.

Vaison-la-Romaine Extensive Roman remains have been uncovered in this small town: a theatre, a large dwelling, a whole street of shops, statues, and an intriguing public lavatory with seating for a large family. The finest works of art, among them a silver bust of a Roman patrician of the 3rd century, have been assembled in an archaeological museum. The church of Notre-Dame-de-Nazareth is a former cathedral and dates from the 6th or 7th century (but rebuilt many times). Beside it are cloisters. The oldest part of the town is the Haute Ville, with 14th-century houses and castle ruins. You reach it by a 2,000-year-old bridge. An obligatory visit.

Vallon-Pont-d'Arc Here the river Ardèche is bridged by a high rock arch, the Pont d'Arc. Take the D290 Pont-St-Esprit road from Vallon for fine views of the Ardèche gorges.

Valréas A road lined with plane trees follows the line of the old town walls. The town centre has many old houses, an 18th-century town hall that was once a palace, a Romanesque church and the 15th-century Chapelle des Pénitents-Blancs (with later additions).

Villeneuve-lès-Avignon When the papacy was established at Avignon, many of the cardinals built their summer residences here. Among the sights are the 14th-century Fort St-André, with its terraces and Italian garden; a Carthusian monastery with an imposing entrance; the Tour de Philippe le Bel, with splendid panoramic views; and the Musée de l'Hospice with "The Coronation of the Virgin" by the 15th-century painter Enguerrand Quarton.

Visan Fortified village with castle ruins. Every year at the end of August or the beginning of September a pilgrimage is made to the 13th-century chapel of Notre-Dame-des-Vignes. Inscribed on the chancel arch are the words *Posuerunt me custodem in vineis*: "I have been placed here as the guardian of the vines".

Viviers-sur-Rhône Small medieval town (which gives its name to the district of Vivarais), built around a 12th-century cathedral.

WINE FAIRS AND FESTIVALS

Beginning of March Côtes du Rhône festival and competition in Vinsobres.

Around 20 April The Fête de St-Marc in Villeneuve-lès-Avignon.

Around 1 May Fête des Vins in Bagnols-sur-Cèze.

Around 20 May Competition for Tricastin wines in La Baume-de-Transit.

Around 15 June Festival of Côtes du

Rhône and "the heritage" in St-Victor-la-Coste.

First week July Fête des Vins des Vignerons in Violès.

Mid-July Fête des Vins in Visan.

Around 14 July Fête des Côtes du Ventoux in Gordes; Fête des Côtes du Rhône-Villages in Vacqueyras.

On 14 July Fête des Vins Canton de Bourg-St-Andéol in St-Marcel d'Ardèche.

Around 20 July Fête des Vins des Côtes du Ventoux in Carpentras; Fête des Vins in Buisson and also in Mondragon.

End of July Fête des Vins des Côtes du Rhône Gardoises, Pont-St-Esprit; a wine festival in Cairanne.

Beginning of August Fête des Vins de l'Enclave and a lavender parade in Valréas.

Around 10 August Fête des Vignerons du Mont Ventoux in Bédoin; wine festival in St-Maurice-sur-Eygues; Fête des Vignerons Ardèchois in Ruoms.

Around 15 August Festival of wine and olives in Mirabel-aux-Baronnies; a Fête des Vins and a Provençal festival in Séguret.

End of August, beginning of September Wine festival in Visan. **Around mid-November** Wine fair

and the Fête des Vins Primeurs in Vaison-la-Romaine.

Around 20 November Festival of wine and music in Ste-Cécile-les-Vignes.

WINE FRATERNITIES

Various fraternities function in the southern Rhône valley: La Commanderie des Costes du Rhône (Côtes du Rhône); La Compagnie de la Côte du Rhône Gardoise (Côtes du Rhône in Gard, on the west bank); La Commanderie de St-Vincent des Vignerons de Visan (Visan); La Confrérie de Vacqueyras (Vacqueyras); La Confrérie des Chevaliers du Gouste-Séguret (Séguret); Les Compagnons de Beaumes-de-Venise (Beaumes-de-Venise); La Commanderie de Tavel (Tavel); and La Confrérie des Vignerons des Côtes du Ventoux (Côtes du Ventoux).

WINE INFORMATION

The Maison du Tourisme et du Vin is in Avignon (41 Cours Jean-Jaurès). In St-Paul-Trois-Châteaux, the Maison de la Truffe et du Tricastin sells wine and other products of the Coteaux du Tricastin and also has a truffle exposition.

▲ Clairette de Die sparkling wine is made in the foothills of the Alps, east of the main Rhône vineyards. The mountains rise up to the east, filling the horizon.

PRODUCERS OF SPECIAL INTEREST

COTES DU RHONE AND COTES DU RHONE-VILLAGES

AUBIGNAN, postcode 84190

Domaine de St-Sauveur: As well as a very good Côtes du Rhône, Lisette Rey and her brother Guy produce a fine Muscat de Beaumes-de-Venise and Côtes du Ventoux.

AVIGNON, postcode 84000, 232 E4

Etienne Bellicard: Sister firm to Gilbey de Loudenne (Bordeaux) and Piat (Beaujolais). Belongs to International Distillers & Vintners and has a large range of Rhône wines.

BOURG-ST-ANDEOL, postcode 07700, 232 C3

Domaine des Amoureuses; Domaine de l'Olivet*: Rudolph Goosens makes a touchstone unfiltered, wood-aged Côtes du Rhône.

CADIGNAC, postcode 30200

Domaine de la Réméjeanne

CAIRANNE, postcode 84290, 232 D4

Cave Coopérative; Domaine Brusset; Domaine de l'Oratoire St-Martin: The wine is called Réserve des Seigneurs de St-Martin.

CHUSCLAN, postcode 30200, 232 D3

Cave Coopérative*: Quality-minded cooperative with up-to-date plant.

LAUDUN, postcode 30290, 232 D3

Domaine Pélaquié; Les Vignerons des Quatre Chemins.

ORANGE, postcode 84100, 232 D4

Domaines Michel Bernard: Sound wines from its own vineyards and from other properties where it has exclusive rights. **Le Vieille Ferme***: Merchant firm established by Jean-Pierre Perrin, offering exemplary red Côtes du Ventoux and white Côtes du Lubéron.

PUYMERAS, postcode 84110

Cave Coopérative*: One of the valley's better cooperatives.

ROCHEFORT-DU-GARD, postcode 30650, 232 E3

Domaine du Père Rocha

ROCHEGUDE, postcode 26130, 232 D4

Cave Coopérative

SABLET, postcode 84110, 232 D4

Domaine de Verquière*: The Chamfort family makes a distinguished Sablet and a very good Côtes du Rhône.

ST-CECILE-LES-VIGNES, postcode 84290

Cave Coopérative; Domaine de la Grand'Ribe*: Pure, charming wine, with fruit. Abel Sahuc is the maker. **Domaine de la Présidente.**

ST-GERVAIS, postcode 30200, 232 D3

Domaine Ste-Anne*: Attractive, slightly spicy red wines and very good whites. This isolated estate belongs to the Steinmaier family.

ST-MAURICE-SUR-EYGUES, postcode 26650, 232 D4

Cave Coopérative

ST-MICHEL-D'EUZET, postcode 30200, 232 D3

Domaine des Riots

ST-PANTALEON-LES-VIGNES, postcode 26230, 232 C4

Cave Coopérative

SAZE, postcode 30650, 232 E4

Domaine de Cabanon

SEGURET, postcode 84110, 232 D4

Domaine de Cabasse*: Séguret and Sablet aged in wood. The owner, Nadine Latour, also runs a hotel with restaurant on the estate (see Travel Information).

SUZE-LA-ROUSSE, postcode 26130, 232 D4

Cave Coopérative; Château de l'Estagnol

TULETTE, postcode 26130, 232 D4

Cellier des Dauphins: Gigantic bottling and marketing concern that processes almost the entire production from nine cooperatives. Among its best wines are the Côtes du Rhône "Carte Noire" and the Côtes du Rhône-Villages "Réserve".

UCHAUX, postcode 84100, 232 D4

Château St-Estève*: Impressive property with a wide range of very good wines, red and white. Large, atmospheric vaulted cellar. The estate is run by Marc Français.

VACQUEYRAS, postcode 84190, 232 D4

Cave Coopérative; Domaine de la Fourmone*: Belongs to the Combe family and makes Vacqueyras and Gigondas (l'Oustau Fauquet) of excellent standard. **Domaine des Lambertins***: Beautiful, typical Vacqueyras from the Lambert brothers. **Château de Montmirail***: Vacqueyras and Gigondas wines for laying down, nurtured by Jacques Bouteiller. **Domaine de Montvac; Pascal***: Small merchant house with excellent wines from the southern Rhône valley, including Gigondas from its own Domaine du Grand Montmirail.

VALREAS, postcode 84600, 232 C4

Romain Bouchard; Domaine des Grands Devers: Based a little way out of Valréas. **Union des Vignerons de l'Enclave des Papes**: Bottling and sales organization for three cooperatives and nearly 20 estates.

VENEJAN, postcode 30200, 232 D3

Cave Coopérative

VINSOBRES, postcode 26490, 232 D4

Cave Coopérative; Château de Deurre; Claude et Nicole Jaume.

VISAN, postcode 84820, 232 D4

Cave Coopérative

BEAUMES-DE-VENISE AND RASTEAU

BEAUMES-DE-VENISE, postcode 84190, 232 D4

Domaine des Bernardins*: Firm, fruity Muscat de Beaumes-de-Venise. **Cave Coopérative***: Aromatic Muscat wine in a distinctive flat bottle. **Domaine de Coyeux***: One of the most elegant Muscat wines of this district from the estate of Yves and Cathérine Nativelle. **Domaine de Durban***: A Muscat de Beaumes-de-Venise with plenty of fruit and class.

RASTEAU, postcode 84110, 232 D4

Cave Coopérative; Domaine du Char-à-Vin: Maurice Charavin's wines include a very successful Rasteau *doré* (Grenache fermented without the skins). **Domaine des Coteaux du Travers; Domaine de la Grange Neuve.**

GIGONDAS

GIGONDAS, postcode 84190, 232 D4

Pierre Amadieu: The biggest landowner in Gigondas; also a négociant. This family concern uses a 160m (175yd) tunnel as a maturing cellar. **Cave Coopérative; Le Mas des Collines; Domaine de la Mavette; Etablissements Meffre**: Firm with a vast amount of land – about 950 hectares (2,348 acres), 110 hectares (272 acres) in Gigondas. One of the best wines is the Gigondas from the renovated Château Raspail. **Domaine Les Pallières; Domaine du Pesquier***: Strong, almost sultry Gigondas, matured in casks. The estate is owned by the Boutière family. **Domaine Raspail-Ay***: Noble, classically made Gigondas, not clarified or filtered. François Ay owns

the estate. **Domaine St-Gayan***: Gigondas that are concentrated and impressive and a masterly Côtes du Rhône from this estate owned by Roger and Jean-Pierre Meffre. **Château du Trignon***: André Roux makes wines of a very high standard, especially the Gigondas, Sablet and Rasteau.

COTEAUX DU TRICASTIN

LES GRANGES-GONTARDES, postcode 26290

Domaine de la Tour l'Elysée: Various *cuvées*; the Syrah is the best. (The "la Tour" in the domaine's name refers to the very modern tower on the estate, in which the wine is made.)

ROUSSAS, postcode 26320

Domaine de Grangeneuve*: Progressive family estate (Mme Bour, daughters and sons-in-law) making pure, charming wines.

LIRAC AND TAVEL

LIRAC, postcode 30126, 232 D3

Château de Ségriès

ROQUEMAURE, postcode 30150, 232 D4

Jean-Claude Assémat*: Energetic, very expert winemaker whose Liracs and Côtes du Rhône are fruity, pure and supple. Assémat works under various estate names, among them Domaine des Causses & St-Eynes and Domaine des Garrigues. **Domaine de Castel Oualou***: An outstanding red Lirac, a fragrant rosé and a refreshing white. Marie Pons-Mure is the owner. **Domaine du Château de St-Roch.**

ST-LAURENT-DES-ARBRES, postcode 30126, 232 D3

Domaine du Devoy*: Elegant but firm red Lirac of top quality. Belongs to the Lombardo brothers. **Charles Pons-Mure.**

The restored château at Suze-la-Rousse in the Côtes du Rhône. It now houses a wine university and stages wine exhibitions. It also acts as a tasting centre for the appellation contrôlée authorities for the entire Rhône valley.

TAVEL, postcode 30126, 232 D3

Château d'Aquéria*: Refreshing, fairly elegant rosé. The château belongs to Paul Bez. **Cave Coopérative; Domaine de la Genestière***: Georges Bernard makes a concentrated, soft and fruity Tavel, and also a quite substantial red Lirac. **Domaine Maby: Prieuré de Montézargues; Château de Trinquevedel***: Powerful, quite stylish Tavel from François Dumoulin, one of the leading growers of Tavel. **Domaine le Vieux Moulin***: A firm, rather fruity rosé for drinking young. The estate belongs to the Roudil family.

COTES DU VENTOUX

LE BARROUX, postcode 84330

Domaine de Champaga

BEDOIN, postcode 84410, 232 D4

Cave Coopérative

MORMOIRON, postcode 84570, 232 D4

Domaine des Anges; Cave Coopérative.

VILLES-SUR-AUZON, postcode 84570

Cave Coopérative

ARDECHE

LAGORCE, postcode 07150

Domaine de Vignier

ORGNAC-l'AVEN, postcode 07150

Cave Coopérative

RUOMS, postcode 07120

UCOVA*: This modern concern bottles and markets almost the entire production from 19 cooperatives in the southern Ardèche. As well as many simple wines it also offers some surprising *vins de pays*, including an excellent Chardonnay and Cabernet Sauvignon.

ST-MONTANT, postcode 07220

Domaine Gallety

ST-REMEZE, postcode 07700

Domaine du Belvezet*: A substantial, intense red wine, one of the best in the whole area.

SE

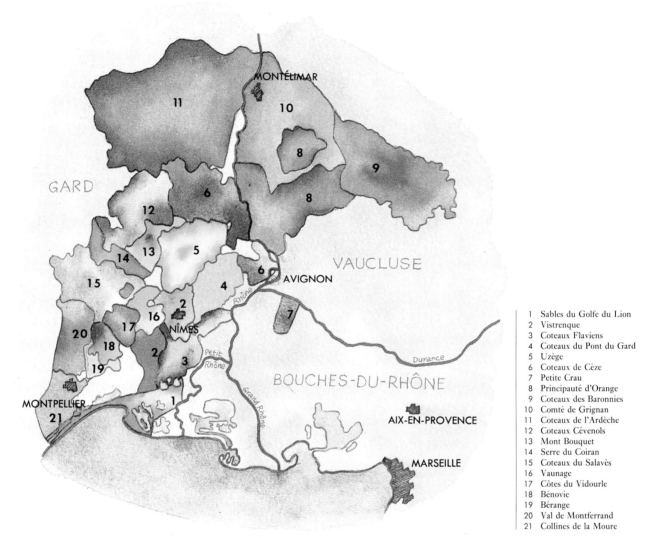

1 Sables du Golfe du Lion
2 Vistrenque
3 Coteaux Flaviens
4 Coteaux du Pont du Gard
5 Uzège
6 Coteaux de Cèze
7 Petite Crau
8 Principauté d'Orange
9 Coteaux des Baronnies
10 Comté de Grignan
11 Coteaux de l'Ardèche
12 Coteaux Cévenols
13 Mont Bouquet
14 Serre du Coiran
15 Coteaux du Salavès
16 Vaunage
17 Côtes du Vidourle
18 Bénovie
19 Bérange
20 Val de Montferrand
21 Collines de la Moure

THE VINS DE PAYS OF THE SOUTHERN RHONE

Vins de Pays represent an enormous volume of wine – around 5.5 million hectolitres (more than 61 million cases) a year – and acquired legal status in the course of the 1970s. Conditions and production standards were clearly defined in a succession of decrees, and dozens of the wines were given names.

The requirements laid down for Vins de Pays are less stringent than those for wines in the VDQS (Vins Délimités de Qualité Supérieure) category, but the regulations do have value: witness the various Vins de Pays that have been promoted to VDQS status which is, of course, a step towards the coveted appellation contrôlée. The rules cover, among other things, the grape varieties that can be used, the yield (from 70 to 90 hectolitres per hectare), minimum alcohol content and – naturally – the area of origin. The wines must also pass analytical and tasting tests.

Wine legislation distinguishes three types of Vins de Pays: regional wines, produced across a number of départements (such as Vin de Pays d'Oc); département wines (Vin de Pays de Vaucluse, for example); and zone wines (Vin de Pays de la Principauté d'Orange). The producer can also put various details on the labels, such as year of vintage, grape variety (if only one kind is used), where bottled, method of production or type or wine (*sur lie*, *vin de primeur*, etc), any awards the wine has won and the name of the estate, cooperative or négociant. Use of the terms "château" and "clos" is not allowed.

By far the most Vins de Pays – some 85 percent – are produced in the Mediterranean départements. Another characteristic feature is that cooperatives provide the overwhelming majority of the wines; indeed, they often have a local monopoly.

The southern Rhône is rich in Vins de Pays. With some, their greatest charm lies in their poetic names, but others can astonish with their quality. At present the best Vins de Pays from this extensive region come from the Ardèche. A dynamic group of cooperatives, with UCOVA of Ruoms in the lead, are making splendid wines from the Burgundian grape Chardonnay, the Bordeaux Cabernet Sauvignon and other varieties. Even the traditional Burgundy firm Louis Latour collaborates with UCOVA in producing a much-lauded Chardonnay Vin de Pays.

South of Nîmes, on the flat, sandy land bordering the sea, stretches the remarkable Vins de Pays des Sables du Golfe du Lion. In these apparently impossible circumstances the Salins du Midi, the giant salt-extraction company which moved into pioneer winemaking in the last century, and is now the biggest wine estate in France, produces surprisingly pleasant wines familiar under the brand name Listel. The Salins du Midi also makes successful use of superior "imported" grape varieties such as Chardonnay, Sauvignon, Cabernet Sauvignon and Merlot.

In terms of quantity, the *départementale* Vin de Pays du Gard comes top in the southern Rhône with an annual 200,000 to 300,000 hectolitres (2.2 to 3.3 million cases). Next come the zone wines Vin de Pays des Coteaux de l'Ardèche, with nearly 200,000 hectolitres, and Vin de Pays des Sables du Golfe du Lion and Vin de Pays des Bouches du Rhône with 100,000 to 150,000 hectolitres (1.1 to 1.6 million cases).

CHATEAUNEUF-DU-PAPE

The history of Châteauneuf is interwoven with religion and wine. In 1309 Clement V (Bertrand de Goth, the archbishop of Bordeaux and founder of the present Château Pape Clément in Graves) was installed as pope at Avignon. After his death a further six popes were to occupy the palace there, among them John XXII. To escape from the bustle of the town, John went looking in the surrounding countryside for a place where he could meditate in peace. His choice was the neglected castle of Châteauneuf, and over the next 15 years the castle was restored for use as a papal summer residence.

During John's reign the papal court was copious in its thirst, with the result that the vineyards around Châteauneuf were greatly increased: in 1333, the year of John's death, there were probably more than three million vines growing in the district, and under later popes even more vines were planted.

At that time sheep farming, wine growing and olives shared the land. But in the eighteenth century the whole emphasis shifted to cultivating vines. In 1727 there was already a rule stating that only grapes from within the boundaries of Châteauneuf could be processed there. This was the forerunner of a series of much stricter regulations drawn up nearly 200 years later, in 1923, on the initiative of Baron Le Roy de Boiseaumarié, the owner of Château Fortia. The present appellation contrôlée legislation here (and indeed throughout France) is based largely on these regulations.

The wine of Châteauneuf-du-Pape (the name only emerged in the nineteenth century) can only be made from 13 permitted grape varieties: eight black and five white. The black grapes are Grenache (that great provider of alcohol), Syrah, Cinsaut, Mourvèdre, Muscardin, Vaccarèse, Counoise and Terret Noir. The white grapes are Clairette, Bourboulenc, Roussanne, Picardan and Picpoul; the white varieties go into the red wine as well as into the small amount of white Châteauneuf-du-Pape that is made. What is actually planted differs from estate to estate. Some growers use only four varieties, whereas all 13 are planted at (for example) the Domaine de Nalys. A further condition is that at the harvest at least five percent of the grapes must be left on the vines – obviously the less ripe or less sound bunches.

The country around Châteauneuf-du-Pape has gentle slopes and wide plateaux, and the most characteristic soil is reddish earth deeply covered with clay and a thick layer of large, smooth stones. During the day the stones absorb the heat of the sun, then radiate it at night, helping to bring the grapes to maximum ripeness. Other soils in this district of 3,000 hectares (7,400 acres) contain gravel, sand and clay. These differences in the soil, in the vines planted – and the various winemaking techniques – mean that Châteauneuf-du-Pape wines come in a variety of styles.

Classic Châteauneuf is "broad-shouldered" with plenty of alcohol: a wine in which the summer sun of Provence seems captured. The best also have elusive nuances: connoisseurs talk of laurel and violets, truffles and plums, cinnamon, herbs and burnt coffee. Traditional Châteauneuf demands patience and often will not reveal its true class for eight to ten years. Other Châteauneuf wines, made by *macération carbonique*, almost resemble Beaujolais: ready for bottling within ten months of the vintage and for drinking within two or three years.

About three percent of Châteauneuf wine is white. Its quality improved greatly during the 1970s; it used to taste heavy and flat, but modern winemaking has increased the freshness and fruit. Today, a good white Châteauneuf can be an attractive alternative to white Burgundy.

Because a great deal of Châteauneuf-du-Pape is sold by négociants, independent estates who do their own bottling have created their own distinctive *bouteille écussonnée*: a bottle with Châteauneuf's crossed-keys insignia on the neck.

▼ Châteauneuf-du-Pape clusters around the ruins of the Papal summer palace. The enormous cellars are intact and are used by the local wine fraternity for banquets and tastings. The vineyards of Châteauneuf are open and rolling, with wide woodlands on the hilltops. Much of the soil consists of the famous large pebbles.

The négociant firm of Père Anselme runs a wine museum in Châteauneuf. The town, with its reminders of past Papal glories and its peaceful streets, is worthy of a wander.
The local headgear (bottom) is optional.

TRAVEL INFORMATION

For hotels and restaurants in the surrounding area see the chapter on the Southern Rhône.

HOTELS

Hostellerie du Château des Fines Roches, 84230 Châteauneuf-du-Pape, tel. 90 83 70 23. A castle flanked by battlemented towers, with seven luxurious rooms, a small terrace, two dining rooms (one in Louis XIII style) and a library. The cooking is excellent, with fresh ingredients (*magret de canard au vinaigre de Châteauneuf-du-Pape*), and the wine list has a good selection of Châteauneuf wines. There is a wine estate here, but run by different owners (the hotel has a good view over the vineyards). Hotel class A; restaurant class B.
Le Logis d'Arnavel, 84230 Châteauneuf-du-Pape, tel. 90 83 73 22. Modern, comfortable hotel, just west of Châteauneuf. It belongs to a wine grower and has a good restaurant and a swimming pool. Class C.
La Mère Germaine, 84230 Châteauneuf-du-Pape, tel. 90 39 70 72. Simple budget hotel with limited plumbing. Terrace and restaurant. Class C.

RESTAURANTS

La Garbure, 84230 Châteauneuf-du-Pape, tel. 90 82 75 08. Good-value country cooking. Class C.
La Mule du Pape, 84230 Châteauneuf-du-Pape, tel. 90 83 73 30. On the first floor of a building in the centre of town. Great care taken with the Provençal-style cooking. A reliable place. Class B.
Le Pistou, 84230 Châteauneuf-du-Pape, tel. 90 39 71 75. Traditional dishes of the region. Class C.
La Porte des Princes, Avenue de la République, 84350 Courthézon, tel. 90 70 70 26. Good, simple restaurant (roast lamb cutlets), but avoid the hotel. Class C.

PLACES OF INTEREST

Châteauneuf-du-Pape The former papal summer palace, overlooking the vineyards, was largely destroyed in 1562 and further damaged in 1944. Nevertheless it is worth walking up to the ruins; the walls still standing indicate the huge original dimensions. What has remained intact is the vast cellar hall, used by the local wine fraternity for its banquets. From the ruins you look out over Châteauneuf and its surroundings. In the centre of the village various producers have their cellars and tasting rooms, and there are also some simple restaurants. At the bottom end of Châteauneuf-du-Pape stands the firm of Père Anselme, which has set up a museum connected with wine; one of the most important of the 500 exhibits is a medieval wine cask with a capacity of 4,000 litres.

WINE ACTIVITIES

The Fête de St-Marc takes place around 25 April; the Fête de la Véraison on the first weekend in August; and in the second half of September there is the festive proclamation of the harvest, the Ban des Vendanges.
In 1967 l'Echansonnerie des Papes, the local wine fraternity, was founded.

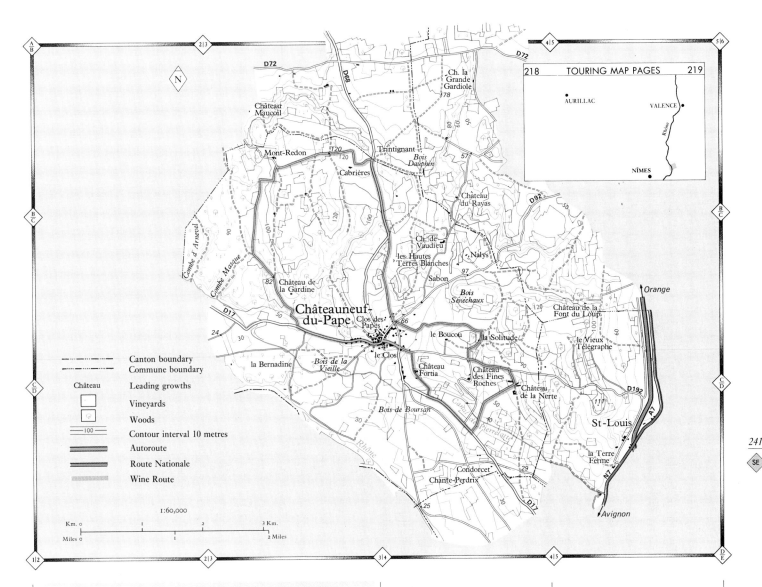

PRODUCERS OF SPECIAL INTEREST

BEDARRIDES, postcode 84370

Bérard Père & Fils*: Merchants with a large estate in Châteauneuf-du-Pape, called Terre Ferme. The red wine is concentrated and full of flavour in the old style.

CHATEAUNEUF-DU-PAPE, postcode 84230, 232 D4, 241 C3

Domaine de Beaurenard/Paul Coulon; Domaine de Cabrières* 241 B3: The Arnaud family guarantee that their red wine will keep for at least 20 years. **Domaine Chante Cigale***: Aristocratic, serious wine for laying down, made by Noël Sabon and Christian Favier. **Domaine Chante Perdrix/Frères Nicolet 241 D4; Domaine Jean Deydiers & Fils/Les Clefs d'Or; Domaine Font de Michelle; Château Fortia* 241 C4**: Red wine of great distinction, frequently with a note of elegance. The white is

marginally less good. The owner is Baron Pierre Le Roy de Boiseaumarié, the son of the man who drew up the appellation contrôlée regulations for Châteauneuf-du-Pape. **Château de la Gardine 241 C3; Domaine du Grand Tinel; Domaine du Haut des Terres Blanches 241 C4; Château Maucoil 241 B3; Clos du Mont-Olivet/Frères Sabon; Domaine de Mont-Redon* 241 B3**: Property of nearly 100 hectares (247 acres) that offers classic red wine and a fragrant, fruity white. **Louis Mousset***: Firm with various excellent Châteauneuf wines. The best is from its own Château des Fines Roches: a monumental but far from clumsy wine. **Domaine de Nalys*241 C4**: The white wine here is excellent; better than the red, which is soon ready for drinking. **Château La Nerte* 241 D4**: The first estate to do its own bottling, in

1785. A traditional rich red wine. **Clos de l'Oratoire des Papes; Clos des Papes/Paul Avril* 241 C3**: Very good, well-balanced red Châteauneuf with finesse and personality. The Avril family have been making wine here for three centuries. **Père Anselme**: A firm that produces various qualities, under a number of names. In general the Châteauneuf-du-Pape is good. **Domaine du Père Caboche***: Delicious and charming white wine and a striking red. The owner is Jean-Pierre Boisson. **Caves St-Pierre**: Concentrates on quantity – but with a good Châteauneuf: Château St-André. **Domaine de la Serrière/Michel Bernard; Domaine de la Solitude/Famille Lançon 241 C4; Château Rayas/Jacques Reynaud* 241 B4**: Well-structured, stylish wine, usually of very high quality. There are many old vines, in sandy soil. The

remarkable Côtes du Rhône from Château de Fonsalette is also made here. **Domaine Trintignant 241 B4; Château de Vaudieu/Gabriel Meffre 241 C4; Domaine du Vieux Lazaret***: Meaty and complete red wine. The energetic owner is Jérôme Quiot. **Domaine de Vieux Télégraphe* 241 C5**: Fermentation in stainless-steel tanks is followed by at most one year in cask. The red wine is broad and complex with a long finish.

COURTHEZON, postcode 84350

Château de Beaucastel*: The Perrin brothers use all 13 permitted grape varieties and ingenious vinification to make one of the very best wines of the district. This is the banker's Châteauneuf-du-Pape.

PROVENCE

▲ The Grand Canyon du Verdon carves its way through the limestone uplands of Provence in a 21km course of considerable grandeur. Until early in this century it | was virtually unexplored, but now two roads, beside the river and along the crest, allow visitors to view the great cliffs and the green waters of the Verdon.

Since World War II no other region in France has attracted more interest than Provence. Every summer an influx of northern Europeans fills an increasing number of flats, hotels and camping sites. The attraction lies in a unique combination of natural factors. Not only is the climate mild and very pleasant (with nearly twice as many hours of sun as London, for example), but the landscape (until the developers descend) is extraordinarily beautiful. The coast – the Côte d'Azur – is a string of beaches, bays, inlets and massed rocks. Inland, rugged mountain massifs are interspersed with plateaux, valleys and occasional spectacular ravines. The vegetation is luxuriant. Hill and mountain sides are often covered with forests; the ground is carpeted with bright flowers, herbs and thick undergrowth. It goes without saying that winegrowing is part of this earthly paradise. As early as the sixth century BC the Greeks were planting vines here. The Romans, who arrived later and stayed about 600 years, also made wine; much of it was exported to Rome.

The Roman heritage is still remarkably strong in Provence: many a farm is on the site of a Roman villa, and the towns display buildings and antiquities to rival those of Italy. Even in the Dark Ages, Provence maintained a hold on civilized life. During the early Middle Ages, Provence experienced a flowering of culture unparalleled in Europe. Troubadours enriched the Provençal language, the tradition of courtly love enhanced a culture and way of life in stark contrast to the beastly conditions then prevailing in "the north". Provence still feels a place apart, reflecting its many centuries of independence: it only became a formal part of France in 1481.

Wine has been and is a natural part of the civilized heritage of Provence, but strangely there is little tradition of excellence. In California – where conditions are climatically very similar – they say that a rich and sophisticated clientele is essential for the growth of a fine-wine industry. Provence has the rich, but – so far at least – it has not got the wine. Gastronomy, by contrast, flourishes. Some superb restaurants take the native olive oil and seafood tradition, modify it according to the tenets of nouvelle cuisine, and produce some superb food. It is a pity that the diners still often have to turn to Bordeaux, Burgundy and the rest of France for refreshment of matching quality.

There are signs, however, of a new spirit abroad in the wine world of Provence. As elsewhere in France – and in the New World – it is people owning relatively small estates who are setting the pace. Such estates can, with modern equipment, investment in quality vines and technical know-how, make excellent wines.

For the wine visitor, Provence offers the chance to combine a visit to the vineyards with a beach holiday. Another aspect of the region is sometimes overlooked. Its clear light and superb climate attracted many of the giants of modern art, and their legacy is a string of remarkable museums. Nice, the capital of the Côte d'Azur, has a museum devoted to Chagall and another to Matisse, and the frescos by Cocteau in the waterfront chapel at Villefranche are much praised.

Geographically and historically, Provence (the name is derived from Provincia Romana) is made up of the départements of Alpes de Haute-Provence, Alpes-Maritimes, Bouches-du-Rhône, Var and Vaucluse. In wine terms it excludes most of the Vaucluse, which is in the Rhône region. Nevertheless, we are still dealing with an enormous territory which has been divided into ten districts.

The largest appellation contrôlée is Côtes de Provence. This is made up of 85 communes around the Massif des Maures which follows the coastline in a north-easterly direction from Toulon. For decades Côtes de Provence has been known mainly for its strong, dry and rather dull rosé, drunk mainly on the spot by easy-to-please tourists. This less-than-interesing wine has not done the wine image of Provence much good and is why enormous efforts have been made since the 1970s to improve the quality and quantity of its red wine. Marked improvements can be noted on both fronts. Red wine now makes up a third of the total harvest – often of surprisingly good quality (especially some of the estate wines). Certain of the rosés should no longer be underestimated, either. White Côtes de Provence is also produced but is often lacking in freshness and liveliness.

There are two smaller appellations contrôlées west of Côtes de Provence. One owes its name to the elegant town of Aix-en-Provence, the second to the picturesque village of Les Baux-de-Provence, built on a rocky outcrop. In some ways, both regions are ahead of Côtes de Provence, although they acquired their appellation contrôlée status years later. Red wines play a more important part here, and Cabernet Sauvignon is used with great success. This Bordeaux grape gives the various red wines a quality that is rarely found in the Côtes de Provence. Georges Brunet of Château Vignelaure (at Rians, Coteaux d'Aix-en-Provence) has done pioneering work with this grape variety.

North of Coteaux d'Aix-en-Provence lies the Montagne du Lubéron, 1,100 metres (3,600 feet) above sea level, now entirely a nature reserve. At the foot of the mountain lie the vineyards of the Côtes du Lubéron. These make mainly red wines. More than 90 percent of the harvest is handled by cooperatives and the wine is supple and uncomplicated. But quality wine with character can also be found from some of the private estates. The Coteaux de Pierrevert district borders the Côtes du Lubéron on the east. This region is still being developed. Up to now the wines (mostly red) have been quite light and not particularly exciting, but the potential for more interesting quality is there.

In 1984 the Coteaux Varois was promoted from Vin de Pays to VDQS, which fulfilled the ambition of some serious wine growers there. As in the Coteaux d'Aix-en-Provence, remarkable results have been obtained with Cabernet Sauvignon. But most of the wines (red or rosé only) are closely related in style to those of Côtes de Provence.

The first appellations to be created in Provence were the four small districts of Palette, Cassis, Bandol and Bellet. Palette is minute and consists mainly of the vineyards of Château Simone. This small estate can be seen from autoroute N7 (on the south side, just east of Aix-en-Provence). The property makes red, rosé and white wines.

The little port town of Cassis is sheltered by steep rocky hills and enjoys a very warm microclimate. Mainly white grape varieties are cultivated in the mostly calcareous soil. The grapes ripen perfectly so that white Cassis always has body and combines beautifully with a strongly seasoned dish such as *bouillabaisse*. The better wines can be more floral than fruity. Red and rosé Cassis are often quite rough.

Bandol, also on the coast, is some 20 kilometres (12 miles) to the east. Bandol is the largest of the four small districts and consists of eight communes or areas. They are surrounded and crossed by mountain ridges, alternating with flat plateaus. Bandol had always been known as a red-wine region, although quite a lot of rosé and a small amount of white is produced. Red Bandol must consist of at least half Mourvèdre, a vigorous, richly coloured grape with a lot of tannin and character and often an aroma of blackberry. Because of its harsh taste when young, the regulations require red Bandol to mature for at least 18 months in wooden casks.

The fourth district, Bellet, is hidden in the hills behind Nice. Because of increasing urban sprawl and other reasons, the appellation status was nearly taken away in 1947. It is thanks to the Bagnis family, owners of the Château de Crémat, that wine growing was revived just in time. In spite of this the district remains small, with less than 50 hectares (124 acres) of vineyards. It produces approximately equal amounts of white, rosé and red wines. On the whole the white – gently refreshing, elegant and subtle – is the best, but some red and rosé wines can also be very pleasant. Its price reflects its privileged location.

TRAVEL INFORMATION

Traditional Provençal cuisine relies heavily on fish from the Mediterranean: anchovies, red mullet, bream, sun fish and so on. Shellfish, vegetables, herbs and garlic also play an important part. The best-known Provençal dish is *bouillabaisse*, described by the gastronome Curnonsky as "the golden soup" (partly because of the saffron used in it). Another famous fish soup is *bourride*. Also well known are *soupe au pistou* (vegetable based with, among other ingredients, garlic, basil and cheese); *pissaladière* (onion tart with anchovy purée and black olives); *ratatouillé* or *ratatouia* and *salade niçoise*. The restaurants below are only a small selection of the innumerable eating places in Provence, and only those in or near wine districts are included.

HOTELS

Le Ventoux, 67 Avenue Victor-Hugo, 84400 Apt, tel. 90 74 07 58. Well-run middle-range hotel with restaurant. Class B.
Hotel Ile Rousse, 83150 Bandol, tel. 94 29 46 86. De luxe beach hotel, with good food. *Demi-pension* obligatory in season. Hotel class A; restaurant Class B.
Bautezar, 13520 Les Baux-de-Provence, tel. 90 97 32 09. Pleasant small hotel. Terrace with view. Restaurant. Class A/B.
Mas de la Bertrande, 13100 Beaureceuil, tel. 42 28 90 09. Well-placed 10km (6 miles) from Aix-en-Provence, near the Montagne Ste-Victoire. Terrace and swimming pool. Regional cuisine with classic and *nouvelle* dishes. Class B.
l'Aiguebrun, 84480 Bonnieux, tel. 90 74 04 14. Near the D943 and a

▶ Right: church in Méounes-les-Montrieux, between Toulon and Brignoles.
▼ Below: the little town of La Garde Freinet, in the Côtes de Provence.

river valley surrounded by trees and flowers. Good cooking. Class A.
Hostellerie Bérard, 83740 La Cadière-d'Azur, tel. 94 90 11 43. One of the best and smartest hotels around Bandol, high up with a fine view. The food is worth a detour and there is a covered terrace. Class B.
La Galinière, 13790 Châteauneuf-le-Rouge, tel. 42 58 62 04. Hotel and restaurant close to the RN7, surrounded by a large park. Riding lessons are available. Class B.
Hostellerie de la Fuste, 04210 La Fuste, tel. 92 72 05 95. One of the best places in the Coteaux du Pierrevert countryside. Flower-bedecked terrace, fine cuisine, luxurious dining room. Hotel class A; restaurant class B.
Hostellerie du Coteau Fleurie, 83360 Grimaud, tel. 94 43 20 17. Charming hotel on the edge of the little town with views over a valley. For good food at low prices try the "menu du marché". Hotel class B; restaurant class C.
Sevan, 84120 Pertuis, tel. 90 79 19 30. Modern complex with chalets, in a

park. Swimming pool; good and reasonably priced food. *Demi-pension* obligatory in season. Hotel class B; restaurant class C.

La Bastide de Tourtour, 83690 Tourtour, tel. 94 70 57 30. Grand hotel in an old fortified building. Good views, park and swimming pool. Excellent restaurant. *Demi-pension* obligatory in season. Hotel class A; restaurant class B.

Les Lavandes, 83690 Tourtour, tel. 94 70 57 11. Pretty hotel in wooded countryside. Swimming pool. *Demi-pension* obligatory in season. Class B.

Le P'tit Hôtel, 83690 Villecroze, tel. 94 70 65 65. Modest, companionable village hotel. Class C.

RESTAURANTS

Arbaud, 19 Cours Mirabeau, 13100 Aix-en-Provence, tel. 42 26 66 88. This restaurant, also a tearoom, was designed and furnished by an antique dealer and deserves a visit for the interior alone – but the food is good too. Class B.

Le Clos de la Villette, 10 Avenue Violette, 13100 Aix-en-Provence, tel. 42 23 30 71. Dishes prepared by a gifted chef. Beautiful garden. Prices at lunchtime are lower than at dinner. Class A/B.

Le Logis du Guetteur, 83460 Les Arcs-sur-Argens, tel. 94 73 30 82. Hotel and restaurant in a quiet location with comfortable rooms. Good food served in a vaulted hall. Class B.

Auberge du Port, 83150 Bandol, tel. 94 29 42 63. Features fish and shellfish. Terrace with a view over the harbour. Class A.

La Réserve, 83150 Bandol, tel. 94 29 42 71. Pleasant restaurant with uncomplicated cooking. Terrace. Class C.

La Cabro d'Or, 13520 Les Baux-de-Provence, tel. 90 97 33 21. Same owners as l'Oustau de Baumanière. This hotel and restaurant has been furnished with solid old furniture and is surrounded by a beautiful garden. Excellent food (*noisettes d'agneau*). Restaurant class B; hotel class A.

l'Oustaû de Baumanière, 13520 Les Baux-de-Provence, tel. 90 54 33 07. Provençal cuisine of the highest calibre. Much of the produce comes from its own garden. The special dishes include *filets de rougets au vin rouge* and *gigot d'agneau en crôute*. Meals are also served on the terrace. Impressive wine list. Also a luxury hotel. Class A.

La Tonnelle des Délices, 83230 Bormes-les-Mimosas, tel. 94 71 34 84. Extremely popular restaurant with contemporary regional dishes and good regional wines. Class B.

Chez Gilbert/Restaurant le Port, 13260 Cassis, tel. 42 01 71 36. Busy

harbour restaurant. Class C.

Le Flibustier, 13260 Cassis, tel. 42 01 02 73. At the harbour entrance. *Terrine du pêcheur*, grilled *rougets* and *filet de morue*. Class B/C.

La Presqu'île, 13260 Cassis, tel. 42 01 03 77. West of the town. Mediterranean fish creatively prepared. Class B.

Castel Lumière, 83330 Le Castellet, tel. 94 32 62 20. Cooking with a regional slant (*daube d'agneau au Bandol blanc*) and an impressive view from the terrace. A few rooms (*demi-pension* obligatory in season). Class B.

La Pergola, 83240 Cavalaire-sur-Mer, tel. 94 64 06 86. Carefully prepared Italian cuisine. Class B.

Grand Hotel Bain, 83840 Comps-sur-Artuby, tel. 94 76 90 06. The ideal place for lunch on the way to the Gorges du Verdon. Lamb and truffle pâté are among the special dishes at this hotel, which dates from 1737. Terrace. Rooms. Class C.

La Brigantine, 83420 La Croix-Valmer, tel. 94 79 67 16. One of the restaurants of the Hotel des Moulins de Paillas, close to the beach. Enjoyable dishes at reasonable prices. *Demi-pension* is obligatory in season. Restaurant class C; hotel class A.

La Calèche, 83300 Draguignan, tel. 94 68 13 97. Not far from the station, offering reasonably reliable Provençal food. Class C.

Auberge Provençale, 13810 Eygalières, tel. 90 95 91 00. Simple dishes perfectly prepared. Terrace. Also a few beautiful rooms. Class C.

Auberge du Vieux Four, 57 Rue Grisolle, 83600 Fréjus, tel. 94 51 56 38. Small establishment with fine cuisine and an interesting wine list. The *patron* cooks and his wife serves the food. Class C.

Bello Visto, 83580 Gassin, tel. 94 56 17 30. The best known of the six restaurants along the promenade at Gassin. Fish dishes and a magnificent view. Class C.

Au Café de France, 83360 Grimaud, tel. 94 43 20 05. Pleasant restaurant with a terrace, on the village square. Adequate to good cooking (but the service can be slow). Class C.

La Réserve, 83380 Les Issambres, tel. 94 96 90 41. Good-value Provençal cooking (basil almost omnipresent). Large terrace. Rooms. Class B.

Auberge Josse, 83510 Lorgues, tel. 94 73 73 55. Fish and lamb cutlets from the grill. Class C.

Hostellerie du Parc, 83340 Le Luc, tel. 94 60 70 01. Prettily appointed hotel and restaurant with a terrace. Good traditional food. Class B.

Les Pignatelles, 83290 La Motte, tel. 94 70 25 70. Creative cooking in a rustic setting. The terrace overlooks

the vineyards. Class C.

Les Sarments, 13114 Puyloubier, tel. 42 29 32 07. Provençal cuisine with flair and inspiration. Class C.

Café des Arts, 83990 St-Tropez, tel. 94 97 02 25. On the Place de Lices with its games of boules. Honest regional dishes. A favourite meeting place for film stars. Class C.

Le Chabichou, 83990 St-Tropez, tel. 94 54 80 00. Favourite eating place for prosperous locals (including film stars). Notable cuisine with fish specialities. Expensive. Class A.

La Romana, 83990 St-Tropez, tel. 94 97 15 50. Italian cuisine, *très Tropézien*, so do not go before 9 or 10 at night. Class A.

Les Chênes Verts, 83690 Tourtour, tel. 94 70 55 06. Small restaurant surrounded by trees, along the road from Tourtour to Villecroze. Refined dishes prepared with fresh ingredients. Class B.

l'Oustau du Vin, 13530 Trets, tel. 42 61 51 51. Attractive menu with seasonal dishes. Expertly compiled wine list. Class C.

Le Concorde, 83550 Vidauban, tel. 94 73 01 19. Good food, friendly service, an extensive wine list and a

view of the village square. Class C.

Au Bien-Être, 83690 Villecroze, tel. 94 70 67 47. Hidden from the road (which goes to Lorgues). Talented owner-chef. Also a few hotel rooms. Restaurant class C; hotel class B.

PLACES OF INTEREST

Only places of interest in towns and villages in the wine districts are mentioned below. Provence is rich in history and art: for example there are works by great artists in Antibes (Musée National Pablo Picasso), Cagnes-sur-Mer (Musée Renoir) and Nice (Musée National Marc Chagall, Musée Matisse). The harbour town of Marseille and the once most elegant Cannes are also, of course, worth visiting.

Aix-en-Provence The Cours Mirabeau, a long avenue shaded by plane trees, runs straight through this university town. In the centre there is a fountain that delivers water at a temperature of 34°C (93°F). Aix owes its foundation to these hot springs which were discovered by the Romans. Besides shops and cafés (especially the famous Les Deux Garçons which was patronized by

▲ Autumn tints the vines in a Provence vineyard, reflecting the hues of the spices — saffron, cayenne — in Port Grimaud's market and on a café sign offering local dishes in Nice. Provence is climatically, culturally and gastronomically Mediterranean. Nice, in particular, cherishes its Italian traditions.

245

Zola and Cocteau) you will notice magnificent 17th- and 18th-century *hotels particuliers* (private residences). The painter Paul Cézanne (1839–1906) was born in Aix, worked there for part of his life and died there. His studio (Avenue Paul-Cézanne) is open to the public. You can see a few of his paintings in the Musée Granet, as well as those of other Provençal artists in the 13th-century Place de St Jean de Malte. The Musée des Tapisseries houses 17th- and 18th-century tapestries (Place des Martyrs de la Résistance); the Musée du Vieil-Aix specializes in the history of the town (17 Rue Gaston-de-Saporta); and the 16th-century town hall contains the 300,000 books of the Méjanes library. Beside cathedral Saint-Sauveur (5th–16th centuries) you will find a romantic baptistry and cloister. The cathedral itself also has many art treasures, including a triptych of the burning bush and 15 Flemish Gobelin tapestries. In contrast, there is a collection of

modern art at the Fondation Vasarely (1 Avenue Marcel-Pagnol). Then 3km (2 miles) north of Aix lies Entremont, the site of a Celtic-Ligurian (3rd–1st century BC) settlement.
Apt Busy town in the Lubéron with the old cathedral of Ste-Anne, which has two crypts, one above the other. Apt also has an archaeology museum.
Les Arcs-sur-Argens Medieval tower, ruins of a 12th-century castle and an early 16th-century altarpiece in the church of St-Jean-Baptiste.
Aubagne Famous for its pottery museum and the French Foreign Legion monument. There is an old quarter in the town.
Aups Some 300 paintings by, among others, Van Dongen and Dufy can be seen in a former chapel.
Bandol Typical holiday town: in winter there are only 7,000 people but in summer numbers swell to 40,000. Visit the exotic garden, with plants from around the world.
Barjols A village full of fountains

and the largest plane tree in Provence. This giant can be found by the *Mairie*.
Les Baux-de-Provence For centuries, a powerful family ruled from the castle here until 1632. The ruins of the castle and the abandoned buildings attract thousands of visitors every year. There is a fine view from the 13th-century castle tower and the Charloun Rieu monument (a Provençal poet). The Baux gave its name to bauxite, discovered here in 1622, from which aluminium is refined.
Ile de Bendor Small island opposite Bandol, with a Provençal village, a few hotels, a zoo, a small maritime museum and a permanent exhibition of 10,000 wine and spirit bottles from all over the world. (Unfortunately, empties can also be seen elsewhere in the region.)
Bonnieux A Lubéron village built on a hillside. In 1983 a bakery museum was opened. Near Bonnieux is the Pont Julien, the only Roman bridge

still intact between Nîmes and Turin.
Bormes-les-Mimosas Picturesque old town with steep streets and flowers everywhere, and the ruins of a 13th-century castle.
Brignoles The Musée du Pays Brignolais is in the palace of the Comtes du Provence. Among the exhibits are the 3rd-century sarcophagus of Gayole (the oldest Christian tomb in France), and an old Provençal kitchen. There is also information about bauxite.
Cassis Much-visited harbour and wine town where several great painters have worked. East of Cassis, Cap Canaille rises 362m (1,200ft) above the sea (panoramic views); while towards the west along the coast you will pass various *calanques*.
Le Castellet Hill village in the Bandol district. Attracts craftsmen who work here. The view is magnificent.
Cogolin Besides wine, this little town produces carpets, cork objects, reeds for wind instruments and pipes. You can see 8,000 such exhibits in the Courieu pipe factory. The old part of Cogolin, higher up the hillside, is worth the short walk.
Draguignan Busy market town (Wednesday and Saturday mornings) with a medieval centre. The Café des Négociants on the market square is ideal for relaxing, where you will also find the 17th-century Tour de l'Horloge and a town museum whose exhibits include a painting of the Battle of Maastricht by Parrocel (1676).
Entrecasteaux The castle towering above the village was bought in 1974 by the Scottish McGarvie-Munn family and restored with much taste and effort. Beautiful modern paintings hang on the walls of the many rooms. Wine lovers will be fascinated by the set of wineglasses designed by Ian McGarvie-Munn. Each wineglass has a bird engraved in the stem.
Flayosc Typical Provençal village with medieval buildings, an old fountain, a wine cooperative and a large church (with an enormous 18th-century painting).
Fréjus The surroundings of this coastal town have been developed in a particularly offensive fashion, and it suffers frequent traffic jams. In the centre of the town, however, there is a group of church buildings including a 13th-century cathedral; a 12th-century cloister; a late 4th-century baptistery, which is one of the earliest in France; and an episcopal palace with an archaeological museum. Fréjus has many Roman ruins: an arena, a theatre, the remains of an aqueduct, a town gate and the Lanterne d'Auguste, a tower with a

hexagonal spire near the harbour. In Caesar's time the quays were 2km (over a mile) long.

Gassin This village, built on the St-Tropez peninsula, is 200m (650ft) above sea level. The centre is for pedestrians only and there is a wonderful view.

Grimaud Now an artists' community, Grimaud is built on a hillside at the foot of a ruined castle. The church is an 11th-century Romanesque basilica and just outside Grimaud there is the pretty Chapelle des Pénitents Blancs (1482).

Iles d'Hyères Three islands that can be seen from various points along the coast, such as Le Lavandou and Cavalaire-sur-Mer. The largest, the Île des Porquerolles, produces a small amount of wine. The islands are a local wildlife reserve.

Lorgues The 12th-century Collégiale St-Martin, and the chapel Notre-Dame-de-Benva with 15th- and 16th-century frescos, are most impressive. There is also a beautiful avenue shaded by plane trees.

Pertuis A quaint centre with its old houses and castle tower. The church of St-Nicolas holds art treasures and its organ is a listed monument. Pertuis is also known as the "Gate of the Lubéron".

Port Grimaud Tasteful and intentionally striking harbour-village with a mooring for nearly every house. Cars are banned. This modern-day Venice is best admired from the village tower.

Ramatuelle Charming village on a hill behind St-Tropez. Many craftsmen and artists have settled here. The road from Ramatuelle to La Croix Valmer offers panoramic views.

St-Maximin-la-Ste-Baume Formerly a place of pilgrimage. The building of the local basilica started at the end of the 13th or beginning of the 14th century. In the 16th century the almshouse, 29m (95ft) high, was built. It has cloisters but no clock tower.

St-Tropez A town irresistibly attractive to tens of thousands of holidaymakers (and film stars). The roads leading to St-Tropez are often blocked by traffic and the harbour is packed with luxurious yachts. The Musée de l'Annonciade has an impressive collection of paintings of the period 1890–1940 (Van Dongen, Dufy, Matisse, Utrillo and so on). The citadel above St-Tropez has the Musée de la Marine, which has a Greek galley among its exhibits.

Salernes Floor and wall tiles are produced here. Salernes has a Romanesque church, three old chapels, a pretty fountain and the ruins of a 13th-century castle.

▲ Top: cork oaks traditionally served the Provence wine industry, although most corks are now imported.

▶ Right: local costume is worn on festival days.

Abbaye du Thoronet Isolated abbey 9km (6 miles) southwest of Lorgues. Sober Romanesque style.

Toulon Important naval centre with various museums such as the Musée de Toulon with mainly modern art (113 Boulevard Maréchal-Leclerc); the Musée Naval with model ships and other items (Place Ingénieur-Monsenergue); and the Musée National du Débarquement with reconstructions of the Allied invasion in 1944 (on Mont Faron, which can be reached by the winding road or by cable car).

La Tour-d'Aigues Castle ruins dating from the 16th century with two regional exhibitions. In the Romanesque church, later enlarged, there is a beautiful group of statues and a throne used by Louis XIII.

Tourtour This "village in the sky" is at the top of a hill. It has a charming square and the post office is in a former castle.

Grand Canyon du Verdon A good 20km (12 miles) long, this river ravine has sheer walls varying from 200 to 1,500m (650 to 4,900ft) in height. Certainly worth a day trip.

Ancienne Chartreuse de la Verne A monastery founded in 1174 with buildings dating from the 16th to 18th century. It is deep in the Massif des Maures, near a spring. Monks returned to live here in 1983.

Villecroze There are caves which can be visited with a guide. The village also has a Romanesque chapel, an ancient clock tower and a park with a waterfall.

Villeneuve-Loubet In the old town centre there is a museum, founded in 1966, dedicated to the legendary chef Auguste Escoffier, with menus, confectionery, a Provençal kitchen, a small wine cellar and many memorabilia commemorating the master himself. Villeneuve-Loubet is west of Nice.

WINE ACTIVITIES

April Wine fair in Brignoles.

Mid-June Wine fair in Pourrières.

July or August *Fête du vin* in Vidauban.

First Sunday after 6 August The *Fête du raisin* in Fréjus.

August Wine festival in St-Tropez.

End of August or beginning of September Wine festivals in Cogolin and La Motte.

Beginning of September Grape harvest festival in Cassis.

Provence has three wine fraternities: l'Orde Illustre des Chevaliers de Méduse (Côtes de Provence), La Confrérie des Echansons de Vidauban (Vidauban wines) and La Confrérie des Comtés de Nice et de Provence (Bellet).

WINE INFORMATION

The Maison des Vins Côtes de Provence is in Les Arcs-sur-Argens.

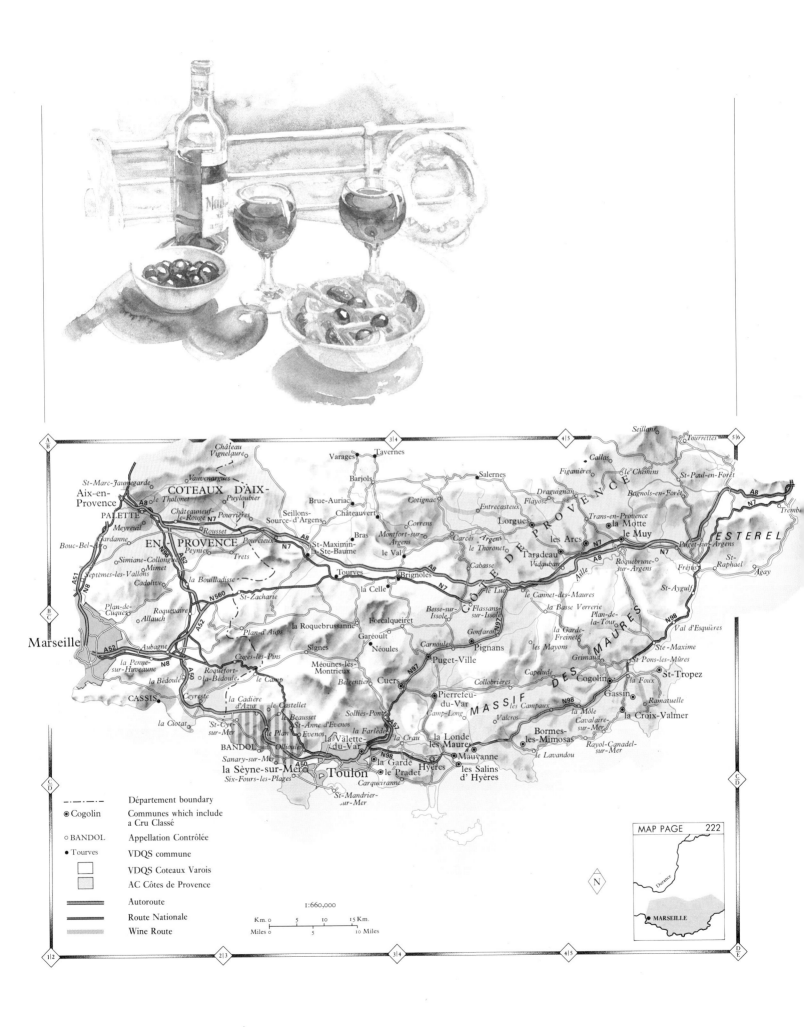

Seillans
Tourrettes

Château
Vignelaure

Varages   Tavernes

Callas
Figanières   le Chênin
St-Paul-en-Forêt

St-Marc-Jaumegarde

Vauvenargues

Barjols   Salernes

Bagnols-en-Forêt

COTEAUX D'AIX-

le Tholonet

Puyloubier

Brue-Auriac

Cotignac

Draguignan
Flayosc

A8
N7
Tremb

Aix-en-
Provence

Châteauneuf-
le-Rouge

Pourrières

Seillons-
Source-d'Argens

Châteauvert

Entrecasteaux

Trans-en-Provence
la Motte

PALETTE

Rousset N7

Correns

Lorgues
les Arcs

le Muy

ESTEREL

Meyreuil

Peynier

Bras

Montfort-sur-
Argens

Carcès   Argens

Puget-sur-Argens

Gardanne

EN-

St-Maximin-
Ste-Baume

le Val

le Thoronet

Taradeau
Vidauban

St-
Raphael

Bouc-Bel-

Trets

Cabasse

Roquebrune-
sur-Argens

Fréjus

Agay

PROVENCE

Simiane-Collongue
Mimet

Pourcieux

Tourves

Brignoles

le Luc

le Cannet-des-Maures

St-Aygulf

Septèmes-les-Vallons

la Bouilladisse

la Celle

N7

la Basse Verrerie

Cadolive

N 560

St-Zacharie

Besse-sur-
Issole

Flassans-
sur-Issole

Plan-de-
la-Tour

Val d'Esquières

Plan-de-
Cuques

Roquevaire
Allauch

St-Zacharie

la Roquebrussanne

Forcalqueiret

Gonfaron

la Garde-
Freinet

Marseille

Aubagne

Plan-d'Aups

Garéoult

Carnoules

les Mayons

Ste-Maxime

la Penne-
sur-Huveaune

Cuges-les-Pins

Signes

Néoules

Puget-Ville

Pignans

Grimaud

St-Pons-les-Mûres

Roquefort-
la-Bédoule

Méounes-les-
Montrieux

Capelude

Cogolin

la Foux

St-Tropez

la Bédoule

le Camp

Belgentier

Cuers

Collobrières

les Campaux

Gassin

Ramatuelle

CASSIS

Ceyreste

la Cadière
d'Azur

le Castellet

Pierrefeu-
du-Var

Camp-Long

la Môle
Cavalaire-
sur-Mer

la Croix-Valmer

la Ciotat

le Beausset

St-Anne d'Evenos

Solliès-Pont

Valcros

Bormes-
les-Mimosas

St-Cyr-
sur-Mer

le Plan
Evenos

la Farlède

la Crau

la Londe
les Maures

Rayol-Canadel-
sur-Mer

BANDOL

Ollioules

la Valette-
du-Var

le Lavandou

Sanary-sur-Mer

N98

la Garde

Mauvanne

la Sèyne-sur-Mer

A50

Hyères

Toulon

le Pradet

les Salins
d'Hyères

Six-Fours-les-Plages

Carqueiranne

St-Mandrier-
sur-Mer

—·—·—   Département boundary

⊙ Cogolin   Communes which include
a Cru Classé

○ BANDOL   Appellation Contrôlée

• Tourves   VDQS commune

▫   VDQS Coteaux Varois

▫   AC Côtes de Provence

════   Autoroute

────   Route Nationale

────   Wine Route

1:660,000

Km. 0   5   10   15 Km.

Miles 0   5   10 Miles

MAP PAGE   222

N

MARSEILLE

PRODUCERS OF SPECIAL INTEREST

BANDOL

LE BEAUSSET, postcode 83330, 247 C3

Domaine de l'Hermitage; Domaine du Val d'Arenc*: Well-made red wines that mature well. The "Cuvée de la Gravière" is especially recommended.

LA CADIERE-D'AZUR, postcode 83740, 247 C3

Domaine Lafran-Veyrolles; Moulin des Costes*: The quality achieved by the Bunan brothers with their red, rosé and white Bandol is only occasionally matched by others. Domaine de la Noblesse; Domaine de Pibarnon*: The highest wine estate in Bandol. Henri de Saint-Victor produces wines that are full of character and often win awards. Domaine des Salettes; Château Vannières.

LE CASTELLET, postcode 83330

Domaine de l'Olivette

LE PLAN-DU-CASTELLET, postcode 83330, 247 C3

Le Galantin; Domaine Ray-Jane; Domaine Tempier: A red wine with character and a charming aroma of fruit; also an invigorating and delicious rosé.

STE-ANNE-DU-CASTELLET, postcode 83330, 247 C3

La Bastide Blanche

STE-ANNE-D'EVENOS, postcode 83330, 247 C3

La Laidière; Château Ste-Anne.

ST-CYR-SUR-MER, postcode 83270, 247 C3

Domaine du Cagueloup; Domaine de Frégate; Château Pradeaux: Traditional wines from old vines, matured in cask for four years.

BELLET

BELLET-DE-NICE, postcode 06200

Château de Crémat*: Leading estate owned by the Bagnis family (who saved the Bellet appellation). Gently refreshing white, red and rosé wines.

ST-ROMAN-DE-BELLET, postcode 06200

Château de Bellet*: Excellent white wine with class. The red and rosé, too, are very successful. Lou Clot de la Touré/Jacques Schneider; Clos St-Vincent/René Gomez.

CASSIS

CASSIS, postcode 13260, 247 C2

Domaine du Bagnol; Clos Boudard; Le Ferme Blanche*: Attractive, refreshing white wines, from a blend of five grape varieties. Mas de Fontblanche; Château de Fontcreuse*: This is the only Cassis château. The white Coteaux Cassidains is the best product. Domaine du Paternel*: An elegant Cassis. Clos Ste-Magdeleine*: Meaty, generous Cassis, made by François Sack.

COTEAUX D'AIX-EN-PROVENCE

LANÇON-DE-PROVENCE, postcode 13680

Château de Calisanne*: A very good "Cuvée Prestige", as well as simpler wines.

PUYRICARD, postcode 13540

Château Grand Seuil

LE PUY-STE-REPARADE, postcode 13610

Domaine Les Bastides*: Sound red "Cuvée Spéciale" matured in wood. Château La Coste*: Château de Fonscolombe*: Important property belonging to the De Saporta family. Very successful red, white and rosé wines, especially the "Cuvée Spéciale".

RIANS, postcode 83560, 247 B3

Château Vignelaure*: Georges Brunet has done pioneering work here – by planting Cabernet Sauvignon, for example. His elegant, characterful red is one of the very best in Provence. Modern art can be admired in the château and cellars. In 1986 an American group acquired a majority shareholding. Château Pigoudet.

ST-CANNAT, postcode 13760, 232 F5

Château de Beaupré*: Baron Double's wines include a delicious, pure rosé. Commanderie de la Bargemone.

VERNEGUES, postcode 13116

Château Bas*: Since 1970 George de Blanquet has produced red wines of a consistently improving quality; his "Cuvée Temple" in particular deserves note. There are ruins of a Roman temple on the estate and a Romanesque chapel.

COTEAUX D'AIX-EN-PROVENCE-LES-BAUX (previously VDQS Coteaux des Baux-de-Provence)

LES BAUX-DE-PROVENCE, postcode 13520, 232 E4

Mas de la Dame; Mas Ste-Berthe.

MOURIES, postcode 13890

Domaine de Lauzières

Château Fonscolombe

ST-ETIENNE-DU-GRES, postcode 13150, 232 E4

Domaine de Trévallon*: Red wine, full of subtlety, the best in the district. The maker is Eloi Dürrbach.

ST-REMY-DE-PROVENCE, postcode 13210, 232 E4

Terres Blanches/Noël Michelin

COTEAUX DE PIERREVERT

PIERREVERT, postcode 04100

La Blaque/Charles Pons-Mure; Domaine de Régusse.

COTEAUX VAROIS

BRUE-AURIAC, postcode 83119, 247 B3

Domaine de St-Estève

GAREOULT, postcode 83136, 247 C3

Domaine des Chaberts

LA ROQUEBRUSSANNE, postcode 83136, 247 C3

Domaine du Loou

ST-MAXIMIN-LA-STE-BAUME, postcode 83470, 247 B3

Domaine du Déffends/Clos de la Truffière*: Exquisite red and rosé wines (including "Rosé d'une Nuit").

VILLECROZE, postcode 83690

Domaine de St-Jean*: Excellently equipped estate where American Alain Hirsch makes exemplary red and rosé wines from Cabernet Sauvignon and other grapes.

COTES DU LUBERON

APT, postcode 84400, 232 E5

Domaine de l'Isolette*: Owner Luc Pinatel repeatedly wins awards with his red and white wines.

BONNIEUX, postcode 84480, 232 E5

Château La Canorgue*: The best estate of the Lubéron, with wines that include a red that could equal a *cru* from the Beaujolais. Jean-Pierre Margan is the owner.

MIRABEAU, postcode 84120

Clos Murabeau [sic]

PERTUIS, postcode 84120, 232 E5

Château Val-Joanis*: Large model estate created from nothing since 1978 by Jean-Louis Chancel. **La Vielle Ferme**: Sound brand of Lubéron wine produced by Jean-Pierre Perrin.

LA TOUR D'AIGUES, postcode 84240

Union des Vignerons des Côtes du Lubéron: Blending, bottling and sales centre for 17 regional cooperatives.

COTES DE PROVENCE

ANTIBES, postcode 06600

Domaines Ott*: Head office of the very active Ott family, who own and successfully manage several well-known wine estates. Among them are Clos Mireille and Château de Selle in Côtes de Provence, and Château Romasson in Bandol. (22 Boulevard Aiguillon.)

LES ARCS-SUR-ARGENS, postcode 83460, 247 B5

Domaine des Hauts de St-Jean*: Henri Pawlowski's wines deserve their countless medals. **Château St-Pierre**; **Château Ste-Roseline***: This estate is a former convent, now listed as a historic monument. Generous red wine, in a striking bottle.

Château Simone

BORMES-LES-MIMOSAS, postcode 83230, 247 C4

Domaine des Campaux; **Domaine de la Malherbe**.

LE CANNET-DES-MAURES, postcode 83340, 247 B4

Domaine Colbert; **Château de Roux**.

COGOLIN, postcode 83310, 247 C5

Château des Garcinières

CUERS, postcode 83390, 247 C5

Château de Gairoird: Count Deydier de Pierrefeu makes an enjoyable and refreshing white, among other wines.

FLASSANS, postcode 83340, 247 C4

Commanderie de Peyrassol: Yves and Françoise Rigord produce an extensive range of wines, among them their excellent special *cuvées*.

FREJUS, postcode 83600, 247 B5

Domaine de Curebéasse*: Jacques Paquette's white wine is one of the best in Provence, and his red and rosé are also good.

GASSIN, postcode 83990, 247 C5

Château Barbeyrolles; **Domaine de Berthaud**; **Les Maîtres-Vignerons de la Presqu'île de St-Tropez**: Association of a dozen quality-conscious estates and a number of cooperatives. **Château Minuty**.

LA LONDE-LES-MAURES, postcode 83250, 247 C4

Domaine de Maravenne; **Domaine St-André de Figuière***: Intensely fragrant, lively, red "Cuvée Spéciale". **Domaine de la Source Ste-Marguerite**.

LORGUES, postcode 83510, 247 B4

Castel Roubine*: M. Hallgren, a Dane, who bought this estate in 1979, has expanded the vineyards and improved quality.

LE LUC, postcode 83340, 247 B4

Domaine de la Bernarde*: Property with modern equipment producing admirable rosé and good red wines. **Domaine Gavoty**.

LA MOTTE, postcode 83920, 247 B5

Domaine du Jas d'Esclans; **Domaine de St-Roman d'Esclans**.

PIERREFEU-DU-VAR, postcode 83390, 247 C4

Domaine de l'Aumérade; **Vignobles Kennel**; **Château Montaud**.

PIGNANS, postcode 83790, 247 C4

Domaine de Rimaurescq*: Estate owned by the Isnard family for three centuries.

PUYLOUBIER, postcode 13114, 247 B2

Domaine Richeaume*: An admirable estate both for its architecture and for its wines. Henning Hoesch is the owner.

ROQUEBRUNE-SUR-ARGENS, postcode 83520, 247 B5

Domaine des Planes*: The wine growers Christophe and Ilse Rieder make exemplary wines. The red Côtes de Provence comes in two styles.

ROUSSET, postcode 13790, 247 B2

Château de la Bégude

ST-JULIEN, postcode 83550

Château St-Julien-d'Aille

TRETS, 13530, 247 B3

Château Ferry Lacombe; **Château Grand' Boise**; **Mas de Cadenet**.

LE VAL, postcode 83143, 247 B4

Château Réal Martin

VIDAUBAN, postcode 83550, 247 B4

Domaine des Féraud*: One of the leading estates: white, red and rosé are all excellent. **Domaine Peissonel***: Pierre Lemaître is a fervent promoter of the wines of Provence. His own red wine is well above average.

PALETTE

MEYREUIL, postcode 13590, 247 B2

Château Simone*: Using a rich range of grape varieties, the Rougier family produces a red wine that in good years creates a veritable symphony of tastes. The château also produces a rosé and two styles of white.

LANGUEDOC

etween the southern spurs of the Massif Central and the sandy beaches of the Mediterranean lies France's largest wine region, the Languedoc. Almost a third of all France's vineyards is concentrated on these sunny fertile plains. The region covers three important départements: Aude, Gard and Hérault. Most of the wine areas in these départements are included in the Languedoc with the exception of the northwest corner of Gard, where the districts of Lirac and Tavel form part of the Rhône wine region.

Although the industry was begun by the Romans (or, indeed, the Greeks), for centuries the wines were only of regional importance and production was much lower than it is now. This changed in the seventeenth century when the Canal du Midi, linking the Mediterranean and the Atlantic, was built and trade increased. Much more important, however, was the introduction of the railways in the nineteenth century. These made it possible for large quantities of Languedoc wine to be transported cheaply to Paris and other northern cities. The availability of cheap wine pushed up demand; the daily glass of wine became the norm. Between 1840 and 1900, consumption in the Paris region alone rose from some 2 million hectolitres to around 5 million hectolitres a year. The Languedoc became France's "wine reservoir". Quantity was everything: the largest possible amount of wine at the lowest possible price.

In this century the tide turned. Wine consumption in France itself went down and competition from other countries increased. There was (and still is) an unsaleable surplus in the Languedoc and the growers protested. How fierce these protests sometimes become is reflected in a simple memorial on one of the approach roads to Narbonne, marking the spot where a grower lost his life. The only solution was to switch the emphasis from quantity to quality, and intensive work has been going on for several years. Organizations such as the Comités Interprofessionnels of Coteaux du Languedoc, Corbières and Minervois have greatly stimulated quality winegrowing, and a new generation of viticulteurs has been trained by the University of Montpellier. The authorities are also encouraging the uprooting of vineyards on flat, overproductive land: Aude and Hérault shed 30,000 hectares (74,000 acres) of unworthy, if not appalling, vineyards between 1976 and 1984. Growers are encouraged to concentrate on the slopes. With lower production per hectare and better techniques, the Languedoc has the potential to become the California of France.

It is symptomatic of these trends that during the 1980s several Languedoc districts were awarded appellation contrôlée status: in 1982 Faugères and St-Chinian; in 1985 Coteaux du Languedoc, Corbières and Minervois: in 1986 Costières du Gard. By far the largest district is Coteaux du Languedoc, with 121 communes between Narbonne and Nîmes. A number of communes and groups of communes have been elevated to the status of Cru and can cite their names on their labels. They include:

Cabrières At the foot of the Pic de Vissous. Supple, pale pink rosé is the speciality, but the red wines can also be very successful.

La Clape Between Narbonne and the Mediterranean. Produces elegant, full-bodied red wines, delicious whites and good rosés.

(Coteaux de) La Méjanelle Southeast of Montpellier. Often rather light reds to drink young, but also more substantial wines.

Montpeyroux In the north of the Languedoc. Sinewy reds.

Picpoul de Pinet South of Pézenas. White wines, refreshing and tart.

Pic St-Loup Named after a high peak. Produces both light and fruity and richly coloured, full-bodied red wines.

Quatourze Southwest of Narbonne. Solid red wines for keeping.

(Coteaux de) St-Christol Between Montpellier and Nîmes. Pleasant, reasonably firm reds and supple rosés.

St-Drézéry Between Montpellier and Nîmes. The smallest Cru. Produces light reds as well as dark, mouth-filling wines with oak and fruit.

St-Georges-d'Orques Northwest of Montpellier. Usually sturdy red wines. In the seventeenth century they were exported to Russia.

St-Saturnin In the northern Languedoc. The only producer, an excellent cooperative, makes full-bodied red wines as well as white and rosé.

(Coteaux de) Vérargues Between Montpellier and Nîmes, near Lunel. Elegant red wines and also refreshing rosés.

▲ Above: the wide sandy beaches and lagoons on the Languedoc coast have provided sites for some futuristic new holiday complexes.
▶ Right: much Midi wine goes into apéritifs.

About half of the extensive St-Chinian district – a good 20,000 hectares (49,400 acres) – produces Coteaux du Languedoc; the other half uses the appellation St-Chinian. The story goes that in the last century wine from St-Chinian was given to patients in some Paris hospitals because of its invigorating qualities. It is easy to understand why: St-Chinian is vigorous, flavoursome and usually deep red in colour. The wine from neighbouring Faugères is similar.

Intertwined with the Coteaux du Languedoc appellation is that of Clairette du Languedoc, an untidy triangle north of Pézenas, producing white wine made from the Clairette grape. Using modern techniques, some growers are making fruity, stylish wines, but the bulk of Clairette du Languedoc is rather boring cooperative wines. The situation is similar with Clairette de Bellegarde, an enclave in the Costières du Gard, which is made up of 24 communes. The better reds have colour, class and tannin. There are also clean, refreshing rosés and whites, but most of the wines lack character.

On the west side of the Languedoc lies the hill country of Corbières, one of the most interesting districts of the south. Planting and winemaking

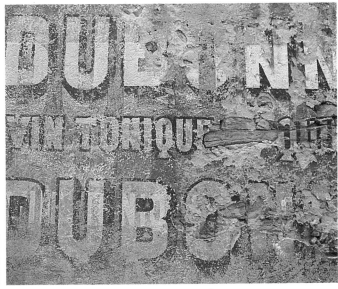

greatly improved during the 1970s and 80s, which has meant a dramatic rise in the quality of many of the red wines and some of the whites. Vast areas of the large region, which stretches from Narbonne and the coast to more than 50 kilometres (30 miles) inland, are quiet and unspoiled. Peaceful villages nestle in the landscape of mountains, hills, valleys and plains, and the drab facades of the houses often hide elegant interiors with beautiful floor tiles, moulded ceilings, imposing fireplaces and antique furniture (Spain is not so far away). Closely related to Corbières is Fitou, a red wine from two enclaves in the Corbières district.

Minervois, like Corbières, has undergone a renaissance. The two districts are separated by the Aude river valley and in the Minervois the terrain is rougher, the climate drier, the wine usually leaner, often livelier. The vineyards are surrounded by hills and plateaux with shrubby undergrowth, wild flowers and fragrant herbs; the tranquility here is even more striking than in Corbières. The many very good red wines, from cooperatives as well as private estates, make the district well worth following. Minervois rosés and white wines can also be good.

Two smaller districts, somewhat overshadowed by Corbières and Minervois, are the VDQS Côtes du Cabardès et de l'Orbiel (whose wines can also be sold as Cabardès), north and northeast of Carcassonne, and the Côtes de la Malepère (on the other side of Carcassonne).

In the Languedoc, with its abundance of red wines, Limoux occupies a special place. A very high-quality sparkling white wine, Blanquette de Limoux, is produced here (and in some 40 surrounding communes). The wine is named after the Mauzac grape, known here as Blanquette (the leaves are dusty white underneath), from which it is made. Clairette, Chardonnay and Chenin are also used, in smaller proportions, giving the wine more fragrance, finesse, fruit and acidity. Like champagne, Blanquette de Limoux acquires its sparkle from secondary fermentation in bottle. Some 80 to 85 percent of the wine is produced by the large modern cooperative at Limoux. A still white, Limoux Nature, is also made, but the quality is far below that of the sparkling wine. The Limoux red, Anne des Joyeuses, is a more interesting proposition.

Muscat wine has been produced in the Languedoc for some 2,000 years: the Roman historian Pliny the Younger thoroughly approved of the Muscat from Frontignan. The only permitted grape is the Muscat à Petits Grains, and fermentation is interrupted by adding five to ten percent alcohol. A certain proportion of the sugar – at least 125 grams per litre – consequently remains in the wine. By law, the minimum alcohol content must be 15 percent. It is, in fact, a Vin Doux Naturel. In France, Muscat wine is often drunk as an apéritif, but it also makes a good accompaniment to a dessert.

There are four districts for Muscat. The largest and best known is Frontignan: Muscat de Frontignan has a good reputation for its reliable (if not remarkable) quality. Muscat de Lunel is slightly more refined; the town of Lunel proudly calls itself La Cité du Muscat. The highest alcohol and sugar content is found in Muscat de Mireval; Muscat de St-Jean-de-Minervois often outdoes the others in fullness and nuance. Production is dominated by cooperatives.

Finally, there are the Vins de Pays. As indicated on the maps on pages 216 and 256, the Aude, Gard and Hérault départements have some 60 areas producing Vins de Pays, with a further five in the Pyrénées-Orientales (Roussillon). In volume, Vins de Pays de l'Hérault and Vins de Pays de l'Aude lead with an annual 800,000 and 700,000 hectolitres (almost 9 million and 8 million cases) respectively. By contrast, less than 1,000 hectolitres of Vins de Pays des Monts de la Grage is produced annually.

The wines also vary widely in quality. The great majority are simple but quite a few makers are producing wines of a sometimes surprising standard. The very fact that the regulations laid down for Vins de Pays are less restrictive than those for VDQS and appellation contrôlée wines means that superior grape varieties from outside the local district can be used. Cabernet Sauvignon, for example, seems to be giving excellent results and Merlot, too, is on the way up. Already some Vins de Pays are easily the match of any appellation contrôlée wine from the area. Given their success, their numbers will undoubtedly grow.

Autoroute

Route Nationale

Wine Route

TOURING MAP PAGES

220
221

NÎMES

MONTPELLIER

MARSEILLE

PERPIGNAN

1:625,000

Km. 0   10   20 Km.

Miles 0   5   10 Miles

TRAVEL INFORMATION

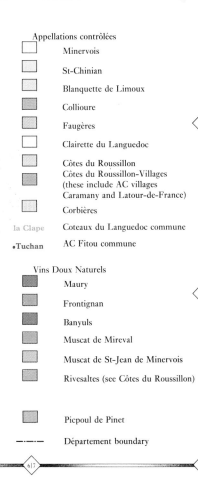

Confits and *cassoulets* are specialities of the Languedoc, as they are all over southwestern France, and these hearty dishes are served in many regional restaurants. Languedoc is also plentifully provided with fish – both sea and freshwater – and the Bassin de Thau produces vast quantities of oysters and other shellfish. Fish soups such as *bouillabaisse* and *bourride* are often found on menus. Charcuterie (various kinds of sausages) and lamb are also popular. Some towns have their own specialities: Nîmes has *brandade* (dry salted cod, pounded with milk, oil, garlic and lemon juice) and Pézenas *petits pâtés* (stuffed minced mutton sweetened with brown sugar).

HOTELS

Hostellerie de l'Evêché, 11580 Alet-les-Bains, tel. 68 69 90 25. Quiet situation near the cathedral ruins. Traditional plumbing. Regional cooking. Hotel class B/C; restaurant class C.

Hotel Lou Tamarou, Route de Pézenas, 34500 Béziers, tel. 67 30 12 76. Very comfortable modern hotel near the entrance to the town. No parking problem. Class B.

Résidence des Aubuns, 30132 Caissargues, tel. 66 70 10 44. On the road to Nîmes airport. Modern comfort, swimming pool and restaurant. Class B.

Domaine d'Auriac, 11000 Carcassonne, tel. 68 25 72 22. Luxury hotel surrounded by a park and vineyards. Excellent restaurant. Swimming pool. Hotel class A; restaurant class B.

Pont Vieux, 32 Rue Trivalle, 11000 Carcassonne, tel. 68 25 24 99. Simple, small hotel, not far from the Cité. Class B.

Le Tassigny, 11200 Lézignan-Corbières, tel. 68 27 11 51. Classically furnished rooms. The restaurant Le Tournedos is much patronized by locals. Hotel class B; restaurant class C.

La Résidence, 6 Rue de ler Mars, 11100 Narbonne, tel. 68 32 19 41. Very pleasant hotel in the centre. Friendly reception. Class B.

Hotel du Cheval Blanc, 30000 Nîmes, tel. 66 67 20 03. Renovated hotel near the Roman arena. The restaurant has an attractive menu. Class B.

Le Relais de Val d'Orbieu, 11200 Ornaisons, tel. 68 27 10 27. Very quiet high-class hotel with good cuisine. Swimming pool. Hotel class A/B; restaurant class B.

Château de Violet, 11160 Peyrac-Minervois, tel. 68 78 10 42. Beautifully furnished château-hotel with park, swimming pool and restaurant. Hotel class A/B; restaurant class B.

Hotel Genieys, 34120 Pézenas, tel. 67 98 13 99. Small town hotel; varying plumbing. Country food. *Demi-pension* obligatory in season. Class C.

Auberge de la Tour, 34290 Valros, tel. 67 98 52 01. The rooms at the back look out over vineyards. Fairly good food. Hotel class B; restaurant class C.

Le Balajan, 34110 Vic-la-Gariole, tel. 67 48 13 99. Functional hotel – its white paint stands out against the green of the Frontignan vineyards. The plumbing varies. Also a restaurant. Hotel class B/C; restaurant class C.

RESTAURANTS

Au Petit Voilier, 11100 Bages, tel. 68 41 38 63. Overlooks the lake of Bages, south of Narbonne. The menu is mainly fish-based: a very typical regional dish is *bourride d'anguilles*. Class C.

L'Oliver, 12 Rue Boildieu, 34500 Béziers, tel. 67 28 86 64. Small bistro-style restaurant, clever and creative cuisine. Class B.

La Madrague, 34140 Bouzigues, tel. 67 78 32 34. Good menu based on fish and shellfish. Class C.

Le Languedoc, 32 Allée d'Iéna, 11000 Carcassonne, tel. 68 25 22 17. Good menu with regional dishes (*cassoulet au confit de canard*). Inner courtyard. Class C.

*Petites Daurades
Friture
Le Kg 51f.too*

Logis de Trencavel, 286 Avenue Général-Leclerc, 11000 Carcassonne, tel. 68 71 09 51. Good cooking and a wide range of regional wines. Also a hotel. Class B.

Auberge du Pont Lévis (just east of the Cité), 11000 Carcassonne, tel. 68 25 55 23. Excellent restaurant, on the first floor (*feuilleté de coquilles St-Jacques, foie gras*). Class B.

l'Art du Feu, 34160 Castries, tel. 67 70 05 97. Good regional cooking at agreeable prices. Class C.

Le St-Anne, 11190 Couiza, tel. 68 74 26 50. Cosy. Order the cheap menu. Class C.

Auberge de la Corneille, 11300 Cournanel, tel. 68 31 17 84. Good cooking at reasonable prices. Class C.

Auberge de Cucugnan, 11350 Cucugnan, tel. 68 45 40 84. *Coq au vin* is a speciality. Class C.

Chez Odette, 11560 Fitou-Village, tel. 68 45 72 89. Regional dishes: *gigot d'agneau au Fitou, poulet au Muscat*. Class C.

Chez Léonce, 34510 Florensac, tel. 67 77 03 05. Old establishment but contemporary cuisine, including many fish-based dishes. Also a hotel. Restaurant class B; hotel class C.

Capion, 34150 Gignac, tel. 67 57 50 83. Regional dishes (two menus) and a good selection of local wines. Also a hotel, *demi-pension* obligatory in season. Class B.

Le Remise, 34800 Lacoste, tel. 67 96 35 76. Strictly regional cuisine, such as home-made *terrines* and *confits*. Class C.

Maison de la Blanquette, 11300 Limoux, tel. 68 31 01 63. Wine growers' wives serve the food and there is cooperative-produced wine with, for example, *cassoulet maison en fricassée de Limoux*. Class C.

Hostellerie du Palais, 34400 Lunel, tel. 67 71 11 39. Traditional food in a rustic setting. Garden and hotel. Restaurant class C; hotel class B/C.

Les Aliberts, 34210 Minerve, tel. 68 91 22 95. An old fortified farm high above Minerve: the wines of the abbey of Fontfroide used to be aged here. Special dishes: lamb and guinea fowl. Class C.

Relais Chantovent, 34210 Minerve, tel. 68 91 22 96. Surroundings full of atmosphere and delicious, inexpensive food. Also hotel rooms. Class C.

Hotel Montpellierain des Vins du Languedoc, 7 Rue Jacques-Coeur, 34000 Montpellier, tel 67 60 42 41. Promotional and information centre for the region, where you can also eat. Class C.

l'Alsace, 2 Avenue Pierre-Semard, 11100 Narbonne, tel. 68 65 10 24. No specialities from Alsace, but excellent *bouillabaisse* and grilled langoustine. Class C.

Le Floride, 66 Boulevard Frédéric-Mistral, 11100 Narbonne, tel. 68 32 05 52. Relaxed atmosphere with *fruits de mer* a speciality (the *coquilles St-Jacques à la Provençale* are famous), as well as *cassoulet* and game. Class B.

Le Réverbère, 4 Place des Jacobins, 11100 Narbonne, tel. 68 32 39 18. Highly thought-of restaurant in the style of the *belle époque* where the cuisine is inventive and of high quality. Class B.

Also in Narbonne: there is a very good Chinese restaurant patronized by the wine men of Narbonne. Ask one of them to show you where it is.

Mapotel Imperator/l'Enclos de la Fontaine, Quai de la Fontaine, 30000 Nîmes, tel. 66 21 90 30. A pleasant old restored house with a charming garden. Good cooking with market-fresh ingredients. Also a hotel. Restaurant class B; hotel class A/B.

La Tour Sarraisne, 34310 Poilhes-la-Romain, tel. 67 93 41 31. Former smithy, modern paintings, light and stylish cooking. Class B.

Lou Flambadou, 34360 St-Chinian, tel. 67 38 13 02. Inn with regional dishes and wines. Class C.

La Palangrotte, 1 Rampe Paul-Valéry, 34200 Sète, tel. 67 74 80 35. Probably the best fish restaurant in the area. Class C.

PLACES OF INTEREST

Aigne Minervois village where the streets wind in a snail-shell pattern around the 12th-century church.

Aigues-Mortes This town "of the dead water", completely surrounded by towers and walls, was built at the end of the 13th century in the middle of salt marshes. A little in front of the town wall stands the Tour de Constance in which there is a chapel, and where there used to be a prison. The vast cellars of the salt and wine company Salins du Midi (Listel) lie just outside the town.

Alet-les-Bains Artists' village south of Limoux.

Béziers Prosperous town and the centre of the wine trade of the Hérault and Aude, but with a tragic history: in 1209, the population was slaughtered by a crusader army. The Musée du Bitterois (7 Rue Massol) is dedicated to local history (some of the exhibits relate to wine) and next to it is the Musée des Beaux-Arts. The former cathedral of St-Nazaire (13th to 15th century) has an impressive fortified façade; the cloister is used as a museum of sculpture. Next to the 19th-century arena, well known for its bull fights, are the ruins of a Roman amphitheatre. The gardens of the

Plateau des Poètes are very beautiful. The Béziers-born Pierre Paul de Riquet (1604–1680) built the Canal du Midi, which links the Atlantic to the Mediterranean, and designed the port town of Sète.

Cabrières Prehistoric caves, a mineworker's grave from the Bronze Age and Gallo-Roman excavations.

Carcassonne A famous profile. The town is made up of two parts. The *ville bas* or "low town" dates from the 13th century and has two interesting churches: the 13th-century cathedral of St-Michel, with some remarkable works of art, and the church of St-Vincent (beginning of the 14th century). The Musée des Beaux-Arts includes works by local and Italian painters, and also by Salvador Dali.

The other (and much more famous) part of the town is the old Cité, which is built on a hill, a stronghold with double defence walls. In the mid-1800s work was begun by the imaginative medievalist Viollet-le-Duc to completely restore the Cité. A castle dating from the 12th century houses an archaeological museum; the church of St-Nazaire is thought to date from the 8th century; the stained-glass windows in the Gothic chancel are impressive. But it is the encircling walls, turrets and moat that leave an impression. Walt Disney could not have done the Middle Ages better – especially at night, with floodlights blazing.

Castries The 16th-17th century château that overlooks Castries is the largest in the Languedoc. It is surrounded by gardens and terraces designed by Le Nôtre, and has an aqueduct 7km (more than 4 miles) long built by Pierre Paul de Riquet (see Béziers above).

Caunes-Minervois Fortified village at the mouth of the Gorges de l'Argent-Double, with houses dating from the 16th and 17th centuries. Near by are the quarries that provided the marble for the columns of the Trianon in Versailles.

Clermont-l'Hérault Old fortified township with medieval walls, gates, eight towers, a 12th-century castle ruin and three large churches. The church of St-Paul (13th–15th century) has the most beautiful rose window in the Languedoc.

Cucugnan Wine village built on a hilltop and written about by Alphonse Daudet. Not far from it is the Château de Quéribus (13th–14th century) with the remains of walls and polygonal keep. A gem, well worth the exercise to reach the top.

Duilhac-sous-Peyrepertuse The Château de Peyrepertuse, overlooking Duilhac, is a splendid example of local military architecture. The ruin

dates mainly from the 13th century.

Oppidium d'Ensérune Archaeological site west of Béziers, that dates from the 6th century BC. The excavation lies along the summit of a hill and there is a marvellous view of the plain below.

Faugères Ruins of a temple and a 12th-century chapel.

Fitou The chapel of St-Aubin-du-Pla, which dates from the 9th century, stands in a bleak spot northeast of the village.

Abbaye de Fontfroide Partly 12th-, partly 13th-century (and later rebuilt) Cistercian abbey of light pink sandstone with a lovely garden. In good shape, and viticulturally in the Corbières.

Frontignan The town museum is housed in a former chapel and also contains wine-related exhibits. The church of St-Paul is mainly 14th century. In Frontignan-Plage, the cellars of the vermouth manufacturer Noilly Prat are open to the public.

Gallician The Musée du Vignoble Boissy d'Anglas has, among other exhibits, a 16th-century wine press and coopers' tools. The collection was put together by a wine grower.

La Grande Motte Tourist town built in the 1970s. It is dominated by pyramid-like apartment blocks.

Laurens Perhaps the oldest commune in France and centre of the appellation contrôlée Faugères. It is famous for its marble.

Lézignan-Corbières Very interesting Musée de la Vigne et du Vin, with wine-related objects, cellar equipment, costumes, relevant art, and so on.

Limoux Every weekend from January to March a unique carnival is held in which participants wear disguise and the sparkling wine flows abundantly. The Musée Petiet is dedicated to the *belle époque* and also exhibits regional art. A colourful tiled wall with illustrations of wine themes stands by one of the approach roads.

Le Livinière Picturesque village in the Minervois with Roman ovens, oil mills and a dolmen. Also an excellent wine cooperative.

Mailhac Due to excavations at the Oppidium du Cayla, the local museum has an important collection of prehistoric objects.

Minerve Perched on a narrow red-rock ledge above where two rivers join, with the ruins of old walls, gates and a castle. A small museum whose collections include prehistoric objects. An altar in the Romanesque church dates from the 5th century, and the small museum includes a collection of prehistoric items. In the early 13th century, Minerve was a stronghold of heresy; in 1210 more than 100 of the inhabitants were burnt at the stake.

Montpellier The busy atmosphere of the crowded centre contrasts strongly with the elegant peace of Le Peyrou, the promenade in the highest part of the town which is flanked by a graceful water tower (*Château d'Eau*) on one side and an equestrian statue of Louis XIV on the other. Next to it there is a magnificent botanical garden, the Jardin des Plantes, and opposite the botanical garden is the 14th-century Benedictine college which houses the

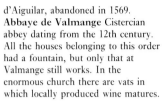
◀ Lavender is an important crop in the Midi, as here at Pic St-Loup.

the country for viticulture.

Narbonne The 13th-century cathedral of St-Just stands out above the centre of the town and contains many works of art. Next to it lies the former episcopal palace with its three massive towers: today it is used as a town hall and also houses the Musée d'Art et d'Histoire (French and Flemish masters). The Maison Vigneronne (8 Rue Flatters) illustrates the history of wine growing in the Aude and is well worth a visit.

Nîmes Possesses the richest stock of Roman buldings in the whole of the south of France. These include an amphitheatre that can hold more than 20,000 spectators (bull fights still take place in the arena in summer); the Maison Carrée, a beautiful rectangular temple – was it the inspiration for La Madeleine in Paris? – containing the Musée des Antiquités; the Temple of Diana (in the pleasure gardens of the Jardins de la Fontaine, at the foot of Mount Cavalier); the octagonal Tour Magne (belvedere); the Castellum Divisorium (for saving and storing water); the ruins of a forum and two town gates.

Also worth visiting in this dusty and busy town are the cathedral of St-Castor (12th and 17th centuries); the neighbouring Musée du Vieux-Nîmes; an archaeological museum (13 Boulevard de l'Amiral Courbet); and the Musée des Beaux-Arts (Rue Cité-Foule) with works by Breughel, Rodin and Rubens as well as a Roman floor mosaic of the "Wedding of Admetes". Whatever you do, don't miss the Jardins de la Fontaine. Perhaps Persia or India contains something so original.

Pézenas With its magnificent patrician residences, the centre of Pézenas is a unique open-air museum. One of the buildings houses

oldest medical faculty in France (derived from the Moorish scholarship of Andalusia), and the Musée Atger (drawings and engravings). Other interesting museums are the Musée Fabre (Boulevard Bonne-Nouvelle) with many French and Italian masters, and the natural history museum (Place Eugène-Bataillou). The cathedral of St-Pierre dates from the 16th century. The university of Montpellier is the most important in

the Musée Valloid-St-Germain. Documents and other objects remind us that Jean-Baptiste Poquelin, better known as Molière, lived in Pézenas from 1650 to 1656.

Pinet In the church there is a crib made by all the inhabitants of this wine village.

Remoulins Near this "cherry capital" stands the Pont du Gard, one of the greatest monuments of Roman engineering, with three tiers of arches built with blocks of stone weighing six tons each. The bridge was part of an aqueduct 50km (31 miles) long which brought water from the Eure to Nîmes.

Rieux-Minervois Wine commune with an unusual seven-sided church.

St-Chinian Remains of a 9th-century monastic house.

St-Guilhem-le-Désert Village built in a rugged valley with a monastic foundation of 8th-century origin. Very old cloister, early Romanesque church and two marble sarcophagi dating from the 7th century. The Gorges of the Hérault, a lovely sequence of rocky rapids in ravishing country, are near by, and so, farther south, are the Grotte de Clamouse (fine crystalline forms) and the Pont du Diable (11th-century bridge).

Sète Praised by Georges Brassens, Sète is a port divided by wine, fishing and pleasure, its centre divided by canals and basins. From the jetty near Le Vieux Bassin there is a good view of this colourful town. In the Musée Paul-Valéry (named after the poet, who was born here) there are paintings by Cézanne, Monet and Renoir. At various times in history, Sète has been notorious for its traffic in bogus wines.

Sigean One of the rooms in the Musée des Corbières has wine as its theme.

Sommières Picturesque medieval village with a Roman bridge over the River Vidourle.

Tuchan One of the centres for Fitou wines. Above the town are the ruins of the 12th-century Château

d'Aiguilar, abandoned in 1569.

Abbaye de Valmange Cistercian abbey dating from the 12th century. All the houses belonging to this order had a fountain, but only that at Valmange still works. In the enormous church there are vats in which locally produced wine matures.

WINE FESTIVALS AND WINE FAIRS

Mid-July Wine festival in Lézignan-Corbières.

End of July Minerve 1210, a song, dance, eating and drinking festival in Minerve.

August *Foire aux vins* in Narbonne, and the *Fête du Muscat* in Frontignan.

Second half of August Wine festival in St-Chinian.

September/October Harvest festival in Carcassonne.

October *Fête du vin nouveau* in Béziers.

First weekend in November Wine fair in Nîmes.

Fairs and festivities are also organized in many other villages and towns of the Languedoc, especially in the summer months.

WINE FRATERNITIES

The Languedoc has a good many of these, although some are dormant. The list that follows is arranged alphabetically:

Antica Confraria de St-Andiu de la Galiniera (Béziers and district); Capitoul des Fins Gosiers de Limoux (Blanquette de Limoux); Les Chevaliers de la Belle Aude et du Languedoc (Aude wines); Les Compagnons du Minervois (Minervois); La Confrérie des Ambassadeurs des Coteaux du Languedoc (Coteaux du Languedoc); La Confrérie de St-Adrien-d'Adissan (Hérault cooperatives); La Confrérie des Tastevins du St-Chinian; Le Consulat de la Septimanie (Narbonne and district); Illustre Cour des Seigneurs de la Corbière (Corbières); Ordre de la Boisson de la Stricte Observance des Costières du Gard (Costières du Gard).

WINE INFORMATION

Information about regional wines can be obtained in various places, including Béziers (Maison Régionale des Vins, 18 Rue du 4-Septembre); Carcassonne (Caveau des Vins d'Origine, in the Porte Narbonnaise of the Cité); Lézignan-Corbières (Les Coteaux Occitans, on the RN 113); Montpellier (Hotel Montpellierain des Vins du Languedoc, 7 Rue Jacques-Coeur, also a restaurant); in Olonzac (Maison du Minervois, Boulevard Blazin); and St-Chinian (Maison des Vins).

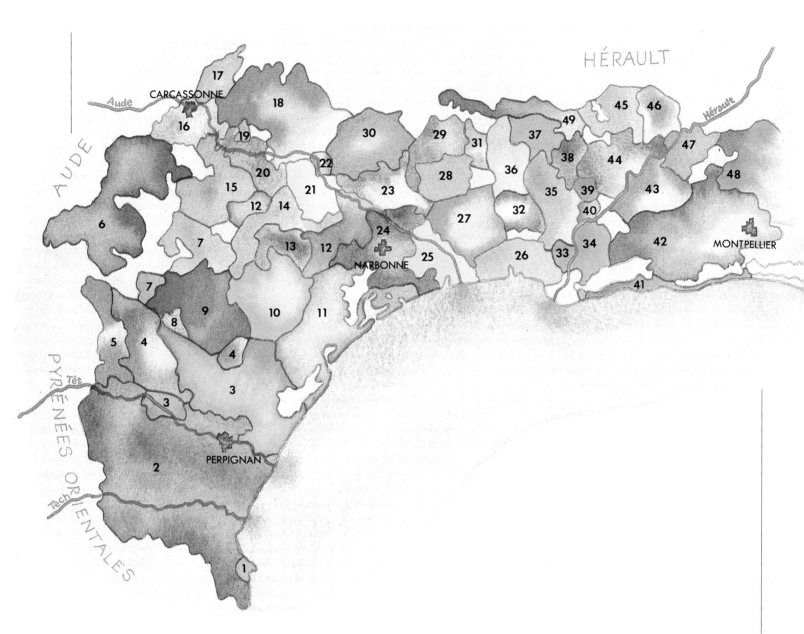

THE VINS DE PAYS OF THE LANGUEDOC AND ROUSSILLON

1 Vin de Pays de la Côte Vermeille
2 Vin de Pays Catalan
3 Côtes Catalanes
4 Vals d'Agly
5 Coteaux des Fenouillèdes
6 Haute Vallée de l'Aude
7 Coteaux du Termenès
8 Cucugnan
9 Coteaux Cathares
10 Vallée du Paradis
11 Coteaux du Littoral Audois
12 Val d'Orbieu
13 Coteaux de la Cabrerisse
14 Hauterive en Pays d'Aude
15 Val de Dagne
16 Coteaux de la Cité de Carcassonne
17 Côtes de Lastours
18 Coteaux de Peyriac
19 Hautes de Badens
20 Coteaux de Miramont
21 Coteaux de Lézignanais

22 Hauterive
23 Val de Cesse
24 Coteaux de Narbonne
25 Côtes de Pérignan
26 Ardailhou
27 Coteaux d'Enserune
28 Coteaux de Fontcaude
29 Monts de la Grage
30 Côtes du Brian
31 Cessenon
32 Coteaux du Libron
33 Bessan
34 Côtes de Thau
35 Côtes de Thongue
36 Coteaux de Murviel
37 Coteaux de Laurens
38 Cassan
39 Caux
40 Pézenas
41 Sables du Golfe du Lion
42 Collines de la Moure

43 Vicomté d'Aumelas
44 Côtes du Céressou
45 Coteaux du Salagou
46 Mont Baudile
47 Gorges de l'Hérault
48 Val de Montferrand
49 Haute Vallée de l'Orb

PRODUCERS OF SPECIAL INTEREST

BLANQUETTE DE LIMOUX

LIMOUX, postcode 11300, 252 B2

Georges & Roger Antech/ Domaine de Flassian; Pierre-Jacques Astruc; Cave Coopérative*: Modern equipment and an emphasis on quality has earned the Blanquette de Limoux produced by this large cooperative a worldwide reputation.

PIEUSSE, postcode 11300

Domaine de Fourn/G.F.A. Robert

CORBIERES

BIZANET, postcode 11200

Domaine de Cave Neuve; Château Gaussan.

BOUTENAC, postcode 11200, 252 C4

Domaine de Fontsainte: Powerful red wine from Yves Labourcarie. Domaine de La Voulte Gasparets*: Corbières with class.

CAMPLONG-D'AUDE, postcode 11200

Cave Coopérative: Very good white wines.

EMBRES-ET-CASTELMAURE, postcode 11360

Cave Coopérative: Remarkably good reds to drink at 1–2 years.

FABREZAN, postcode 11200

Château de la Boutignane; Domaine de Jérémie.

▼ Gastronomes will find plenty of fresh fish to enjoy on the Midi coast.

GRUISSAN, postcode 11430, 252 D4

Château le Bouîs*: Superior red, a successful white and a slightly sparkling rosé. Pierre Clément.

LAGRASSE, postcode 11220

Château St-Auriol*

LEZIGNAN-CORBIERES, postcode 11200, 252 C4

Château Etang des Colombes*: Excellent red and white wines. The tasting cellar is also a small museum. Château du Grand-Caumont.

MONTSERET, postcode 11200, 252 C4

Château Surbéry-Cartier (formerly Château les Ollieux)

PORTEL-DES-CORBIERES, postcode 11490

Château de Lastours

RIBAUTE, postcode 11220

Domaine de Pech-Latt*: The red and white Corbières produced by Jean Vialade are both commendable. Also a number of other wines.

STE-ANDRE-DE-ROQUELONGUE, postcode 11200, 252 C4

Domaine de Villemajou*: Top-class Corbières from Georges Bertrand, one of the most energetic and talented wine makers.

ST-LAURENT-DE-LA-CABRERISSE, postcode 11220, 252 C3

Château de Caraguilhes; Cave Coopérative; Domaine de Montjoie, Château les Palais.

COSTIERES DU GARD AND CLAIRETTE DE BELLEGARDE

BELLEGARDE, postcode 30127, 232 E3

Domaine de l'Amarine*: Aromatic white wine. Mas Carlot*: The best all-round estate in the area. Domaine St-Louis-la-Perdrix.

CAISSARGUES, postcode 30132

Château de Belle-Coste*: A range of award-winning wines.

MANDUEL, postcode 30129, 232 E3

Château de Campuget; Domaine de Rozier*: Beautiful red wine.

NIMES, postcode 30000, 232 E3

Domaine de Mourier; Château de la Tuilerie*: Delicious rosé and good red wine.

FAUGERES

FAUGERES, postcode 34480, 252 B5

Cave Coopérative: Several good Cuvées, including a rosé. Gilbert Alquier.

LAURENS, postcode 34480

Cave Coopérative; Château de Grézan*: Walled castle dating from the 12th century, where the Luvac family make a good quality Faugères.

LA LIQUIERE, postcode 34480

Château de la Liquière*: Jean Vidal is a committed and quality-conscious wine producer, as his wine demonstrates. Domaine de St-Aimé*: Sinewy Faugères with a lot of character. Bernard & Claudie Vidal: Husband and wife team, very successful with their Faugères.

COTEAUX DU LANGUEDOC AND CLAIRETTE DU LANGUEDOC

BEAULIEU, postcode 34160, 232 E2

Château de Beaulieu

CABRIERES, postcode 34800, 252 B6
Cru Cabrières

Cave Coopérative; Domaine du Temple*.

CLARET, postcode 34270, 232 E2

Domaine de Lavabre*: Estate owned by the Georges Bonfils firm from Sète. Supple, fruity red Coteaux du Languedoc.

CAUSSES-ET-VEYRAN, postcode 34490, 252 B5

Domaine de Guiraud-Boyer

FONTANES, postcode 34270, 232 E2
Cru Pic St-Loup

Domaine de la Roque

257

SE

◄ The Etang de Bages is typical of the lagoons along the coast.

GRUISSAN, postcode 11430, 252 D4
Cru La Clape

Château Rouquette sur Mer*: An outstanding estate. Jacques and Dominique Boscary have won medals with their red, rosé and white wines.

LAVERUNE, postcode 34880

Château de l'Engarran

MONTPELLIER, postcode 34000, 232 F2, 253 C7
Cru Coteaux de la Méjanelle

Château de Flauguergues*: Beautiful château, on the road to Mauguio, producing good red wines. **Château Rastouble**.

NARBONNE, postcode 11100, 252 C4
Crus La Clape and Montpeyroux

Château Moujan (La Clape); **Château Notre-Dame***: Yvon and Georges Ortola make the best red and rosé Quatourze. **Château de Pech Redon***: Extremely reliable, rich-tasting red and rosé La Clape. Chardonnay is adding class to the already interesting white. **Vignerons du Val d'Orbieu***: Quality-conscious group who advise many estates and cooperatives in the Languedoc, and also bottle and sell their own wine. **Domaine de Vires**.

NIZAS, postcode 34320

Château Carrion-Nizas*: Bernard Gaujal uses 20% Merlot in his red Coteaux du Languedoc.

PAULHAN, postcode 34230, 253 C6

Château de la Condamine Betrand*: Perfect Clairette du Languedoc and delicious red and rosé wines. Bernard and Marie-José Jany.

PEZENAS, postcode 34120, 252 C6

Château St-André*: A fragrant, invigorating Clairette du Languedoc and a good red Coteaux du Languedoc, produced by expert wine grower Jean-Louis Randon.

PINET, postcode 34850, 252 C6
Cru Picpoul de Pinet

Domaine Gaujal*: Recommended for its white wine and also its Merlot (Domaine de la Rouquette, a *vin de pays*).

ST-CHRISTOL, postcode 34400, 232 E2
Cru St-Christol

Cave Coopérative

ST-DREZERY, postcode 34160, 232 E2
Cru St-Drézéry

Domaine du Mas de Carrat

ST-GEORGES-D'ORQUES, postcode 34680, 253 C7
Cru St-Georges-d'Orques

Cave Coopérative

ST-SATURNIN, postcode 34150, 253 B7
Cru St-Saturnin

Cave Coopérative*: The only producer of this *cru*, with good red and rosé wines.

SALLES-D'AUDE, postcode 11110
Cru La Clape

Château Pech de Céleyran

COTES DU CABARDES AND DE L'ORBIEL

CONQUES-SUR-ORBIEL, postcode 11600

Domaine de Rayssac

COTES DE LA MALEPERE

MALVIES, postcode 11300

Château de Malvies-Guilhem

FITOU, 252 D3

TUCHAN, postcode 11350, 252 D3

Cave Coopérative; Château de Nouvelles*: Fitou and Muscat de Rivesaltes with class.

MINERVOIS, 252 B4

AZILLANET, postcode 34210

Domaine du Pech-d'André

BAGNOLES, postcode 11600

Château du Donjon

BIZE-MINERVOIS, postcode 11120, 252 C4

Château de Cabezac*

BLOMAC, postcode 11700

Château de Blomac*: A 100% Carignan and an interesting rosé.

CAUNES-MINERVOIS, postcode 11160, 252 B3

Cave Coopérative; Château de Villerambert-Julien*: Concentrated, classically made wine. **Château de Villerambert Moreau***: Minervois with class.

GINESTAS, postcode 11120

Château de Vergel

LAURE-MINERVOIS, postcode 11800, 252 B3

Cave Coopérative

LA LIVINIERE, postcode 34210, 252 C4

Cave Coopérative*: Excellently equipped cooperative; the wines (some are aged in cask) are in keeping. **Domaine Ste-Eulalie***: Delicious Minervois, rich in fruit.

OLONZAC, postcode 34210, 252 C4

Château de Gourgazaud

PARAZA, postcode 11200

Château de Paraza*: Rosé and red (the Special Cuvée) are excellent.

POUZOLS, postcode 11120, 252 C4

Domaine Meyzonnier*: Jacques Meyzonnier has repeatedly produced the best Minervois of the year. **Château de Pouzols**.

RIEUX-MINERVOIS, postcode 11160, 252 B3

Domaine des Homs; Cave Coopérative.

TRAUSSE-MINERVOIS, postcode 11160

Daniel Domergue*: A Minervois that can accompany even game dishes. **Château de Paulignan***: The Tallavignes family has made white Minervois a speciality.

MUSCAT

FRONTIGNAN, postcode 34100, 253 D7

Cave Coopérative*: Firm Muscat de Frontignan from one of France's first cooperatives. **Château de la Peyrelade***: One of the very best *vins doux naturels*.

LUNEL, postcode 34400, 232 E2

Domaine de Belle Côte*: Generous, almost sultry, Muscat de Lunel, from vines on the highest slopes of the village.

MIREVAL, postcode 34840, 253 C7

Cave Coopérative*: Fairly small cooperative producing a sturdy Muscat de Mireval, rich in sugar.

ST-JEAN-DE-MINERVOIS, postcode 34360, 252 B4

Cave Camman*: Pleasantly fragrant Muscat de St-Jean-de-Minervois. **Cave Coopérative***: Responsible for about 90% of the local production.

VERARGUES, postcode 34400, 232 E2

Cave Coopérative*: Well-balanced Muscat de Lunel, matured for three years. **Domaine du Grés St-Paul**: Also red Coteaux du Languedoc.

ST-CHINIAN

BERLOU, postcode 34360, 252 B5

Cave Coopérative*: Meaty, deep red wines made by traditional methods, using three grape varieties.

CAZEDARNES, postcode 34460

Domaine des Calmette

CEBAZAN, postcode 34360, 252 B5

Union des Caves Coopérative du Secteur de St-Chinian: Sells the wines from five cooperatives.

MURVIEL-LES-BEZIERS, postcode 34490, 252 C5

Château Coujan

PRADES-SUR-VERNAZOBRE, postcode 34360

Jean-Claude Grasset; Domaine des Jougla*: Leading family estate making exemplary wines.

ST-CHINIAN, postcode 34360, 252 B5

Clos Bagatelle*: A vigorous St-Chinian and also a delicious Muscat de St-Jean-de-Minervois.

VINS DE PAYS
(See also the map on page 256)

ANIANE, postcode 34150, 253 B7

Mas de Daumas Gassac*: Famous estate with complex soil similar to that of the Côte d'Or and using Bordeaux vineyard techniques. The result is superb wine: the Latour of the Midi. Also an excellent rosé and a rare, fascinating white.

AIGUES-MORTES, postcode 30220, 232 F2

Listel/Salins du Midi*: The most important cellars of France's largest vineyard owners, Salins du Midi (the salt company), are here. In the south they produce mainly *vins de pays* with the Listel label. The wines from individual grape varieties (Cabernet, Chardonnay, Chenin Blanc, Sauvignon) are particularly interesting.

LEZIGNAN-LA CEBE, postcode 34120, 252 C4

Domaine d'Ormesson*: Charming red wine made from seven grape varieties, matured in wood.

MARSEILLAN, postcode 65350

Domaine de la Fadèze*: Excellent Syrah.

PEZENAS, postcode 34120, 252 C6

Prieuré de Saint-Jean de Bébian*: Fragrant red wine, expertly made by Alain Roux.

STE-ANASTASIE, postcode 30190

Domaine Gournier

SERVIAN, postcode 34290

Domaine du Prieuré d'Amilhac*: Very attractive wines from, for example, Chardonnay/Sauvignon and Cabernet Sauvignon.

THEZAN-LES-BEZIERS, postcode 34490

Domaine de Ravanes*: Firm, fragrant Cabernet Sauvignon.

VIAS, postcode 34500

Domaine du Bosc

ROUSSILLON

For about four centuries, until 1642, Roussillon was part of the kingdom of Mallorca, or Majorca. Spanish influences are still clearly present: the language spoken in this area (now the département of Pyrénées-Orientales) is the Catalan of Catalonia, and old fortified villages still mark the former frontier with France.

Around the capital Perpignan and behind the long sandy shoreline stretches a large plain where fruit and vegetables are grown: strawberries, apricots and apples, asparagus, raspberries, cherries, pears and peaches. And grapes. Grapes are the most common fruit in Roussillon: some 40 percent of all agricultural land is planted with vines.

In the 1960s – much earlier than in neighbouring Languedoc – growers in Roussillon began aiming for quality. Their efforts were rewarded in 1977 when appellation contrôlée status was granted to Côtes du Roussillon and its superior version, Côtes du Roussillon-Villages. These mainly red wines are ripe, rich and powerful. A large proportion of the grapes, especially the abundant Carignan, are processed by *macération carbonique*, the method traditional in Beaujolais, in which the grapes are left on the bunch and fermented whole, stalks and all, to extract maximum fruit and flavour. Ageing in wood is also gaining ground.

Caramany and Latour-de-France are two of the most reputed villages. Rivesaltes is also produced in the greater part of the Côtes du Roussillon (in 86 of the 118 communes). In volume this is France's biggest producer of Vin Doux Naturel, a fortified apéritif and dessert wine that comes in three styles: white, red, and one made solely from Muscat grapes. The third style, called Muscat de Rivesaltes, is far and away the best; it can often make an ideal accompaniment to fruit, sweet desserts or blue-veined cheeses.

Banyuls, also a Vin Doux Naturel, originates from an isolated district along the rocky coast. Steep, slaty hillsides and an obligatory period of ageing contribute to the character of Banyuls, which is halfway between that of madeira and port. The best (and most mature) is Banyuls Grand Cru, most of it sweet but there is also a rather drier version. Banyuls is one of the very rare wines that can successfully be served with chocolate.

Collioure, from the same district, can be regarded as a sort of unfortified Banyuls. It is a firm, rounded wine that undergoes at least nine months' ageing in wood.

The Pyrenees rise superbly above the Roussillon vineyards. From Fourques in the Côtes du Roussillon the Massif du Canigou fills the western sky above the autumn vines. Spain is just over the horizon: the people here speak Catalan.

TRAVEL INFORMATION

Roussillon cuisine features fish from the sea, game from the nearby forests and mountains, and vegetables and fruit from the fertile plain. Thus there is a wide range of regional dishes – sometimes with a Spanish touch to them. The best-known speciality is *cargolade*: snails roasted over vine twigs and eaten with *aîoli* (a powerful garlic mayonnaise).

HOTELS

Le Catalan, 66650 Banyuls-sur-Mer, tel. 68 88 02 80. Modern, built in a semicircle on the rocks. Swimming pool. *Demi-pension* obligatory in season. Class A/B.
Les Elmes, 66650 Banyuls-sur-Mer, tel. 68 88 03 12. Comfortable beach hotel where you can eat well. *Demi-pension* obligatory in season. Hotel class B; restaurant class C.
La Casa Pairal, 66190 Collioure, tel. 68 82 05 81. Luxuriously appointed in a park full of flowers. Swimming pool. Class A/B.
Athéna, 1 Rue Quays, 66000 Perpignan, tel. 68 34 37 63. Central but reasonably quiet. Class B/C.
Le Mas des Arcades, Rue d'Espagne/RN 9, 66000 Perpignan, tel. 68 85 11 11. Modern complex on the edge of town, with swimming pool and restaurant. Class B.

Alta Riba, 66600 Rivesaltes, tel. 68 64 01 17. Pleasant, very adequate hotel and restaurant. Class B/C.

RESTAURANTS

Le Sardinal, 66650 Banyuls-sur-Mer, tel. 68 88 30 07. In the large dining room you can enjoy *marmite de filets de poisson* and *sole braisée au vieux Banyuls*. A fine wine list. Class C.
Château de Jau, 66600 Cases-de-Pène, tel. 68 64 11 38. You can lunch here in the summer by prior arrangement. Class C.
l'Hostal, 66300 Castelnou, tel. 68 53 45 42. Famous for *cargolade* and other regional dishes. Class C.
Le Baroque, 66530 Claira, tel. 68 28 23 17. Excellent selection of Roussillon wines. Class C.
La Bodega, 66190 Collioure, tel. 68 82 05 60. In a former wine cellar. Regional cooking of a good standard: try the *rougets*. Class B/C.
La Frégate, 66190 Collioure, tel. 68 82 06 05. Garden-like interior and a terrace outside. Also a good hotel. Restaurant class C; hotel class B.
Les Templiers, 66190 Collioure, tel. 68 82 05 58. Great artists such as Dufy, Matisse and Picasso paid their bills here with their art. Some 3,000 works hang in the premises: enough

to make your mind wander from your wine or your meal (for example, fish soup, various fish dishes). Also a hotel. Restaurant class C; hotel B/C.

Le Quéribus, 66460 Maury, tel. 68 59 10 26. Game and local wine. Class C.

Henri Delcros, 68 Avenue Maréchal-Leclerc, 66000 Perpignan, tel. 68 34 96 05. Talented chef, famed for his fish recipes and his desserts. Class B.

Le Festin de Pierre, 7 Rue du Théâtre, 66000 Perpignan, tel. 68 51 28 74. Noted for fish and poultry. Class B/C.

Le Rallye, 8 Place des Variétés, 66000 Perpignan, tel. 68 35 16 16. Authentic regional cuisine. Class C.

Relais St-Jean, 1 Cité Bartissol, 66000 Perpignan, tel. 68 51 22 25. Contemporary cuisine in the shadow of the cathedral. Good wine list, with wine by the glass. Class B.

Le François Villon, 1 Rue de Four-St-Jean, 66000 Perpignan, tel. 68 51 18 43. Inspired regional cuisine (e.g. *foie gras de canard au Banyuls*). Class C.

Park Hotel/Le Chapon Fin, 18 Boulevard Jean-Bourrat, 66000 Perpignan, tel. 68 35 14 14. Progressive cooking and a large dining area. Also a quite luxurious hotel. Class B.

Le Vauban, 29 Quai Vauban, 66000 Perpignan, tel. 68 51 05 10. Brasserie-style bistro, always busy. Good food (*carpaccio de magret de canard*) and wine (by the glass). Class C.

PLACES OF INTEREST

Baixas One of the most pleasant villages of the plain, with the remains of defensive walls, a Gothic church with a Baroque chapel and art exhibitions in the Cellier Dom Brial.

Banyuls-sur-Mer Seaside resort and wine town. Just outside the town is the Métairie Maillol, where the great sculptor Aristide Maillol (1861–1944) worked and lies buried.

Cabestany The church has a greatly valued Romanesque tympanum with the figure of the Virgin.

Canet-en-Roussillon A marine aquarium and the Musée du Père Noël (Father Christmas).

Cases-de-Pène Exhibitions of modern art in summer in the Château de Jau. Near the village is a 17th-century hermit's chapel.

Castelnou Picturesque walled hamlet where painters and craftsmen live. An 11th-century feudal stronghold rises above it.

Céret The museum of modern art includes a room full of Picassos and 14 works by Matisse.

Collioure Once an important commercial port. The harbour is dominated by the Château Royal,

where exhibitions are held in summer. Next to the church (built 1691) a former lighthouse serves as a belfry; the church itself is richly endowed with Baroque art. Some 3,000 works, many by famous artists, hang in the hotel-restaurant, Les Templiers (see Restaurants).

Elne For centuries Elne was more important than Perpignan and was the seat of a bishop. The cathedral of Ste-Eulalie was begun in the 11th century and beside it are splendidly preserved cloisters which, with a chapel, house a museum (sculpture, hand-thrown pottery, pre-Roman finds and a sarcophagus with grape motifs).

Espira-d'Agly The church (*c.* 1200) is striking for the use of the natural colours of the stone and the special masonry techniques.

Ermitage de Força Réal A hermit's chapel (and, beside it, a TV station) and a panoramic view.

Montalba-le-Château Fortified village at the foot of a large castle that dates back to the 10th century; also a wine museum.

Perpignan In the old, atmospheric centre there is the palace of the kings of Mallorca surrounded by its defensive walls, a number of chapels and a two-storey church. Also in the centre of town is the 14th- to 16th-century cathedral of St-Jean (well worth seeing) and the Loge de Mer (1397), formerly a stock exchange and marine court. On the square in front of it is Maillol's Venus (see Banyuls above); the Sardana is danced here in the summer. An attractive museum of folk art is housed in Le Castillet, a large 14th- and 15th-century town gate. Other interesting museums are the Musée Hyacinthe-Rigaud (paintings) and the Musée Joseph-Puig (coins, medals and a cultural documentation centre).

East of Perpignan is Castel-Roussillon, where extensive excavations are taking place and a

Romanesque church has been restored. There is an aeronautical museum on the road to Elne.

Port-Bacarès On the waterfront a packet boat, the *Lydia*, now houses a casino, and also on the beach there is an open-air museum of sculpture, the Musée des Sables.

Salses the fort at Salses, between the vineyards and beside the railway, is Roussillon's most-visited monument.

It dates largely from the 15th century and could accommodate 1,500 men and 100 horses. Built half underground, its red brick walls are 6m (20ft) thick.

Tautavel Here in 1971 the skull of *Homo tautavelensis*, some 450,000 years old, was discovered. The local museum of prehistory is excellently appointed. Overlooking the village and close to the cavern where the skull was found is the ruin of a

PRODUCERS OF SPECIAL INTEREST

▲ Mending nets in Port-Vendres on the Côte Vermeille.

medieval tower.

Thuir Famous for the cellar belonging to Byrrh (apéritifs) with the world's biggest barrel: capacity one million litres. Thuir also has the remains of its surrounding walls, a fine marble fountain, a 12th-century statue in the church and a reference centre for local wines and crafts (Cellier des Aspres). A chocolate factory can also be visited.

WINE FESTIVALS AND FAIRS

June Fête de la St-Bacchus (the great festival of the Maîtres-Tasteurs fraternity) and the Salon des Vins et de la Gastronomie, both in Perpignan.
July Fête de Rivesaltes in Rivesaltes and Fête du Vin et des Fruits in Elne.
Beginning of August Wine festival in Estagel.
Mid-October Fête du Vin Nouveau in Perpignan.

WINE FRATERNITIES

La Commende Majeure de Roussillon and Les Maîtres-Tasteurs du Roussillon promote Roussillon wines; Les Templiers de la Serre promote the wines of Banyuls.

▲ Barrels stand in the open air at a maker of Banyuls wines above the historic little town of Collioure. The citadel and fortified quayside church recall the time when the town was a stronghold of the Kings of Majorca.

Roussillon is included with the map of Languedoc on pages 252–253, and is also on the Vins de Pays map on page 256.

BAIXAS, postcode 66390, 252 D3
Cave Coopérative

BANYULS-SUR-MER, postcode 66650, 252 F3
Domaine du Mas Blanc*: Produces excellent Banyuls (including one that is fruity and bottled early) and a very fine Collioure. Owned by Dr André Parcé & Fils. **Domaine de la Retorie***: Banyuls full of character (first vintage 1984) from Marcel and Thierry Parcé.

BELASTA, postcode 66720
Cave Coopérative

CANET-ST-NAZAIRE-EN-ROUSSILLON, postcode 66140
Château de Rey*: Renowned Muscat de Rivesaltes, Cabernet (*vin de pays*) and Côtes du Roussillon.

CASES-DE-PENE, postcode 66600, 252 D3
Château du Jau*: Robert Doutres' large estate produces excellent Côtes du Roussillon, Muscat de Rivesaltes and Banyuls. There are art exhibitions at the château in summer, and a restaurant (but book ahead – see Restaurants page 259).

ELNE, postcode 66200, 252 E3
Mas Chichet*: Paul Chichet's speciality is a wood-aged Cabernet *vin de pays*.

MAURY, postcode 66460, 252 D2
Cave Coopérative; Paul Lafage & Fils; Mas Amiel*: The owner, Charles Dupuy, matures his remarkable, elegant Maury for five to nine years in cask.

PASSA, postcode 66300, 252 E3
Domaine St-Luc*: Luc-Jérôme Talut's best wine is his Muscat de Rivesaltes.

PERPIGNAN, postcode 66000, 252 E3
Domaine Sarda-Malet, 134 Avenue Victor-Dalbiez; **Vignerons Catalans***: A group set up in 1965. Some 50 cooperatives and various individual estates are now associated with it. More than any other concern, Vignerons Catalans has striven to raise the standard of quality of Roussillon wine – with great success. The group's large range includes red Villages from Caramany, Latour-de-France and from Château Cap de Fouste, Château St-Martin and Mas de la Dona. Many of the white wines are also to be recommended, for example the Taïchat; and the rosé from Rasiguères is one of the best in the district.

PORT-VENDRES, postcode 66720, 252 F3
Cellier des Templiers/GICB*: Group of five cooperatives that produce more than half of all Banyuls (and Collioure). The group has a good range of many excellent wines.

RIVESALTES, postcode 66600, 252 D3
Cazes Frères*: André and Bernard Cazes make a wide range of wines, notably Muscat de Rivesaltes, Côtes du Roussillon Villages and both red and white *vins de pays*.

ST-JEAN-LASSELLE, postcode 66300
Jaubert & Noury

TAUTAVEL, postcode 66720, 252 D3
Cave Coopérative

TRESSERE, postcode 66300, 252 E2
Etienne Amouroux; Serge Bourret.

TROUILLAS, postcode 66300, 252 E2
Domaine de la Casenove; Domaine de Canterrane.

VILLENEUVE-LA-RIVIERE, postcode 66610
Salvat Père & Fils

VINGRAU, postcode 66600
Cave Coopérative

CORSICA

When the Phoenicians discovered this island in the 6th century BC they called it Koraî, meaning "covered with forests". The description is still partly true today, for more than a quarter of Corsica's surface is covered with woodland, some of it of superlative pines, and the brushwood and low trees of the *maquis* are everywhere. Corsica is also mountainous: a massif rising out of the sea. It has a score of peaks, and only along the east coast is there a large area of flat land. Other peoples, both before and since the Phoenicians, have inhabited the island, among them the Etruscans, the Syracusans, the Carthaginians and the Romans; evidence of their presence is displayed in the local museums.

In 1347 the Genoese took possession of the island – but only of the coastal areas; they did not venture into the interior. Genoese watch towers still stand at various points around the coast. With one short interruption, Italian domination lasted for almost four centuries. This is why in many respects Corsica, the Ile de Beauté, is more Italian than French. The dialect – teaching it is compulsory in the schools – is closely related to Italian; the houses and churches look Italian; the names of towns and villages are Italian; the food features pasta and other Italian specialities; even the grape varieties are Italian.

The Sciarcarello and the Nielluccio are always prescribed as the basic grapes for Corsica's red and rosé wines. The two varieties complement each other excellently: one gives light-red wines with good acidity; the other deep-coloured, full-bodied wines. All Corsican white wines must be from at least 75 percent Vermentino grapes. As this variety gives wines with a lot of alcohol and not much acidity, an increasing number of producers now pick the grapes before they are fully ripe.

An impetus was given to winegrowing by the Genoese: in 1572 every family was ordered to plant four vines. But it was only under French rule, especially after the Revolution, that viticulture became really important. Around 1870 Corsica had some 15,000 hectares (37,000 acres) of vineyards and three quarters of its income came from wine. The arrival of phylloxera put an end to this period of prosperity; it was not until the 1960s that restoration really began. This was due largely to repatriates from Algeria who, with government help, soon reclaimed the malarial eastern plains and planted them with vines. Once again wine became Corsica's most important agricultural product.

Unfortunately, quantity prevailed over quality. The greater part of production was concentrated on cheap *vins de table*, which were used to strengthen light wines from the south of France. In second place came the somewhat better Vins de Pays; and wines with an appellation contrôlée came distinctly last. For many years AC wines represented less than three percent of the total output. The proportion has now risen to about five percent – not because the production of quality wine has increased but because the amount of bulk wine has decreased: since 1976 a third of the vineyards have been uprooted.

Corsica's recent wine history has thus been similar to that of the Languedoc and other mass-production areas of France. It has been an unfortunate involuntary participant in the battle to stem the flow of bad wine into the European "wine lake". Corsica has plenty of good vineyard sites in the hills and along the coast, so the potential for quality is there. The island seems set to return to the pre-phylloxera past, with concentration on the hill vineyards.

The prevalence of bulk wine has meant that Corsica has not enjoyed a very illustrious reputation as a winegrowing area. Nevertheless, the island does yield a respectable amount of very good wines, full of character, from independent, quality-minded growers. The tourists who annually journey to Corsica drink the largest part of the vintage – and the Corsicans are not slow to help. Only a small proportion is shipped to the mainland or elsewhere.

Winegrowing is mainly in the coastal areas, often in isolated districts. The most northerly fields are those of Coteaux du Cap Corse. The best dry wine of the island, Clos Nicrosi, is made at the end of this wild limestone peninsula. That there is an apéritif with the name Cap Corse is confusing for, apart from its name, it has nothing to do with this wine district. In the southwest of the peninsula the beautiful little district of Patrimonio produces some excellent red wines. Rosé used to be a speciality here and is still made; at its best it is a refreshing summer wine. Come down the west coast and you reach La Balagne, the largest quality-wine district. Its wines are sold under the name Calvi. Its often gravelly vineyards yield attractive reds and an increasing amount of fresh, fruity white wines. Coteaux d'Ajaccio, around the capital, is one of the most active districts. The black Sciacarello grape predominates for red wines; the Vermentino is the basis of a number of pleasant white wines.

The old, fortified town of Sartène on its hillside is the centre of a district whose wines are mainly firmly structured reds. The southernmost wine area, Figari, is suffering a decline. The local cooperative is going to great lengths to win recognition for its supple wines, particularly the reds. Not far from Figari is Porto-Vecchio, a busy holiday resort. Thanks to the grower Christian Imbert, it is still numbered among the wine districts.

The east coast is dominated by its low-lying area, where the best wines are offered under the name Vin de Corse. Large estates and a number of cooperatives set the pace. Considerable advances have been made in quality so that today there are pure, pleasant red and rosé wines to enjoy. In central Corsica, near Ponte Leccia, there is a tiny district that also produces Vin de Corse.

Finally, there are the sublime Muscat wines that are made on Cap Corse and in Patrimonio – golden in colour, luxurious in taste and almost stunning in their perfume. Of their kind they are among France's best – but as there is no appellation for them, they cannot officially be exported.

TRAVEL INFORMATION

Corsican cuisine is closely akin to the Italian, so many restaurants serve a rich variety of pastas (or pâtes). The local charcuterie is tasty and one of the most common pâtés is made from blackbirds. The meat of young goats and lambs is often served and the interior produces a lot of game (including wild boar). Naturally fish is frequently on the menu, both from the sea and from the mountain streams, and tomatoes, peppers, garlic, olive oil and fennel feature as flavourings. A good deal of the sheeps'-milk cheese goes to the mainland to be made into Roquefort.

HOTELS

The addresses below are just a small sample of the many hotels, apartments, chalet parks and camping sites available on Corsica.

Columbia, 2 Avenue de Paris, 20000 Ajaccio, tel. 95 21 12 66. Simple, pleasant hotel for budget-conscious visitors. Class C.

Eden-Roc, Routes des Sanguinaires, 20000 Ajaccio, tel. 95 52 01 47. By the sea, about 7km (4½ miles) south of the town. All the rooms have a terrace. Swimming pool. *Demi-pension* only. Class A.

Resch, 7 Rue Cardinal-Resch, 20000 Ajaccio, tel. 95 21 43 08. Comfortable hotel in the centre of Ajaccio. Class B.

Napoléon, 4 Rue Lorenzo-Vero, 20000 Ajaccio, tel. 95 21 30 01. Rather colourless but adequate. Class B.

Posta Vecchia, Rue Posta-Vecchia, 20200 Bastia, tel. 95 32 32 38. Near the old part of town and just behind the waterfront. Businesslike. Class B.

l'Abbaye, Route de Santore, 20260 Calvi, tel. 95 65 04 27. Conveniently situated and comfortable, in a former monastery. Class B.

La Pietra, 20220 l'Ile-Rousse, tel. 95 60 01 45. Incomparable view of the sea and modern furnishings. Restaurant. Class B.

Le Maquis, 20166 Porticcio, tel. 95 25 05 55. Opposite Ajaccio across the bay: an old manor converted into a very comfortable hotel with excellent food and service, and a beautiful swimming pool. Perhaps the best hotel in Corsica. Hotel class A; restaurant class A/B.

Dolce Notte, 20217 St-Florent, tel. 95 37 06 26. Quiet location near the sea. Terrace. The restaurant serves dinners only. Class B.

RESTAURANTS

Palm Beach, Route des Sanguinaires, 20000 Ajaccio, tel. 95 52 01 03. Modern Corsican cuisine. The owner is a wine grower. Also a small hotel. A good view. Class B.

Pardi, 60 Rue Cardinal-Fesch, 20000 Ajaccio, tel. 95 21 43 08. Corsican cooking in a Corsican setting. Class C.

Point U, 69bis Rue Cardinal-Fesch, 20000 Ajaccio, tel. 95 21 59 92. Great pains are taken with the cuisine and wine cellar. Class B.

St-Hubert, 3 Rue Colonel-Colonna-d'Ornano, 20000 Ajaccio, tel. 95 23 23 78. As the saint's name (St. Hubert is patron of the hunt) and the décor suggest, there is a good deal of game on the menu. Class C.

> Right: fishing is the concern of many of Corsica's people. The island is blessed with many natural harbours and bays.

▼ Below: Corsica makes much of its most famous son, Napoleon Bonaparte. The statue in Ajaccio shows the Emperor in classical guise.

Chez Assunta, 4 Place Fontaine-Neuve, 20200 Bastia, tel. 95 31 67 06. Renowned restaurant (*cabri rôti*) in a large vaulted room with a terrace. Class B.

Lavezzi, 8 Rue St-Jean, 20200 Bastia, tel. 95 31 05 73. Classic and local cuisine, the best in Bastia (try the anchovies) and a fine wine list. Covered terrace. By the old harbour. Class B.

La Romantique, 4bis Rue du Pontette, 20200 Bastia, tel. 94 32 30 85. Fresh *fruits de mer*; the décor lends atmosphere. Terrace by the old harbour. Class B.

Comme Chez Soi, 20260 Calvi, tel. 95 65 00 59. Feast on fish here with a view over the harbour. Class C.

U' Spuntinu, Route de Bonifato, 20260 Calvi, tel. 95 65 07 06. In a country setting, traditional cooking, garden and a covered terrace. Class C.

Le Vieux Moulin, 20238 Centuri-Port, tel. 95 35 60 15. The fresh fish and *bouillabaisse* make this an excellent place for lunch on Cap Corse. Rooms (*demi-pension* in season – when the disco is in operation). Class B.

l'Albibu, 20253 Patrimonio, tel. 95 37 07 69. Set among the vineyards with a backdrop of mountains. Sea and freshwater fish. Class C.

Auberge du Prunelli, 20129 Pisciatello, tel. 95 20 02 75. Very Corsican in all respects; covered terrace by a river, on the road from Ajaccio to Sartène. Class C.

Le Bistrot du Port, 20137 Porto-Vecchio, tel. 95 70 22 96. Enjoy

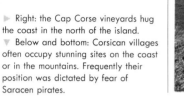

▶ Right: the Cap Corse vineyards hug the coast in the north of the island.

▼ Below and bottom: Corsican villages often occupy stunning sites on the coast or in the mountains. Frequently their position was dictated by fear of Saracen pirates.

pastas and fish dishes on a terrace here by the harbour. Class C.
Le Lucullus, 20137 Porto-Vecchio, tel. 95 70 10 17. The no-nonsense dishes are best here: roast or baked lamb or goat, charcuterie, etc. Rustic furnishings. Class B.
La Chaumiere, 20100 Sartène, tel. 95 77 07 13. Simple, tasty food at low all-in prices. Class C.

PLACES OF INTEREST

Corsica is an arid, rocky island, but it offers far more than that description suggests. Its coast is spectacular, with many sandy beaches and coves. The mountains and forests are superb walking country. There are many fascinating towns and villages with reminders of the island's warlike past. Corsica is quite unlike anywhere else in France, with a character that owes much to Italy but also stems from the island's own past. Corsica is, and feels, a very independent place.
Ajaccio Napoleon Bonaparte, born here in 1769, is still very much present. The main street is called the Cours Napoléon and you come across his name in many other places. The house where he was born (Rue St-Charles) is a museum and the town hall houses a museum wholly devoted to him, the Musée Napoléonien. In the Place Maréchal-Foch, the square in front of the town hall, a white marble statue of Napoleon as first consul stands above a fountain with four lions and there are other statues of him in various places in the town. Most of the members of the Bonaparte family are buried in the Chapelle Impériale (Rue Cardinal-Resch).
Beside the chapel the Musée Fesch has an admirable collection of Italian primitives and Corsican painting has been brought together in the Musée du Capitellu, opposite the Citadel (the Citadel is closed to visitors). Ajaccio cathedral is 16th century and built in Venetian Renaissance style. Napoleon was baptized here and his last words are chiselled on a column to the left of the entrance.
About 12km (7½ miles) northwest of Ajaccio is the imposing 19th-century Château de la Punta, which can be visited. Behind the façade, with its two rows of columns, there are richly decorated rooms and an enormous fireplace.
Aléria This town was founded by the Phoenicians around 565 BC and later inhabited by the Etruscans, Romans and others. The Jérôme-Carcopino museum, with local archaeological finds, is housed in the Matra fort. Among the most remarkable items are drinking vessels from 480 BC in the form of a dog's and a donkey's head. The excavations

are also open to visitors. In a nearby lake whole islets of empty oyster shells have been found, tipped there by the Romans.

Aregno Village in the Balange with a church built from multicoloured stones and containing splendid 15th-century frescos.

Bastia The island's largest commercial centre and port. The district around the old harbour has a great deal of atmosphere and the terraces along the 300m (330yd) open space opposite the new harbour can be very convivial in the summer. Above Bastia there is a 14th-century Genoese fortification, the bastion from which the town's name is derived. Within its walls are the former cathedral of Ste-Marie (it has an Assumption of the Virgin, in silver); the chapel of Ste-Cros; and the Musée Ethnographe de Corse (a governor's palace with vaulted rooms full of local history).

Bonifacio A fortress town on a spectacular site at the very south of the island. Ramparts, church and arched, cobbled streets survive from medieval times.

Calenzana The Couvent d'Alzipratu is at the foot of Monto Grosso. A former religious house, it was founded in 1509 and is partly in ruins but frescos and an impressive library can still be seen.

Calvi Columbus was born here in 1441 (a wall plaque in the Rue Columbo commemorates the fact) and the French Foreign Legion has barracks here, but Calvi is first and foremost a holiday resort, with a harbour for pleasure craft and fishing boats. The enormous citadel above the town contains, among other things, a museum of religious art (Oratoire St-Antoine) and the church of St-Jean-Baptiste (13th and 16th century). At the foot of the citadel, by the harbour and the colourful La Marine district, there is an old round Tour du Sel.

Cap Corse The northern tip of the island is a rugged peninsula jutting into the Mediterranean. It offers dramatic scenery, fine sheltered beaches and some fascinating hill villages. The area has its own wine, AC Cap Corse.

Corte Once the island's capital, now the largest inland town. The Foreign Legion garrisons the citadel which dates from medieval times. The old streets and shady courts are charming. Corte is a centre for exploring the wild interior of the island.

Evisa Mountain village and a centre for fine walks in the hills and forests, including the 3-hour descent of the Gorges de Spelunca.

Figari Northwest of this wine village

a mountain called l'Omo de Cagna has a rock in the form of a man.

Filitosa Prehistoric religious and cultural monuments have been found here, including carved menhirs. Filitosa has a museum.

l'Ile Rousse Resort with a casino on the west coast.

Macinaggio In this Cap Corse village, 19th-century wine warehouses have been converted into a museum for Roman archaeological finds, including a great deal of pottery.

Patrimonio The very photogenic 16th-century church of St-Martin stands amid the vineyards.

Porto-Vecchio Just north of this busy resort, to the right of the N198, is the hamlet of Torre. This has given its name to a people who lived on the island around 1500 BC and left behind many monuments. Torre itself has a burial site and just a little farther south, across the N189, is Castello d'Arraggio, the remains of a primitive fortification.

Propriano The little port, at the head of a gulf in the southwest of the island, dates from classical times. It is now a thriving seaside resort.

Roccapina On the road from Sartène to Bonifacio you can see the Rocher du Lion, a rock with the shape of a recumbent lion. Beside it stands a Genoese watch tower.

Rogliano One of the prettiest villages of Cap Corse with many old houses, a ruined castle and the church of St-Agnel (the Empress Eugénie donated the chancel balustrade).

St-Florent Resort and old harbour town in the north of the island, close to Cap Corse. Nearby is a 12th-century cathedral, all that remains of a city destroyed by the Saracen pirates.

Sartène The town centre is medieval and pure Corsican. A former prison now serves as a museum of prehistory. As in many places in Corsica, the Holy Week celebrations include a spectacular procession.

WINE INFORMATION

Although Corsica has no Maison du Vin, there are two bodies that actively promote the island's wines: CREPAC (at Casa Corsa, 22 Boulevard Dominique Paoli, 20000 Ajaccio) and GIVC (6 Rue Gabriel Péri, 20200 Bastia). There is also an energetic group of the better independent wine estates, called UVACORSE (Chambre d'Agriculture, Residence Castel-Vecchio, 20000 Ajaccio).

PRODUCERS OF SPECIAL INTEREST

CALVI

CALENZANA, postcode 20214, 266 C2

Domaine de Cantone*: Owned by the Discala brothers; the red, made from four grape varieties, is one of the best in the district. **Cave Coopérative**: Fresh white wine made in the modern style and pleasantly fruity. **Couvent d'Alzipratu***: Sturdy, deep-red wine from an isolated estate (see Places of Interest, Calenzana).

CALVI, postcode 20260, 266 B2

Clos Landry

MURO, postcode 20225

Clos Regina

COTEAUX D'AJACCIO

MEZZAVIA, postcode 20167

Domaine Comte Péraldi: Very

good Sciacarello rosé, and reds that promise very well, with the singular dusty/herby fragrance of this remarkable grape.

PISCIATELLO, postcode 20129

Clos Capitoro; Domaine de Paviglia.

COTEAUX DU CAP CORSE

ROGLIANO, postcode 20247, 266 B3

Clos Nicrosi*: On his estate on the high slopes, Toussaint Luigi produces the island's best dry white wine (100% Vermentino) and a grand Muscat (Muscatellu), but the yield of both is very limited.

FIGARI, 266 D3

PIANOTOLLI, postcode 20131

Cave Coopérative

PATRIMONIO

PATRIMONIO, postcode 20253, 266 B3

Cave Coopérative: Clos de Bernardi; Clos Marfisi.

ST-FLORENT, postcode 20217, 266 B3

Dominique Gentile*: Produces one of Corsica's very best red wines, with a lively taste and supple, rounded quality. Fermentation is in stainless-steel tanks.

PORTO-VECCHIO

PORTO-VECCHIO, postcode 20137, 266 D3

Domaine de Torraccia*: Christian Imbert is one of the most dynamic and expert winemakers on the island, producing a substantial, balanced red, an aromatic white and a pleasant rosé.

SARTENE

PROPRIANO, postcode 20110, 266 D3

Domaine Fiumicoli

SARTENE, postcode 20100, 266 D3

Domaine de San-Michèle

VIN DE CORSE

ALERIA, postcode 20270, 266 C3

Union de Vignerons de l'Ile de Beauté: Active coopérative with several good wines, especially reds. The best is Domaine Marquillant, aged in new oak barrels.

ARENA, postcode 20215

Cave Coopérative; Domaine de la Ruche Foncière: The Filippe family have a large store where fruit, vegetables, charcuterie and other produce of the island is sold, as well as wine.

CATERAGGIO, postcode 20270

Cave Coopérative

MAP PAGE 223

AJACCIO

PATRIMONIO — Appellation Contrôlée

Wine-producing area

Route Nationale

Wine Route

1:1,585,000

Km. 0   10   20   30   40   50 Km.

Miles 0   10   20   30 Miles

ACKNOWLEDGMENTS

It must be evident to readers that books of the complexity of this one (and books as beautifully designed as this) are far from being the unaided work of their authors. They depend on devoted and highly experienced editors and designers to bring together their diverse elements, to compile maps, commission artists and photographers, sift and check thousands of references – and, perhaps hardest of all, to provide authors with the right mixture of encouragement and discipline.

The firm of Mitchell Beazley has become famous for its skills in presentation. The authors of this Atlas owe a special debt to the individuals who have nursed this long and complex work so smoothly and rapidly from manuscript to finished book.

Chris Foulkes as Executive Editor combines flair and unflappability in balancing the demands and needs of his colleagues. Di Taylor is the editor every author feels he deserves: a wise and kindly friend who knows when to coax and when to be firm, who can anticipate problems and somehow massage words to fit funny spaces and make sense at the same time.

Eljay Crompton, the designer of the book, and Anita Wagner, who has handled the maps, have both worked devotedly and meticulously to produce such a handsome and practical volume.

To them and to their colleagues in both the editorial and production departments we warmly acknowledge our gratitude.

In compiling this Atlas the authors have also called on the services of many wine producers, négociants, committees, etc, and are particularly indebted to the following who have recommended hotels and restaurants in their areas:

Alsace

Marcel and Philippe Blanck	Blanck/Domaine des Comtes de Lupfen	Kientzheim
Rémy Gresser	Domaine André Gresser	Andlau
Léonard Humbrecht	Domaine Zind-Humbrecht	Wintzenheim
Pierre Seltz	A. Seltz & Fils	Mittelbergheim

Bordeaux

Christopher Cannan	Europvin	Bordeaux
Jean-Michel Cazes	Château Lynch-Bages	Pauillac
Herman Mostermans	Les Vins de Crus	Bordeaux
Hamilton Narby	Château Guiraud	Sauternes
Alain Querre	Château Monbousquet	St-Emilion
Hélène Sicet	Agence Expression	Bordeaux
Alan Spencer		Bernadas-Ste-Terre
Jean-Louis Viaut	GIE du Médoc	Bordeaux

Burgundy

Jean-François Bouchard	Bouchard Père & Fils	Beaune
Jean Durup	Domaine de l'Eglantière	Maligny
Jean-François Delorme	André Delorme	Rully
Georges Duboeuf	Les Vins Georges Duboeuf	Romanèche-Thorins
Olivier Kooman	Albert Bichot	Beaune
Rolland Mathelin	Les Vins Mathelin	Châtillon-d'Azergues
Jean Vachet		St-Vallerin

Champagne

G. Frémaux	Société de Producteurs	Mailly-Champagne
Pierre Horiot	Horiot Père & Fils	Les Riceys
Christian Pol-Roger	Pol Roger & Co.	Epernay

Corsica

Comte Louis de Poix	Domaine Comte Péraldi	Mezzavia

Jura

Rolet Père & Fils		Montigny

Languedoc

Guy Benin	Domaine de Ravanès	Thézan-les-Béziers
Andrée Ferrandiz	D. F. Services	Coursan
Ludovic Gaujal	Domaine Gaujal	Pinet
Peter Geerts		Arques
Bernard Jany	Château la Condamine Bertrand	Paulhan
Alain Jougla	Domaine des Jougla	Prades-sur-Vernazobres
Jérôme d'Ormesson	Domaine d'Ormesson	Lézignan-Lacèbe

Loire

Henri Marionnet	Domaine de la Charmoise	Soigns
The Sauvion Family	Château du Cléray	Vallet

Massif Central

Paul Lapandéry		St-Haon-le-Vieux
Gérard Pétillat	Domaine de Bellevue	Meillard

Provence

Georges Brunet	Château Vignelaure	Rians
Laurent Bunan	Moulin des Costes	La Cadière-d'Azur
Claude Dieudonné	Domaine de Régusse	Pierrevert
Eloi Dürrbach	Domaine de Trévallon	St-Etienne-du-Grés
A. M. Hirsch	Domaine de St-Jean	Villecroze
Henning Hoesch	Domaine Richeaume	Puyloubier

Jean-Pierre Margan	Château La Canorgue	Bonnieux
Jean Paquette	Domaine de Curebéasse	Fréjus
Françoise Rigord	Commanderie de Peyrassol	Le Luc
François Sack	Clos Ste-Magdeleine	Cassis
J. S. de Taisne	Château Fonscolombe	Le Puy-Ste-Réparade

Rhône

Paul Avril	Clos des Papes	Châteauneuf-du-Pape
Jean-Clause Assémat		Roquemaure
Georges Champetier	UCOVA	Ruoms
Max Chapoutier	M. Chapoutier	Tain-l'Hermitage
Marc Français	Château St-Estève	Uchaux
Marcel Guigal	E. Guigal	Ampuis
Gérard Jaboulet	Paul Jaboulet Aîné	Tain-l'Hermitage
Jean-Claude Raspail		Saillans

Roussillon

Dr André Parcé	Domaine du Mas Blanc	Banyuls-sur-Mer

The Southwest

Alain Brumont	Domaine Bouscassé	Maumusson
André Duboscq	Union de Producteurs Plaimont	St-Mont
Patrick Germain	Château Bellevue La Forêt	Fronton
J.-M. Hébrard	Les Vignerons Réunis des Côtes de Buzet	Buzet-sur-Baïse
M. Rigal	Rigal & Fils	Parnac

In addition the following bodies have been extremely helpful in supplying detailed information:

Comité Interprofessionnel des Vins d'Alsace	Colmar
Union Interprofessionnelle des Vins du Beaujolais	Villefranche-sur-Saône
Comité Interprofessionnel des Vins de Bourgogne en Mâcon	Mâcon
Comité Interprofessionnel de la Côte d'Or et de l'Yonne	Beaune
Conseil Interprofessionnel du Vin de Bordeaux	Bordeaux
Comité Interprofessionnel des Vins de la Région de Bergerac	Bergerac
Comité Interprofessionnel du Vin de Champagne	Epernay
Comité Interprofessionnel des Vins des Côtes de Provence	Les Arcs-sur-Argens
Comité Interprofessionnel des Vins des Côtes du Rhône, Côtes du Ventoux, Coteaux du Tricastin	Avignon
Conseil Interprofessionnel des Vins de Fitou, Corbières et Minervois	Lézignan-Corbières
Comité Interprofessionnel des Vins de Gaillac	Gaillac
Comité Interprofessionnel des Vins d'Origine du Pays Nantais	La Haye-Fouassière
Comité Interprofessionnel des Vins de Touraine	Tours
Conseil Interprofessionnel des Vins d'Anjou et de Saumur	Angers
Comité Interprofessionnel des Vins Doux Naturels	Perpignan
Groupement Interprofessionnel des Vins de l'Isle de Corse	Bastia
Bureau National Interprofessionnel de l'Armagnac	Eauze
Bureau National Interprofessionnel du Cognac	Cognac
Conseil des Vins du Médoc	Bordeaux
Syndicat du Cru Corbières	Lézignan-Corbières
Syndicat des Coteaux du Languedoc	Lattes
Syndicat des Costières du Gard	Nîmes
Société de Viticulture du Jura	Lons-le-Saunier
Syndicat de Défense des Vins du Jurançon	Pau
Syndicat de Défense et de Contrôle des Vins du Madiran	Maubourguet
Syndicat du Cru Minervois	Olonzac
Syndicat Viticole de Pouilly	Pouilly-sur-Loire
Union Viticole Sancerroise	Fontenay
Syndicat Régional des Vins de Savoie	Chambéry
Syndicat Viticole et Agricole de St-Emilion	St-Emilion

Special thanks are also due to Madeleine Zaffarano of SOPEXA in The Hague, Holland, who with her staff has gone to considerable trouble in assembling a great deal of wine information. The same kind efforts were made by Bernard Crouset of Services Officiels Français du Tourisme, Amsterdam, in the area of tourism, and Pierre Davesne of the Office National Interprofessionnel des Vins who provided excellent, up-to-date information concerning Vins de Pays.

INDEX

269

271